OXFORD READINGS IN CLASSICAL STUDIES

The series provides students and scholars with a representative selection of the best and most influential articles on a particular author, work, or subject. No single school or style of approach is privileged: the aim is to offer a broad overview of scholarship, to cover a wide variety of topics, and to illustrate a diversity of critical methods. The collections are particularly valuable for their inclusion of many important essays which are normally difficult to obtain and for the first-ever translations of some of the pieces. Many articles are thoroughly revised and updated by their authors or are provided with addenda taking account of recent work. Each volume includes an authoritative and wide-ranging introduction by the editor surveying the scholarly tradition and considering alternative approaches. This pulls the individual articles together, setting all the pieces included in their historical and cultural contexts and exploring significant connections between them from the perspective of contemporary scholarship. All foreign languages (including Greek and Latin) are translated to make the texts easily accessible to those without detailed linguistic knowledge.

OXFORD READINGS IN CLASSICAL STUDIES

All available in paperback

Oxford Readings in Classical Studies

Horace: Satires *and* Epistles

Edited by
KIRK FREUDENBURG

OXFORD
UNIVERSITY PRESS

OXFORD
UNIVERSITY PRESS

Great Clarendon Street, Oxford OX2 6DP

Oxford University Press is a department of the University of Oxford.
It furthers the University's objective of excellence in research, scholarship,
and education by publishing worldwide in

Oxford New York

Auckland Cape Town Dar es Salaam Hong Kong Karachi
Kuala Lumpur Madrid Melbourne Mexico City Nairobi
New Delhi Shanghai Taipei Toronto

With offices in

Argentina Austria Brazil Chile Czech Republic France Greece
Guatemala Hungary Italy Japan Poland Portugal Singapore
South Korea Switzerland Thailand Turkey Ukraine Vietnam

Oxford is a registered trade mark of Oxford University Press
in the UK and in certain other countries

Published in the United States
by Oxford University Press Inc., New York

© Oxford University Press 2009

The moral rights of the author have been asserted
Database right Oxford University Press (maker)

First published 2009

British Library Cataloguing in Publication Data
Data available

Library of Congress Cataloging in Publication Data
Library of Congress Control Number: 2009926744

Typeset by SPI Publisher Services, Pondicherry, India
Printed in Great Britain
on acid-free paper by
CPI Antony Rowe, Chippenham, Wiltshire

ISBN 978–0–19–920353–6 (Hbk.)
978–0–19–920354–3 (Pbk.)

1 3 5 7 9 10 8 6 4 2

Acknowledgements

I wish to thank all those who contributed to this volume, especially those who agreed to update their bibliographies and supplement their original publications with a few further thoughts. To those who delivered their papers to me quickly, I apologize for the delay in seeing them into the light of day.

For their technical assistance, special thanks are due to Anke Rondholz, who helped at an early stage, and Christopher Simon, who made a mammoth effort to bring things together at the end. I also wish to thank Dorothy McCarthy at OUP for keeping me informed and on-task, and Michèle Lowrie for allowing me to sound her out about numerous matters both technical and scholarly.

Contents

Note on Translations

Five of the articles in this volume (Klingner, Labate, Pasoli, La Penna, Traina) appear here for the first time in English translation. All translations are mine (K.F.), but I had much help along the way. Klingner's massive 'Horazens Brief an Augustus' was a remarkable challenge, and I am especially thankful to Anke Rondholz for her very helpful first draft. Professor La Penna set me straight on several points of translation in his article. For helping clarify other mysteries of the Italian language (or for assuring me that the Italian writing was indeed mysterious) I wish to thank Andrea Cucchiarelli, Irene Peirano, and Tommaso Gazzarri. Vorrei ringraziarvi tutti per la vostra gentilezza.

Introduction: The Satires and Letters of Horace in Recent Scholarship

Kirk Freudenburg

The articles included in this volume have been chosen for their capacity to summarize, to inform, and to provoke. They do not represent, nor do they add up to, a recognizable consensus about Horace's hexameter poems, his two-books-each of satires (*Sermones*) and epistles (*Epistulae*). Rather, they represent a small fraction of the many fine resources that are now available for the study of these poems. In drawing this sampling of scholarship together, I have included articles that have been especially influential on recent Anglo-American scholarship, as well as several older and by now 'classic' articles that I think deserve a fresh hearing. Some of these works have, until now, been difficult to access because they are hidden in hard to find books or journals, or because they pose rather formidable linguistic challenges to students whose German or Italian has fallen on hard times. I have included yet other articles that are personal favourites; articles that taught me things that I did not manage to learn from any other source.

Despite their differences, all of the articles contained in the volume are remarkable for the way they do their work at multiple levels, moving from the basics of grammar, vocabulary, and syntax to issues of genre, socio-politics, and beyond. They underscore and exemplify the value of close reading, and of paying strict attention to detail, when those activities are not philological (dead-) ends in themselves. Instead, working from the specifics of the poetic page, these articles take us into the various complex and overlapping discursive systems (aesthetic, political, philosophical, sociological) that Horace's poems both arise from and seek to address. Even the oldest articles in this set concern themselves with the varied contexts of the poems' production, and therefore with the things that these poems express but do not, necessarily, say.

Though much of the best recent work on Horace has come in the form of monographs, the emphasis of this collection is, by necessity, upon free-standing articles that have appeared in the last thirty years. The result is that some really fine work has had to be left out. Another type of study that I have chosen to avoid, though I have thought it best to make certain exceptions to the rule, is that of the already-anthologized article. Such articles are widely available, as are volumes of general essays on Horace. Of these the most significant now are Rudd (1993b), Harrison (1995a), Woodman and Feeney (2002), and Harrison (2007a), as well as Martindale-Hopkins (1993), which is now the standard work on the reception of Horace in British writing from the sixteenth to the twentieth centuries. A further companion to Horace is slated to appear in 2009 (edited by Gregson Davis). Also widely available, and thus left out of this volume, are chapters in general volumes on the genres in which Horace wrote. I will have more to say about the contents and impacts of these below.

Since the early nineties the first book of Horace's *Sermones* has received a good deal of attention from critics, perhaps exceeding that received by the rest of his hexameter works combined. In fact, much of what is said about Horace as satirist tends to be based rather narrowly on observations drawn from his first book, with Book 2 being thought, at least since Fraenkel's *Horace* (1957), to contain less heart, and less Horace, and therefore to be less worth studying. Helping pierce the dark of Book 2 is Frances Muecke's (1993) commentary and translation, which is loaded with fresh observations on all the poems, besides gathering up and distilling the best observations and further possibilities contained in the commentaries that have come before. In addition, Paolo Fedeli's (1994) commentary on both books also produces refreshing new results by breaking poems down differently, in connected series of thematic sections, rather than line-by-line. Among recent general studies of Roman satire that have featured chapters on Horace, especially thorough and insightful are Hooley (2007) and Gowers (2005). Muecke (2007), though more limited in scope, provides an excellent survey of recent scholarship on the *Sermones*. Together these are the best short introductions to the *Sermones* now available in English. Among works that address Horatian satire within larger generic surveys, Rudd (1986) works out a taxonomy of themes, and Plaza (2006) looks at satire's mechanisms of humour, largely in Bakhtinian terms. This work provides a useful survey of the current lie of the land of humour theory, mapping certain currents in the analysis of Roman satire against those theories. Plaza's bibliographical survey includes dozens of studies from disciplines well outside the field of Classics. Keane (2006) observes the behaviour of Rome's moralizing satirists over time, watching how they adjust the authoritative poses they strike to help us make sense of the genre as a composite of multiple systems of criticism, moral correction, and entertainment.

One of the articles most responsible for spurring the recent upsurge in interest in the *Sermones* is Ian DuQuesnay's massive 1984 study of the 'propaganda value of *Sermones* I' (reprinted with fresh translations of the Latin in Chapter 2 below), an article that drew a strong critical response from Kennedy (1992). DuQuesnay sees Horace in his *Sermones* seeking to defuse suspicion of, and hatred towards, the new regime, by giving us tell-tale glimpses into the non-threatening and sunny reality of an enlightened administration, thus helping to make an utterly radical state of affairs seem somewhat less terribly radical. Despite the optimistic packaging of this argument, and a tendency to treat propaganda as the point of the book, DuQuesnay has unquestionably shown that, in its ethical argumentation, *Sermones* Book 1 is highly attuned to certain explosive political issues of Horace's day, and that these are slyly layered into the speaker's moral discourse under various, seemingly innocuous, ethical headings, such as *clementia, amicitia*, and the all-important *libertas*. Whether Horace does this to propagandize, or to obfuscate and provoke, is a question that I began asking in Freudenburg (1993), a book that owes much to DuQuesnay's basic idea that there is a good deal of the political that hides uncomfortably inside the ethical and aesthetic tenets of Book 1. That work, *The Walking Muse*, was concerned primarily with the philosophical (especially Greek rhetorical) background of Horace's theories of comedy and style in Book 1. My subsequent work in Freudenburg (2001) was much more about the social poetics of those tenets as ideas that played, smartly, uncomfortably, or otherwise, in the culture wars of late Triumviral and post-Actian Rome. In *Satires of Rome* I was concerned to show how Horace wrestles against his genre's past, both in his theorizing, and in the way he stages his own failure to speak. The poet's promotion of Greek aesthetic considerations, I argued, as refined as that may superficially seem (and we commonly do use this refinement to rescue Horace *qua* satirist from his detractors), does as much to provoke criticism as it does to defuse it. It was John Henderson who, in a series of articles on Roman satire, beginning with his classic 'Gendersong' in 1989, argued that the task of authorizing the satirist's voice as that of a 'real satirist' or not is one that we take upon ourselves, as we rush in to support whatever good cause we happen to see him fighting. That this cause is also always, and especially, 'ours', and that our rushing in to defend that cause (criticism as an act of authorization, highly invested in, and defined by, ideology) has the potential to tell on us (criticism as self-revelation, showing us our insides) has been the consistent message of Henderson in his various works on satire throughout the nineties, and now helpfully republished in Henderson (1998a) and (1999). His study of the mirroring of Poet/Pest in *Satire* 1.9 is included as Chapter 7 below.

Of the dozens of articles and book-chapters that have been written on Horace's first book of *Sermones* in recent years, I have chosen to include a rather early piece by James Zetzel (1980) on the structure of the book. Despite what Zetzel says in his postscript on p. 40–1 below, this piece has had an enormous impact on the current state of Horatian scholarship, as seen most recently, for example, in Cucchiarelli (2007) on the accrual of various senses of the book's structure in the epodes. Zetzel's article took a decisive step away from old (largely classical grammatical and nineteenth-century Germanic) paradigms of what constitutes a book's structure, focused as these were on overall architecture (as if seen from outer space rather than from the inside), on solid lines and symmetry, to focus on the book as something that unfolds its structure in the process of reading, offering images and ideas that accumulate as we move from one poem to the next. Reading it this way, we have to find our 'structural' bearings in other places, such as in our sense of the person who preaches or tells stories or otherwise converses from the written page. This is a person, Zetzel shows, who reveals himself to us slowly, first as a moral voice, seemingly alone and quite distant from his discerning patron; then as a literary thinker, a man with a political past, laughably colourful in many of his features; and finally as an insider, a man with many powerful friends, including the book's addressee, Maecenas. In several significant ways, Zetzel's approach to structure resembles Pasoli's (1965, reprinted as Chapter 17 below) 'connotative' approach to the poet's literary language in *Epistles* 2.2, because he shows how images accumulate meaning as one reads along. For example, he demonstrates the way that a moral valence accrues to the aesthetic description of Lucilius as 'muddy' (*lutulentus*) in *Satire* 1.4 by way of our encounter with a greedy fool who drowns in a swirl of mud in *Satire* 1.1.55–60. And it is exactly this slippage between aesthetic and moral (and political, philosophical, cultural, etc.) categories that is at the heart of much recent scholarship on the book.

Since Zetzel's ground-breaking study, many have taken up the question of how the speaker reveals himself in the course of Book 1, and as what. Gowers (2003) provides a full bibliographical survey of recent studies of the Horatian persona in her study of the poet's evasive autobiographical representations in *Sermones* Book 1. To the sources she cites, one can now add Barchiesi-Cucchiarelli (2005), on the satirist's body as a self-referential and cleverly generic symbol, and Harrison (2007b), who covers all the most significant autobiographical moments in the works of Horace, demonstrating that they consistently combine fantasy not with reality *per se*, but with contrived effects of realism (Barthes' 'reality effect'). The one 'persona' article featured in this volume is that of Turpin (1998, Chapter 4) which argues that the speaker of the diatribe satires (*Satire* 1.1–1.3) is not just an Epicurean, but a parody of an Epicurean insofar as he is comically obsessed with food, friendship, and sex. Nor is he just Maecenas' lesser friend in these poems, or a respected adviser to his 'king'. Rather he is easily taken for a hanger-on, a hungry parasite, who is humorously swept up into some very high company. The evidence that Turpin brings together to support his thesis is compelling, and at the very least it suggests that the moralist of these poems is tricked out in some fairly awkward colours. His performance leaves us to consider who he is, what we are to do with him, and what we are to make of these poems as . . . if not moral discourse, then what? Related to the topic of the poet and his self-performance is the '*Libertino patre natus*' piece by Gordon Williams (1995, Chapter 5), which fashions a good social-historical case for Horace's true experience being stretched in the claim 'I am the son of a freed slave'. Since the time of Fiske (1920) it was recognized that the claim has a literary and philosophical precedent in the words of Bion of Borysthenes to Antigonus Gonatas. Moles (2007) provides a complete analysis of the Bion analogy in Horace and is now the best short introduction to the philosophical contents of Horace's poetry in its many forms.

Emily Gowers's (1993b) study of *Satire* 1.5 (Chapter 6) takes up the issue of the speaker's humorous failings, his political reticence, and his evasiveness, in a poem that is as surprising for what it does not say as it is for the roads it does not take. Gowers carefully works through the social and emotional details of the poem not to prove, yet again, that Horace dodges what we want to know, but to probe into why we want to know it, and thus to analyse the kinds of interrogations we make of Horatian *Sermo* more generally. The problem, and the paradox, of the un-satiric satirist of *Sermones* Book 1 has been further explored by Schlegel (2005). The programmatic import of *Satire* 1.5, as the second half of a set with 1.4 (as practice to theory), has been fully analysed by Cucchiarelli (2001), a study that also shows the rich iambic and Greek Old Comic trappings of the poem, as well as of the theories that inform it. Labate (1996, Chapter 3), puts us in the shoes of the ancient grammarian as he attempts to categorize the *Sermones* according to existing theories of genre. He shows that the special problem of satire, in its super-abundance (its *saturitas*) of suitable material (fables, preaching, anecdotes, etc.) forced the ancient theorists of satire to shift away from strict categorization according to content and metrical form, and to look to the special shaping, and integrating, of content to form that comes from the speaker's self-performance, especially through his strong, continuous presence in the poems, his conversational self-exposure, and his combativeness, which are the two poles of the satirist's performance that Horace took from Lucilius. This means that, for Horace, his best means of remaking the genre into a more polished entity was to be found in refinements to the attitudes and contours of the self he projects. Zetzel (2002) has subsequently shown that Horace is both Callimachean and anti-Callimachean in his brushing up of satire, and, much as I tried to do in *Satires of Rome,* he shows that 'Callimachean satire' is a very odd notion indeed; that it was not, in fact, what Horace was after nor what his *Sermones* can be taken to represent. These poems, he shows, are well on their way to being 'Augustan', and this at a time when Octavian is not yet Augustus. Scodel (1987) reached some strikingly similar conclusions in her analysis of the Callimachean background of *Satire* 1.10. Scodel's article, included in updated form as Chapter 8, shows that, in picking a fight with his critics over issues of linguistic purity, Horace imitates Callimachus' thirteenth *Iamb* in a creative, and largely anti-Callimachean way, in order to prove a solidly Callimachean point about how creative imitation differs fundamentally from slavish adherence to an original, even when that original happens to be Callimachus (or, by extension, Lucilius). In other words, Horace can show his Callimachean credentials only by departing creatively from Callimachus in his imitation of Callimachus' famous fight in defence of *polyeideia* ('multiformity') and the mixing of dialects. This is a fight that Horace wages against purists of a different sort; namely, those Late Republican neoteric fans of Catullus and Lucilius who were loudly claiming to know Callimachus best. *Satire* 1.10, Scodel shows, is full of glib, Callimachean clichés, and Horace overdoes and mishandles some of the theories he draws from Callimachus in order to let us hear just how hackneyed post-Catullan Callimacheanism had come to sound. This 'whither Roman Alexandrianism' idea comports well with Zetzel's thesis. Above all, both articles show that one has to be awfully careful in approaching theorist-Horace with expectations of orthodoxy, authority, and easy answers, especially when that theory is itself cast in the form of satire.

Scholarship on Book 2 of the *Sermones* has tended to focus on three poems in particular (1, 6, 8), with much recent attention paid to the bookends of poems 1 and 8. These are, as it were, the New York and California of the book that critics visit to structure their sense of the whole. A notable exception to this bi-coastal, 'fly-over' approach is Oliensis's (1998a) chapter on the 'self-incriminating satirist of satires 2' which prompted some of my own observations about the lost and searching nature of the book in Freudenburg (2006).

The conversation with Trebatius in 2.1 has awakened much recent interest in the topic of satire and the law. The most rigorous and legally informed among these studies are the recent contributions of Muecke (1995), McGinn (2001), and Lowrie (2005). But I chose to include in this volume a short article on the topic by Jeffrey Tatum (1998, Chapter 9), and I did so not only because it is suitably concise, but especially because it is very good at showing the interpenetration of the legal with the aesthetic and cultural-moral in *Satire* 2.1, which is largely the most serious point that pokes through the poem's concluding pun. That interpenetration, Tatum shows, is the poem's rather nasty, albeit playfully nasty, point, and it may just signal that jurisprudence no longer matters in the way it once did in a new world where one man's aesthetic, legal, and moral judgement trumps all. Other useful studies concerning satire and the law are Cloud (1989), Mazurek (1997), and Ruffel (2003), with the last of these being exceptionally well informed on the matter of poetic aggression in Late Republican poetry more generally. As mentioned, second in line to *Satire* 2.1 in terms of the scholarly attention it has recently received is the book's concluding poem, 2.8, the Dinner Party of Nasidienus. This poem, besides being important to its book, is important to the history of Roman satire for the several remakings it underwent, most notably, as Bodel (1999) shows, by Petronius in the *Cena Trimalchionis* and by Juvenal in his fifth satire. On the latter, see Braund (1996: 304–5). Studies focused more tightly on the poem's programmatic function, its literary allusiveness, and its metapoetic potentials include Freudenburg (1995), Caston (1997), Oliensis (1998b), and Marchesi (2005), all of which owe a great debt to Gowers (1993a), a work that, within its grand scope, fully explores the food imagery of Book 2 (which far exceeds that of Book 1) and the literary-cultural and philosophical ramifications of the 'satire as feast' analogy.

Some of the best new work on Horace's epistles has come in the form of commentaries: Mayer (1994) on Book 1; Rudd (1989) on Book 2 and the *ars Poetica*; Fedeli (1997) on both books; Horsfall (1993a) on *Ep.* 1.7 and Citti (1994) on *Ep.* 1.5. A great mass of scholarship has been devoted to individual poems and themes, but Kilpatrick has written informative book-length introductions (1986 and 1990) to both books. These, along with Ferri (2007), the volume introductions of Mayer and Rudd, as well as the insightful chapter of

Armstrong (1989), are rich in bibliographical resources and summary analysis that will help orient the reader in the main issues of scholarship up to the early nineties. Ferri (1993) presents a more particular approach to the book, reading *Epistles* Book 1 as a deliberate retreat from hard Epicurean didactic, with each letter a tentative experiment in talking to friends, and in teaching them, that finds Horace stepping back from certain of his earlier Lucretian sureties, and from the harder convictions of his youth, in friendly discourses spoken in self-consciously quiet and uncertain tones. An alternate approach to the topic of Lucretian didacticism in Horace's first book of letters is Morrison (2007), who draws on Fowler (2000a) and dePretis (2004) to argue that the engagement of these letters with Lucretius extends well beyond their frequent allusions to the lessons and rhetorical tones of the *De Rerum Natura* to include its sense of temporal sequence in the plot it implies of a student's moral progress. Horace, Morrison argues, stars in the role of the backslider searching for right living and spiritual peace. Johnson (1993) saw similar plot lines running through the book, especially in the poet's ongoing struggle to achieve *libertas*. But Johnson's study is unusual for the way it downplays the issue of the poet's philosophical allegiances to let him speak as a personal poet, and thus to let him have his way when he tells us not to try to pin him down. That, the poet's chafing against restrictions, against our boxing him into already settled notions of genre, society, metre, self, is a thread that runs through Horace's hexameter works, and through the whole of his poetry more generally. Johnson provides a lively and illuminating analysis of the poet's struggle for freedom, in his philosophy, in his friendly relations, and his art, as he performs that struggle as an ongoing and open-ended enterprise in *Epistles* Book 1.

The articles on the first book of the *Epistles* included for republication in this volume are primarily concerned with the book's philosophical character and purpose. All of them take seriously the philosophical programme announced in the first poem, and the earliest of these, a well-known piece by Macleod (1979a, Chapter 10), takes to heart the idea of Horace's 'conversion' to philosophy as the truth of his later life. This article sets out, helpfully, to defamiliarize us in our reading of the book by taking us into an alien world where the study of moral philosophy was much less the technical and academic concern that it is today, and much more a lived pursuit, and a way of arming oneself intellectually and emotionally for the task of living a decent life. Moral philosophies were systematized and preached by thinkers who were thought to have achieved higher levels of insight and contentment. Their doctrines were trafficked in by the Roman elite, sometimes very seriously as we see in the case of Cicero, but more often as lessons once learned in school and easily cheapened by the demands of real life, or simply left behind. It is largely to men such as these, Macleod argues, the young, second-tier captains of commerce, poetry, and statesmanship who could not be bothered with taking time for their inner selves, that Horace, from his own flawed and wobbly perspective, addresses himself in his first book, in letters of 'subtle diplomacy' that are his own best means of self-improvement. Harrison (1995a) finds precedent for this project, and for the writer it projects as fallible but trying, in earlier books of letters from philosophers to students and friends, and he demonstrates that there is a telling consistency between ancient epistolographical theory and what Horace actually does in *Epistles* Book 1: both put a high value upon concision and simplicity, and both are antipathetic towards engaging in dialectical hair-splitting, or adopting a dogmatic tone. Harrison describes the particular advantages of the letter form for philosophical protreptic, locating this especially in the letter's ability to package lessons in very personal terms, and to express hard philosophical truths through home-spun metaphors, and by reference to colourful snatches of daily life (a lopsided haircut, an ill-fitting shoe); all of which will have a profound impact on Seneca in his letters to Lucilius.

The last two decades have been particularly rich in studies attempting to trace the precise provenance of Horace's philosophical lessons in Book 1. Some scholars have sought to demonstrate that Horace, despite the protestations of *Ep.* 1.1, is heavily invested in the teachings of a particular philosopher or school. Traina (1991, Chapter 12), in a new English translation, is an excellent recent example of this trend, which now includes works by Ferri (1993), Moles (1986 and 1995), and Armstrong (2004). Traina provides a complete survey of the doxographical sources on Aristippus to argue that, in the first book of his epistles, Horace is, at heart, an Aristippean who is subject to episodic bouts of Stoic fancy. A fuller study of the topic that owes much to Traina's nuanced, intertextualist methods while respectfully disagreeing with his results is Moles (2002, Chapter 13). This article demonstrates how specific tenets and sayings of particular philosophers and schools are woven deeply into the very fabric of these poems, encountered in much the same way that earlier epic materials are encountered as meaning-filled allusions in Virgil's *Aeneid.* The main points of contact, Moles shows, are with Cicero, Aristippus, Diogenes, Epicurus, Socrates, and especially with the softer (Middle) Stoicism of Panaetius. But he uses this evidence not to argue, as many have, that Horace's adaptability, his failure of orthodoxy, constitutes a failure to deliver serious philosophy. Rather, he argues that his failure to be boxed in is his way of being philosophical in these letters, and of taking to heart (by showing it in action) the letters' core message of *autarkeia* (self-determination). Such philosophical adaptability allows the poet to address the many different needs of his friends by availing him of whatever philosophical perspective(s) that each man's individual needs dictate. Moles further argues that, when it comes to the topic of the poet's withdrawing from city life, and his trying to become himself in the company of powerful men such as Maecenas and Augustus, the distant and philosophical becomes much more immediate, politically relevant, and grim.

Horace's long, epistolary musings on literature, in his letters to Augustus (*Ep.* 2.1), to Florus (2.2), and to the Pisones (the *Ars Poetica*) constitute some of the least studied and worst accounted for poems in the Horatian corpus. For that reason I have included in this volume several older, and by now 'classic' pieces, originally in German and Italian, that provide excellent summaries of the contents, structures, and basic arguments of these poems, even as they introduce some of their own approaches that we would still do well to consider. Klingner (1950, Chapter 14) was the first major study of the epistle to Augustus since Vahlen and Heinze. The nineteenth-century analysts, he shows, had done violence to both the letter to Augustus and to the *Ars* in their attempts to make them conform to classical notions of seamlessness and structural solidity. Klingner, refreshingly, argues that the letter to Augustus is a *sermo*, as Horace himself seems to indicate, and that its structure should therefore be read conversationally, as an unfolding mix of spontaneity and calculation. Klingner takes us through this conversation, paying special attention to its sudden directional shifts. He teases out the unspoken or hinted at threads that connect one thought to the next and bind the whole together, showing that often it is the mention of a single word that causes the poet to drop one topic and take up another. But he also regards the conversationalist of the poem as an ironist and a rogue whose attitudes and assumptions shift in unforeseen directions as his conversation proceeds. Klingner's observation that the presence of Orbilius, the poet's sadistic old schoolmaster (in line 71), sends a shudder through the theoretical argument itself, causing Horace to play, momentarily, the respectable schoolboy who is properly reverential towards the grand old masters of Roman poetry, is just one of the many gems that make this article timeless and well worth having in English. La Penna's (1950, Chapter 16) article of the same year focuses more narrowly on the interaction between the *Ars* and the letter to Augustus, and it explains their overly strong emphasis on drama as conditioned by, and a commentary upon, Augustus' programme of restoring the Latin theatre. This is a conclusion that Klingner came to, in his own way, as well. Both articles make clear that Horace's assessment of that project, and of the Rome and the Romans of Augustus' aesthetic remaking, is anything but rosy.

Feeney (2002a, Chapter 15), republished with minor updates, takes up the topic of the interplay between the poet and the *princeps* in the letter to Augustus, elaborating on an idea that he first made in Feeney (1992) on free speech under the principate. Informing the later piece on *Ep.* 2.1 are two landmark studies by Fowler (1995) on the aesthetics of politics in Rome (now freshly republished in the companion volume to this one, Michèle Lowrie (ed.), *Horace: Odes and Epodes*) and Barchiesi (1993) on Horace's *Ep.* 2.1 and Ovid's *Tristia* Book 2. Feeney analyses the thorough interpenetration of the political with the aesthetic in the letter to Augustus in matters of authority and canonization, creativity, *libertas*, and so on. And he shows just how uncannily enmeshed and inseparable Horace and Augustus have become: both have sought immortality through their efforts. Both have struggled to please and to improve a fickle, and sometimes recalcitrant, populace. And, by now, both are struggling alone. Feeney shows Horace miming Augustus once again in his struggles to deal with a recalcitrant literary-historical tradition that put things into ready-made boxes (generic canons, hierarchies, pithy one-line distillations of a poet's entire life's *oeuvre*) that could not begin to contain achievements such as his own that were bold and genre-defying. Like Horace in the realm of his 'immortal' poetry, Augustus cannot be shoved into existing canons of 'human' achievement. Nor could Horace write of those achievements in the ways that others, such as Choerilus and Cicero, had tried, only to have their pages end up as fish-wrap. Much of the theorizing of this letter, Feeney shows, is itself genre-defying, unique to Horace, and terribly funny. Lowrie (2002) delivers an acute analysis of some of the same issues, working back from the poem's mock-Ciceronian conclusion to show that Cicero is a strong ghostly presence throughout *Ep.* 2.1, and that the relationship of author to statesman in the poem is figured through Cicero, and significantly complicated by his (in-)famous example.

In her chapter on the *Ars Poetica*, Oliensis (1998a, Chapter 19) takes up an idea introduced by Armstrong (1993) that treats the *Ars* as referencing, and extending from, Republican educational practices that sought to produce solid young men of the right kind. This '*De Officiis* in aesthetic dress', Oliensis argues, finds the poet addressing the 'Piso boys' on matters of literature by means of sententious quips and chestnuts of right thinking that the Roman elite used to keep their world straight, and to make sure that everything kept its proper, hierarchical place. This casting of literary theory as bound to the old rules of social decorum finds the speaker both teaching his lessons to his wards, as it were, and satirizing them both (lessons and wards) at the same time. But it also finds him being less than polite in a poem obsessed with *politesse*, and often breaking his own rules (especially with his indecorous leech at the poem's tail-end) as he goes. It was largely based on my reading of this chapter, as well as the fine summary introduction to *Ep.* 2.2 of Pasoli (1965, Chapter 17), that I came to write on the odd configuring of the censor-critic in the letter to Florus in Freudenburg (2002b, Chapter 18). In this article I look to the issue of how themes and theories are tugged at and shaped by the unseen gravitational forces of the letter's various further audiences and addressees, especially by Augustus himself. The idea that letters, theorized as they were in antiquity as one side of a conversation, actively incorporate their addressees not as blank screens that receive whatever information is projected against them, but as active participants in the arguments they formulate, was recently taken up by Griffin (1995) and Leach (1999) in their studies of Cicero's letters to his friends. Although I was unaware of these studies when I first wrote the piece, their findings comport well with the main point I argue: that the letter to Florus is focalized through Florus, or at least to some degree shaped by his obsessions and legal mindset. Figured in this way, Horace's lessons invite us to have a look around that mindset, to get comfortable with it if we can, and thus to consider how poetic and political matters are strangely construed therein—exotically, idiotically, or otherwise.

Readers will not all find the same value in these articles that I have. Still, having them all together in this single volume should help students of Horace gain a representative sense of how his hexameter works have been received in recent criticism, thus laying the ground-work for future studies in which they will say something new for themselves.

Part I

Horace's *Sermones*

1

Horace's *Liber Sermonum*: The Structure of Ambiguity

James E. G. Zetzel
D. M. Eric Guttmann

Order, structure and unity, in dealing with a book of poems, are concepts notoriously difficult to define. If one speaks of the structure of an individual poem—except in those portions of Catullus or Propertius where one can never be quite certain where one poem begins and the other ends—there is at least the reassuring fact that the poet meant it to have some unity. While critics may debate about whether there is logical argument, continuity of imagery, ring composition or some other form of deliberate patterning designed by the poet, there is usually no doubt that there is something, and that, whatever it is, it has an important effect on the meaning of the entire poem. In dealing with a book of poems, unfortunately, that is not the case. Even apart from the difficulty of determining whether the arrangement—or an arrangement—was the creation of the poet or merely of a subsequent editor or scribe (and for Latin poetry the recent debate over the *Liber Catulli* comes to mind),[1] it is rare that the poet provides clear indications of arrangement or continuity. The persona of the poet may vary, the overt subject may change, and only rarely (as, for instance, in the case of Propertius 1.7 and 1.9) does the author provide a clear and objective link between one poem and another, a link visible enough to allay the doubts of those scholars

---

[1] See most recently Clausen 1976 with references to the previous literature.

who feel that such structures are more often in the mind of the critic than in the intention of the poet.

One or two books of poems do provide objective assurance to the critic, in the form of numerical patterns. Virgil's *Eclogues* and the *Monobiblos* of Propertius, both investigated by Otto Skutsch, are the clearest examples; but even in those striking cases not all scholars are willing to recognize the overwhelming evidence of the calculator nor, even if it is accepted, is the interpretation of the numbers as obvious as one might wish.[2] I do not intend here to discuss those patterns and their possible interpretations; it is, however, important to accept them as being there, because they alone provide evidence that the poet intended a structure. We may not agree on the interpretation, but we cannot deny the fact. And it is the obvious structural labor of Virgil in the *Eclogues* that provides the model against which to examine the arrangement of Horace's *Liber Sermonum*.[3]

Structure, at least as far as modern critics have been concerned, has never been a major element of Horace's book. The two major critical works of recent years that deal with the *Satires* devote little space to the arrangement of the first book;[4] and while a complex structure for Book 2 was recognized long ago, the critical appreciation of the first book as a book is very recent and has for the most part been limited to the crude structure of the triadic arrangement or to the

[2] See Skutsch 1963 on Propertius 1 and Skutsch 1969 on the *Eclogues*. The numerical structure of the *Eclogues* is rejected by the most recent editor, Coleman 1977: 18f.; for a thorough review of the question see Van Sickle 1978: 17–37.

[3] I have not here attempted to analyze in detail parallels between the *Eclogues* and the *Sermones*, although it is a topic of some importance. Most critics agree that Horace took the number 10 from Virgil as well as the division at poem 6 marked by a renewed invocation: so Port 1926: 288, Kiessling-Heinze 1961: xxii, Fraenkel 1957: 112, Büchner 1962: 123, Ludwig 1968: 321–2, and even Coffey 1976: 81 who, however, also remarks that 'it would have been inappropriate for the writer of an informal *libellus* to assemble his conversation pieces with the contrived artifice that was a mark of some of the major books of Augustan poetry'. Both Witte 1923 and Van Rooy 1973 believe in the close dependence of the *Satires* on the *Eclogues*, but the former's argument is based in part on vague structural similarities, in part on a mistaken belief that both books of *Satires* were published together, after the *Georgics* had been published; the latter's attempt to find precise correspondences between each Satire and the parallel Eclogue is, not surprisingly, unconvincing.

[4] Fraenkel 1957 and Rudd 1966. Rudd 1976: 142–4 discusses structure, but finds that the evidence demonstrates 'texture' rather than 'architecture'.

connections between two or three poems.[5] What is offered here is consequently tentative; and as my view of the structure of the whole book necessarily involves some differences in the interpretation of individual poems, some portions of the argument will have to be reserved for future detailed exposition.[6]

In many ways, of course, comparison with the *Eclogues*, whose similarities to the *Sermones* have long been recognized, has led scholars to belittle the conscious artistry of Horace's book. Pastoral poetry is by its very nature artificial, elegant and in many ways precious, and Virgil's book is the supreme example of that genre. The poetic skill apparent in every verse uttered by Virgil's alleged rustics leads the reader, by the very incongruity between art and its setting, to expect all the artifice that a great poet can produce. There is less shock, therefore, in accepting not only elaborate numerical patterns, but the whole delicate counterpoint between the different ways of aligning the poems, kaleidoscopic variations of emphasis that make the stress fall on now one, and now another poem. The book of the *Eclogues* is, as Clausen has said, one of the few perfect books.[7]

The *Liber Sermonum* could scarcely be credited with the supreme literary elegance of the *Liber Bucolicon*. In part, that is a matter of its genre. While bucolic poetry was an Alexandrian form, and had to have all the attendant felicities of style and wit, *sermo* had none of that tradition. It is derived from the two traditions of Lucilian satire and Hellenistic diatribe, both of which prided themselves on plain

---

[5] On the structure of Book 2 see below, n. 43; also Boll 1913 and Port 1926: 288–91. The latter's article is still a useful survey of the subject of arranged books of poetry. While Boll believed in a complex structure for Book 2, he thought (45) that the poems of Book 1 were not conceived with any structure in mind and therefore could not be arranged symmetrically. On the triadic structure of Book 1 see Kiessling-Heinze 1961: xxii, Wili 1948: 72. Van Rooy's seven articles constitute the most significant attempt to progress beyond that, but by seeing too much pattern he obscures what is important; he is also less interested in interpretation than in pure pattern. For a summary of work on the subject to 1968, see Van Rooy 1968: 38–40; since then, other than his own articles, the most important works are Ludwig 1968 and Rambaux 1971.

[6] As I am not dealing in any detail with the contents of individual poems, I wish to record here my great debt to the work of W. S. Anderson, who is the first modern critic to take the *Satires* seriously as poetry (for a firm statement, see Anderson 1963a: 29). While I differ with him on the interpretation of many poems, and in general take them less seriously than he does, I do so with considerable hesitation.

[7] Clausen 1964: 193.

speech—that is the basic meaning of *sermo*—and personal state-ment.[8] The wit that these forms exhibited was in the funny story or in parody, not in the allusive humor and delicate reminiscence that characterizes the Alexandrian tradition. Horace himself describes Lucilius' works as revealing his life as if spread out on a votive tablet (2.1.32–34):

> quo fit ut omnis
> uotiua pateat ueluti descripta tabella
> uita senis,

by which it comes about that the old man's whole life lies open as if laid out on a votive tablet

and he goes on to say that Lucilius is his model in writing satire. It is therefore not entirely unreasonable to consider satire in general, and the *Liber Sermonum* in particular, not as literature at all, but as autobiography. And artful literary structure is not what we are usually taught to expect in an autobiography, even less in a diary or votive tablet. Hence, the *Satires* are normally read not only as discrete poems—many modern critics to be sure are not guilty of this fallacy to the same degree as Fraenkel and Rudd—independent of any arrangement in their book, but as naive and totally unironic state-ments; not, finally, as poetry, but as diary.[9]

Some of this may sound overstated, or at best elementary, but the fact remains that analysis of the *Satires*—of all ancient satire—is far less advanced than analysis of other, more obviously 'literary' works. And while it is rare nowadays to find the occasional ostrich who still worries about the order of composition of the *Eclogues*,[10] questions

---

[8] For a summary of the traditions see Coffey 1976: 68–9, 92–6.

[9] Coffey 1976: 90 believes that Lucilius' work was 'an unabashed exposé' of his life, while Horace's was 'a calculated defense of his career and way of life' embodying some fiction; Fraenkel 1957: 104–5 took the description of Lucilius at 2.1.32–4 to be applicable to Horace as well as Lucilius. It is, of course, doubtful that Horace literally meant that Lucilius' verse was his diary; it too was literary artifice, although to what degree must remain uncertain; cf. Anderson 1963a: 18–19. As far as autobiography is concerned, it may be salutary to recall that it too is a highly artificial form: Edward Gibbon's famous and detailed account in his *Memoirs* of the inspiration for *The Decline and Fall of the Roman Empire* exists in no less than three versions, while his Journal, to which he refers, contains no such passage. See Gibbon 1966: 136, 304–5.

[10] Notably Coleman 1977: 14–21.

of fact and date still occur with depressing regularity in dealing with the *Satires*, and even with the *Epodes*.[11] Before one can deal with the organization of the *Liber Sermonum*, it is necessary to show briefly once more that it is a work of literature, not of history, that it is not necessary—indeed it is harmful—to take the poems as straightforward statements with only a surface meaning, and that one can not, under any circumstances, accept as objective truth anything in the poems. The reality of the book, as of all books of poetry, *may* represent objective reality, but there is no reason for that to be the case. And in the case of *Satires* 1, indeed, acceptance of everything said in the book as fact can only lead to the conclusion that Horace is the most careless and absent-minded of poets, or that he is at best a half-wit.

On the very simplest level—normally disregarded by biographical interpreters—one must consider the first-person singular in the book. One begins in the first poem with a first-person address to Maecenas. That first person is thought to represent the ideas of Horace; likewise, the literary history and judgments of the fourth poem are the thoughts of that same Horace; the autobiographical narratives of 5, 6, 7, and 9 are reports of the real Horace's real life, and so on. But what then of the eighth poem? (1.8.1–3):

> Olim truncus eram ficulnus, inutile lignum,
> cum faber, incertus scamnum faceretne Priapum,
> maluit esse deum. deus inde ego...

Once I was a fig-tree trunk, a useless piece of wood, when a carpenter, uncertain whether to make a stool or Priapus, preferred it to be a god. Since then I am a god...

It is a trivial observation to point out that Horace was never a tree trunk, nor a god, nor was he permanently attached to the Esquiline Hill. This poem is the most elementary sort of personification, and no one would dream of taking it as autobiography. But why, then, should we assume that the persona of the rest of the book is any more autobiographical? Those speakers, to be sure, are human, and bear some resemblance to what we think we know of the real Horace; but it might also be pointed out that Priapus' egotism and cowardice are

[11] On the *Satires* see most recently Coffey 1976: 66–7.

not unlike that of the speaker of the ninth poem,[12] and his incontinence (in this case farting) has some relationship to that of the fifth. I need not labor the point: 'Horace' like 'Priapus' can only be examined as a literary fiction in the context of the book; they are no more accurate representations of Horace himself than Tityrus and his friends are of the real Virgil. What is misleading is that the conventions of satire demand that the fictional speaker be given the mask of the real author, while those of bucolic demand that it be a shepherd.[13]

We should also look skeptically at what Horace says about his own background and about his reasons for writing satire. In the fourth poem, Horace emphasizes the didactic and moral element in his poetry; he writes this type of verse, he says, because his father used to form his character by proposing specific individuals as examples to be followed or shunned (4.105–30). It is mildly troublesome to note that in the same poem (4.1–7, 51–52), he implies that he is doing so as the direct heir of the Old Comedy *via* Lucilius, and that there is a high public moral purpose to his and their poetry. These passages have been harmonized by some modern critics, as giving two different partial explanations, one personal and one poetic, for the same phenomenon,[14] but it is surely not coincidental that the Lucilian explanation follows immediately upon a series of poems that appear to be public moral homilies, while the personal motive precedes two poems that concern the speaker's own life. It should also be noticed that the public moral tone disappears almost entirely from the book at this point. Even more inconsistent, of course, is the obviously ironic reason for writing satire that is given at the end of the book, in the tenth poem: there, he says, he took up satire because it was the only genre that had not had a successful modern

[12] On the character of Priapus see Anderson 1972: 8–12, Stahl 1974: 38.

[13] On this convention, see Kernan 1959 chapter 1, particularly 14–18, Anderson 1963a: 16–17, Dessen 1968: 6–9. In many respects, it is possible to see Horatian satire as first-person pastoral, employing the word in the sense used by Empson, who speaks (1974: 22) of 'the pastoral process of putting the complex into the simple.' Note also Kernan 1959: 18: 'Somehow the satirist seems always to come from a world of pastoral innocence and kindness.'

[14] So Van Rooy 1968: 66; cf. also Kiessling-Heinze 1961: 68–9, who say that Horace only implies his descent from Old Comedy in order not to obscure the origin in 'Erlebnis und Bedürfnis'.

exponent.[15] And as for Horace's father, whose portrait in the sixth satire was so dear to the hearts of Sellar and Fraenkel,[16] need it be pointed out that that poor freedman, who seems to have had to struggle to put his son through school, was wealthy enough to leave his son the census of a Roman *eques*?[17]

As a final example of the non-factual nature of the *Sermones*, one should consider what is at least implied about Lucilian satire and his own in the fourth and fifth poems. The implicit background of the fourth satire is that Horace has been criticized for personal attacks, as represented by poems 1–3, and one of his replies is that in so doing he is following the moral purpose of Lucilius, who is himself follow-ing the Old Comedy. But, although every section of this summary has been taken as objective truth by at least some modern critics, in context none of it is true. The attacks on public figures were not the sole aim of Aristophanes and his contemporaries, nor do they seem to have been Lucilius' only interest—and that is surely the only possible translation of *hinc omnis pendet Lucilius* (4.6: 'all Lucilius hangs from this')—nor is personal attack in the Lucilian mode of any great importance in the first poems of Horace's book.[18] While there is some merit in comparing Lucilius' attacks on Lentulus Lupus and others with Aristophanes' on Cleon, nothing in Horace has either the sharp wit or the sustained vitriol of either of them.[19] And, as if to underline the falsity of his own statements about Lucilius in the

---

[15] Stahl 1974: 27–28, like Wili 1948: 82–83, appears to take seriously two explan-ations, one based on the moral tradition and the other on what he calls 'den formal-poetologischen, dass im Kreis der Dichter um Maecenas ihm die Pflege der Satire nach der anspruchvollen Mass-Staben der Neuen Dichtung zugefallen sei'. He does, however, seem to recognize the inconsistency of the two explanations in 4.

[16] Fraenkel 1957: 103 citing with approval the opinion of W. Sellar.

[17] See Taylor 1968: 477–9 with reference to her previous discussion of the subject.

[18] This is often taken as a genuine piece of Varronian literary theory, which it may be (but see Lejay 1911: xlvii–xlviii), meant seriously by Horace; so Fraenkel 1957: 126, Brink 1963: 156–7. Others who do not accept this view of its origin still take it as a serious self-defense; so Lejay 1911: 96, Kiessling-Heinze 1961: xxi, Wili 1948: 71, Rudd 1966: 88–9, Van Rooy 1968: 60.

[19] Despite the fact that most of the persons named in the first three poems are either dead, fictional or insignificant, it is still repeated (e.g. by Rudd 1966: 88) that Horace had to defend himself against the charge of having made personal attacks. Fraenkel 1957: 88–9 rightly remarked of the characters of 1.3 that 'they are...mere ghosts'; even Rudd 1966: 133–8 can find Sallust alone to be a major figure, to which van Rooy 1968: 70 added Fausta. She was probably alive, but was notorious for her

fourth poem, the next one, which is the most obvious imitation of Lucilius, has nothing to do with the tradition of personal attack.[20]

In short, while any statement in Horace's book taken out of its context may sound perfectly reasonable, it cannot be assumed that it represents the considered opinion of the poet. All relevant information must be included. At times, the context of the individual poem shows a motivation for the statements—as about his father's advice in 4 or his poverty in 6—which should at least cause some hesitation in the critic's mind. And at times, the larger context of the book casts doubt on the significance of individual statements or poems. Horace is perhaps the most ironic and contradictory poet of antiquity; to take anything that he says as completely sincere is to ignore his style and his intention. As Reuben Brower rightly said, 'Horace can be convincingly serious only when it is certain that no one will take him quite seriously.'[21]

The question of the significance of the fourth satire, and of the criticism of Horace's first poems included in it, leads directly to the first problem concerning the arrangement of the book. It will be obvious that I do not consider historical chronology to be of any use, but once again it is necessary to set forth a few observations, and to draw the logical conclusions. I regard it as axiomatic in dealing with the arrangement of books of poetry that one can not speak of relative chronology within the book. In the case of the *Liber Sermonum*, the fact that the seventh poem refers to events of the late 40s BCE does not mean that the poem was written then, not only because there are elements in it designed to be read with both the third and fifth poems (at least), poems whose dramatic date is clearly later, but because once it is recognized that the book is arranged with some intention by the author it is clear that the poems, even if preliminary versions

adultery (cf. Syme 1964a: 278–80)—including an affair with Sallust, on whom see below, n. 26. Coffey's observation (1976: 91) seems apt: 'In general no living person of note was pointed out as an example of immorality.'

[20] Most scholars recognize that Lucilius is the link between 4 and 5, but fail to see any contradiction between the two views of Lucilius; so Port 1926: 289. Kiessling-Heinze 1961: 88–9 suggest that 5 was written with greater care in order to contrast with the sloppiness of Lucilius criticized in 4.

[21] Brower 1959: 162; his chapter on Horace remains the best introduction to the *Satires* in English.

were written at various times, must have been revised together to make the book. Thus, the question about *Satire* 7 is not when it was written relative to the other poems, but why the poet chose to include a poem referring to events of the Civil Wars in a book published in or after 35 BCE. So also in dealing with the vexed problem of the *Fourth Eclogue*: granted that the dramatic date of the poem is 40 BCE, the actual date cannot be proven to be earlier than the date of publication. Any interpretation based on isolating the poem from its context is doomed from the beginning.[22] The only significant chronology in a *liber* of this sort is that of unrolling the book: that we are to read the first poem before the second, the second before the third. The order of reading creates its own dramatic time, and neither the *Eclogues* nor the *Satires* ever violate it. Any interpretation that takes the poems out of order separates them from the literal unrolling of time and ignores the poet's clear intention.

What, then, are we to make of the criticisms of *Satires* 1–3 that are embedded in *Satire* 4? In that poem, while defending his satire against supposed critics, Horace quotes one verse from the second poem and alludes to portions of the first three.[23] In the same way, the tenth poem summarizes the opening of the fourth, and deals with implicit criticisms of his view of Lucilius.[24] The usual critical response has been to believe that the first three poems had been read and criticized for the personal attacks in them, and that the fourth poem is a real reply to real criticisms.[25] And yet, is there any objective evidence that such criticisms ever took place, that the first three

---

[22] The same is clearly true of the sixteenth Epode, in a book which was not published until after Actium. The whole *Prioritatsfrage* between the fourth Eclogue and the sixteenth Epode is misleading: the dramatic date tells us nothing, and the only safe basis for investigation is the date of completion of the book. Horace *must* have known the fourth Eclogue before 30, while Virgil *may* have known of the sixteenth Epode by 35. On the internal chronology of the Eclogues see now Van Sickle 1978: 24–7.

[23] Thus 4.26ff. seems to refer to the first two satires; 4.48–9 to 2.20, 4.81–4 to 3, 4.92 is a quotation of 2.27, Horace's father's advice at 4.107ff. refers to 1.73ff., 2.7ff., 2.55–6, 2.31–2, while 4.130 refers to 3.20. Not all these allusions are precise, but they make 4 in some ways a summary of 1–3.

[24] 1.10.1–4.

[25] See above, n. 18. On 10 as a reply to critics of 4, see Lejay 1911: 250, Kiessling-Heinze 1961: 155–6, Brink 1963: 165, Rudd 1966: 92, Van Rooy 1970a: 8, Coffey 1976: 80.

poems had been known to any large public? Horace himself disposes
of the possible answer, that he had recited them publicly (4.22–3):

> cum mea nemo
> scripta legat, uolgo recitare timentis...

since nobody ever reads my writings, as I am afraid to recite in public...

But even if we ignore that, it is clear, as I suggested above, that the
comparison of the brief attacks against largely unknown or unim-
portant figures in *Satires* 1–3 to Lucilius' onslaughts on the major
political figures of his day is absurd, and cannot be taken as fact. It is
also worth observing that the most important figure attacked in
Satire 2, Sallust, is accused of excessive attention to freedwomen
and of pride in not being an adulterer; in fact, the other well-
known anecdote about the historian's sexual life suggests the exact
opposite: that he was famous as an adulterer.[26] I suspect, although
I cannot prove it, that Horace has deliberately reversed the story to
make a joke of the personal attack. Why, then, the imagined criticism
in 1.4? Comparison with the *Eclogues* offers a parallel to these self-
referential comments. In the fifth *Eclogue*, Virgil refers back to the
second and third, and in the ninth he quotes putative earlier poems
that are not now found in the *Liber Bucolicon*, but are similar to
extant passages.[27] One purpose of these allusions is to provide
coherence and continuity within the book, to create an imagined,
not a real sense of time, to make self-sufficient the poetic universe of
the work within the limit of ten short poems.[28] In the same way,
Horace, by imagining a dialogue with his critics, draws the reader
into the poet's world and helps him accept and enter the poetic
reality and poetic time of the book itself.

[26] See Gellius *NA*. 17.18, citing Varro's *Logistoricus, Pius de pace*. The difficult
question of the identity of Horace's Sallustius is well discussed by Syme 1964a: 280–4,
who believes that, if it is the historian and not his heir, then Horace's allusion refutes
the legend of Sallust's adultery, precisely because he is there accused of excessive
interest in freedwomen: 'If in fact the name of a Sallustius was attached to a known
and notorious case of adultery, the poet would be fogging the issue, and guilty of
sheer incompetence. That is not Horace's way' (281). Not Horace's way, but that of
the speaker; and it is surely no coincidence that Fausta, with whom Sallust was
allegedly involved, is named in the same poem.

[27] *Ecl.* 5.86–7, 9.23–5, 27–9, 39–43, 46–50.

[28] Thus Büchner 1962: 123: 'Nach dem Vorbild der Eklogen ist darin eine Welt von
Dichtung bewusst zu einem Kosmos von 10 Gedichten zusammengefügt worden.'

In one sense, therefore, the major structure of a book like the *Satires* or the *Eclogues* is simply the order of the poems and the changing impressions made by each in relation to what has come before. In that kind of structure, there is no one central poem, no key to the book, except in so far as the development between the first poem and the last permits us to see one. And, as we shall see, there is a striking development from the beginning to the end of Horace's book. In another way, however, there is pattern as well as order in the *Sermones,* and the patterns that one can find are complementary, in some sense, to the linear order that is the basic structure of the book.

A number of schemes have been suggested by scholars to show the connections among the poems, and it is probably as easy to create confusing charts of inter-connections among the *Satires* as it is among the *Eclogues.*[29] Before looking at such patterns, however, it is worth looking at the poems one at a time to show how each is linked to those around it. Such links take a number of forms: they can be structural, thematic, or merely involve the repetition of proper names. But, taken together, they do show that the order of the poems is by no means haphazard; and one suspects that Horace, like Virgil, inserted some of these allusions only in the final stage of writing the book, for exactly that reason.[30]

The first poem, whether one considers the topic to be greed, unhappiness with one's lot, or some combination of the two, is closely connected to the second. This is done not only by the repetition of the name of Fabius at the beginning of the first (1.14) and the end of the second (2.134), but by the general topic of moderation, the fact that each begins with an introductory section of 22 lines, and, most important, the continuity of the subject between the end of the first and the beginning of the second.[31] The third poem, likewise, follows directly from the second: the figure of Tigellius is prominent at the opening of each, the theme of moderation is further elaborated, and the argument concerning sex and love, a major part of the second, is used as a lesser example of the third.[32] The grouping of

---

[29] e.g. Van Rooy 1968: 40.

[30] On Virgil's insertions see, for example, Clausen 1972: 201–2.

[31] Cf. Port 1926: 290, Fraenkel 1957: 96. For a detailed analysis of the relationship between 1 and 2, some of which is incomprehensible to me, see Van Rooy 1968: 41–56.

[32] On 2 and 3 see Van Rooy 1968: 55 n. 28.

the first three poems together, finally, is accomplished by the general similarity of topic and style, but also by the repetition of the address to Maecenas at 1.1 and 3.64 (his absence from 2 has nothing at all to do with an early date), and the presence of Crispinus at the end of the first (1.120) and the third (3.139).[33]

The first major break in the book apparently comes with the magisterial opening of the fourth poem, which seems to represent a total change of topic, from ethics to literary criticism, from almost impersonal diatribe to personal statements of the poet. And yet that break is by no means total. It has been observed, for instance, that the vices which at 4.3–4 the Old Comedy is said to attack are precisely the same as those mentioned in 3.106;[34] in the same way, Horace's detractors (4.26ff.) suffer from the flaws pilloried in the first two poems of the book.[35] This, of course, is the result of the fact that 1.4 is made to appear to be an answer to the criticisms of Horace's personal attacks in the first three poems. Even more important, it should not be forgotten that there is careful alternation in 4 between moral themes based on the first three poems, and stylistic ones which lead to the later discussions of satire and proper style. Van Rooy has also made the interesting observation that this balancing of Lucilius' virtues (of content) with vices (of style) is exactly the procedure recommended in evaluating one's friends and oneself in 1.3.[36] Thus, even though a new division of the book seems to begin here, there are so many links between the first three poems and the fourth that one would be justified in seeing 1.4 as a conclusion to the first set as well as the beginning of another.

[33] On the links among the first three poems as a group see Armstrong 1964, Rudd 1966: 1–35 and Van Rooy 1968: 51. Fraenkel 1957: 90 viewed the appearance of Crispinus at 1.120 as merely preparatory to his appearances at 3.139 and 4.14.

[34] Cf. Van Rooy 1968: 59. On 3 and 4 in general see Wili 1948: 93 and Kiessling-Heinze 1961: 45–6.

[35] Van Rooy 1968: 61–2; see also above, n. 23. The best recent study of Horace's father in 4 is that of Leach 1971; see p. 631 on the connection with 1 and 2. See now also Anderson 1974: 38–9 who still, in my view, admits too much autobiography into art. Kernan 1959: 18 cites 1.4.116ff. as 'a good description of the moral ideals of all satirists.'

[36] Van Rooy 1968: 61–71; see also Fraenkel 1957: 127. Note the superficial link created by the naming of Tigellius Hermogenes at 3.129, 4.72 and 10.90; cf. Van Rooy 1968: 55 n. 28.

Like the fourth poem, the fifth, the Journey to Brundisium, is on one level a total change of subject from the previous poem, and is also linked to it by various unobtrusive means. Horace apparently changes from a discourse on the nature of satire to a personal narrative, the first narrative poem in the book. On the other hand, the personal element in the Journey is anticipated by Horace's description of his father's advice at the end of 4; even more important, the whole fifth *Satire* is a close imitation of Lucilius, the poet whom in 4 he claimed as his exemplar. The fact that the 'Lucilius' of 4 is totally different from the 'Lucilius' of 5 is a topic to which we shall return. There is also a smaller link between 4 and 5: both end with references to *Iudaei* (4.145, 5.100).[37] Between 5 and 6 the links are again more obvious: both are 'autobiographical', both concern Horace and Maecenas. The whole triad is also tied together by the descriptions of Horace's father in 4 and 6.[38]

The seventh *Satire*, which is both the shortest and the earliest in dramatic date, does not have any of those overt small links with other poems that characterize the first six. In a sense, however, it is an elaboration of both the preceding poems: it is an expansion of the mock-epic battle of Sarmentus and Messius Cicirrus at 5.53ff.,[39] and it is also an incident from that career as a military tribune which Horace had mentioned in 6. There is far less connection between the seventh and the eighth, a fact which tends to cast doubt on the usual grouping of 7–9 as a triad. Indeed, the fact that they are all tales, *ainoi*, is the only real connection between them. The eighth does not fit easily into any grouping: it is the only poem that is not narrated by 'Horace'. But the fact that both 7 and 8 are jokes (and not very good ones at that) leading up to a punch-line does relate them.[40] Narrative form, likewise, connects 8 and 9, but those two are linked also by the presence of Maecenas (implicit in 8.14–15) and by the character of the speaker. The Priapus of 8 is cowardly and helpless, except for

[37] Van Rooy 1970b: 45–6 also takes the *breuitas* of 1.1.1ff. as an implicit contrast to Lucilian verbosity.

[38] On the structure of 6 itself see Rudd 1966: 41–2 and Van Rooy 1970b: 47–9; on the relationship of 5 and 6 see Van Rooy 1970b: 50–9; on the triad see Wili 1948: 95–6.

[39] Cf. Schröter 19.

[40] On the connections between 7 and 8 see Hanslik 1937: 21–3, Anderson 1972: 10–13.

luck; so is the Horace of 9.[41] As for the link between 9 and 10, it is clearly the circle of Maecenas, the list of friends and associates that appears in both of them.[42] And the last poem, in fact, looks back specifically to 4, and in general to the entire book to which it serves as a conclusion.

The simple fact that each poem is linked to its context, however, by no means exhausts the structures of the book. There is, as I have mentioned, the triadic grouping favored by most critics, with the last poem serving as a general conclusion. But, as we have seen, many of the groupings and divisions that this involves are somewhat arbitrary: the fourth poem belongs with the first three as well as with the fifth and sixth; the ninth poem is far more closely connected with the tenth than with the seventh and eighth. Still, the grouping by threes is there, and its importance in Horace's eyes has recently been made clearer by Ludwig's study of the structure of the two books together.[43] Other divisions and patterns, however, have also been seen, and many of them are no less valid than the triads. Van Rooy, for instance, sees the book as composed in pairs; but while many of his points are valid, I suspect that most of his connections are merely the result of the links binding each poem to its neighbors. And while grouping by two does fit in very well with the last part of the book, it unnaturally severs the third from the first two.

Yet another division that has been observed in the book is into halves. Just as one of the major patterns of the *Eclogues* is a division of the book at the sixth poem, marked by the second preface at the

[41] On 8 and 9 see Van Rooy 1971: 84–5 and Anderson 1972: 12. Buchheit 1968 sees both 7 and 9 as Homeric parodies involving literary criticism in a somewhat Alexandrian vein. While many of his observations are useful, he badly over-reads 9 and his interpretation of 7 is unconvincing.

[42] On 9 and 10 see Van Rooy 1972a with whose arguments about the 'moral significance' (52) of 9 I find it impossible to agree.

[43] Ludwig 1968 has shown clearly that Book 2 not only has an independent structure, somewhat different from that seen by Boll 1913, but is also linked to a triadic arrangement of Book 1. But that Horace used the triadic structure of 1 as the basis for joining it to 2 does not mean that it was the only (or even the primary) arrangement of 1 in Horace's mind when he completed it. Ludwig 1968: 317 also recognizes the division of each book into halves. To this may be added a numerological argument (the only mathematical pattern I was able to discover in the *Satires*): the number of lines in the first half of Book 1 (deleting 1.2.13) is 643, the same as the number of lines in the first half of Book 2.

opening of 6 and the repetition of the motif of the slender reed
and song at 1.2 and 6.8, so too the first lines of *Satires* 1 and 6 both
contain an address to Maecenas,[44] and the last lines of 5 and 10
both contain references to the book of the satires as a written work,
chartae at 5.105 and *libello* at 10.92, the last word of the book. We are
thus reminded at these critical points of the significant fact that this is
a work of literature, not of life. It does not seem to me, however, that
there is any other substantive change between the first half of the
book and the second that would mark this as more than a purely
formal articulation.[45]

It is also possible to recognize patterns of responsion that do not
involve adjacent poems only. Thus, 4 and 10 are clearly related in
topic and so, in some ways, are 5 and 9; thus we can see two pairs in
chiastic order.[46] This pattern, however, does not seem to extend any
further: I can see no valid connection between 6 and 8, nor is there
any obvious one between the groups of poems 1–3 and 6–8. In some
ways, also, 6 and 9 seem to be contrasting portraits of petitioners to
Maecenas, 4 and 6 portraits of Horace's father, 5, 7 and 9 mock-epic
scenes. But none of these patterns seems to embrace the entire book;
they merely add to the texture of cross-reference and allusion that is
created by a reading of the poems in order.

There is, however, one significant pattern embracing the entire
book that does not seem to have been given much attention, and
which is shared by the *Eclogues* and the *Satires*. That is a pattern of
responsion around the fifth poem: 4 balances 6, 3 7, 2 8, and 1 9.[47]
Thus, in the *Liber Sermonum*, the fourth and sixth poems both
concern Horace's father, the third and seventh both involve jokes

[44] See Fraenkel 1957: 101 and above, n. 3.

[45] Van Rooy 1972b argues that *auaritia* and *ambitio* were chosen as opening topics
for the two halves of the book because they are the two 'cardinal vices', but I find
many of his arguments very forced.

[46] On these pairs see Port 1926: 289, Büchner 1962: 124, Rudd 1976: 142–3; on 4
and 10 see Van Rooy 1970a.

[47] Rambaux 1971, the only scholar who has discussed this pattern, sees quite
different (and in my view rather vague) connections between the pairs; we agree
only on the erotic connection between 2 and 8. Rambaux summarizes the purpose of
the pattern as follows: 'Le recueil répond donc, dans sa structure même, au problème
majeur posé dès les trois premiers vers: comment sortir de l'insatisfaction' (204). The
pattern is denied by Ludwig 1968: 321–2 and not noticed by Van Rooy 1973.

on the nature of kingship, and each has the word (or name) *rex* in the last line (3.142, 7.35). The second poem and the eighth are linked by their erotic themes and their concern with the less romantic aspects of love (prostitution/adultery, magic)—and it is perhaps not coincidental that the second and eighth poems of Virgil's book are also concerned with love—while it is in fact the first, not the fifth or sixth, which is most closely linked to the ninth in describing two sides of an approach to Maecenas. But of that particular correspondence, which is of some importance in the interpretation of the book, we will say more later.

All the patterns that we have discussed so far are purely structural, and no attempt has been made to explain them except in so far as they show that Horace did place his poems in a deliberate order, and that we are supposed to see the book not merely as a collection of discrete items but as a whole and, presumably, as a progression. It is not, however, a single progress, not the gradual revelation of a consistent persona. For the whole book, it should be apparent, is controlled by an ironic doubleness of vision, a permanent doubt as to the intention of the poems, arising from the initial *ridentem dicere uerum* (to tell the truth while laughing). Horace has so constructed the book that there must always be a question as to what the *uerum* is, what the source of *risus*. Horace is not only ambiguous in many of the individual poems—a topic that we will not examine in detail here—but the entire aim of the book's development is left double. On one level, we see a serious progress from philosophy to literary criticism, as well as from theoretical ethics to their practical application. The latter is obvious: from the sermons of the first three poems we progress to Horace's father's precepts in 4, to Horace's moderate way of life as described in 6, to the description of the amicable and unstrained existence of the circle of Maecenas in 9. As to the former development, in the first group of poems we receive maxims on moderate life, in the fourth satire they are modulated to questions of literary style, and the entire last poem is concerned less with life than with literary propriety. In one sense, a major portion of the book is taken up with the relationship between manner of life and literary style, endorsing *mediocritas* in both spheres. Thus, for example, we may see the metaphor of the muddy river, used in the first poem to illustrate the dangers of greed (54–60):

> ut tibi si sit opus liquidi non amplius urna
> uel cyatho et dicas 'magno de flumine mallem
> quam ex hoc fonticulo tantundem sumere.' eo fit,
> plenior ut si quos delectet copia iusto,
> cum ripa simul auolsos ferat Aufidus acer.
> at qui tantuli eget quanto est opus, is neque limo
> turbatam haurit aquam neque uitam amittit in undis.

As if you should need no more than a jug or a ladle of liquid and should say 'I would prefer to take the same amount from a large river rather than from this little spring.' The result is that the fierce Aufidus carries away, torn off along with the bank, those whom a quantity larger than what is right pleases.

In the fourth poem, the muddy river is applied, in proper Callimachean fashion, to the sloppy style of Lucilius (11):

> cum flueret lutulentus, erat quod tollere uelles

since he flowed muddy, there were things you would like to remove

and this image is repeated in 10.50, with further elaboration (61–63):[48]

> Etrusci
> quale fuit Cassi rapido feruentius amni
> ingenium.

Such as was the talent of Cassius the Etruscan, boiling more than a raging river.

In a similar fashion, Callimachus is paraphrased, along with Philodemus and Terence, in the second *Satire* (105–8), but it is an amatory epigram that is adapted (31 Pf); in the last poem, Callimachus is again adapted, but this time it is the famous Proem to the *Aetia* that is fitted to a Roman context (10.31ff.).[49]

The other way in which the progression of the book is apparent is through the personal development of the speaker. We begin with a voice that is all but disembodied, except for the fact that he is addressing Maecenas on a philosophical topic. This lack of detail lasts through the first three poems, but from the introduction of Horace's father in the fourth, through the explicitly autobiographical

---

[48] On the connection of 1.54ff. with the later passages see Herter 1951: 29, Wimmel 1960: 156–62, 227 and 1962: 15 n.14, Brink 1963: 159. Note also the use of *turgidus* in 10.36–7; see Van Rooy 1970a: 14–15.

[49] Fraenkel 1957: 130 n. 4, Wimmel 1960: 152.

narratives of 5–7 to the statements about Maecenas and his friends and their social and literary beliefs that occupy the last two poems, we gain an increasingly vivid idea of the speaker. In a sense, the book is a progressive revelation, a development of a persona, and also a description of the speaker's progress from outside the circle of Maecenas to inside it. Thus, as a whole, the book fulfills artistically the description of Lucilian satire in 2.1.30ff., as a votive tablet setting forth a life; what Horace has done is to contract that real life—if indeed the self-portrait of Lucilius was in any sense real—into a single book of short compass and simultaneous publication; an imagined life, not a true one.

But to see the book as a straightforward progression from philosophy to life and literature, from outside to inside the circle of Maecenas, as the growth and development of the character 'Horace', is to miss most of the humor and irony of the book. The speaker of the book is not a good philosopher at the beginning, nor a particularly good literary critic in 4; the image of the circle of Maecenas as, for instance, it is described in 9, seems to be belied by the tone of the speaker in that poem, as well as by the narrative of 5. The book, in short, is filled with contradictions, of Horace making fun of himself.

Consider, for instance, the first poem, which is surely intended to establish much of the tone of the book, and must serve as a guide to our reading of the rest of the poems. The speaker begins colloquially: *qui fit* and *nemo* are not poetic words;[50] the first lines of the poem are also filled with the vocabulary of philosophy—*fors, sors, ratio*[51]—and progress to one of the tritest sets of commonplaces, on man's discontent with his own lot. Clearly, the speaker must be imagined to be one of those street-corner philosophers in the manner of Bion, with whom every intelligent Roman must have been all too familiar.[52] That it is a highly literary presentation, however, not one aiming at

[50] On *qui fit* see Lejay 1911 *ad loc.*, on *nemo* Axelson 1945: 76. There are, of course, colloquialisms throughout the poem; see, for example, Kiessling-Heinze 1961 on lines 17, 19, 20, 21, etc.

[51] On the terminology see Palmer *ad loc.*; note also the Lucretian *cetera de genere hoc* and *praeterea* at 1.13 and 23, with the notes of Lejay 1911 and Kiessling-Heinze 1961.

[52] On the diatribe see Fraenkel 1957: 92–3, Rudd 1966: 17–20. I do not understand how Coffey 1976: 71 can say: 'In a conversation piece addressed to Maecenas Horace cannot pontificate like an itinerant preacher.'

great verisimilitude, is shown by the verse itself: unlike a Bion or Menippus, Horace is writing in hexameters. They are not as elegant, to be sure, as Virgil's, but more so than Lucilius'. The effect may have been something similar to that of the *Mimiambi* of Herodas.[53]

The irony of the singing philosopher is further enhanced by the name of Maecenas in the very first line. On the one hand, its presence is an implicit dedication of the whole book, and suggests that Maecenas was already well aware of Horace, and did not disapprove; this impression is that which emerges from the fifth poem and later. On the other hand, in the context of these specific verses, we are forced to imagine our philosopher buttonholing the great man in the street, attempting to gain his attention—and perhaps his patronage. And in this aspect of the relationship, it is clear that the speaker is not successful. Consider, for example, the ineptitude of his philosophy. The examples of men unhappy with their fate are not well chosen: each man wishes for a life that is carefully shown by Horace to contain exactly the problems that he already hates, the slowness and toil of the soldier's and merchant's existence, the early rising of the lawyer and the farmer. Although commentators are prone to cite the other examples of this type of argument, those works do not contain these contradictions.[54]

As the poem continues, moreover, our speaker's tact and logic both fail him. If he is addressing Maecenas in the hope of obtaining patronage, then why does the second person singular change from Maecenas in line 1 (and, presumably, 14) to the greedy man of line 38? To say that Horace has forgotten whom he is addressing is no answer;[55] in the dramatic situation, it is clear that the speaker

---

[53] See Cunningham 1971: 14. The effect of the mellifluous verses of the *Eclogues* would have been quite different: shepherds, unlike Cynics, were supposed to sing, and Theocritus provided a clear literary precedent. Virgil's hexameters merely reinforce the obvious artificiality of the form. Lucilius, of course, does provide a model for Horace, but to what extent that is supposed to be evident in the first poem, which is more Lucretian than Lucilian, is hard to tell.

[54] Note, for instance, that in Ps.-Hippocrates *Epist.* 17.30, 40–1 (cited by Fraenkel 1957: 93) the pairs are general and obvious: the public official longing for private life, the islander for the continent. The same is true of Horace's own use of the theme in *Carm.* 1.1. On the topos in general see Silk 1966.

[55] Coffey 1976: 70 is typical: 'The recipient of the discourse [is] no longer Maecenas but an imaginary listener.'

'Horace', not the poet, has forgotten where he is. The same may be said of the argument. Despite the quantity of scholarly agonies, the break in the argument at line 20 is still as evident as it was to Palmer: 'There are in reality two subjects, discontent and avarice, but Horace tries to treat them as one, and the suture is apparent.'[56] And, when we return to the subject of the *auarus* in line 108, the awkwardness (both of language and thought) is equally clear. At the end of the poem, therefore, it should come as no surprise that the speaker borrows from Lucretius Book 3, and then breaks off, fearing to be thought to have borrowed from the writings of Crispinus—a Stoic.[57]

It is not my intention to examine the arguments of the diatribes in any detail, but any inspection of the secondary literature will show how hard it has been for scholars to construct a logical and coherent argument in any of them. 'The logic of conversation' is the best explanation that is offered,[58] and while that is to a certain extent true, it does not explain everything. What is important is the very fact that scholars have had to struggle to find the logic; the fact that it is not immediately apparent—as it is, for example, in Lucretius— itself says something about the characterization of the speaker. The same, indeed, is true of the literary satires. In poem 4 Horace claims that he is not a poet—but at the end of the poem it is the band of poets, of which he is a member, that will come to his aid.[59] The inconsistent view of Lucilius in the fourth and fifth *Satires*, mentioned above, is equally apparent. In the tenth poem, Horace modulates from criticism of mixing Greek and Latin to criticism of writing verses in Greek alone, without seeming to perceive the difference.[60] In none of these cases, or in others that might be adduced, are we to

---

[56] Palmer 1883: 113 cited by Fraenkel 1957: 90; see also Wimmel 1962: 9. The major (longest) modern attempt to harmonize the poem is that of Herter 1951; see also Fraenkel 1957: 90–7. Bodoh 1970 argues for different reasons that the bad logic of the poem is deliberate, while Wimmel 1962 believes that 1.1 is a slightly awkward stage in the development from 'true' diatribes (1.2, 3) to dialogue (2.3, 7); note p. 44: '...alles verrät die Unsicherheit eines Autors, der die alte Form verlassen, die neue noch nicht gefunden hat.'

[57] Crispinus' Stoicism is attested not only by the scholia, but by Horace himself at 3.139.

[58] Lejay 1911: 1 and 60 and elsewhere, followed by others down to Coffey 1976: 70.

[59] 1.4.39–40, with 141–2.

[60] Fraenkel's attempt (1957: 130) to resolve the dilemma is unconvincing.

think that Horace was unaware of what he was doing; from his entire poetic career, it is evident that he was the most careful and painstaking of writers. Rather, it is a constant feature of the book that even those literary and philosophical views that are clearly serious—not to say trite—are presented as contradicted by either the logic or the context. The purpose of these poems is not to expound philosophy or literary theory: it is to create a portrait of the speaker. It is that constant tension between the ideas presented and the incoherence of the voice that presents them that is a major element in *ridentem dicere uerum.*

The sense of irony and ambiguity inherent in the contrast between the conscious artistry of Horace and the inability of his persona[61] informs the order of the poems as well: not only the obvious contradiction between 4 and 5, but in the placement of *Satires* 7 and 8 as well. After firmly placing himself in the circle of Maecenas in 5 and 6, and establishing himself as a modest, subtle and unassuming figure, Horace proceeds to tell the story of Rex, which appears to date from a time in his life that it would obviously be more tactful to forget, and he tells a joke that, despite Fraenkel, is singularly lacking in humor.[62] Furthermore, the story of Priapus on the Esquiline is, at least in its implications, singularly tactless: Maecenas had rehabilitated the paupers' graveyard, and yet we are shown a Priapus, obviously a part of Maecenas' gardens, having to deal with witches collecting bones from the Esquiline's past, which Maecenas has not succeeded in burying completely.[63] By placing these two poems here, Horace is casting doubt on the intellectual and social progress that the preceding poems seem to imply.

[61] Inconsistency of this sort is basic to the rhetoric of satire; cf. Kernan 1959:14ff. It should, however, be observed that Horace's persona differs markedly from that of Juvenal and later satirists in that it is not primarily anger and prurience, but rather bumbling incompetence, that is the major character trait.

[62] Fraenkel 1957: 118–21. Van Rooy 1971: 82 describes it as 'one of the most artistic and most subtle satires written by Horace'; for a better assessment see Rudd 1966: 64–7. Hanslik 1937: 21, Buchheit 1968 and Van Rooy 1971: 67–83 see larger relevance in 7 to the literary theories of 10; there may be something in this, but I am doubtful.

[63] Against Fraenkel 1957: 123–4, Buchheit 1962: 64 and Anderson 1972—with whose approach I am otherwise in agreement—and others, I do not see how the putative presence of witches in the new gardens could be other than embarrassing to Maecenas.

It is the ninth poem, however, that famous encounter with the pest, that most clearly exhibits the structural ambiguities and variations of the book. On the one hand, it offers a charming portrait of life in the charmed circle of Maecenas: no ambition, no backbiting; the true exemplar of friendship. But seen in its context in the book, it can be made to yield quite another meaning. As was suggested above, there is a striking pattern in which the first poem and the ninth are intended to be read as a pair, and in fact they bear the same relationship to one another as do the first and ninth *Eclogues*. Both of these poems involve the problems of the outsider and the insider: the first shows Horace on the outside, the street-philosopher attempting to break into Maecenas' circle. The ninth, on the other hand, reverses the position. Here Horace is on the inside, attempting to fend off the pest who is making an assault on the group. This is certainly like Virgil's poems, in which Tityrus, in 1, keeps his land and Moeris, in 9, does not. But seeing the ninth *Satire* as a counterpart to the first casts a somewhat different light on the speaker. Granted that the pest in 9 is far more violent in his attempt than Horace in 1, and that his literary ideas are far more offensive than the philosophy of 1, still the Horace of 9 is not altogether an admirable character. It is not merely that he is describing his state of social and intellectual bliss in a hyperbolic way; he is smug, elitist and rude, with no sympathy for the man who is in the position in which he himself once was. Thus the ninth poem does not just cast a bright light on Maecenas and his companions, as Fraenkel thought, it questions their self-satisfaction as well.[64]

That such a double view is intended by the poet is confirmed by a reading of the central poem of this structure, the famous Journey. For the poem is central to the book, and not only structurally. It is the first serious portrait of Maecenas; it introduces Virgil and other literary lights of the day. It is in itself a journey, and as such mirrors that journey of the speaker into the circle of Maecenas which the entire book describes. And yet it is a heavily ironic poem. Granted that we hear praise of Virgil that is presumably heartfelt (31–34):

> postera lux oritur multo gratissima: namque
> Plotius et Varius Sinuessae Vergiliusque

---

[64] Fraenkel 1957: 116.

> occurrunt, animae, qualis neque candidiores
> terra tulit neque quis me sit deuinctior alter.

The next day starts, the most pleasing of all: for Plotus and Varius and Virgil appear at Sinuessa, souls than whom earth has born none more splendid nor to whom anyone is more devoted than I.

But what are we in fact to make of these great characters, the leaders of the political and literary world of the day, on a mission of major political import? We learn nothing of literature, nothing of politics. We learn that Maecenas likes to play ball, that Horace has eye trouble, that Virgil suffers from indigestion. We hear of the mock-epic fight of Sarmentus and Cicirrus, of a kitchen fire, of Horace's wet dream. Throughout the poem there is an immense contrast between the importance of the characters and the triviality of their actions.[65] It is all done, of course, with the greatest artistry, but the speaker of the poem remains blissfully unconscious of the world around him.

How then, finally, are we to take the contradictory structures of the book, its creation of a unified sense of disorder, of a speaker who is consistent only in his lack of logic and consistency? No one answer is readily available, and the last poem is, if anything, more whimsical than the others. After sketching in a few brilliant verses his view of the proper poetic style (7ff.) and attacking those post-neoterics (perhaps including Virgil himself) who revelled in Alexandrian style, he gives as a reason for his choice of poetic form the fact that it was the only unoccupied type of poetry, a statement that we are surely not intended to take seriously. And after giving a long list of those whose judgment he respects—the circle of Maecenas—he ends the book:

> i puer atque meo citus haec subscribe libello,

hurry up, boy, and write this at the end of my book

a verse which not only marks the end of the work *(subscriptio)*, but denies all his statements in the poem about slow and careful composition, implying that he, like Lucilius, writes standing on one foot, dictating to a slave.

---

[65] This is seen, for instance by Coffey 1976: 76. My interpretation differs from that of most critics (recently Classen 1973 and Stahl 1974), who see the poem as a celebration of friendship.

This is not the place to offer a full-scale reinterpretation of the *Liber Sermonum*, although it should be clear that one is badly needed. It is not easy to determine what, if anything, is the real intention of the book. There is no one philosophic or literary motive apparent, although I would suggest that one of the major purposes is a highly ironic critique of the state of poetry at the time, particularly the fancy and inane imitators of Catullus. One important fact, however, should have emerged. Like the *Eclogues*, the *Liber Sermonum* is a highly organized work of literary art. The poems are carefully ordered, so that the interpretation of each one is in some way affected by its position in the book, and conscious irony and ambiguity are the hallmarks of the work as a whole and in its parts. For by the arrangement of his work, Horace has created a coherent pattern of incoherence, an order which at every stage both makes positive statements and contradicts them by the context. Whatever we feel the final aim of the poet is, it is surely not simple-minded moral or literary judgments; it is, among other things, the creation of a complex and demanding poetic world.[66]

ADDITIONAL NOTE, 2007

It is now nearly thirty years since the oral version of this paper was delivered at a panel on the poetic book organized by John Van Sickle at the APA Annual Meeting for 1977, and there has been so much valuable criticism of the *Satires*, both of the individual poems and of the book as a whole (not least by the editor of this volume), that it would be impossible to bring it up to date without completely changing its contents. As a result, I have made only minor and cosmetic changes, and have not attempted to add references to more recent scholarship, significant portions of which are included

---

[66] I have taken advantage of the lecture format for which this paper was originally composed to state without argument a number of controversial positions and to pass over some important topics, including the argument of a number of the poems. I owe much to the suggestions of my colleagues and students, particularly Dr William H. Lowe Jr. of Brown University, whose discoveries about the *Liber Sermonum* have greatly clarified my own ideas.

in this volume. I wrote it as an attempt (following the work of William Anderson) to apply to the *Satires* some of the criticism written about modern satire, notably by Reuben Brower and Alvin Kernan (to conversation with both of whom and with Michael Putnam, I owe much); in retrospect, it seems to me more dated as literary criticism (in which a great deal of more interesting work has been done since) than as literary history, as an attempt to remedy the nervous silence about the *Satires* that was pervasive in accounts of the development of Latin poetry from the 50s to the 20s BCE. That argument only emerges in the last paragraphs of the present article; I have made the case in more detail in Zetzel 2002.

2

Horace and Maecenas:
The Propaganda Value of *Sermones* I

I. M. Le M. DuQuesnay

The satires of Horace are generally read as if they were apolitical poems or even as if they implied a complete and conscious rejection of any concern with public life.[1] Yet it is also widely believed that Maecenas had quite deliberately gathered round himself a number of talented poets who would celebrate the glories of Octavian and help to rally support for his policies.[2] Horace's *Sermones* Book 1[3] is the earliest work to be dedicated to Maecenas, the first fruits of this patronage. Simply to juxtapose like this these two widespread assumptions is to reveal the inherent, puzzling contradiction. In this paper it will be argued that once the satires are considered in relation to the political context in which they were written, and read with an awareness of the terms in which the contemporary propaganda war was being waged, then they can be seen to possess a political

[1] For example Rudd (1966: 37); McGann (1973: 59–72).

[2] For example Williams (1982: 13); Coffey (1976: 65); Syme (1939: 242). My own views on the relationship of Horace and Maecenas are very close to those of Horsfall (1981a) and very different from those of Lefèvre (1981). For a variety of views on Maecenas as a patron of literature see further Dalzell (1956); Reckford (1959); André (1967); Williams (1968) and Nisbet-Hubbard (1970) and (1978), indices s.vv. Maecenas, patronage.

[3] The title of the collection as such is *Sermones,* not *Satirae.* The word *satura* in the singular denotes either the genre of satire or else an individual poem, and in the plural it denotes any group of separate poems considered as separate pieces rather than as parts of a single collection or *libellus.* See Horsfall (1981b: 108), on which this note depends.

dimension and relevance that have gone unnoticed. In what follows, space will not allow me to do more than explain the possible significance of the individual satires and some of their various details in relationship to the contemporary political situation. It is obviously not possible to give here a full and completely balanced account of each poem. Sometimes the political dimension of a poem is not the most important and it should be emphasised that the approach suggested in this essay is intended primarily to complement rather than to replace more traditional approaches[4] and to redress the balance by concentrating almost exclusively on this neglected aspect of these multi-faceted poems.

Horace does not in these poems overtly praise Octavian as Triumvir or as victor in the *Bellum Siculum*. Nor, perhaps more surprisingly, does he exploit the traditional function of satire in times of civil war and social and political division to denigrate the opposition systematically and in detail.[5] His technique is both less direct and more positive. His basic strategy is to present an attractive image of himself and his friends as sophisticated, cultured and intelligent men who are humane in their attitudes to others and mindful of the *mos maiorum*. Above all he exhibits a concern with moral issues. But for the contemporaries of Sallust the distinction between morality and politics was not a meaningful one.[6]

DATES

The clear meaning of the last line of *Satire* 1.10 is that this collection of ten poems was published as a single *libellus*, independently of the second book. It also implies that the tenth poem was the last to be written. The poem itself has every appearance of being composed as a formal epilogue in that it carefully defines Horace's position in the tradition of Lucilian satire and his place on the contemporary literary scene. Horace introduces a Bibulus as a member of his audience at

---

[4] See, especially, Fraenkel (1957: 67–135) and Rudd (1966: 1–124).
[5] See Jal (1963: 201–8).
[6] See the valuable discussion by Williams (1968: 619–33).

Rome (1.10.86) whose approval he seeks. This man is plausibly identified with Brutus' stepson L. Calpurnius Bibulus, the Antonian admiral who had taken a fleet to Sicily in 36 to help Octavian. He spent the winter of 36/35 at Rome before returning to govern Syria for Antonius. It seems safe to assume that *Sermones* 1 was 'published' in that same winter.[7]

Few of the other poems can be dated. There is no reason to tie the seventh to the dramatic date of the incident which it describes (43/42); the fifth is obviously later than the spring of 37 and the preliminaries to the Treaty of Tarentum. As to relative chronology, it is certain only that the second satire precedes the fourth and the fourth the tenth. It is, however, important to emphasise that the common belief that Horace had composed some satires before he joined Maecenas is utterly without foundation. If it is supposed that Maecenas was not content with the *commendatio* of Virgil and Varius Rufus and that he must have required written evidence of Horace's skill as a poet, there is still absolutely no reason to suppose that these early specimens have survived at all, much less that they were satires.[8] All ten poems were judged worthy of and suitable for inclusion in a *libellus* dedicated to, and so publicly associated with, Maecenas: obviously, then, all of them could have been composed after the beginning of their *amicitia*. Certainly the absence of Maecenas' name from any poem proves nothing, as a glance at any book of Augustan poetry reveals. It is incredible that *Satire* 1.2 should have shocked either Maecenas or Octavian, hard to believe that they gave anything less than wholehearted approval to this first onslaught on adultery.[9] In *Satire* 1.4 Horace could not have invoked his friendship

---

[7] All dates in the text are BCE unless otherwise indicated. For Calpurnius Bibulus, see Broughton (1968: 401 and 404). 36/35 is generally accepted as the date for *Sermones* 1. It has been challenged (unconvincingly) by Williams (1972: 20). The precise nature of publication at this time is still far from clear. I assume that the *Sermones* became available to a much wider audience and readership than Horace's immediate circle of friends and that Maecenas used his considerable resources to promote their dissemination. See now Zetzel (1981: 232–7); Kenney (1982: 15–22) and Wiseman (1982a).

[8] *Pace* Fraenkel (1957); Coffey (1976: 66–7) and others.

[9] For the *Romana simplicitas* of Octavian see Mart. 11. 20. Octavian had tried to legislate against adultery as early as 28 and actually did so in 18: see Brunt (1971: 558–66); Csillag (1976: 29–35 and 219–20); Galinsky (1981); and Wallace-Hadrill (1981).

with the powerful Maecenas without substantially affecting the argument.[10] In short, there is no reason to think that the satires are anything but what they appear to be, ten Lucilian poems for Horace's *amicus* Maecenas, written between the years 38, when their *amicitia* began, and the winter of 36/35, when they were 'published'.

THE HISTORICAL CONTEXT

The years 38 to 36 delimit almost exactly a distinct and important phase in the history of the second Triumvirate. It is the period of the *Bellum Siculum*.[11] Since it formed the unspoken context and implicit backdrop to *Sermones* 1, some understanding of the nature of this conflict and the issues involved is fundamental to any attempt to assess the potential of the satires as propaganda.

The younger son of Pompeius Magnus, Sextus Pompeius, proclaimed his devotion to his father's cause and his determination to emulate him by styling himself Magnus Pompeius Pius. Outlawed himself in 43 by the *lex Pedia*, he became a thorn in the side of the Triumvirs by providing a rallying-point and refuge, first, for the victims of the proscriptions and, later, for the survivors of Philippi. His success may be judged from the terms of the Treaty of Misenum (the peace of Puteoli) concluded between himself and Octavian and Antonius in 39. Sextus was conceded control of Sardinia, Corsica, Sicily and the Peloponnese (Achaea); he was promised a consulship and an augurate. In effect he was recognised as the virtual equal of Octavian and Antonius. More important in the long term, the exiles, the refugees from the proscriptions and Philippi, were allowed to return, some of them to be honoured at once with tribuneships,

---

[10] A major theme in S. 1.4 is the *libertas* of the satirist. The truth of the matter is that what a humble man like Horace could say with impunity depended on how powerful his friends were: cf. Crook (1967: 255). Horace admits as much at S. 2.1.83–6. This reality is neglected by LaFleur (1981).

[11] There are basic accounts in: Syme (1939: 227–42); Carter (1970: 131–53); Huzar (1978: 129–47 and 290–2) (not free from error); Hadas (1930) and Yavetz (1969: 22 and 86–8). On the details Broughton (1968: 386–410) provides full references to the sources.

praetorships and priesthoods. Only those directly implicated in the murder of Caesar remained in exile.[12]

The peace was short-lived. No sooner had Antonius returned to the East than hostilities broke out between Octavian and Sextus. In 38 Octavian suffered some humiliating setbacks and defeats. Indeed one of the reasons for the nine-month hiatus between Horace's interview and final acceptance by Maecenas was that the latter had to undertake an urgent diplomatic mission to Antonius in the East to secure his backing and reinforcements for the imperiled Octavian.[13] Horace's silence is tactful and significant. The next year was one of consolidation and preparation. Finally, on 3 September 36 Octavian's forces defeated those of Sextus at Naulochus. The fears and anxieties of those years are only too imaginable. For a second time in two decades Rome had witnessed a power struggle between a Caesar and a Pompeius which had run from *amicitia* through civil war to a victory for Caesar. There must have been grave doubts about the future.

The task facing the young Octavian, if he was to avoid the fate of Julius Caesar, is simply defined. He had to build upon his hard-won success, to increase his real power and his reputation without seeming to be a tyrant, and to increase and broaden the basis of his support. With the full and concerted support of his friends this delicate and complex task was so successfully accomplished that within two years he had transformed his position from one of relative weakness to one of indisputable equality with that of Antonius.[14]

Octavian entered Rome with an *ouatio* in November 36, having meticulously observed Republican protocol and thereby proclaiming his respect for the *mos maiorum*.[15] He was showered with honours, many of which he declined. But the anniversary of his victories was to be celebrated with annual sacrifices; a golden statue was erected in the forum with a legend advertising the restoration of peace; and the Italian cities set up statues of him in their temples.[16] So much for

[12] The main sources are App. *Bell. ciu.* 5.84–5; 5.67–74; 143; Dio 48.36–8 and Vell. 2.72 and 77.
[13] Broughton (1968: 393); App. *Bell. ciu.* 5.92–3 with Gabba (1970: ad loc.).
[14] See Syme (1939: 227–42).
[15] Dio 49.15.3.
[16] Dio 49.15; App. *Bell. ciu.* 5.530.

reputation and honour. The army needed attention. Some veteran legions were discharged, although few were settled in Italy and for them the land was purchased not confiscated. This action was calculated to secure the support of the Italian landowners and avoid another Perusine War. The rest of the army were promised rich booty from the coming Illyrian campaigns.[17] These new wars would serve a number of objectives. They provided an opportunity for Octavian to consolidate and enhance his reputation as a military man. The war would be glorious, for at last the might of Rome was to be turned against a ferocious foreign foe which for ten years had threatened the borders of Italy, and the standards captured from A. Gabinius in 48 were to be recovered.[18] Both factors would be useful propaganda if Antonius succeeded against the Parthians. These campaigns were to provide Octavian, his friends and supporters, and the legions with valuable battle experience; the booty was to be used, in time-honoured fashion, to adorn the city and to benefit the people. These new buildings and repairs would be a physical manifestation of the benefits to come from the end of civil war and the renewed pursuit of the traditional Roman goals. More immediate benefits to the people of Italy lay in the swift and effective campaign to clear out the bandits and brigands which infested the countryside, perhaps a similar campaign to rid Rome itself of thieves and robbers, and the remission of various taxes and debts.[19]

All these activities were clearly designed in the first place to increase the power and prestige of Octavian and to win him support. But Octavian made a number of other moves which show him to have been anxious to avoid the trap into which Caesar had fallen: he had to convince people that this time the better cause had won, that the new Caesar respected the *mos maiorum* and that he was not aiming at *regnum* or *dominatio* but simply emulating the achievements of the great heroes of the Republic to the incalculable benefit of the state. The first step was to discredit totally Sextus Pompeius. The victory, it was insisted, was not over the proud remnants of the

[17] App. *Bell. ciu.* 5.528.
[18] Aug. *RG* 29.1; Wilkes (1969: 48–9).
[19] Main sources: App. *Bell. ciu.* 5.127–9; Dio 49.13–15; Vell. 2.81 (see Woodman (1983: ad loc.)); Aug. *RG* 25.1.

Republican cause, over the last defenders of the *mos maiorum* and
libertas but 'against brigands and a band of slaves' (*contra latrones
atque seruilem manum, Epode* 4.19), and it was not the Triumvirs
who threatened the liberty of Rome but Sextus who 'threatened the
city with the chains that he, as their friend, had removed from
faithless slaves' (*minatus urbi uincla, quae detraxerat | servis amicus
perfidis, Epode* 9.9–10).[20] The words were underscored with brutal
action. In spite of earlier pledges to the contrary, the runaway slaves
with Sextus were ostentatiously returned to their masters and those
alleged slaves whom no master claimed were impaled in the towns
and cities from where they had absconded.[21] This attack on Sextus
was counterbalanced by a more positive presentation of the case of
Octavian and the Triumvirate. This was, at long last, really the end of
civil wars. Such was the claim of Octavian, for at this time there was
no public admission of even the slightest disagreement between
Antonius and Octavian.[22] The task for which the *Triumuiri Rei
Publicae Constituendae* had been appointed was virtually complete
and Octavian professed his willingness to relinquish his special
powers: he was confident that Antonius felt the same. They would
do just that, as soon as the Parthian campaign was successfully
completed. In the mean time, as evidence of his good faith and his
intentions, most of the administration of the state would be seen to
be carried out by the annual magistrates in accordance with the *mos
maiorum*. In order to induce forgetfulness of the bitter struggles of
the recent past, Octavian caused the propaganda writings of the civil
wars to be burned. To ensure that his own views prevailed and that
his intentions were not misunderstood he delivered speeches to the
senate and the people, detailing his achievements and explaining his
aims and his policies since the murder of Caesar. These speeches were

[20] Cf. Vell. 2.73, especially his description of Sextus as *libertorum suorum libertus
seruorumque seruus;* and Aug. *RG* 25.1: *mare pacaui a praedonibus.*

[21] App. *Bell. ciu.* 5.131; Dio 49.12.4–5.

[22] App. *Bell. ciu.* 5.128; 130; 132 (*bis*); cf. Dio 49.13.2 (which is inconsistent with
13.3–4) and 49.15.2–3. Their statues were erected in the temple of Concordia in 35
(Dio 49.18.6; cf. 49.15.1). This earlier propaganda helps to explain why, when the
break did come, so much importance was attached to depicting Antonius as the
aggressor, to the domination of Cleopatra and to the fact that his alliance with her
constituted a threat from the barbarian East.

then written up and published.[23] It is surely hardly credible that amid all this activity, when Octavian clearly could and did expect his friends to support his cause in every way that they could, Maecenas, his closest friend and adviser, should publish and distribute a work which was irrelevant to the needs and the preoccupations of himself and his friends.[24] It is also difficult to believe that Horace could have lived day by day amid all this activity and yet have remained aloof from and immune to it all.

HORACE, *AMICUS MAECENATIS* ('FRIEND OF MAECENAS')

Horace's friendship with Maecenas is a historical fact, movingly guaranteed by the latter's famous words to Augustus: 'be as mindful of Horatius Flaccus as of me' (*Horati Flacci ut mei esto memor*).[25] But it began as a professional friendship.[26] Early in 38 Maecenas was evidently recruiting poets and had already befriended Virgil and Varius Rufus, both of whom were established poets.[27] They introduced Horace and, presumably, vouched for his skill and potential as a poet. Maecenas was following impeccable precedents, from Alexander and his successors through Scipio Aemilianus to Asinius Pollio. His personal motives are nowhere recorded: he may have wanted a status symbol, an entertainer, a propagandist or an encomiast. Most

[23] App. *Bell. ciu.* 5.132. This is useful evidence that the concept of written propaganda and the means to disseminate it were available.

[24] Cf. Syme (1939: 242): 'Maecenas had been [i.e. by 33] working more quietly and to set purpose. It was his task to guide opinion gently into acceptance of the monarchy, to prepare not merely for the contest that was imminent but for the peace that was to follow victory in the last of all civil wars.'

[25] [Suet.] *Vit. Hor.* 2.2 Klingner. I see no reason to infer from Horace's courtesy to his patron in his poems any coolness in their relationship.

[26] See especially White (1974) and (1978). Saller (1982) agrees with him that a poet hoped for support and publicity for his work from his patron but stresses that 'the traditional rewards for poets were *pecunia* and *honores*' and that poets were different from other *amici* in that they offered their poems as part of the exchange. See also the valuable papers of Horsfall (1981a) and Wiseman (1982).

[27] Virgil's *Eclogues* had appeared in late 39 and Varius Rufus' *De morte*, which is echoed in *Ecl.* 8, perhaps as early as 43 (see Hollis (1977)).

likely he never analysed his motives and all these factors played their part. It would be impossible to deny that Maecenas simply had an enthusiasm for poets and poetry.[28] Having said that, it is important to stress that Maecenas did not just employ Horace as a poet but made him a 'friend', an *amicus*.

On Horace's own testimony the formal interview was no less concerned with his qualities as a man and his suitability as an *amicus* than with his quality as a poet. Maecenas evidently found him stimulating company: Horace became his *conuictor* ('companion') and accompanied him on journeys. In addition he presumably performed such services for Maecenas as lay within his power, including those of a private secretary. But above all, Maecenas could expect from his *amicus* public support whenever the occasion arose: Horace's status as a poet did not exempt him from the normal obligations of *amicitia* ('friendship'). Poetry was almost the only means available to Horace to make public statements which commanded attention. He could not be expected to let pass this opportunity to support his friend.[29]

What Horace hoped for from the *amicitia* with Maecenas is easy to imagine. He had returned from Philippi with sufficient wealth to buy the post of *scriba quaestorius,* which was often held by *equites* ('knights') like himself and this probably guaranteed him a (minimum) annual income of 24,000 sesterces.[30] He could have lived in comfortable obscurity.[31] But, as he later said, 'reckless poverty drove

[28] White (1978: 82) rightly insists that 'poets were *amici* and *sodales,* like anyone else'. But that does not mean that a Roman would not befriend someone precisely because he was a poet; all the acceptable reasons for so doing are assembled by Cicero in the *Pro Archia.* Although Archias was a Greek by birth, Cicero insists that he was a *ciuis Romanus,* and it may be assumed that if anything which he said about Archias had been felt to be unworthy of, or inapplicable to, a *ciuis Romanus,* then he would not have said it.

[29] Cf. White (1974: 49–50), esp.: 'To Statius' mind it [sc. the publication of a poem] has the overtones of a public avowal, by which he testifies to the virtues and friendship of the person concerned.'

[30] See Fraenkel (1957: 14–15) and White (1978: 89). I am assuming that since *equites* frequently found it worthwhile to purchase this post it probably yielded an income at least comparable to that which would come from investing their census in another way.

[31] A legionary soldier in the thirties received 900 sesterces p.a. and that was presumably at least a bare living wage. At the other end of the social scale, Cornelius Nepos assures us that Atticus lived frugally on 36,000 sesterces p.a. (*Vit. Au.* 13.6) but

me to make verses' (*paupertas impulit audax* | *ut uersus facerem,* *Epistles* 2.2.50–1). In that same poem he acknowledged that his poetry did bring him wealth. In both this poem and in the *Epistle to Augustus*, Horace quite clearly attributes his wealth to the fact that he was a poet and not simply to his being a friend of Maecenas and Augustus (they befriended him just because he was a poet) and his public acknowledgement of this fact makes it clear that there was nothing unusual, inconceivable or dishonourable in such a relationship for either the poet or his benefactor. Maecenas may have marked the beginning of their *amicitia* with a large cash gift, but of that nothing is said.[32] Horace certainly derived many other advantages from their *amicitia:* he lived with Maecenas and travelled with him;[33] he was introduced to other *principes uiri* ('leading men', including Octavian) from whom he could expect *beneficia* ('benefits') in exchange for the 'fame, praise, and immortality' (*gloria et laus et aeternitas*) which he conferred upon them by mentioning their names in his poems.[34] Above all, he received access to scribes and papyrus, books, audiences for his recitations and, presumably as an extension of this, the 'publication' of his poems.[35]

Contemporary readers of Horace did not need to be told about the nature of *amicitia*. They could be relied upon to understand the

Cicero, who allowed Marcus 80,000 a year (*Ad Att.* 16.1.12.32), is proud to claim that he can live on less than 100,000 while the rich man with extravagant tastes cannot manage on 600,000 (*Parad. Sto.*). Cf. Shatzman (1975: 11–98, esp. 47–74 and 94–8).

[32] Such gifts were not uncommon. Maecenas had apparently freed Sarmentus, the *scurra* of *S.* 1.5, and given him sufficient money to purchase the *scriptum quaestorium* (Treggiari (1969: 271–2)). It is not likely that he was less generous to Horace.

[33] *S.* 1.9.48; 1.5.

[34] For these *beneficia* see White (1978: 90–2). For the generosity of Augustus see [Suet.] *Vit. Hor.* 219–20 Klingner; Hor. *Epist.* 2.1.245–50 and Macrob. *Sat.* 2.4.31 where a poet receives an exceptionally generous payment of 100,000 sesterces. In 29, Varius Rufus received 1,000,000 from Augustus for his *Thyestes* and Virgil died leaving ten times the minimum senatorial census which he had received *ex liberalitatibus amicorum*.

[35] White (1974: 44 n. 15 and 55 n. 60) questions the belief that the dedicatee assumed responsibility for the publication. Each case must be judged on its merits: Cicero's *Academica* and *De finibus* were published by Atticus but dedicated to Varro and Brutus respectively. In the absence of evidence, it seems reasonable to assume that Maecenas was responsible for the publication of Horace's work, either by his own scribes or, less probably, through a friend (as one may speculate that Cornelius Nepos secured Atticus as a publisher for Catullus). See also Marshall (1976: 252–63 and n. 7 above).

realities of Roman society and to read the poems accordingly. But
Rome was not a totalitarian state and there was no mechanism by
means of which Maecenas could have compelled Horace to act as his
amicus. It defies probability to suppose that he would have wished to
do so. Nor did there exist any means by which Maecenas or even
Octavian could have compelled Horace, simply by virtue of his being
a Roman citizen (*ciuis Romanus*), to write in support of the regime or
could have prevented him from writing if he criticised it. Horace
could have remained independent, if he had chosen to do so, and
lamented the defeat of the Republican cause to the end of his days.
Instead, as he openly avows, he had freely accepted the friendship of
Maecenas with all its material advantages and social obligations. If he
had then gone on to express in his works distaste for or disapproval
of what Maecenas stood for at that time he could not have expected
this to be taken as a sign of a praiseworthy independent spirit or the
fulfilment of some mystical duty as a poet to be subversive and to
question the nature of his society. It would have been taken simply as
a sign of impudence and churlish ingratitude. But Horace does no
such thing. He dedicates the *Sermones* to Maecenas (1.1.1 and 1.6)
and so fulfils his obligations as an *amicus* by giving something in
exchange for the *beneficia* which he has received. He also states quite
openly that he sought the approval of Maecenas as of other friends
for what he wrote (*Satire* 1.10.81–90). It may be supposed that
Maecenas even suggested themes and discussed work in progress as
Atticus did with Cicero.[36] That is not to suggest that Maecenas vetted
every line for its doctrinal purity: for there was no doctrine in that
sense. But Horace makes much of his a*micitia* and encourages the
reader to suppose that there exists between the two men 'that in
which a friendship's full force lies: a complete consensus of wants, of
enthusiasms and of thoughts' (*id in quo omnis uis est amicitiae,
uoluntatum studiorum sententiarum summa consensio,* Cicero, *De
amicitia* 15). Moreover Horace's contemporaries must have been

---

[36] Cf. White (1974: 54) and (1978: 88); *De Amic.* 4; *Ad Att.* 15.4.3; Virg. *Ecl.* 8.11
(to Pollio) and *G.* 3.40–1 (to Maecenas). If the idea of a commission were ill-
mannered, Virgil would never have used the word *iussa,* which would then be a
rebuke to his dedicatee. Everyone knows of Cicero's quest for an encomiast for his
consulship. Unsolicited dedications were in fact a much more delicate problem (e.g.
Cic. *Ad Att.* 13.12 etc.). Cf. Horsfall (1981a: 14–16).

eager to learn what they could about Maecenas. He was at this time the second most powerful man in Rome; yet he remained an elusive and enigmatic figure, a *priuatus* and an *eques* whose power resided in his *amicitia* with Octavian. Horace does all that he can to encourage his readers to interpret the poems as the work of an *amicus* of Maecenas and so invites them to draw what inferences they can about himself and his friends.

To suppose that Horace's technique in the satires is not deliberate and that the effects are not intended would be to underestimate grossly the skill of Horace as a poet and his self-consciousness as an artist. Yet nowhere in *Sermones* 1 does he adopt any conventional poetic stance such as those adopted in *Epodes* 7 and 16. He even pretends to deny the status of poetry to his satires (*Satire* 1.4.39–42) and so, by implication, the status of poet to himself. He even suggests that his poems were not intended for publication.[37] All this helps to create and foster the impression that the reader is hearing the authentic voice of the historical character of Q. Horatius Flaccus, who has a claim on our attention not as a poet but simply as a fellow citizen who is also a friend of the powerful Maecenas. Nothing is done which would allow the reader to feel conscious of any gap between the image presented in the poems and reality. Certainly it cannot be demonstrated that anything which Horace tells us in the satires is actually untrue. There is obviously the question of selectivity and omission, but the fact remains that the picture which Horace presents of himself and his friends is completely plausible and clearly intended to be so. This is a technique which Horace has taken from Lucilius, of whom he later said (*Satire* 2.1.30–4): 'he used to entrust secrets to his books as if they were his closest friends . . . and so it happens that the old man's entire life is laid out, as if painted on a votive tablet' (*ille uelut fidis arcana sodalibus olim* | *credebat libris . . .* | *. . . quo fit ut omnis uotiua pateat ueluti descripta tabella* | *uita senis. sequor hunc . . .* cf. *Satire* 2.1.57–60). But it is also a technique which has interesting affinities with those employed by ancient biographers, who were well aware that 'it is not always in the most glorious actions that virtue or badness are revealed; indeed often a little action, a saying or a jest reveals character more clearly

---

[37] *S.* 1.4.71–8; 1.10.72–5. The claims are disingenuous: see Brink (1963: 156–71).

than battles etc.' (Plutarch, *Alexander* 1.2). In a similar way, Horace allows us to witness the apparently trivial actions of himself and his friends, and to overhear their conversation. He does not preach at his readers, he does not comment on the significance of what he portrays and he does not draw attention explicitly to the virtues of his friends. Instead he allows the reader to draw the inevitable conclusions for himself: as a result the reader is more easily persuaded and less inclined to object or protest that the image Horace is presenting is at odds with their preconceived prejudices (see also below, pp. 61–2, 71). If the modern reader is concerned with understanding Horace's skill and tact and with recapturing the initial impact of his poems, then it is surely a mistake to ignore the fact that the satires are so finely tuned to their historical context or to suppose that either Horace or Maecenas was unaware of the impression which they would make on contemporaries. Maecenas was well enough pleased with the efforts of his *amicus* to present him with the Sabine farm shortly after the publication of the *Sermones*.

'LUCILIUS... NOSTRUM... DELAPSUS IN AEVUM' ('WERE LUCILIUS TO SLIP DOWN TO OUR OWN DAY...')

Horace's choice of Lucilius as a model is in some respects a curious one. His fullest account of his relationship to his model (1.10) serves to highlight one consequence of that choice. Having explained that he abandoned an earlier desire to write in Greek because it would offer little chance of originality (1.10.31–5), Horace concedes that by taking Lucilius as his model he can only be 'less than the (genre's) discoverer' (*inuentore minor*) and he adds: 'for my part, I would not dare pull off the crown that clings to his head to general acclaim' (*neque ego illi detrahere ausim | haerentem capiti cum multa laude coronam, Satire* 1.10.48–9). The fact that the language and the imagery are completely traditional in the poet's claim to originality serves only to emphasise the inversion of the claim to originality here.[38] It is worth considering at least briefly Horace's possible motives in making this choice. That means in effect considering the more important question of the possible significance of his choice.

At 1.10.40ff. Horace briefly catalogues those friends and contemporaries who had achieved pre-eminence in various genres: Fundanius in comedy, Pollio in tragedy, Varius in epic and Virgil in bucolic. This is by no means an exhaustive list of the recognised genres and so Horace cannot be intending to imply, as is sometimes suggested,[39] that he started to write satire simply because that was the only genre available. At most this passage could be taken to imply that he did not take up any of the actual genres specified because he felt that they were already well treated by his friends. However, if availability had been his sole or even chief concern then he could have simply pressed on with the *Epodes* or the *Odes* and if he had wanted variety (which is not a motive he indicates either explicitly or implicitly) then he could have turned for models to archaic elegy or some other genre. The only reason which Horace does give for writing satire is: 'this was the genre that I could write it better than Varro of Atax, who had tried in vain, as well as certain others, though with less distinction than its inventor' (*hoc erat, experto frustra Varrone Atacino | atque quibusdam aliis, melius quod scribere possem | inuentore minor* etc., 1.10.46–8). This seems to mean no more than that Horace could see no living person who had achieved outstanding success in satire and he felt that it was a genre in which he could surpass all others—except Lucilius. The reason that Horace must be content to remain *inuentore minor* is that Lucilius was a Roman and not a Greek poet and as a result Horace could not lay claim to being the first to practise the genre at Rome. This willingness to sacrifice the claim to originality is striking and underlines the curiousness of choosing Lucilius as a model.

There is no doubt that in the first century Lucilius enjoyed a very considerable reputation. Cicero even bestows upon him the coveted epithets *doctus et perurbanus* ('learned and sophisticated')[40] and

---

[38] For *corona*, see Kambylis (1965: 173–6; 155–62) (for *inuentor*). Cf. Wimmel (1960), index s.v. primus-Motiv. For *audere* cf. Enn. *Ann.* 7 prologue; Lucr. 1.66–7; Catull. 1.5; Virg. *G.* 2.175; Manil. 2.10; 3.1; Hor. *Epist.* 1.3.11; also below, p. 236 n. 136. [The reference is to Cairns on Propertius 4.6 which was in the same volume as this essay.]

[39] Cf. Fraenkel (1957: 130–1); Rudd (1966: 95); Coffey (1976: 80).

[40] Cic. *De or.* 1.72 = 2.25.

Satires 1.4 and 1.10 make it clear that many shared that high estimation. It is precisely this aspect of Lucilius' reputation which Horace
calls into question. He concedes that Lucilius' standards were very
high by those of his own day, that his task was made more difficult by
having no Greek model and that he would have done better if he had
lived in Horace's day (1.10.64–71). In other words, he would have
written like Horace. In effect then, Horace reserves his real contempt
and scorn for the poetic standards of the latter-day defenders and
imitators of Lucilius. He calls his style 'muddy' (*lutulentus*, 1.4.11;
1.10.50) in a clear allusion to Callimachus' Assyrian river (*Hymn to
Apollo* 108–9) and accuses his defenders of judging his poetry not by
its art but by 'the Persian chain' and of being insufficiently indifferent
to the standards of popular taste.[41] In short, Horace is challenging
the right of Lucilius to the epithet *doctus*.

The standards by which Horace and his coterie judge poetry are
clear enough. They are the standards of Callimachus which had been
established at Rome in the previous generation, by the Neoterics.[42]
Unfortunately the attention of modern readers has been distracted
from this simple point by Horace's description of Hermogenes and
'that monkey' (*simius iste*) as 'skilled at singing nothing but Calvus
and Catullus' (*nil praeter Caluum et doctus cantare Catullum*,
1.10.17–19). Horace says that these men have not read their Greek
models. Such an accusation could not possibly be levelled at either
Calvus or Catullus. Neither could the implied charge of lacking
variety. The names of Calvus and Catullus serve to highlight by
contrast the absurdity of Hermogenes and his partner in aspiring
to the epithet *doctus*. However, it is surely not as exemplary Neoterics
that Calvus and Catullus are brought in but as masters of lampoon
and invective.[43] But while the context almost obliges the reader to
make the assumption that Hermogenes and his fellow poet are
devotees of invective it may be doubted that they were actually
given to reciting Calvus and Catullus: one of Calvus' lampoons was
directed against Hermogenes himself.[44] By using the names of Calvus

[41] Cf. Brink (1963: 156–71); Wimmel (1960: 154–62); Williams (1978: 85–92);
Callimachus, *Aetia* fr. 1.18 and *Epigr.* 28.4 Pf; Catull. 95b.

[42] See now Lyne (1978: 167–87).

[43] e.g. Suet. *Iul.* 73.

[44] Cic. *Ad fam.* 7.24.1–2; Porph. on Hor. *S.* 1.3.4. This interpretation depends on
acceptance of the view that there is only one Hermogenes Tigellius or, *mutatis
mutandis*, that the two are very closely related (cf. Treggiari (1969: 269–70)).

and Catullus, whose Callimachean ideals he shares, instead of speci-
fying invective, a genre in which they had gained pre-eminence,
Horace has scored a stinging hit against his opponents

Be that as it may, this slight digression has brought us indirectly to
a most important feature of the reputation of Lucilius in the first
century. For the contemporaries of Horace the name of Lucilius was
synonymous with personal abuse and invective.[45] That was the
meaning of 'Lucilian character' (*Lucilianus character*). The name
which they gave to this quality was simply *libertas*. Horace's reaction
to this aspect of Lucilius' reputation was again complex. He praises
him for it at the beginning of both the fourth and tenth satires. But
he is very careful to distinguish the sort of invective which he
characterises by the verb *notare* ('to stigmatise') and which has a
basic moral and exemplary justification from mere backbiting and
vicious personal abuse designed merely to raise a laugh. He emulates
the *libertas* of Lucilius only to a limited extent and only to provide
negative moral *exempla*. He is critical of personal abuse which serves
no moral purpose and his criticism is here aimed as much at the
latter-day supporters of Lucilius as at Lucilius himself. Horace seems
to be implying through his own practice something which is also
suggested by the remaining fragments, that the almost exclusive
identification of the name of Lucilius with invective in the first
century was in fact a distortion of the true nature of his poetry.
The new evaluation of Lucilius which is implicit in Horace's own
practice, the broader scope of his satire and the clear allusions to
Lucilian models precisely when his poems are least concerned with
invective, all combine to persuade the reader that Horace is a truly
modern Lucilius.[46] The question of why Horace chose as his model
the poet so closely identified with invective and then chose to play
down precisely that aspect of his model still remains. The answer
perhaps lies in the word *libertas*. As applied to Lucilius the word

---

[45] See Coffey (1976: 35–64 (esp. 63–4)); Anderson (1963b: 73).

[46] Contrast Fraenkel (1957: 124–35); Rudd (1966: 86–124); Brink (1963: 156–71),
who all see Lucilius as Horace's prime target. Fiske (1920) remains fundamental: his
detailed arguments do not all command assent, but it would be wrong to underesti-
mate the amount of imitation of Lucilius in Horace. In all probability his imitations
are based on theme and structure at least as much as upon the detailed verbal echoes
still dimly perceptible from the fragments.

denotes primarily freedom of speech. But *libertas* itself is a much broader concept and it was never a more emotive or powerful concept than during the forties and thirties.[47] Both Pompey and Caesar had claimed to be the champions of *libertas,* but from the death of Cato Uticensis the word became the rallying cry of the anti-Caesarians, the Pompeians and the Republicans. Caesar was killed in the name of *libertas* and it was the watchword of Brutus and Cassius at Philippi. At first sight there may seem to be little connection between the two types of *libertas.* But the freedom of speech which was exemplified by Lucilius was essential to the aristocratic conception of *libertas*[48] and the inseparability of the two concepts is well illustrated by a letter of C. Trebonius, one of the Liberators, which was written to Cicero in 44 (*Ad familiares* 12.16.3):

uos quid ageretis in republica, cum has litteras dabam, non sciebam. audiebam quaedam turbulenta, quae scilicet cupio esse falsa, ut aliquando otiosa libertate fruamur; quod uel minime mihi adhuc contigit. ego tamen nactus in nauigatione nostra pusillum laxamenti, concinnaui tibi munusculum ex instituto meo, et dictum, cum magno nostro honore a te dictum, conclusi et tibi infra subscripsi. in quibus uersiculis si tibi quibusdam uerbis εὐθυρρημονέστερος ['risqué'] uidebor, turpitudo personae eius, in quam liberius inuehimur, nos uindicabit. ignosces etiam iracundiae nostrae, quae iusta est in eiusmodi et homines et ciues. deinde, qui magis hoc Lucilio licuerit assumere libertatis, quam nobis? cum etiamsi odio par fuerit in eos, quos laesit, tamen certe non magis dignos habuerit, in quos tanta libertate uerborum incurreret.

In writing this letter I was not sure what part you were playing in public affairs. I heard about certain upheavals, which naturally I hope are false, so that at some point we may enjoy our freedom away from the fray—something I haven't had the least chance of to this point. And yet, I found just a slight measure of relaxation in the course of my journey. Thus, according to my usual practice, I have put together a pretty little gift for you, and I have versified one of your sayings, one spoken with high esteem for me. And I have written it out for you below. If in these verses, given certain words that I use, I seem to you too *risqué*, the foulness of the person against whom I am inveighing so freely will vindicate me. You will also overlook my rage, which is justified against men and citizens of this type—still, why should Lucilius

---

[47] See Wirszubski (1950); Syme index s.vv. *Libertas,* Freedom of Speech; MacMullen (1967: 1–45); Weinstock (1971: 133–62).

[48] See esp. Syme (1939: 152); MacMullen (1967: 298 n. 17).

have more a right than I to lay hold of this level of freedom? Though he may
have been a match (for me) in the loathing he felt towards those whom he
castigated with such great freedom of speech, his victims were certainly no
more deserving (sc. of such treatment than mine).

Here we find Trebonius celebrating his first taste of that *libertas*, which
he evidently hoped that the murder of Caesar had restored, by composing an invective in the manner of Lucilius as a concrete demonstration of his new-found *libertas*. The target of his invective was
probably M. Antonius, his former friend and the future Triumvir.

Sallust makes it clear that to many, not only those who supported
Sex. Pompeius, the second Triumvirate was a tyranny and incompat-
ible with traditional *libertas*.[49] It is difficult to believe that in this
context Horace's choice of Lucilius as a model was politically naive.
When Horace, who proclaims himself to be the *amicus* of Maecenas
and so a supporter of the Triumvirs, also sets himself up as the New
Lucilius, he is surely inviting us to see the Triumvirs as the friends of
libertas, not its enemies. His own redefinition of Lucilian *libertas* as
something morally responsible invites the inference that the Triumvirs are opposed not to true *libertas*, which is traditional and responsible, but rather to licence, the irresponsible, malicious and divisive
exercise of freedom with which true *libertas* is wrongly confused by
those who oppose them.[50] At all events the lack of invective in Horace
is striking and requires some explanation. It cannot be seriously
maintained that the main reason is that Horace was only the son of
a freedman and so not powerful enough to attack important living
contemporaries. It was never probable that anyone would seek retri-
bution from Horace. His friends were too powerful, as Horace
himself concedes, albeit jokingly, at the end of *Satire* 2.1.[51] That is
why it is better to look for a positive reason for his handling of this
key feature of Lucilian satire.

There is some reason to think that Lucilius was exploited for
propaganda purposes by the Republican cause and that he was

[49] Syme (1964a: 121–37; 214–39) and, esp., Sall. *Iug.* 3.3.

[50] For *licentia* vs. *libertas*, see Wirszubski (1950: 7–8). Cf. Hor. *Odes* 3.24.25–32;
4.15.9–11.

[51] See above, n. 10.

associated in particular with the Pompeians.[52] Lucilius was the great-
uncle of Pompeius Magnus and two of the friends of Pompeius, his
freedman Pompeius Lenaeus and Curtius Nicias, wrote exegetical
works on Lucilius. It may well be, although the evidence does not
allow a definitive conclusion, that in fact most of the *defensores* and
imitators of Lucilius were friends of Pompey and hostile to Caesar. If
so, the trend seems to have survived the death of Pompeius Magnus.
His freedman, Pompeius Lenaeus, composed a Lucilian invective
against Sallust in reply to his treatment of Pompey in his *Histories*.[53]
The case of Trebonius has already been noted. If this assumption is
correct and the Pompeians had indeed been able to make capital out
of their association with Lucilius as the poet of Republican *libertas*[54]
then one of Horace's motives must surely have been to issue a
counter-challenge: he was the true successor to Lucilius, his friends
the true champions of *libertas*. The technique is familiar. In the
forties and thirties, Antonius had made propaganda both from his
claim to be the new Dionysus and from his alleged descent from
Hercules through the eponymous ancestor of his *gens*, Anton son of
Hercules. In the run up to Actium the supporters of Octavian did
their best to counter these claims. But they were obviously effective as
propaganda and after Actium the Augustan poets simply transfer
them to Augustus himself and Hercules and Dionysus become familiar prototypes for the *princeps*.[55]

There may however be a more positive side to Horace's choice of
Lucilius as a model. He was closely identified with one of the greatest
heroes of the Republic, P. Cornelius Scipio Africanus Aemilianus.
Simply because of the pre-eminence which he had achieved, Scipio
provided useful precedents to the great men of the first century who

[52] So Coffey (1976: 64) and esp. Anderson (1963b), who overstates a basically
sound thesis (understandably, in view of the novelty of his idea, of its importance and
of the frustrating nature of the evidence).

[53] See Treggiari (1969: 119).

[54] Contrast Anderson (1963b: 74).

[55] See Huzar (1978), index s.vv. Heracles, Dionysus: this led to the attacks on
Antonius as a drunkard and a glutton (see Scott (1929: 133–41 and 1933: 7–50)). For
Augustus-Heracles, see esp. Virg. *Aen.* 8 with Binder (1971: 146–7); and for Augus-
tus-Dionysus, see Virg. *Aen.* 6.791–805; Hor. *Odes* 3.3.9–15; *Epist.* 2.1.5–17; this was
part of Augustus' attempt to replace Antonius as the new Alexander, cf. Kienast
(1969: 430–56). See also Woodman (1983) on Vell. 2.82.4.

attained extraordinary positions of power and influence: the sole
consul Pompeius, the dictator Caesar and the Triumvir Octavian.
The 'Scipionic Circle' is an important part of the idealisation of
Scipio and the growth of the Scipionic myth. The reality is less
impressive.[56] Yet through his patronage of Polybius, Panaetius, Terence and Lucilius he established himself as an important patron of
the arts. Pompeius also had literary friends and encouraged, apparently, work on Lucilius. But he was less happy in his choice of writers.
The next major patron was Maecenas and it is hard to believe that he
was unconscious of the predecent. Horace's claim to be the new
Lucilius certainly invites the reader to compare the two circles.
Even though in *Sermones* 1 he nowhere makes the parallel explicit,
it is clear from the first satire of Book 2 that he was leaving the reader
to draw the inference for himself. In that poem he has Trebatius
accepting the equation of Lucilius and Horace and naturally extending it to equate Scipio with Caesar (Octavian).

This brief survey will, it is hoped, have made it clear that Horace's
choice of Lucilius as a model is potentially much more significant
than has generally been realised.[57] It is true that Lucilius had acquired
a considerable reputation as a poet. But Horace makes it plain that he
had chosen him as his model in spite of and not because of his purely
literary achievements. The reader is confronted with a Horace who
proclaims himself to be the *amicus* of Maecenas and at the same time
the modern equivalent of the poet who had inescapable associations
with Republican *libertas*, with Scipio and the Scipionic Circle and
with Pompeius. For the most part the reader is left to draw what
inferences he will from this combination. But he is surely intended to
leave the *Sermones* with the impression that Horace and his friends
cherish the true Republican ideal of *libertas;* that this circle of friends
is characterised by its cultured interest in Hellenistic philosophy,
blended with a deep respect for the *mos maiorum,* and by its interest
in literature which conforms to the highest contemporary standards,
a circle in fact remarkably reminiscent of the legendary Scipionic

---

[56] See Astin (1967: 294–306).
[57] Compare Horace's choice of Archilochus as his model in the *Epodes*, Nisbet
(1984: 2).

Circle; and, finally, that in this latest war between a second Caesar and a second Pompeius it is the champions of *libertas* and the *mos maiorum* who have won, not their oppressors.

THE REMAINING *SATIRES* OF BOOK 1

The initial dedication to Maecenas (1.1.1) establishes at the outset Horace's friendship with him and so with the new rulers of Rome. But the prime function of *Satires* 1, 2 and 3 is to set the tone for the collection and to establish the *persona* of the poet. While the themes themselves are the commonplaces of Hellenistic philosophy, what is striking and novel is that these poems treat moral issues seriously and at length in a style which matches the highest standards of Neoteric art. In this respect they contrast sharply with the poetry of Catullus and the other Neoterics and even with Virgil's *Eclogues*. The only precedent is offered by the Epicurean poets, Lucretius and Varius Rufus (*de morte*). The philosophy of the satires is eclectic and, for the most part, commonplace. But there is a slight bias towards Epicureanism in the quietism of the first satire and in the value attached to friendship in the third. In the second, it is unexpectedly, and perhaps pointedly, revealed that the teachings of Philodemus and the Elder Cato are in harmony in preferring the brothel to adultery. This general impression is reinforced by the constant verbal echoes of Lucretius.[58] But Horace appears as a typical Roman Epicurean, neither doctrinaire nor dogmatic. It was a popular philosophy at the time and it is important to remember that Maecenas, the dedicatee, was an Epicurean.[59]

The only school, however, which Horace does reject is that of extreme and dogmatic Stoicism. The most influential Roman Stoic had been the younger Cato. His ostentatious Stoicism and his uncompromising Republicanism were dramatically combined in his

---

[58] For example, *S.* 1.118–19 and Lucr. 3.938–9; the theme of discontent, Lucr. 3.1053–75; *S.* 1.2 and Lucr. 4.1058–83; *S.* 1.3.43–54 and Lucr. 4.1160–70; 1.3.98–112 and Lucr. 5.780–94; 925–1160. The possibility of echoes from Varius Rufus' *De morte* should not be forgotten.

[59] André (1967: 15–61).

suicide. He had rapidly become the hero of the Pompeian and Republican cause and it seems likely that his example very quickly established austere Stoicism as the proper and fashionable philosophy for those opposed to Caesar and his successors, a cause which it was to serve for more than a century.[60] The explicit rejection of extreme Stoicism at the end of the opening triad may thus be intended to highlight a simple point: the Stoics and the Pompeians have no monopoly of concern with morality and they do not even have the most satisfactory answers.

In these first three satires Horace presents himself deep in conversation with his friends, of whom the most prominent is Maecenas, urging a strong moral stance on a variety of issues. No one will suppose that Maecenas needed to be persuaded by Horace. There was a convention by which advice and exhortation could stand as an alternative to encomium: the speaker urges his addressee to do or believe that which he already intends to do or does believe.[61] The advantage of this indirect approach is that it virtually prevents the audience from accusing the speaker of base flattery or the addressee of tyranny. This is probably why Cicero adopted this technique in the *Pro Marcello*. By adopting what is clearly a very similar technique, Horace creates a favourable impression not only of himself but also of Maecenas and the nature of the *amicitia* which he extends to Horace. It is worth recalling Cicero, who introduced the section on the evils of flattery at *De amicitia* 91: 'therefore, just as to warn and to be warned is a key feature of true friendship, and one [sc. of the friends] should do so freely but without being hurtful, and the other should receive criticism patiently and without resentment, so one must think that there is no worse blight upon friendships than adulation, flattery, and toadyism' (*ut igitur et monere et moneri proprium est uerae amicitiae, et alterum libere facere, non aspere, alterum patienter accipere, non repugnanter, sic habendum est nullam in amicitiis pestem esse maiorem quam adulationem blanditiam assentationem*). By using this approach Horace is able to convey two highly significant impressions: first, that Maecenas is no tyrant and Horace no flattering courtier; second, that his *amicus* Maecenas. and

---

[60] MacMullen (1967: 1–94).
[61] Nisbet-Hubbard (1978), and index s.v. paraenesis.

his other *amici* (including inevitably, but implicitly, Octavian), share his own views on the evils of discontent, *auaritia* and adultery, which is an example of *luxuria* which leads to debt and so (the argument was commonplace) to civil war.

The full significance of this can only be appreciated when the nature of the contemporary hostile propaganda against the Triumvirs is recalled. The Pompeians and Republicans will have called the Triumvirate a tyranny, *dominatio, potentia paucorum* and *regnum* ('tyranny', 'control by a few', 'kingship'). A letter ascribed to Brutus accuses Octavian of *cupiditas* ('lust') and *licentia* ('licence', *Ad M. Brutum* 2.1) and faithfully reflects contemporary propaganda: 'No condition of our enslavement will be so favourable as to deter me, for my part, from waging war against the state itself; that is, against this kingship and these extraordinary military powers and tyranny and control that aim to stand above the laws' (*ego certe, quin cum ipsa re bellum geram, hoc est cum regno et imperiis extraordinariis et dominatione et potentia, quae supra leges se esse uelit, nulla erit tam bona condicio seruiendi, qua deterrear, Ad M. Brutum* 25.6).[62] According to Plutarch, Brutus said much the same about the Triumvirate (*Brutus* 28.2–3) and Sallust echoes the same propaganda (*Bellum Iugurthinum* 3.3 *potentia paucorum*).[63] It may also be assumed that the Pompeians alleged that the Triumvirs (principally, of course, Octavian who was in Rome) were motivated by *auaritia, ambitio* and *luxuria* ('greed', 'ambition', 'profligacy') since these were the conventional and established characteristics of those who waged civil war.[64] Sextus could and, doubtless, did argue that Octavian was the aggressor.[65] It must not be assumed that it was only an insignificant minority who were hostile to the Triumvirs at this time. Sextus enjoyed considerable popular support: Etruria had risen in arms to support him in 36 (Dio 49.15). Many in the higher levels of society were in his debt, especially those who had been proscribed or who had fought for the Republic at Philippi and then found refuge with Sextus

---

[62] Shackleton Bailey (1980: 10–14), has argued that this letter is a forgery.

[63] Syme (1964a: 218); not all, however, agree upon the reference: Koestermann (1971: 36).

[64] Jal (1963: 377–91): cf. Suet. *Aug.* 68 (Sex. Pompeius called Octavian *effeminatum*).

[65] Cf. Tac. *Ann.* 1.10: *Pompeium imagine pacis (deceptum)*.

until their return in 39.[66] On the other hand the proscriptions of 43–42, the Philippi campaign and the Perusine War of 41–40, and the land confiscations had all created hostility towards the Triumvirs in general and Octavian in particular. Sallust's testimony is particularly important. He had been a supporter of Julius Caesar and remained hostile to Pompeius Magnus. Yet he clearly loathed the Triumvirs and insisted that Rome's moral decline and its concomitant political corruption had reached its nadir under the Triumvirs.[67]

Against this background it is significant that Horace presents Maecenas and his friends as being as much concerned with moral standards as Sallust himself and equally hostile to the vices of *auaritia, ambitio* and *luxuria*. Satire 1.1 attacks discontent with one's lot. Sallust complains: 'all shifts in affairs portend slaughter, flight, and all the other effects of war' (*omnes rerum mutationes caedem, fugam aliaque hostilia portendant, Bellum Iugurthinum* 3.2); and, as a part of his contrast of an idealised past with the corrupt present, says: 'human life was conducted without lust: each man was satisfied with what he had (*uita hominum sine cupiditate agitabatur: sua cuique satis placebant, Bellum Catilinae* 2.1). Horace also turns to an attack upon greed, *auaritia*, which he, like Sallust again (*Bellum Catilinae* 10–11), sees as the source of present ills. In the next satire, Horace attacks sexual depravity. Sallust had listed among the characteristics of the supporters of Catiline: 'a lust for sexual depravity; women openly selling their chastity' (*lubido stupri; mulieres pudicitiam in propatulo habere*); and had inferred: 'these were the things that, once their friends were broke, made the youth burn hot for villainy' (*haec iuuentutem, ubi familiares opes defecerant, ad facinora incendebant, Bellum Catilinae* 13.344 and, more bluntly, 14.2: 'with his dick he squandered his father's goods', *pene bona patria laceraverat*).

Given the general and commonplace nature of such complaints, it would be rash to insist that Horace had Sallust in mind (but see

[66] Vell. 2.77 and App. *Bell. ciu.* 5.72.
[67] Syme (1962: 121–37; 212; 214–39; 280). Little is known of his great-nephew, adopted in 35. He is mentioned with Dellius and Cocceius by Seneca (*Clem.* 1.10.1) as among those who joined Augustus *ex aduersariorum castris*. They were Antonians, and Syme (1964a: 275) makes him 'a partisan of Antonius' also. If so, Seneca is being careless in his use of the plural. He may have supported, rather, the Republicans and/or Sextus.

above, pp. 59, 65). But the historian does not escape unnoticed (*Satires* 1.2.47ff.).[68] He had been ejected from the senate in 50 by the censor, Ap. Claudius Puicher, and subsequently accused by Varro (in *Pius aut de pace*) of adultery and, also, of extortion. Inevitably men contrasted his life with the moral fervour of his writings.[69] Horace does not repeat these crude slanders: instead he repeats Sallust's own defence: 'I touch no matron' (*matronam nullam tango,* 1.2.49).[70] And then he mischievously accuses him of taking this (acceptable) preference for freed-women (*libertinae*) to an excess where it is as reprehensible as adultery itself.

Satire 1.3 deserves special comment. The thematic words *aequum, iustum* and *ignoscere* ('fair', 'just', 'to pardon') establish the theme of the poem as not an attack upon any individual or vice but a recommendation of the moral virtue, *aequitas* ('fairness'). In the language of political morality this word is closely related to *clementia* ('clemency') and, as such, was doubtless a topical theme at the conclusion of the war with Sextus, if not also during the war.[71] It is worth recalling that in the war between Pompeius Magnus and Julius Caesar, the Pompeians had repeatedly been accused of *crudelitas* ('cruelty') and of desiring *regnum* ('royal authority') and Cicero claimed: 'at times not only men in arms, but private persons as well were threatened' (*non modo armatis interdum etiam otiosis minabantur, Pro Marcello* 18).[72] Caesar, of course, had preferred 'a new procedure of victory, so that we should protect ourselves with mercy and generosity' (*noua ratio uincendi ut misericordia et liberalitate nos muniamus, Ad Atticum* 9.7c.1). Caesar's *clementia* however was hated as the virtue of a tyrant, and two of its beneficiaries (or

[68] The view, accepted here, that Sallustius at *S.* 1.2.48 is the historian and not the great-nephew (which would cause chronological problems) is accepted, on balance, by Syme (1964a: 280–4) and Rudd (1966: 135–6).

[69] For example, Aul. Gell. *Noct. Att.* 17.18 (Varro) and Suet. *Gramm.* 1 (Pompeius Lenaeus).

[70] Ps.-Acro on *S.* 1.2.49 seems to contain at least the seeds of the truth: that Sallust had defended himself against the charge of adultery made by Varro—probably not in the senate however—with some unfortunate remark that his critics could wilfully misinterpret and use against him, as Horace does here.

[71] See Hellegouarc'h (1963: 261–7); Weinstock (1971: 238; 245–6).

[72] See Seager (1979: 176–7), for the evidence and a realistic discussion. Cf. Weinstock (1971: 237).

victims), Brutus and Cassius, led the conspirators.[73] Octavian, understandably, began his career by refusing to show clemency either in the proscriptions or to those captured at Philippi.[74] In the *Res gestae*, however, he claimed: 'often I waged wars on land and at sea, against citizens and external foes throughout the whole world, and as victor I spared all those citizens who sought my pardon' (*bella terra et mari ciuilia externaque toto in orbe terrarum saepe gessi uictorque omnibus ueniam petentibus ciuibus peperci*, 3.1).[75] The shift in attitude seems to have started after Naulochus in 36: Appian states that he pardoned the Pompeian generals (*Bellum ciuile* 5.127), although Dio suggests that his *clementia* was not indiscriminate (49.12.4–5).[76]

Horace handles the theme with subtlety and caution. He begins with a humorous portrait of Tigellius ('there was nothing steady about that man', *nil aequale homini fuit illi*, 1.3.9) who serves as a foil to the one and only direct appearance of Octavian in this collection of satires. Unobtrusively, Horace establishes the link between Octavian and his *pater*, Julius Caesar, and reminds the reader of his power ('he who could compel', *qui cogere posset*, 1.3.4–5), even while he shows him pardoning the fault of his friend, Tigellius. The virtue displayed by Octavian is *aequitas*, not *clementia*. The next section of the poem expands upon the significance of this as a virtue which is desirable among friends, that is among equals, rather than as a quality to be desired in a tyrant's behaviour to his subjects. The whole section is marked by repetitions of its key verb, *ignoscere* (1.3.23 and 4), and summarised: 'this is what binds men together and keeps them bound as friends' (*haec res et iungit, iunctos et seruat amicos*, 1.3.54). Having established the importance of *aequitas* in dealings with friends, Horace moves on to a discussion of crime and punishment in the wider context of society. He now links the concepts of *aequitas* and *iustitia* together. His own position is illuminated by contrast with that of the doctrinaire Stoics: they insist on equal treatment for 'thefts' and 'villainies' (*furta* and *latrocinia*): 'you

[73] For Caesar's *clementia*, see Weinstock (1971: 233–43); Hellegouarc'h (1963: 261–3); and for the hostility which it inspired see Jal (1963: 464–8) and Syme (1939: 159–60).
[74] Dio 47.13.3 and Suet. *Aug.* 13; 27.
[75] The crucial word is *petentibus*: cf. Vell. 2.86.2. On the *clementia* of Augustus, see Weinstock (1971: 240).
[76] Cf. Dio 48.3.6 and Sen. *Clem.* 1.11 and Suet. *Aug.* 27.2 on his *paenitentia saevitate*.

threaten to mow down small offences with the great, using a similar
scythe, if men should grant royal authority to you' (*magnis parua
mineris* | *falce recisurum simili te, si tibi regnum* | *permittant homines,*
1.3.122–4).[77] The link between the Republican-Pompeian cause and
doctrinaire Stoicism has been noted above; it was standard practice to
label the Pompeians 'brigands' (*latrones, Epode* 4.19); Octavian certainly accused Sextus of aiming at *regnum* (*Epode* 9.9–10); and perhaps the old accusations of *crudelitas* had been revived against the
Pompeians. Such a context would lend point to the sentiment: 'how
recklessly we sanction laws that are unfair against ourselves' (*quam
temere in nosmet legem sancimus iniquam,* 1.3.67). Horace ends the
poem, as often in the satires, by using himself as an example: 'and my
dear friends will forgive me if I have stupidly done wrong' (*et mihi
dulces ignoscent, si quid peccaro stultus, amici,* 1.3.139–40). The language resumes the earlier argument. But among his *amici* were Caesar
(Octavian) and Maecenas; among the faults which they pardoned, the
reader will recall, Horace's adherence to the Republican cause at
Philippi. He himself is an example of Octavian's *clementia* or, to use
the preferred terminology, *aequitas.* The poem thus ends by recalling
implicitly the theme with which it began, the *aequitas* of Octavian.[78]

The only poem which gives a direct and detailed picture of the
Republican side is *Satire* 1.7. Horace here gives an apparently
straightforward account of an incident in Brutus' camp in Asia in
43/42. The tale is told with gusto, seemingly for its own sake or,
rather, for the sake of the commonplace pun at the end. But what
makes the poem really interesting is simply the fact that it is included
at all in a collection dedicated to Maecenas. There is no overt malice
against Brutus. In the eyes of the Triumvirs his possession of Asia
was no doubt illegal.[79] He presumably claimed to be a proconsul

---

[77] The collocation of *furta* and *latrocinia* may echo the language of contemporary
political polemic: cf. Sall. *Iug.* 4.7 (a reference I owe to Prof. Woodman).

[78] The elasticity of the Latin words helps Horace to treat an important issue
suggestively while only treating one aspect or part of it in detail: cf. Cic. *Marc.* 21
*omnes enim, qui fuerunt inimici, aut sua pertinacia uitam amiserunt aut tua miser-
icordia retinuerunt, ut aut nulli supersint de inimicis aut qui fuerunt sint amicissimi.*
Note also *Odes* 1.12.57 (Augustus) *latum reget aequus orbem.*

[79] Cf. *RG* 2 *qui parentem meum trucidauerunt, eos in exilium expuli iudiciis
legitimis ultus eorum facinus et postea bellum inferentis rei publicae uici bis acie.* The
reference is to the tribunal established by the *lex Pedia* in 43.

(perhaps with *maius imperium*).[80] Horace calls him imprecisely a *praetor* (18) which suits his judicial function in this scene.[81] The joke about Caesar's murder is told in the bluntest language ('you cut the throat', *iugulas*, 3) and with no sign of embarrassment. This creates the overwhelming impression that the friendship of Maecenas has imposed no inhibitions on Horace about freely recalling his earlier allegiance. The implicit message must have been reassuring to other former Republicans who had either just returned to Italy or who were still hoping to return after the defeat of Sex. Pompeius. If Horace, the freedman's son, could find such complete acceptance, there was hope for the others.[82]

On reflection, however, the scene seems rather less innocent. The Republicans are depicted at each other's throats in litigation,[83] which seems peculiarly appropriate, when one recalls the unending series of trials and prosecutions which were the hallmark of the last years of the Republic and the laments of the Republicans like Cicero when Caesar had deprived him of his favourite occupation.[84] Both contestants are characterised by their fond devotion to the arts of vituperation. Horace invites us to share his evident and typically Roman distaste for litigation.[85] These exemplars of *libertas* are also described in language comparable to that used by Horace of the imitators of Lucilius.[86] Finally, the pretensions of the litigants and

---

[80] See Broughton (1968: 346–7; 361).

[81] See, e.g., Crook (1967). For the legal background to this poem, see Burton (1975: 92–106). It should also be noted that Brutus had been appointed *praetor (urbanus)* by Julius Caesar in 22. The ingratitude was duly noted and helped to swing public opinion against the conspirators (App. *Bell. ciu.* 2.146).

[82] Cf. Odes 2.7 (to a Pompeius). It is not known precisely when or how Horace returned to Italy after Philippi—via Domitius Ahenobarbus in 40 (Brundisium); via Sicily and Sex. Pompeius in 39 (Misenum); or by some other route.

[83] Cf. Cicero's complaint about the atmosphere in the camp of Pompeius Magnus (*Ad fam.* 7.3.2): *reliqui primum in ipso bello rapaces, deinde in oratione ita crudeles, ut ipsam uictoriam horrerem; maximum autem aes alienum amplissimorum uirorum.* See further Gelzer (1968: 238–9).

[84] For the trials, Gruen (1974: 260–357). For Cicero's complaints, see, e.g., *De off.* 2.2–4.

[85] Note the charge against Horace at *S.* 1.4.78–9 *'laedere gaudes'* | *inquit 'et hoc studio prauus facis'*. Cf. Cic. *De off* 2.51. Defence speeches were, of course, a different matter. See further Wiseman (1971: 120–1); Kelly (1976: 93–111).

[86] Compare: *durus*, 1.7.29 and 1.4.8; *tumidus*, 1.7.7 and *turgidus*, 1.10.36; *ruebat flumen* and *multo fluenti*, 1.7.26–8 and 1.4.11; 1.10.50–1; 61–2; *salso*, 1.7.28 and *sale*, 1.10.3; *ridetur*, 1.7.22 and 1.4.82–3 and 1.10.7–8. See also Bernardi Perini (1975: 1–24).

even their profession of *uirtus* (1.7.14)[87] are first mocked by the comparison with Hector and Achilles[88] and then punctured by the more realistic comparison with the gladiators Bithus and Bacchius.

At the centre of all this activity is Brutus. The poem culminates in the reference to his murder of Caesar and his pride in his family tradition of opposition to tyranny.[89] The murder of Caesar had taken place on the day when, so it was rumoured, it was to be proposed in the senate that Caesar should be given the title *rex*, perhaps only for use outside Italy in his forthcoming campaign against the Parthians.[90] In view of this, it is at least ironic that Brutus who is now in charge of Asia is addressed by Persius as 'Asia's sun' (*solem Asiae*) and his companions as 'health-giving stars' (*stellas salubres*, 1.7.24). This is the conventional language of encomium of Hellenistic kings. It is also reminiscent of Caesarian propaganda about Caesar's star (the *Caesaris astrum*).[91] Suddenly the claims of the liberators ring hollow. Perhaps the real motive for the murder is contained in the description of Brutus as 'the praetor controlling wealthy Asia' (*praetore tenente ditem Asiam*, 1.7.18–19).[92]

---

[87] *uirtus* was the key word for the Republicans: cf. *Odes* 2.7.11 *uirtus fracta*, with Porphyrio ad loc. (*uirtute se Cassius et Brutus praecipue iactabant*) and Nisbet-Hubbard (1978: ad loc.).

[88] 'Identifications and comparisons with Homeric heroes were always fashionable', Weinstock (1971: 199). But Horace may be mimicking a fashionable way of talking among the Republicans: see Plut. *Brut.* 23 (Brutus and Hector); 24 (Patroclus); 34 (a quarrel between Cassius and Brutus compared to that between Achilles and Agamemnon. Plutarch's account of this episode also illustrates the *parrhesia* cultivated among the Republicans). Earlier, Domitius Ahenobarbus had maliciously nicknamed Pompey 'Agamemnon' (Plut. *Pomp.* 67; *Caes.* 41).

[89] Commentators seem to forget that these included not only L. Iunius Brutus who expelled the Tarquins but also C. Servilius Ahala (Plut. *Brut.* 2; Cic. *Ad Att.* 13.40.1, cf. 2.24.3)—an ancestor through his mother and adoptive father—who killed Sp. Maelius for aiming at *regnum* in 439 (Liv. 4.13–14).

[90] Cic. *De diu.* 2.110 with Pease (1963: ad loc.). See also Weinstock (1971: 340–1) and Rawson (1950: 149–50).

[91] Cf. Fraenkel 121 n. 2; Weinstock (1971: 381–4); Doblhofer (1966: 17–21). Note that Plutarch says that when Cassius was hailed by the Rhodians as 'Lord and King', he retorted angrily: οὔτε βασιλεὺς οὔτε κύριος, τοῦ δὲ κυρίου καί βασιλέως φονεύς καί κολαστής 'neither lord nor king but punisher and killer of your lord and king': *Brut.* 30. (Cf. Val. Max. 1.5.8 and App. *Bell. ciu.* 4.65–7.)

[92] Cf. Kiessling-Heinze (1968: ad loc.). For the reputation of Asia as a province, see Cic. *Mur.* 11–12. Cf. Nic. Dam. *Vit. Caes.* 19.

Horace is subtle enough to leave the reader to draw his own conclusions. He cannot be accused of malicious invention: every reader knows he was there and that the anecdote has all the authority of an eyewitness account. In any case, we are assured that the tale is well known (1.7.3).

Satire 1.8 complements 1.7 perfectly. It deals with the transform-ation of the burial ground on the Esquiline into the magnificent gardens (*horti*) of Maecenas.[93] Horace forgoes the opportunity to compose an extravagant and encomiastic description in the manner of, say, Statius, *Siluae* 1.3 or 2.2. The contrast with Persius' extrava-gant encomium of Brutus in 1.7 is complete and, presumably, inten-tional. The whole poem is spoken by Priapus, not by Horace *in propria persona*, and the name of Maecenas is not even mentioned. The avoidance of fulsome flattery and the good humour are typical of the friendship with Maecenas. But it would be a mistake to infer that the compliment is not serious. The poem concentrates on the foul deeds of the witches Canidia and Sagana, but the contrast of *nunc-prius* ('now-before') which dominates the poem reminds us of the benefit which Maecenas has conferred upon the city by ridding it of such nuisances.

The theme of magic and witchcraft is literary and conventional.[94] On one level it illustrates the thoroughly Hellenistic literary tastes of Maecenas' circle.[95] But the subject was also topical (see also above, p. 46). In 36 C. Calvisius Sabinus (cos. 39) was appointed to rid Italy and the city of Rome itself of the thieves and robbers which infested it (Appian, *Bellum ciuile* 5.132). A little later Agrippa expelled astrolo-gers and witches from Rome (Dio 49.43). But it was Maecenas, according to Dio (49.16.2), who was in charge of affairs in Rome and the rest of Italy at this time. He seems to have instituted some kind of precursor of the Vigiles, a sort of police force cum fire service (Appian, *Bellum ciuile* 5.132).[96] His services to Rome in

---

[93] See Fraenkel (1957: 123–4); Rudd (1966: 70). For the *horti Maecenatis,* Grimal (1943: 50–3) (for Priapus, gardens and graveyards) and 152–5.

[94] See now Tupet (1976).

[95] Buchheit (1962: 63 n. 2 and 66 n. 2 refers to Maecenas *als Priapeendichter,* citing Sen. *Epist.* 101.1 but without explanation).

[96] See Gabba (1970: ad loc.). Permanent arrangements do not seem to have been made before 7 BCE see *CAH* 10.200 and, for earlier arrangements, Lintott (1968: 89–106).

this unfamiliar capacity were recalled a quarter of a century later by a
lesser poet than Horace:[97]

> num minus urbis erat custos et Caesaris obses?
> num tibi non tutas fecit in urbe uias?
> nocte sub obscura quis te spoliauit amantem,
> quis tetigit ferro, durior ipse, latus?

Can it be said that he was any less a guardian of the city and Caesar's stand-
in? Can it be said that he did not make the city's streets safe for you? Who
robbed you in the dark of night, on your way to make love? Who struck your
flank with his sword, himself more cruel than its iron?

Horace's poem is probably intended to recall this side of Maecenas'
career as well.

   It would be strange if the propaganda of Octavian had not associated the activities of these thieves and brigands, astrologers and
witches with Sex. Pompeius. Canidia and Sagana are practising
necromancy: they gather up the bones from the graveyard and
summon the spirits of the dead (1.8.29).[98] Such activities were
especially associated with Pythagoreans.[99] The most famous of
these was Nigidius Figulus who was an ardent supporter of Pompeius
Magnus and the only man known to have been tried and exiled for
magical practices in the Republic.[100] The addiction of the Pompeians
to this sect seems to have survived the death of Nigidius in 45. His
famous prophecy that Octavian was *dominus terrarum orbi natus*
('born to be master of the world') may have been originally used by
Pompeians and Republicans in hostile propaganda against Octavian.[101] But there is another interesting incident involving Sex. Pompeius. The elder Pliny (*Natural history* 7.178) says:

bello Siculo Gabienus Caesaris classium fortissimus captus a Sex. Pompeio
iussu eius incisa ceruice et uix cohaerente iacuit in litore toto die. deinde
cum aduesperauisset, gemitu precibusque congregata multitudine petiit uti

---

[97] *Eleg. in Maec.* 27–30; cf. 14: *Romanae tu uigil urbis eras.*
[98] See Tupet (1976: 299–300).
[99] See MacMullen (1967: 95–162); Liebeschuetz (1979: 119–39).
[100] Liebeschuetz (1979: 130–1).
[101] Suet. *Aug.* 94.5 (see further Dio 45.1.3–5) and compare ibid. 40.5 and 53.1:
(Augustus) *domini appellationem ut maledictum et opprobrium semper exhorruit* etc.
For the hostility of Nigidius to Caesar, see e.g. Weinstock (1971: 21; 52 and 341).

Pompeius ad se ueniret aut aliquem ex arcanis mitteret, se enim ab inferis remissum habere quae nuntiaret. misit complures Pompeius cum amicis, quibus Gabienus dixit inferis diis placere Pompei causas et partes pias, proinde euentum futurum quem optaret.

During the Sicilian War, Gabienus, the bravest man in Caesar's fleet, was captured by Sextus Pompey. At Pompey's order his throat was cut, nearly sliced all the way through, and he lay on the shore for an entire day. Then, after evening had arrived, a crowd was drawn together by his groaning and his entreaties. He asked that Pompey come to him, or that he should send one of his inner-staff, because he, having been sent back from the nether-world, had news to tell him. Pompey sent several of his friends. Gabienus told them that Pompey's cause, and his pious party, were pleasing to the gods below, and that accordingly the outcome would be what he desired.

This version of the story seems to have been a part of Sex. Pompeius' own propaganda.[102] It is not hard to imagine the retort from Octavian. Cicero, with far less to work on in his speech against Vatinius, had said (*In Vatinium* 14):

te Pythagoreum soles dicere . . . cum inaudita ac nefaria sacra susceperis, cum inferorum animas elicere, cum puerorum extis deos manes mactare soleas.

You are accustomed to calling yourself a Pythagorean . . . whenever you take up rites that are unheard of and unspeakable, whenever you draw up the souls of the dead, whenever you sacrifice to the shades with the entrails of boys.

Finally, it may be noted that another direct descendant of Pompeius Magnus, M. Scribonius Libo, was accused by Tiberius of necromancy and meddling with magic and put to death. As in 33, astrologers and magicians were expelled from Italy.[103]

If this hypothesis is correct, then Horace's light-hearted poem is not only a compliment to Maecenas on the building of the *horti*, but an expression of relief at the removal of various undesirables from the city and the end of Sex. Pompeius and his nefarious crew.

Satires 1.5 and 6 provide a much more explicit and detailed picture of Maecenas and his circle. The journey to Brundisium described in

---

[102] See Aid (1976: 130–49); Grenade (1950: 28–63).

[103] See further Seager (1972: 89–93); MacMullen (1967: 126 and 325 n. 30). Note esp. Tac. *Ann.* 2.28: *Iunius quidam [sc. a Libone] temptatus ut infernos umbras carminibus eliceret.*

1.5 was a preliminary to the negotiations between Octavian and
Antonius in the summer of 37, negotiations which were a turning-
point in the history of the thirties.[104] Octavian had suffered major
defeats in his war with Sex. Pompeius in the previous year. The
administration of politics was in chaos and Italy was infested with
brigands, its ports blockaded and afflicted with famine. When Antonius returned to Italy with three hundred ships, yet another civil war
must have seemed the inevitable prospect. It was narrowly avoided,
and, 'resentful and suspicious, the dynasts met at Tarentum'.[105]
Horace is notoriously reticent about the political context and his
account is noticeably free of all tensions. That is surely deliberate.

   The journey, then, which Horace is describing certainly took place,
as his contemporaries would be only too well aware. Yet of all the
satires, this is the one most obviously modelled on a famous poem by
Lucilius.[106] Horace has deliberately selected the incidents and the
details which would remind his readers of the journey described by
Lucilius. The effect is underlined by echoed phrases, evocative parallels and pointed contrasts.[107] Lucilius' journey had no political
purpose of any kind: it was simply an account of a rich Roman
eques paying a visit to his estates in Sicily in the golden years of
Rome's history. The main effect which Horace achieves by harmon-
ising these two journeys is to transform a recent moment of threat
and crisis into something familiar, ordinary and amusing. The poem
exudes an atmosphere of good-natured humour and co-operation. It
makes it hard to believe that there ever was a real danger of war
between Octavian and Antonius. In other words the poem justifies
the propaganda of the Triumvirs, who advertised their continuing
friendship after Tarentum. That also was the public image through 36
and 35.[108] It is not easy to date this poem precisely, but it does not
have the air of being written immediately after the event it describes.
In one respect only is distortion of the truth really apparent. It is
hard to believe that in 37 Maecenas could have travelled through a

   [104] See Broughton (1968: 396).
   [105] Syme (1939: 225).
   [106] The problem has taxed the critics: Fraenkel (1957: 105–12); Rudd (1966:
54–64); Williams (1968: 569–70).
   [107] For the details, see Fiske (1920: 306–16).
   [108] See esp. Dio 49.18.6–7 on the statues erected in the temple of Concordia.

brigand-infested Italy without a heavily armed bodyguard. Yet of these there is no sign. Perhaps the intention is to encourage the reader to reflect that the military successes of Octavian and his generals in 36 had made travel in Italy safe once again: like Lucilius one could again travel safely, even as far as Sicily, which until recently had been in the control of Sex. Pompeius.[109]

The journey which Horace described took place at a most delicate time. The Triumvirate had legally expired on the last day of 38.[110] It was renewed at Tarentum and the second term was made to run retrospectively from 1 January 37. The agreement reached between the Triumvirs was legally ratified only afterwards. A recent writer has rightly insisted on the 'brute fact that the triumvirs in the first part of 37 by continuing to exercise their triumviral functions were acting in a way that contemporaries would consider a usurpation, whether justifiable or unjustifiable, a usurpation that in fact went unchallenged, except, presumably, by Sextus Pompey and his supporters.'[111] This account does, however, overlook the fact that Sex. Pompeius' challenge is reflected in Appian's account and that Octavian at least made some show of respecting the constitutional niceties without, of course, going so far as to relinquish his army.[112]

Horace's poem must he viewed in the light of this background. The position of Maecenas, Fonteius and Cocceius is described with great care: 'they were dispatched, each of them, as ambassadors on

---

[109] For brigands, see App. *Bell. ciu.* 5.132 and Suet. *Aug.* 32.1–2. But it was common practice to omit mention of slaves and menials at all times.

[110] For a recent discussion of the problems, with full citation of the evidence, see Gray (1975), 15–29.

[111] Gray (1975: 20).

[112] Cf. Gray (1975: 21): 'Engaged in a life and death struggle with Sextus Pompey, Octavian felt all the more strongly the need to conciliate conservative and republican elements in Italy by a display of constitutionalism.' I accept his argument that it was Octavian who secured the comitial validation of the renewal of the Triumvirate and thereafter duly styled himself TRIVMVIR RPC ITERVM (unlike Antonius). The claim that the Triumvirate was renewed 'without again asking the people' (App. *Bell. ciu.* 5.95) I believe to come from a hostile source, ultimately reflecting the propaganda of Sex. Pompeius. I would also suggest, tentatively, that Octavian did not campaign against Sex. Pompeius in 37 because (at least in part) he wished to show his respect for his constitutional position. It is also worth noting that M. Oppius, the son of a *proscriptus*, was elected 'by the people' in 37 (Broughton (1968: 396–7). But see also Millar (1973: 50–67): he doubts the ratification of the renewal (53) and entertains the hypothesis that Octavian was Triumvir in 32 (58).

matters of great importance, well accustomed to reconciling feuding friends' (*missi magnis de rebus uterque | legati, auersos soliti componere amicos*, 1.5.28–9). The last phrase is a masterpiece of understatement which minimises the tension and makes inevitable the successful outcome of the negotiations. The first phrase emphasises the importance of the mission but is vague about its exact nature. The three men are called simply *legati*, a suitably ambiguous word since it is used of both private and public embassies.[113] Nothing is in fact allowed to spoil the impression that this is a party of private individuals going about their business. Maecenas and his party travel in the manner of ordinary citizens of their class: the sustained parallel with Lucilius reinforces this impression.[114] Maecenas is, like Lucilius, just another rich Roman *eques*. Horace's desire to create this impression is perhaps the most important reason for his omission of all mention of a bodyguard. It is hard to imagine a more complete contrast than that between the impression made by Maecenas' party on the move and that which Caesar made on Cicero when he visited him in 45 accompanied by two thousand soldiers![115] At the small estate (*uillula*) near the Campanian bridge they are provided with the bare essentials, a roof, fuel and salt. That is their due as travellers.[116] The skinny thrushes being prepared for them at Beneventum never arrive and the party survives being almost burned to death only to endure the 'teary smoke' (*lacrimosus fumus*) at Trivicum. They buy water at one place, bread at another and take in the tourist attractions as they go. There is no sense of urgency or crisis. It is an ordinary journey such as any Roman might have made. The only respite from the hardships is afforded by the hospitality of friends and relatives.

Horace cleverly emphasises the complete absence of all pomp and ceremony. The poem begins with himself and the equally lowly Heliodorus setting out from Rome. But the hardships which they endure do not change with the arrival of the *legati*. As just noted, the journey goes on in exactly the same way as before. The point is subtly

[113] Cic. *Ad Att.* 1.11.1, with Shackleton Bailey (1965: ad loc.).

[114] For a convenient account, see Balsdon (1969: 213–17; 224–43).

[115] Cic. *Ad Act.* 13.52.

[116] Cicero was similarly proud of not making demands when he was travelling (*Ad Att.* 5.10.2; 5.16.3).

underlined by the account of the visit to Fundi, the first place to be reached after the arrival of Maecenas. Here the *praetor* Aufidius Luscus (One Eye), with all the fussiness of the small town mayor greeting royalty, provides the only ceremonial reception of the journey. The reaction of the party is significant. Nothing could be further from the self-congratulation and pride of Cicero when similarly welcomed on his return from exile:[117] 'we leave, laughing insanely' (*linquimus insani ridentes*, 1.5.35). The message is plain: Maecenas and his friends are not behaving like Hellenistic monarchs or tyrants or their self-important courtiers and they do not expect to be treated as such.[118]

The relationships within the group are also instructive. When the *legati* arrive, the introductions are carefully handled. First, Maecenas: Horace conveys the nature of his personal and intimate friendship by giving him no epithet and pays him the compliment of needing no formal introduction. It is assumed that the reader will know who he is and that he is the *amicus* of Octavian. Next, L. Cocceius Nerva: Horace associates him firmly with Maecenas and gives him the polite and enthusiastic epithet 'noblest/best' (*optimus*). Both Maecenas and Cocceius had taken leading parts in bringing about the agreement at Brundisium in 40. At that time Cocceius had owed his first duty to Antonius but was the key figure in the negotiations because he was a friend of both men (Appian, *Bellum ciuile* 5.64). The reader is carefully reminded of their role on that earlier occasion (*soliti* 'accustomed'), 1.5.29) and this reminder acts as a guarantee of a second success. Finally, C. Fonteius Capito: he is carefully set off against the other two. Unlike them he had not been at Brundisium. Asinius Pollio had represented Antonius on that occasion.[119] As the newcomer he receives a fuller description, both *nomen* and *cognomen* and the vital designation 'friend of Antonius' (*Antoni... amicus*). The passage suggests (perhaps deliberately), or at least reflects, a shift in the balance of power between Octavian and Antonius from 40 to 37.

---

[117] See Cic. *Ad Att. Sest.* 131; *Pis.* 51–2.

[118] Note esp. that when Suetonius assembles a number of details to show that Augustus did not behave like a tyrant, he records (*Aug.* 53.2) *non temere urbe oppidoue ullo egressus aut quoquam ingressus est nisi uespera aut noctu, ne quem officii causa inquietaret.*

[119] See Broughton (1968: 378) and Syme (1939: 217).

The careful balance between the two sides of the group as well as the atmosphere of mutual goodwill and co-operation is further suggested by the simple record that at Formiae Murena, presumably the brother-in-law of Maecenas, provided the accommodation and Fonteius the food (1.5.38). Cocceius, the mutual friend, provides both at his villa near Caudium.[120] Here too the party enjoys the verbal banter of Sarmentus and Messius. This episode (1.5.51–70) is the high spot of the journey. It serves to dissolve all tensions within the group and to dispel all the reader's anxieties. None of the *legati* is mentioned again. Their mission has in a sense ceased to matter for no one can any longer have any doubts at all about the outcome.

The poem also tells us much about Horace's friendship with Maecenas and by showing us how he treats his friends illuminates his character. While waiting for Maecenas, Horace occupies his time rubbing ointment on his sore eyes. By the time he has finished ('meanwhile', *interea*, 31) Maecenas has arrived. As if to emphasise that this point is significant, it is made again. While the party are resting at Capua, we are told: 'Maecenas goes off to play, Virgil and I to sleep, for playing ball is inimical to both the blear-eyed and the dyspeptic' (*lusum it Maecenas, dormitum ego Vergiliusque;* | *namque pila lippis inimicum et ludere crudis,* 1.5.48–9). What is striking here is the complete absence of any sign that Horace is obliged to dance attendance on his powerful friend. There is no show of flattery or adulation. The effect is reinforced by the intervening account of the warm and effusive welcome which is given to Plotius Tucca, Varius Rufus and Virgil when they arrive (1.5.39–44). There should be no temptation to misconstrue Horace's behaviour. His ailment serves to excuse him for not welcoming Maecenas and for not joining him at sport.[121] It would clearly be wrong to infer that Horace's affection for Maecenas was less than wholehearted. The warmth of the friendships within the group is illustrated by the welcome of Virgil and his companions and made explicit in the generalisation: 'While in my

---

[120] Cf. Syme (1939: 225), who suggests that Cocceius was 'still perhaps a neutral'. Horace seems to suggest that he has crossed the line (cf. Sen. *Clem.* 1.10.1). For Murena, see Nisbet-Hubbard (1978: 151–7).

[121] For illness as an excuse, see Dio 44.8.1–4 (on Caesar's discourtesy to senators: cf. Gelzer (1968: 317); Cic. *Phil.* 1.11–12 (cf. 1, 11–12); Hor. *Epist.* 1.7.1–13 and [Suet.1] *Vit. Hor.* 2.13 etc.

right mind, there's nothing I would compare with a friend for giving pleasure' (*nil ego contulerim iucundo sanus amico,* 1.5.44). Maecenas, of course, is included in the *amici* of Horace. At the same time these incidents reveal the humane consideration which Maecenas shows to his friends. This is significant. The Romans were always acutely sensitive about the way in which the rich and powerful treated their friends and clearly considered it to be indicative of their true nature.[122] It was precisely because of the arrogant and imperious manner in which he treated those whom he wished to consider him as a friend, that Julius Caesar inspired such hatred. That was the behaviour of a tyrant.[123] Contemporary attitudes to the Triumvirs may be judged from the bitter comments of Sallust: 'for to rule by violence over one's homeland, or one's subjects, even when the power is yours and you are chastening faults, is nonetheless oppressive' (*nam ui quidem regere patriam aut parentes, quamquam et possis et delicta corrigas, tamen importunum est,* Sal. *Iug.* 3.2). And he describes their supporters as those 'possessed by a dishonourable and pernicious passion to give away their own honour and freedom to the control of a few men' (*inhonesta et perniciosa lubido tenet potentiae paucorum decus atque libertatem suam gratificari,* 3.3). Horace's skilfully contrived portrait of the friends of Maecenas gives the lie to this conception. The impression he wishes to create can be usefully summed up in the words of Cicero: 'let courtesy be present, and may toadyism, the helpmate of vice, be far removed as unworthy not only of a friend, but of a free man: life is lived one way with a tyrant, another way with a friend' (*comitas adsit, assentatio—uitiorum adiutrix—procul amoueatur quae non modo amico, sed ne libero quidem digna est; aliter enim cum tyranno, aliter cum amico uiuitur, De amicitia* 89).

---

[122] For example, the lover conventionally contrasts his concern for his beloved with his rich rival's lack of concern. This motif of concern for the sick was probably a commonplace of Hellenistic philosophical treatises on friendship as suggested by Yardley (1973: 283–8). Biographers also note with some regularity how men treated their sick friends: for example, Suet. *Caes.* 72 (to illustrate that *amicos tanta semper facultate indulgentiaque tractauit*); *Aug.* 53.3 (again in the section intended to show that he did not behave tyrannically); see further Millar (1977: 112) and Woodman (1977) on Vell. 2.114.1.

[123] See Gelzer (1968: 323–4); Cic. *Ad fam.* 6.14.2 *omnem adeundi et conueniendi illius indignitatem et molestiam pertulissem; Ad Att.* 14.1.3; 2.3.

Satire 1.6 is a complex and difficult poem. But since it is explicitly concerned with Maecenas, his friendship with Horace and their attitude to contemporary politics, it demands careful scrutiny. It also occupies a key position in the collection and serves to dedicate the book to Maecenas.[124] The ostensible purpose of the poem is to express the gratitude which Horace feels at being accepted as an *amicus* of Maecenas, a theme which is established in the first six lines. Instead of emphasising their equality as *amici* and Roman *equites*, Horace emphasises the very great difference in their social status.[125] The encomium of Maecenas is impressive and includes two of the standard topics, his homeland (*patria*, 1–2, especially *Lydorum*) and his ancestors (3–4). It culminates in the assertion 'no one is better born than you' (*nemo generosior est te*, 2). In view of what follows, it seems that this bold phrase is intended to use Maecenas' distinction among the municipal aristocrats (*domi nobiles*) to obscure or, rather, to compensate for the fact that he was not a Roman *nobilis*.[126] In view both of this and of the current political climate it is worth stressing that his ancestors are for once not called *reges* ('kings') but 'those who once commanded large legions' (*olim qui magnis legionibus imperitarent*, 4).[127] This description matches the claims of the Roman *nobilitas* precisely in the terms of their own aristocratic code of values.[128] This information is an implicit justification of the extraordinary position which Maecenas held from 36 to 33 when, although a *priuatus*, he was entrusted as *amicus Caesaris* with the administration of political affairs in Rome and Italy.[129] But Horace immediately insists that he does not exhibit the usual arrogance of the *nobilis* (5) and he cites his own case as

[124] Cf. Virg. *Ecl.* 4; Tibull. 1.7; Prop. 3.9 and 4.6. It is important not to be dogmatic about the placing of the dedicatory poem: Horace certainly wrote *Odes* 4 for Augustus (5 and 15) and not for Paullus Fabius Maximus.

[125] White (1978: 81) shrewdly observes that *'amici* rarely could be and rarely considered themselves peers'. The problem was recognised by theorists from Aristotle on (e.g. *Nic. eth.* 8.14). The best general discussion of *amicitia* is Brunt (1965).

[126] See Wiseman (1971), index s.v. *domi nobiles*.

[127] Contrast *Odes* 1.1.1; 3.29.1; Prop. 3.9.1; *Eleg. in Maec.* 13.

[128] On the importance of military success to a Roman aristocrat, see esp. Harris (1979: 9–41).

[129] Dio 49.16.2.

proof:[130] *ignotos* ('unknowns') contrasts with *generosior* and *libertino patre* ('freedman father') with the glorious ancestors of Maecenas.

The first main section after this prelude (7–44) elaborates on this attitude of Maecenas. It is clear that the views expressed are at least as much those of Maecenas as of Horace: 'when you say it doesn't matter', 'you rightly convince yourself', 'what are we to do?' (*cum referre negas,* 7; *persuades hoc tibi uere,* 8; *quid oportet | nos facere,* 17–18). A contemporary would have been more interested in Maecenas' views on these questions than in those of Horace: he was not only rich and powerful but a friend of Octavian, and the Triumvirs had the power to appoint the magistrates.[131] At the same time elections still took place and apparently not all the magistrates were chosen by the Triumvirs: M. Oppius, the aedile of 37, had been impoverished by the proscriptions but was the choice of the people.[132] The result of this confused situation was political chaos, in 38 there were sixty-seven people who held the praetorship in this first year after the return of the refugees and the proscribed (Dio 48.43.2). In 36 there were no aediles at all owing to a lack of candidates (Dio 49.16.2). A *puer* (Dio 48.43.2) was chosen as quaestor, and a slave was detected when about to assume the same office, while another was detected while actually serving as praetor. These irregularities and abuses are at their height in the years 38–36. There is no doubt that they inspired contempt and disgust and it is worth stressing that after the defeat of Sex. Pompeius there is a sharp decline in the number of such incidents.[133] The bitterness, felt no doubt

[130] For the conventional *superbia nobilium,* see, e.g., Hellegouarc'h (1963: 439–41); Sall. *Iug.* 31 and 85.

[131] See Millar (1973: 51–4), who notes that 'the right of patronage was extended even beyond the Triumvirs' (52), citing Dio 1.23.1 on Statilius Taurus. The role of Maecenas in these appointments was perhaps only informal but he was doubtless part of the *consilium* of Octavian.

[132] This incident seems to show that Octavian kept a low profile in 37, after the lapse of the Triumvirate and before it was officially renewed (see n. 112). App. *Bell. ciu.* 4.41 and Dio 48.53.4–6 do not make it clear whether both the son and the father or the father alone had been proscribed (Appian, incidentally, compares the son's action to that of Aeneas: see above p. 70 with n. 88). The popular support for Oppius was demonstrated in the Theatre of Pompeius, an obvious site for a display of pro-Pompeian sympathy (cf. Vell. 2.79.6); the masked *kakourgoi* who donated money were then presumably Pompeian sympathisers of some means, not eager to be identified by the Triumvirs. Dio duly notes that the 'senate' disapproved of the popular devotion to this man.

[133] Millar (1973), 50–4.

by many, is reflected by Sallust: 'magistracies and commands, in short all care for the state, seem to me little to be desired in times such as these, seeing that neither is honour awarded to virtue, nor are those who have gained power through deceit are neither safe, nor any more honourable because of it' (*magistratus et imperia, postremo omnis cura rerum publicarum minume mihi hac tempestate cupiunda uidentur, quoniam neque uirtuti honos datur, neque illi quibus per fraudem eis fuit uti, tuti aut eo magis honesti sunt,* Sall. *Iug.* 3.1).

Horace begins by stating Maecenas' view: 'you say it makes no difference what sort of parent anyone has, as long as he is freeborn' (*referre negas quali sit quisque parente natus, dum ingenuus,* 7–8). The qualification is highly significant. Maecenas would not condone the slave who stood as quaestor or the one who had been executed for taking the office of praetor. It was a constant theme of contemporary propaganda that slaves and freedmen were promoted far beyond their station by Sex. Pompeius.[134] The sensitivity of Octavian to this accusation is reflected by the fact that when Menodorus (alias Menas) defected to him from Sextus he would not even dine with him until he had been promoted to freeborn status (*assertus in ingenuitatem,* Suetonius, *Augustus* 74). It is significant that the story was reported by the patrician Valerius Messalla.

There follows a simple and emphatic assertion of Maecenas' belief in the ideology of *nouitas,* the claims of the *noui homines* (the 'new men', i.e. members of a family first to attain curule office).[135] That is hardly surprising. The *noui homines* flourished, as never before, under the Triumvirs.[136] Sallust, predictably, reflects the jaundiced view: 'even new men, who in former times would outperform the nobility by their virtue, strive for commands and offices through intrigue and outright villainy rather than through the skills befitting good men; in fact, it is as if the praetorship and the consulship, and all other things of the sort, are illustrious and magnificent in themselves, with no consideration for the virtue of those who hold them' (*etiam homines*

---

[134] Hor. *Epod.* 4.19–20; Vell. 2.73.1. Cf. Syme (1939: 201 and 236) who acidly remarks on 'freedmen, of which support Pompeius had no monopoly, but all the odium'.

[135] See Wiseman (1971: 107–22).

[136] See Wiseman (1971: 8–9; 171–3); Syme (1939: 227–58).

*noui, qui antea per uirtutem soliti erant nobilitatem anteuenire, furtim
et per latrocinia potius quam bonis artibus ad imperia et honores
nituntur; proinde quasi praetura et consulatus atque alia omnia huius-
cemodi per se clara et magnifica sint, ac non perinde habeantur ut eorum
qui* ea *sustinent uirtus est,* Sall. *Iug.* 4. 7–8). Horace insists that
Maecenas' view of *nouitas* is every bit as elevated as that of Sallust:
he too believes that *uirtus* is the basis of their claim to *honores* (*probos*,
11). This theme will be developed later.

It is possible that the reference to Servius Tullius has a pointed
significance. Suetonius records of the Octavii: 'this family was admitted into the lesser families of the senate by king Tarquinius
Priscus. Soon thereafter it was brought over to the patrician side by
Servius Tullius. With the passing of time it went back to the plebs,
then Divine Julius returned the family once again to the patriciate
after a long interval of time' (*ea gens a Tarquinio Prisco rege inter
minores gentis adlecta in senatum, mox a Seruio Tullio in patricias
traducta, procedente tempore ad plebem se contulit ac rursus magno
interuallo per Diuum Iulium in patriciatum redit, Augustus* 2.1). The
story may have been particularly prominent, if not actually invented,
in the years immediately following Octavian's marriage to the patrician Livia (17 January 38).[137] For it was at this time that he showed
himself eager to secure the support of the *nobiles*.[138]

It is Maecenas' attitude to the *nobilitas* and to the *populus* which is
the subject of the following lines (12–22). The argument is subtle.
Maecenas does not reject the claims of the *nobiles*. But he does insist
that *uirtus* is the most important qualification for office and that
maiores ('ancestors') alone are not sufficient. The fact that even the
populus adhered to that principle in the case of Laevinus confirms
that his attitude is traditional and in accordance with the *mos
maiorum*. The most striking confirmation that Maecenas recognises
the claims of the *nobiles* as legitimate comes with the reference to
Appius the censor (20–1): to qualify for the senate, a man should not
only be himself *ingenuus* (8) but the son of an *ingenuus* (21). This
attitude to the *nobiles* is not really surprising.[139] Most of them were

---

[137] It was presumably invented when the Octavii were made patricians 'again'.
[138] Cf., e.g., Syme (1939: 238–9).
[139] Cf. Syme (1939: 229–40).

not supporters of Octavian but of Antonius or, even, Sex. Pompeius. At the same time he wanted their support. His marriage to Livia in 38 gave him a link with a patrician family. By the end of 36 he has three supporters from noble families: Appius Claudius Pulcher (cos. 38), whose uncle is the censor mentioned with approval at 1.6.20–2 (especially *uel merito*); Paullus Aemilius Lepidus (cos. 34) whose family receives a passing honorific mention at 1.6.41; and M. Valerius Messalla Corvinus (cos. 31) whose family is similarly mentioned at 1.6.42. In respect of Messalla it is worth noting that the claims of the Valerii to have expelled from Rome the tyrannical Tarquinius Superbus are also prominently displayed (1.6.12–13).[140] This sounds like a refutation of Brutus' claim[141] and is perhaps intended to highlight the impeccable credentials of Octavian's new supporters. The impressive encomium of Maecenas with which the poem began and his own obvious pride in his ancestors guarantees the sincerity of his sympathy with the claims of the *nobiles*.

Maecenas' views may be briefly summarised: the promotion to high office of *noui homines* is entirely justified by their *uirtus*. Yet birth also is important: to hold public office, a man should be at least *ingenuus ingenuo patre natus* ('freeborn, the son of a freeborn father'), while the Laevinus story suggests that a *nobilis* may be disqualified from taking up his birthright by lack of *uirtus*. This attitude must have given hope and encouragement to both the *noui* and to those *nobiles* wanting to return to Italy after the war with Sextus or those who had returned after the treaty of Misenum in 39. To inject a cynical note, it was presumably the surest demonstration of *uirtus* for a *nobilis* to renounce the Pompeian cause. At the same time the insistence on *uirtus* is intended to allay the fears and prejudices of those who shared the view of Sallust.

Horace does not, of course, deny that the *indigni* ('undeserving') have achieved high office. But the blame for this is laid quite firmly

---

[140] Kiessling-Heinze (1968) on *S.* 1.6.12 say that the Messallae did not trace back their line to P. Valerius Poplicola, cos. 509. This is certainly untrue if *Catalepton 9* is addressed to P. Valerius Messalla Corvinus and of this there can now be little doubt (see Richmond (1978: 189–201)): see *Cat.* 9. 35–40 and cf. Hor. *S.* 1.10.28 (?).

[141] Cf. Plut. *Brut.* 1 'those who felt hatred and ill will for Brutus on account of the murder of Caesar say that his father's family does not go back to the man who threw out the Tarquins', etc.

on the 'people, who often, in ignorance, award offices to the un-deserving, and who are bumbling slaves to reputation, and who are dumbfounded by portraits with inscribed achievements' (*populus qui stultus honores | saepe dat indignis et famae seruit ineptus, | qui stupet in titulis et imaginibus*, 1.6.15–17). This is prefaced by the remark that the *populus* is 'the judge whom you've come to know' (*iudice quo nosti*, 15). Horace seems to have something specific in mind. Appian records (*Bellum civile* 5.99) that in 36 Octavian sent Maecenas to Rome 'on account of those who were still under the spell of the memory of Pompey the Great, for the fame of that man had not yet lost its influence on them'. It seems probable that the *fama, tituli* and *imagines* are those of Pompeius. Certainly the verb *seruit* would aptly describe their support for Sextus. Horace is then trying to suggest that the *indigni* have been given office by the *populus* and not by the Triumvirs, and that the *indigni* are the supporters of Sextus. The argument is at least credible: the runaway slaves, both the one who stood as quaestor and the one who was elected as praetor, were presumably alleged to be Pompeians, like the *tribunus militum* attacked by Horace in *Epode* 4. There is little doubt that many of the sixty-seven praetors of 38 were freshly returned from Sextus.

The rest of this first main section focuses on Tillius. His identity is unfortunately not certain.[142] He is accused of being the son of a freedman (1.6.38–41). He had been expelled from the senate (1.6.25 with Porphyrio's comment: 'for previously he had been expelled from the senate', *nam pulsus ante senatu fuerat*). The context would nat-urally suggest that he had been expelled by Appius Claudius. He later re-entered the senate and became a tribune. It is subsequently revealed that he also became a praetor (1.6.108). Porphyrio says simply that he was readmitted to the senate 'after the death of Caesar' (*post Caesarem occisum*). His name inevitably recalls that of the assassin of Caesar, L. Tillius Cimber, whose origins and career are obscure. He had a brother for whose return from exile he was pleading at the moment Caesar was killed. It has been suggested that this was Horace's Tillius, but that is improbable. It is possible that he was the son of a freedman of the Tillii. In any case it is hard to believe that any bearer of that hated name was anything other than a

---

[142] See Wiseman (1971: 266).

supporter of Sextus Pompeius. His poverty (1.6.107–11) suggests
that he may have been proscribed. Perhaps he was one of the sixty-
seven praetors of 38.

In spite of this uncertainty it is clear that Horace is using the case
of Tillius to bolster his argument that birth is of importance in
politics and ought to be. But in endorsing one tenet of the aristocratic code Horace firmly rejects another: 'but Glory drags them in
chains behind her gleaming chariot, the unknown no less than the
well-born' (*sed fulgente trahit constrictos Gloria curru | non minus
ignotos generosis*, 1.6.23–4). The pursuit of *laus* and *gloria* lay at the
heart of the Roman aristocratic code.[143] The inherited *uirtus* of the
aristocrat was recognised by the *honores* ('offices') conferred upon
him by the *populus*. These were valued, primarily and increasingly, as
a prelude to military commands which provide scope for acquiring
gloria. The result was an intensively abrasive and competitive society.
By the middle of the first century attitudes to *gloria* were ambivalent.
Sallust, for example, asserted that Rome owed her greatness and
success precisely to 'a lust for glory' (*cupido gloriae, Bellum Catilinae*
7.3). However, Polybius had already predicted that 'the craving for
office and the sense of shame which comes from obscurity together
with increasing ostentation and extravagance will usher in a period of
general decline' (6.57.5–6). Neither Cicero nor Sallust could bring
himself to reject the ideal of *gloria:* both recognise that a 'struggle for
glory' (*certamen gloriae*) was destroying the state and tried to distinguish true *gloria*, resting on *uirtus* and won only by serving the state,
from the false, which set the interests of the individual and his own
dignitas above the welfare of the state.[144] Horace has gone further and
rejects the ideal of *gloria* altogether. His striking image personifies
gloria as a *triumphator*. It was an appropriate choice: the triumph was
the surest means of winning *gloria*. But in Horace's image those who
pursue *gloria* are shown not as *triumphatores* but as prisoners of war
dragged along in chains by the triumphal chariot of *Gloria*. This vivid
and crushing image gives memorable expression to an attitude that
was to find repeated expression under Augustus. But this revaluation
of *gloria* was surely not due entirely to Horace. More probably,

[143] See esp. Harris (1979: 17–40); Earl (1967: 44–79).
[144] Cf. Hellegouarc'h (1963: 380–3).

Horace here reflects a reaction of Maecenas and Octavian to contemporary feelings: Dio (48.53.1–2) records the anxiety caused in 37 by the rapid turnover among magistrates eager 'not so much to hold office at home for very long as to be counted among the ex-magistrates and so to obtain the honours and powers of serving abroad'.

This rejection of *gloria* is balanced by the positive description of the true significance of holding public office (1.6.34–5): 'he who promises that the citizens and their city will be the objects of his concern, together with the empire and Italy, and the shrines of the gods' (*qui promittit ciuis, urbem sibi curae, imperium fore et Italiam, delubra deorum*). The division of the *res publica* into its component parts solemnly parades the full range of a magistrate's responsibilities. But the emphasis falls on the key word, *curae*. It is because of this that it is proper to insist on birth as a qualification for a magistrate (*iniciat curam*, 32; *curare*, 37). The concept of government as 'care for the state' (*cura reipublicae*) had some precedent in the language of Republican politics.[145] But it is especially characteristic of the empire. Together with *custodia* ('custodianship') and *tutela* ('safekeeping') and related concepts, it conveys the notion of government as a heavy responsibility, undertaken out of a sense of duty and not merely as an opportunity to win personal wealth and glory.[146] It is clear from Cicero that this concept had some currency under Caesar: 'when we were languid from inactivity and the condition of the state was such that it had to be governed by the judgment and care of a single man' (*cum otio langueremus et is esset rei publicae status ut eam unius consilio atque cura gubernari necesse esset, De natura deorum* 1.7). It was doubtless echoed in the propaganda of the *triumuiri rei publicae constituendae*.

In the second main section of the poem (45–88), Horace focuses attention on himself. He is a positive counterbalance to Tillius: like him he has been a tribune (*tribunus*, 25) and has incurred envy (*inuidia*, 50 and 26) and jibes about the status of his parent (46 and 36). But Horace has now come to see the error of his ways and the reader will recall that he served as military tribune (*tribunus militum*)

---

[145] Cf. Hellegouarc'h (1963: 252–3).

[146] See Béranger (1953: 186–205): cf. Plin. *Epist.* 3. 20. 12: *sunt quidem cuncta sub unius arbitrio qui pro utilitate communi solus omnium curas laboresque suscepit.* Also Woodman (1977) on Vell. 2.104.2, 105.3, 106.3.

in the Republican army under Brutus. But Horace is now a *priuatus* (cf. 26) and simply *amicus Maecenatis*. The main purpose of this section is to demonstrate from the example of Horace himself the way in which Maecenas puts into practice, even in choosing his personal friends, his belief in the prime importance of *uirtus*. Maecenas is described at the outset as 'especially careful to take on those who are deserving, well free of crooked ambition' (*praesertim cautum dignos adsumere, praua* | *ambitione procul,* 51–2). The friends of Maecenas, exemplified by Horace, are to be contrasted with the *indigni* on whom the *populus* bestows its favours (16), exemplified by Tillius. The phrase *praua ambitione procul* (51–2) echoes and confirms the rejection of *gloria* as a goal (23–4). Primarily it describes Horace but it also hints that Maecenas is free from *ambitio* in his own choice of friends.[147] In view of his enormous power and wealth, the only friendship which Maecenas could be accused of cultivating out of *ambitio* was that with Octavian. Horace obliquely refutes the slander.

   In what follows Horace gives a detailed account of himself which emphasises his high moral character. This is not intended primarily as self-praise but as praise of Maecenas, as is clear from the conclusion: 'I myself consider it a great achievement that I pleased you, you who separate the honourable from the foul not on the basis of a famous father, but a life and heart that is pure' (*magnum hoc ego duco,* | *quod placui tibi, qui turpi secernis honestum,* | *non patre praeclaro sed uita et pectore puro,* 62–4). Having begun by saying that it was the fact that his father was *libertinus* which quite properly debarred him from a political career, he next explains that it was because of his father that he had received an education such as would have met the stringent standards of a Cato and had become a person of such moral integrity and rectitude that he was chosen as an *amicus* by Maecenas. Horace's *uirtus* derives from a very traditional education and is evidently *prisca uirtus*. But his father was not only responsible for inculcating this *prisca uirtus* which made him *dignus amicitia Maecenatis* ('worthy of Maecenas' friendship'), but did so without any expectations that Horace would have his *uirtus* recognised by being given public office. For him *uirtus* is its own reward.[148]

---

147 Cf. Rudd (1966: 41; 279 n. 5).
148 See Otto (1890: 373–4) s.v. *uirtus* (1).

But while not seeking *gloria* and ensuring that his son is free from *praua ambitio* he has earned *laus* (88): the point which Horace is making is proverbial—'glory is the shadow of virtue, whom she even accompanies against her will' (*gloria umbra uirtutis est, etiam inuitam comitabatur*).[149]

Having illustrated his own *prisca uirtus* and so expanded on the attitude of Maecenas to birth and *uirtus*, Horace concentrates in the final section (89–131) on describing the 'life of those who are free of wretched and weighty ambition' (*uita solutorum misera ambitione grauique*, 129). Again the generalisation is significant. Horace is using himself as an example of a class of people which has the approval of Maecenas (51–2). At the outset Horace insists on the sincerity of his claim to lack *ambitio:* he now believes that even if free to choose he would not want 'parents distinguished by fasces and curule chairs' (*parentes... honestos* | *fascibus et sellis*, 95–7). Horace now views public office not as an *honos* but an *onus* ('burden').[150] He goes on to justify his position by referring to the expenses incurred by those in public life. The issue has topical relevance. Dio (48.53.3–6) records that there were some who had to abandon office altogether because of their poverty and cites the example of M. Oppius who was, however, enabled to carry on as aedile because of the generosity of the public. Horace quotes again the unfortunate Tillius. It should be stressed that Horace's underlying assumption is that *cura rei publicae* is an *onus* which requires considerable expenditure and is not simply an *honos* which will provide opportunity to win glory and amass wealth. It is worth recalling that this same conception justified Augustus imposing a property qualification for senators and constantly increasing it.[151]

From these negative considerations Horace turns to a delightful and attractive account of the 'leisure', *otium* (*otior*, 128) and the 'freedom', *libertas* ('by whatever way I fancy', *quacumque libido*

[149] Otto (1890: 155) s.v. *gloria* (1).

[150] Cf. Varro, *Ling. Lat.* 5. 73 *honos ab onere: itaque honestum dicitur quod oneratum et dictum: onus est honos qui sustinet rem publicam.* The idea is commonplace: cf. Otto (1890: 167) s.v. *honos*.

[151] See, e.g., Suet. *Aug.* 41 (the details are problematic). Note also Suet. *Aug.* 29.4 *ceteros principes uiros saepe hortatus est ut pro facultate quisque monimentis uel nouis uel refectis et excultis urbem adornarent.* Many of the buildings which he lists belong to the thirties. Also Vell. 2.89.4.

est, 111) which he enjoys as a *priuatus*. The section is framed by expressions of relief that the onerous responsibilities of government rest with others. This high value which is set on *otium* and the demonstration that it can be combined with *libertas* need to be viewed in the context of contemporary opinion.[152] Cicero, finding that the *cura rei publicae* was in the hands of one man, complains of his enforced *otium* and consoles himself with writing philosophy in the hope that in this way he may still be able to serve his country and win *gloria* for Rome. Sallust, under the Triumvirs, confessed that he, like Horace, had in his youth been seized 'by corrupt political ambition' (*ambitione corrupta*) and that 'a desire for office plagued me with the same ill-repute and hatred as the rest' (*me... honoris cupido eadem qua ceteros fama atque inuidia uexabat, Bellum Catilinae* 3.4–5). Again he asserts, like Horace, 'I myself believe that there will be those who, because I have decided to pass my time away from the state, will refer to this toil of mine, so great and so useful, as laziness. To them the greatest assiduous effort seems to be saluting the rabble and seeking their favour by hosting parties' (*ego credo fore qui quia decreui procul a re publica aetatem agere, tanto tamque utili labori meo nomen inertiae imponant, certe quibus maxuma industria uidetur salutare plebem et conuiuiis gratiam quaerere, Bellum Iugurthinum* 4.3). But he like Cicero wishes still to serve his country and to win *gloria* from his writings, and, unlike Horace, he justifies his withdrawal from political life by expressing his contempt for triumviral government. Horace ironically echoes the complaints of men like Cicero and Sallust when he says 'I take consolation in these things' (*his me consolor*, 130) but his next words, 'bound to live more pleasantly' (*uicturum suauius*), show him endorsing the views not of these disgruntled aristocrats but of the Epicureans. Twenty years earlier Lucretius had denounced 'lust for offices' (*honorum cupido*, 3.59–89) and taught that it was 'pleasant and grand to view another's toil' (*suaue... magnum alterius spectare laborem*) and 'it is sweet to behold evils from which you yourself are free' (*quibus ipse malis careas... cernere suaue est*, 2.1–4).[153] It was above all the Epicureans

---

[152] See Wirszubski (1950: 91–6).

[153] Cf. also Lucr. 2. 7–14, esp. *despicere... alios contendere nobilitate | noctes atque dies niti praestante labore | ad summas emergere opes rerumque potiri.*

who had belittled the concept of *gloria* and praised *otium*. In doing so they were challenging traditional Roman values.

Horace ends with another reference to his ancestors: 'I take consolation in these things, bound to live more pleasantly than if my grandfather had been a quaestor, and my father and uncle as well' (*his me consolor uicturum suauius ac si quaestor auus pater atque meus patruusque fuisset*, 130–1). The form of the last line is clearly intended to recall the opening lines on Maecenas: 'and not because your mother's father, and your father's as well, once commanded mighty legions' (*nec quod auus tibi maternus fuit atque paternus | olim qui magnis legionibus imperitarent*). The contrast suggests that just as Horace's present life is a consequence of birth, social status and education so is that of Maecenas. For Horace it was improper that 'a Roman legion took orders from me as tribune' (*mihi pareret legio Romana tribuno*, 48). By implication the *cura urbis et Italiae* which Maecenas has undertaken is now seen not only as justified by his birth and social status but even an obligation imposed by them. But that is not all. At the beginning of the last section Horace had said that if (96–9):

> ... meis [sc. parentibus] contentus honestos
> fascibus et sellis nollem mihi sumere, demens
> iudicio uolgi, sanus fortasse tuo, quod
> nollem onus haud umquam solitus portare molestum.

Content with these my ancestors, I'd rather have them than choose for myself parents distinguished by fasces and curule chairs, a madman in the judgment of the rabble, though perhaps sane in your judgment because I'd be unwilling to carry a nasty load that I am by no means used to.

Porphyrio shrewdly observes: 'this is rightly spoken to Maecenas who, wanting nothing to do with senatorial office, remained at the level of an equestrian' (*hoc ad Maecenatem recte dicitur, qui abhorrens senatoriam dignitatem in equestris honoris gradu se continet*). To put it differently: when Horace once again draws attention to the contrast between the views of Maecenas and those of the *uolgus*, he is deliberately reminding his readers of the most unconventional of all Maecenas' characteristics, his complete refusal to accept any *honores*. As a result Horace's account of his own preference for being a *priuatus* and enjoying *otium* is seen as mirroring and justifying the behaviour of Maecenas.

It is evident from both the admiration of Velleius and the malicious slanders of Seneca that Maecenas' contemporaries would have found his behaviour as enigmatic and curious as modern historians.[154] This poem of Horace provides a coherent and important commentary on his life. Maecenas accepted, as every reader knew, the *cura* or *custodia urbis et Italiae*. But he accepted it as an *onus* imposed on him by the *fortuna* of his birth and his wealth (contrast 1.6.100–11) and, it may be supposed, by his *amicitia* with Octavian. But he remained ostentatiously a *priuatus* and *otiosus* even, according to Seneca, 'when he was fulfilling Caesar's role in his absence ... on the tribunal, the rostrum, and in every public gathering' (*cum absentis Caesaris partibus fungeretur ... in tribunali, in rostris, in omni publico coetu*, *Epistles* 114.6). Seneca attributes this to moral degeneracy, a charge which Horace has been careful to refute. The real reason lies in the rejection of *gloria*. Maecenas is exemplifying through his own behaviour a new concept of government as service to the state: he accepts the 'burdens' (*onera*) but is not motivated by a personal craving for *honores* or *gloria*. In this way he both serves his country and demonstrates his loyalty to Octavian by refusing to enter a 'struggle for glory and office' (*contentio gloriae dignitatisque*). Again, this idea has further contemporary relevance: in 37 Agrippa refused to celebrate a triumph for his victory in Gaul because he thought it disgraceful to make a display while Octavian was faring badly against Sex. Pompeius (Dio 48.49.4).[155]

This poem, carefully constructed and well argued, provides valuable information on the political attitudes of the most powerful man in Rome apart from the Triumvirs. It also provides an explanation of his eccentric and, at that time, unconventional behaviour. The indirect and allusive method adopted by Horace reinforces the central theme: it would be obviously inappropriate to give explicit and fulsome praise to a man who rejected *gloria*. As in *Satire* 1.8, the 'praise and thanks' (*laudes gratesque*) are conspicuous by their absence.

---

[154] Vell. 2.88.2 and Woodman (1983: ad loc.); Sen. *Epist.* 114, etc.

[155] For a more cynical view of Agrippa and the quest for *gloria*, see Dio 49.4.2–4. Perhaps the example of the traitor Salvidienus Rufus prompted a re-evaluation of *gloria: qui natus obscurissimis initiis parum habebat summa accepisse ... nisi in id ascendisset e quo infra se et Caesarem uideret et rem publicam* (Vell. 2.76.4).

Satire 1.9 is, by comparison, straightforward and can be dealt with briefly. It relates in lively and dramatic style Horace's encounter with an anonymous pest. This man is not, of course, hostile to Maecenas but he has a completely incorrect idea of what he is like. He so far misunderstands the artistic standards of Maecenas and his friends that he believes that his claim 'who can write more verses than I, or more quickly?' (*quis me scribere pluris | aut citius possit uersus*, 24–5) will secure his admission into the circle of Maecenas (*in numerum amicorum Maecenatis*). He undervalues the sincerity of the friendships within the group (22–3) and believes that they admire the 'softness' (*mollitia*) of effeminate dancing and the singing of the degenerate Hermogenes (25).[156] He characterises Maecenas as 'a man of few men' (*paucorum hominum*), a phrase which can have sinister and ominous overtones,[157] and clearly believes that he is eager for personal power and position ('no one has made more opportune use of fortune', *nemo dexterius fortuna est usus*, 45).[158] He believes that Maecenas is to be won by fawning flattery (8–60) and that the members of the group are motivated by personal ambition. His own *ambitio* is cleverly revealed in his resolve: 'I will bribe his slaves with gifts' (*muneribus seruos corrumpam*, 57). In this enterprise he will show a perverse *industria* (58–9).[159] His failure to appear in court is an indication that he lacks *fides* and the fact that he puts his personal interests above his civic duty and the law is a further sign of his *ambitio*. In answer Horace simply asserts that the lifestyle of the group is marked by its moral integrity and that the relations within it are entirely free of *contentio gloriae dignitatisque* (48–52). Finally, he reasserts the importance which Maecenas attaches to *uirtus* (4).

The reaction of the pest is 'you are telling a tall tale, hardly believable' (*magnum narras, uix credibile*). Surely no reader of the

---

[156] But even Velleius (2.88.2) describes Maecenas as *otio ac mollitiis paene ultra feminam fluens*. Dancing is a stock item of abuse: see Cic. *Pis.* 18 with Nisbet (1961: ad loc.), Woodman (1983) on Vell. 2.83.2.

[157] Cf. Syme (1964: 218) 'In the prologue of the *Bellum Jugurthinum* "potentia paucorum" denotes three men, precisely (3. 4)'.

[158] Not really a flattering phrase: Fortuna was proverbially *indignorum fautrix* (Plin. *Nat.* 2.22). Cf. Rudd (1966: 41).

[159] Sallust would have characterised such *labor/industria* as *dolis atque fallaciis*: see *Cat.* 11.1–2 with Earl (1961: 10–11).

satires can suppress a smile: he knows, now, that Horace is indeed speaking the truth. Yet a moment's reflection will reveal that many contemporary readers must have begun to read the satires with just such beliefs about Maecenas and his friends as those entertained by the pest. Many would in fact have shared the much more contemptuous and derogatory attitudes reflected in Sallust. The anonymous interlocutor in 1.9 performs in fact a function similar to that of the maudlin mourner in Lucretius 3.894–911, namely to represent vividly views which the poet has been trying to discredit.[160] Horace was obviously sufficiently confident of the effectiveness of his presentation of the *amicus Maecenatis* in the preceding satires to risk placing this contrary view in this penultimate position in the book.

SOME NAMES AND TARGETS

It is absolutely certain that Horace made a number of real and living people the butts of his humour and the targets of his criticism. The precise identity and even the number of the people who fall into this category are uncertain and the problem is aggravated by the fact that some of the names are taken from Lucilius and others are simply fictitious type-names.[161] The reader might naturally expect, given the contemporary historical circumstances and the nature of Roman society, that they would not belong to the same socio-political 'pyramid' as Horace (that is, the one headed by Octavian, Maecenas and Agrippa and made up of their families, relatives, friends and dependents) and that they would be known to be hostile to the Triumvirs. He might further expect them to belong to the most obvious of such groupings, the proscribed and the active adherents of the Republican and Pompeian forces. Some of Horace's targets, like Rupilius Rex (1.7), presumably do fall into this category. Others, like Sallust, may have been well known as opponents of the Triumvirs without being supporters of the other side. The situation is further

---

160 But this is not to suggest a direct debt. Both poets found the device in diatribe: see e.g. Wallach (1976), index s.v. interlocutor, imaginary.

161 See Rudd (1960: 161–89); Rudd (1966: 132–59) (with reference to earlier work); Treggiari (1973: 245–61).

complicated by the fact that many, like Valerius Messalla and Horace himself, had changed their allegiance during the early thirties.

Caution, then, is necessary. It must also be borne in mind that the names of only about one hundred of the proscribed and sixteen of those condemned by the *lex Pedia* are known and that the sources put the total numbers at from one hundred and thirty to three hundred senators, and two thousand equites.[162] It is therefore worth noting that Appian describes in some detail the adventures of a Balbinus and a Pomponius, two of the proscribed who fled for refuge to Sex. Pompeius.[163] He was presumably following an almost contemporary source, since the notoriety of Balbinus and Pomponius was surely shortlived. When Horace makes passing hits at a Pomponius (1.4.52) and a Balbinus (1.3.40), it is natural to link them with their notorious homonyms: stories of escapades in the proscriptions presumably enjoyed a vogue with the return of the *proscripti* in 38. Others may fall into this category: another passing hit is directed against Sex. Villius Annalis, the lover of Fausta (1.2.64), and one relative, at least, was proscribed, L. Villius Annalis.[164]

The political allegiance of most of the other targets is difficult to ascertain. Fabius the Stoic (1.1.14; 1.2.134) 'a follower of the Pompeian party' (*Pompeianas partes secutus*), according to Porphyrio, who also tells us that the *nomen* of that other Stoic, Crispinus, was Plotius: that fact suggests the possibility of a link with another of the proscribed, L. Plotius Plancus.[165] Both these scraps of information tend to support the earlier speculation that Stoicism had a special connection with the Pompeian Republican cause. Unfortunately the scholiasts are not always to be trusted: for example, Cassius Etruscus (1.10.62) who is dead in 35, cannot be, as they

[162] Syme (1939: 191): they are listed conveniently with full reference to the sources by Drumann-Groebe (1899), 1. 470–4.

[163] App. *Bell. ciu.* 4.45 and 50. For Balbinus, see Wistrand (1958: 43–5). The *latrones* Caelius and Birrus (1.4.69) may also have been Pompeian supporters: cf. *Epod.* 4.19.

[164] App. *Bell. ciu.* 4.18; Val. Max. 9.11.6.

[165] Porphyrio identified Hypsaea (1.2.91) as a Plautia Hypsaea. What connection she might have had with P. Plautius Hypsaeus is unknowable. He had once been a legate of Pompeius Magnus but was abandoned by him in 52 and convicted *de ambitu*: no more is heard of him. Porphyrio also identified Nomentanus (1.1.102; 1.8.11) as L. Cassius Nomentanus; but see Rudd (1966: 142); Syme (1964a: 283) and Wiseman (1971: 115).

say, Cassius Parmensis, the assassin and a loyal adherent of Sex.
Pompeius whose death did not occur before Actium.[166] But it is
worth noting that they tend to search for the identity of the man
behind the name in the ranks of the proscribed: even Sagana (1.8.25)
was said by Helenius Acro (according to Porphyrio) to be real: 'in
Horace's day there was a witch by the name of Sagana who belonged
to Pompeius the senator who was proscribed by the triumvirs'
(*Saganam nomine fuisse Horati temporibus Pompei sagam senatoris
qui a triumuiris proscriptus est*, v. l. 'the freedwoman of Pompeius the
senator', *temporibus libertam Pompei senatoris*).

Two other groups of names deserve comment. In *Satire* 1.10 a
number of the literary figures who are mentioned disparagingly are
known to have been hostile to Caesar or to Octavian. Laberius the
mime writer had been humiliated by Caesar in 46 and had retaliated
with such famous lines as 'henceforth, citizens, we are losing our
freedom' (*porro, Quirites, libertatem perdimus*) and 'the one whom
many fear must fear the many' (*necesse est multos timeat quem multi
timent*, 34–5 Diehl).[167] Pitholeon was identified by Bentley with the
Pitholaus who wrote poems of invective (*carmina maledicentissima*)
against Caesar.[168] Alpinus (1.10.36) is plausibly identified with Furius Bibaculus who certainly lampooned Octavian and may also have
attacked Caesar; he is, however, usually credited with an *Annales Belli
Gallici* which is supposed to have been an epic in praise of Caesar's
Gallic Wars.[169] The dilemma is clear: it is therefore worth noting that
Ps.-Acro in his note on *Satire* 2.5.40 gives the title of this work as
pragmatia Belli Gallici (i.e. πραγματεία vel sim.). This becomes
suggestive when it is recalled that in *Satire* 1.10, in the lines preceding
the parody of Alpinus, Horace's complaint had been directed precisely against those poets who mixed Greek and Latin. Since it is
hard to believe that anyone did this in a serious epic, the possibility
must be considered that Bibaculus' poem was a satirical parody,
a mock-epic on Caesar's campaign. Finally, there is also Sp. Maecius

[166] For the death of Cassius Parmensis, see Vell. 2.87.3 and Woodman (1983: ad
loc.); Val. Max. 1.7.7. Cf. Syme (1978a: 52).

[167] Cf. Beare (1964: 155–8).

[168] See Rudd (1966: 120; 147); Treggiari (1969: 118–19), who prefers not to accept
the identification of Pitholaus with M'. Otacilius (vel sim.) as proposed by Lewis
(1966: 271–2).

[169] For a full survey of the problems connected with Furius Bibaculus, see
Wigodsky (1972: 148–50); and cf. Rudd (1966: 289–90); Lyne (1978: 171).

Tarpa (1.10.38) who had been appointed by Pompeius Magnus to select the plays to be performed in his theatre: even in the thirties the theatre retained its association with the Pompeii.[170]

The second group consists of people who share their *nomina* with notorious opponents of the Triumvirs. Cassius Etruscus (1.10.62) shares his with three of the assassins: C. Cassius, L. Cassius Longinus and Cassius Parmensis; Trebonius (1.4.114) with C. Trebonius and Tillius (1.6.24 and 107) with, L. Tillius Cimber, two more assassins. There is also Fannius (1.10.80) who shares his *nomen* with C. Fannius, the most honoured and faithful adherent of Sex. Pompeius.[171] Again the evidence is simply not adequate to make it certain that there is any connection or relationship between these men. But in the circumstances it is hard to believe that there is no significance at all in these coincidences and harder still to believe that Horace expected his readers not to associate these men with their notorious homonyms.

There are three possible counter-examples who could disturb this dim and uncertain outline of a neat and expected pattern. Alfenus *vafer* (1.3.130) was identified by Porphyrio with P. Alfenus Varus, cos. suff. 39. Almost no scholar has accepted this: not only was Varus eminent, but he had been honoured by Horace's friend, Virgil (*Eclogues* 6 and 9) and he was also a supporter of Octavian.[172] But if Horace expected his readers to avoid this error, his Alfenus must have been well known. The only other Alfenus on record is apparently P. ALF(enus) Primus, known from an inscription to have been *legatus pro praetore* in Achaea in the late Republic or early Augustan period.[173] It will be recalled that Achaea had been granted to Sex. Pompeius in 39: it is possible (no more) that he was acting for Sextus.[174] If that suggestion is not accepted then the problem must be left unsolved.

[170] See Cic. *Ad fam.* 7.1.1, who also is disparaging about his literary standards. For the theatre and the Pompeii in the thirties see Vell. 2.79.6 and n. 132 above.

[171] App. *Bell. ciu.* 5.139. One could perhaps add Demetrius (1.10.79; 90) who shares his (very common) name with a notorious freedman favourite of Pompeius Magnus (for whom see Treggiari (1969: 184–5)).

[172] See Rudd (1966: 137; 292); Nisbet-Hubbard (1970: 227–8); Syme (1964a: 281).

[173] See Broughton (1968), Supplement 4; Wiseman (1971: 279 no. 521). The restoration of the *nomen* is not certain.

[174] It is not however clear when Pompeius actually took charge of Achaea: App. *Bell. ciu.* 5.77; Dio 48.46.1.

At *Satire* 1.2.36, Horace refers to 'Cupiennius, an admirer of high-class cunt' (*mirator cunni Cupiennius albi*). To some scholars the name has seemed too good to be true; but it may have been.[175] Porphyrio at least thought he could be identified with C. Cupiennius Libo 'famous for his close relationship with Augustus' (*Augusti familiaritate clarus*). That would be, in fact, a good reason for supposing him not to be Horace's target. But Libo's friendship with Augustus may have belonged to a later period or even to an earlier one: the *cognomen* suggests the possibility that he was related to L. Scribonius Libo who had been briefly the brother-in-law of Octavian (40–39) during the latter's marriage to Scribonia. But Scribonius Libo was also the father-in-law of Sex. Pompeius and one of his most faithful supporters.[176]

In this respect, as in others, the most difficult problem is posed by Hermogenes Tigellius.[177] In *Satire* 1.2, the death is reported of Tigellius the Sardinian; in the later poem, *Satire* 1.10, Hermogenes Tigellius seems to be alive and well. The discrepancy has convinced some that there must be two people:[178] the Sardinian featured in the opening lines of *Satires* 1.2 and 3, and a Hermogenes Tigellius who appears elsewhere (1.3.129; 1.4.72; 1.9.25 and 1.10.18; 80; 90). But the fact that variations on his name are clearly used in 1.10 as a structural device makes it difficult to believe that the same technique of ring-composition is not being used in 1.3. Moreover, whatever form of the name is used, he always appears as a singer (*cantor*).[179] There is no obvious solution.[180] For present purposes the real problem is caused by the fact that in *Satire* 1.3 it is clearly stated that

175 Rudd (1966: 143 and 145); Wiseman (1971: 114); Syme (1964a: 115–16).

176 App. *Bell. ciu.* 5.139.

177 See Treggiari (1969: 269–70).

178 Notably Fraenkel (1957: 86) and Rudd (1966: 292–3).

179 Note the verbal echoes and variations in: 1.2.3: *cantoris... Tigelli*; 1.3.1–8: *cantoribus... cantare... Tigellius... citarer... resonat*; 1.3.129: *Hermogenes cantor*; 1.4.72–6: *Hermogenisque Tigelli... recito recitent... resonat*; 1.9.25: *Hermogenes... canto*; 1.10.18–19: *Hermogenes... doctus cantare*; 1.10.80: *Hermogenis... Tigelli*; 1.10.90: *Tigelli.*

180 With more or less improbability, unitarians can suppose that Horace wrote 1.2 in response to a premature report of Tigellius' death; that the opening lines of 1.2 are a last-minute addition or rewriting prior to publication; that Tigellius had held a mock funeral, like Trimalchio! Separatists may suppose that the living Hermogenes is the dead man's son or freedman.

Tigellius had enjoyed the *amicitia* of both Caesar and Octavian. This raises the question of why Horace is attacking a friend of his patron's patron. One possibility is that Tigellius had defected to Sex. Pompeius. What makes this a possibility is that Tigellius was a Sardinian and in 39 Sardinia had been granted to Sex. Pompeius. If that is so, and if there is only one Hermogenes Tigellius, and if the Fannius of 1.10.80 is related to or even identical with C. Fannius, the adherent of Sextus, then the reference to him as 'dinner-guest of Hermogenes Tigellius' (*Hermogenis... conuiua Tigelli*) could be a humorous allusion to their billeting arrangements. An alternative and rather easier solution could be offered, if it is assumed that there are two persons involved. Then there would be no reason to consider the living Hermogenes an *amicus Caesaris* and he could even be a Pompeian.[181] The dead Tigellius would then have been singled out for extensive criticism, perhaps because, rather than in spite, of his being an *amicus Caesaris*. In that case Horace would be reinforcing the conciliatory tone of the satires by a characteristic admission of (past) imperfections on his own side.

CONCLUSION

At first sight the satires defeat those expectations generated both by the contemporary historical situation and by traditional associations of Lucilian satire with invective. There is neither overt praise of Octavian nor abuse of Sex. Pompeius. As a result the genial and conciliatory tone of the satires makes all the more impression. But these are not the poems of a man who has turned in on himself in disgust at the contemporary political scene or of one who has rejected the current would-be leaders and whatever solutions they have to offer. On the contrary, after Philippi, Horace changed sides.

---

[181] The names in this group—Hermogenes, Demetrius and Pantilius (1.10.78–80)—sound like the names of freedmen and of course Sextus was particularly associated with freedmen in contemporary propaganda. They are also distinct from and opposed to both the immediate friends of Maecenas (1.10.81–3) and the distinguished political supporters of Octavian and Antonius (1.10.85–6).

He joined Maecenas and that means that he committed himself to support of the Triumvirs and of Octavian. The satires are dedicated to Maecenas and in them Horace talks as his friend. Every reader takes away from the poems an impression of what Maecenas and his friends are like as people: very human and humane, witty, cultured and morally serious. In short, they are the ideal Roman citizens. Maecenas and his friends were real people and in reality they occupied the very centre of the political stage. No contemporary reader could forget that or fail to bring to his reading of the poems the historical context and the political dimension. Moreover, the poems constantly deal with topics—*auaritia, luxuria, aequitas, libertas, ambitio*—which are the very moral issues which are at the heart of contemporary analysis of Rome's problems. There is adequate evidence to allow a reconstruction, at least in broad outline and with some detail, of the nature of that political debate and its terminology, of the claims and counter-claims of the groups competing for power and of the ways in which they tried to discredit their rivals. When the satires are considered against this background, it becomes clear that they constantly reflect and echo this debate, both in their choice of themes and in small details (more, probably, than can now be detected), and that they consistently contribute to it from one particular point on the political stage. Horace, it must be emphasised, is not writing as a detached observer, but as the friend of Maecenas. It also becomes clear on reflection that the image of Maecenas' friends which emerges from the poems is so precisely suited to the political requirements of the mid-thirties and so exactly calculated to allay the fears and anxieties of Horace's contemporaries about the intentions, ambitions and moral character of their new leaders that it is just not possible to suppose this effect to be accidental.

This is the propaganda value of the satires. They are more rather than less effective for avoiding the crude, the obvious and the strident. But the word propaganda has ugly connotations and it is well to be clear. There is no reason to think that Horace did not intend to win the sympathy and support of his readers for his powerful *amici* and to present persuasively their own view of themselves. But there is also no reason whatsoever to think that Horace was insincere, that he did not believe genuinely that Octavian represented the best, even the only, hope of achieving peace, prosperity, and freedom. He may have been wrong but, equally, given the available choices—which were not (let it be remembered) between democracy and totalitarianism or fascism—he may have been right. Hostility to Octavian is fashionable among modern scholars, who also tend to idealise the Republic. Whatever justification there may be for this view, it is logically ridiculous to expect the supporters and friends of Octavian to share it. One final point may be made. There is no need to suppose that Horace was merely entrusted with giving verbal form to themes devised by his masters. He wrote as a friend who sympathised with and understood their intentions and who had every reason to feel grateful and unwilling to offend or hurt his friends. Rebellion and independence, even supposing that they were available alternatives, may have been more Romantic but they would have been less *utile urbi*. For it seems reasonable to think that the poets may have helped to shape the way in which Octavian progressed from the bloody and ruthless pursuit of power in the late forties to the enlightened self-interest of the principate. They presented their readers with an acceptable image but that image in turn set a standard for the new ruler to live up to. *Sermones* 1 is an important first contribution to that *lene consilium*.[182]

---

[182] I am most grateful to Prof. E. J. Kenney and Mr R. Seager for their comments and encouragement. They are not, of course, to blame for any errors of fact and judgement which may remain.

3

Horatian *Sermo* and Genres of Literature

Mario Labate

The classification of literature in the grammatical and literary-critical traditions of antiquity followed a wide array of principles that were the fruit of complex stratification. The results it produced are almost always judged disappointing by modern critics.[1] The case of satire is *sui generis*, and particularly interesting. Let us, for a moment, put ourselves in the shoes of a Latin grammarian. In setting about to classify the genre, this man would find himself facing a series of authors—authors undoubtedly famous—whose works were entitled, or at least commonly designated, 'satire'. But the classification of that genre must have seemed awfully problematic to him. In this case he had no recourse to a model from the Greek grammatical tradition, for in the map that Quintilian traces to compare Greek literary genres to Roman, the only discrepancies we find are the lack of a slot on the Greek side to match the genre of Latin satire (which he locates between elegy and iambic), just as there is no slot on the Latin side to match the genre of Greek Old Comedy (located between lyric and tragedy): 'Satire', he says, 'is entirely ours' (*satura tota nostra est*). It was, moreover, a case far from simple, because no simple criterion (metrical, thematic, or otherwise) could ever really be enough to classify it.

In the end, the Latin grammarians did not fare too badly, seeing that the distinction they drew between the two strands (and thus between the two 'genres') of satire is still widely used even today: on

---

[1] Cf., above all, Rosenmeyer (1985: 74–84). I take up the question more fully in Labate (1993: 155–60).

one side, in the stronger line, are Lucilius, Horace, Persius, and Juvenal. On the other side, we have a line more ragged and uncertain, leading from Ennius-Pacuvius to Varro.[2] The criterion of identification will have been primarily of a formal kind: the Lucilian strand was the one that fixed the hexameter as the metre of formal verse satire, while variety and a lack of formal restraint seemed to be the most obvious characteristics of the second group (Varro emphasized the pursuit of experimentation even at the level of form. Not content with emphasizing polymetry, he dared to attempt the prosimetry of Menippus: 'that second type of satire is even earlier. Terentius Varro wrote it, but his was mixed not only with a wide array of poems', *alterum etiam prius saturae genus, sed non sola carminum varietate mixtum condidit Terentius Varro,* Quint. *Inst.* 10.1.95). However, the classification based on metre was not without its problems, if for no other reason than that Lucilius himself, the genre's *inuentor,* settled on writing in hexameters only in the course of production, so he continued to exist in non-hexametric form as well.[3] Moreover, given all that the Alexandrian writers had done with it, the hexameter was definitely the least specific and the most general of metres. As in the case of didactic poetry or bucolic, a vivid sense of generic identity required that elements of 'content' be linked to the element of form.

But even in taking this two-pronged approach to the genre, our ancient grammarian must have found himself at a loss, since the very name 'satire' (etymology was frequently invoked as the guarantor of a specific vocation of a literary form) referred to the idea of variety and mixture, and it brought with it negative connotations of irregularity or 'mish-mash'. These were matters not only of satire's forms but also of its themes.[4] In fact, even from the scant traces of the satires of Ennius and the fragments of Lucilius, we have a sense of

---

[2] For the history of Latin satire we now have a number of excellent syntheses: besides Knoche (1982⁴), especially valuable is Coffey (1976). See also Classen (1988). For a clear picture of critical issues, with useful bibliography, see Citroni (1991) and (1989).

[3] Cf. Diomedes, G.L. I, p. 485Keil: *apud Romanos Lucilius et Catullus et Horatius et Bibaculus.* It is significant that Quintilian, who is the critic more attached to this scheme of classification, omits Lucilius from his list of iambic poets.

[4] The most incisive treatment of the problems concerning the origin and the name of Latin satire is that of Van Rooy (1966). Useful further developments are in Citroni (1989) and (1991).

how wildly varied their materials were: social commentary, autobiography, moral reflections, diatribe, investigations into nature and dialectic, literary discussions, grammatical and linguistic discussions, Aesopian fables, anecdotes, dialogue, comparisons, diaries, current events, letters, polemic, caricature, invective.

Faced with such difficulties, I think that even an ancient critic would have been urged to take a more sophisticated approach, to look for features further characterizing the genre not only in terms of subject-matter, but especially in terms of the poet's behaviour, in the ways he presents himself to his addressee, and modulates his themes according to a characteristic code; he would focus, in other words, not on the contents, but on the form of the contents: 'what we call satire is a poetic work belonging to the Romans that now, at any rate, is written to abuse and to attack the vices of men in the manner of old comedy, the sort that Lucilius wrote, then Horace, then Persius (*satira dicitur carmen apud Romanos nunc quidem maledicum et ad carpenda hominum uitia archaeae comoediae charactere compositum, quale scripserunt Lucilius et Horatius et Persius,* Diom. G.L. I, p. 485K). Since the subject-matter was so varied and uncertain, the genre's characterizing feature had to be found in the critic's polemical attitude, and his arguments' moral motivations.

It is here that the expertise of literary-critical analysis (and one generally supposes that the problem was put in these more complex terms by Varro in his *de poematis*) and the satiric poets' own self-consciousness merge. As is well known, already Lucilius may have claimed a Greek ancestry for his poetry ('familiarize yourself with those more ancient poems that have given rise to all these', <*nosce*> *archaeotera* <*illa*> *unde haec sunt omnia nata,* 1111Marx = 1122Krenkel), and Horace, in his turn, will show no hesitation in referring to it as decisive (*S.* 1.4.1–8):

> Eupolis atque Cratinus Aristophanesque poetae
> atque alii quorum comoedia prisca uirorum est,
> si quis erat dignus describi, quod malus ac fur,
> quod moechus foret aut sicarius aut alioqui
> famosus, multa cum libertate notabant.
> hinc *omnis* pendet Lucilius, hosce secutus
> mutatis *tantum* pedibus numerisque; facetus
> emunctae naris...

The poets Eupolis, Cratinus, and Aristophanes, and all the other 'real men' of Old Comedy, if anyone deserved lampooning, either because he was wicked, and a thief, or because he was an adulterer, or murderer, or notorious in some other way, they would brand him with abundant freedom of speech. Lucilius depends on them *totally*. These are the ones he follows, changing *only* their metres and rhythms. He is clever and sharply perceptive...

It is especially significant that, in this case, Horace manages, more or less, to reverse the principles of classification that privileged metre as the crucial indicator of literary identity: a type of dissociation of metre from mind, *numeri* from *animi,* is underscored by the contrast *omnis/tantum* (highlighted above). In another famous programmatic passage, Horace marked as a further characterizing feature of Lucilius' satiric persona his tendency to treat satire as a literary space suited to representing himself (a trait present already in Ennius, but obviously taken much further by Lucilius). Satire 'in the Lucilian manner' (*Lucili ritu*) thus meant for Horace satire in the manner of a 'votive tablet' (*votiva tabella*), holding sketches of the poet's life, accurately drawn; and not just his activities, but also his deepest thoughts; a diary, but also a model of existence.

When an author exists in fragmentary form, it is more or less inevitable for him to be understood by way of his literary and cultural heirs. Such conditioning becomes even stronger the more those heirs look to the problem of his connection to a model of their own (and thus the image they assign him is pre-packaged). A Lucilius too 'Horatian' (or 'Ciceronian'), for example, is the shortcoming of one of the richest and most intelligent books written on Lucilius (and Horace), a book with much to teach us concerning Late Republican Latin culture, M. Puelma Piwonka's *Lucilius und Kallimachos.*[5] To pass judgement through Horace's eyes (that is, to take one's start from his programmatic poems), we have to admit that satire owes to Lucilius not only the definitive fixing of a trait as fundamental as its metrical form, but that in establishing a form for its contents, just as he did, between the poles of aggressiveness and autobiography, Lucilius gave to Latin satire a structure that remained relatively stable. The assessment of Horace, posing as the 'Augustan' follower of the *inventor*, Lucilius, is subsequently confirmed by Persius, and it will be further reinforced by Juvenal.

[5] Puelma Piwonka (1949).

At any rate, I think that the study of Latin satire has more than once been found to suffer from an approach that we might define as more static than dynamic, one that looks to 'themes' and 'motives' and 'attitudes' rather than to their disposition into a meaningful form.[6] From this static point of view, there is no doubt that one can discover in Lucilius varied potentials that are, as it were, contained in his satires, and that will unleash their 'shaping' potential in different directions as the genre subsequently develops. A biting critical disposition unites the different representatives of satire, but we all know that it is the divergent inflection of this fundamental feature that profoundly alters the persona of the satirist and the form of his satire. Something similar can be said for autobiography. But perhaps it will be easier to understand what I have in mind here if one thinks of the risk that comes of confusing different functions. For clarity's sake, I schematize as follows: there is one function (we will label this function A) represented by the 'diatribal' role of the guide, the preacher and teacher. The Lucilian satiric persona can adopt this role within the ambit of *sermo,* but one risks confusing it with a very different function (B) that develops from the promptings of didactic in the first book of Horace's *Sermones.* The teacher's role will differ again in Book 2 of the *Sermones* (function C), and in his *Epistles* (function D), and yet again in the *Satires* of Persius (function E). It is dangerous, therefore, to confuse the presence of dialogue in the *Satires* of Lucilius with Horace's choice of dialogue as a formal device in the second book of his *Sermones* (dialogue will undergo further changes in function in Persius and Juvenal). And it is dangerous to confuse the epistolary experiments of Lucilius with the epistolary form that, in Horace, will mark the last phase of his *Sermo.* Naturally, I can only make a few gestures towards disentangling the complexities of this material here. A good place to begin is with the configuration of the satiric genre that one derives by analysis from the first book of Horace's *Sermones.*[7] The poems in which Horace dwells

[6] The recent study of Rudd (1986) featured this critical approach in its title: *Themes in Roman Satire.* It is to Rudd that we owe one of the most significant studies of the satiric poetry of Horace, in his Cambridge book of 1966, *The Satires of Horace.*

[7] Here and in what follows I develop certain ideas that I presented already in Labate (1981). My translation owed an obvious debt to a number of earlier works. Among these, of particular significance are: Anderson (1963a/1982); Rudd (1966); La Penna (1968/1993); and McGann (1973).

explicitly on the topic of satire (1.4 and 1.10, as well as 2.1, which is 'retrospective' in looking back on Book 1 instead of laying out the poetics of Book 2) present us with a poet who is the heir of the Lucilian satiric persona in its two basic poles: he writes poetry with critical bite, as well as poetry that is personal-autobiographical. In particular, aggression and named verbal abuse (ὀνομαστὶ κωμωδεῖν) are linked in Horace to diatribe settings where the poet's persona develops broad arguments on certain grand moral themes (human discontent and avarice, sexual vice, clemency and friendship), while satire as an image of the author's life is a feature common to the poems of the second book. In these, the satiric voice no longer argues, for the most part, but he recalls, represents, and describes persons and events that, in one way or another, have something to do with his own life. Whether in *S.* 1.4 or 1.10, Horace knows that he must distinguish himself polemically from Lucilius in the form of his expression (new demands of a modern style have by now rendered the unkempt ease of Lucilius' style impracticable). But as far as divergences in the form of his contents are concerned, Horace either has left these differences unspecified, or he has preferred to entrust them to a more subtle, meta-literary discourse. That said, were we to read a satire of Lucilius side-by-side with a satire of Horace, I believe that we would measure their differences not merely in terms of style.[8]

For Horace, claiming his own identity as a satirist means giving a better definition of the genre's identity. The satiric genre will now be the point where disparate drives converge, yet where all are essential because they are reciprocally defined in scope and function, each delimited by the others: satire must operate in such a way that comic representation and autobiographical occasion enter into a meaning-ful and organic relationship with a moral search that is, at once, based in lived experience and informed by philosophical study. Had he been born in the generation of the Augustan poets, Lucilius would have given suitable polish to the form of his expression (*S.* 1.10.67–71): but 'filing off a great deal from his verse' (*deterere sibi multa*) is a principle that holds for the form of his contents as well. In other words, as far as Horace is concerned, one has to let die those traits of the satiric tradition that now seem superfluous, and

---

[8] For acute observations on *S.* 1.10.9–14, see Fraenkel (1957:128ff.).

that are no longer functional for the genre's organic design. The principle that unifies and characterizes the satiric persona of Horace is, as I have said, that of a moral search. Clearly Lucilius had some interest in posing moral questions in his *Satires*. But, as far as we can tell, that interest probably did not have the same 'formative' function; in other words, it did not represent the principle from which all the other elements derived their meaning and their motivation.

This way of conceiving satire, first of all, imposes a responsibility on the satirist to disavow attacking for pleasure, i.e. that feature of lively, exhibitionist aggression that the comic hero of Aristophanes shares with the protagonists of iambic poetry, and that to Horace must have seemed perfectly suited to the 'iambic idea' (ἰαμβικὴ ἰδέα). And thus it was instead in his iambic *Epodes*, written at the same time as his *Sermones*, that Horace found the appropriate venue for such impassioned polemics, and for other forms of the 'poetry of excess'. And yet, compared to Lucilius, who was himself a student of Greek Old Comedy, the moral function of the satirist's polemical attack in Horace has undergone a shift as well.

The poet basically tells us this himself. Named abuse (ὀνομαστὶ κωμῳδεῖν), he says, served above all to 'unmask', that is, 'to strip off the skin in which each paraded stylishly before us, though ugly inside' (*detrahere pellem, nitidus qua quisque per ora | cederet introrsum turpis, S.* 2.1.64–5). In a certain way, then, this is a 'public' function: the citizen-poet, 'keen of scent' (*emunctae naris*), uses his polemical whip to expose hidden vice to public scrutiny. In a famous chorus of his *Wasps* (verses 1009ff.), Aristophanes claimed a heroic role for his comic poet within the *polis*: it is he who dared attack those in power (μέγιστοι); a modern-day Hercules, he took on the terrible monsters that were infesting the city, beginning with Cleon: thus he merited the title 'defender and liberator of our land' (ἀλεξίκακον τῆς χώρας τῆσδε καθαρτήν, v. 1043).

If Lachmann was right in his reconstruction (a reconstruction subsequently rejected by Marx, but taken up again by Krenkel), Lucilius imagined a publicly 'engaged' role for his satiric poet as well: *rem populi salute et fictis versibus Lucilius | quibus potest, impertit, totumque hoc studiose et sedulo* ('with passion and diligence Lucilius involves himself in the *res publica*, sharing good wishes and verse, the best he can write', 688–9Marx = 735–6K). From this point of view, it matters that the targets of Lucilius' attacks were, above all, the city's leaders (*primores populi*). And it is not by chance that the quality by which Lucilius is commonly defined (just as for the authors of Old Comedy) is a quality eminently political: his 'freedom' (*libertas*) as a citizen to stand toe-to-toe with his fellow citizens, and to deal with them on a level plane.[9] Likewise the mark that both Old Comedy and satire use to brand their targets has a political dimension: *notare* is the term used of the censor's 'mark'.[10]

Given that his political and social circumstances differed so widely from those of Lucilius, it is clear that Horace could not have taken on Rome's leading men (*principes viri*). But his taking aim at lesser figures on the city's cultural scene presupposes an important change in the function of satiric aggression. It has been rightly observed that satire needed to defy canons and systems of codification in order to conquer terrain that could accommodate themes outside the scope and moral reach of the traditional genres: accommodated by this new terrain, above all, was 'the observation of the moral and social problems posed by social connections'.[11] It is no wonder, then, that it is actually in the definition of the poet's connection to his society that satire concludes the search for a form of its own.

The satiric persona constructed by Horace does not engage in exposing the wicked and attacking his enemies. His satire is armed, but he prefers to leave his sword in its sheath: 'but this stylus of mine will attack no living thing without being provoked, and it will protect me, like a sword stowed in its sheath' (*sed hic stilus haud petet ultro | quemquam animantem et me veluti custodiet ensis | vagina tectus,* S. 2.1.39–41). Lucilius, in contrast, will be imagined by his poetic successor with his sword unsheathed: 'as often as Lucilius blazed and bellowed, as if with drawn sword...' (*ense velut stricto quotiens Lucilius ardens | infremuit...*, Juv. 1.165–6). But, for Horace, the weapon of choice for striking an enemy is actually that of iambic poetry: 'watch out, watch out: evildoers catch hell from me, and my

---

[9] Hor. *S.*1.4.5, *multa cum libertate notabant*; cf. Quint. *Inst.* 10.1.65, *antiqua comoedia...facundissimae libertatis et...in sectandis vitiis praecipua.*

[10] Cf. Lucil. fr.1033Marx = 1103Krenkel, *quem scis scire tuas omnes maculasque notasque*; Cic. *Brutus* 224, *homo simillimus Atheniensis Hyperboli, cuius improbitatem veteres Atticorum comoedia notaverunt.*

[11] See Citroni (1989), especially pp. 315ff.

horns are raised and ready' (*cave, cave: namque in malos asperrimus* |
parata tollo cornua..., *Epod.* 6.11–12). To simplify, then, we might
say that instead of attacking persons in their vices, the satirist now
criticizes vices in persons.

For Horace, the critique of moral deviations is a tool for moral
research (in the manner of Aristotle, via the observation of opposite
extremes). To serve that function, the satirist's criticism must have
not only targets of its own that differ from those of Lucilius and Old
Comedy, but above all it must have its own addressee (in the sense of
an internal addressee, the one imagined by the text itself as the
'beneficiary' of the satiric discourse). Those benefiting from satire
for Horace are neither the city nor its inner-workings (the city might
have better arms to wield against malefactors), nor are they the same
malefactors as before (who might rediscover virtue's path once they
are exposed to its proper form), nor a populace characterized by
moral choices that lack definition (they might now be guided along
and urged towards the good). Horace presents himself neither as a
polemical 'defender of the state' (*defensor civitatis*) nor as one who
preaches and instructs. His portrayal shows him comically coerced by
the defects of others, and content to find in the world a road just
wide enough for himself and his restricted group of friends. And thus
one could say that what we have here is not a true search as much as
we have, rather, a demand for confirmation and self-recognition. The
road sought, in other words, has already been discovered: for the
select group whose moral choices the satirist shares, the distortions of
society are like a negative surface that permits the group's own
positive image to be reflected, and thus to be recognized and become
recognizable. The satiric form of Horace's first book imagines a
triangular relationship among poet, friends, and society, and it
takes for granted that a discerning and intelligent man can live with
the distortions of others; that he can get past them, or even have
dealings with them, without losing (and thus to better recognize) his
own moral identity.[12]

It is worthwhile to watch how the motif of 'unmasking' develops
over the course of the *Sermones*. Horace, who had rejected such a
function in book one, lets others deploy it in Book 2, the 'inept

---

[12] Best in developing this point has been McGann (1973).

professors'. Though in charge of satiric speech, these *doctores inepti* cannot understand the contradictions and ambiguities of Horace's moral view, and thus the poet who was unwilling to unmask in Book 1 is shown as the one who becomes unmasked in Book 2:[13] 'but you, though you are what I am, and perhaps even worse, should you attack me without provocation, as if you were my better, and wrap your vice in lovely words?' (*tu cum sis quod ego et fortassis nequior, ultro | insectere velut melior verbisque decoris | obvolvas vitium? S.* 2.7.40–2). In the *Epistles* it will again be the poet, the voice guiding the *sermo,* who will have both the need, and the ability, to tear aside the lovely mask of vice. But that activity there will be a function of his new diatribe-role, as the teacher who aims to cure the ills of those still far away from the goal of *sapientia*: 'but the entire house, the whole neighbourhood sees him, gorgeous in his fancy skin, but ugly inside' (*sed videt hunc omnis domus et vicinia tota | introrsum turpem, speciosum pelle decora,* Hor. *Ep.* 1.16.44–5). The same function, coupled to a more radical therapeutic plan, will be taken up again by Persius who, from the art of demystification, will produce his satire's central concern. Satire, for Persius, is the lens through which the student of philosophy manages to see (and to make visible) the infected sore that hides under the belt: 'you have a wound hiding beneath your loins, but it is covered over by a wide belt of gold' (*ilia subter | caecum vulnus habes, sed latus baltes auro | praetegit,* P. 4.43–5); '(save your) fancy trappings for the mob! I know the you that's inside and hiding under your skin' (*ad populum phaleras. Ego te intus et in cute novi,* 3.30); 'yet if you, though you've just become a grain in our basket, still hold onto your old skin and, while shining on the outside, you keep a clever fox inside your vapid heart' (*sin tu, cum fueris nostrae paulo ante farinae, | pelliculam veterem retines et fronte politus | astutam vapido servas in pectore vulpem,* 5.115–17).[14]

   The organic link that binds comic aggression to the satirist's moral search (just as that binding his autobiographical portrayal to his moral search), in sum, the link between satire and philosophy, made it inevitable that Horace (even more so than Lucilius) should engage with both the form of diatribe and with its didactic and

---

[13] See n. 26 below.
[14] See Bramble (1974: 153ff.); also La Penna (1981), esp. pp. 53–60.

exhortatory impetus. Beyond his 'public' role as 'defender of the state', Lucilius had been able, with sufficient calm, to take up the role of a moral guide, one who addresses his interlocutor (whether generic or a friend) to deliver him from error and to teach him rules of conduct. A healthy number of fragments provide us with appeals to a second person that are typical of a teacher seeking a didactic touch, e.g. in demanding that his student pay attention in order to make him as receptive as possible: 'I insist that you investigate the matter with me and pay attention to my words' (*rem cognoscas simul et dictis animum adtendas postulo,* 693Marx = 707K); 'moreover that you would please attend to and apply your mind to my words' (*praeterea ut nostris animos adtendere dictis | atque adhibere velis,* 851–2Marx = 874–5K); 'but if you would, just for a moment, take hold of these things and consider them' (*quod si paulisper captare atque observare haec volueris,* 696Marx = 705K); 'if you will let these things flow through your ears to water your heart' (*haec tu si voles per auris pectus inrigarier,* 610Marx = 677K).[15]

In the first book of his *Sermones* (especially in the so-called 'diatribe satires'), the poet keeps separate his own *persona loquens* from that of a diatribe-preacher.[16] This separation happens all the more urgently when the changing philosophical and moralizing registers of his own satiric language push him into close, objective alignment with the diatribe-preacher.[17] Significantly, however, the preacher's admonitory gestures find a home in the second book of the *Sermones,* when the voice conducting the discourse is no longer that of the poet.[18]

---

[15] Because he was too preoccupied with his own thesis, neatly separating Lucilius from diatribe, Puelma Piwonka (1949: 62, 88 n. 4, 180 n. 3) denied the didactic and exhortatory function of these fragments by arguing that their chief function would have been to present the poet of the *Sermones* as a lecturer (drawing attention that would serve to entertain, not to preach, rather like the appeals to spectators that we find in comedy, e.g. *ad* Plaut. *Cas.* 9, *aures vocivae si sunt, animum adtendite*). But cf. esp. Lucr. 1.948–50: *si tibi forte animum tali ratione tenere | versibus in nostris possem, dum perspicis omnem | naturam rerum*; and 4.912: *tu mihi da tenuis auris animumque sagacem*.

[16] See for example *S.* 1.1.13–14, *cetera de genere hoc, adeo sunt multa, loquacem | delassare valent Fabium*; 1.1.120–1, *ne me Crispini scrinia lippi | compilasse putes, verbum non amplius addam*; cf. 1.3.126ff.

[17] Cf. *S.* 1.2.37–8, *audire est operae pretium, procedere recte | qui moechos non voltis.*

[18] For example *S.* 2.2.1–4, *quae virtus et quanta, boni, sit vivere parvo | (nec meus hic sermo est, sed quae praecepit Ofellus | rusticus, abnormis sapiens crassaque Minerva) |*

In the *Epistles* Horace again speaks in the first person, in the voice of one who instructs, a teacher who is, at once, weak and inconstant, but who is also aware of the urgent necessity of advancing towards *sapientia*. He is a teacher who, above all, teaches himself.[19] But he is ready to urge his friends to recognize and profit from the learning he has acquired and the progress he has made.[20]

The revival of the teaching function of satiric language will be even more decisive in Persius: 'learn, you wretches, and investigate the causes of things' (*discite, o miseri, et causas cognoscite rerum*, P. 3.66).[21] By this point, caricature of philosophers and contempt for their lessons is the prerogative of ignorant rubes, the 'goatish tribe of centurions' (*gens hircosa centurionum*).[22]

One could also follow the course that I have summarily traced here by studying an important formal variation of *sermo*: namely, the function and characterization of the 'you' addressed by the *persona loquens*, and the ways in which a varied use of the second person suggests a multiplicity in the satiric discourse's levels of address. This is a topic that has attracted attention especially from scholars of Horace (from Cartault, Heinze, and Lejay to, more recently, C. Codoner and M. Citroni). From Citroni's analyses one has a good sense of how satires that are 'monologic' (thus, all the satires of Book 1 and, in particular, *Sermones* 1.1 and 1.2) are characterized by a complex play of interlocutors.[23] I simplify as follows: on the one

discite; 2.3.32–3, *si quid Stertinius veri crepat, unde ego mira | descripsi docilis praecepta haec*; 2.3.77–81, *audire atque togam iubeo componere, quisquis | ambitione mala aut argenti pallet amore, | quisquis luxuria tristive superstitione | aut alio mentis morbo calet: huc propius me, | dum doceo insanire omnis, vos ordine adite*; also 2.4.1ff., 88ff.; 2.5.10; 2.7.44ff.

[19] Hor. *Ep.* 1.1.23–7: *sic mihi tarda fluunt ingrataque tempora quae spem | consiliumque morantur agendi nauiter id quod | aeque pauperibus prodest, lucupletibus aeque, | aeque neglectum pueris senibusque nocebit. | restat ut his ego me ipse regam solerque elementis.*

[20] Hor. *Ep.* 1.1.48: *discere et audire et meliori credere non vis?*; 1.2.5, *cur ita crediderim, nisi quid te detinet, audi*; 1.6.67–8, *siquid novisti rectius istis, | candidus imperti; si nil, his utere mecum*; 1.8.16, *praeceptum auriculis hoc instilllare memento*; 1.17.3–4, *disce, docendus adhuc quid censet amiculus, ut si | caecus iter monstrare velit*; 1.17.16, *doce vel iunior audi*; 1.18.67, *protinus ut moneam* (*siquid monitoris eges tu*).

[21] See also P. 5.91–2 *disce, sed ira cadat naso rugosaque sanna, | dum veteres avias tibi de pulmone revello.*

[22] P. 1.127ff.; 3.77ff.; 5.189ff.

[23] Citroni (1993), recommended also for further bibliographical sources.

hand, we have a 'you' who is sane and reasonable, i.e. the satirist's friend who shares his immunity from the vice that is the object of criticism; on the other hand, we have the adversarial 'you' typical of diatribe, one who plays the devil's advocate and stands up for the false values that are to be laughingly refuted (for example, the avaricious man addressed in *S.* 1.1.38ff.).

None of these second persons is the addressee actually targeted by the speaker's precepts: the doltish 'you' is not refuted to be won over, and the sane 'you' does not need to be. Citroni writes: 'through the play of interlocutors and grammatical persons, the satirist points out to interlocutors who are of like mind the objectionable behavior of the fools he puts on stage. He addresses his speech to these fools. He converses with them, in a certain sense, right before the eyes of that other audience...'[24]

In the dialogue satires of Book 2, the play of interlocutors can become completely baffling. An extreme case is that of Damasippus, who treats Horace to the sermonizing that Stertinius had used to rescue and convert him. Here we have a 'you' that is Horace, one that is Damasippus, or any of the several 'you's' conjured up by his argument (Oppidius, Agamemnon), or again a more generic 'you' addressed by moral instruction, or one that is simply a function of the diatribe's argument. We have here an intersection of discursive planes that is difficult to sort out, and it is perhaps wrong to want to do so. What is certain and significant is that the reasonable 'you' of Book 1 has disappeared, and this disappearance makes it more or less pointless to make neat distinctions among the other 'you's', all of whom are, in fact, at this point potential patients of philosophical therapy (adversaries to be refuted, students to be instructed, lost souls to be saved).

The 'you' that represents a friend (Maecenas, Aristius Fuscus, and others like them) returns as the addressee of the moral discourse in the *Epistles*, but with the important difference that this person is no longer constituted as having no need to be convinced, i.e. as one who is already a positive model to be lived up to. In contrast to *Sermones* Book 1, in the *Epistles* the *persona loquens* allows for differences with his friends, and he presents those friends as participants in the

[24] Citroni (1993: 123).

far-flung errors of Roman society, or at least as distracted and lacking awareness. In those instances where a homogeneity can be established between the one leading the *sermo* and the friends who are addressed by it, this homogeneity ends up being a matter of the weakness of the teacher's voice: the teacher-corrector puts himself among those needing correction, and the scolding he directs at a friend can, at the same time, be directed at himself. Thus, the 'we' of the *Epistles* is, in the end, different from the reasonable and elite 'we' of *S.* 1.1.119 or 1.6.18.

The *Satires* of Persius are dominated by a 'strong' teaching voice. It goes without saying that there is no trace in them of the 'you' who needs no correction. Persius' *persona loquens* is precisely that of a teacher, and Persius assumes this persona even when he addresses his own teacher, Cornutus, to show him how the student has, in turn, learned to become a teacher. As a teacher, Persius is not heeded, but he is confident in his own doctrine, which he persists in preaching even to a society that does not care.[25]

We have seen how the triangle of satiric voice/friends/society breaks down as we move from Book 1 of the *Sermones* to Book 2, signalling profound changes in the form of satire's contents. In choosing a conversational mode, that is, in drawing back and ceding to others the role of conversational-guide, with the subsequent proliferation of satiric *personae* who are diverse in their credibility, Horace stages a crisis of satire, or at least of the structure given to it in Book 1. He displays to his reader the upsetting of satire as a site for an empirical moral search, as the mirror in which reasonable men of like mind can recognize their own moral physiognomy, positively reflected. Left to take over the scene in Book 2 are the contradictory opinions and diverse truths of society at large. Some of these opinions are more plausible, others more bizarre or excessive, and yet others are downright objectionable. But none is completely without a trace of reasoned thought, not even Catius or Teiresias.[26] If I had the time, I would try to show the entire intertextual thread that links the

---

[25] This aspect has been well illuminated by Ferri (1993), esp. pp.145–87.

[26] I made a case for this in Labate (1981: 35–9), with an emphasis that diverges in part from Anderson (1982: 41–9). See now also La Penna (1993), and Lefèvre (1993: 111–40).

doctores inepti of Book 2 not only to the satiric *persona* of Book 1, but also to the thoughtful and self-aware teacher of the *Epistles*.[27]

What I especially want to underline here is how, in his three collections of *sermones*, Horace has located in strategic central positions certain poems that contain, so to speak, the key to the form of *sermo* itself (the form of its contents). In each of these three poems (*S.* 1.6, *S.* 2.6, and *Ep.* 1.7) the poet addresses Maecenas and defines his relationship to Maecenas. There is a metaliterary significance to these poems that seems largely to have escaped notice. In *S.* 1.6 we have the poet's admission to a homogeneous group that not only determines the 'triangular' structuring of his satiric discourse, but establishes the very possibility of satire's functioning as an empirical moral search: the awareness of belonging to an elite group chosen on the basis of intellectual and moral values (*prava ambitione procul*) is a necessary precondition of satire because that sense of belonging allows one to 'live along with' (*convivere*) the distortions of the majority, criticizing them with the indulgence of one who does not feel his own identity threatened. Such criticism is thus a tool of smiling affirmation of the satirist's own identity: one thinks, for example, of his encounter with alternative paradigms of living in the 'pest' satire.[28] To put this in 'philosophical' terms, we find here a delicate balance between 'independence' and 'moderation' (αὐτάρκεια and μετριότης) that has been recognized as characteristic of 'Horace's moral view'.[29] Such independence does not manifest itself in bitter social isolation, but in involvement in life that is cordial and ironic, and coupled to the preservation of interior freedom. The amazing account of a day in the city that concludes *S.* 1.6 represents, emblematically, the possibility of urban αὐτάρκεια (the sort that Maecenas can give to his friends). This is an independence realized amid the multicoloured realities of a metropolis crowded with people who are hard at work and not at all disposed towards *sapientia* (shopkeepers, soothsayers, con artists, money-lenders, penny pinchers).

In *S.* 2.6, on the other hand, the balanced corresponsion of life-to-text is thrown off: the mechanism jams, and αὐτάρκεια in the city is

---

[27] I give a set of examples (by no means exhaustive) in Labate (1981).
[28] Cf. Rudd (1966: 81ff.); see also Latacz (1980), with additional bibliography.
[29] See esp. La Penna (1993), particularly pp. XLIV–LIV.

no longer possible. This represents the impossibility of satire itself. 'With ambition nowhere in sight' (*ambitione procul*) was key to the poet's relationship to Maecenas in Book 1. There he lived with the city's great men without getting involved in career ambitions (as the pest intended to do), in social obligations, and in political affairs (as so many of the general populace must have intended). Lucilius, who engaged in free and relaxed play with Laelius and Scipio while waiting for the cabbages to cook, symbolized for Horace a paradigm of social rapport, in a relationship that was gratifying and encouraging, but capable of leaving one's choices in life undamaged and one's values undistorted. Just as Terence before him, Horace held that, for an intellectual of modest means, 'pleasing the great' was an important acknowledgement of one's own qualities, an affirmation of *virtus*. But one had to keep the role of a great man's friend neatly separated from the terrain of public life, and from the 'business dealings' (*negotia*) of the rich and powerful. The 'leisure' (*otium*) of those who were educated, reasonable, and refined clearly had need of serious interests. Varro advised that their friends should be dedicated to literature, at once, both useful and delightful (sat. Men. 340, *quae sint βιωφελῆ et delectent*); that they should be versed in 'matters relevant to a shared enjoyment of life' (*de rebus ad communem vitae usum pertinentibus*), topics that have no place 'in business and the forum' (*in foro atque negotiis*, Men. 338–9). But Horace, as mentioned before, insists on an intimacy that is more frivolous and quotidian (talk of the weather, trivial matters and insubstantial concerns), as we see at *S.* 2.6.42–6:

> ... dumtaxat ad hoc, quem tollere raeda
> vellet iter faciens et cui concredere nugas
> hoc genus: 'hora quota est?' 'Thraex est Gallina Syro par?'
> 'matutina parum cautos iam frigora mordent',
> et quae rimosa bene deponuntur in aure.

(Maecenas includes me) only insofar as he might want someone to ride along when he takes a trip, someone with whom to entrust chit-chat for safe-keeping, as follows: 'what time is it?' 'You think that Thracian Cock is a match for the Syrian?' 'The mornings are already cold, and they bite if you're not careful', and such things that are safely deposited in an ear that leaks.

Horace's concern here is not just with modesty, but with a threat to his mode of life (in the sense of Lebensführung), and even to his work as a poet. The 'intellectual friend of great men' was, in fact, a cultural paradigm already set: Ennius had defined it in his famous portrait of the friend of Servilius (*Annales* 268–86Sk.).[30] There, according to Aelius Stilo, the poet painted his own image, in his relationship to his noble protectors.[31] The 'good companion' of Ennius is characterized by many qualities that Horace would not object to (his *ingenium,* his vast culture, *comitas,* sense of moderation, and uncorrupted morality). But there is one place where Horace senses a discrepancy between the Ennian paradigm and his own cultural exigencies, at the point where Ennius' good companion had picked up Hellenistic features from the official friend and confidant of the king:[32] to his modest but worthy friend Servilius is completely open, and he confides in him completely. He shares with him not only matters that are slight and meaningless, but also matters of importance (*res magnas*). In the company of his friend, Servilius frees himself from some of the distressing weight that oppresses him (*evomeret*). Answering to such great credibility are the friend's suitable qualities: he keeps the weightiest secrets safe (*tuto locaret*), because he is characterized by 'a stinginess of language' (*linguae parsimonia*), 'the right timing of speech' (*loquendi opportunitas*), and a 'scrupulous regard for keeping and guarding a secret' (*servandi tuendique secreti religio*).[33] Horace, in contrast, admits to being incapable of self-control and unable to keep secrets safe: he speaks of having *rimosa… aure* ('an ear that leaks'). And with the barbed oxymoron *concredere nugas* ('to entrust with trifles for safe-keeping'), he tells us that he can only be trusted with matters of no account.

The crisis of αὐτάρκεια in the city, and in satire, arises from the failure to maintain a distinction between cultural models that are closely related: the good companion of Ennius tends to be superimposed on, and to trump, Horace's friend of the great. The problem is

---

[30] A famous piece by Mariotti (1951: 127–30 = 1991³: 80–1) rightly returned this epic fragment of Ennius to the same cultural, intellectual, and literary climate that gave rise to the *Satires.*

[31] Cf. Norden (1915: 132–33); Leeman (1958: 318–21).

[32] Cf. Skutsch (1968: 92–4); see also Skutsch (1985: 447–462).

[33] Gel. 13.4.4.

one of social communication: the Horatian model struggles to find a language that can make him recognizable to his society. The poet presents us with his failure by way of a lively mime (*S.* 2.6.32–9 and 51–8):

> at simul atras
> ventum est Esquilias, aliena negotia centum
> per caput et circa saliunt latus. 'ante secundam
> Roscius orabat sibi adesses ad Puteal cras.'
> 'de re communi scribae magna atque nova te
> orabant hodie meminisses, Quinte, reverti.'
> 'inprimat his cura Maecenas signa tabellis.'
> dixeris: 'experiar': 'si vis, potes,' addit et instat.
>
> quicumque obvius est, me consulit: 'o bone—nam te
> scire, deos quoniam propius contingis oportet—,
> numquid de Dacis audisti?' 'nil equidem.' 'ut tu
> semper eris derisor.' 'at omnes di exagitent me,
> si quicquam.' 'quid? militibus promissa Triquetra
> praedia Caesar an est Itala tellure daturus?'
> iurantem me scire nihil mirantur ut unum
> scilicet egregii mortalem altique silenti.

But as soon as I reach the Esquiline Hill, a hundred items of other people's business come bounding through my head and about my side. 'Roscius was insistent that you be on hand for him before ten o'clock, tomorrow, at the Well.' 'About that matter, the big new one that concerns all of you, the scribes were insisting that you remember to come back later today.' 'Make sure that Maecenas puts his seal on these tablets.' If you say, 'I'll try,' he keeps pushing and adds 'If you want to, you can.'

Someone comes up to me and asks for advice (**Stranger**): 'O my good man, for it behoves you to know this, since you are in close contact with the gods, have you heard anything regarding the Dacians?' **Hor:** 'Not a thing.' **Str:** 'Oh what a clever dodger you will always be!' **Hor:** 'But let all the gods harry me if I know anything at all!' **Str:** 'Then what about this? Will Caesar give the spoils he promised to his soldiers from Sicily or Italy?' He is amazed when I swear I know nothing, looking at me as some creature of exceptional and deep silence.

When others require favours or intercessions, when they ask him about affairs of the state, it does no good for Horace to deny that he has power and connections: understatement, reserve, and discretion are exactly the qualities that characterize an 'influential friend of the powerful'. After denying that he is one, Horace remains, in practice, an 'influential friend of the powerful'. In the end, the friend of Servilius would in fact have comported himself in exactly the same way.

As a friend of the great, Horace is a prisoner of his society: he cannot withdraw from the 'diligence to duty and the petty tasks of the forum' (*officiosaque sedulitas et opella forensis, Ep.* 1.7.8). He has no comeback to the one who looks upon him as the 'running slave' (*servus currens*) of Maecenas: 'you'll knock down all that stands in your way if you are running back to Maecenas with something to tell him' (*tu pulses omne quod obstet | ad Maecenatem memori si mente recurras, S.* 2.6.30–1). By receiving him into his group of friends, Maecenas was making satire possible. But this same Maecenas (that is, as he was typecast by Roman society) produces a crisis for satire insofar as he makes satire's very space, the city of Rome, un-navigable by the poet. And yet, at the same time, Maecenas constantly promises a way to escape satire in the gift of the Sabine villa, a place set apart and remote, where the poet will regain control over *sermo*. But he will do so there (in *Epistles* Book 1) without comic aggression, and without studying others from a privileged point of view.

Ep. 1.7 concludes my metaliterary triptych by confirming that the place of the *Epistles* is the 'nook' (*angulus*), which is to say that the new form of *sermo* presupposes a distance from the city and from social life: the letters are discourses of someone absent who reflects upon himself (the letter as 'image of one's own soul', εἰκὼν τῆς ἑαυτοῦ ψυχῆς), and who communicates the wisdom he gains with his friends (the letter as the philosopher's letter).[34] Here again it is Maecenas who guarantees the conditions of the literary-educational project, and he must continue to guarantee them by refraining from drawing the poet back to the space that belonged to satire. This is something that even Maecenas needs to be educated about. With all due courtesy, he has put to him in *Ep.* 1.7 a kind of 'mirror of a friend in power' (*speculum potentis amici*): he must steer clear of the 'Calabrian host' (*Calaber hospes*), but he must also avoid the

---

[34] Heinze (1919: 305ff = 1938: 236–54), later republished in the appendix to Kiessling-Heinze (1959⁶: 367–80).

mildly sadistic caprice of great noblemen, the sort that Philippus represents.

One of the most acute definitions of Horatian satire we owe, as is well known, to Horace's successor, Persius (P.1.116–17):

> Omne vafer vitium ridenti Flaccus amico
> Tangit et admissus circa praecordia ludit.

Flaccus applies an expert's soft 'touch' to his laughing friend's every vice and, once let inside, he jibes close to the heart.

For my part, I think that the textual reference of this famous characterization is to be sought (as Harvey suggests) specifically in the *Epistles*, starting in particular with those letters that are addressed to Maecenas.[35] But if Persius was able to regard this form of *sermo* as 'satiric', it is because his own satire (as he hints) has fully recovered that didactic and educative impetus that, for Horace, stood outside the range of what authentic satire was supposed to be.

---

[35] Harvey (1981: 50).

4

The Epicurean Parasite: Horace,
Satires 1.1–3

William Turpin

I. INTRODUCTION

We have learned a great deal in recent years about reading Horace's satires; there is now widespread agreement that the speaker of the satires is himself a character within them, a persona.[1] Such a persona may be most effective when it has obvious connections with its creator, but that fact does not preclude the exaggeration of reality, or even its complete inversion. For Horace the implications of this approach are exciting: instead of a poet discoursing with cheerful earnestness on morality, on poetry and on his daily life, we have a fictional character, whom we do not have to take seriously at all.

The three diatribe satires present us with a character so absurd that they have been taken, I think rightly, as parodies. Although the poems were once appreciated as effective moralizing sermons,[2] even their admirers found it hard to justify the lack of intellectual coherence, to say nothing of the astonishing vulgarity of the second satire. As parodies, however, the poems are wonderfully successful.

---

[1] Anderson (1982); Zetzel (1980); Freudenburg (1993). For a good discussion of persona (or, as she prefers, 'face') see Oliensis (1998a: 1–16).

[2] Rudd (1966: 1): 'Horace was no Gandhi. But he did see that a great many people who were, by their own standards, sufficiently well off never quite managed to enjoy what they had. And he made bold to point this out in poems which for good humour, lightness of touch, and absence of priggishness have never been surpassed.' See also Schrijvers (1993: 41–90).

The speaker trots out a series of banalities: 'people should be content with who they are'; 'people should not go to extremes'; 'people should be consistent'. But he invariably gets distracted, goes off on tangential rants, and makes a fool of himself. The moralist of the first three satires is, to put it bluntly, a jerk.[3]

This paper will argue that there are additional dimensions to this ridiculous moralist. I suggest that the speaker of the satires is supposed to be understood both as a committed Epicurean and as a contemporary version of that stock figure of Greek and Latin comedy, the parasite, or professional guest. These two characterizations might be thought quite distinct, but for those hostile to Epicureanism or willing to be amused by it there was clearly a connection, and it is central to the character that Horace has created.

Although much of the humor in the first three satires arises from the creation of an incompetent Epicurean, philosophy is only part of the joke. The creation of a parasite persona brings us face to face with the question of Horace's relationship with Maecenas. It is usually assumed that the address to Maecenas is there simply as a sort of dedication, and that the many subsequent uses of the second person singular imply a sort of generic listener.[4] But the humor of these satires is more effective if we regard the second person singulars as directed at Maecenas himself; it is Maecenas who listens to the ranting about avarice, who gets advice about what kinds of women to seduce, and who is told about forgiving friends their faults. Some of this is straightforward exaggeration: Maecenas was filthy rich, notorious for his love affairs, and of course the archetypal friend of poets.[5] But the depiction of Maecenas as a Stoic opponent of Epicureanism, complete with the beard and staff of the professional

---

[3] Freudenburg (1993: 17): 'I maintain that the diatribe satires are completely detached from the true spirit and intent of the ethical treatises they imitate. They are, in fact, a burlesque of Greek popular philosophy, which had grown fully ripe for parodic treatment by Horace's day and certainly long before.' For the structural similarities of the first three satires see especially Armstrong (1964: 86–96).

[4] e.g. Brown (1993) ad loc.: 'Horace now abruptly rounds on a specific imaginary opponent from the ranks of the discontented (te 38, tibi and te 40).' See, however, Lyne, (1995: 142): 'It is difficult to sever most second persons from Maecenas (though, given the grammatical ambiguity, no-one can insist upon the connection).'

[5] For the Roman use of the language of friendship for what we normally describe as patron/client relationships see White (1993: 13–14). For the historical Maecenas in general a good starting place is Lyne (1995: 132–8).

philosopher (*S.* 1.3.133–4), is not exaggeration but inversion. In his recent book on Aristophanes, Michael Vickers observes that a figure can be lampooned not only by exaggerating known character- istics, but also by depicting features which are the opposite of the obvious ones.[6] Vickers observes that the technique is discussed in a rhetorical textbook attributed to Hermogenes, and it is employed by modern comedians of today: one example might be the cockney ladies in Monty Python sketches, with their strong opinions about Descartes and Heidegger.[7] The real Maecenas was a notorious he- donist, and may in fact have been an Epicurean.[8] To portray him as an austere Stoic is broad humor indeed, but we should remember that the satirist speaking in the first person is not the only fictional character in these poems.

II. THE SATIRIST AS EPICUREAN

The question of Horace's own commitment to Epicureanism is a persistent one, but does not need to be resolved here; we need only remember that Horace likes to say that he is, or once was, an Epicurean of some kind, at least in theory.[9] The speaker of the first three satires, however, is a much more committed, even professional, Epicurean: he attacks individual Stoics and makes heavy-handed allusions to Lucretius, he quotes Philodemus by name, and he con- cludes the third satire with a sustained Epicurean attack on a Stoic doctrine.[10] Scholars have sometimes regarded the speaker as a Cynic, or as eclectic.[11] In part this is because Horace himself says that his model is Bion the Cynic, and if my argument here is right we should see this as a comment on genre rather than on substantive

---

[6] Vickers (1977: 14).

[7] Hermogenes, *Meth.* 34, ed. Hugo Rabe, *Hermogenis Opera* (Leipzig 1913), 451–2.

[8] On the question of Maecenas' Epicureanism see André (1967: 15–61); Evene- poel, (1990: 99–117, at 106–7).

[9] See esp. de Witt (1939: 127–34); Nisbet and Hubbard (1970: 376–9).

[10] For reminiscences of Lucretius see Murley (1939: 380–95); Merrill (1905); Freudenburg (1993: 19–20).

[11] Freudenburg (1993: 11) calls him a Cynic; Rudd (1966: 21–2) argues that he is eclectic.

philosophy.[12] But the main reason for denying that our speaker is an Epicurean is that his Epicureanism is simply not very impressive. This is a problem if we take him seriously as a moralist, but it makes perfect sense if we are supposed to be amused.

Philosophers have been ridiculed since Thales. Aristophanes and other writers of Greek comedy clearly got a lot of mileage out of philosophers' various foibles, and the tradition was continued in Rome by Plautus, Terence, and in mime and Atellan farce.[13] Perhaps the single best text on the subject is Lucian's comic sketch 'Philosophies for Sale', itself reminiscent of some of the jokes in Monty Python: philosophers of various persuasions are auctioned off, some at very low prices.[14]

Epicureans, however, made particularly good targets.[15] Though Epicurus himself protested that his doctrines were misunderstood, it is clear that many people understood him to be talking primarily about purely physical pleasures.[16] The most prominent charge was that Epicureans were far too interested in food and drink, and it is this, as we shall see, that provides the most obvious connection with the figure of the parasite.[17] But the other important charge was that Epicureans were sexually promiscuous.[18] This was partly because the

[12] Horace, *Ep.* 2.2.60 refers to the *sermones* of Bion, for which see Kindstrand (1976).

[13] On Epicureans in Greek comedy see Frischer (1982: 55–60); I have not been able to see A. Weiher, *Philosophen und Philosophenspott in der attischen Komödie* (Diss. Munich, 1913). For Roman comedy see Cèbe (1966: 115–16 and 370–1).

[14] Lucian, *Vit. Auct.* (Loeb vol. 2, 451–511); for jokes about philosophers in Latin literature other than comedy see Cèbe (1966: 169–71).

[15] DeLacy (1941: 49–58); David Sedley (1976: 119–60). For Epicurus and his followers in Italy see now David Sedley (1998).

[16] Epicurus, *Letter to Menoecus*, in *D.L.* 10.131–2 (Loeb translation): 'By pleasure we mean the absence of pain in the body and of trouble in the soul. It is not an unbroken succession of drinking-bouts and of revelry, not sexual love, not the enjoyment of the fish and other delicacies of a luxurious table, which produce a pleasant life.' Also in Long and Sedley (1987: no. 21.B).

[17] See esp. fragment 2 of Damoxenus, in Kassel and Austin (1986: 2–6 = Athen. 3. 101f–103b), where Epicurus' cook argues that only Epicureans make really good cooks. So also Lucian, *Vit. Auct.* (Loeb, 2, 451–511), ch. 19.

[18] See esp. Cleomedes, ed. H. Ziegler (Leipzig 1891), 2.92: 'Shouldn't you, most audacious and disgraceful man, quit philosophy and betake yourself to Leontion and Philaenis and the rest of those hetairai, and to those sacred pontifications with Mindyrides and Sardanopolis and the rest of your devotees? Don't you know that philosophy demands Hercules, and men like Hercules, and not, by God, catamites and pleasure.' Notice also Alciphron 3.17.2: where the Epicurean dinner-guest 'took

worst possible construction was placed on the fact that women mixed freely with men in Epicurean circles.[19] But even more important was Epicurean doctrine, which was easy to misrepresent; Epicurus replied to a friend asking what to do about sexual urges that as long as he did no harm he should gratify himself as much as he wanted.[20]

It is the popular association of Epicureanism with sex that lies behind the extraordinary transformation of the argument in *Satire* 1.2, from a sententious statement about moderation into the vulgar and obsessive pontification about adultery. As we shall see, the speaker of *Satire* 1.2 is obsessed with the question of sex in general, and is all too willing to provide pseudo-Epicurean advice on the subject.

III. THE SATIRIST AS PARASITE

The figure of the parasite is most familiar to us, as perhaps he was to Horace, from the comedies of Plautus and Terence, where he is a relatively one-dimensional character, interested almost exclusively in food.[21] But in Greek literature the parasite (or his predecessor, the *kolax*) had a wider range of interests and activities, often only hinted at in the Latin comedies.[22] The parasites of Greek literature were of course devoted to food and drink, but they were also interested in sex.[23] Moreover one special type of parasite was the philosopher, who could be seen so easily as a professional friend and dinner

the harp girl in his arms, gazing upon her from half-closed eyes with a languishing and melting look, and saying that this was "tranquillity of the flesh" and "consolidation of pleasure" ' (Loeb translation). For a discussion of Epicurus' actual views see Nussbaum (1994: 149–54).

[19] *D.L.* 10.7 quotes Timocrates as saying that Epicurus consorted with a number of hetairai, whose names are suspiciously appropriate to their calling.

[20] Epicurus, *Sent. Vat.* 51 = Long and Sedley (1987: no. 21.G.3).

[21] For the Roman evidence see esp. Damon (1997); for Horace's interest in one of Plautus' parasites see *Ep.* 2.1.170–4.

[22] For the Greek evidence see most recently, Damon (1995: 181–95). The evidence is collected in Ribbeck (1883).

[23] Note esp. Alicphron III.31, where the parasite falls in love; notice also that the names of parasites in Latin comedy can be significant: Ergasilus (Captivi) means 'whore' and Penulus (Menaechmi) means 'little penis' as well as 'little brush'; see Corbett (1986: 16–18).

companion. Eupolis in the *Kolakes* made fun of sophists in general for their flattery of the wealthy Callias.[24] It seems that Plato, too, was accused, especially in the spurious 13th letter, of having cultivated Dionysius of Syracuse for sordid motives.[25] A similar charge was leveled against Aristotle for spending time with the tyrant Hermias, leaving the Academy for the sake of 'his insatiable stomach' (*D.L.* 5.11). More generally, Alciphron's strange collection of fictional letters from parasites includes an amusing account of how a group of philosophers once came to dinner and beat the professional parasites at their own game (Aliciphr. 3.17.2).

As philosophers who put pleasure first, Epicureans were particularly liable to the charge of parasitism. The connection is made explicitly by Lucian, who in his comic dialogue on the parasite argues that Epicurus had exactly the same goals as parasites, but that parasites came first and practice the art in a purer form:

As to Epicurus, quite shamelessly filching the end of Parasitic, he makes it the end of his conception of happiness. That the thing is plagiarism, and that pleasure does not concern Epicurus at all, but does concern the parasite, you can assure yourself from this line of reasoning. I for my part consider that pleasure is first of all the freedom of the flesh from discomfort, and secondly, not having the spirit full of turbulence and commotion. Now then, each of these things is attained by the parasite, but neither by Epicurus. For with his inquiries about the shape of the earth, the infinitude of the universe, the magnitude of the sun, distances in space, primal elements, and whether the gods exist or not, and with his continual strife and bickering with certain persons about the end itself, he is involved not only in the troubles of man but in those of the universe. The parasite, however, thinking that everything is all right and thoroughly convinced that it would not be better if it were other than as it is, eats and sleeps in great peace and comfort, with nothing of that sort annoying him, flat on his back, with his arms and legs flung out, like Odysseus sailing home from Scheria.[26]

Here the obvious similarities between the Epicurean and the parasite are that both are devoted to food, and to taking things easy. Horace,

---

[24] Kassel and Austin (1986: vol. 5, 380–99).

[25] See the fictitious 13th letter of Plato, on which Gaiser (1981: 71–94).

[26] Lucian, *Par.* (Loeb, vol. 3, 235ff.), ch. 11 (Loeb translation); see also ch. 12, where it is argued that since Epicurus has to work for a living it's better to be a parasite. See Nesselrath (1985: 311ff.).

William Turpin

as we shall see, chooses in addition to focus on their shared interest in sex.[27]

Even more important for Horace is the fact that both parasites and Epicureans are particularly interested in their friends. Although Epicureans were not alone in treating friendship as a central concern of ethics, they were famous for their special commitment to it.[28] Epicurus held that friendship was the most important of the pleasures that made life worth living: 'Of the things which wisdom provides with a view to blessedness in the whole of life, much the greatest is the acquisition of friendship'.[29] But his view of friendship, at least in theory, was strikingly utilitarian: 'All friendship is desirable for its own sake; but it has its beginning in usefulness.'[30] It is easy to see, therefore, how opponents could treat the Epicurean conception of friendship as coming suspiciously close to parasitism. Cicero accused Philodemus of being Piso's flatterer (*Pis.* 70), and it is perhaps no coincidence that Philodemus devoted a significant portion of his *On Virtues and Vices* to a discussion of how flattery was the opposite of friendship.[31] His interest in the subject seems to be a direct response to opponents such as Cicero, who argues (*Fin.* 2.85) that if utility was all that mattered, as the Epicureans claimed, a wealthy man would do better to trust his money than a friend; even a rich man should put a friend ahead of money, though he needs to make sure that his friend doesn't love him just for his money. He needs, in other words, to beware of the parasite.

The question of friendship is of central importance in the satires, and indeed throughout Horace's work.[32] The friendships between poets and great men of affairs had always been open to the

[27] Lucian elsewhere associates Epicureans with sex, see *Vit. Auct.* 19 (Loeb, vol. 2, 486), where the Epicurean is said to eat 'sweets, honey-cakes, and above all figs'; for the sexual associations of figs cf. Aristoph. *Pax* 1350 and J. N. Adams (1982: 113–14).

[28] Bollack (1969: 221–36), rpt. in Bollack (1975: 565ff.); Mitsis (1988: 98–128).

[29] *Rat. Sent.* 27 = *D.L.* 10.148 = Long and Sedley (1987: no. 22.E.1).

[30] *Sent. Vat.* 23 = Long and Sedley (1987: no. 22.F.1).

[31] Gargiulo (1981: 103–27); Plutarch, in 'How to tell a Flatterer from a Friend' 50 C–D and 54B (Loeb, vol. 1, pp. 270–2 and 290), distinguishes between the parasite and the flatterer, but his point is that the parasite is a more obvious example of the flatterer, and can therefore be detected easily.

[32] Maguiness (1938: 29–48); Kilpatrick (1986).

unflattering interpretation that the poets were essentially parasites.[33] Augustus himself, as we shall see, jokingly puts this construction on Horace's relationship with Maecenas. And Horace accepts this picture of his relationship with Maecenas for his own humorous purposes in *Epistles* 1.17 and 1.18, where he pretends to give advice on how to be a successful parasite.[34] In the first three satires this humorous interpretation of their relationship is the basis for sustained and rather heavy-handed parody.[35]

IV. THE THREE SATIRES

The parasitic and Epicurean dimensions to the speaker's persona emerge only gradually. As so often in Horace, we see the point properly only when we get to the end.

The first satire is ostensibly about why people are never happy with their own jobs and instead envy other people. The answer, unconvincing though it is, turns out to be greed; this conclusion provokes a long tirade on the futility of avarice and an argument that money ought to be spent. The speaker's philosophic loyalties are signalled by polemical attacks on Stoics, at least if we accept the identifications of the ancient commentators (lines 14 and 120), and by parodies of Epicurean doctrines: you should take pleasure in the fact that you don't have the problems other people have (111–12), and you should live so that you will have pleasures to think back on when you die (117–19).

But the issue of parasitism is not far from the surface. The first poem of a book is almost by definition a dedication, and it is addressed to Maecenas by name. In this context an attack on avarice is suspiciously self-serving: poets from Pindar on have talked about generosity as a way of dropping heavy hints about payment.[36] Moreover the poem manages to combine the issues of parasitism and

[33] White (1993: 29 and 280 n. 47).

[34] Damon (1997: 135–40); cf. also Hunter (1985: 480–90).

[35] On the role of Maecenas in *Satires* Book 1 see Seeck (1991: 534–47) and Oliensis (1998a: 17–41).

[36] For Pindar and Theocritus see Gold (1987: 26–32).

Epicureanism just before its end, by comparing the man who has lived a happy life with the guest who has dined well:

> inde fit ut raro qui se vixisse beatum
> dicat et exacto contentus tempore vita
> cedat uti conviva satur, reperire queamus   (*S.* 1.1.117–19)

That's why it's so rare to find a man who says he has lived happily, and departs from life when his time is up, like a guest who is satiated.

As scholars have long recognized, the comparison is derived from Lucretius:

> cur non ut plenus vitae conviva recedis
> aequo animoque capis securam, stulte, quietem? (Lucr. 3.938–9)

why don't you depart like a guest, full of life, and enjoy a quiet tranquillity with a peaceful mind, you fool?

and

> et nec opinanti mors ad caput adstitit ante
> quam satur ac plenus possis discedere rerum. (Lucr. 3.959–60)

and death is hovering unexpectedly over your head, before you can retire satiated and full.

Horace, however, goes out of his way to call attention to the implications of this comparison for an Epicurean who is also a parasite. In combining *conviva* with *satur*, which Lucretius kept apart, he makes more obvious the connections with a parasite at the dinner table. His very use of the word *satur*, especially as he brings his first satire to a close, inevitably reminds us of his chosen genre.[37] But the pun depends in part on the supposed derivation of *satura* from words for 'stew' or 'sausage'.[38] The poem thus ends with the parasite's favorite subject, dinner.

The second satire begins by advocating the sensible, if hackneyed, view that one should avoid extremes. Our satirist, however, cannot stick to that point for long: he soon comes to the issue of extremes in love affairs (28ff.), after which he launches into a long lecture on why,

---

[37] Freudenburg (1993: 112): 'Horace, the conviva satur of line 119, is able to say "enough now", or better yet, "it's satire now", and happily leave off writing.'

[38] Coffey (1976: 11–18). For the importance of the gastronomic connotations of *satura* see Gowers (1993: 109ff.).

in chasing women, one should choose the middle way (38ff.). This sounds sensible enough, at first, but the speaker turns out to be advocating the ludicrous position that one should sleep neither with well-born women nor with prostitutes, but with freedwomen (47–9). Aside from the absurd literalness of this view of the golden mean, we might wonder why the son of a freedman (and presumably a freedwoman) should think this an acceptable position. But as he continues to lecture on the subject of women and sex, we become aware that our speaker is suspiciously experienced in these matters: by the time we have reached the high comedy of the talking *mutto* (68–71), we realize that our speaker is far too interested in the physical aspects of his subject.

Broad sexual humor of this sort might seem to have little to do with philosophy, but our speaker's rantings in fact have a distinctly Epicurean flavor, apparently owing a good deal to Philodemus.[39] We are offered a distorted, and purely sexual, version of the Epicurean doctrine that one needs to make decisions about which pleasures to choose (111–13).[40] But even more significant is the distortion of Epicurean views about avoiding the physical discomforts of sexual desire. As we have seen, Epicurus himself had a practical approach to the problem, and Lucretius offered both a dramatic description of the problem and a notoriously down-to-earth solution:

> ulcus enim vivescit et inveterascit alendo,
> inque dies gliscit furor atque aerumna gravescit,
> si non prima novis conturbes volnera plagis
> vulgivagaque vagus Venere ante recentia cures
> aut alio possis animi traducere motus.   (Lucr. 4. 1068–1072)

For the wound gets more intense and more intractable if you feed it, and day by day the madness grows more intense and the pain gets worse, unless you disturb the original wounds with new ones, and take care of them while they're still fresh by wandering with a wandering Venus, or unless you can direct your thoughts elsewhere.

Lucretius' views, and his articulation of them, seem extreme, but he is presumably quite serious; that did not stop less philosophical poets

[39] Kiessling-Heinze (1957: 24); Tait (1941: 66–7); Cataudella (1950: 18–31); Gigante (1993).

[40] Hor. *S.* 1.2.111–13; cf. de Witt (1939: 130).

from writing parodies.[41] Horace's satirist apparently suffers from an even more extreme form of Lucretius' physical afflictions, and he is even more direct about his solution:

> tument tibi cum inguina, num si
> ancilla aut verna est praesto puer, impetus in quem
> continuo fiat, malis tentigine rumpi?
> non ego: namque parabilem amo venerem facilemque.   (*S.* 1.2.116–19)

When your organs start swelling, and if there's slave girl or a maid or a boy available, I bet you don't choose to bust your balls. Not me, anyhow: what I like is love that is easy and willing.

The Epicurean flavor of this unromantic approach is underscored when the speaker goes on to quote an epigram of Philodemus in support of his views:

> Illam: post paulo: sed pluris: si exierit vir'
> Gallis, hanc Philodemus ait sibi quae neque magno
> stet pretio neque cunctetur cum est iussa venire.   (*S.* 1.2.120–3)

As Philodemus says, she of 'Later' and 'More money' and 'If my husband goes out' is for the birds,[42] and what we want is one who doesn't cost much and isn't slow to come when she's called.

We learn, indeed, that this practical approach to love and sex is based on bitter experience; the end of the poem, with its breathless description of the dangers of adultery, is surely meant to sound like advice from someone with a first-hand knowledge of the subject. And the speaker's Epicurean loyalties are confirmed in the last line, with his passing dig at a Stoic.

The third satire makes more explicit the connection between the speaker's parasitic and Epicurean dimensions. The argument is initially about the need to avoid extremes. But the speaker again goes off on a tangent, in this case on the need for friends to forgive small faults. What follows is a passionate argument for forgiveness in friendship, though the speaker claims to be confident that Maecenas himself would never resent the speaker's own foibles (63–6). It emerges that the speaker sees himself as, in particular, a potential

---

[41] See, in general, Brown (1987), esp. 60ff. On parodies see Sommariva (1980: 123–48); see also Watson (1984: 389–95).

[42] I translate Galli very loosely; for the probable pun see below, n. 50.

dinner guest. He hints at this first when he mentions the example of a slave who slips up while serving at table (80–3). But his interest in dinner becomes more obvious when he describes all the faults in a friend that he himself thinks should be forgiven:

> comminxit lectum potus mensave catillum
> Evandri manibus tritum deiecit, ob hanc rem,
> aut positum ante mea quia pullum in parte catini
> sustulit esuriens, minus hoc iucundus amicus
> sit mihi? (S. 1.3.90–4)

If a man gets drunk and pees on the couch or knocks an antique cup off the table, or grabs a piece of chicken from my part of the dish because he's hungry, will such a friend be less a pleasure to me?

For our speaker, clearly, there is by definition a link between friendship and dinnertime. The answer to his question about bad behaviour at dinner is actually in the affirmative: a friendship can no doubt survive bad manners, but such outrageously bad manners as this would surely test it to its limits. Our speaker is too dim to see this; he is not only a parasite, but a nightmare of a parasite.

V. PHILOSOPHER KING AND PARASITE *REX*

The third satire closes with a polemical attack on the Stoic doctrine that all faults are of equal weight (96ff.). It is here that our speaker's Epicureanism is most obviously on display, though as a bad philosopher what he attacks is an outrageous caricature, not the real thing.[43] But the question of parasitism does not, I think, disappear. The speaker comes to the conclusion that the successful Stoic philosopher, whom Stoics claimed to be the true king, will have hardly any friends at all, because he is obliged to treat all faults equally:

> ne longum faciam: dum tu quadrante lavatum
> rex ibis neque te quisquam stipator ineptum
> praeter Crispinum sectabitur, et mihi dulces
> ignoscent, si quid peccaro stultus, amici,

---

[43] Note esp. *S.* 3.1.99ff., a parody of Lucretius' account of the origins of society, Lucr. 5.780–1457.

> inque vicem illorum patiar delicta libenter,
> privatusque magis vivam te rege beatus.   (*S.* 1.3.137–42)

To make a long story short: while you go forth as a two-bit *rex* and have no followers except Crispinus, my dear friends will forgive me, if like an idiot I make mistakes, and I in turn will happily put up with their mistakes, and will live more happily as a private citizen than you will, for all that you are *rex*.

The Stoic concept of *rex* no doubt lent itself to parody for its own sake, but I would like to suggest that the word is used in a second sense as well, providing a rather dreadful punch line. The words *rex* (and *basileus*) were technical terms in comedy and elsewhere for a parasite's host and patron.[44] Plautus plays on this meaning of *rex* when the parasite Ergasilus says 'Now I'm not a parasite, I'm more regal than the king of kings'.[45] And Augustus made the same joke when he suggested that Horace himself might want to leave Maecenas and work for him: 'So let him come from that parasite's table to this regal one'.[46] Thus in wrapping up his three moralizing lectures, it seems, our satirist returns in a single ambiguous word to the issue of the poet and patron, parasite and *rex*.

The pun on *rex* provides a surprising conclusion to the diatribe satires, but it is apparently foreshadowed in the two preceding poems. In the first satire this added dimension seems to add some elegance to what is otherwise simply a heavy-handed joke. The satirist warns his listener that he had better spend some of his money, lest he end up like a certain Ummidius:

> denique sit finis quaerendi, cumque habeas plus
> pauperiem metuas minus, et finire laborem
> incipias, parto quod avebas, ne facias quod
> Vmmidius quidam: non longa est fabula: dives
> ut metiretur nummos; ita sordidus ut se
> non umquam servo melius vestiret; adusque
> supremum tempus ne se penuria victus
> opprimeret metuebat. at hunc liberta securi
> divisit medium, fortissima Tyndaridarum.   (*S.* 1.1.92–100)

---

[44] White (1993: 29 and 280 n. 47); see also the *Oxford Latin Dictionary*, s.v. *rex* 8.
[45] Pl. *Capt.* 825: 'Non ego nunc parasitus sum, sed regum rex regalior.'
[46] Suet. *Poet.*, *Vita Horati* (Loeb Suetonius, vol. 2, p. 486): 'Veniet ergo ab ista parasitica mensa ad hanc regiam, et nos in epistulis scribendis iuvabit.'

And so put an end to acquisitions, and be less afraid of poverty now that you have more, and begin to put an end to your labors, spending the things you're so avid for, and don't be like a certain Ummidius. The tale is a brief one: he was so rich that he counted his money by the bushel, and so cheap that he dressed no better than a slave; and he was afraid to his dying day that he would be overwhelmed with poverty. But he got split in two by a freed-woman, toughest of the Tyndaridae.

The freedwoman is compared, of course, to Clytemnestra, murderer of Agamemnon. But when uttered by a parasite the allusion has a particular point: the freedwoman killed her patron, and Clytemnestra killed a king.

Kings are referred to more explicitly in the second satire, though in this case the joke is more difficult. One of the advantages of chasing a prostitute, we are told, is that her physical charms are not hidden under a lot of respectable clothing:

> adde huc quod mercem sine fucis gestat, aperte
> quod venale habet ostendit, nec si quid honesti est,
> iactat habetque palam, quaerit quo turpia celet.
> regibus hic mos est: ubi equos mercantur opertos
> inspiciunt, ne si facies ut saepe decora
> molli fulta pede est emptorem inducat hiantem,
> quod pulchrae clunes, breve quod caput, ardua cervix.
> hoc illi recte: ne corporis optima Lyncei
> contemplere oculis, Hypsaea caecior illa
> quae mala sunt spectes. 'o crus, o bracchia!' verum
> depugis, nasuta, brevi latere ac pede longo est.   (S. 1.2.83–93)

Add in the fact that she flaunts what she's got without any faking, she displays her wares openly, and, if she's got some good features, she doesn't boast about them and put them on display, while trying to hide the bad ones. Here's what *reges* do: when they're buying horses they examine them covered up, so that if (as often happens) a pretty face sits on a soft hoof it does not entice the buyer as he is smitten by the lovely haunches, the compact head and the arching neck. And they're right to do this: so don't you drink in bodily attractions with the sharp eyes of a Lynceus, while you look on the ugly parts with the blindness of Hypsaea. 'What an amazing leg! What incredible arms!' you say, but she's got no hips, a long nose, a short waist, and big feet.

The comparison with horse-trading is surprising, not least because the speaker initially regarded the scanty clothes of prostitutes as a positive advantage; covering them back up, on the analogy of the horse-buying kings, would make them rather like respectable ladies, whose decent clothes present their own problems. More important, of course, is the obvious ludicrousness of the parallel: what features, on a woman, are analogous to a soft hoof, and what's wrong with noticing her attractive features anyway? One wonders if the far-fetched parallel is not in fact prompted by the pun latent in *regibus hic mos est*; the parasite drags in the real kings, complete with their strange horse-buying techniques, as an elaborate compliment to his own *rex*: 'here's what you big-shots do'.

Puns have traditionally been held in low esteem. In recent years, however, a number of scholars have drawn attention to the use of puns in Latin authors, including Horace.[47] The Romans could employ various kinds of word-play, and even had a technical term, paronomasia, for the most prominent of them, involving the contrast between similar, but not identical, words. Puns of the kind I am suggesting here, based on double meanings of individual words, were also a standard feature of Roman comedy, and of Cicero's political wit.[48] Often they were prompted by proper names: the cognomen Rex, in fact, was particularly tempting, prompting obvious puns from Julius Caesar, and from Horace himself.[49]

Puns seem to have been specially important to Epicureans. The epigram of Philodemus, which as we have seen is 'quoted' in the second satire, depends on a pun on Galli.[50] And puns mattered a great deal to Lucretius; whatever the precise shape of Epicurean doctrine on the origins and nature of language, it is clear that Lucretius regarded language as a useful analogue for creation in general, and went out of his way to demonstrate in his poetry just

[47] Ahl (1985); id. (1988: 17–43); O'Hara (1996); Reckford (1997: 583–612). Henderson (1998), esp. 89.

[48] Holst (1925).

[49] Suet. *Jul.* 79.2. For Horace, see *S.* 1.7; another obvious pun, on the name Porcius, occurs at *S.* 2.8.23–4. See, in general, McCartney (1918–19: 343–58).

[50] Brown (1993) is the only commentator I can find who explicitly identifies the joke as a pun, though the word Gallus was notoriously ambiguous, as noted by Quintilian, *Inst.* 7.9.2: 'ut Gallus avem, an gentem, an nomen, an fortunam corporis, significet incertum est.' It is an interesting coincidence that Cicero makes a pun on the supposed Gallic origin of Philodemus' patron at *Pis.* 67: 'Vbi galli cantum audivit,

how flexible words could be.[51] The connection between Epicurean theory and puns is easier to see in the case of paronomasia, and it is presumably no coincidence that this is by far the most common kind of pun in Lucretius. But Lucretius could also make puns based on the double meanings of words: the example that comes closest to Horace's pun on *rex*, perhaps, is a pun on the obvious historical and political overtones of the adjective *superbus*.[52] Since the pun at the end of Horace's third satire comes as the climax to an attack on the Stoics, complete with an invocation of the Epicurean theory of language,[53] it seems possible that the puns on *rex* are another manifestation of our speaker's Epicurean identity.

It is worth remembering that some Romans seem to have shared the traditional disdain for puns; Quintilian (*Inst.* 6.3.47) objected to one of Cicero's more atrocious puns, though not because they were bad in themselves, but because they were weak. It is Trimalchio—another atrocious Epicurean—who goes so far as to name his carver Carpus, so that 'whenever he says 'Carpe' he names the man and gives the order in the same word'.[54] Horace's satirist is the same kind of character: it is some comfort that when Horace makes dreadful puns he is not really himself.

The puns on *rex* are important not so much for their own sake, as additions to the corpus of bad Horatian jokes, but because they confirm that the reading proposed in this paper is on the right lines. The depiction of Horace and Maecenas as a philsophizing parasite and his *rex* may take some getting used to, but the puns force us to confront, and perhaps help us accept, the high comedy of Horace's parody.[55]

avum suum revixisse putat.' More significant, perhaps, is that fact that Philodemus himself constructs an entire epigram around a pun on his own name, *AP* 5.115 = Sider (1997), Epigram 10.

[51] See esp. Snyder (1980).

[52] Lucr. 5.1136–7: 'Ergo regibus occisis subversa iacebat | pristina maiestas soliorum et scep tra superba.'

[53] Hor. *S.* 1.3.103–4: 'donec verba, quibus voces sensuque notarent, | nominaque invenere.'

[54] Petr. 36; note also the pun on *esse* at 34; the tables are turned on Trimalchio when one of his slaves reveals a similar aptitude for obvious puns, Petr. 41.

[55] I am grateful to my colleagues Peter Aronoff and Martin Ostwald for helpful discussions and comments.

5

Libertino patre natus: True or False?

Gordon Williams

I offer this paper as a tribute to my friend of forty years, Robin Nisbet. The topic is particularly appropriate, since it was to Robin Nisbet that I first suggested this hypothesis in 1957, a few weeks after Eduard Fraenkel's great book appeared. On that occasion, as on many others, Robin gave me helpful advice and suggestions, though I did not then pursue the idea. It was only many years later that I discovered that Niebuhr had anticipated me in a single sentence in a lecture on Horace.[1] The idea was also put forward in a brief footnote by E. T. Salmon in his book *Samnium and the Samnites* (1967).[2] I tried the idea very informally on an audience at a Liverpool Classical Seminar led by Francis Cairns in 1981, and again on an audience at a lecture in the Institute of Classical Studies in London in 1986; and I am most grateful to both audiences for helpful comments.

I

We know about Horace's father: Suetonius tells us, and, if that were not sufficient, Horace tells us himself. His father was an ex-slave, a *libertinus*. In fact, however, Suetonius had no other source of

I am very grateful to friends and colleagues for reading this essay and making useful suggestions, especially to Ramsay MacMullen, Elizabeth Meyer, and Susan Treggiari.
    [1] Niebuhr (1848: 133).
    [2] Salmon (1967: 369 n. 5).

information; his wording clearly shows that he was interpreting quite literally what the poet says in *Satires* 1.6—a normal procedure for ancient literary biographers when other sources failed. Yet it is routinely taken as an unquestionable fact that Horace's father had been a slave. So the interesting question becomes: where did Horace's father come from? Otto Seeck in 1902, who did not think highly of Horace's poetry, compared him with Heine and asserted that the father was a Jew.[3] This thesis had been argued extensively by Guglielmo Braun some twenty-four years earlier;[4] he traced many parallels between Horace's poetry and various books of the Old Testament, and he concluded that the poet's father was an enlightened Jew from Alexandria. He even interpreted one of Augustus' jokes at the poet as a reference to his circumcision. Karl Mras set himself to refute this in a paper published the year after the anniversary of the poet's 2000th birthday in 1935.[5] But Mras then went on to assert that the father was clearly a slave from Asia Minor or Syria. He started from an examination of the rare word *flaccus*—which refers to large pendulous ears, characteristic of certain breeds of dog—and quoted Rudolf Martin, who published a second edition of his handbook of anthropology in Jena in 1928. After an analysis of length of ears in various peoples, Martin concluded: 'The longest ears are found in Mongols and in the Semitic peoples' (1928: 1.572). So, not a Jew, but from the Middle East and, in particular, from 'the Eldorado of slave-hunters and slave-dealers, Asia Minor and Syria' (1928: 1.73). He then went on to demonstrate a close affinity between the attitudes and outlooks of Horace and Lucian.

II

But the so-called 'fact' needs to be called into question. Was Horace's father really what we mean by a slave in Italy? Horace tells us quite a lot about his father and, though what he tells us is likely to be tailored to his particular purpose in each passage, much of it sounds very odd about a former imported slave. The status of his father as a *libertinus*

[3] Seeck (1902: 134).   [4] Braun (1877–8).   [5] Mras (1936).

depends on a phrase that is repeated three times in one poem. It is a metrically discordant phrase that draws emphatic attention to itself: *libertino patre natum* (*Sat.* 1.6.6, 45, 46). In all occurrences the phrase is used in a way that can only properly be signalled by enclosing it in quotation-marks: that is, the words do not represent the poet's own description of himself, but that used derisively by others (the derision is signified by 5 *naso suspendis adunco* and 46 *rodunt*). The phrase is only once repeated elsewhere, in the σφραγίς, that closes *Epistles* I, which the poet offers to the book/slave as advertising copy. Here the word-order is slightly altered to *me libertino natum patre*, but the phrase clearly recalls its earlier occurrences and deserves quotation-marks here too, as the context makes clear:

> cum tibi sol tepidus pluris admoverit auris,
> me libertino natum patre et in tenui re
> maiores pennas nido extendisse loqueris
> ut quantum generi demas virtutibus addas.
>   (*Ep.* 1.20.19–22)

When a gentler sun shall have collected a larger number of ears around you, you will be found announcing that I, 'born of a freedman father' and in straitened circumstances, spread wings too big for my nest, with the result that, to the extent that you detract from my family, you add to my virtues.

He means that a work on practical ethics will attract more customers the humbler the author's beginnings and the less his physical attractiveness (as he goes on to elaborate in his own case), because the greater then will be his own moral strength and authority. There is no hint of his father's servile status anywhere else. So what the evidence amounts to is that men who wished to deride the poet described him as born of a freedman father, and in both passages where this phrase is offered the poet had a special interest in representing himself as suffering from a major social disadvantage (the better to emphasize the value of his own moral qualities).

Those moral qualities, he acknowledges, he owes to his father; and in *Satires* 1 he uses his father's method of moral instruction as an explanation and justification of his own type of social satire (in which the poet claims to be a moral instructor like his father). His father brought him to Rome to school (I will come back to the implications of this later), and the poet gives a picture of his father walking down the streets of Rome with him, exemplifying the various types of behaviour to avoid by pointing out prominent Romans—of whose private life he shows a remarkable knowledge. Is this a former imported slave? How has he gained his information about upper-class Romans? How often has he come to Rome?

How could this—apparently deeply heartfelt—portrait be made plausible to Horace's readers? As if this were not difficult enough, note the very words that the poet puts into his father's mouth:

> sapiens vitatu quidque petitu
> sit melius causas reddet tibi; mi satis est si
> traditum ab antiquis morem servare [possum].
> (*Sat.* 1.4.115–17)

A philosopher will give you the theory of what should be avoided and what aimed at; for me it is sufficient if I am able to maintain the moral code handed down by our ancestors.

If this is a former slave speaking, then it is most reminiscent of Plautine jokes in which slaves refer to their ancestors. But if it is to be understood seriously (as it certainly seems to be), then this is the portrait of a man who has a strong sense of tradition—and a very practical homespun sense of tradition that regards typically Greek theoretical debates on ethics as superfluous. Centuries of living in the same stable society, with lovingly preserved traditional values, are surely to be understood to lie behind such attitudes. Inheritance, and the preservation of it, is important to such a man, and Horace represents his father as saying:

> nonne vides Albi ut male vivat filius, utque
> Baius inops? magnum documentum ne patriam rem
> perdere quis velit.
> (*Sat.* 1.4.109–11)

Don't you see how wretchedly Albius' son lives, how poverty-stricken is Baius?—a powerful lesson against anyone's dissipating his inheritance.

By the time Horace wrote this satire, he had not only acquired a theoretical training in ethical philosophy at Athens, but he had also lost his inheritance (*Ep.* 2.2.43–52). In *Satires* 1.6 he represents his father as a *coactor* (86–7), a type of banker who specialized in the financing of auction sales, and as a small farmer (line 71). That style of life—combining a profession with the running of a farm—strikes one as entirely typical of life immediately below the level of the upper class in Italian towns.[6] The provincial aristocracy might despise the profession, but it played a very significant role in the economy of Italian towns,[7] and its considerable profits (for all Horace says) could be invested in land.[8] Such, I suspect, was the lifestyle of Horace's grandparents, so that Horace's father had good reason to value the prudent management of inheritances.

III

It is hard to see Horace's father as a former imported oriental slave, haphazardly sold in Venusia, through which town the Via Appia conveniently meanders on its way north from the east-facing port of Brundisium. But it is equally hard to see the poet as the son of such a man, for he constantly gives expression to feelings of pride and joy in belonging to a particular region of Italy, and those feelings also appeal to a sense of long-established tradition. That love of place appears everywhere.[9] In *Sat.* 1.5.77–8, where the Via Appia begins to lift steeply south of Beneventum into the mountains of Apulia, the poet writes '*incipit ex illo montis Apulia notos ostentare mihi quos torret Atabulus*'; this detail is surrounded by verbs in the first-person plural, but this moment of joy is private to the poet (as is the local name for the Sirocco). It appears in the σφραγίς to *Odes* 1—in the pride of the poet that his fame will reach to his own native region (*Odes* 3.30.10– 12; cf. *Odes* 4.6.27 *Dauniae defende decus Camenae*, referring to the *Carmen Saeculare*).[10] It appears in his account of the miracle that saved him in infancy on Mt Voltur, when he wandered away from his nurse Pullia, and which became the talk of the little towns around:

> mirum quod foret omnibus
> quicumque celsae nidum Acherontiae

---

[6] See e.g. D'Arms (1981: 50, 102, 157).
[7] See Rauh (1989).
[8] Mommsen (1877).
[9] For collections of passages see e.g. Canter (1930–1); Sirago (1958).
[10] See the analysis by Fraenkel.

saltusque Bantinos et arvum
　　pingue tenent humilis Forenti　　　(*Odes* 3.4.13–16)

so that it was a miracle for all who dwell in the nest of lofty Acherontia and
the glades of Bantia and the rich loam of low-lying Forentum.

An intense pride and joy in the region are expressed in the economical and vivid descriptions of the three little towns, unknown otherwise to history. But I want to mention an example where I can now correct a regrettable error of my own. It is *Odes* 3.6.33–44:[11]

> non his iuventus orta parentibus
> infecit aequor sanguine Punico,
> Pyrrhumque et ingentem cecidit
> Antiochum Hannibalemque dirum,
> sed rusticorum mascula militum
> proles, Sabellis docta ligonibus
> versare glebas et severae
> matris ad arbitrium recisos
> portare fustis, sol ubi montium
> mutaret umbras et iuga demeret
> bobus fatigatis, amicum
> tempus agens abeunte curru.

Not from parents like that did the youth arise who stained the sea with the blood of Carthage and slew Pyrrhus and great Antiochus and fearful Hannibal, but a masculine race born of rustic warriors, trained to turn the turfs with Sabellian spades and, at the bidding of an austere mother, to bring home cut wood when the sun altered the shadows of the mountains and took yokes off weary oxen, bringing the friendly time with his flying chariot.

In 1969 I carelessly translated *Sabellis* as 'Sabine'. But the poet is thinking of the contributions to Roman forces so often made by the tribes of Samnium, and, in particular, he is thinking of the steadfast loyalty of Venusia when Hannibal attacked southern Italy and most other towns went over to him. That military contribution is signalled by the prominence of the high-principled mother (the father being away at war).

---

[11] Williams (1969) ad loc.

Horace specifically represents himself as a Sabellian.[12] Hence the terrifying prophecy given to him as a child that he suddenly remembers when he cannot escape from the pushy social climber (neither poison nor sword nor illness will be the end of him, only a compulsive talker); this prophecy was given to him by an old Sabellian woman (*Sat.* 1.9.29). In *Ep.* 1.16.49 the interlocutor (*Sabellus*) is a transparent disguise for the poet himself. Of the Sabellian tribes, his own, the Apulians, are especially selected for mention: they are praised as *impigri* (*Odes* 3.16.26) and, when the poet wants to epitomize the shame caused to Roman soldiers in Parthian captivity, he selects the Marsi and the Apuli (*Odes* 3.5.9)—cf. *militaris Daunias* (*Odes* 1.22.13). The admiration for and identification with the people of the region around Venusia find purest expression in the superb portrait of the farmer Ofellus, a neighbour of Horace's family whom the poet has known since boyhood (*Sat.* 2.2.112) and whose property was confiscated in 42 BCE at the same time as Horace's— though Umbrenus, the soldier who was the beneficiary, put Ofellus back on the property as a tenant farmer paying rent in kind (perhaps the same happened to Horace's estate; he never says). Ofellus is portrayed unsentimentally with loving admiration as an ideal human being, like the poet's father, a natural philosopher of sturdy homespun wit; and, to some extent, this portrait can be read as fleshing out the portrait of his father (who, if he was alive in 42 BCE, suffered the same fate as Ofellus).[13]

During his consultation of Q. Trebatius Testa in *Satires* 2.1, the poet reflects on his own identity in a particularly interesting way:

> sequor hunc, Lucanus an Apulus anceps:
> nam Venusinus arat finem sub utrumque colonus,
> missus ad hoc, pulsis, vetus est ut fama, Sabellis,
> quo ne per vacuum Romano incurreret hostis,
> sive quod Apula gens seu quod Lucania bellum
> incuteret violenta.

I take him [Lucilius] as my model, uncertain whether to call myself a Lucanian or an Apulian, since the Venusian settler ploughs right up to the territories of both; he was sent there—and the Sabellians, as the old story

---

[12] Sonnenschein (1898).

[13] He was almost certainly dead, since Horace represents the loss of the estate as being his own loss (*Ep.* 2.2.50–1).

goes, driven out—to prevent an enemy invading through a territory unguarded by Romans, whether the violence of the Apulian or of the Lucanian tribe should threaten war.

The source of the uncertainty here is surely not, as Kiessling and Heinze appear to have thought, because Horace's 'father, the slave, belonged to those *quorum nemo queat patriam monstrare parentis* (Juvenal 8.45)', but because his father's property was in a part of the territory of Venusia that could originally have belonged either to the Apuli or to the Lucani. That is, when land was seized for the original colony, it was taken from a region that lay partly in Apulia and partly in Lucania, but in such a way that the original boundary was now impossible to trace. This seems the most reasonable interpretation if no assumptions are made about the father's servile status. That is, the poet regards himself as belonging to one of the pre-Roman Sabellian tribes, who, of course, re-established themselves in Venusia under Roman occupation. In fact, Oscan culture remained strong in Venusia even after it became a Latin colony, and fresh Roman colonists had to be sent out to the town on a number of occasions.

But this passage arouses a further puzzling question. How is it relevant for Horace to treat so explicitly the problem of border territories and of tribal identities in the course of consulting the jurist about writing satire? The disquisition cannot just be designed to show that Horace was endowed with a pugnacious frontier spirit, suited to satire.[14] The question admits of a different explanation.

In 89 BCE the rebel forces had great success in Apulia under a certain Trebatius (Appian, *BC* I.228–9), until he was finally defeated by C. Cosconius. This Trebatius may well have been the grandfather of C. Trebatius Testa,[15] just as Herius Asinius, commander of the rebel forces of the Marrucini till he was killed in action, was the grandfather of C. Asinius Pollio.[16] Trebatius Testa, as Cicero's letters to him show, had estates and relatives in Velia in Lucania, where Cicero happened to have been visiting (*Fam.* 7.19); but he was also the patron in Rome of the people of Ulubrae. If the rebel Trebatius was his grandfather, then the family, although they had extensive

[14] Kiessling and Heinze (1914–30) ad loc.
[15] Salmon (1967: 357 n. 4).
[16] Ibid. 356.

property elsewhere, may have been Venusian (which would explain the prominence of Trebatius as a Sabellian praetor). In that case, the special point of the legal consultation of C. Trebatius Testa in *Satires* 2.1 was that the families of the poet and the jurist had been friends of long standing and shared in common the same puzzle over tribal identity, carefully posed here as a parody of proper judicial deliberation (and sharpened for Trebatius by the fact that he had important links to Lucania). Trebatius Testa was probably born about 85 BCE, Asinius Pollio was born in 76 BCE, and Horace in 65 BCE. I should guess that these two important men were patrons to the poet (and to his father) when he first came to Rome, and that Pollio, who held the consulship in 40 BCE, used his power as consul to appoint the poet to the prestigious post of *scriba* after his disastrous flirtation with the Republican/senatorial cause at Philippi (from which, for all he says about his poverty, Horace returned sufficiently wealthy to be able to purchase the highly profitable post).[17] Trebatius was then rewarded with *Satires* 2.1, and Pollio with the splendid *Ode* 2.1 (both highly conspicuous poems). Both men were supporters of Julius Caesar, the patron of both, though Trebatius, unlike Pollio, shifted his support to Octavian—which made him the right person to be represented as offering the poet the Lucilian advice to write epic in support of Octavian.

The question can now be asked: what did Horace's grandfather do in the Social War? But unfortunately it cannot be answered. It would be interesting to know if the grandfathers of Trebatius, Pollio, and Horace all had one conspicuous thing in common—service for the rebel cause in the Social War, a cause for which all three suffered and died.

When he talks of his father in *Satires* 1.6, Horace says that his father refused to send him to the local school run by a teacher called Flavius:

> causa fuit pater his, qui macro pauper agello
> noluit in Flavi ludum me mittere, magni
> quo pueri magnis e centurionibus orti,
> laevo suspensi loculos tabulamque lacerto,

---

[17] For details of the purchase and operation and profits of the apparitorial office of *scriba* see Badian (1989); Purcell (1983).

ibant octonos referentes Idibus aeris.
sed puerum est ausus Romam portare, docendum
artis quas doceat quivis eques atque senator
semet prognatos. vestem servosque sequentis,
in magno ut populo, si qui vidisset, avita
ex re praeberi sumptus mihi crederet illos.
ipse mihi custos incorruptissimus omnes
circum doctores aderat. quid multa? pudicum,
qui primus virtutis honos, servavit ab omni
non solum facto, verum opprobrio quoque turpi;
nec timuit sibi ne vitio quis verteret olim
si praeco parvas aut, ut fuit ipse, coactor
mercedes sequerer; neque essem questus, at hoc nunc
laus illi debetur et a me gratia maior.   (*Sat.* 1. 6. 71–88)

For this [my moral strength of character] my father was responsible; he, though of modest means with a meagre little farm, refused to send me to the school of Flavius—to which hulking boys born of hulking centurions used to go, hanging their satchels and writing-tablets over their left shoulders and paying their fee of eight asses in the middle of every month. Rather, he had the audacity to take his boy to Rome to be taught the same subjects that any equestrian or senator would teach those born of his own blood. If anyone should have noticed—seeing that the crowds were dense—my clothing and the slaves at my heel, he would have assumed that the expenditure lavished on me came from ancestral inheritance. He used to escort me himself in person around all my teachers, a guardian of most steadfast integrity. And so he kept me chaste (and that is the prime distinction of virtue) not only from any disgraceful act but even from rumour. And yet he did not act out of fear that someone at some time might blame him were I to pursue a modest income as an auctioneer or, as he was himself, as a banker—and I would not have reproached him. So, for this reason, I now owe him even greater praise and gratitude.

It was clearly a bold and surprising move for Horace's father to take his son to school at Rome, and it is usually assumed that he did this to provide the boy with the best education possible. But more analysis is worthwhile here. The emphasis on the size of the centurions and the size of their sons should remind us that Horace describes himself as *corporis exigui*, 'of diminutive physique' (*Ep.* 1.20.24). (It is worth recalling in this context that about 1,500 Sabellian skeletons were found at Aufidena and that they belonged, almost without exception, to dolichocephalic individuals of medium height.[18]) Perhaps in a Sabellian town Romans—and especially Roman soldiers—were instantly distinguishable from natives by their height and bulk. Further, the schoolmaster's name, Flavius, seems Roman. So this may have been a school in Venusia especially designed for the practical needs of sons of Roman soldiers. But Horace's father had higher aspirations for his son. Also, if there was one single origin for the ugly phrase *libertino patre natum*, it may have been the mockery of the poet by sons of the Roman veterans (who would have had access to the background information).[19] The bullying of the diminutive Horace by such ruffians may have been another strong motive for his father to go to such extraordinary lengths to avoid the local school.[20]

Further speculation is possible. Horace elsewhere tells us the name of probably the most famous of his teachers, Orbilius (*Ep.* 2.1.71).[21] L. Orbilius Pupillus came from Beneventum. He was aged 50 when he went to Rome in 63 BCE to set himself up as a teacher—previously he had held the post of local magistrate's clerk (*apparituram magistratibus fecit*), and he had then served very successfully in the Roman army. Unlike Venusia, Beneventum did not join the rebel cause in the Social War, though the two towns are only fifty or sixty miles apart. Since Beneventum lies on the Via Appia north of Venusia, I should speculate that Horace's father had come to know the slightly older Orbilius (perhaps on journeys to Rome) before he moved to the capital; and it was that acquaintance and his knowledge of the man's talent and moral strength (he had suffered the loss of both his parents, who had been murdered by enemies on the same day) that persuaded him to make his very bold and expensive move and take his son to Orbilius' school in Rome. Orbilius was a man of such distinction in his home town that, after his death at the age of one hundred, a statue was erected on the Capitol in Beneventum representing him seated, dressed in a *pallium*, with two book-boxes by his

[18] Salmon (1967: 57).

[19] Fraenkel (1957: 3).

[20] For schoolboy mockery and bullying see the anecdote of Cassius and Faustus, son of Sulla (Val. Max. 3.1.3; Plut. *Brutus* 9), or schoolboys fighting as 'Pompeians' and 'Caesarians' (Cassius Dio 41.39.4).

[21] Biograph in Suet. *De gramm. et rhet.* 9.

side. Incidentally, the fact that Horace's father did not hire a talented private tutor for his son suggests that he did not have the resources of a Cicero and that he probably took his profession as *coactor* and practised it in Rome, perhaps preceding his son in the *decuriae* of the *apparitores,* in addition to practising as *coactor argentarius* privately.[22] Just to be in Rome enabled father and son to meet and form useful relationships with important people, and, if I am right about Pollio and Trebatius, Horace's father possessed influential friends in Rome who could introduce him to others.

Another father who took his son to Rome to be educated was Cicero's. However, Marcus and Quintus received their education in the house of Crassus, and that type of education was beyond the reach of Horace's father. Cicero's own son Marcus, who was also privately educated at Rome, was the same age as Horace, and we next meet the two of them, together with various other young upper-class Romans, in Athens, seeking the higher education in philosophy and rhetoric that was normal for wealthy young aristocrats. Among those young men was L. Bibulus, the nephew of Brutus, whom Horace later mentions as being a friend and valued reader of his poetry (*Sat.* 1.10.86). Horace was therefore not excluded from this group by being 'of lower station' (Syme 1939: 198). Brutus joined them all in Athens and attended philosophical lectures with them. He concealed his military preparations but recruited many of them to his cause, including Marcus Cicero and Horace. He made Horace a *tribunus militum,* as was his right as commander. But that post normally went to young equestrians or senators starting on a career. Why did Brutus do it?[23] In the case of young Cicero there was some reason: he had already seen military service as a cavalry commander with the forces of Pompey (*De off.* 2.45). I suspect that Horace likewise had had military experience in similar circumstances before Brutus recruited him. But Brutus' act shows that Horace's father was most unlikely to have been an ex-slave—perhaps he was even by now *equestri censu.*

[22] For the opportunities that opened up to a man who became an *apparitor* see Purcell (1983: 147–8).

[23] See Suolahti (1955); he gives the explanation 'due to the necessity of admitting to the service in times of war elements rather weak in social origin, one typical example being the above mentioned son of a freedman, Q. Horatius Flaccus' (117). But other cases are very hard to find; for one see Treggiari (1969: 64–5).

Where, then, did the well-remembered insults to Horace as *libertino patre natus* originate? I suspect that the answer lies in what happened at Venusia during the Social War.

IV

Venusia was the only Latin colony to join the rebels in the Social War. It is recorded specifically by Appian (*BC* 1.42), together with 'Canusia and many other towns', as attaching itself to Gaius Vidacilius, the rebel commander in the region. He killed the chief Roman citizens, but enrolled the ordinary people and slaves in his army. The town is not mentioned again until late 89 BCE, when the Roman praetor Gaius Cosconius, after defeating Trebatius, the rebel commander, overran the territories of Asculum (?Ausculum), Larinum, and Venusia; but Venusia itself, which is in a very strong position, clearly held out till 88 BCE. In that year, Diodorus recounts, 'Metellus [i.e. Q. Caecilius Metellus Pius, probably proconsul in 88 BCE—he had been praetor in 89] took by storm Venusia in Apulia, a very important city that was held by many soldiers, and he took captive more than three thousand prisoners' 2.10). My hypothesis is that Horace's grandfather and father were among those prisoners. What happened to such captives?

In November of 89 BCE the consul Gnaeus Pompeius Strabo took Asculum. This town had been the scene of the slaughter of the Roman praetor Servilius and of his legate Frontinus and then of all Romans in the town (Appian, *BC* 1.38). The only evidence for what happened after its capture is a curt epitome by Orosius: 'After Pompeius entered Asculum he beat with rods and beheaded the prefects, the centurions, and all of the chief men, the slaves and all the loot he sold by auction, the rest he ordered to leave, free certainly but naked and needy' (5.18.26). The wholesale executions were clearly in reprisal for the slaughter of Roman citizens. The auction of slaves and loot was routine—but were only slaves auctioned, and all others sent away free? There are two cases that strongly suggest otherwise.

M. Aurius Melinus, a prominent citizen of Larinum (itself a rebel town), was captured at Asculum and bought by a senator Q. Sergius and placed in his *ergastulum* in the Ager Gallicus. When his presence there was finally discovered, he was then murdered by scheming relatives to prevent his inheriting his mother's estate (Cic. *Pro Cluentio* 2.1–25). Aurius had probably been serving with the rebel army, been shut up in Asculum, and then captured when the town fell.

Another very interesting case is that of P. Ventidius Bassus. He was captured by Pompeius Strabo at Asculum and was carried in chains by his mother in the triumph (A. Gellius 15.4; Cassius Dio 43.51.5). His romantically successful later career, culminating in the consulship, is told by Aulus Gellius. What about his father? He could have been killed in the siege; but he may have been among those executed. The son was enslaved, but later enrolled as a Roman citizen.

That is what I suspect happened to the three thousand prisoners taken after the capture of Venusia. Reprisals are sure to have been exacted for the slaughter of Roman and prominent citizens (not to speak of the stubborn resistance of the town). Horace never mentions his grandfather: he may have been executed. The father may have been spared, like Ventidius, because of his youth, but sold into slavery. Even as late as 25 BCE, under the authority of Augustus, when the Salassi revolted, all males of military age were sold into slavery.[24] But to Romans, in any case, *captivitas* was a form of *servitus,* and how were such prisoners subsequently enrolled as Roman citizens? In the case of the Italians after the Social War, there was a considerable delay in the granting of *civitas,* certainly to 86 BCE and possibly to 84 BCE. Since they were not yet citizens, they could not regain their status by exercise of *ius postliminii.* They may well have had to undergo manumission in order to gain *civitas.* But, of course, they would then have been registered as full Roman citizens. Therefore, to call Horace's father *libertinus* was a gross travesty of the facts; but that is the essence of insult. This would be enough in itself to explain the sneers of military men that Horace recalls in *Satires* 1.6.

---

[24] Strabo 4.6, 7.

V

What all this amounts to is that Suetonius relied only on a very literal
interpretation of that satire for his statement that Horace's father was
a freedman. He had no independent evidence for it. His reliance on
literal interpretation is clear when he adds, after saying that Horace's
father was a freedman and auction-banker: 'It has been believed that
he was a salted-fish merchant, since someone in a quarrel once
insulted him by saying: "How often have I seen your father wiping
his nose with his arm." This pretty story was clearly invented on the
basis of Bion's famous reply when the king enquired about his
origins;[25] and it was stimulated by Horace's own description of his
satires (*Ep.* 2.2.60) '*ille Bioneis sermonibus et sale nigro*', where *sale
nigro* is a pun derived from Bion's *bon mot*. The likeliest motive for
the invention lies in the ironic response of a disingenuously literal
reader (that is, a reader who knew that Horace's father had not really
been a slave) to the repeated *libertino patre natum* of *Satires* 1.6,
repeated as a prized anecdote sufficiently often to come to Suetonius'
attention (who was by nature a literal reader).

A more responsive interpretation of *Satires* 1.6 is needed. Horace
represents himself in the *Satires* and in the σφραγίς to *Epistles* 1 as the
homespun philosopher, with a disadvantaged background, who had
learnt life's lessons the hard way, and whose words are therefore
worth taking seriously. *Satires* 1.6 is central to this self-portrait. He
never says that *libertino patre natum* is true; the words are always in
quotation-marks. He opens the satire by saying to Maecenas:

> ... [non] naso suspendis adunco
> ignotos ut me libertino patre natum.   (5–6)

You do not turn up your nose at unknowns like me, born of a freedman
father.

We are at first inclined, with Suetonius, to take that literally, but
doubts are aroused by what immediately follows:

> cum referre negas quali sit quisque parente
> natus, dum ingenuus, persuades hoc tibi vere...   (7–8)

[25] Fraenkel (1957: 6–7).

When you assert that it does not matter from what sort of father any man was born, provided he was free-born, you rightly persuade yourself of this...

Now we feel forced to take *dum ingenuus* as modifying *quisque,* since we apparently already know that Horace's father was not *ingenuus.* This seems universally accepted—except that Schütz wanted to take the word in its moral sense (which is impossible in view of 21, '*ingenuo si non essem patre natus*'). But Schutz properly recognized the awkwardness of having Horace allow Maecenas to dismiss his father with contempt. Also the run of the Latin here, where the emphasis is heavily on *quali... parente,* properly requires *dum ingenuus* to modify these words rather than *quisque.* Palmer cheerfully explains that Maecenas is here following the example of Augustus: 'Maecenas would not, for instance, have associated with Horace's father.' But if we read on, suspending judgement and recognizing that the reference of *dum ingenuus* is ambiguous, we soon come to this:

> censorque moveret
> Appius, ingenuo si non essem patre natus—
> vel merito quoniam in propria non pelle quiessem.   (20–2)

And [let us suppose] Appius as censor would have expelled me if I had not been born of a free-born father perhaps rightly, because I had not been content to stay inside my own skin.

There is double irony here: Appius had notoriously admitted freedmen to the senate in 312 BCE, while a descendant had carefully expelled them in 50 BCE, and the possibility that Horace's father was not free-born is framed as an impossible condition. The truth—that the words *libertino patre natum* are spoken only by enemies who wish to injure (and whose words consequently have the status of what Demosthenes says about Aeschines' mother)—finally emerges at lines 45–6, where the poet reviews the circumstances of his friendship with Maecenas in preparation for describing at length what a wonderful father he had—such that, were he given his life to live over again, he would not choose any other.

One important rhetorical strategy of *Satires* 1.6 is to display the poet as starting life with no advantages whatever, except for a father of strong moral character. But he burdens that father with a disability reminiscent of Bion's (and Bion was clearly in the poet's mind) that

had a tenuous basis in a reality that went back to the Social War half a
century earlier. We should not follow Suetonius in using the satire as
evidence for the social status of Horace's father, any more than we
should accept Horace's protestations of his father's or his own poverty. A combination of disadvantaged birth and poverty too perfectly
suits the pretensions of a moral philosopher. Horace's father was, in
fact, a proud native-born Sabellian whose family had suffered for
supporting the rebel cause in 90 BCE, though he had been able to lift
the family's fortunes again in a short time, after he gained Roman
citizenship.

This hypothesis removes any need for surprise that Horace,
labouring under the social disadvantage of being a freedman's son,
chose two such aggressive genres as *Epodes* and *Satires* for his earliest
poetry. It also leaves us free to accept what Suetonius tells us about
the mirrors in Horace's bedroom (since Sabellians were reputed to be
especially prone to lechery!)[26]—a detail that Eduard Fraenkel
asserted was 'filthy', 'a *locus communis*', and 'based on nothing but
rumores'. Hostius Quadra will not have been the only wealthy Roman
to indulge his special tastes in this way (Sen. *NQ* 1.16).

Another of the delicate rhetorical strategies in *Satires* 1.6 is
designed to portray the poet's relationship to Maecenas in such a
way that due deference and gratitude to the patron can be expressed,
but only together with a strong sense of the client's—or rather, the
friend's—self-sufficiency and independence (which are seen especially in the lengthy sketch of the poet's lifestyle that ends the
poem). The topic of the relationship between inferior and superior
dominates both books of *Satires* and the first book of *Epistles*. The
trouble was that, just as the poet could be insulted by the envious or
hostile as *libertino patre natus*, so could he also be represented as the
scurra of Maecenas.[27] He deals defensively with the latter insult by
making Damasippus and Davus come right out and say so: that is,
the defence consists in creating a setting in which the charge must
appear ridiculous—if only for the reason that the poet would not
dream of giving it such publicity if there were the slightest truth in it.
The use of the ugly phrase *libertino patre natum* should be viewed in

[26] Salmon (1967: 59) defends them against the charge.
[27] On this aspect of *Satires* 2 see Oliensis (1998a).

the same light. Of course, expressed in such blunt terms, the phrase was indeed a mere insult that misrepresented Horace's birth. Nevertheless, there was a sufficiently significant grain of truth in it for Horace to feel injured by it and therefore compelled to deflect its sting by publishing it in a setting where its essential falsity would be immediately apparent. The extraordinary attack (*Epodes* 4) on the unnamed ex-slave who has (like Horace) become a *tribunus militum* is emphatically represented as a personal vendetta on the part of the poet (1–2, '*lupis et agnis quanta sortito obtigit | tecum mihi discordia est*'), as if he had a special personal interest in the case. This too can be read as a defensive gesture: if the poet selects such a man as a target, that fact in itself demonstrates that he can have nothing whatever in common with the man. Horace's father had not been a slave.

Eduard Fraenkel put two entries in the index to his *Horace* under the rubric 'Horace—never lies'; one concerns his interpretation of *Odes* 1.38, the other 3.25. The argument in this essay has not been to expose Horace as a liar, but to make the point that interpreters cannot accept what the poet seems to say as simple statements of historical fact.

Note. I have not said anything about the name 'Horatius', mainly because I am inclined to regard it as a Latinized form of an Oscan name. But it may be a Roman/Latin name, and the family may have been sent to Venusia as settlers. They will have had no connection with the patrician *gens Horatia* which died out earlier. But the fact that the new citizens of Venusia after the Social War were enrolled in the *tribus Horatiana* may suggest an influential family of Horatii in Venusia who thought that choice of tribe appropriate. If the family was indeed Roman, and if Horace's grandfather was therefore a Roman citizen (though this is a less likely hypothesis in view of the interpretation of *Sat.* 2.1.34–9 offered above), why would he join the rebel cause? He may have married a Sabellian woman and been caught by the provision of the *lex Minicia* (perhaps of 91 BCE) which decreed that the children of marriages between a citizen and a non-citizen should take the lesser status.[28] That would have meant that Horace's father would suddenly have lost Roman citizenship.

---

[28] See Salmon (1967: 338 n. 4).

6

Horace, *Satires* 1.5:
An Inconsequential Journey

Emily Gowers

'If I were to waste your time with a long conversation (*si longo sermone morer tua tempora*), I would be damaging the public interest.'[1] So Horace begins his *Epistle to Augustus*, typically selling himself short. He does not pause for breath for 270 lines. Equivocations like this about the sound of his own voice had been a particular characteristic of Horace's earlier books of 'Conversations', the *Satires* or *Sermones*, a teasing mixture of seemingly directionless rambling and forceful short cuts.[2] Nowhere is this mixture more evident than in the fifth satire of the first book, a short story which apologises for being a long one, where Horace compensates his readers for a long haul with an ending that must leave them feeling short-changed.

The poem is about a journey Horace made or says he made from Rome to Brundisium: he starts off on the Via Appia, takes a sidetrack through the mountains to the Via Minucia on the other side, then carries on down the coast.[3] Horace's account inspired many later travel-writers to follow in his footsteps. Gibbon made the journey for rather pedestrian reasons, in order to measure Horace's speed; Addison's motive was more aesthetic, to compare what he called 'the face of this country' against Horace's poetic landscapes. And in the 1960s

---

[1] *Ep.* 2.1.4.

[2] On equivocation as a feature of the *Satires*, see in general Zetzel (1980: 59–78).

[3] On the route see Mazzarino (1968: 174–96). I am grateful to John Patterson for this and other references.

Charles Lister was paid £50 by Chatto and Windus to relive Horace's adventures with local beauties of another kind.[4]

The sense that this journey really happened is generated by the number of random details Horace includes along the way—fleeting remarks about foundation myths, a pompous mayor, a kitchen fire, the buzz of mosquitoes or the price of bread.[5] These have tempted several armchair travellers to fill in the background for themselves. Horace's remarks seem deliberately unaesthetic, yet Fraenkel insists that the description of Anxur on its shining rocks is the first landscape-painting for its own sake in Latin literature; and that Horace's sparse but suggestive complaints about mosquitoes and love-songs capture the melancholy feel of the Pomptine marshes.[6] Perhaps the most extreme example of this kind of infilling is Harold Nicolson's golden reconstruction of Horace's and Maecenas' journey in the *Spectator* of 1944, against the backdrop of Montecassino:[7]

> Horace and Virgil packed their little bundles and waited rather shyly until the great men were ready for the road. And then they would start off in single file, the sun flashing on the armour of Maecenas's guard, the mules picking their way through rocks and arbutus bushes with obstinate delicacy, climbing high among the eagles and the peaks. And then on again above the valleys, until they reached the end of the day's marching and would be met by the slaves who had preceded them and prepared fire and bedding and warm water and rows of little thrushes upon sticks.

All this from Horace's meagre asides about skinny thrushes, stabled mules and bad water.

More sceptical readers know that the poem is part of a literary tradition of travel-writing. An ancient scholiast tells us that Horace is himself following in the footsteps of his satirical predecessor Lucilius, who described a journey from Rome as far as the Sicilian straits, via Capua and his estates around Tarentum.[8] The

---

[4] Gibbon (1814: 335–54); Addison (1705: 186); Lister (1991). Cf. Dosch (1904), cited by Rudd (1966: 60).

[5] Calp. Sic. *Ecl.* 1.28 describes the literary style of the traveller (*uiator*) as *triuiali more.*

[6] Fraenkel (1970: 110 'Anxur'; 109 'marshes').

[7] Nicolson (1944: 54).

[8] Porph.: *Lucilio hac satyra aemulatur Horatius iter suum a Roma Brundisium usque describens quod et ille in tertio libro fecit, prima a Roma Capuam usque et inde fretum Siciliense* ('Horace rivals Lucilius in this satire, tracing his journey from Rome

unsuccessful erotic encounter, the session of animal abuse and the grouses about the journey itself have all been linked with scattered fragments ascribed to Lucilius' third book.[9] The trail of quotations continues from Horace to Rutilius Namatianus, whose account of a journey from Rome to Luna includes another periphrasis for a name that will not fit into the metre and more laughter at Jewish superstition.[10] Even one Victorian traveller has to be suspected of intertextual imitation when he spies on a mock-heroic battle between muleteers and landlords, scoffs at a miraculous spring ('I could match it with many equally superstitious notions in Ireland'), and espouses a self-consciously bathetic style: 'the Muse...kept far from my prosy brain'.[11]

Horace's own prosy brain has helped to keep the poem underrated too. The miserly Pococurante gives it a special mention in the index of third-rate literary works he recites to Candide—which may of course be a negative recommendation—but his sentiment there is typical of how the poem has been received by most of its critics: 'I see nothing extraordinary in his journey to Brundisium.'[12] Quite so: the poem seems designed to annoy us. Horace lets slip that he is travelling in the retinue of Maecenas, who seems to be bent on an important diplomatic mission, and they are joined by some of the most interesting literary figures of the day. Yet all we learn about Virgil is

to Brundisium, something Lucilius too did in his third book, starting from Rome and travelling to Capua and from there to the Sicilian strait').

[9] Fiske (1920: 306–16). On ancient journey poems: Lejay (1966: 140–3); Grupp (1953); Illuminati (1938). Possible other candidates for a genre of Latin travel poetry include: Varro's Menippean satires, *Marcipor, Periplous* and *Sesculixes,* ed. Astbury (1985); the *praetexta* by Cornelius Balbus cited at Cic. *Fam.* 10.32, in imitation of the *presbeia* in *Iliad* 9; J. Caesar, *Iter* (Suet. *Jul.* 56: *reliquit poema quod inscribitur* Iter... *fecit dum ab urbe in Hispanium ulteriorem quarto et uicensimo die peruenit,* 'He left a poem entitled "The Journey"...which he wrote in the course of a twenty-four day journey from Rome to Farther Spain'); Valgius (Morel, *Frag. poet. Lat.* 106); Persius, *Hodeporicon* (a possible textual reading in the *Vita*); Ausonius, *Mosella,* ed. Green (1991); Rutilius Namatianus, *De reditu suo siue Iter Gallicum,* ed. Doblhofer (1972). Cf. also the prose epistle of Sidonius (*Ep.* 1.5) with its echoes of Horace on friendship (2); laughter (3): and filthy water (6, 8).

[10] Rut. Nam. 1.419–20; 1.387–94.

[11] Ramage (1868). Ted Kenney has kindly drawn my attention to *Hogarth's Peregrination,* ed. Mitchell (1952).

[12] Voltaire, *Candide,* ch. 25. I owe this reference to Neil Hopkinson. See Sallmann, (1974: 179–206); for a catalogue of disgruntled readers (180–1).

that tennis did not agree with his digestion, and a few muffled asides about the embassy take second place to Horace's own bodily ail-ments. Maecenas' arrival is reduced to a subordinate 'meanwhile', somewhere out of the corner of Horace's sore eyes. World events—*magnae res*—are off the edge of his map altogether. Gibbon was disgusted by Horace's egotism, his obsession with his 'offensive infirmities', his diarrhoea and his wet dream ('the nasty accident that befell him in the night'), and concludes: 'The maxim that everything in great men is interesting applies only to their minds and ought not to be extended to their bodies.' Travelling with a cynical satirist with his ear to the ground and friends in high places should have been more illuminating.

Reading between the lines can tell us a great deal about contem-porary politics and patronage,[13] but the ending of the poem con-tinues to frustrate anyone in search of historical verisimilitude. Three separate peace treaties from the Second Triumvirate have connec-tions with Brundisium: the Treaty of Brundisium of 40 BCE; the Treaty of Tarentum of spring 37; and a meeting in Athens between Octavian and Antony in 38 BCE. But none of them is quite consistent with Horace's account. 40 BCE is too early for Horace to have known Maecenas: so even if he says he ends up at Brundisium, we have to rule it out as the obvious destination. However, if Horace was heading for Tarentum, a route via Brundisium is perversely indirect. As for the third option, it would certainly make sense to sail to Greece from Brundisium, but the time of year is possibly wrong, at least in the eyes of those who know the habits of mosquitoes and frogs. Stuck at this crossroads, one reader in the 1950s decided to abandon the whole problem and talk about 'poetic fiction' instead: he decided that Horace was not much bothered about history, so his embassy was probably a loose conflation of all three.[14]

But Horace is so very precise in all the other details of his route that it is hard to accept that he is suddenly being vague at the end of it all. This journey may never have happened, but it is still a simulation of a real adventure. On the other hand, Brundisium is clearly the

---

[13] See DuQuesnay (1984: 19–58; esp. 40–3).

[14] Musurillo (1954–5: 159–62), where the arguments for each treaty are set out; modified by Anderson (1955–6: 57–9).

wrong ending: a deliberate ending but the wrong one, and inexplic-
ably abrupt. The people who want to pin the treaty down and the
ones who do not care which one it is are both on the wrong track.
A new explanation is needed for why Horace is being so perverse,
one that keeps the unexpected ending in sight.

While I have suggested that the poem asks to be read literally, I do
not mean by this that it is a transparent invitation to us to follow in
Horace's footsteps. It would be a mistake to read the poem in the
context of works like the itineraries or Julius Caesar's lost *Iter,* which
sounds like a logbook of a Roman route. Horace has something else
on his mind. This is in quite another sense a poetic fiction: not so
much a conflation of journeys as an exercise in writing Horatian
satire.[15] That means, as so often with Horace, a series of negative
choices. The roads not taken on this journey are as much part of the
picture as those that are. Of the former the most important is the
road from Rome to Tarentum described by Lucilius, which took up a
whole book in the process. Lucilius, in Horace's eyes, was a sloppy
traveller, with a great deal of unwanted mud clinging to his boots.
Although Horace starts off following in his footsteps, his route, as far
as we can tell, diverges along the way, and the economy of his journey
is quite different too.

The journey is a milestone in Horace's book: it marks the half-way
point in his 'Conversations', *Sermones,* which until this point have
been a series of unstructured, sceptical discussions on how to live life
in the difficult world of modern Rome. This poem comes as a breath
of fresh air: Horace escapes from Rome on to the open road, and
after all his knotty musings we sense that there is to be some action at
last. But in its way the journey is yet another kind of conversation, a
conversation on wheels; it is a more literal version of all the tangled
ramblings, the stops and starts, asides, resumptions and suspended
endings that make up Horatian satire.

Horace does not make the comparison explicitly—not here anyway. But there was already a long tradition in the ancient world of
comparing conversations or narratives to journeys. Demetrius, for

---

[15] See Lowe (1979: 135): 'This Horatian journey is essentially a conceptual journey, at once a real action and a metaphoric device, the theme of a poem, and an
illustration of the way to write such a poem.'

instance, when be wants to break up a particularly dense Thucydidean sentence into something clearer, if more diffuse, makes his point plain with a metaphor from travelling:[16]

If the phrasing in the sentence is varied, there will be many more resting-places (*anapaulai*) in the narrative, although something of its stateliness will be destroyed. Just as long journeys are shortened by a succession of inns, so desolate paths, even when the distances are short, give the impression of length.

Perhaps a historian's style is not the best analogy for Horace. A more likely ancestor for Horace's *sermo* is another dialogue, one in prose, Cicero's *De oratore*, which needs to be linked much more closely with this poem. There is a significant moment in Book 2 where M. Antonius pauses, turns to Julius Caesar Strabo, and tells him that, although he has a little left to say, he is tired of speaking:

et Antonius, 'perpauca quidem mihi restant,' inquit 'sed tamen defessus iam labore atque itinere disputationis meae requiescam in Caesaris sermone quasi in aliquo peropportuno deuersorio.'

His rambling talk has been like a long and tired journey; he wants to hand over to Strabo and be able to rest in his conversation (*sermo*) as if in a convenient wayside inn (*deuersorium*, literally a turning off from the road). Strabo modestly replies:

'atqui' inquit Iulius 'non nimis liberale hospitium meum dices; nam te in uiam, simul ac perpaulum gustaris, extrudam et eiciam.' (Cic. *De or.* 2.234)

Antonius will hardly think his hospitality generous: as soon as he has had the slightest taste of it he will be thrown out on to the road again.[17]

Sermo, in Cicero's metaphor, then, becomes a road with *deuersoria*, places to turn off. The comparison works very naturally, because the diminutive of *deuersorium, deuerticulum*, has a double meaning in Latin: not just a detour or a roadside inn, but also an evasion or a

---

[16] *De elocutione* 47.
[17] See Fantham (1972: 153–5), who points out that the metaphor is an appropriate one for the dialogue, which relies for its existence on the hospitality of friends. The same is, of course, true of Horace's journey.

periphrasis.[18] Evasion and periphrasis are the single central themes, metaphorically and literally, of Horace's poem; all the way through, he is playing on the parallels between talking and journeying, especially the kinds that involve roundabout routes. This connection had already been made in satirical travel-literature. In his *Periplous*, Varro fusses about on behalf of his readers: 'In case we stray, we shall have plenty *of ektropai* (i.e. *deuerticula*), or resting-places, to make the road safe but dense, full of stops.'[19] Later Rutilius Namatianus, deciding to split his journey-narrative in two, marks the dividing point between the books with the image of the milestone that cheers a jaded traveller.[20] Sixty lines later, he apologises for a short digression with a suitable pun: forgive me for that long-winded detour, he says: let us get back to the road again.[21]

Can Horace's poem be understood, then, as a diversion, or, more paradoxically, as a wayside inn in the middle of a book of real conversations, a breathing-space punctuated by internal stops and starts like the journey it describes? A network of inns is a good metaphor for picaresque narrative, as is plain from a much later example, in Fielding's *Joseph Andrews*. Again at the beginning of the second book, the author gives his reader a break while he compares the pause in the narrative to one of the inns along his hero's route:[22]

Those little spaces between chapters may be looked upon as an inn or resting-place where he may stop and take a glass of any other refreshment as it pleases him. Nay, our fine readers will, perhaps, be scarce able to travel farther than through one of them in a day. As to the vacant pages which are placed between our books, they are to be regarded as those stages where in long journeys, the traveller stops some time to repose himself and consider

---

[18] *OLD* s.v. *deuerticulum*: 1(c) a circumlocution; (2) a loophole, means of evasion; (3) a digression.

[19] Var. *Men.* 418 (Astbury): *et ne erraremus, ectropas esse multas; omnino tutum esse, sed spissum iter.*

[20] Rut. Nam. 2.1–4: *nondum longus erat nec multa uolumina passus,* | *iure suo poterat longior esse liber;* | *taedia continuo timuit cessura labori,* | *sumere ne lector iuge paueret opus...*; 7–10: *interualla reor fessis praestare uidetur* | *qui notat inscriptus milia crebra lapis* | *partimur trepidum per opuscula bina ruborem,* | *quem satius fuerat sustinuisse semel.*

[21] Rut. Nam. 2.61–2: *sed deuerticulo fuimus fortasse loquaces:* | *carmine propositum iam repetamus iter.*

[22] H. Fielding, *Joseph Andrews*, Bk. 3, ch. 1.

of what he hath seen in the parts he hath already passed through; a consideration which I take the liberty of recommending a little to the reader; for, however swift his capacity may be, I would not advise him to travel through these pages too fast; for, if he doth, he may probably miss the seeing some curious production of nature, which will be observed by the slower and more accurate reader.

All these writers are aware that the length or shortness of a journey, as it appears on paper, is measured not by the mile, but by the number of stops and diversions along the way. How long or how short, then, is Horace's journey, how fast or how slow? He is apparently interested in making us think about this question, or rather about its ambiguities. The shortest poem in the book so far is signposted in the last line as a 'long journey' written on a 'long piece of paper':

> Brundisium longae finis chartaeque uiaeque est. (104)

Brundisium is the end of a long journey and a long piece of paper.

How long it is on the map depends partly on where we think Horace was going. He may be choosing a short cut from Rome to Brundisium, but even that is disputable: in the *Epistles,* Horace says it is a toss-up whether the Via Appia or the Via Minucia, the road he branches on to, is the faster route between the two cities.[23] If the expected destination is Tarentum, on the other hand, it is certainly the long way round. And yet Horace cuts his account short. Either way, it is not long compared with Lucilius' journey to the Sicilian Straits—at least, as the crow flies.

On paper, of course, it is in Horace's power to make this journey just as long or as short as he chooses. And the same applies to its psychological effect on the reader. The last line looks like a contribution to the Callimachean debate about whether or not to measure poetry by the mile.[24] In the previous poem Horace had taunted Lucilius with having an average writing speed of 200 verses an hour, but complained about being bogged down in the trail of muddy waste he left in his wake. Could his own long piece of paper (his *longa charta*) be read as a charter for Callimachean smoothness and brevity?

---

[23] *Ep.* 1.18.20: *Brundisium Minuci melius uia ducat an Appi.*
[24] See Wimmel (1960); Clausen (1964: 181–96); and the survey of Latin references in Hopkinson (1988: 98–101).

Not on the surface, at any rate. If Horace were putting his poetic principles into practice on the road, what would the result be? On the evidence of the prescriptive satires, 4 and 10, smooth roads, speedy transport (cf. *ut currat sententia*, 'so that the thought flows', 1.10.9), drinkable water, first-class comfort. Instead there is polluted water, bread full of stones, and endless noise: mosquitoes, croaking frogs, and the wailing of love-sick bargemen. Muddy, polluted, garrulous: those were the very criticisms Horace offered us of Lucilius' style, yet here all those negative metaphors are translated into the practical hazards of his own journey. And Horace makes a point of telling us that sometimes he positively chose to take his time. What is he saying, then, about his relationship with his predecessor on the road?

Horace's reply to Lucilius is an ironic one.[25] In *Sat.* 1.9, he is led on a wild goose chase by the pest, and says desperately: 'There's no need for you to go out of your way' (16–17 *nil opus est te | circumagi*), yet they end up zigzagging across Rome. In this poem he goes out of his way to offer us diversions. First on the map: half-way through he seems to be heading straight for Beneventum (*tendimus hinc recta Beneuentum* 71), then we find out long after the event that the mules have left the main road for an untrodden path, leaving us to join the dots of a fuzzy, unsignposted narrative. The nameless town that will not scan to fit line 87, based on a similar joke in Lucilius, may well be a hoax for the sake of it, another kind of satirical circumlocution.[26] The journey is punctuated with detours and delays that become diversions in their own right: travellers get stuck in the mud, and boats do not leave on time. Each random-seeming comment on the towns passed through looks like an aside or an irrelevance. But Horace manages somehow to make light of the obstacle course, make delays brisk, skim over unprepossessing surroundings. He is showing Lucilius that he has a different approach to getting through material; he can make a slower journey faster on paper.

Lucilius, in his depleted state, is in a poor position to put his side of the case, but one fragment does survive from the first stages of his journey, which coincided with Horace's:

[25] Cf. Barnes (1988: 57–9); Freudenburg (1993: 202).

[26] Lucil. 228M. The most recent attempts to identify the town are in Desy (1988: 620–5, Ausculum) and Radke (1989: 54–72, Herdoneae).

uerum haec ludus ibi, susque deque fuerunt,
susque et deque fuere, inquam, omnia ludus iocusque:
illud opus durum, ut Setinum accessimus finem,
αἰγίλιποι montes, Aetnae omnes, asperi Athones.   (1.10–13 M)

That part was really child's play, I'd say, up down, down up, all the way, all
fun and games. The next bit was hard going, when we got to Setinian
territory, mountains all no-go for goats, steep Everests all the way [Mount
Etnas and Mount Athoses].

This could be seen as a display of his charming deficiencies: the
seesaw, singsong repetition of *susque deque*, the jumble of Greek
and Latin words. Yet Lucilius clearly saw the need for variety quite
as well as Horace: the first part of his journey was a doddle, the
second an uphill struggle. His ramblings are just a more exaggerated
simulation of the ups and downs of chit-chat.

Horace's style is more terse and limited. With careful packing, he
gets more into a smaller suitcase. He chooses out-of-the-way routes
and makes a continuous narrative snappy. But there are still reasons
why this could never be a perfect Callimachean journey: it is also a
satirical one, and a satirical one is necessarily a journey gone wrong,
one that mixes the rough with the smooth, and is prone to disasters.
We cannot enjoy or laugh at a smooth journey; what we need is a bit
of *Schadenfreude*, the kind provided by a jaded vision of travelling.[27]
On the surface this looks nothing like one of Fielding's blank pages, a
vacation or rest-cure. Horace, as he himself suggests, is a most
splenetic traveller, a proto-Smelfungus (*haud animo aequo* 8), grous-
ing about the weather, the roads, the food and his bodily complaints.[28] So even in this poem the satirical need for ups and downs
works against any obvious appearance of consistency.

Many of the details of Horace's route that look straightforward
and literal, bolstering up the illusion of reality, can be translated into
statements about the specifically satirical nature of the journey. This
is most obvious in the first lines:

[27] See Rudd (1966: 61).
[28] Freudenburg (1993: 203–5) argues that Horace is playing the role of a disgruntled comic parasite, and compares *Ep.* 1.17.52–7 on the disasters that befall a hanger-
on on his journey to Brundisium (cf. *Ep.* 1.11.11: *sed neque qui Capua Romam petit
imbre lutoque | aspersus uolet in caupona uiuere*).

egressum magna me accepit Aricia Roma
hospitio modico...   (1–2)

On leaving great Rome I was received by Aricia in a modest hostelry.

Horace leaves Rome and washes up in a modest little inn at Aricia. Or,
on a poetic level, he opts out of the demands of monumental poetry (or
his own satirical material so far), and plumps for modest hospitality
and evasion instead.[29] His companion, he says, was the rhetorician
Heliodorus, by a long shot the most learned of the Greeks (the first of
several puns in the poem on the idea of length). Most of the commentators agree that Heliodorus must be a pseudonym for the philosopher
Apollodorus, who taught Octavian.[30] But Horace does say he was a
rhetorician, and a more plausible candidate as a cicerone on a sight-
seeing tour might be the Heliodorus who wrote a poem called *Thea-
mata Italica*, 'Sights of Italy' (or *Thaumata Italica*, 'Miracles of Italy').[31]
It is even more probable that Horace means that he did not take a man
at all, but a book, a kind of 'Companion Guide to Southern Italy'.[32] In
other words, he is giving us some idea of the pedigree of this poem as a
piece of travel-writing. Of course, as a satirist, Horace is not interested
in the usual kind of sight-seeing, but in the very opposite, things like
black eye-cream and dirty dreams (84 *immundo uisu*); as an Epicurean
sceptic, he pours scorn on local miracles. Heliodorus is the first of
Horace's red herrings: he wants to make his readers expect castles in the
air, but lets them down with a bump.

On from Aricia to Forum Appi, at the gateway to the Pomptine
marshes, Rome's perpetually embarrassing swamp. The clientele of
this town are distinctly more dubious, sailors and cheating landlords:

differtum nautis, cauponibus atque malignis   (4)

Stuffed with sailors and cheating landlords

---

[29] On the poem as a *recusatio* see Ehlers (1985: 69–83; esp. 82) and Lowe (1979: 130).

[30] See Frank (1920: 393).

[31] See Kiessling and Heinze (1921: ad loc.). Twelve hexameters of this poem
survive in Stobaeus *Anth.* 100.6 (= III 344.17 Meineke), describing a miraculous
spring that cured eye-disease near Cicero's villa at Puteoli (cf. Plin. *N.H.* 31.3).

[32] At *Sat.* 2.3.11–12 he names four Greek writers as his 'companions' on a writing-
trip: *quorsum pertinuit stipare Platona Menandro,* | *Eupolin, Archilochum, comites
educere tantos?* Cf. Mart. 14.188 on a parchment volume *of* Cicero: *si comes ista tibi
fuerit membrana, putato* | *carpere te longas cum Cicerone uias*; and *OED* s.v. 'cicerone'.

A bit of local colour perhaps, but these are old acquaintances, too; sailors and landlords were part of the scum of the earth Horace and Maecenas looked down on in Satire 1 from their high ground of Epicurean stability.[33] The town itself, *differtum*, stuffed, with its tight squeeze of filth and refinement, doubles as an image of Horatian satire, the suspicious sausage that bulges with all types, and is good only in parts.[34] This balance is reflected in the dramatis personae of the rest of the poem: along the way Horace falls in with his ideal audience, the poets of modern Rome, and an equal measure of riffraff—drunken bargemen, mule-drivers, clowns, cooks, slaves, and of course a deceitful woman.

Horace spends a long time at Forum Appi, waiting impatiently for his travelling-companions to finish dinner, and then for the barge to leave. Another town on the marshes, Ulubrae, features in the *Epistles* as an example of the ultimate dump, and Forum Appi is one of the lowest points of an uneven journey.[35] Why does Horace dwell on it? For an answer we have to go back to Cicero's *De oratore*, and rejoin Strabo after the long digression or *deuersorium* his friend requested. He tells him that he must be regretting his decision to stop. Instead of basking in the wayside inn of his conversation, he might as well have paused somewhere in the Pomptine marshes, hardly a beautiful or salubrious spot; he must be dying to get back to the road again:

sed iam tu, Antoni, qui hoc deuersorio sermonis mei libenter acquieturum te esse dixisti, tamquam in Pomptinum deuerteris, neque amoenum neque salubrem locum, censeo, ut satis diu te putes requiesse et iter reliquum conficere pergas. (Cic. *De or.* 290)

On the surface, then, Horace's *deuersorium/sermo* presents itself as a Pomptine fleapit for his readers, from which, like him, they will be only too glad to escape.[36]

---

[33] *Sat.* 1.1.29: *perfidus hic caupo, miles nautaeque per omne | audaces mare qui currunt.*

[34] On the etymology *satura* see Coffey (1989: 12); Diomedes 1.485 *GLK: siue a quodam genere farciminis, quod multis rebus refertum saturam dicit Varro uocitatum*; and cf. Martianus Capella 9.997–8: *miscilla…doctis indoctis adgerans, | fandis tacenda farcinat, immiscuit.*

[35] *Ep.* 1.11.29–30: *quod petis hic est, est Vlubris, animus si te non deficit aequus.*

[36] Cf. *Ep.* 1.15.10: *mutandus locus est deuersoria nota | praeteragendus equus.*

The journey so far has taken two days, Horace tells us, down the
Via Appia, the main artery of Italy and a very un-Callimachean
highroad:

> hoc iter ignaui diuisimus, altius ac nos
> praecincti unum: minus est grauis Appia tardis.   (5–6)

This part of the journey we split in two, a one-day haul for express travellers;
the Via Appia is easier for slowcoaches.

More express travellers, he says, could get through it in only one, and
indeed we can tell from the fragment above that Lucilius did. Who
are these men in a hurry? *altius praecincti* literally means 'with tunics
hitched up for fast walking'.[37] This disturbs at least one commentator: how could Horace possibly inflict a walking tour on the elderly
Apollodorus?[38] Perhaps he means that the slaves went on foot,
carrying their masters in litters?[39] Apart from the fact that this may
be Heliodorus or a book anyway, there is another explanation.
Walking is the natural pace for satire. Take Horace's evening stroll
round the Forum and the Circus Maximus in *Sat.* 1.6, in search of
vegetables and fortune-tellers, or his ramblings down the Via Sacra in
Sat. 1.9, a journey that is simultaneously a conversation, and can
teach us a great deal about the significance of pace in this poem.
More specifically, in *Sat.* 2.6 Horace tells us that the muse of satire is
none other than the *musa pedestris*, the pedestrian or prosy muse.[40]
A walking pace, even if it gives us a distorted picture of Roman
methods of transport, is an appropriate start for a pedestrian satire.

Altius ... praecinctis, literally, 'more girt-up', also has a military
flavour: it conjures up ideas of being well-prepared for battle. This
is where the paths not taken fit in: not just Lucilius' route, but also,
looming above plodding satire, the panoramic range of epic, the kind
of treatment that Horace always managed to avoid. Satire as a
hexameter form always had a suppressed epic potential (according

---

[37] Porph. *id est, expeditius et agilius*; cf. Serv. ad *Aen.* 1.210: *accinctos enim
industrios dicimus*. The phrase has roughly the same meaning as English 'with sleeves
rolled up'.

[38] Testorelli (1977: 29, n. 62).

[39] As suggested by Palmer (1885).

[40] 2.6.16–17: *ergo ubi me in montis et in arcem ex urbe remoui, | quid prius illustrem
satiris musaque pedestri?*

to Cicero, Ennius gave the name *uersus longus*, 'long verse', to the metre, so to achieve brevity in hexameters was something of a long shot anyway).[41] Horace makes room for mock-heroics along the way in the form of periphrases for the time of day and gods' names for fire and love. Above all, the oldest journey poem in the world was an epic: the shadow of Odyssean *nostos* is one we travel with throughout this satire almost as a matter of course.[42] The first line, for example, seems to be an echo of the beginning of Odysseus' journey narrative in Book 9: Horace leaves Rome as Odysseus leaves Troy; and there are more Odyssean themes to come.[43] A third kind of fast traveller would be the courier, the marathon runner on state business—the kind of person who might be persuaded to shed an official secret or two. But Horace clings stubbornly to a lazy pace: the Via Appia, he repeats, is *minus... grauis*, less of a nuisance, or, less weighty, less grand, if you take it slowly.[44] Unified epic would make an unbroken journey; Lucilian satire was an easy ride; political news would go by express; but the best place for Horace, a man not in a hurry, is the crawler lane, with plenty of stops.[45] The pace of his journey, full of banalities and asides, goes hand in hand with the freedom of the small man; he follows his own vagaries, not dictates from on high.

Perhaps the best text to read alongside this poem, apart from Cicero's *De oratore*, is, again, Horace's *Epistle to Augustus* (*Ep.* 2.1), his most transparent refusal to write epic. There he says that, if he had the power, he would abandon satire and write about the emperor's exploits, cataloguing the sites of lands and rivers, castles on mountaintops, the kingdoms of the barbarians, world wars, and Rome itself:

> nec sermones ego mallem
> repentes per humum quam res componere gestas,

[41] Cic. *Leg.* 2.68: *herois uersibus, quod longos appellat.*

[42] On the poem as epic parody see Sallman (1974: 200–6).

[43] See Ehlers (1985: 80–1): Homer *Od.* 9.39–40: Ἰλιόθεν με φέρων ἄνεμος Κικόνεσσι πέλασσεν | ἰσμάρωι; cf. Virg. *Aen.* 3.210: *seruatum ex undis Strophadum me litora primum | excepit.*

[44] In the light of Rutilius' explicit comparison between the divisions of his book and those of a journey (n. 20), it is also possible to read lines 5–6 as a statement about the place of 1.5 as a half-way stopping-point in Book 1.

[45] Ps.-Acron: *Appia uia non est molesta tardioribus, quia habitaculis frequentatur ubi possunt manere, quocumque peruenerint.*

> terrarumque situs et flumina dicere, et arces
> montibus impositas et barbara regna, tuisque
> auspiciis totum confecta duella per orbem...
> et............... Romam...   (*Ep.* 2.1.250–4, 256)

I would not compose conversations that crawl along the ground rather than important narratives: descriptions of lands and rivers, citadels perched on hilltops and foreign kingdoms, and wars carried out under your auspices across the world, and...Rome.

In other words, the great geographical-historical narrative this journey might have been.

In its own way, the journey poem does follow this prescription, but always on a mundane, satirical level. There is a war early on, for instance; but it is the war Horace declares on his queasy stomach as the result of an attack of typhoid (*uentri* | *indico bellum* 7–8). The sites he visits are duly catalogued, but these are not epic rivers and landscapes so much as mosquito-ridden canals and one-horse towns that stink of fish and superstition. There is one hill-top citadel, gleaming Anxur, which should be the highpoint of the poem, coinciding as it does with the arrival of Maecenas. Yet Horace finds it all too dazzling for his sore eyes. There are two quasi-Homeric duels— one between bargemen and the other between two buffoons, conjured up with an appeal to the epic muse, who is really the pedestrian muse in disguise. Meanwhile, the only explicit treaty of the poem is a tryst made with a girl who lets Horace down and causes him to have a wet dream. Both the mock-war and the mock-treaty focus on Horace's dirtied stomach, the most appropriate part of the body for stained, ignoble satire.

One further link between the two passages is that, in the *Epistle to Augustus*, Horace actually uses a metaphor from travelling to classify his satires: not the pedestrian muse this time, but something not much better. He describes them as satires that creep along the ground (*sermones...* | *...repentes per humum*)—humble, humdrum satire moving at a snail's pace. Small wonder, then, that twice in the journey poem—symmetrically from the centre—the verb used to describe the travellers' pace is *repere*, to creep—*repimus* (25), *erepsemus* (79)—we crawled along.[46] Working against the idea of constant speed, though,

---

[46] Cf. *Ep.* 1.4.4: *reptare*.

is the satirical need for variety, a range of extremes: at one point the travellers bowl along in carriages (*rapimur raedis* 86); on the canal they come to a complete standstill (*nil cum procedere lintrem | sentimus* 20–1, 'when we felt the boat wasn't moving'). Variations in pace help literally to break the journey up. In *Sat.* 1.9, similarly, Horace's Roman journey begins at walking pace, then starts to vary: *ire modo ocius, interdum consistere*, 'sometimes moving faster, sometimes standing still' (9). On the whole, Horace presents himself as a very passive traveller, swallowed up by inns and villas (*accepit* 1, *recepit* 50, *recepisset* 80), swept along (*rapimur* 86), thrown out (*exponimur* 23), carried away by sleep (*aufert* 83) or diverted from it (*auertunt* 15). We never learn anyone's motive for stopping in a particular place or choosing one route over another. Another word that is symmetrically repeated is *supinus*, 'flat on one's back', used once of a bargeman (19), once of Horace himself (85), suggesting laid-back indifference. If we are looking for a sense of direction in this poem, he seems to be saying, we are bound to be frustrated.

So much for pace and direction. What about modes of transport? Apart from the brief luxury of carriages, much of Horace's travelling is done on muleback, and a mule pulls the barge along the canal. The detour through the mountains was, Strabo tells us, specifically a mule-track.[47] Can we see mules as the other proper vehicle for Horatian satire? In the next poem, Satire 6, where Horace basks in the freedom of a humble and obscure life, he prides himself on being able to ride to Tarentum on a gelded mule (instead of travelling like a provincial governor with all the paraphernalia of slaves and portable lavatories).[48] Other people are able to visit their Tarentine estates on horseback, or rather on an old hack—*caballo*.[49] This sounds like a joke at Lucilius' expense: as an *eques* he was entitled to a horse, however ramshackle; he had all the advantages and disadvantages of social connections; and his journey poem took him past his estates around Tarentum. Roly-poly Horace, with his down-to-earth narrative on muleback, is like Sancho Panza to the master who careered

---

[47] Strab. C282–3.
[48] *Sat.* 1.6.104–5: *nunc mihi curto | ire licet mulo uel si libet usque Tarentum.*
[49] *Sat.* 1.658–9: *non ego circum | me Satureiano uectari rura caballo.*

along on a broken-down nag.[50] If Horace's journey turns out to be smoother on paper, that is in spite of the bumpy ride.

But it is still often hard to decide where the longs and shorts of this narrative begin and end. Horace's greatest feat is to give his readers a taste of delay, then whisk them off on another tack. The snatch of bargemen's dialogue, for example, is both a specimen of Horatian compression and a prescription for it: Bring her over here; you've got three hundred in there already; whoa, that's quite enough (the familiar catchphrase *iam satis est*).[51] Another dig at Lucilian verbosity, his 200 verses an hour, is slipped cheekily into a narrative of delay. Expressions like *tandem* ('at last', 17), *uix demum* (23 'even then'), *iamque* (21, 'and now') help to spare us delays as well as telling us that they happened (cf. *tota abit hora* 14, 'a whole hour passed'). The longest digression, the central duel between two buffoons, is told not with 100 tongues but *pauca* (51), a few words: many jokes, *multa* (65), *permulta* (62), are condensed into a sample. So should we regard this as a long passage—considerately pared down—or a short one, because we lose most of the details? Horace tells us that the whole session was spun out for hours: *prorsus iucunde cenam producimus illam* (70). A journey of delays and asides is telescoped into a whistlestop tour: in line 34 we arrive at Fundi to find ourselves already kissing it goodbye. Horace would have subscribed to Sterne's philosophy in *Tristram Shandy*: ' "Now before I quit Calais", a travel-writer would say, "it would not be amiss to give some account of it".—Now I think it very much amiss—that a man cannot go quietly through a town, and let it alone, when it does not meddle with him.'[52] The poem's provocative last line sums up the ambiguities of length and brevity Horace has been experimenting with all along. How we view a stretch of road or deal with a given distance is ultimately a matter of perspective.

Is there anything, then, that gives a sense of breadth or purpose to this tall story? Two lines of latitude in a longitudinal poem—the

[50] As a hybrid, and a form of transport half-way between horseback and Shanks's pony, the mule would suit Horace's pedestrian poetics. Cf. Lucian, *Bis acc.* 33, where Dialogue claims to be a paradoxical mixture, neither pedestrian nor mounted on the back of metre (οὔτε πέζος εἰμι οὔτε τῶν μέτρων βέβηκα). Freudenburg (1993: 206–7) also believes that mules are a metaphor for satire.

[51] 12–13: '*huc appelle!*' '*trecentos inseris: ohe | iam satis est!*'

[52] L. Sterne, *Tristram Shandy*, Vol. VII, ch. 4.

far-shining rocks of Anxur and the broad stripe on a provincial mayor's toga[53]—only remind us how much the wider world is excluded. The conclusion *didici* (101, 'I have learned'), said of an Epicurean truism with which Horace must have started out, makes a mockery of the idea of travelling as an empirical education.[54] The Italian landscape is less of a sight in itself than a sentimental backdrop to Horace's emotional life. The real peak of the poem is Horace's reunion with his poetic friends: on such a footloose journey, friendship is the only bond[55] (*neque quis me sit deuinctior alter* 42, 'no one else is more tied to me'), from the boatman's wistful song for his *absentem amicam* (15, 'absent girlfriend') to the tragic split from Varius at Iliadic Canusium (*flentibus hinc Varius discedit maestus amicis* 93, 'at this point Varius departed sadly from his tearful friends'), signalled in advance by the teary smoke from a damp fire (*lacrimoso non sine fumo* 80, 'together with tearful smoke').[56]

Yet most of Horace's details are included for humorous reasons, and the dominant mood is laughter: the travellers laugh at the buffoons' show (*ridemus* 57), at the pompous mayor of one-horse Fundi (literally 'the pits'), with his municipal regalia (*ridentes* 33), and at the treasured local miracle of Gnatia (*risus iocosque* 98). It is a kind of Epicurean laughter prompted by disdain for the representatives of the irrational (like the witches in Satire 8 or the fortune-tellers in Satire 6). The final sentiment of the poem represents the gods as laid-back creatures, as supine as Horace himself, up in the

---

[53] 26: *impositum saxis late candentibus Anxur*; 36: *latum clauum.*

[54] See Fussell (1965: 262–82), 'The open and ironic road', on 'empirical tourism' in eighteenth century English literature.

[55] On friendship as the poem's theme see Classen (1973: 235–50). However, there are hints throughout that Horace's release is only temporary: the *scriba* Messius is described as a runaway slave (656, 68); mules are loose, then tied up again (18–19); Aricia (1) was connected with a runaway slave who became the priest of Diana; Feronia (24) protected freedmen (Serv. ad *Aen.* 8.564). With one bound Horace is free (*egressum* 1) after the mock-threats of the press-gang of poets at the end of Satire 4, but he is eventually forced back to Rome.

[56] Varius leaves his friends wearing a tragic mask (by contrast with his comic persona at Sat. 2.8.63–4: *Varius mappa compescere risum | uix poterat*); these lines look like a reference to a lost epic or tragedy, or possibly to his Epicurean poem *De morte*, given the double meaning of *discedere*, 'to leave' or 'to die' (Richard Janko has suggested to me that the poets met Horace at Sinuessa because of the associations of the Bay of Naples with Epicurean philosophy). Savage (1959–60: 1–4, 4–10) sees an allusion to the myth in which Diomedes' friends were metamorphosed into birds.

great hotel (*tecto* 103) in the sky.[57] Only a credulous Jew would believe in miracles, Horace concludes, quizzically challenging us to believe or not in his own traveller's tale. In Gibbon's view the laughter was too humble: 'The gross language of a boatman and the ribaldry of the buffoons surely belong only to the lowest species of comedy. They might divert travellers in a mood to be pleased with everything; but how could a man of taste reflect on them the day after?'

These comic interludes may, as Gibbon says, be just another kind of diversion or evasion, but the level of humour is more carefully pitched than it looks, and possibly the only driving force behind this apparently serendipitous journey. Throughout the *Sermones*, Horace has expressed an uneasy nostalgia for the Italians' old native wit, what he calls Italian vinegar,[58] which is now only to be found in rustic hedgerows, away from the suspicious city. In *Sat.* 1.7 he records the exchanges of abuse between a vine-dresser and an anonymous traveller (*uiator*). This shadowy traveller crops up again as the *uiator* engaged in a duet with one of the bargemen on the Pomptine canal (16, 17). Is Horace perhaps telling us that he is on a quest for the banished traces of Roman satire (the *uestigia ruris*, 'traces of the countryside', of *Ep.* 2.1.160)?

The central diversion of the poem is the comic duel staged between an Oscan, Messius Cicirrus (cock), and a clown, Sarmentus (bundle of sticks), an exchange of ritualised bantering insults. Horace is by now in Campania, Oscan territory, and Atella, home of native Roman farce, is just down the road.[59] This duel is another of the unsolved problems of the poem, mysterious, to say the least. Sarmentus taunts Messius for looking like a unicorn, an *equus ferus*, which was apparently an insult for rustic origins,[60] and tells him that, with the ugly scar on his head left by the mysterious 'Campanian disease', he might as well do the Cyclops dance, as he will need no stagey mask or tragic buskins (64). Messius retorts by teasing

---

[57] See Sallmann (1974: 197, n. 52): Ps.-Acron: compares Pl. *Amph.* 863: (*Iuppiter*) *in superiore qui habito cenaculo.*

[58] *Sat.* 1.7.32: *Italo... aceto.*

[59] Cf. Lejay (1966: 139). Strabo C250 notes that the Campanians used to invite gladiators in pairs to perform at dinners.

[60] Isid. *Etym.* 12.1.54 on *equiferus: qui ad urbanam dignitatem transire non potest.*

Sarmentus for being a runaway slave with a tiny appetite.[61] The whole episode has been read as a political allegory for the threat posed by Sextus Pompeius to the Italian grain supply.[62] This seems possible, but wide of the mark. Here is a duel that plays out some of the obsessions of the oldest Roman satire, with its hints of cuckoldry, farce and animal abuse. By rejecting tragic boots and introducing his protagonists with mock-heroic grandeur, Horace gives a slap in the face to high poetry. In the *Epistles,* he mentions Cyclops and Satyr dances in the same breath, so perhaps satyrs are the hidden ingredient in this performance.[63] In the *Ars poetica* Horace claims that, when suppressed by law, satyr-plays 'migrated with their humble dialogue (*humili sermone*) to obscure taverns'.[64] 'What a threat you would pose if you were not mutilated', says Sarmentus cryptically. Does this mean that Horace is really on the hunt for a boojum: even in Southern Italy the old verve has been emasculated, and innocuous laughter has replaced the ancient sting?

This brings me in a roundabout way to the poem's unexpected ending. There are many reasons for Horace's detour to Brundisium via the Via Minucia coming as a surprise. First of all, it is a deviation from the obvious route past Lucilius' Tarentine estates. Secondly, we have been geared up all the way for an Odyssean *nostos*, which means a return to Venusia, Horace's own Ithaca. He starts with an escape from the sinking city; he passes through Formiae, home of the Laestrygonians; then restages burning Troy as a farcical kitchen fire, in language that Virgil is thought to have filched for his own epic narrative in the *Aeneid*.[65] And of course Horace meets a

[61] There may well be an element of self-ridicule in the characters of Aufidius Luscus and Sarmentus, both described as *scriba* (35, 66). Horace's native river was the Aufidus, he was a *scriba quaestorius*, like Luscus ('One-Eye') he had something wrong with his vision (*lippus* 30), and his satirical physique is puny (*Sat.* 2.3.308: *longos imitaris, ab imo | ad summum totus moduli bipedalis*; cf. *pusillo* 69). I have not been able to see Doblhofer (1980: 52–67), which apparently makes this point.

[62] Savage (1962: 410–42).

[63] Ep. 2.2.124–5: *ut qui | nunc Satyrum, nunc agrestem Cyclopa mouetur.* Barnes (1988: 59, n.12) points out that Messius' joke about Sarmentus' physique is an echo of the Cyclops' description of Odysseus at *Od.* 9515: ὀλίγος τε καὶ οὐτιδανὸς καὶ ἄκικυς.

[64] *Ars* 229.

[65] See Austin (1964: 141 on *Aen.* 2.310–11), where the two passages are compared, especially the phrase *flamma culinam | Volcano [sic] summum* (Hor. *Sat.* 1.5.73–4) against Virgil's *ampla ruinam | Volcano superare.*

Cyclops in the shape of Messius Cicirrus. Finally, after Beneventum, we catch sight of *montis notos* (77)—well-known mountains. *notus*, until now a sinister word in the Satires, smacking of branding and proscriptions,[66] at this point suggests reassuring familiarity. But this is where the mules leave the beaten track, and there is no faithful Penelope waiting for Horace. *intentum Veneri* (84), bent on Venus, is a red herring: instead, a deceitful girl fails to show up and Horace has his 'nasty accident in the night'. As sleep carries him away (*somnus tamen aufert* 83), we learn that we too have been diverted from Venus: her town, Venusia, lies *far away* on the Via Appia. Thirdly, for reasons mentioned earlier, Tarentum was a more likely site for a peace treaty, the one in 37 BCE, if we have to abandon the treaty of Brundisium on grounds of chronology. Plutarch tells us that Brundisium was in fact planned as the original location for what became the treaty of Tarentum; Antony had blockaded the town with 300 ships and the inhabitants had refused to let him moor there, so the mission was diverted along the coast instead.[67] All this might help to explain why Horace took such a circuitous route, but it does not tell us why he fails to finish that particular story.

There may be yet another reason why we seem to be destined for Tarentum. In *Sat.* 1.6, Horace speaks of Lucilius riding round his Tarentine estates on a local nag. The adjective he uses is *Satureianus* (*Satureiano caballo* 59). Satyrion was the name of the original Greek settlement next to which Tarentum was later founded. An oracle (Strabo C279) presented it as a rich soil on which to found a city, and Virgil puns on the name in Latin: *saturi Tarenti* (*Georg.* 2.197)—Satyrian Tarentum, or rich, fat Tarentum, as in the etymology of *satura*, satire. So could Tarentum, the city that gave us the tarantula and the tarantella, also claim to be the home of Roman satyr-plays and satire?[68] Do we expect Horace, instead of an *Iter*

---

[66] e.g. *Sat.* 1.3.24; 1.4.5.

[67] Plut. *Ant.* 35.

[68] Wiseman (1988: 1–13), in considering the evidence for Roman satyr-plays, lists a number of connections between Italian place-names and satyrs (7: e.g. Satricum in the Pomptine marshes, comparing Virg. *Aen.* 7.801 *Saturae palus*), but he does not mention Satyrion. As he point out (12), Odysseus' wanderings were a rich source of satyr-play plots with Italian connections.

Brundisinum, to be giving us an *Iter Satureianum*? If we go back to the poem's ancestor, Cicero's *De oratore*, the digression so firmly signposted with travelling metaphors is, after all, a digression on wit.

But Brundisium, not Tarentum, is the end of the road. There is no doubt about that. Horace names it as his terminus in what is perhaps the most emphatic ending in Latin literature: *Brundisium longae finis chartaeque uiaeque est* (104).[69] Paradoxically it is also one of the most open-ended and unsatisfying endings possible. On any journey, we might reasonably expect the final destination to be the climax, but Horace rushes the last stages, covering the longest stretch of the journey so far, 44 miles, in one line, and pretending that there is no more room on the paper. A long sheet is the name he gives his shortest poem so far; a long journey is what he calls a route which may be longer than the way the crow flies or the straight and narrow of the Via Appia, but which is still, with all its detours, shorter than we had expected.[70] It should have been obvious: Horace is up to his usual tricks in this satire, erring on the side of discretion in deciding when to call it a day. Even before he hurtles to the close, the longeurs creep in: bread is described as *longe pulcherrimus* (89, 'by far the finest'); the journey becomes a *longum iter* (94–5, 'long journey'). Such a prematurely shortened ending is both consistent with Horace's other satires, where asides like *ne longum faciam* (1.3.137)—'to cut a long story short'—signal instant breaking-off,[71] and with this satire so far, which has been one long string of truncations and curtailments.

For a start, Horace's body has gone through a series of parallel frustrations: he has to starve himself out of dinner, after the attack of water poisoning; then gets a cold welcome at Beneventum, where a fire in the kitchen separates the greedy guests from their skinny thrushes; sexual disappointment ends in a wet dream; and, all along, conjunctivitis blinds Horace to the sights on his route. *lippus,* the word he uses of his sore eyes (30), is usually an insult he levels at deranged Stoics, gossips in barber shops, or people who cannot see

[69] On the endings of Latin poems, see Fowler (1989a: 75–122). Line 104 might recall Ennius, *Annals* 542W, *Brundisium pulcro praecinctum praepete portu,* and momentarily excite hopes that a topographical description is to follow.

[70] Barnes (1988): at *Od.* 3.4.2 Horace uses *longum . . . melos* unironically of a long poem.

[71] Cf. 1.1.95: *non longa est fabula.*

their own faults.[72] Is Horace telling us here that he himself is an imperfect Epicurean or, ironically, that he is not going to leak any gossip about his friends in high places or recall the sights of the journey, despite dropping names like Maecenas and Heliodorus?

It is a strange coincidence that many other people involved in this story are in some way deformed or impaired, particularly in their vision. The man who built the Via Appia was blind; along the way, Horace meets the one-eyed mayor, Luscus, and of course a Cyclops. The narrator of Cicero's digression on wit was called Strabo, the Squinter, a name he shares with the geographer who helps us plot Horace's route. The last figure in the poem is a circumcised Jew.[73] *olim truncus eram*, 'Once I was a trunk', says Horace, posing as Priapus in Satire 8. Is he still a truncated satirist in these poems, mutilated like Messius Cicirrus, a cock without his coxcomb? If I choose, I can ride to Tarentum on a mule, he says in Satire 6, but the mule in question is a clipped or castrated one.

All these images are meant to warn us that we are not destined to leave Horace's satires like the contented dinner-guest in Satire 1, the *conuiua satur* (1.1.119). In his last Satire, 2.8, frustrated guests leave the table unfilled, in a poem that is constructed as an unfinished play.[74] Horace will always leave us prematurely disappointed. As a satirist he is disarmed, unable to fulfil his proper function. The journey poem is a chart full of circumscriptions, suggesting all the constraints that have led modern satire to be rerouted.

The poem deceives us by stopping short, but it is a false ending in another sense too. The book does not end here, and this line is followed immediately by a recapitulation, as if after a digression. Horace seems to have complete freedom of movement, but it is really as though he has been released on bail: at the end of the poem he must go back to Rome and face his civic responsibilities.[75] He begins

---

[72] Cf. 1.1.120; 1.7.3; 1.3.25.

[73] See Pisani (1953: 18) on Apella (100) as a name that means 'circumcised'.

[74] See Gowers (1993: 178–9).

[75] See above n. 55 on examples of ties and bonds in the poem. Bail is one aspect of the shadow of the law-courts that hangs over the satires as a whole: cf. 1.1.11 *datis uadibus qui rure extractus in urbem est*; 1.9.36–7 *et casu tunc respondere uadato | debebat.*

Satire 6 and the second half of his *Sermones* with a throwback to
Satire 1: *Non quia, Maecenas*..., 'It's not because, Maecenas...'.[76]
The miniature Odyssey of Satire 5[77] is followed immediately by a
longer satire, as Horace plays with his own principles about
keeping within limits.[78] So the finality of the ending is ironic in
two opposite ways.

For the Romans, it is true, Brundisium existed primarily as a point
of departure. But if the embassy that the poem records is meant to be
Maecenas' journey to Greece in 38 BCE, it still leaves us and Horace
stranded in a cul-de-sac. Even today this port is not worth the detour,
it may have been full of eastern promise (Aulus Gellius tells us he
rummaged in second-hand shops there, and picked up scruffy old
books of real travellers' tales, of men with heads beneath their
shoulders),[79] but on its own it was the ultimate blind alley—an
appropriately indefinite ending for a poem that stops short of its
full potential and turns out to have been a shaggy dog story all along.
Like the anonymous town whose longs and shorts are too bumpy
even for prosy satire, there are things Horace cannot name in verse,
only point to by signs. If there is to be a Magna Charta, he is saying, it
is too big for this small piece of paper, and *ars breuis, uia longa* will be
his motto.[80]

---

[76] Cf. 1.1.1: *Qui fit, Maecenas*...; cf. 1.1.108: *illuc unde abii redeo*; and Cic. *Fam.*
12.15.5: *redeamus unde diuertimus.*

[77] The endings (*-que...-que* 104) are mock Homeric. For the *Odyssey* as a
proverbially long-winded narrative, see Leutsch-Schneidewin, *Corpus Paroem.
Graec.* I 210.8, II 13.79 and Barnes (1988).

[78] Cf. 1.1.106: *sunt certi denique fines | quos ultra citraque nequit consistere rectum*;
1.1.92: *denique sit finis quaerendi.* The joke may have been improved by the visual effect
of seeing this very definite ending followed at once by a new beginning on the same page
of the next one (John Henderson points this out to me). Cf. *uerbum non amplius addam*
(*Sat.* 1.1.121), followed immediately by Satire 2. Van Sickle (1980: 4–42) suggests that
an ancient book-roll could be as long or as short as the author wanted (7) and that the
last column of a poem was usually shared with the beginning of the next poem (6).
I cannot see any particular reason for the length of 1.5 (104 lines), though the number
is almost an average of the total length of the 10 satires (1,030 lines).

[79] Gell. *A.N.* 9.4.1.

[80] I am grateful for the criticisms and suggestions from the audience at the
Philological Society meeting at which this paper was first delivered, and to Ted
Kenney and Edmund Thomas for advice and encouragement at various stages.
I should like to thank Richard Hunter and the anonymous referee for their very
helpful comments.

POSTSCRIPT, 2008

In a more recent paper I have adjusted and supplemented some of the views stated here. See 'Horace, Satires I: the Ends of the Beginning', in *Perceptions of Horace: A Roman Poet and his Readers*, ed. L. Houghton and M. Wyke, Cambridge (forthcoming).

7

Be Alert (Your Country Needs Lerts): Horace, *Satires* 1.9[1]

John Henderson

You see me on the street you always act surprised
You say howareyougoodluck but you don't mean it

When you know as well as me you'd rather see me paralysed
Why don't you just come out once and scream it?[2]

1. THE GR*IN OF THE P**T'S V*CE: SATIRE[3]

Who is that man with the handshake? Don't you know...
He is an onlooker, a heartless type,
Whose hobby is giving everyone else the lie.[4]

This chapter returns to the triumviral traumas of the 30s, focussing on the last piece proper in Horace's first poetry collection, *Satires* 1, just the retrospective epilogue to come. In this poem 9 (too lengthy to reproduce here), Horace writes down an anecdote starring Horace, which also releases a controlled 'leak' from the palace (of Octavian Caesar's closest associate Maecenas); and leaves readers an ironical but pithy reflection on buttonholing and social climbing, as moral

---

[1] 'No. We have too many lerts—be aloof', etc.: Nash (1985) 46. 'Don't be afraid! Your country doesn't need fraids!': Chiaro (1992) 36.

[2] Dylan (1971 = 1965) 'Positively Fourth Street'.

[3] After Barthes (1981) + Goldhill (1991).

[4] MacNeice (1966 = 1941–4) 210, 'The Satirist'.

182   *John Henderson*

(ized) *vademecum*—the kit a networker needs to negotiate the baffling circuitry of power at Rome. This text, besides, composes a poetic
(of 'anti-aesthetic' plebeian vigour adapting Callimachean angularity
and litotes, not without paradox).[5] But this is also programmed as
Satire, made from the dia-logic-al exchange of *sermo*, the conversational interaction presented within the story. And in the political
stake of its legibility are wagered the purchase of discourse and
conversation analysis, pragmatics, narratology, new rhetoric, social
semiotics, patronage theory, and a welter of cultural history concerns
and techniques. Satire in its element, out casing the streets, frames
civic discourse as the (in)effectual *locus* of cultural politics;[6] it checks
out (reads) our reading of sociality—challenges us to do our worst.
These days, the piece is commonly seen as a '*Schwätzersatire*' that
progressively reveals itself to be, rather, an '*Erfolgsjägersatire*': the
once traditional 'Bore' has (significantly) been re-dubbed 'Pest'.[7]
But nothing ventured, nothing gained: only if the *jeu* of the exchange
within the poem between its characters is circuited into the exchange
between the narration and its reader(s) will it bite. In construing
Roman culture, we are positioned by *our* construal of 'culture', and
the provocation of Horace's writing-and-thinking means to commit
us, within our contestation of cultural stakes.

In *sermo* (no, don't mock), social actors liaise civic relations in the
polity, their discourse dares read people, and the way that people read
each other—reading *this* Rome, they and we check out reading—and
reading-culture:

Until around the beginning of the twentieth century, laughter is generally
treated as a response to other people's 'minor' faults.... The 'we'
who dissociate ourselves from faulty 'comic' characters are regarded as a

---

[5] Freudenburg (1993) 208–11, after Buchheit (1968); cf. ch. 5. On 1.9: esp. Latacz
(1980), Anderson (1982 = 1956), Rudd (1961), Lefèvre (1993) 52–4.

[6] Shotter (1993). 'Politics partly consists in the disputes and struggles which occur
in language and over language' (Fairclough (1989) 23). Gender politics: Henderson
(1999) ch. 7; triumviral politics: DuQuesnay (1984) 52f.; Henderson (1998a) ch. 3,
on *Serm.* 1.7.

[7] *Erfolgsjägersatire*: Büchner (1961 = 1962), cf. Di Benedetto (1980–1) 396, Latacz
(1980) esp. 16 n. 32. *Bore*: Rudd (1961); but Rudd (1982[2] = 1966) 74, 'I shall call him
"*the pest*"'. Shackleton-Bailey (1982) 20 produces 'The "bore", who is really a vulgar
place-hunter'; Latacz (1980) works reflectively through a century's readings of the
poem's sketch of a '*Karrierist*'.

pre-existing, not discursively constituted, unified group. The position of the audience is assumed to be singular, their interest in what constitutes 'good society' identical, the correctness of their views an absolute given, not a constructed confirmation. Within these approaches the ideological effectiveness of comedy is clearly indexed, but not treated as a dynamic process requiring interrogation.[8]

In short, Satiric othering of The Pest by The Poet stains (us) more than 'we' used to acknowledge. They have more in common, much more, than class-status once allowed; and we have, too:

Since critics commonly refer to Pope's victims as 'The Dunces,' it is worth emphasizing that few of them actually deserve that name, or at least they deserve it no more than most modern academics.[9]

Out on the block, there is no guaranteed, secure or authorised closure, so, yes, this performance *is* jovial jollity, but it turns on the unpleasantness of pleasantries, and raids the mall of self-promotion for the swag of malice. The charming 'Pest satire' tells how A Funny thing happened to poor dear Flaccus on the way to the Forum, but it also fills your head with an inner monologue of suppressed contempt, over-dubbed so we can only hear the sound-track of our own self-congratulation. We're out there, but screaming inside.

(This) *Satire* centres on 'innuendo and squint', the body-language of impolite *inuidia* (spite; vv. 64f., *nutans,* | *distorquens oculos*). It 'bespeaks (showcases ~ signifies more and other than can be named?) malicious wit (naughty wit ~ nasty salt in wounds?), sarcastic mockery (cheerful grin ~ withering derision?), and fake innocence (averting the gaze ~ hiding everything, even hiding hiding)' (65f., *male salsus* | *ridens dissimulare*). At core, the satiric world gets your goat, as 'visceral pain' bursts through civilised repression (66, *iecur urere bilis*). All is *Angst, ennui,* nausea: 'sickening evil eye' and 'noisome petomania' (25, *inuideat,* 70, *oppedere,* 70). 'Whispered imprecations, raging madness' (11f., *o te cerebri* | *felicem, aiebam tacitus*). Names hound victims, tongues wag death-wishes (11, 25, *Bolane, Hermogenes*; 38, 47, *interearn, disperearn*). Scarring the

---

[8] Purdie (1993) 150.
[9] Damrosch (1987) 123. Cf. Freudenburg (1993) 208, 'The satirist is not far from the pest whom he despises.'

memory, black-magic witchery-pokery palms off 'gypsy curses on another bright spark' (29f., *puero cecinit... anus... dira*): 'poison is in, knives are out—plague, racking pestilence and maiming impend, spiked feet for another Oedipus' lingering demise' (31f., *uenena... ensis... laterum dolor... tussis... tarda podagra*). We join in, pelt Aunt Sally, get rid of our hate: our nastiness. (Just love it.) Here we go, hitting the Sacred Way, where citizens at large treat each other as aliens, the enemy within (32, *hosticus*). On Desecration Row, the sweet-talking veneer peels away in a trice, to expose 'sour abuse and yelled insult as the reality behind all the billing and cooing of social graces' (4f., 38, 41, 72; 76f., *dulcissime rerum... suauiter; si me amas; sodes; ignosces; tu turpissime, magna | inclamat uoce... clamor*). The satirist prowls his own backyard, the city-centre public space owned by masculist prerogative; patrimony of the free (adult, citizen, Re-public).[10] *He* sees, neither 'blocks or parishes', the living landmark details around which communities come into being, nor the wonders of the imperial 'metropolis', Rome's cosmocratic totality (13, *garriret, uicos, urbem laudaret*), but specimens from the human menagerie, the denizen who steps from the crowd, cranky and idiosyncratic as all the rest. One under every stone...

...and one in every skull. Not saccharine ecphrasis, not pleasant encomium, but tough-talking rudeness, hard-boiled hypocrisy. Face it: in this modernity of rat-race cynicism, unabashed elbowing up the heap, poetry is, exactly, prostitution, snobbery and social climbing. The system is a scrabble for patronage, the reclusive billionaire targetted by jail-bait hoodlums, petty crime as first training for, then route to, the top of the laureate pops. The stupidity of self, self, self. And fame. All ends badly, in unsavoury scenes of riot, public outcry, scandalous publicity: black maria ignominy and pantomime farce (77f.).

To write (literature), one must serve. One must ingratiate oneself, pay court, display oneself, show off one's stylistic muscles... suck up to, wheedle, and wait upon, one has to sell oneself. Disgusting!... Who knows whether it is

---

[10] 'The impassive stroller (who) symbolizes the privilege or freedom to move about in the public arenas of the city observing but never interacting, consuming the sights through a controlling but rarely acknowledged gaze': Pollock (1988) 67–75, cf. Henderson (1989) and below. Horace promenades through the Forum: 6.113f.; contrast the displaced persons and outlaws of 1.7, the furtive females abashed in 1.8.

not worse than normal, straightforward prostitution, which at least does not put on airs, pretending to high condition, untouchability, precious virtue![11]

There! Civility is a veneer, those manners that make Man. Or, rather, that's the veneer of Satire, and we know it to be critical, hypercritical, bad criticism—way off-beam. We know that, whatever else, Satire satirizes the satirist and satirizes the genre of Satire, turns on itself and on the consciousness of its voice and its readers. Its mark and mask is *self-*mockery. It would matter if the rictus of Satire spoke true, but the distortion of its perspective always risks (courts) objection: it is, before all, a matter of reception whether 'Satire' is an apt ascription, diagnosis, or denigration of any particular representation.[12] The *modality* of a performance so accused (= 'The set of ways that the meanings of texts are keyed in to structures of meanings outside them in such a way as to command or disclaim belief')[13] is the all-important determinant.

2. THE WA*KING MUSE[14]

My evil twin bad-weather friend he always wants to start when
    I want to begin...
I know he looks like me hates work like me and walks like me he's
    even got a twin like me
My evil twin bad-weather friend I know some day I'll meet him
    but I don't know where or when[15]

In the case of Lucilian *satura,* in or out of Horace's velvet hands, 'if the cap fits, wear it' (1.1.69f., *mutato nomine de te | fabula narratur*). Satire is forever 'in denial', since its scapegoat victims, chosen because they threaten, or threaten to threaten, our identity by looking all too like us, are *eo ipso* handed a power over our thoughts that we

[11] Lem (1979) 114f., 'Raymond Seurat: *Toi'.*
[12] Cf. Purdie (1993) 115, Howes (1986).
[13] Hodge (1990) 10, cf. 143–51, 'Problematizing modality'.
[14] After Freudenburg (1993).
[15] They Might Be Giants (1992) 'My evil twin'.

must refuse to acknowledge: as we hug our discontent, we are sure (worried) there will be no changing places here (1.1.16–19). Our dis/ like is normally projected away against *the name* as reification, objectivisation and control of the other, and Satire dares name names or is not Satire:[16] but this sketch precisely flags the name as absent, withheld, silenced (3, *quidam notus mihi nomine tantum*). The skit *à deux* leaves just the one who need never have their name declared: namely, oneself. All attempts to nominalize, categorize, classify, label, fix the Other must outdo the narrative, which entirely eschews sobriquet, nickname or brickbat, and tellingly dramatizes the stigmatization by epithet which it refrains from authorizing (v. 75, *turpissime*: from the lips of the extra). Readers regularly isolate tight-lipped Horace on his cloud, taking *nescioquid meditans nugarum* (2), to include or indicate a 'reverie of creativity' issuing in (verse such as) this very (self-deprecating, Callimachean) slip of a poem. The poem dreams up a *quidam* 'A. N. Other', and Horace will point him out exclusively, and no less than seven times over, as plain *ille* / (6, 12– 13—where the mannerism is underlined, 21, 41, 61, 74).[17]

Horace, then, fights with his shadow[18]—and fans (keeps live-feeds-tends-nourishes) the 'bad press' of *phthónos*, that price of fame, that (sometimes) deadly game of paparazzo power playing around, and playing around with, social charisma:

> (Whispered voices)
> —Heh, heh, heh. This is a story about *your friend and mine*.
> —Who is it?
> —Who is it?
> (Sung)

---

[16] Contrast Henderson (1989) on 1.2, esp. 126, *do nomen quodlibet illi*, Henderson (1998a) chapter 3 on 1.7. Poem 3 is even *on* naming ∼ name-calling (esp. 42–54); 1.1 at once *practises* naming as the core of enculturation, (e.g. 103f., *auarum ... uappam . . . ac nebulonem*). Cf. LaFleur (1981). A gremlin in the press systematically erased one word wherever it appeared in the original of this essay, and once or twice my proof-reading failed to restore it: the word was ... 'Horace'!

[17] This is self-reflexivity incarnate and engrossed, large as life: *totus in* '*ille*"s! (*illis* |, 2). For *ill-* |, cf. esp. 7.25, 2.126, 3.57, in a distribution of: 1.1 × 2, 1.2 × 7, 1.3 × 5, 1.4 × 4; *vs.* 1.5 × 1, 1.6 × 1, 1.7 × 1, 1.8 × 0, 1.10 × 1; *vs.* 1.9 × 10. On name-calling as sticking like napalm, cf. Sornig (1989) 100. Horace's 'determined thinking before he writes—and mum's the word': 4.137f.

[18] Oliensis (1991) 119 compares Horace's epodic fight out of his paper bag Canidia, and *her* twin *carmina*, to boot.

There you stand with your L.A. tan
With your New York walk
And your New York talk... [19]

Who was it 'wormed his way in' to the world run by the winners (the World)? Not 'Honest John' Horace, he insists: a P**t you could hardly confuse with a P**t![20] Truly, this relationship is symbiotic as language. Language, that is, in its contemporary ('Bakhtinian') understanding as a saturated dialogism in which 'we imagine to ourselves what the speaker wishes to say', always oriented to the uttered move, and already anticipating its reply. Framed by our placing of who is speaking and what is speaking them—a matter beyond individualising 'characterisation' or ethopoeia; rather, the valorization of a topology of social/political relations.[21] In the zero-sum tussle of verbal interaction, 'the speaker listens and the listener speaks', together modelling respect through attention, or subjugating the lumpen other by infringing their (your) proper turn to speak. We negotiate the exchange of the power of identity, running the gauntlet between our competing wishes to be given our head, and be given approval. Life, cackles Satire, is the inept collision of oral with anal, the big-talking P**t who takes too much, gives and has too little for return, opposite the 'loof P**t who holds back from exchange, just acquires and hoards.[22]

The poem—it is *Horace*'s poem—constructs for its caricature a 'stylistic physiognomy', a personal vo*ce; but this within a specific arena of rank, distance, affinity. A régime of politesse speaks through both actors. Self-denial and restraint promise weak solidarity as acknowledgements of each other's importance; but in the same move the minimal parade of affinity ensures that difference in status

---

[19] John Lennon (1974) 'Steel and glass', a (deadly) self-caricature, as hero/target.

[20] Worming: Shackleton-Bailey (1982) 20. The Horatian *qui s'excuse s'accuse*: Bernstein (1992) 41. Swallowing the self-exoneration: e.g. DuQuesnay (1984) 53, Braund (1992a) 21.

[21] *Bakhtin*: e.g. (1986) 95, cf. Leith and Myerson (1989) 12, Pechey (1989) 47, Tannen (1989) 12. ~~Characterization~~: Holquist (1990) 63.

[22] Quote: Holquist (1986) 63, cf. Tannen (1989) 12. Turn-taking/turn-infringing: Pocock (1984) 35. Brown and Levinson (1987) 13, on 'Negative face' and (wait for it) 'Positive face'; cf. Goffman (1972), Kendon, Schlegoff, etc., in Drew and Wootton (1988). Runs/hoards: Purdie (1993) 105.

is, all along, at issue.[23] This clash or buzz of personality is (also) a
scorpion-dance of rhetorical strategy: conversation boxes the polity
into stereotype crates, as it norms and polices the terms for orderly
behaviour.[24] So can we tell the score? Does *ille* get it right (like 'us'),
since 'our' discreet silence is a life-form denied him and every would-
be climber? Or is *our* evasive anti-language just one (more) way not
to face up to thinking out loud, and is *his* pesky self-declaration
engagingly up front—along the lines of: 'Yippee I'm a poet and I
know it | Hope I don't blow it'?[25] To defer peremptory diagnosis of
The Pest as a cartoon Mr Ambition,[26] be a lert, and *listen*:

Through the fiction of the 'virtual offence', or 'worst possible reading',
politeness presumes as it disarms potential aggression: by orienting to the
'virtual offence', an offender can display that (they have) the other's interests
at heart.[27]

An approacher must make the running, opening the sequence with a
liaison-hungry greeting formula to elicit a first, functional return to
make a non-committal 'adjacency pair'; then, or already, feelers are
put out: 'Do I know you/am I talking to you/are you one of us? And:
What do you want/do we have business/is this an offer? At once, the
stakes of 'reading': was that a put-off/do you want me to be more
direct/is this something we need to *say*?[28]

I have looked all over the town for the Autodidact. He can't possibly have
gone home. He must be walking about at random, filled with shame and
horror, that poor humanist whom men don't want any more.[29]

[23] See Hodge and Kress (1988) 45, 123.
[24] Cf. Quasthoff (1989) esp. 186. Conversation as 'practical metadiscourse': Taylor (1992) 11.
[25] Dylan (1964) 'I shall be free no. 10'. Cf. Jaworski (1992) 122–5, 109 on these silences: 146—they can be walls/bridges, and/or gad-flies, 49. Hodge and Kress (1993) 77 on defensive shutters. Connor (1987) 103 for the Pest as 'disarming' and 'wry' to *tell* Horace that he's after Maecenas *through Horace*.
[26] e.g. DuQuesnay (1984) 52: *industria*, no *fides*, self-interest above law and before civic duty; Rudd (1982) 78.
[27] Brown and Levinson (1987) 1, after E. Goffman.
[28] 'Illocutionary structure': Hatim and Mason (1990) 76–8, 82–92. Greetings and adjacency: Leith and Myerson (1989) 120f., Jaworski (1992) 56, Brown and Levinson (1987) 40. What is assumed: Holquist (1990) 61. The *cliché*: Zijderveld (1979) esp. 50.
[29] Sartre (1965) 228.

3. TELLING TALES OUT OF COURT: *SERMO*

When he had gone, I thought of a splendid answer I ought to have
given him.[30]

There are two batches of dialogue. The latter, with A Dear Friend (vv.
62–72), recapitulates in momentary miniature the former, an exchange with The Other, but Horace now takes the lead, where earlier
he was the one approached (4–60). The second discourse effectively
terminates the first, though only as a fluke, and despite itself! In the
exchange with *ille*, five 'rounds' are scripted. We now explore them,
up close: see the whites of their eyes (our 'I''s).

1. The 'greeting' is plain/colloquial (v. 4, *quid agis…?*). Of itself
neither clearly a phatic nod requiring just reciprocation, nor de-
claredly a pre-sequence 'feeler'; but when *are* greetings formulaic,
'just' greetings—and not, for instance, anticipatory seizure of the
initiative, promising 'face-threatening' push in the turn-taking
ahead?[31] Honorific name, or hypocorism, is lacking (contrast
Horace's own, inaugural version of The Approach, *Qui fit*, Maecenas,…, 1.1.1), but the routine phrase is topped up with a heartily
individualised flourish of superlative affect: 'Howyadoin', my fave in
all the world' (v. 4, *dulcissime rerum*). The reply is immediate, but
calmer, 'Nicely' (5, *suauiter*), and superstitiously, formulaically, unassuming—but warning in undertone that the exchange is momen-
taneous, over before it is begun, a memo to self: '—right now' (5, *ut
nunc est*). To make up for the un-called superlative, Horace throws in
an under-whelming but verbally unreserved blessing on the person's
houses, 'And I wish you all you want' (5, *et cupio omnia quae uis*): all-
embracing, all-, that is, *except* the actual person and his actual
priorities! Horace's supplementary 'Nothing I can do for you?' (6,
num quid uis?) repairs his first reaction's lack of even lip-service
interest in the other's existence—yet the strongly negative phrasing,
and salient rhyme with the first reply, at once undo any such gesture.
 A dozen words, by now, for four, but nine of them are monosyllables: nothing to set next to the carting over of the generous chunk

---

[30] Grossmith (1945: 1892) 13f.   [31] See Bodenheimer (1984) 264–75.

dulcissime + *rerum*. *Ille* now heeds the interrogative form of Horace's preemptive leave-taking formula, not its sense: brisk-and-brusque, he sums himself up in two shortest of phrases in apposition, no frill, no approach-work, just zero-degree verbiage: 'You know us, we're a PhD' (7, *noris nos . . . docti sumus*). He risks mockery for failing, or refusing, to understand Horace's drift, but means to bind his language to his would-be fellow's: his grammar proposes that they become a 'we', indeed they already 'are a we', *sumus*. Horace's second over-and-out matches, echoes, drowns these four words, while his final word, the verb 'to be', shifts the present away into deferral, and open dissolve: 'All the more for me you'll be' (7f., *pluris* | *hoc, inquam, mihi eris* ∼ 7, *noris nos, inquit, docti sumus*). Posing as if joining the other with encouragement, shared enthusiasm, he puts him down: he wasn't noticing at all (*hoc*), but detaching himself, as if *ille* had meant his *nos* to continue, *minus Horace*, in an exclusively 'royal we' (*nos . . . -i sumus*). This is rudeness: imputing the worst construction.

2. The second joust arises out of a pantomime of one-way communication and counter-communication. *Ille* tells Horace all about Horace, sees/is not fooled: what he is at and what he has on his mind (14–16, *cupis* ∼ *cupio, nil agis* -◡ ◡-◡ | ∼ *quid agis* -◡ ◡-◡ |), he seizes the future (*tenebo . . . persequar* ∼ *eris*), seizes the moment (*nunc . . . est* ∼ *nunc est*), masters Horace's ironic 'to me' with his emphatic jab 'well, for you' (*mihi* ∼ *at tibi*). Horace fights fire with fire: *his* initial *nil* out-emphasises the other's *nil*; then he hands *ille* something he 'doesn't know' (17, *non tibi notum*); if Horace has been 'wanting to run, for ages now', that is beggared by the 'long' hike ahead (*longe*), and the mighty river to cross. *Ille* will stick to Horace, so Horace (says he) will stretch his, or their, legs—and in the process *tells* his butt he is 'pulling' one of *his* ('conning' him: 18, *circumagi*). *Ille* serves back all he has received: re-doubles the exchange of 'nothings' with 'and no' (14–19, *nil, nil, nil, nil . . . et non*); he repeats his 'doing's, answering for himself the friendly question that was never put back to him (15, 19, *agis, agam* ∼ 4, *quid agis?*); he is not deflected by Horace's run-around (15, 19, *usque, usque*), but 'chases' him by 'chasing up' his own words (16, 19, *persequar, sequar*). To pay Horace back for starting with (satirical) echo of his (satirical) finish, in the depersonalized phrasing that holds an addressee a thing at

arm's length, he now ends by clobbering Horace's final monosyllable with his own staccato (16–19, *nunc iter est tibi* ∼ *nil opus est te* | ∼ *sequar te* |). Horace made no denial of the other's reading of his rudeness, clear as a book: he didn't bother to comment; his partner made no bones about it, coming on like a pimp from the pages of Plautus, or a fan dogging Socrates' every Platonic step. But if this is jovially strenuous 'courting' (= determined self-promotion), it is also his attempt to get Horace to 'know' him, to speak what he is, how he wants to be seen. Just as he had promised from the word go (*docti sumus*). And the poet has just handed him his chance to prove he means it, challenged his stickability. Just how 'close' will he get to those faraway royal gardens, the true destination of Horace's lie with the truth, over the bridge to Caesar and apotheosis? (v. 18) Who could the mysterious, magnetic invalid be, to draw Horace clean out of Rome? Worth tagging along for the ride, just on the off-chance? *Ille* keeps his counsel, concentrates rapid-fire phrases on the *dynamics* of the encounter, 'You/me/you/me/you . . . I/I/I/I/ You' (14–19). Horace's words look far, far away, to find a scene minus *ille*; mean time, *ille*—who do you think 'I am'?—lets us see that someone round here is 'feebleness' on legs, and it isn't him! (19, *non sum piger*).

3. The third snatch of dialogue has the man try again, risking an approach behind the genteelness of a conditional . . . brag ('If I know me', v. 22, *si bene me noui*). He returns to his theme, the offer of his 'acquaintance' (*me noui*), takes over Horace's own words and bends them to spell their opposite: not a never-never future, and a bogus offer to value the guy, but a strenuously meiotic promise to win his esteem, in a strictly concrete future (7f., *pluris* | *hoc . . . mihi eris* ∼ 22f., *non V. pluris amicum* | *non V. facies*). Obstinate ass's ears hear him cap this with yet 'more' fom his file (more extravagant litotes), the man with the mostest: 'just you wait for churning out poetry against the clock, come groovy dancing, crooning past Crosby' (22–5). This *Egito* blurts in musical tricolon, puts his hero (Hermogenes) up alongside Horace's poet-friends and -geniuses, rolled into this one *victor ludorum*: call me Mr Vers(e)atile. The same words show he has *both* much *and* zilch in common with Horace—'who more?' (22–5).

Horace interrupts before any gesture of liaison gets made, for *Ille* has answered his own pseudo-questions, cashing them out as exclamatory in force. Horace butts in to take his turn, hooking onto the final flourish of self-plumping (*ego canto* |). But his abjection of *ille* into some more indirect phrasing is at once dismantled, with a firm 'I'—'I am power, I can kill, I decide who lives' (16, 27, *est tibi...* ~ *te...est opus* ~ 27f., *haud mihi...composui*). Whatever Horace was leading into, a switch of topic harking back to greetings and leave-taking, perhaps some information, *gratis*, perhaps a health warning, the pre-launch signal of a tirade in the offing, or even murder in mind, who can tell?[32] The other says no and no it is, Horace's lead is peremptorily nullified: 'No way' (*haud*), and *ille* has taken total control, with his end-of-the-line kiss of 'death' (*omnis composui*).

4. Automatic-fire interchange comes next (vv. 38–41). A second conditional overture-formula introduces an imperative, a brief request for 'brief assistance' (38, *si me amas...paulum hic ades* ~ 22, *si bene me noui...amicum*): this is uncompromisingly refused in another grammatically conditional locution (*interam si*). *Ille* is blocked with a rash of cop-outs which say he must make allowances for wetness, he doesn't 'know' where Horace is at, he does 'know' he can't stop even for a moment (39f.). Now for a momentary *pas de deux*, as the nuisance will not take no for an answer. He opens up his 'dilemma' to the other, but only to sweep doubt aside, in another strong negation sure of the future—almost in the same breath (*quid faciam* ⌣- |, *non faciam* ⌣- |). He puts his foot down, expressing momentary uncertainty before bossing his victim, in no uncertain terms. Horace is still his mark.

5. From the point of Horace's 'submission' (v. 43, *sequor*), the fifth and final colloquy runs in a block of solid speech (vv. 43–60: spaced by just 44, *hinc repetit*, introducing the tableau, and 50, *inquam*, underlining a 'strong' point). The two voices intertwine and even run together.[33]

---

[32] Cf. Bogaert (1963), Rudd (1961) 81 n. 9, Shackleton-Bailey (1982) 21. Most akin are 26f., *est tibi mater,* | *cognati, quis te saluo est opus* ~ 1.84f., *non uxor saluum te uult, non filius...*(cf. 20f., 59f., *ut...asellus* |*...onus, nil sine magno...labore* ~ 1.88–90 *nullo...labore...ut si quis asellum* |*...*, cf. 6.99, *onus*).

[33] Especially in a text with neither modern punctuation nor speech-marks: apportioning lines in vv. 44–5 is an ancient crux (Rudd (1982) 285 n. 54).

Ille now takes the lead, and at once gets to the point, the 'name' he homes on *through* Horace (tecum), Maecenas. No call to spell it out or beat about the bush. The new topic educes compliments, and a comprehensive assertion in another negated comparative under-statement (44f., *nemo dexterius* ∼ 22, *non... pluris*); then comes a suitably tentative, unpushy application for an entrée, set out as a hypothetical conditional with attractively energetic *anastrophae* (twisted word-order: *haberes... uelles si; posset qui... hunc hominem uelles si*). Banging his own drum, he offers 'himself as heroic aide' (46). Horace should take a tip from Maecenas, realise what a stroke of luck he is handed on his plate, and look no further for his own Man Friday. Once he has reached for his conditional, he follows up with an asseveration modelled on Horace's riposte to his first request, for assistance in person (47, *si... dispeream ni* | ∼ 37, *si... interean si* |). In his categorical way, he sees his new boss cutting emphatic swathes through the also-rans, levering himself, and of course his new protégé, 'past all-comers': leaving all for dead (48, *summosses omnis*, 48 ∼ 28, *omnis composui*).

'Maecenas—how're you with him?' (43) is where *ille* gets the anecdote to its point. There is no warrant *in the text* for the traditional assumption that Horace has all along been just the smart way to the Great Man, so that storming Horace is just the preliminary objective, and only now do we move on to the master-plan. If, but only if, *ille* knows as much about Horace as *vice versa*, then (we readers through poems 1–8, and chapter 7, must presume) he has to know the answer already (*viz.* Horace belongs to (= has captured) Maecenas), and must be letting Horace know that he is set on storming the salubrious Esquiline. Anyhow, the reply blanks out the interlocutor and his (derisory) notions, as mention of Maecenas, and imputation to Horace of brazen ambition, make this 'Priapus' put his foot down, with his own emphatic volley of 'No, no way, nowt!' (48–50, *non, nec... ulla... | nec, nil*). He gets the Second Person out of the reckoning, and dwells instead on the *domus*. Away from verbal arm-wrestling with *ille*, to visions of the ambience where only the great and the good hang out, where the mentality of grubby scrabbling is anathema: the in-crowd. The thought sends Horace down a row of three assertions about his world (*est, est, est*), to a final nugget of gnomic authority, 'each person is a cog in the wheel' (= ~~rivalry~~ and ~~competition~~). In Maecenas' palace (and through the topic of Maecenas' place), obstacles such as The P*st that get in Horace's sacred path cease entirely to figure.

This has all been downright rude finger-wagging: pretending to admire 'a Grand Theme, a modern marvel', *ille* labels it 'a Tall Tale— pull the other one' (52, *magnum narras, uix credibile*). As satirist, as voice of spite, as Mr Commonsense, he and we know it stinks, for all the forthcoming asseveration from Horace (53, 56, *habet, habet*: both last words). *Ille* wants in Horace's dream, he's just learned that Nirvana is round the next bend, and exclaimed 'A heroic Saga! How amazing!' Not unnaturally, he had supposed like everyone else that the éminence sat atop a stratified pyramid of staff, interposed between the vertical grades from serf up to courtier. Now he's being assured that he can skip all that, if only he can get his toe in the door (54–6). He is 'egged on', as he spots (53, *accendis*), and for a second time is promised a future of success dependent only on his own positive qualities (54f., *uelis tantummodo... expugnabis*). Horace greases his compliments, no matter how (in)sincere, but actually he's promising more 'instant rebuffs', as modelled in the poem by the stone-walling P*et (56, *difficilis aditus primos*). *Ille* walks onto the punch—because his persistence has paid off, he has finally winkled Horace's secret out of him. He's thrilled: he is now off Horace's case because (he believes) he has been shown how the normal 'broking' system of commendation (47, *tradere*) can be finessed.[34]

This syncopated exploration of the negotiations between the two Poets means to bin securely antithetical and polarized readings which entirely miss the dialogical charge of the poem in order to whitewash Horace ('with infinite patience and tact'), and blackball The Pest ('a tiresome and insistent acquaintance').[35] Courtesy of Satire, we have seen, the twosome share their limelight/prey on each other. This is so in *ille's* last stand, still. Which is also his finest hour. Confident as ever, he maps out his future, in a rhythmically intensified spate of enthusiasm, a fourfold chain of assertion (57–60, *corrumpam* -∪∪-- |, *quaeram* |, | *occurram, deducam* -∪∪--|) and triply downright negation (*haud, non... desistam* -∪∪--|, *nil*).[36] The meiosis at work in *non... desistam* stands finally as the 'motto' of the entire representation of *ille*: 'to leech forever'. He is 'at one, still, with his

---

[34] Johnson and Dandeker (1990) 226.
[35] Copley (1969) 150.   [36] Cf. Rudd (1982) 78.

autonomous *Egito'* (56, *haud mihi deero*). With more litotes (*nil sine* ...), he puts on heroic style again (59, *magno* ~ 52, 62, *magnum*), and winds up with spick-and-span gnomic self-authorisation of his own (59f. ~ 51f.).

What this Well-Respected Man about Town has said may prove he has taken the satirist's bait; but it is good bait, *by Horace's own lights*. To bribe the slaves, keep on keeping on through whatever rejections, waiting for the right moment, bumping into the great man on walkabout, to dance on him along his (sacred) way (57–9). All this is, true, what *ille* has just been through *with Horace*, whether we *or* Horace see this as successful or not. The words put in his mouth are *not* pretty talk, but they read as self-mocking banter as easily as self-condemnatory awfulness. We *know* it's 'true'—an accurate précis, couched for sure in vigorously straight street-fighting terms, but sensible and as culturally 'true' as any of Horace's representations of Rome. Just the way it is, the nub of the social system. (Dis)count the pugnacity as 'humorous', just like the ?nastiness and smugness? from Horace's own lips. It is not difficult to hear Horace's voice, as well as his, in the Pest's final flourish: 'Without a struggle Life gives Man— Nothing' (59, *nil*, cf. 15, 19)—along with those of Horace the author of the book (1.40, 62, 2.28, 3.9, 17, 18, etc.), of his caricature in 1.9 (16), and of Horace its narrator (14). This is the 'nothing' unresponsiveness which generates the next surge of 'nothing' dialogue in the text, sweet nothings to plug the face-threatening act of keeping stony silence.

Similarly, to select a few of the traces, *ille* joins in with the narrator's voice-print, the verse-*cum*-verbal 'tic' of *ille* | (53); knowing *ille* spoke what the narration was telling us was going on in the character Horace's head (14, *misere cupis... abire* | ~ 8, *misere discedere quaerens* |); he knew of Crispinus' daft challenge to scribble *à la* Lucilius (23f., *quis me scribere pluris* |... *possit uersus* ~ 4.16, *uideamus uter plus scribere possit* |); the glimpse of Horace's coterie shadows Horace's own earlier rhapsody (21f., *non Viscum pluris amicum* | *non Varium* ~ 5. 41f., ... *Varius... Vergiliusque* | *occurrunt, animae qualis neque candidiores* |... *neque quis me sit deuinctior alter.... amico* |); and the flourish of the 'last stand'—which has clinched the uncrossable divide between 'us' and 'them' for (I think all) readers who have risked print—is modelled heavily on the book's most ringing of Horace's own didactic professions of resolve:

* Pest's promise: 'I shan't let myself down, I'll turn the slaves with bungs, if I get left out today I shan't give up, I'll look for good moments, I'll join him at a traffic light, I'll see him home. Without a struggle...' (56–60).

*Protreptic from Poet's dear old Dad: 'I don't let myself down: this is truer, doing this I'll live a better life, this is how sweetly I'll join my friends, this is not good from somebody, well I'll never do anything as stupid as him, now will I?' (56–9).

The verbal-conceptual fit is unmistakable (esp. *haud mihi deero... occurram in triuiis* ~ 4.134–9, esp. *neque enim... desum mihi, ... sic dulcis amicis | occurram*).

At a grander level, too, at two stages the narration and its 'direct speech' blur together inseparably: at 11–13, Horace's exclamation is audible to us, though spoken silently, while the other's twopenny-worth of chatter about this and that, plus his hymn to Rome, are noted but not heard (12, *quidlibet*, cf. 2, 10, 67, *nescioquid*); and from 28–37, first Horace is exclaiming, ordering, narrating to the dead, to himself and to the Pest, in *direct* speech, then the narrator slides into *oratio obliqua* when reporting what the P**t is to be supposed to have explained to him by the time that they reached the next piece of 'dialogue' (37, ... *quod ni fecisset, perdere litem*, cf. 38–47, *si, si, si, si, ni...*, etc.). Narration has these two as much entwined as polarised.

To terminate the dialogue with the P**t, unbeknown to the *character* Horace, we have already been reading how the introduction of *Maecenas* to the discourse at once slams *Horace*'s door on *ille* for him, gets him out of Horace's sentences and off his back. *This* 'servant', Horace, has turned down *ille*'s 'gift-horses' ('slaves with bungs'); *ille* is, right now, dumped out in the cold ('left out today'); he has had his informal, unpressured opportunity, stepped forward boldly to honour Flaccus with his attendance, the obeisance of *deductio* ('good moments', 'join him', 'see him home'). We've been here all along, at one remove: struggling for adherence, precedence, ascendancy (6, *adsectaretur* ~ 16, 19, *persequar, sequar*, 'comically' inverted in 42f., *praecedere...*, *sequor*). The story is a tussle for the prize of an 'introduction' (47, *tradere*). To *Maecenas*. And, very simply, because Pest dares blurt the name 'Maecenas', Poet *un*names Pest, watching over Maecenas' good name, round the clock.[37]

But now (60–74), the entrance of Dear Aristius Fuscus further sidelines *ille,* as the two 'friends' lock horns and shut him out of discussion (62, *consistimus,* excludes him). Finally (74–8), once the débâcle of the dialogue has died its multiple death, citizen's arrest summarily expels *ille* from the scene, 'drowning out' all conversation, ending the *sermo* (75f., *magna* | *inclamat uoce*). The Law intervenes, to unplug the socializing, unless 'twas (it was) Poetry that finished him and 'his' poem off (78).

The more 'dialogical' the world is (your world), the harder it must get to *write* others *down* and off without thereby attacking your own being, for mutual ascription of roles must consolidate communication, and fill out humanization;[38] and (as 1.3 intuited) there is a feedback loop from liking to reading compliment where insult lurked, back to liking some more and . . . so on.[39] Sociality even consists in such reciprocal investment, indeed the point of getting to know others is that we can scarcely hope to tell if a stranger is, exactly, naïve, *faux naïf,* deeply scheming, genially ironic, woundingly sarcastic, a 'bore', a 'pest', whatever.[40]

4. THE 'SHAGGY GOD' STORY: ANECDOTE

For the Snark *was* a Boojum, you see.[41]

But this poem is *not* a mime, not even an urban mime. For sure, the levels of narration are a complex tangle where 'many modes of

---

[37] *Adsectatores* make themselves useful all day: Wiseman (1982) 29f., nominating Horace's *ille* 'a familiar character in Latin literature . . . the *ardelio*' [*sic*]. On *ardaliones*: Henderson (1976) 31f.

[38] Cf. Pocock (1984) 39–42.

[39] Cf. Brown and Levinson (1987) 16.

[40] A first impression of the order of 'talkativeness' must be fine-tuned from the arena of performance to the range of underlying personality traits: Cohan and Shires (1988) 75. When would-be poet Lycidas pesters bard Moeris on *Eclogue* 9's perambulation in the presence-to-thought of 'Menalcas' (∼ Maecenas), Varius is dragged in, with a further luminary, as top poet of the day (vv. 35 ∼ 23): *Satires* 1.9 walks in the shadow of its elder sibling: *et me fecere poetam* | . . . *sunt et mihi carmina, ne quoque dicunt* | *uatem pastores . . .* (vv. 32–4; cf. Henderson (1998c)). So does the book of *Satires:* Van Rooy (1973), Freudenburg (2001).

[41] Carroll in Gardner (1967) 96.

discourse are included in the poem';[42] but this is fundamentally a solo performance by its narrator, whose double mediation ventriloquizes both his characters and his own narration. To insist on the point: he shows their actions, supplies their thoughts, glosses the ensemble; he profiles his own performance, enacts his own focalizing intellection, and glosses the ensemble. In 'improving' the story, he takes control, gilds and repairs; re-reads and re-writes, in short, (re-) interprets what he narrates. Story-tellers offer interpretations, they explore interpretivity, the terms of social and discursive legibility. And story-tellers are performers, they monopolize attention and must therefore deal with their audience in an exchange of a hearing for an acceptable presentation: narration is itself always a social act which calls for interactional receptivity. Horace, Horace's story, relates how someone, Horace, relates to A. N. Other, and as he does so we his audience relate to his account, and relate his reading to our own understanding and experience of relationships.[43]

There is always the likelihood that terms for reception will be addressed through the tale, and that there will be slippage between the various 'levels' of reading or interpretation involved in the narration/narrative. Thus the short story will advertise its (considerate, modest, *piquant*) brevity; its poetic scorns *longueurs*. So loquacity and pomposity entwine when the mock-oracular gipsy plays epical prophetess (29, *Sabella* for *Sibulla*), to determine Horace's existence as flight for his life from every chatterbox, from all talkers, and an ultra-painful death that beggars 'slow foot gout' (29–34). Meantime, Horace the *raconteur* monopolizes the entire (book-)length of all the proceedings which he has by now all but succeeded in unrolling along his reader's path. His pun on *rex* took its time in the shortest poem of all (1.7); his *Priapeum* was long for its genre, but occupied neither more than fifty hexameters nor less (1.8); this trip creeps (stealthily) down the Sacred Way toward the size of the earlier poems, but insists

---

[42] Rudd (1982) 76.

[43] Ventriloquism: Leith and Myerson (1989) 226, Cohan and Shires (1988) 104–12. Improving: Moore and Carling (1988) 164–72, 'Telling stories and telling the truth'; 'exploration' of a story's import: Leith and Myerson (1989) 176. 'Over-dramatization' in 1.9: Connor (1987) 103. Receptivity: the teller and jokester get privileged long turns, Leith and Myerson (1989) 27, Purdie (1993) 128. Relating: Chambers (1984) 4 and *passim*.

throughout that it is syncopating tedium, abbreviating and summar-
ising irritation away so that readers are insulated from the drag of
being stuck in its story. The management then preaches 'obligatory
brevity' (10.9). But, you know, they are just selling tickets...

So too with the rest of the self-awarded traits, such as 'humble Joe'
non-violence and belonging on the side (*our* side) of the Law! For
storytellers fatten their fame as they create their fictions. Quotation is
a route to the sense of an encounter, dialogue an involving strategy
for dramatizing the burden of any narrative—even *ipsissima uerba*
are appropriated strictly to promote the narration. Horace the narrator is the master of the discourse, dissimulating to strut his stuff.
The character Horace reinforces this author-ity by orbiting the tale
around his own centrality (from start, *sicut meus est mos* to finish, *sic
me seruauit*), and othering his interlocutor from the audience. The
butt's turn is to be a joke, just language, while the narration 'takes
off' (both) its victim(s), works its way with detail, pacing, reticence,
image, nudge and wink... For his cultured audience and us their
clones, this ironic social commentator trades on the solidarity of an
in-crowd élite.[44] The opaque and ambiguous modality of the anecdote cancels, disarms, disowns any propositional content it may
sketch; it works in denial and double-think, for those who need or
want no such thing. You can't claim any 'validity', let alone 'universal
validity' for it, indeed the anecdote sits up and begs us to work
(dialogically) between the utterances in the context it provides, and
the narration as a whole.[45]

Thus, 'It so happens I was going along the Sacred Way when...' is
a virtuoso design for careful casualness. It plots coincidental hap-
penstance (1, *forte*, 36, *casu*, 60, *ecce*, 74, *casu*, 74; contrast 6.53f.,
non...casu, nulla...fors on Horace's entrée to Maecenas) on a grid
of 'poetic' necessity-*cum*-divine justice (1, *uia Sacra*, ~ 74, 78,

---

[44] The insiders line up in the lines 10.81–6: the mob of heavies he can call out to
deal with trouble-makers like you, 4.140–3. Self-promoting narration: Leith and
Myerson (1989) 26–31. Law-abiding narrators *vs.* bungling, fouling, discursively
inept butts: Purdie (1993) 59. 'Constructed dialogue', forever veiling its fictive status:
Tannen (1989) ch. 4. Conversation analysis has discredited 'reported' or 'indirect
speech' as presentational phenomena that aspire to a false autonomy. Butt = joke on
legs: Purdie (1993) 67.

[45] ~~Validity~~: *pace* Rudd (1982) 80; cf. Brown and Levinson (1987) 28, Hodge and
Kress (1993) 151.

obuius... Apollo) that brings the narrative full circle (*accurrit, quid agis, dulcissime, arrepta, adsectaretur, in aurem* ∼ *aduersarius, quo tu turpissime, auriculam, rapit, concursus*). The jest is a tease, however: a malformed *anti*-narrative, a 'Shaggy Dog' *anti*-joke.[46] It tells of a reluctant duel, the abortive story of a failure to escape from the story (from 8, 14–19, *discedere quaerens, cupis abire, usque tenebo,* | *persequar, usque sequar,* to 34, *uitet,* and all the sack-race way to 73, *fugit*). This consists of a staggered series of blocked non-events, rising through a non-intervention from a fraud Helper, to a to-all-intents gratuitous... anticlimax. The task set Horace is to get rid of The Horror; and the story of the story is to get rid, too, to get shot of the story and save us all from further punishment and a chattering death. As in 1.7 and 1.8, the narration covers the tracks of its pleasurable violence in disposing textually of one more hapless victim by caricature: code-name *Horaceshow.* 'Good humour' half-hides and half-shares (dis/simulates) the unpleasantness, as if it really could be at Horace's expense and ours. Blame Vesta, instead, her oasis was a mirage (35)! By Apollo! *He*'s the one that took so long to save us all from the funk.

Why did the monkey fall out of the tree? Because it was dead.

5. TRIUMVIRAL PURSUITS: TEXTUAL POLITICS

> You came hangin' round me
> I'm not so glad you found me
> You're still doing things that I gave up years ago.[47]

'I'll scratch your back and you knife mine.'[48] Many readers have, not unreasonably, heard in Horace's hotly dissentient blurt about life *chez* Maecenas *the* message of the poem: 'No, life there *isn't* the way you

---

[46] Shaggy dog: Legman (1972) 118f., 'hostility against the listener', Purdie (1993) 39, Nash (1985) 118–23, 'The defective exchange'.

[47] Reed (1972) 'Hangin'' round.

[48] Lennon (1974), 'Nobody loves you (when you're down and out)'.

think...'. (vv. 48–52)[49] The lines have often been taken as prime evidence for relations between (a) Maecenas and (a) Horace, and a confirmation from the *Horace's* mouth that poets were on a par with other members of a Roman Emir's retinue. This is, need I say?, perfectly unreflective. The Poet *wrote the lines*. Poets write patrons and think the City—poets *write down Rome*. They could legitimate themselves as oddities, but *bona fide Quirites* (Romans), by writing themselves into the heart of the Roman value-system and institutional apparatus. As we remarked, the satirist scripts himself into the role of the cockney sparrow strolling with the healthy disrespect of the free citizen through the streets he knows like the back of his hand.[50] In his patch, his viewpoint is intimate, even definitive:

It is here that the values of civilisation are gathered and condensed: spirituality (churches), power (offices), money (banks), merchandise (department stores), language (agoras, cafés and promenades); to go... to the city-centre is to encounter the social 'truth', to participate in the proud plenitude of 'reality'.[51]

'I'm walkin' down streets that are dead. | Walkin' walkin'—with you in my head':[52] 'A stroll of perhaps three hundred yards (along the) Via Sacra between the Velia and tribunal of the Forum',[53] to reach the focal point of Vesta's temple, the heart(h) of Rome, at the centre of the poem; from there onwards to explore law, religion, and poetry, the Trojan legacy of Rome and the patron divinity of Octavian The Son of the Deity (Caesar)—so many *Apollo's* waiting for us at, and as, the finale. The separateness of The Sacred, boundaried off from the mess of mundane confusion, haunts the anecdote, whose blocked narrative of difficulty, restriction and barred access to the great precisely militates against social fluidity. Excursions of Apollo's

---

[49] Signalled by the strong negative opener, and by the re-affirmation of its truth-value that succeeds it (*est*..., *nil*... *est quia, est*).

[50] Poets on a par: esp. White (1978) 78: see Griffin (1984) 204 and n. 43. Self-legitimation: Wallace-Hadrill (1990a) 10.

[51] Barthes *cit.* Duncan and Duncan (1992) 31. As we noted in Henderson (1989) and above, The *Flâneur* has stalked far and wide through recent criticism, cf. McGann (1973) 61, Ulmer (1989) 167, Brand (1991), Rignall (1992), Fer (1993) 167f., essays in Caws (1993).

[52] Dylan (1997) 'Love sick'.

[53] Dudley (1967) 78.

Poet in the social domain suggest paradigms of general application.
So what *is* at stake in Horace's stroll?

The foundational myth of Republican Liberty, and still more its
triumviral masquerade, enshrined civic power-relations of 'coopera-
tive interaction between equals'. Both relatively informal and explicitly stipulated networks of vertical liaisons mediated access to power
and regulated competitive flow of symbolic capital and other resources, in nexuses of 'friends', and patron—client dyads.[54] Negotiations between (a) Horace and (the inimitable) Maecenas, however
trivial in themselves, sport the tensions and contradictions that breed
between these axiological imperatives; they implicate *both* the general
(izable) run of relations radiating through the community, *and* the
specificity of relations between (a) Maecenas and the (precarious
unless massively historicized) Caesarian *juntà*. So this is more than
anecdotal word-to-the-wise, this is a honed and calculated artwork
that intercedes against crude social climbing, in order to advertise a
political order proof against contestation. The triumviral gang would
sell revolutionary détente as (if) a settled system of priorities
and channelled procedures. Where the diatribe poems that fronted
the book press on us a moralized mapping of public life, along the
coordinates of a strife-stripped culture aspiring to consensus, the Pest
poem now accredits a chaotic and destabilizing tyranny in the wake
of *coup d'état*.[55] In the thirties, it required energetically false consciousness, not least from the dissembling courtiers of the newly-

[54] Wallace-Hadrill (1990a) 74, 80. Historians have now focussed their analysis
of patronage on the jockeying of individuals in their variously proliferating and re-
negotiated social relationships around liaisons of specifically constituted/contested/
invisible/obfuscated superiority, inferiority, solidarity and affect. More than
this, however, Horace's melodramatics (along with other texts neglected as literary,
so ... atypical, purblind, slippery?) can point to the glaring prospect that the historicity of patronage consisted in the discourse of patronage, ranging between cultural
traces of discussion of patronage such as *Sermo* 1.9 and documents of patronage such
as *litterae commendaticiae*, and oral communication, formal or otherwise, both at the
meta-discursive level and in speech-acts such as *traditio*. This ensemble of 'talk' was
the reality of patronage, far from both neatly systematised analytical models with
conventional notation and agreed codings for nomenclature, and far from any
analytic extra-discursive 'reality'.

[55] For such strategies of de-politicisation: Connolly (1984) 139. Cf. Fairclough
(1989) 10. Crowley (1989) 76f. explains the totalizing power of the myth of equality
(haven of unity, stability and security of definition).

adopted Caesar, Jr., to persuade anyone that an egalitarian core was the political 'truth' of Rome. *We* need neither collude in normalizing the triumviral *Putsch*, nor duck the satiric venom that seeps from Horace's sunny story.

Sermones 1 models Horace as the (poet-)friend of the great, and articulates this in a cumulative series of tableaux which resonate together thematically—a fragmented narrative. Getting to know Horace (this is his first public appearance), hearing his story, proves to be the story of him, and so us, getting to know *Maecenas*. Getting to know that 'Maecenas' is the horizon for a new cognition, under a new sociopolitical sky. And this written reading of self, culture, politics comes courtesy of Maecenas, via his *scriptorium*, and thanks to Octavian. Horace progressively teaches himself the lessons he preaches on polite self-restraint from the twin besetting sins of greed and ambition (esp. 1.1.103, 4.26, 6.51, 68, 128, 10.84). He turns from a 'rough diamond' outsider's broadside street-philosophy to the undersold obliquities of his off-key but witty jests. Along the (consecrated) way, he fastens on, promotes and performs reticent confidentiality (esp. 4.84f.; so 1.5 forecloses on its politicking; 1.9 suppresses a name for *ille*, cf. *nescioquid*, 2, 10, esp. 67).[56] In poem 7 he approached directly the cardinal scene for public display of *fides* by telling of a *quasi* law-court trial in caricature, withholding the verdict for readers to judge for themselves: 1.9 still more discreetly contents itself with jumped bail and pre-trial procedures, underscoring how friends and clients drew on solidarity at law, just the way that *ille* prematurely acts out in his request to Horace (38); when the long arm of the law reaches out to whisk Mr X off to face the music, its formulaic language (76, *licet antestari?*) brooks no discussion, but arrests the dialogue in a staccato volley of note-form summaries.[57]

---

[56] The squeeze between civic *libertas* and discreet *amicitia*: Hunter (1985a) esp. 487f., cf. Freudenburg (1993) 86–92, 209. 'The antithesis of freedom of speech is not censorship but excommunication: the denial of the right to participate.' (Harris (1990) 159).

[57] Cloud (1989) 65–7, 'The problem of the pest', counsels incisively that the law plays an 'emblematic role' here, rescuing Horace for order from outrage. The stirring citizen's arrest may serve for 'comic insulation', humorously overdone to make sure it amuses us more than it hurts *ille* (Purdie (1993) 61; cf. Cloud, loc. cit. 66). Solidarity at law: Wallace-Hadrill (1990a) 66.

In court, *ille* must 'reply' (36, *respondere* ~ 14, 63, *respondebam*, *respondet*), but may speak only when Society bids and must otherwise hold his peace, on pain of contempt. Where spite would ask of a fellow 'How did he keep that out of court?' (4.99f.), Horace's jolly story parades its veiling as humorous repartee of 'the power which lay behind the good taste and relaxed civility of the circle', Big Brother's triumviral hold on Rome not invisibly patrolling the Forum.[58] The iron grip in Horace's velvet glove will be re-veiled/revealed again in the (un)funny drollery that closes 2.1, laughing offence under the holy laws against slander and libel out of Caesar's court.[59] Horace has friends, he there lets you see. He even spins the present yarn exactly to show off 'power before the law (skill to plead, stamina to represent)', (and) his 'understanding of the condition of the citizen (obligations, rights, terms)' (39, *ualeo stare... noui ciuilia iura*). The narration proclaims what the character disclaims, in a mock-innocent parable of the power of spite to do down a fellow-citizen the length and breadth of the City. Horace brags, too, how he came to blow the whistle on an acquaintance, for all his bashful agoraphobia: this is one of those cases he thought about before, where some 'comrade *ille* or another got out of line' and instead of 'cheerful tolerance' from Mr Nice, faced hostile witness from the Laureate—the sort of 'daft boob' it would take a real 'sweetie of a pal to understand' (3.139–41). To cap all, Horace now crows about it, just the way Tom, Dick and Harry's spite had just known he was itching to—from the rooftops, for fun, behind fall-guy's back, all fertile fantasist and court-jester (4.78–85). Wake up, and make like Horace: 'lend an ear..., get a move on with your verdict, listen to both sides, approach the thing from every direction' (77f.) Above all, one last reminder. 'That's the way: find yourself a decent Minder' (78, *sic me seruauit Apollo*).

The poem is also framed within the book.[60] In the story of the transformative influence of Maecenas taking Horace under his wing,

---

[58] So McGann (1973) 70, 'Is the poet, unconsciously no doubt, pointing to the power etc.?' *Caesar qui cogere posset...* (1.3.4, to Maecenas) reads as easily with *Maecenas qui...*

[59] Satire in 2.1: Freudenburg (1990). *Recusatio*: Clauss (1985).

[60] Cf. Henderson (1989) and (1998a) ch. 3, Zetzel (1980) 69, Rambaux (1971) esp. 179.

Horace has now 'come of age', as programmed (34, *simul atque adoleuerit aetas* | ~ 4. 119, *simul ac durauerit aetas* |). His maturation measures from his buttonholing of Maecenas in 1.1, to his insider's 'leak' about Life around Maecenas to 1.9's man in the queue. In parallel, Lucilian satire melts into Horatian, the theorizing in 1.4 (of 1–3) re-forming in 1.10 (in the light of 5–9).[61] All the traits we have got to know *en route* are now available to us for Horace the old pro on the corner (his consciousness as narrator, character and artist), whereas we're never to get to know the new kid on the block (*pace* 7, *noris nos*).

Most compellingly of all, the triptych of anecdotes 1.7–9 reads as serial progression, from the past and distance of Brutus' vitriolic Asia, war-torn by extremists of hyper-cultural smarm and primitive crudity; through the pivotal work of re-construction of Rome under way in Maecenas' Esquiline gardens, the mass grave reclaimed from the poisonous talons of pre-cultural hexing; to the forensic present of Maecenas' cosmopolis, and the well-tempered moderation of Terentian gentility. From imprecatory invocation of the 'great gods'; self-incarnation as a god ('I'm a god'); the pilgrimage to Apollo. Third-person narration, with Horace deleted from the cast of figures at the scene, in favour of anonymous narrators from the crowd; first-person narration, displaced from citizen Horace through the silly *alias* of the scarecrone guarding the phalace grounds; the full reality of Q. Horatius Flaccus, *ciuis, poeta, amicus*, sauntering through the telling of the tale of his sauntering in broad daylight and all his glory: his own first-person, the one-man show! Yells end 1.7 and 1.9, the one all names and trial, the other nameless and halted by arrest and taking into custody. The victims of 1.8 flee Maecenas Gardens' final fart, dash for cover into 1.9's cityscape, which wends its sacred way toward The Gardens of Caesar (18), but winds up talking more 'farts' and 'commotion' (78, *concursus* ~ 8.47, *currere in urbem*; 70, *oppedere* ~ 8.46, *pepedi*).

This matrix for the poem in a metamorphic sequence strongly frames 1.9 as a processual meditation on the socio-politico-cultural business of changing places. If getting across the underlined 'point',

---

[61] Freudenburg (1993) esp. 198–211. Horace coming in from the cold: Zetzel (1980) 69.

on the rhythms of admission to, and afterlife in, the magic circle of
Maecenas (vv. 48–52, 55–6) is the purpose of the poem, nevertheless,
our reading of the unfolding story of Horace's revisionary account to
the latecomer of the terms for application, probation and full admission is bound to be received in the light of his earlier telling in 1.6 of
his own experience of the process: *ille* stands now in the shoes that
Horace wore then. So the question is whether there is *anything* to
distinguish Horace's successful approach to the approach from the
way The Impertinent One now shapes up to the same task. Anything,
that is, besides success in angling the wangling. Or rather, the (easier)
question is whether Horace represents the candidate Horace with
feeling, but candidate *ille* without! Let's see.

The P*st has tried to approach the best Po*t he could find; worse
luck for him, it was a twisted débutant satirist he picked, not one of the
stars of the heroic hexameter. All Horace told us before was that it
wasn't luck, but 'supreme Virgil, with his no. 2, Varius' that shoved
Horace under Maecenas' fastidious nose (54f.). How Horace had
fastened onto Virgil, other than by buttonholing him in the street
and showering him with compliments for Viscus and...Varius, he
does not recount to us. Only that they came through with verbal
commendatio on his behalf (55, *dixere quid essem* ∼ 9. 47, *tradere*).
The account of the fateful interview is *not* an object lesson in good
technique in sucking up and greasing. Far from it. Horace lines up one
of his many ostensive demonstrations of confidentiality: 'Once I got
close...' (56). Not much to go on there: '...after a few brief words'
(56, *pauca locutus*). So the secrets stay safe with Horace (57, 'childlike |
dumb modesty stopped more declarations'). If Ho*race* is anything to
go by, 'Don't wave your pedigree; don't take him for a ride hacking
round the shires of deepest Gloatcester' (58–60, *non ego me claro
natum patre, non ego circum | me Satureiano uectari rura caballo...
narro*). If busking your wares is *infra dig.*,[62] then how quite is a
budding poet to get a break? Surely Horace is doing just what satiric
spite would be sure he would, namely pulling up the draw-bridge after
himself? His blocking of communication with *ille* works to maintain
distance between the safely arrived Horace and his would-be emulator.

[62] This is scotched at 4.74f.; *ambitio* included *any* form of canvassing or blowing
your own trumpet.

Down this not-so-Sacred Way, Horace is blocking his *alter ego*'s apotheosis. Showing us, despite the character Horace, that the law of the urban jungle is that Every 'Pest' will eventually turn into a 'Bore': 'smug, elitist and rude'.[63] Just as his earlier narration of his own hand in his meteoric rise of fame, all the eloquence and persuasion he would muster to tell us of all the eloquent persuasion he could muster, thinned down the communication so successfully that it could never be pirated. For Horace's blue-print ran, and runs, as economical with the truth as it is tight-lipped and secure: 'I told him what I was' (60, *quod eram narro*).[64]

6. ISN'T HE A BIT LIKE YOU AND ME?[65]
VADEMECUM

Particle Man Particle Man doing the things a particle can
What's he like? It's not important: Particle Man.

Is he a dot or is he a speck? When he's under water does he get wet?]
Or does the water get him instead? Nobody knows: Particle Man.[66]]

'Society is now one polish'd horde, | Form'd of two mighty tribes, the *Bores* and *Bored*.'[67] Besides the names of Caesar and Maecenas, one Augustan brave does take a bow here, everybody's favourite, the poet-grammarian Aristius Fuscus ('supreme Fuscus', between 'Varius, Maecenas and Virgil' and 'both the Viscuses' on the list of worthies and heavies at 10.82f.: cf. 9.22f., 'Viscus and Varius').[68] Not only are you

---

[63] Zetzel (1980) 71: i.e. 'questions . . . the self-satisfaction' of Maecenas' coterie.

[64] Cf. Petron. *Sat.* 83.9, 'I'm a poet, and, as I hope, not the flattest gusto around'; 'Aesop blessed the poet fishing for applause: he *should* blow his trumpet—no one else is going to' (Phaedr. *Appendix* 9, cf. Henderson (1976) 366–70, 'His own best critic').

[65] J. Lennon and P. McCartney on The Beatles (1965) 'Nowhere man'.

[66] They Might Be Giants (1990) 'Particle Man'.

[67] Byron (1970) 819, *Don Juan* XIII, xcv.

[68] His name would make him: 'Best' of (comic) poets (*aristos = optimus*)-*cum*-'poker-faced schoolmaster' (cf. McGann (1973) 89). Fuscus (= Bardon (1956) 115 n. 5) was automatically on Horace's list of *doctos . . . et amicos* (10.87 ~ 9.7, 22, *docti sumus . . . amicum*), his twin and complement, as un/like him as could be, at home in Rome where for Horace the Sabine nest was best (*Epp.* 1. 10. 1–5, *uetuli notique columbi* ~ 9.7, *noris nos*).

bound to cross his path in town and face his 'obfuscatory sense of humour' (65, *male salsus | ridens dissimulare*), but he 'won't let you or your compositions go without a flea in your ear' (*Epp.* 1.10.45, *nec me dimittes incastigatum* ∼ 15, *usque tenebo*). He is the you that wants to laugh off the satirical teeth behind this poem's smile: mind you find yourself joining in. Through Fuscus, the positions of Horace and Hooray Henry triangulate for the reader: Horace's approach to 'Dark Horse' Fuscus briskly re-cycles the Shadow's approach to Horace. The *proxemics* (body language) of Fuscus and Pest say(s) so (61, *occurrit* ∼ 3, *accurrit*; 64, | *et pressare manu* || ... *bracchia* ∼ 4, | *arreptaque manu* || ...; 62, *consistimus* ∼ 9, *consistere*; 65, 73f., *eriperet...ac...linquit* ∼8, 14, *discedere...abire*); power-relations are acted out again (73f., *fugit...ac...linquit* ∼ 16, 19, 42f., *persequar...sequar...praecedere..* . *sequor*); the relationships are noted (61f., *mihi carus et illum | qui pulchre nosset* ∼ 3, *notus mihi nomine tantum*); the conversations proceed in tandem (62f., *unde uenis...quo tendis?* ∼ 4, *quid agis?*; 63, *respondet* ∼ 14, *respondebam*).

That Funny thing happening on the Sacred Way to the Forum, 'Zero' Fuscus is putting on a comic caricature of Horace the satirist, along with all his derision and dissembling, the whole shooting match in a cameo. (Be there.) When Horace is 'aggressively/intimately pushy' with the bodily contact at the 'greetings' phase (63f., *uellere... et pressare*), and tries to invade Fuscus' space by telling the world 'in no uncertain terms what special esteem he held Horace in' (67f., *certe...te | ...mecum*), he blabs, before a third party, that Fuscus has a (dark!) secret, gloats over the huddle in prospect. But his threat to usurp his would-be victim's self-determination *by forging his authorization* is at once repulsed: Fuscus bows to no one, he 'owns his own mind, runs his past, present and future' (68f., *memini...dicam...hodie*). He defers Horace into an expressly indeterminate 'never-never' (68f., *meliore | tempore dicam*), oriented around 'his own priorities, his own culture' (69, *tricesima sabbata*): yes, it takes all sorts to make a Republic.

Then he turns on him the classic baiting by stereotype of Satire's Wa*king Muse (73, *ac me* |), the unpardonably crude voice of the disavowed bodily function, all that sociality declines to 'know' about each other of every us: 'You wouldn't wanna fart in Jewish faces?'

(69f., *uin tu | ... Iudaeis oppedere?*). Common scents, let's say, from an Emasculate Muse.[69]

Horace's rude 'no' (70, 'No problem for *me*') gets smothered by Fuscus' thick spray of impregnably opaque Horatian self-irony (71f., 'Well, *I* do, I'm a teeny bit weedy, one of the millions'). He reaffirms his declaration of intent to 'defer', as his last word, on this or on any other subject for that matter (69, *dicam* ~ 72, *loquar*). He underlines that 'this is a rebuff', and one he is enjoying delivering, too, with or without apology (72, *ignosces*). His words put Horace off and down from his coat-tails. His four pointed 'stilettos' of speech line up in parataxis—to other Horace (72, *alias*). I pass over the rhetorical figuring of Fuscus as the incarnation of *occultatio* in his practice of rhetoric here: his staccato and laconic brevity already speaks loud and clear the message which his polite frankness needs no privacy to smuggle into the discourse.[70] Fuscus' rebuff contrives to be pleasantly, disgustingly, comically, vague but effective, as he plays the religion ace—whereas, earlier, Horace's own curt shooing had lapsed into circumstantial bluffing and insulting oneupmanship:

* 16–18, 'the bedside emergency beeping now, the Tiber to get past, then mighty Caesar's front lawn, way out of your league'.

* 67–70, 'the umpteenth Sabbath, those poor Jews, funny I dare say but it's a rule of mine, a creed you might say, some better moment, by all means'.

A pretty curtsey, from Mr Courtesy. In person. As a brief reprise of the earlier saga of Approach met by Resistance (non-cooperation and withdrawal), this pantomime scene brings to the surface of the text

[69] The comedy of 'contempt by breaking wind in the direction of someone else. The terms are *katapérdesthai* and *prospérdesthaî*': Henderson (1975) 197. Fuscus' 'disclaimer' *ignosces* (v. 72) 'calls Horace's bluff', since 'Horace himself is on trial—to see if he will put his charitable theories from 1.3 into practice', e.g. 3.21–3, *ignoras ... ignotum ... ignosco* (Emily Gowers, *per litteras*). Rhetoric of obfuscation: Usher (1965). Feldman (1993) 510 n. 103, 558 n. 41, sees satirical victimisation appropriating circumcision for its self-constituting image (morselization of the social fabric or body politic; masculist symbolic power set over phallic virility) in the linkage of '*Fuscus left me under the sacrificial knife*' with 'docked' and, *credat Iudaeus Apella*, of Apollo with Apella (*a-pellis, 'Les Foreskin' ?) at 5.100.

[70] Contrast Horace's own crassly billboarded signals that circumscribe 1.1–3, curtailed at 'Not to filibuster', at 3.137, with six verses yet to come, before 140, *ignoscent ... amici.*

the common humanimality of P**t and P**t, shared now with Fuscus, *à trois*. More pointedly, Fuscus' expostulation to Horace smuggles into the narrative its own formation. ~~Displaced under denial~~, paraded for all to see and rub in, Satire's very own constitutional weakness for the taboo gratification of foul slanguage, and vicious menacing of the socially abject. Fuscus' 'farting at docked Jews' hits the spot, if we would prefer to disavow any such desire, to talk dirty and torture the defenceless a bit. But only provided we can keep the self-deception going. For this, the stock-in-trade of Satire, is the fascination of our disgust, however we may prefer not to face the fact, and however the suppressed violence is turned back on our selves and our favourite poet(s). 'Docked' accuses nullified potency: contrast that farting *ruber... phallus* of 1.8 (of maple, mind, not rubber) which persecutes and routs the dispossessed and demonized females; recall 1.7 dumping a renegade hillsman's coarse insults on an effete oriental trader, who pulls down the curtain by calling down bloodcurdling slaughter on him—the 'cut throat' of the sacrificial victim which Fuscus fixes Horace to become, 'under the knife' (73f.).

'Pity the poor parvenu' or 'Poke the puny poet': either way, this is (you have been warned) 'the "*pet-en-gueule*," or "fart-in-the-face"' that images the desire of lovers of satire: literary flatophily ('*flatophilology*').[71] The bad mouth *Egito* Horace may choose to portray himself as one more 'docked Jew', too civilised to 'look after' himself (*seruare*), disarmed by his rise up the social ladder, but that is only Horace the satirist-narrator whipping up pleasurable spite in us, against one more hung-up person in the whole wide universe. Watch Fuscus, more than catalyst, no simple observer. Aristius plays a sub fusc. blackness, a satiric Apollo (72f., 'Such a black sunrise for me' ~ 4.85, '*He* is black', 100, 'the ink of the black cuttle': of spite). Fuscus 'saves his own skin'—Horace must pray for Apollo to 'save' his (73, *fugit* ~ 65, *eriperet*, which translates the verb whisked away from the closing Homeric tag by paraphrase: 78, *sic me seruauit Apollo* = *tòn d' exérpaxen Apóllon, Il.* 20.443). Alert or malicious, we

---

[71] '*Pet-en-gueule*': 'the fetichistic interest in the farting and flatus of the erotic partner, which it is desired to see and smell as close up as possible' (Legman (1978) 1012, cf. 1006–17).

leave him where he leaves his new pal, in the lurch, Satire into Comedy won't go?

The point for citizens, the preciousness, of dialogue, *can* be glimpsed through the thick modal screen of this *sermo*. To explore the anecdote, resist/escape the élitist chauvinism that locks into the prejudicial monologism of the narration, and blocks out the ironic oscillations staged in the flurry of interaction as it unfolds, in however flawed a mutuality, *both* between the conversationalists, *and* also in the dialogue between their representation and our reading. Put your own worst construction up for inspection—alongside my 'virtual offence' against Horace, and against you. Join Horace with his shadow, then join *in* with them, too: only, do listen! 'Do we talk only when we are speaking? . . . Can I remain silent when talking?'[72]

'You're so vain you probably think this song is about you'.[73]

> I wish that for just one time you could stand inside my shoes
> And just for that one moment I could be you
> Yes I wish that for just one time you could stand inside my shoes
> You'd know what a drag it is to see you.[74]

---

[72] Jaworski (1992) 25, 28.

[73] Simon (1991 = 1972), 'You're so vain'.

[74] Dylan (1971) 'Positively Fourth Street': cf. Herdman (1981) 23, 'the ultimate in gestures of rejection. . . . The refined cruelty of this is remarkable. The repetition of the proposition keeps the listener in suspense, perhaps hoping for a more sympathetic line . . . "could stand inside my shoes" might be expected to mean "understand my point of view" rather than what it does mean, "see you as I do"; and in the light of that expectation "And just for that one moment | I could be you" could even seem to express an outgoing impulse instead of the sneer which it later proves to be.' As in Horace, the victim's anonymity makes the song satire on the poet's fix of 'negative capability'.

8

Horace, Lucilius, and Callimachean Polemic

Ruth Scodel

Satires 1.10, though its underlying thematic unity is fairly clear, is difficult to understand as a sequential argument. Ostensibly, at least, it is a response to criticism leveled at Horace for 1.4, with its critique of Lucilius. Its real concern is the poetic program of Horace himself, as is to be expected in the final poem of the book. The two subjects are, naturally, closely related, for it is by refusing to ignore the faults of his predecessor that Horace defines his own goals. But while the basic unity of subject may not be problematic, the choice of issues, the amount of detail with which different aspects of the subject are treated, and transitions from one section to the next show Horace's characteristic elusiveness. Horace begins by defining the importance of variety, brevity, and the use of the *ridiculum* ('comic' or 'absurd') in preference to the *acre* ('harsh') in satire (1–15). Although at first the reader expects these qualities to comprise the *cetera* ('other qualities', 5) Horace denies Lucilius possessed, the criteria are general and could apply to any poet as well as to Lucilius; it seems clear that they are primarily the goals of Horace himself. The poem here moves away from Lucilius, and does not specify how he would be judged on these criteria: he was obviously too prolix, but could be defended on the score of variety. The argument obliquely returns to Lucilius in claiming that the poets of Old Comedy possessed the qualities Horace has just praised, and are to be imitated in this respect (*hoc*

For this volume, I have added some references to more recent scholarship and rewritten a few sentences that I found either poorly framed or inaccurate. I have not, however, made significant revisions.

stabant, hoc sunt imitandi, 'they adhered to this, in this they should be imitated', 17).[1] The echo of 1.4 (1–7), where Lucilius is said to have depended entirely on Old Comedy, changing only the meters, links Lucilius with these poets without making it clear whether Lucilius is indirectly praised for imitating them or criticized for failing to meet their standards.

In any case, it is doubtful that Horace really places himself in the critical tradition that regarded Old Comedy as the model of urbane wit; Cicero (*De off.* 1.104) commends Old Comedy and Plautus—not an object of Horace's admiration—in the same sentence.[2] That does not mean that he does not mean what he says or that he is incoherent; he uses the available literary theories eclectically and manipulates them for his immediate needs, but always with an end in view—his own practice. In 1.4 Horace exaggerated the relationship between Old Comedy and Lucilius.[3] He works similarly here: the praise of Old Comedy serves as a transition between the criteria for good satire and the attack on Hermogenes and the *simius, nil praeter Calvum et doctus cantare Catullum* ('the ape with no learning except at singing Calvus and Catullus'), who have never read the masters of Old Comedy. The issue has decisively changed from Horace's justification for criticizing Lucilius to the critical qualifications of literary figures Horace evidently dislikes, who lack the learning necessary to evaluate either Lucilius or Horace. The explicit characterization of these figures—Hermogenes, Tigellius, and a devotee of the neoterics— places this work in a frame of reference quite different from that of 1.4 (where Tigellius appeared in a different role, pawing over books at the shops, 71–2). While 1.4 includes both criticism of Lucilius on neoteric principles, for writing too much (9–13), and material re- mote from or opposed to neoteric concerns and positions, such as

---

[1] For the dispute about which of the preceding qualities Horace means here see Brink (1963: 166 n. 2); Fraenkel (1957: 129).

[2] Rudd (1966: 94) reveals the problem in his paraphrase of the lines, which tries to avoid it by introducing the qualifications Horace has so notably omitted: 'But the facetiae of Lucilius tended too often to be crude and harmful. Admittedly Aristopha- nes and the others were not wholly free from these defects, but their lapses were less frequent and should certainly not be imitated.'

[3] For Horace's 'coat-trailing' in *S.* 1.4, see Newman (1967: 283–9). A convincing attempt to make sense of Horace's various theoretical affiliations is Freudenburg (1993: 52–108).

the moral claims made for satire or the choice of Ennius as exemplary poet at 60–2, neoteric questions are not prominent in that poem. In 1.10, on the other hand, opinions about Lucilius appear directly alongside wider literary issues, and the question inevitably arises whether they are merely juxtaposed or are integrally connected. Hermogenes and the ape are mocked for not having read Old Comedy, the 'source' of Lucilius, and their ignorance would be really telling only if they are imagined to have presumed to judge Lucilius (and no doubt Horace also).[4] Immediately after they are mentioned the poem presents an imaginary interlocutor (or interlocutors) who praises Lucilius. Just as the learning of the ape is extremely limited, the interlocutors are *seri studiorum* ('literary Johnnies-come-lately', 21). Lucilius' admirer and the ape are certainly representatives of the same type, and a reader could easily assume them to be the same person.

The interlocutor commends Lucilius for using Greek words in his Latin, and receives a fierce answer from Horace. In this section, there is some suggestion, marked by the use of a generalizing second person (*cum versus facias*, 'when you compose poetry', 25), that contemporary practice is as much on Horace's mind as that of Lucilius. This issue of Latinity is the only stylistic question to be treated specifically and at length in the poem (20–30), but the argument used is not a strong one. Horace points out that nobody would speak other than pure Latin in the courts, and implies that one should not do otherwise when composing verse; but the conclusion does not necessarily follow, and Horace does not entirely refrain from the use of Greek words himself.[5] As with Horace's treatment of Old Comedy, some exaggeration is present: a matter of degree is treated with a vehemence that makes it sound more absolute than it is. More important than the argument itself are its underlying

---

[4] A. Kiessling and R. Heinze (1959: 156) argue that Hermogenes and Demetrius are critics of Horace himself, not defenders of Lucilius. The tone in which Hermogenes and Tigellius are mentioned is certainly sharper than that of the surrounding lines, but it is hard to see the point of stressing their ignorance of Old Comedy, the standard by which Lucilius is found wanting, if they are not concerned with Lucilius.

[5] e.g., *hybrida* ('half-breed'), *pharmacopolae* ('potion-peddlar'). Lucilius himself satirized the excessive use of Greek words. An extensive discussion in Rudd (1966: 111–124) argues for similarities between Neoteric and Lucilian usage of Greek, but we are still left with obvious exaggeration by Horace.

assumptions. The argument is patriotic—*patriae, patris Latini, patriis* ('fatherland, father Latinus, ancestral') all occur in 27–9— but also purely aesthetic: Horace insists that using Greek is not *difficile et mirum* ('hard and awesome', 22), giving the impression that these are poetically desirable qualities.

Horace's narrative of how Quirinus came to him in a dream is presented as if it were going to clinch the argument against the use of Greek words, but in fact the god warned the young Horace against composing Greek verses (31–5).[6] The Roman divinity naturally links the advice to write in one's own language with the preceding passage about writing pure Latin, but Quirinus' argument is not that Romans should write Latin, but rather that there are so many Greek poets already that trying to become one more is a perverse undertaking. The dream moves the argument away both from the earlier issue of Greek words in Latin and, once again, from Lucilius to Horace's own practice, but it continues an implicit theme of the preceding passage: writing Greek verses appears to be the obvious, easy choice, the beaten track of the Callimachean original of the passage (*Aetia* 1.21–29 D'Alessio/Pf), just as writing impure Latin is not hard and awesome. The poem continues to glide from subject to subject; it now refers briefly to what Horace does not do—write bad epic or look for publicity (36–40):

> turgidus Alpinus iugulat dum Memnona dumque
> defingit Rheni luteum caput, haec ego ludo...

While swollen Alpinus is murdering Memnon and shaping the yellow source of the Rhine, I play at this . . .

On the surface the transition is abrupt, although Horace has followed the dream's advice and become a Latin poet. But there may again be a connection beneath the surface: Horace has responded not only to the recommendation of Quirinus, but also to the advice Apollo gives in the Callimachean scene on which Horace's dream is modeled, avoiding 'fat' by keeping away from the epic genre. At the same time, the insistence on Horace's poetry as 'play' may serve to counter a possible implication of the choice of Quirinus as inspiring god—

---

[6] See again Fraenkel (1957: 130).

one might have expected the deified Romulus to advocate patriotic, epic themes, particularly in opposition to Greek *versiculi* ('verselets').

By this point the poem appears to have dropped Lucilius completely, as it elaborates Horace's own poetic choices.[7] There is, however, no real opposition between criticism of Lucilius and personal statement, since they will be linked near the end of the work, when it is claimed that the stylistic perfection Horace aspires to, and does not find in Lucilius, demands a limited audience (72–5). The following tongue-in-cheek description of how Horace came to choose satire (40–7) slips back to Lucilius at its close, for Horace claims that he sought a genre which had no successful recent practitioner, but did not thereby imagine himself superior to its inventor (47–9). But while the disappearance of Lucilius from this section is not a problem, the close of Horace's *recusatio* (39), *nec redeunt iterum atque iterum spectanda theatris* ('and [works that] don't come back to be viewed in the theaters again and again'), provides a difficult transition. In context it reads like a dismissal of such composition, a declaration of preference for 'playful' poetry addressed to a small group, but it is immediately followed by praise for a theatrical poet, and the tragedian Pollio and epic poet Varius are next in the list.

What appeared to be a refusal on poetic principle suddenly appears rather as a practical strategy. Horace's refusal to compose in any area where a master was already at work could represent an expression of the Alexandrian rule of avoiding the beaten path, but the famous Alexandrian rejection of the major genres has no place here. As he did in the dream, Horace invites a false assumption about his poetics, and then reveals that his rejection of certain genres is a matter purely of personal style. The relation between 38–48 and 1.4 is an odd one, too; the same topics are discussed (avoidance of publicity, 1.4.71–72; choice of genre, 1.4.103–6), but with a completely different emphasis. In 1.4, Horace's not putting his work before large audiences was a reason for potential objects of satire not to fear him; now it is a poetic principle, or an expression of

---

[7] *Pace* Rudd (1966: 101–2). Lucilius did seek a less restricted and sophisticated audience than Horace claims for himself at 81–8 (fr. 593 Krenkel) and Horace probably implies criticism in distinguishing himself from Lucilius there (cf. Brink (1963: 167–9)), but while the issues are related, there is nothing here to bring Lucilius to mind, and no reason to regard him as a publicity-hound.

aesthetic modesty; in 1.4 Horace seemed to have been inclined to satire by his father's example, and it is a by-product of efforts at moral self-improvement, while here he has chosen the genre for purely aesthetic reasons.

The remainder of the satire is relatively straightforward. Horace first insists on a general right to criticize other poets, exemplified by Lucilius himself (50–5), then repeats and amplifies his objections to Lucilius' style, giving a final summary which concludes with the claim that Lucilius would follow different standards now (56–71); this leads directly to Horace's general statement of the need for care and effort in composition, and the corresponding willingness to accept a small but discerning audience, which is then catalogued, while Demetrius and Tigellius are scorned (72–91).

The poem goes back and forth between discussing Lucilius and presenting Horace's position on the appropriate tactics for the contemporary satirist, but since the connection between these themes is close, there is nothing inherently difficult in this movement. The modulations appear to be deliberate, marked by transitions that overturn a reader's expectations. But Horace, while modulating from Lucilius to himself and back again, seems with equal emphasis to put forward Callimachean themes only to move away from them again. The poem is characterized by its repeated evocations of the clichés of Augustan Callimacheanism. Both the criticisms of Lucilius and the self-characterizations in the poem repeatedly echo the favorite passages of Roman Callimacheans, the close of the *Hymn to Apollo* (105–12) and the proem of the *Aetia* (frs. 1 and 2, especially 1.21–9).[8] The dream is a humorous adaptation of Callimachus' warning from Apollo which gives what is, in effect, Callimachean advice. The description of *turgidus Alpinus'* epic (on a great and muddy river); the complaint that Lucilius is *lutulentus* ('muddy'); and the comparison of Cassius Etruscus to a wild stream all point unmistakably in this direction. Horace's avoidance of the theater and his emphasis on learning in the first part ('not . . . learned', 19, 'literary Johnnies-come-lately', 21), and his emphasis on revision and hard work in composition, with a corresponding preference for a small

---

[8] All citations from Callimachus are from D'Alessio (1996). On the frequent use of these passages in Augustan poetry, see Wimmel (1960) *passim*.

number of discerning readers, in the second (67–90) point to the same aesthetic without direct allusion.

Yet much in the satire seems quite independent of Callimachean-ism, or even opposed to it. The opening emphasis on the importance of variety in satire, avoidance of the *acre* ('harsh'), and use of the masters of Old Comedy as models, while not anti-Callimachean, are not explicit principles of Callimachean poetics.[9] Callimachus' *Iambs* provide an example of how a genre can be made both gentler and more varied, but do not overtly teach these points.[10] Since no precepts for satiric style were available within that tradition, Horace was forced to seek elsewhere if he wished to offer rules rather than vague advice about craftsmanship; but his choosing to do this is striking in a poem whose Callimacheanism is so prominent. He praises equally authors in all genres, epic included, and suggests that his own choice was determined entirely by what was as yet unoccupied (40–3), immediately after he has satirized bloated epic. The satire obviously seeks to define Horatian satire in respect to Lucilius, and slips from passages relevant to the judgment of Lucilius to passages where he is forgotten, but it seems equally concerned with a definition in respect to Callimachus, and moves toward and away from Callimachean allusion in the same way. The allusion to the neoterics Hermogenes and the ape, sandwiched between comments on Old Comedy as the standard for satire and on Lucilius' use of Greek words, suggests that the link may lie in the opponents of Horace: Lucilius' defenders are neoterics, and their admiration for Lucilius is somehow an expression of their neotericism. Yet the standards of fine craftsmanship to which Horace appeals in the poem are precisely those he might be expected to share with admirers of Calvus and Catullus. His repeated appeals to these standards both suggest that Horace sees the issues of Lucilius and Callimacheanism

---

[9] Wimmel (1960: 154–6) stresses the basically Callimachean quality of the prin-ciples of *brevitas* and *varietas*, but points out that these appear along with the profoundly unCallimachean description of the satirist's taking on the role of a *rhetor* (12); Callimachus enunciated no theory of the γελοῖον ('comic'), and would have been unlikely to prefer the *ridiculum* on the grounds that it *melius secat res* ('is better at surgery', 15).

[10] Cucchiarelli (2001: 168–79) shows how Callimachus' re-invention of Hipponax is a model for Horace's reimagining of Lucilius.

as linked, and raise the question of what distinguishes the Callimacheanism of Horace from that of his opponents.

According to the spurious lines affixed to the opening of the poem,
Valerius Cato, the *grammaticus,* neoteric poet, and doyen of neoterics, was a champion of Lucilius. While the lines are spurious, they
probably reflect genuine information, for the connection between
admiration of Lucilius and neoteric modernism they make in the
figure of Cato is an unlikely invention.[11] Cato may have defended
Lucilius for a number of reasons, stylistic or political.[12] His followers
may have joined him in defense of Lucilius simply because his
prestige made it the party line. At any rate, he provides an external
connection between Lucilius and neotericism. The persistence with
which Horace affiliates himself with the basic principles he must have
shared with Cato is, of course, a way of attacking his opponents (real
or imagined) on their own ground. It is not entirely obvious why
Lucilius' apparent supporters should have admired him: the only
positive praise of Lucilius Horace puts in their mouths is his use of
Greek words, which, whatever its place in neoteric practice, is not a
central tenet of neoteric poetics (unlike the Callimachean passages
Horace recalls), while Horace insists that his stylistic objections are
irrefutable (2–3) and implies that objections to his criticism of
Lucilius as *lutulentus* ('muddy') have been based solely on the opponents' feeling that Lucilius should be above the criticism of one
such as Horace (51–6). The attack and the defense against it, in other
words, are not on obviously neoteric ground, as far as substance goes;
Horace has put them there.[13]

---

[11] The overwhelming consensus regards the lines as spurious; the most important
defense of them remains that of Hendrickson (1916) and (1917).

[12] The political claim is made by Anderson (1963b: 64–9), following the suggestion of Marx (1904, vol. 1: li).

[13] So Shackleton Bailey (1982: 30): 'As remarked by Cicero, the "neoterics" did not
think much of Ennius, or presumably of early Latin poetry in general. Why should
people who had no time for anything written much over thirty years ago (for the
"ape" will have been more or less representative) be up in arms about Horace's
strictures upon an early poet? Surely not because of any special affinities with
Lucilius.' Rudd (1966: 119–23) argues for such affinities, but they appear convincing
only on the basis of a historicist-literal reading of the satire, which almost demands
that they exist.

But while it does not seem that the defense was necessitated by a response to Horace which made straightforwardly Alexandrian claims on behalf of Lucilius, the strategy does not seem to make sense either if the defense of Lucilius were entirely independent of the opponents' neoteric affiliations. Horace had considerable latitude in how he chose to characterize and define the opponents within his satire, and it is indeed possible that the hostility to which he replies is partly (or even largely) fictive.[14] He chose to define his opponents as admirers of neoteric poetry, while expending great effort to claim a certain Callimachean ground for himself. Simultaneously he defines himself in contrast to some aspects of Callimacheanism, declaring himself a Callimachean in his insistence on stylistic perfection but otherwise independent of neoteric tradition; the attitude is one which will be typical of Horace.[15] The satire has two targets, super-ficial Callimacheanism and excessive admiration for Lucilius, and the precise self-definition Horace seeks can be achieved only by his establishing himself in respect to both. The two were connected externally by the activity of Cato, and more profoundly by Horace's dislike of all schools and of uninspired imitation. Appropriately, he is explicit about his relationship to the forthright Lucilius, and subtle in alluding to the allusive Callimachus, but the position he takes is similar. On both sides, the satire declares simultaneously allegiance and independence.

I would like to suggest, however, that there is yet a further con-nection between Lucilius and Callimachus, an association between the satires of Lucilius and the *Iambs* of Callimachus, and that, in particular, Horace has in mind the 13th *Iamb* as a parallel for Lucilian practices, which he counters by evoking the central passages of Callimachean aesthetics. Callimachus' *Iamb* 13 defends his use of mixed dialect and his *polyeidea* ('multiformity'); Lucilius has similar

---

[14] The historicity of the attacks to which Horace replies used to be taken for granted: so Kiessling-Heinze (1959: 155); Grube (1965: 233): 'In any case, the criticism of Lucilius obviously annoyed some literary circles in Rome.' Without denying that there was a real basis for Horace's defense, I think it not unlikely that he exaggerated the hostile response in order to close his book with an appropriately programmatic-polemic finale.

[15] Wehrli (1944: 67–76); Wimmel (1960: 153–62, 187–92, and *passim*); on *S.* 2.1, see Clauss (1985).

qualities, and his satire probably owed something to the model of Callimachean iambic.[16] The comparison between Lucilius and Callimachus may have been drawn by Cato, or it may have been Horace's own idea, but, though nowhere made explicit, it provides an underlying reason for Lucilius to serve as the vehicle for Horace to define himself against contemporaries defined as neoterics, and it links the Lucilian subject-matter of the poem with its structure of continual shifting in attitude towards Callimachus. Through play on this identification, the critique of Lucilius enables Horace to establish himself simultaneously as an adherent of Callimachean standards of composition and as an independent who does not follow Callimachus slavishly.

Horace, as the author of the *Epodes*, was thoroughly familiar with Callimachean iambic. The 13th *Iamb* was probably, like *Sat.* 1.10, the last poem in a book, though Horace probably used an edition which included four additional poems in the collection (and modeled his book of *Epodes* on it).[17] It too is a defense against critics real or imagined. It also resumes elements from an earlier poem in the collection: its opening line, Μοῦσαι καλαὶ κἄπολλον, οἷς ἐγὼ σπένδω ('Lovely Muses and Apollo, to whom I make libations'), recalls the mention of Apollo and the Muses in the first poem (8), it returns to the pure choliambic meter of 1, while the intervening poems have used choliambics in combination with other meters or other meters entirely, and it returns to literary polemic and complaints about excessive poetic rivalry, as in 1 Hipponax harangued the φιλόλογοι ('literary scholars', the term used in the *Diegesis*, 1.3) against poetic envy (8 ff.). Horace at *Sat.* 1.4.34–5 echoes *Iamb* 1.78–9, and it would be typical Horatian technique, in returning to the theme of the earlier poem, to return also to the Callimachean equivalent.

Where the mutilated papyrus of *Iamb* 13 becomes reasonably legible, the critics are attacking Callimachus for his use of a mixed dialect (11–21):

---

[16] Puelma Piwonka (1949).

[17] This is a controversial issue. Pfeiffer (1949) calls these poems Μέλη ('Lyrics'). Arguing for thirteen *Iambi*, Dawson (1950: 132–3); Clayman (1976: 29–35); Puelma Piwonka (1949: 232–3); Kerkhecker (1999: 271–82). Favoring thirteen but cautious: Acosta-Hughes (2002: 9–13). For 17: Ardizzoni (1963: 257–63); Cameron (1995: 167–73); D'Alessio (1996: 43–7); Lelli (2005: 1–27).

ἐκ γὰρ ......[. οὔτ'] Ἴωσι συμμείξας
οὔτ' Ἔφεσον ἐλθών, ἥτις ἐστι.αμ.[
Ἔφεσον, ὅθεν περ οἱ τὰ μέτρα μέλλοντες
τὰ χωλὰ τίκτειν μὴ ἀμαθῶς ἐναύ|ονται·
ἀλλ' εἴ τι θυμὸν ἢ 'πὶ γαστέρα πνεϝα.[
εἴτ' οὖν ἐπ... ἀρχαῖον εἴτ' απαι.|[..].[
τοῦτ' ἐμπ[έ]πλεκται καὶ λαλευσ|[..].[
Ἰαστὶ καὶ Δωριστὶ καὶ τὸ σύμμικ|τον[
τ[ε]ῦ μέχρι τολμᾷς; οἱ φίλοι σε δησ|ουσ[
κ[ἢ]ν νοῦν ἔχωσιν, ἐγχέουσι τὴν[κρᾶσιν
ὡς ὑγιείης οὐδὲ τὤνυχι ψαύεις

Not mingling with Ionians, nor going to Ephesus, which is...Ephesus, where those who plan to compose in limping meter not incompetently light their fires. But if at all...blows (?) on spirit or belly, whether...ancient or...this is woven in and talking Ionic and Doric and mixed. To what point will you have the nerve to do? Your friends will imprison you, if they are sensible, and will pour out the mixture, since you do not touch Health even with your fingernail.[18]

Callimachus' first-person reply is unfortunately badly mutilated. He may possibly use legal language to insist that the case will not be lost without a hearing,[19] and he seems to accuse the opponent of some kind of dishonest business. But at line 30 his argument becomes clear again; the issue has shifted from Callimachus' dialect to his writing in various genres (30–4):

τίς εἶπεν αυτ[....]λε..ρ.[....].
σὺ πεντάμετρα συντίθει, σὺ δ' η[ρῷο]ν,
σὺ δὲ τραγῳδε[ῖν] ἐκ θεῶν ἐκληρώσω;
δοκέω μὲν οὐδείς, ἀλλὰ καὶ το.δ..κεψαι

Who said...you compose pentameters, you epic, and you have gotten tragedy as your lot from the gods? I believe, nobody, but even...

The poem appears to have continued with the theme for some time. According to the *Diegesis* (9.335–8), Callimachus adduced the example of Ion of Chios as a poet who was successful in many genres (43–7), and compared poets to carpenters, who are not blamed for

18 'Pour out the mixture': either of medicine or the libation to Health. See Pfeiffer ad loc. for support for the supplement [κρᾶσιν and parallels for the proposed allusion to the *poculum Sanitatis*.
19 Pfeiffer ad loc.

making different kinds of goods. It is not clear whether *polyeidea* refers to the collection of *Iambi* alone, whose poems encompass a wide range of tones, subjects, and meters, or the Callimachean corpus as a whole; the first alternative fits better with the preceding theme of dialect mixture, where choliambics are explicitly mentioned; the issue is not just how to write verse but how to write in this genre. But the denial that there is a 'one poet, one genre' rule and the example of Ion of Chios fit the second better, for Ion is praised for his work in different genres, not for expanding the boundaries of these forms.[20]

The connection between the two topics is somewhat unclear (as are so many of Horace's transitions); the complaint of πολυείδεα, 'multiformity', may have appeared in the lines missing at the opening of the poem, and the link may have been clearer in the opponent's speech. At any rate, they are linked by a general theme of poetic license versus control. To write in pure dialect appropriate to the genre, and to observe fixed generic boundaries, whether within a single book or in one's whole poetic activity, are both acts of loyalty to conventions and rules and mark an acceptance of limits. Mixing dialects, on the other hand, and refusing to follow circumscribed generic limits or to define oneself exclusively as a particular type of poet, are both forms of independence. Furthermore, the linguistic peculiarities of Callimachus' choliambic would naturally serve as evidence that the poet who fluttered from genre to genre had failed to observe the rules proper to each. The envious—probably the specialists in one form or another—objecting to such a wide sphere of activity as poetic πολυπραγμοσύνη (not minding one's own business), and resentful of their inability to escape competition by selecting a particular genre, would be particularly annoyed that Callimachus, the 'dilettante', takes liberties with the tradition. But the complaint about *polyeideia* shows more openly the personal motives of the complainer than that about language and so leads into the following section.

---

[20] Clayman (1980: 48–51) argues that the term refers 'directly and exclusively' to the *Iambi* (Horace's *Epodes* illustrate this type of *polyeideia* precisely) but does not confront the problem this creates for the example of Ion. The issue continues to be debated: Lelli (2004: 126–7).

The poem then returns to the theme of poetic rivalry which dominated the first poem (52–3):

.]..να | οιδος ἐς κέρας τεθύμωται
κοτέω]ν ἀοιδῷ κἠμὲ δει..ταπραχ ...]

A singer is angry as a bull, furious with a singer, and me, too...

The legal context (re-)appears, as a poet τὴν γενὴν ἀνακρίνει ('questions the birth', 54) of another, presumably Callimachus, and accuses him of being a tattooed runaway slave (55–6). The Muses themselves are frightened (58–9):

φαύλοις ὁμι[λ]εῖ[ν ....].ν παρέπτησαν
καὐταὶ τρομεῦσαι μὴ κακῶς ἀκούσωσι·

to associate with the bad ... have flown by, and trembling themselves for fear they get a bad reputation

Poets as a result do not eat well, but scrape with their fingernails like visitors at Delos who take tiny bits from the sacred olive tree (60–2):

τοῦδ' οὕνεκ' οὐδὲν πῖον, ἀ[λλὰ] λιμηρᾷ]
ἕκαστος ἄκροις δακτύλοις ἀποκνίζει,
ὡς τῆς ἐλαίης, ἣ ἀνέπαυσε τὴν Λητώ.

For this reason each one scrapes off with the tips of his fingers nothing fat, but pieces of starvation, as if from the olive-tree that gave rest to Leto.

Backbiting has presumably led to disillusionment and lack of support by patrons. In the final surviving lines Callimachus seems to take over the words of his imagined adversaries (63–6):

μηθ.[..] ....ν ἀείδω
οὔτ'[Ἐφεσο]ν ἐλ[θὼ]ν οὔτ' [Ἰω]σι συμμείξας,
Ἔφεσον, ὅθεν περ οἱ τὰ μέτρα μέλλοντες
τὰ χωλὰ τίκτειν μὴ ἀμαθῶς ἐναύονται

Nor...I sing, not having gone to Ephesus nor mingled with Ionians—Ephesus, where those who are going to give birth to lame meters intelligently light their fires

The resemblances between this poem and Horace's satire should not, of course, be exaggerated. The basic situations in which the poems are set are quite different, for Horace's self-defense is presented as a defense of his criticism of his predecessor, while Callimachus' is a straightforward response to complaints about his own work. But there is a striking coincidence of theme between this poem and sections of Horace's which do not echo the more famous programmatic passages of Callimachus. In each case Horace, handling a theme similar to that of Callimachus, takes the opposing position. Callimachus defends himself against critics who object to his use of mixed dialect. Horace, on the other hand, attacks those who admire Lucilius for mixing Greek words in his Latin. The issue is not quite the same, but the analogy is there, and in each case the issue is one of linguistic purity; the charge against which Callimachus defends himself is the Greek equivalent of the complaint Horace makes against Lucilius. Callimachus' opponents implicitly accuse him of ignorance, for the poet who wishes to compose choliambics 'not ignorantly' gets his fire at Ephesus, as Callimachus has failed to do; Horace accuses his opponents of being poetic late learners for believing that it is a good thing to mix Greek and Latin.[21] Furthermore, each poet employs the image of wine-mixing. For Horace's opponent, Greek and Latin combined produce a mixture that is *suavior, ut Chio nota si commixta Falerni est* ('sweeter, just as the Falernian brand is mixed with Chian', 24); Callimachus' friends, conversely, will have to mix the wine for his libation to Hygieia, for his linguistic behavior is an evident mark of insanity and shows that he has not had any dealings with this goddess.

Horace at 40–9 defends his choice of genre on purely poetic grounds, with no apparent need to do so, since nobody (in this satire) has criticized the choice. The implied accusation, that Horace considers himself better than Lucilius (and has presumably chosen to write satire for this reason), has no parallel in Callimachus. But while there is no relationship between the passages at a deep level, Horace chooses to explain his choice by implying that there is room for only one first rate practitioner of a genre in a generation, and that each poet is attached to a particular genre. In the case of Virgil, the generic choice is described as determined by the Camenae (44–5): *molle atque facetum | Vergilio adnuerunt gaudentes rure Camenae* ('The

---

[21] I take μὴ ἀμαθῶς ('not unintelligently') with τίκτειν ('to give birth'), but the implication is still present if it is taken with ἐναύονται ('they light their fires'): those who do not get their inspiration from Ephesus are composing stupidly.

Camenae who rejoice in the countryside granted the soft and elegant
to Virgil'). This is exactly what Callimachus, defending his composition in many genres, denies takes place: nobody is given a form of
poetry, be it elegy, epic, or tragedy, by divine ordinance and required
to keep to it. In 44–7 or 49 he enumerates the areas where Ion of
Chios was outstanding: τραγῳδοὺς ... π]εντάμετρον ... Λυδὸν] πρὸς
αὐλὸν λ .... καὶ χορδάς: 'tragedies ... pentameter ... to the Lydian
pipe ... and strings'. Ion is a particularly significant example, since he
was not the only major practitioner of his time in these genres, and
his work is apparently described as perfect (48–9):

$$] \ \hat{\eta}\nu \ \gamma\grave{\alpha}\rho \ \grave{\epsilon}\nu\tau\epsilon\lambda\acute{\epsilon}\varsigma \ \tau\epsilon \ \tau\grave{o} \ \chi\rho\hat{\eta}\mu\alpha$$

For the work was complete

Horace declines to follow the iambic Callimachus even as his underlying argument takes a Callimachean position; in seeking the Calli-
machean goal of originality (ἑτέρων ἴχνια μὴ καθ᾽ ὁμά | δίφρον ἐλᾶν,
'Do not drive your chariot along the same tracks as others', *Aet.* fr.
1.26–7), he rejects the Callimachean authority to attempt many
genres. Of course Horace is disingenuous here: he surely did not
believe that divine powers had allotted a single genre to each poet,
and was indeed composing *Epodes* and *Satires* in the same period, but
by claiming that he was obliged to find a single poetic form for
himself, he not only removes the issue of his choice of satire from
the moral ground on which he justified it in 1.4, but presents the
generic choice as evidence of his dedication to ideals of poetic
excellence which are appropriate to his situation as a Roman poet.
Although the restriction to a single genre shows the poet's modesty,
for he does not attempt a form already handled by a poet he admires,
it places him firmly within a catalogue of poets who among them
bring a new excellence to Roman poetry in all genres. Horace's
contemporaries have a task to perform for Latin poetry, and playful
experimentation in each other's genres would interfere with it.

Callimachus proceeds to attack excessive poetic polemic as Horace
likewise treats the issue of poetic polemic, though here, as before, his
argument is the reverse of Callimachus', as he defends his right to
criticism of other poets, a right which depends on the implied claim
that perfection does not exist. His tone is completely unlike that of

the enraged poets of Callimachus. Horace makes no claims to be better than Lucilius and reminds the reader that he has surely found flaws in Homer himself, while Lucilius criticized the weaknesses of Accius and Ennius, likewise without pretending to be superior to them. Whereas Callimachus depicts a world in which poetic rivalry is fueled by envy and has reached a level which is destructive to poetry itself, Horace depicts a world of courteous poet-critics motivated only by their high standards and humble in their own pretensions.

The entire middle section of Horace's poem thus bears a general resemblance to Callimachus' in its sequence of themes-linguistic purity, choice of genre, and the appropriateness of poetic po-lemic—which strongly suggests that in this part of the satire he is following Callimachus. But in each case Horace takes a decisively un-Callimachean attitude, even though the transition between the first and second of these topics (the dream and the attack on Alpinus) is a positive, if humorous, evocation of Callimachean poetics. The first issue places Callimachus and Lucilius on the same side, in opposition to Horace, as linguistically impure. The second implies no connec-tion between Callimachus and Lucilius; the third, on the other hand, appropriates Lucilius as a model for the reasonable poetic polemic he espouses, so unlike the vicious style of the poets depicted by Cal-limachus. It appears that the satire may be as much about Callima-chus as about Lucilius. While one recurring element is the criticism of Lucilius for failing to meet the standards of Callimachus' non-iambic pronouncements, a second is an implied criticism of Callima-chus' iambic practice, one which significantly begins from a point at which Callimachus and Lucilius resemble each other. Horace is not just using neoteric standards against neoteric critics; he is employing one side of Callimachus against the other. Callimachus' general ideals demand a rejection of some elements of his iambics, and Lucilius in those respects in which his work resembles or follows Callimachus' iambic practice is not to be praised or imitated. Just as Greek words are not to be taken directly into Latin, but need to be translated, as Horace translated the Greek term ὀψιμαθεῖς into *seri studiorum,* so critical principles are not to be taken over wholesale and indiscrim-inately applied.

The Callimachean poem stands in a complex relationship to other Callimachean programmatic statements, and Horace's relationship

228 *Ruth Scodel*

to it is similarly complex. Callimachus' image of the poor poets scratching for food because the Muses refuse to associate with them recalls and reverses Pindar's Archilochus (*P.* 2.55–6), fattened on hatred. But their state is created by the absence of the Muses, and should therefore be poetic as much as economic. The image of their scraping with their fingers recalls the earlier complaint that Callimachus has not touched Hygieia (the goddess Health) with his finger-nails, as evidenced by the madness of his poetry. In the famous speech of Apollo in the *Aetia* preface, it is the poet who feeds the Muse and should avoid making her fat; in the *Iamb*, the Muse feeds the poet, who would like more fat than he gets. The presence of the Muse would mean a richer diet for the poets; but poetic diet is inevitably associated with poetic style. The *Iamb* thus seems almost to contradict one of the central images of Roman Callimacheanism by expressing a desire for fat rather than famine, but 'fat' here is probably not the stylistic excess and bombast condemned in the *Aetia*, but poetic resources and imagination, which the poets have lost along with patronage through their obsessive squabbling.

The imagery of Callimachus' poetic program, in other words, is not as simple as Roman Callimacheanism made it, and in any case, the basic rule of Callimachus was to avoid whatever was stale or hackneyed. Horace was not interested in a poetic dogma, and, fur-thermore, must have felt that nothing could be less in the spirit of Callimachus than an attempt narrowly to imitate Callimachus.[22] His satire asserts that the basic principles of Callimachean art require above all that weaknesses should not be defended because they have analogues in the master's practice, and that Latin poets must find a way to imitate Greeks without trying to be Greeks. Horace refuses to imitate Callimachus literally, but advocates a more profound kind of imitation. The *Iamb* is itself a defense of poetic liberty and a revolt against too slavish a form of imitation, for Callimachus insists on his right to compose within the Hipponactean genre without confining himself to Hipponax' dialect or taking his inspiration from Ephesus. In imitating a model, he does not give up his own identity, neither his style nor his place of origin. Similarly, Horace is a Callimachean who

[22] Barchiesi (2001), examines the dynamics of Horace's imitation of both archaic iambic and Callimachus in the *Epodes*.

does not write in Greek or a Latin that imitates Callimachus' Greek and who emphasizes his own Romanness. But while for Callimachus the mixed dialect marked the independence and freedom of a cosmopolitan self, the Roman poet's linguistic situation is different, and impurity makes him less himself and more like Pitholeon of Rhodes or a resident of Canusium.

Too narrow a view of Callimacheanism is the flaw that the satire uses to link the defenders of Lucilius and their neoteric program, and it is by rejecting such a view that Horace at once places himself on Callimachean ground and declares his originality and independence. This underlying goal may help explain the transition between the argument that the poet who writes in Latin should write pure Latin (21–30), and the dream in which Quirinus warns Horace against writing Greek verses (31–5). Both are slavish forms of imitation, which avoid the real task of making Greek poetic achievements fully and originally Latin. The dream exemplifies what that task is by thoroughly romanizing a Greek original. The opening of the poem, with its list of qualities desirable in satire and its repetition of the emphasis on Old Comedy of 1.4, has a similar effect. The lines point to a completely non-neoteric model, but one that demands real learning rather than mere fashionable imitation from its followers, and that is hence more truly in the best Callimachean tradition—and the model, incidentally, followed by Callimachus in *Iamb* 1 in bringing back Hipponax from the Underworld. Callimachus himself repeatedly cites classical poets as his authorities, so that Horace's use of Old Comedy is in the master's spirit. Moreover, the kind of satire Horace recommends, which emphasizes the *ridiculum* over the *acre*, is hardly based on Old Comedy, but is in fact exactly the mode of Callimachean iambic (which is milder than Callimachus' polemic style elsewhere). While Horace rejects specific elements of Callimachean practice, he still composes in the spirit the *Iambs* recommend. In insisting on his right to engage in poetic criticism, he completely avoids the malicious spirit that is Callimachus' real target; in explaining his choice of satire as the result of a 'one poet, one genre' rule, he contradicts the actual assertions of the *Iamb* but also implies a desire for high standards and a membership in a friendly brotherhood of writers of different types that is in the spirit *Iamb* 1 recommends with its anecdote of the Seven Sages, each deferring to the next. In

composing satire, as later in pursuing philosophy, Horace was constantly determined to emphasize his independence, but although
nullius addictus iurare in verba magistri ('not obligated to swear
according to the text of any teacher') and consistently scornful of
those who were mere followers—thus placing himself firmly on the
side of basic Callimachean principles—he implies that the true
carrier of a tradition is not the slavish imitator but the poet who
adapts his master in the same spirit in which the master adapted his
own predecessors.

9

Ultra Legem: Law and Literature in Horace, *Satires* 2.1

Jeffrey Tatum

The first poem in the second book of Horace's *Satires* represents a dialogue between the satirist and the eminent jurist, Gaius Trebatius Testa.[1] The presence of the jurist, it has been observed, is remarkable. Likewise the literary shape of this opening poem, which departs from the monologues of Book One. The subject, or at least the ostensible subject, of the conversation between the two men is the degree to which the poet's compositions have exposed their author to legal hazard and how best to address Horace's potential vulnerability. Recent critical scrutiny has complicated (and thereby improved) our appreciation of *Sat.* 2.1 by concentrating on three important yet controversial distinctions: (i) How does this poem negotiate the difference between law and literature encapsulated in the expression *ultra legem*, found in the opening lines? (ii) Which constitutes the true programmatic matter of this opening satire, moral (or legal) issues or stylistic and compositional ones? (iii) Is this satire serious or ironic? These three questions, clearly related to one another, introduce concerns so crucial and so obviously fruitful to any understanding of Horace's early poetry that it seems difficult to elude the conclusion that the dynamic of their competitive claims is, in no

---

[1] Trebatius was 'the most important lawyer of the period' in the opinion of Bauman (1985: 2; cf. 123–36). For a brief characterization of Trebatius, who had been the friend of Cicero (cf. Cic. *Fam.* 7.5–22) and was in good standing with Octavian, see F. Muecke (1993: 99–100), with further references.

small measure, itself a vital aspect of this poem.[2] In other words, *Sat.*
2.1 may fairly be said to exhibit that characteristically Augustan
'multiplicity of resonances' which, in the words of one influential
study of the period, 'can be experienced on several levels, depending
on the intellectual and social horizon of the reader'.[3] All of which
urges us to pay special attention to the poem's conclusion, which at
least holds out the prospect (however problematic) of a resolution to
the various oppositions that are operative throughout the piece. For,
in the end, all readings of Horace's satires, whatever their divergences
from one another, must nevertheless yield to a single reading: the one
entertained by Caesar.

In the opening lines of *Sat.* 2.1 the satirist observes to Trebatius:

> sunt quibus in satira videar nimis acer et ultra
> legem tendere opus.

In my satires I appear to some to be excessively acrid and to be stretching my
work beyond what is legitimate.

The jurist, quite reasonably, takes the expression *ultra legem* to be a
reference to what we may here conveniently call the law of libel. The
satirist, however, because he goes on to defend his habit of versifica-
tion mainly in literary terms, is ordinarily taken to have meant the
phrase as a reference to a generic or stylistic principle. This ambiguity
is the essential point of departure for the entire dialogue, one consequence of which has been a majority consensus amongst commentators that the interlocutors of *Sat.* 2.1 simply speak different
languages. W. S. Anderson, for example, insists that 'the satirist and
Trebatius converse on two entirely different levels'. N. Rudd observes
that aesthetic principles are 'cleverly confused with the law of libel',
and E. Fraenkel speaks of 'the blending of two different elements'.
F. Muecke, who insists on an even sharper division than her prede-

---

[2] It should be said at the outset that no one fails to recognize the humorous tone of
Sat. 2.1. That the poem nevertheless addresses serious political concerns represents the
view of Smith (1951: 169–79); Fraenkel (1957: 145–53); LaFleur (1981: 1790–1826);
Muecke (1995: 203–18); McGinn (2001: 81–102). Ironic interpretations include
Anderson (1984: 35–42); Harrison (1987: 38–52); Freudenburg (1990: 187–203), the
last of whom concentrates on stylistic issues raised by specific terms and expressions
employed in *Sat.* 2.1.
[3] Galinsky (1996: 229).

cessors, argues for 'the autonomy of these two distinct and independent voices'.[4] Only A. D. Leeman, so far as I know, discerns a
significant interpenetrating of legal and literary matters, and that is
because in his view the two subjects find common ground in the
rhetorical construction of their argumentation.[5] In reviewing these
approaches one cannot but recollect the strictures of Richard Posner,
who, in his opposition to contemporary theorists seeking to establish
a strong commonality between literature and law, insists upon their
complete separateness.[6] This modern dialogue is not wholly irrelevant to the dialogue between Horace and Trebatius: after all, literary
criticism luxuriates in multiple readings of a given text, be they
complementary or competitive, in full awareness that the interpretation of a text alters it forever for subsequent readers (at least for
those in the know); although the actual application (i.e. interpretation) of a legal text also transforms the law that is being applied in a
particular legal situation, this process does not normally lead to
multiple and competing readings of the same legal text, else its just
application should fail.

   The conversation between the dignified yet reductive jurist and the
clever but irrepressible poet has often been felt to be so one-sided in
favor of the latter that it has been described as 'shadow-boxing', a
common conclusion that tends to give rise to the idea that the poem is
too playful to be engaging serious or political matters.[7] But DuQuesnay's study of the first book of *Satires* has demonstrated how effectively Horace can exploit ironic and even self-deprecating verses to
explore topics 'which are at the heart of contemporary analysis of
Rome's problems'.[8] In light of the apparent continuity between the
closing poem of Book One and the opening satire of Book Two (in
despite of the change in form from monologue to dialogue), one can
hardly be blamed for at least considering the possibility that *Sat.* 2.1

----

   [4] Anderson (1982: 118); Rudd (1966: 130–1); Fraenkel (1957: 147); Muecke (1995:
203). A similar distinction is drawn by Littlewood (2002: 59–63).
   [5] Leeman (1982: 159–63).
   [6] Posner (1988). The common relationship between law and literature is stressed
by (amongst others) Eagleton (1986); Jardine (1996); Kornstein (1996).
   [7] The expression is employed by Rudd (1966: 128).
   [8] DuQuesnay (1984: 19–58, the quotation is from p. 57). Horatian irony and self-
deprecation: Zetzel (1980).

is at some level serious when it incorporates into its text the themes of law, of *amicitia* and of *Caesar invictus*.[9] Some of that seriousness, it is here proposed, has been missed because too sharp a dichotomy has been established between the poem's interlocutors, a severe division that has tended to distract from their common satisfaction (and the basis of that satisfaction) at the poem's end. For though they unquestionably commence their conversation from different perspectives, it becomes increasingly difficult, as the poem progresses, to sustain the view that the spheres and sensibilities of the jurist and the poet are so extremely distinct as is ordinarily maintained. Each displays an awareness of the realities of literature and of the realities of Roman life, and each is representative of a category of intellectual endeavor that confronts Roman society with a demand for moral excellence.

Let me make my case briefly. Trebatius enters the poem as the advocate of silence, unsurprising advice from an Epicurean (Cic. *Fam.* 7.12; Gell. 7.12.1) but a recommendation that would, obviously, annihilate Horace the poet. But Trebatius, in historical fact as well as in the world of *Sat.* 2.1, is adept at literature.[10] He is quite familiar with the hierarchy of genres: filling in for Apollo, it is he who encourages the poet to turn to epic, a proposition the poet rejects by resorting to *recusatio* (lines 10–15).[11] The jurist then suggests that the poet write of Caesar within the domain of satire, as Lucilius did of Scipio (lines 16–17). This our satirist will perhaps do—but he must find the proper, specific opportunity:

> . . . nisi dextro tempore Flacci
> verba per attentam non ibunt Caesaris aurem
> cui male si palpere, recalcitret undique tutus   (18–20)

. . . unless the time is right, Flaccus' words will not find Caesar's ear attentive; if you stroke him the wrong way, he will kick out in all directions to keep himself safe.

---

[9] *Sat.* 1.10, like *Sat.* 2.1, deals with Lucilius, with genre, with friendship and with aesthetic matters. Furthermore, the poems alluded to at *Sat.* 2.1.1–4 are clearly the satires of Book One. Cf. Rudd (1966: 128) 'the links with Book 1 are obvious'.

[10] Cic. *Fam.* 7.6; 7.12; 7.16. The reductive reading of Trebatius is sustained by McGinn (2001: 98–9).

[11] Fundamental on *recusatio* is Wimmel (1960, *Sat.* 2.1 is discussed at 162–7). Horace and Augustan *recusatio*: Lyne (1995: 31–9). For the suggestion that this *recusatio* makes specific allusion to Callimachus' *Hymn to Apollo*, see Clauss (1985: 197–206).

Horace proceeds to describe once more his humble origins, making it explicit that his lineage is inferior to Lucilius' (lines 28–9 and 34–78). Trebatius then anticipates the satirist's main line of defense: his powerful friends. If the poet continues in his current vein, the jurist worries:

> ... o puer, ut sis
> vitalis metuo et maiorum ne quis amicus
> frigore te feriat   (61–2)

... my dear boy, I am afraid that you will not last long and that any one of your powerful friends will give you the cold shoulder

a warning that seems not to affect the satirist:

> infra Lucili censum ingeniumque, tamen me
> cum magnis vixisse invita fatebitur usque
> Invidia   (75–7)

Although I am inferior to Lucilius in status and talent, nonetheless Envy will grudgingly concede that I have constantly lived amongst the great.

And, like Lucilius, Horace expects the safety and support of his powerful friends.

This was not by any means an uncontroversial resource. Book One of the *Satires* celebrated the poet's *amicitia* with Maecenas: it was in this atmosphere of friendship that the poet could create poetry that inscribed 'true *libertas*, which is traditional and responsible'.[12] But that same friendship was (and is) susceptible to alternative constructions: Zetzel, for instance, sees in the poet of Book One a persona that is 'smug, elitist and rude', a total insider envied for his social and political adroitness and opportunism.[13] That there existed ancient parallels for this construction is implied inescapably by the poet's own 'image-management'.[14] Yet, for all that, critics have probably been right to emphasize the charming and attractive dimensions of the poet's *amicitia* with Maecenas as it is represented in Book One, a representation that, as DuQuesnay has argued, permitted Horace to offer oblique support to Octavian, not least because, whatever his

[12] DuQuesnay (1984: 30).
[13] Zetzel (1980, the quotation is from p. 71).
[14] See Lyne (1995: 12–30).

position in terms of the realities of power, Maecenas could be
delineated primarily as a man of culture (and of public spirit) and
not as a political figure formidable in his own right. *Sat.* 2.1 represents a significant shift, since *Caesar invictus*, be he triumvir or
budding Princeps, could never be simply a man of good taste. His
power and station made that impossible. Indeed, as A. Wallace-
Hadrill has stressed in a study surveying the whole of the Principate,
the emperor could never actually be just like any other (even powerful) *amicus*.[15] The lesson required some time to sink in, but this poem,
in raising the issue of *amicitia* in the context of putative legal threats,
introduces, perhaps for the first time in Rome, the problematic nature
of post-Actium *amicitia* with Caesar. It should not go unnoticed that,
in our poem, it is Trebatius who introduces the *praemia* of epic and
the merits of Lucilian panegyric: the jurist knows the *leges* of literary
forms. He also recognizes the poet's reliance on his estimable associates and concedes the protection that one can enjoy by dint of having
powerful *amici* (line 89). But that is a pragmatic resource—extra-legal
and extra-literary—that the poet, not the jurist, deems an appropriate
recourse. We shall return to this.

Finally, Trebatius make his last point:

> sed tamen ut monitus caveas, ne forte negoti
> incutiat tibi quid sanctarum inscitia legum.
> si mala condiderit in quem quis carmina, ius est
> iudiciumque.   (80–3)

Nevertheless you have been warned to take care lest your ignorance of our
sacred laws cause you trouble. 'If anyone will have composed harmful verses
against someone else', there is recourse to the law and the courts.

Here the jurist makes syncopated allusion to the XII Tables. I agree
with J. D. Cloud in seeing here an antiquarian reference that underscores the jurist's (and of course the author's) erudition.[16] In the
matter of libel, the provision of the XII Tables had by Horace's day
been superseded by legislation *de iniuria*, whatever the details.[17] The

---

[15] Wallace-Hadrill (1982: 32–48). See also Feeney (1992: 1–25, esp. 7–9).

[16] Cloud (1996: 569; cf. 677–721).

[17] Smith (1951: 169–71); LaFleur (1981: 1790–1826); Cloud (1996: 679). Already
in Cicero's day, most people believed that the praetor's edict, and not the XII Tables,
was the source of law: cf. Cic. *Leg.* 1.17.

actual language of the XII Tables, in its latest reconstruction, distinguished evil spells from invective song:

qui malum carmen incantassit... <quive> occentassit Carmen<ve>
cibd<issit>...

whoever cast a magic spell... <or whoever> sing in enmity <or> compose
a song...

Horace's reformulation eliminates the issue of black magic, so that
mala carmina are, in Trebatius' application of the statute, vitupera-
tive verses. The satirist, however, reads the law differently: for him,
mala signifies the verses' aesthetic quality, not their content, which is
to say, not their generic category. The two characters' interpretations
of the legal text differ, but they are not wholly antithetical. And what
must be noted is that both Trebatius and the satirist are applying a
legal statute in terms of its relevance to literature, if to different
aspects of literature.[18]

   Who is to adjudicate between their cross readings—and the critical
readings of Horace's detractors? The poet's judges in lines 1–4 were
the anonymous and universal *sunt quibus* and *altera pars*. By the
poem's end, however, the universal estimation has become irrelevant.[19] One man's reading of Horace's verse is what matters:

> ...Esto, si quis mala; sed bona si quis
> iudice condiderit laudatus Caesare? Si quis
> opprobriis dignum latraverit integer ipse?   (83–5)

...So be it, if anyone composes bad verses. But what if he composes good
verses and is praised for them, with Caesar as judge? What if he barks at
someone who deserves criticism, so long as he himself is blameless?

The aesthetic quality of his *carmina*—as well as their aptness to the
particular situation—will be the evidence entertained by Caesar and
not the rules of the hierarchy of genres. Under those circumstances,
Trebatius immediately concedes, the satirist need have no fear for his
legal safety (line 86).

---

   [18] Jurists as interpreters of archaic texts: Rawson (1985: 205–8).
   [19] Although it is worth observing that the laughter in which this poem dissolves
implicates Horace's audience in the view that he is rightly regarded as innocent: cf.
Plaza (2003: 355).

Freudenburg has enumerated in impressive detail the aesthetic implications of the language of *Sat.* 2.1 and is correct to include stylistic concerns in the poem's programmatic agenda.[20] However, it is not often enough observed that the poet's introduction of literary quality as a matter of legal concern is not wholly facetious. Let us leave aside for the moment the question of literary invective. Suetonius informs us that Augustus encouraged literary talent in every genre; however, he was jealous of his public image and took offense when he was made the subject of *inferior compositions.* He even went so far as to warn the praetors not to allow his name to be cheapened at public performances:

ingenia saeculi sui omnibus modis fovit. recitantis et benigne et patienter audiit, nec tantum carmina et historias, sed et orations et dialogos. componi tamen aliquid de se nisi et serio et a praesentissimis offendebatur, admonebatque praetors ne paterentur nomen suum commissionibus obsolefieri. (Suet. *Aug.* 89.3)

He nurtured the talents of his age in every way. He listened with kindly patience to those who recited not only their poems and histories but also speeches and dialogues. However, he was offended when anything was written about himself unless it was both serious and from the pen of the most distinguished authors. And he regularly admonished the praetors not to allow his name to be debased at public events.

This item is undatable as it stands in Suetonius, nor does the biographer tell us on what specific legal grounds the praetors were to regulate the proper presentation of the Princeps' name (praetors, of course, acted as the chief administrators of the Roman games).[21] The item can hardly be unrelated to the question of libel, but as it stands it has far more to do with literary standards for laudatory references than with political toleration for invective. In other words, this passage suffices to show that Trebatius' earlier advice to the satirist (to switch to epic) was out of touch with the political realities of his and Horace's time. Quality, not genre, is what mattered to Caesar. Hence the poet—not the literal minded jurist—emerges as the realist.

The question of libel, the opinion of a jurist and the personal judgment of Caesar combine to establish the problem of *ad hominem*

---

[20] Freudenburg (1990).
[21] Talbert (1984: 59–64).

justice as a motif subtending the whole of *Sat.* 2.1. Libel in Rome was a status issue: the elite were immune; a member of a vulnerable class, such as Horace, himself lampooned, so he claims at *Sat.* 1.6.45–6, as the freedman's son who was friend to the great Maecenas and had once been a military tribune, could not speak out against his betters with impunity. Libel, then, was an *iniuria* depending on who said what to whom. The exercise of free speech, of *libertas*, has been much discussed, and its standing as a class privilege during the Roman republic is well established.[22] And it is clearly as a class issue that libel (and by implication *libertas*) are configured in *Sat.* 2.1.

One of the more obvious failings of Roman justice during the republican period was its *ad hominem* quality, which naturally favored the privileges of the elite and underlined the disadvantages of the lower orders, who had to accept justice as it was meted out by their superiors. It was just this state of affairs that necessitated legislation that forbade praetors any divergence from their own edicts (the *Lex Cornelia* of 67 BCE).[23] Hitherto praetors had not scrupled to dispense justice on the basis of their friendship with or hostility toward the parties of suits.[24] The senate did not approve of this corrective measure, since the undispassionate execution of praetorian responsibility has served as a valuable source of *gratia* (Asc. 59C), but the law was very appealing to the rest of Rome. Indeed, Bruce Frier has proposed that one factor in the emergence of Roman jurists was the desire to achieve a rule-oriented approach to litigation that would lessen the advantages held by the senatorial grandee.[25] The age of Augustus led to the (relative) triumph of *aequitas*. But, in the triumviral period, a period of proscriptions and confiscations, the exercise of law preserved a distinctly *ad hominem* quality (cf. Virg.

[22] In addition to Smith (1951) and LaFleur (1981) see Momigliano (1942: 120–4); Daube (1951: 411–50).

[23] *Lex Cornelia*: Asc. 59C; Dio 36.40.1–2; cf. Frier (1985: 75); Lewis (2006: 264). On the intellectual methods of jurists, cf. Rawson (1985: 201–14).

[24] Frier (1985: 73). Cf. also Kelly (1966: 31–68) and Johnston (1999: 124–6) on the inequities of the late republic. The resources available to the plaintiff of low rank (essentially patronage and compelling public pressures in response to an enormity) are discussed by Garnsey (1970: 189–92), who concludes that 'the situation of the weaker plaintiff improved with the end of the republic and the coming of the Empire' (p. 192).

[25] Frier (1985: 256–65).

Ecl. 1). Consequently, in the aftermath of Actium, as the Principate slowly began, even hesitantly, to take its form, anxiety over the administration of justice could hardly be escaped by a majority either amongst the traditional elites or by the new men whom the perturbation of the triumviral period had carried to some prominence.[26]

Who Trebatius actually was in Roman society matters to a proper appreciation of this literary dialogue just as much as does Horace's carefully constructed literary identity. In *Sat.* 2.1 Trebatius embodies the principles of jurisprudence. The satirist, on the other hand, who is exactly the sort of inferior person who should be attracted to the advantages of the jurists' approach to law, instead challenges Trebatius' principled view of things by appealing to the very system of *ad hominem* justice that the jurists sought to eliminate. That a person of Horace's ilk could benefit from old style connections was a reflection of the disintegration of the senate's old domination and of the instability of the 30s, marred by civil war, social unrest and legalized murder—and of the clear pre-eminence of invincible Caesar, established at Actium, in whom the future stability of Rome was clearly to be fixed.[27] That our poet should subject the contradictions inherent in his status and position to such an ironic analysis comes as no surprise after the poems of Book One. But what matters here is that the satirist's appeal to Caesar, the poem makes clear, does not depend on his inherited status but on his personal merits as a poet and on the actual validity of his poetry's moral claims.[28] Nor does his standing as a poet depend on the literary tradition in which he situates himself but rather on the appropriateness and on the sheer quality of whatever he writes. Horace's particular literary achievement—phrased just so, timed just so—will afford him the security that he could likewise obtain by adhering to Trebatius' advice, if he could deny his own *ingenium*. All of which requires a revision of the dichotomy that has been read into *ultra legem* at the poem's beginning: aesthetics and legal safety are not by any means easily or conveniently distinguish-

---

[26] Narrative treatments of the triumviral period and the early Principate: Pelling (1996: 1–69) and Crook (1996)—each with abundant references to scholarly literature.

[27] Griffin (1993: 3).

[28] Augustus liked, or at least made quite a show of seeming to like, moralizing literature: Suet. *Aug.* 89.2. But see Galinsky (1996: 265).

able in this satire, especially when the favor of Caesar can cause any legal complaint, whatever its basis in the impersonal principles of statute law, to be laughed out of court. The satirist, diverging from the conformity to the rule of law which constitutes the genius of jurisprudence, strives for individuality.[29] Still, the differences between the jurist and the poet must not be exaggerated, especially as they tend to collapse under the social pressures of the 30s or in the presence of the victor at Actium.

Nevertheless, it is important that Caesar's verdict be neither capricious nor simply the result of Horace's being well connected. The poet's personal qualities and the propriety of his moralistic verses make him the right sort of *amicus* for Caesar, despite their disparities in class and origin. Though his status is modest, no faction can silence Horace so long as Caesar will protect his legitimate rights. In this reality, Trebatius concedes the poet's safety. But this is not merely a recognition of Caesar's irresistible power. If the conditions of lines 83–5 are actually met, Horace deserves to speak his mind. Freedom of speech is no longer, in the world of *Sat.* 2.1, the prerogative of the *nobilis* or of the senatorial class. Nor is the poet obligated to play the panegyrist: indeed, he must take care not to do so except under exactly the right circumstances. Invincible Caesar, that 'challenge to Roman powers of definition',[30] though he is a judge whose authority threatens to transgress the claims of jurisprudence, becomes the powerful *amicus* who, in the end, delivers true *libertas* and true justice, the quest for which was the basis of the science in which Trebatius excelled. Thus the dialogue between these two talented Italians[31] of different generations concludes in reference to agreeable laughter. Law and literature alike can thrive in the Rome of *Sat.* 2.1 owing to the excellent judgment of the victor at Actium.[32] Still, our own response to the poem's final line depends on our estimation of Horace's description of himself and of Caesar. The captious might observe that the issues of Book One, the topics on

[29] A different view is put forward by McGinn (2001: 99–103).

[30] Feeney (1992: 2).

[31] Muecke (1993: 107): Horace represents himself as Lucanian at line 38 in order to identify himself more closely with Trebatius, who was from Velia in Lucania.

[32] McGinn (2001: 101) is right to point out that one function of this satire is to offer oblique instruction to Caesar on how to be a good Princeps.

which the poet claims a right to speak and for which he anticipates Caesar's protection, are hardly those characteristic of stirring senatorial debates. Just so. Hence the abiding question of whether, in the end, Caesar's protection is a good thing or a bad thing. That, however, is a controversy that remains most unlikely to be resolved, least of all with a laugh.

Part II

Horace's *Epistles*, Book One

10

The Poetry of Ethics: Horace, *Epistles* 1

Colin Macleod

In 23 BCE the first three books of Horace's *Odes* appeared. In the years which followed, up to the completion of *Epistles* 1, his work took a new direction, and the ethical themes which had had a marked place in his lyric verse became his entire concern: in his own words (*Ep.* 1.1.10–11),

> nunc itaque et versus et cetera ludicra pono;
> quid verum atque decens curo et rogo, et omnis in hoc sum.

And so it is that now I am setting aside verses and other playthings. My concern is with what is true and fitting; that's what I ask, and it is what I am all about.

What Horace describes in this context, at the very beginning of the book, is a kind of conversion to philosophy;[1] and so the reader is at once drawn to ask what philosophy means to the poet. Before considering this question by scrutiny of the poems, two more general ones should be raised: first, what are the dominant features of ancient ethics as a whole and how far does it differ from modern ethical systems or moral thinking?[2] Second, what part did moral philosophy

---

[1] On this phenomenon in antiquity see Nock (1933: ch. 11). Horace's account of his conversion is an unusual one in not conforming to the dogmatic pattern that Nock traces; it need be no less genuine for that, though it is clearly meant to signal a new departure in his *poetry*. For a sensitive account of Horace's mobility of belief and mood in *Ep.* 1, see Perret (1959: 149–53).

[2] A very helpful general treatment of ancient ethics, to which I am indebted in many respects, is Dihle (1966: 646–796 [s.v. 'Ethik']); the article includes a select bibliography.

play in the life of Romans in Horace's time? The answers I shall give to these very large questions are pragmatic and limited: they are meant simply as preparation for considering Horace's *Epistles*.

There are, of course, different schools of thought in Greek ethics; but for all of them the summit of moral aspiration and the centre of ethical reflection is the good man and the good life. The vocabulary of the *Epistles* reflects this concern: the key terms are words like *sapientia, virtus, aequus animus, nil admirari, recte vivere*, ('wisdom', 'virtue', 'a steady mind', 'to be astonished at nothing', 'to live rightly') all of which refer to a habit of mind or a manner of living. In modern times ethics has become both more abstract and more specific. Philosophers have tended more and more to the analysis of moral concepts and judgements.[3] At best, this tendency is actuated by more than curiosity about language; it follows from the inquiry into the possibility of knowledge which begins with Descartes and is reforged and reinforced by Hume, Kant and others. Thus ethical problems have been the cognitive ones: how far, if at all, is morality rational or objective? Can judgements and valuations be distinguished from mere whims or fancies, and if so, wherein lies the distinction? And if to judge or evaluate is not simply to describe, what relation do they bear to the world, or to the body of experiences which goes by that name? These problems are known to antiquity too; but the answers to them in modern times have been designed to satisfy a subject who is because he thinks. If we turn to more popular moral thinking, it seems that the scope of morality has narrowed since ancient times. If ordinary English usage tells us anything, 'ethics' is something associated with a particular profession: there is a code which governs the behaviour of doctors or solicitors as such and makes infringements of it 'unethical', but beyond that the word has no widely recognized application.[4] 'Moral' extends further; but the stuff of morality is particular duties (or rights) and actions. Morality enters into life where there are 'questions of principle' concerning a possible

[3] The most striking exception to this generalization is existentialism. It is no surprise to find that its progenitor, Kierkegaard, is a profound and subtle connoisseur of Greek ethics. Another exception is 'attualismo': see Calogero (1960 and 1962) (also a fine connoisseur of Greek philosophy and a pupil of Socrates).

[4] I do not count as ordinary usage the sense in which I have used 'ethical' in this context, i.e. 'pertaining to moral philosophy'.

decision; and that phrase implies that such questions are not always present. At this point the popular and the philosophical lines of thought converge; for both tend to isolate and limit the realm of morality.

But ancient ethics is at once more general and more concrete. The question which animates it was posed by Plato, who with his teacher Socrates brought ethics to birth in the West: how ought I to live? (cf. *Rep.* 352D; *Gorg.* 500C). In other words, the ancient moral philosopher was also a moralist, and his moralizing is an attempt to define the art of living,[5] an art being a method with a goal, which must be learnt: the starting-point of this enterprise is naturally an account of the human condition. Moreover, to him, happiness and goodness are one; for to live well cannot but be to fulfil oneself. Thus his task is not to separate right from expedient, but rather to prove their identity: the project of Plato's *Republic*, for example, is 'to define how each of us may lead his whole life most profitably' (344E); this is how Plato goes about showing that morality is not a chimera. To that extent, then, ancient ethics is self-centred: it is focussed on what is good for each of us; and indeed much of what for the ancients was moral philosophy would now be called psychotherapy, since its business was with the well-being or wholeness of the inner man. This is offensive to any who think of duty or altruism as the heart of morality; it does not mean that duty or altruism were notions neglected by ancient ethics.

What, then, was the place of philosophy in Horace's environment, and how for him and men like him did it identify and face the problems of living? In the first century BC there were well-established schools of thought; and the study of philosophy was part of a full education. Horace himself went to Athens as a young man where, as he puts it (*Ep.* 2.2.43–51)

> adiecere bonae paulo plus artis Athenae,
> scilicet ut vellem curvo dinoscere rectum
> atque inter silvas Academi quaerere verum.

Dear Athens added a good deal of her art, which is to say that I was eager to distinguish the straight from the curved, and to seek out the truth among the trees of the Academy.

---

[5] Besides Plato, *passim*, cf. Plut. *Mor.* 613B and the Loeb editors' note ad loc.

But philosophy was not merely an academic discipline in our sense.
Philosophers were esteemed and cultivated by some public men, or
even maintained by them as advisers or tutors;[6] and their ethics
found many applications to everyday life. This fact is implicitly
clear in Cicero's philosophical writings, especially the *De officiis*;
and we have lively illustrations of it from his letters.[7] Thus he thanks
Lucceius for a letter of condolence as follows (*Ad fam.* 5.13.1–2):

Quamquam ipsa consolatio litterarum tuarum mihi gratissima est (declarat
enim summam benevolentiam coniunctam pari prudentia), tamen illum
fructum ex iis litteris vel maximum cepi, quod te praeclare res humanas
contemnentem et optime contra fortunam paratum armatumque cognovi;
quam quidem laudem sapientiae statuo esse maximam, non aliunde pen-
dere nec extrinsecus aut bene aut male vivendi suspensas habere rationes.
quae cogitatio cum mihi non omnino excidisset (etenim penitus insederat),
vi tamen tempestatum et concursu calamitatum erat aliquantum labefactata
atque convulsa; cui te opitulari et video et id fecisse etiam proximis litteris
multumque profecisse sentio.

Although your letter's consolation is most welcome to me (for it shows the
utmost of goodwill bound together with an equal amount of foresight),
nonetheless the greatest benefit I took from your letter was that I recognized
you, with clear distinction, despising human affairs, nobly prepared and
fully armed against fortune. This is what I take to be wisdom's greatest
distinguishing hallmark: to let nothing depend on what's outside oneself,
nor to keep one's reckoning of life, whether it is lived badly or well,
contingent on external circumstances. This idea, although I had not lost it
completely (for it was deep within me), nonetheless had been weakened, and
uprooted to some degree, by the violence of the times with its onrush of
disasters. I see that you are lending the idea support, and I feel that you have
actually done this in your latest letter, and that you have been most helpful.

  Consolation was one of the major tasks of philosophy because it
taught how to face something no-one can avoid in life, suffering and
bereavement; and the many consolatory letters and treatises which
survive reveal that its teachings were taken seriously and found
valuable. Here it is in particular the Stoic doctrine that the only

---

  [6] e.g. Scipio and Panaetius (*RE* 18.2.422–43); Tiberius Gracchus and Blossius (*RE*
3.571); Piso and Philodemus (*RE* 19.2445); Cicero and Diodotus (*RE* 5.715);
Octavian, Athenodorus and Arius (*RE* Supp. 5.49–51).
  [7] For another one, see Fraenkel (1957: 361).

good is virtue or wisdom[8] which comforts Cicero. Or again, this is how he writes to his predecessor as governor of Cilicia, Appius Claudius Pulcher, who was complaining that Cicero had failed to meet him (*Ad fam.* 3.7.5):[9]

Illud idem Pausania dicebat te dixisse: 'quidni? Appius Lentulo, Lentulus Appio processit obviam, Cicero Appio noluit?' quaeso, etiamne tu has ineptias, homo mea sententia summa prudentia, multa etiam doctrina, plurimo rerum usu, addo urbanitatem, quae est virtus, ut Stoici rectissime putant? ullam Appietatem aut Lentulitatem valere apud me plus quam ornamenta virtutis existimas? cum ea consecutus nondum eram quae sunt hominum opinionibus amplissima, tamen ista vestra nomina numquam sum admiratus; viros eos qui ea vobis reliquissent magnos arbitrabar. postea vero quam ita et cepi et gessi maxima imperia, ut mihi nihil neque ad honorem neque ad gloriam adquirendum putarem, superiorem quidem numquam, sed parem vobis me speravi esse factum. nec mehercule aliter vidi existimare vel Cn. Pompeium, quem omnibus qui umquam fuerunt, vel P. Lentulum, quem mihi ipsi antepono; tu si aliter existimas, nihil errabis si paulo diligentius, ut quid sit εὐγένεια [quid sit nobilitas] intellegas, Athenodorus, Sandonis filius, quid de his rebus dicat attenderis.[10]

Pausanias told me that you said this as well: 'Well, what did you expect! Appius went out to greet Lentulus, and Lentulus Appius, but would Cicero be willing to greet Appius?' Oh, please! Such nonsense from you as well— you who are, in my opinion, a man of deep foresight, of great learning, with loads of practical experience and, I will add, urbanity, which is a virtue, as the Stoics are right to insist? Do you think that 'Appian-ness' and 'Lentulity' counts more with me than distinctions of virtue? Even when I had not, as yet, achieved those distinctions that the opinions of men judge most eminent, still I was never astonished at these grand names of yours. I used to think that those who left you these names were great men. But later, once I had taken up and exercised the highest command, such that I thought that I had nothing more to add to my honour and glory, I hoped to have become never, surely, your superior, but your equal. By god, that's exactly the estimation that Cn. Pompeius had of me, whom I put ahead of anyone who ever lived, and P. Lentulus, whom I rank ahead of myself. If you think differently, you won't be too far off if you attend more carefully to what

---

[8] Shackleton Bailey ad loc. compares *Tusc.* 3.37 and 5.36. See further *SVF* 3.49–67.

[9] On going to meet (ἀπάντησις and ὑπάντησις) as a conventional honour, see Pearce (1970: 313–16).

[10] On *urbanitas* and εὐγένεια as philosophical topics, see Shackleton Bailey's notes. Chrysippus labelled as virtues εὐπαντησία, εὐτραπελία, and ἐπιδεξιότης (*SVF* 3.255).

Athenodorus, son of Sandon, has to say about these matters, so that you might understand what 'nobility' actually consists of.

Here Cicero is anxious to calm Appius' wounded pride; at the same time, as a *novus homo*, he wants to keep up his self-esteem against the anger of a *nobilis*. By appeal to philosophic teachings he can both soothe and scold his addressee with detachment and as an equal, implying that they should both act as what they are, men of quality and urbanity; and since it is Cicero who recognizes this, he can even feel himself—without saying so, of course—to be the superior.

This much to indicate how Horace's *Epistles* are by no means an oddity in their application of philosophical teaching to daily affairs. In them too, ethics belongs in every kind of situation because its business is life as a whole. Thus in *Epistle* 5, in inviting Torquatus to dinner, Horace introduces a topic discussed by Aristotle and Zeno, whether the wise man will ever get drunk.[11] This is not a trivial matter because it implies a deeper and broader question, whether the good life is rigidly consistent or admits of relaxation and even abandon;[12] and so it comes to be asked if drunkenness is a natural release or a vicious distortion. Or again, *Epistle* 9 is a letter of commendation, like those in *Ad familiares* XIII. Here too there is a problem of ethics and etiquette (two things the ancients did not sharply distinguish): is Horace to recommend his friend Septimius to the great Tiberius and risk defeating his purpose by presuming too far? Or is he, for fear of that, to do nothing and cut the figure of a selfish hypocrite? Naturally the questions behind many of the *Epistles* cover larger areas of life than these do, but they exemplify a major theme of the book, how to behave in society and to consort with the great. This theme is nowhere more exhaustively treated than in *Epistles* 17 and 18.

These poems address two different men on the same topic: that is, in effect, how to make a career, since friendship (*amicitia*) with the

---

[11] Cf. Macleod (1977: 361). Further *SVF* 1.229; 3.643–4, 712. Plut. *Mor.* 613B–C is illuminating in general on the ethics of symposia, a theme treated by Horace himself in the *Odes* (esp. 1.18 and 3.21) and the *Satires* (2.665–76). Some Peripatetics wrote περὶ μέθης; see Wehrli on Chamaileon frag. 9–13; later, note Philo. *Ebr.* 91; Sen. *Ep.* 838–27; Dio Chrys. 27.1–4.

[12] See further McGann (1969: 29 [on *Ep.* 1.18.59–64]) and Kiessling-Heinze (1957: ad loc.).

powerful was a normal and indispensable path to success.[13] But such a choice of life imposes a severe discipline. The dependent has to restrain, or at least refrain from expressing, the desire to get rich that is naturally one of his motives: not only because he might obstruct his own aims by putting off his patron or causing squabbles with other dependents, but because if the great man does satisfy his wishes, that may lead him to debauchery and bankruptcy (17.43–51; 18.21–36). He must in conversation be neither slavishly obsequious nor gruffly obstinate (18.1–20),[14] he must be adaptable in company without being indiscreet or disloyal (18.37–71), and so on. Behind the rich humour of these poems, their sometimes gaily satirical treatment of what can go wrong in the careerist's life and the sometimes gently mocking tone of their precepts, lie an ideal of how to live in society, the man who has the self-knowledge to be simply what he is with others. By recognizing the limitations of his status, as the philosopher Aristippus did (17.13–32), he accepts them with dignity; and he feels no need to assert himself by acting the pontificating pundit (18.15–20), the retiring *littérateur* (18.39–66)[15] or the extravagant playboy (18.31–6). In short, the dependent cannot find favour with his patron if he is not himself worthy of respect, if he does not, in the way proper to his choice of life, live rightly.

In effect, in these *Epistles* Horace has written in his own manner a *De amicitia*, in the tradition that flows from *Nicomachean Ethics* VIII–IX; the type of friendship concerned is what Aristotle calls φιλία καθ' ὑπεροχήν.[16] It is natural, then, to find Horace towards the end of *Epistle* 18 (96–103) telling Lollius to study philosophy:

> inter cuncta leges et percontabere doctos
> qua ratione queas traducere leniter aevum:
> num te semper inops agitet vexetque cupido,
> num pavor et rerum mediocriter utilium spes,

[13] In general on Roman *amicitia* and its ethics, see Brunt (1965: 1–8). For an attractive account of Horace on friendship see Maguinness (1938: 29–48). Note also White (1978: 74–92).

[14] More relevant to this section than Aristotle ap. Stob. *Ecl. Eth.* 2.7.25, mentioned by Kiessling-Heinze (1957: ad 18.9), is *EN* 1126[b] 11–16.

[15] On this section, see further Macleod (1976: 41–3).

[16] Cf. Maguinness (1938: 33–4). For thoughtful remarks on *Ep.* 18 as a whole, see Rohdich (1972: 261–88), though he rather underrates the humorous and satirical elements in the poem.

> virtutem doctrina paret naturane donet,
> quid minuat curas, quid te tibi reddat amicum,
> quid pure tranquillet, honos an dulce lucellum
> an secretum iter et fallentis semita vitae.

Amid all this, you will read learned men, and make inquiry of them, asking by what method you may pass your life serenely. Does lust, always a pauper, drive and harass you? What of fear, and of hope for things of middling use? Does teaching give birth to virtue, or does nature give it as a gift? What diminishes worry? What renders you a friend to yourself? What brings undisturbed repose? Is it honour, a pleasing bundle of cash? Or is it a secluded journey, and a path to a life unnoticed?

The last line echoes Epicurus' 'Live in secret' ($\lambda \acute{\alpha} \theta \epsilon \ \beta \acute{\iota} \omega \sigma \alpha s$: frag. 551 Usener); the same phrase was recalled in 17.10:

> nec vixit male qui natus moriensque fefellit.

Nor has he lived badly who has lived unnoticed from birth to death.

In both places it indicates that there is an alternative to a career in high society; and the person who embodies that alternative is the poet himself, living and studying in the seclusion of his Sabine farm. Now Horace had had such a career: the words which encourage the faint-hearted man in 17.35

> principibus placuisse viris haud ultima laus est

to have found favour with princely men is hardly the pinnacle of distinction

are very like those applied to Horace's own life in 20.23:

> me primis urbis belli placuisse domique.[17]

In war and peace, I found favour with the city's leaders.

So behind the advice to careerists is first-hand knowledge; and in the argument of *Epistle* 18 it is the recommendation of philosophy which connects the counsels to Lollius with Horace's account of his own position. In other words, both men alike need philosophy; and Horace also shares with Lollius the need for some material goods (18.107–10). Likewise in *Epistle* 17 he recognizes, as Epicurus did,[18]

---

[17] On the meaning of this line see Wistrand (1958: 38–9 = 1972: 326–7).
[18] See frags. 555–7 Usener; cf. Kiessling-Heinze (1957: ad loc.). Cf. Cic. *Off.* 1.110 (Panaetius); Sen. *De Tranqu.* 7.2.

that a life of simplicity and retirement like his own cannot satisfy everyone. Thus the poet's philosophic detachment does not cause him to look down with pity or contempt on other people;[19] he tries rather to see what all men, and what each individual, needs in order to live well, and to share his insight with his readers so that they can use it in their own way.

In neither *Epistle* 17 nor 18 does it emerge that Horace is the *amicus* of Maecenas. But this is not an evasion, since that aspect of his existence is the subject of *Epistle* 7. (To observe how the poems in *Epistles* 1 complement and contrast with each other adds greatly to the appreciation of each one; this cannot, of course, be achieved by positing a single 'structure' for the book.)[20] The beginning of the letter reveals that Horace has delayed returning to Maecenas at Rome; and the whole is an excuse for his not doing so. But the form of the excuse takes us deep into the ethics of gratitude and friendship. Friendship was a major topic in ancient philosophy:[21] in part because it was seen as a kind of informal contract for the exchange of benefits, so that the rights and obligations of friends could seem worth defining; in part because friendship manifests the need for others that exists in us all and so must be included in any account of how to live well (cf. below on 10.49–50). So in *Epistle* 7.20–4 we find a compressed statement of how favours should be given and taken:

> prodigus et stultus donat quae spernit et odit:
> haec seges ingratos tulit et feret omnibus annis.
> vir bonus et sapiens dignis ait esse paratus,
> nec tamen ignorat quid distent aera lupinis;
> dignum praestabo me etiam pro laude merentis.[22]

The dullard wastrel makes gifts of what he despises and hates: such a field yields thankless men, and will continue to do so year after year. The good man who is wise will say he is available to deserving men, and yet he is no

[19] Contrast Lucr. 2.1–13 and the passages quoted in Bailey's 'Addenda' (1997: 1751).

[20] McGann (1969: ch. 2) tactfully indicates a wealth of connections in *Ep.* 1.

[21] For a thoughtful and comprehensive treatment see Fraisse (1974); he helpfully explains why friendship is a 'lost problem' of philosophy and why it need no longer be.

[22] On the philosophical background to these lines see Fraenkel (1957: 330–2); Hiltbrunner (1960: 298, n. 12); McGann (1969: 13). On the whole I find the most satisfactory account of the poem and their place in it is Büchner (1940: 64–80 = 1962: 139–57).

fool when it comes to separating stage money from bronze. I will prove to be
deserving, even when one takes into account the glory of my benefactor.

The delicate balance in the phrasing of the last line pictures the
equality Horace claims in fact. Maecenas has shown himself a good
and wise man by giving the poet something truly valuable. Horace
will return the favour by being not merely grateful, as is implied by
line 21 and stated by lines 37–8,[23] but 'worthy' as Maecenas is. That
means that if Maecenas were to devalue his gifts by using them to
restrict the poet's freedom, or if Horace himself were in danger of
becoming a slave to them, then he would 'give back everything' (34,
cuncta resigno). This is a critical moment in the argument of the
poem: Horace threatens, if only in theory, a complete break. But the
crisis is overcome by an implicit distinction. What Horace would give
back is the luxury and grandeur of city-life; but his country retreat,
Maecenas' most valuable gift, and his freedom are bound up with
each other. So to have bestowed independence on the poet is Maecenas' merit as a giver; and Horace's staying out of town is therefore
the right response on the part of the receiver.

   This is subtle diplomacy; it also sketches an ideal relationship
between a superior and an inferior, in which generosity on the one
side and gratitude on the other are guaranteed by equality and
respect. The story of Mena and Philippus which follows fills out
this ideal by portraying a debased giving and taking of favours.
Philippus' envious and restless egoism is at first contrasted with the
healthy and contented self-love of Mena; but it then corrupts
the lesser man and brings him unhappiness, because it betrays his
true wishes. Mena's mistake, and what Horace means to avoid, is a
failure of self-knowledge. All this too is diplomatic, because the bad
relationship of patron and dependent is represented only by the two
men in the story, not by Maecenas and Horace. But it also shows with
painful clarity and blunt humour what could go wrong between
them; and the ethical reflections of the earlier part of the poem are
thus an insurance as well as an ideal. Now we cannot say whether
Epistle 7 was prompted by anything that passed between Horace and
Maecenas, nor, if it was, what passed between them. But Horace is

---

[23] On line 38, see Macleod (1977: 327–73); cf. further Epic. frag. 589 Usener; Ter.
Ad. 73.

not inviting his readers to reconstruct a part of his biography,[24] but to see how the philosophy which governs his existence applies to life, how it can interpret conflicts between people and resolve them by combining a moral pattern with a natural fact, the duties of the friend with the needs of the individual.

Some readers think of Horace as complacent, and it is true that in the poems so far considered here he presents his own way of life, however unassumingly, as an ideal, offering what he is to his readers to help them as he has helped himself. But that does not mean he cannot look sharply into his own life and character. Indeed, one peculiar *finesse* of the *Epistles* is how Horace voices for the benefit of friends more or less jocular self-criticism. Then in *Epistle* 4 he ends with the words (15–16)

> me pinguem et nitidum bene curata cute vises,
> cum ridere voles, Epicuri de grege porcum.[25]

For a laugh, you will come see me all fat and glistening in my meticulously tended skin, a pig from Epicurus' flock.

This confirms, even as it humorously softens, the Epicurean message of lines 12–14:[26]

> inter spem curamque, timores inter et iras,
> omnem crede diem tibi diluxisse supremum:
> grata superveniet quae non sperabitur hora.

In the midst of hope and worry, amid outrage and fears, trust that each day that has shown its light on you is your last; the hour that comes unexpectedly will be received with gratitude.

Tibullus clearly needs not only the comforts of the right kind of philosophy, but also someone to laugh at and with; and it is that role which Horace tactfully assumes. In *Epistle* 8 Celsus risks being carried away by the good fortune that has made him 'companion and secretary' (2) to Tiberius. This point is delicately stressed by the pun

---

24 Cf. Becker (1963: 23 [on *Ep.* 14]): 'Was an der "Situation"... des Briefes real und was erdichtet ist... lässt sich nicht entscheiden; für das Verständnis des Briefes hängt davon auch nichts ab. Die Alternative: real oder fiktiv, wird dem literarischen Charakter eines solchen Briefes nicht gerecht.' Similarly McGann (1969: 89–100).

25 On the force of these lines, see McGann (1969: 44).

26 See Kiessling-Heinze (1957: ad loc.).

on his cognomen (*celsus* = 'lofty') which is emphatically placed at the beginning of line 1 and separated from his *nomen, Albinovanus*.[27] In order to warn him of the danger, but without giving offence,[28] Horace describes his own condition: unlike Celsus he considers himself far from 'well' (*recte*: 4, 15), and yet he knows that the trouble is in his own mind (4–12), whereas Celsus may fall for a purely outward success;[29] likewise, Horace knows he is disagreeable to his friends (9–10), which is what Celsus needs to realize he may be himself (17). Now the self-criticism in these poems is not only a matter of 'good form'; it is also part of the ancient ethical tradition,[30] embodied, like so much of that tradition, in the teaching and behaviour of Socrates. This is how Nicias in the Laches (187E–188B) describes the effect of talking with him:

> You don't seem to know that whoever is nearest Socrates and joins with him in conversation cannot avoid, even if he starts talking first about something else, being continually dragged around by him in discussion until he falls into examining his whole life, past and present; and that when that has happened, Socrates will not let go of him until he has thoroughly scrutinized it all ... And I think it no harm to be reminded of what we have done or are doing wrong. Rather, you cannot but face the future with more awareness if you do not run away from that experience, but want and demand, in Solon's phrase, to learn as long as you live, free of the delusion that old age brings wisdom in its train.

Here we see how Socrates brings others to be their own critics; he is, of course, that to himself too. Thus in the *Phaedrus* (229E–230A) he says that his aim is to know himself, an aim pursued by the whole

---

[27] The stilted word-order may be meant to recall Hesiod, frag. 211. 7 M.-W.: τρὶς μάκαρ Αἰακίδη καὶ τετράκις ὄλβιε Πηλεῦ (a *makarismos*, as *Ep.* 8.1–2 are a salutation). If so, this emphasizes still further the mock-solemnity of the opening. For puns on names, see Horsfall (1976: 422); Nisbet (1978: 8).

[28] Also tactful is delivering the whole message through the Muse, a device which at the same time, since it unnaturally elevates the tone of the letter, gently mocks Celsus' pride in his success.

[29] The words *gaudere et bene rem gerere* in line 1 already suggest that there is a kind of happiness or success better than Celsus'; the greeting which conventionally begins a letter is given an ethical form and meaning, as in [Plato] *Ep.* 315A–B; Epic. frag. 95 Usener.

[30] On self-examination as a daily practice, see Chadwick (1978: 1056 [s.v. Gewissen]); also Horace himself, *Sat.* 1.4.133–8.

dialogue in its analysis of the human soul; and in the *Apology* (38A) he, no less than others, is the object of that 'scrutiny' which is the purpose of his life. Later, Arrian's Epictetus says (2.11.1):

The beginning of philosophy, if we are to enter it properly, by the front door, is to be aware of our own weakness and incapacity where the essentials of life are concerned.[31]

This is the beginning of philosophy for Horace too. So let us take *Epistle* 1 to consider further that aspect of his ethics.

That poem, like *Epistle* 7, is an excuse and a refusal. Horace, despite Maecenas' insistence, will not take up poetry again. Such refusals (*recusationes*) are frequent in Augustan poetry,[32] though this form is unusual. What is most common is that one kind of poetry (generally epic, cosmology, or high themes) is rejected for another (lyric, pastoral, elegy, or private themes). That often creates an ambiguity because in saying no to the grand subject the poet does in fact deal with it, though in a small compass and without committing himself to a style of writing that would not suit him. There is an ambiguity in *Epistle* 1 too, and a more thoroughgoing one. Horace has given up poetry for ethics; yet this is a book of poems, and highly finished and artistic ones. But this is not a merely frivolous irony, any more than Plato's attack on writing in the *Phaedrus.* The word he uses to describe poetry is *ludus.* It is, then, a game, or more precisely, a gladiatorial show or school: the metaphor of sport and combat stretches over the first fifteen lines of the poem. The poet is an entertainer; but the time has come for Horace to stop entertaining others and attend to his own soul. Philosophy, on the other hand, is a cure: a medical metaphor runs from line 28 to 40 and recurs at the end of the poem (101–3). So poetry is an obstacle to sound living, because art is not life, and because the artist, as such, cannot but be appealing to a public rather than improving himself. This severe view of poetry emerges elsewhere in *Epistles* 1, notably in 3 and 19; but it is

---

[31] Cf. also 2.17.14–18, 2.26.4, 3.23.34 with Hor. *Ep.* 1.1.97–100 (a sense of conflict within the self as the beginning of philosophy). Socratic philosophy likewise starts by revealing contradiction in the interlocutor: e.g. Plato *Gorg.* 457E, 460E–461A, 487B. Contradiction among men in general is also a beginning of philosophy: cf. Hor. *Ep.* 1.1.70–80 and Arr. *Epict.* 2.11.13, 2.17.10–13, 2.24.15.

[32] See Nisbet and Hubbard (1970: 81–3 [on *Od.* 1.6]).

there accompanied by a distinctly contrasting one. Writing is a part of life, and as an art is like ethics, the art of living; so good or bad qualities of the work—for example, sober independence, or slavish imitation and ambitious overreaching—correspond to moral achievements or failures of the man.[33] The contradiction in this double view of poetry is never resolved; or rather, the only resolution is the *Epistles* themselves. They are that because their controlled and polished verbal art is a fine instrument for probing moral problems. This claim is in fact implicit in *Ep.* 1.1.12:

> condo et compono quae mox depromere possim.

I store up and arrange things that I may at some point fetch from storage.

Condo and *compono* mean in the first instance 'store up, lay down'; but are also both words regularly used of poetic composition.[34] So in the same breath as Horace renounces poetry, he announces that that is what he is writing, and that its purpose is to supply 'provisions' for his new life. This conception of the moral value of poetry is further expressed in what he says of Homer in *Epistle* 2. However, by the same token, to write is not to have achieved wisdom; and that Horace has not achieved it becomes plain in what follows. His aspirations to philosophy are those of a restless, helpless and indecisive human being. 'The storm snatches' him from place to place, he 'drowns in the surge of public life' (the metaphor here is a striking contrast to Epicurean calm, γαλήνη, or Stoic smooth sailing, εὔροια); he 'slides back' into hedonism and individualism; he is impatient as a tricked lover, a reluctant labourer or a mischievous boy. And what stops Horace getting on with the job is not Maecenas' pressure, but his own indecision; indeed, his attitude is that of one who fails to undertake philosophy like the man he berates in another protreptic, *Ep.* 1.2.32–43.[35] Compare too Epicurus, *Vatican Sayings* 14 (= frag. 204):

We have been born once, we cannot be born twice; and we must exist no more for infinite time. But you, though tomorrow is outside your control,

---

[33] Cf. Macleod (1977: 359–76, esp. 362–3).

[34] A point drawn to my attention by Mr Stephen Instone. *Compono* is further stressed by the wordplay with *pono* (10) which it echoes antithetically; on this type of pun see Macleod (1979: on *Od.* 1.20).

[35] Cf. Sen. *Ep.* 1.1–3. For other similar passages, see La Penna (1956: 192–3).

put off the moment. Everyone's life is wasted in shilly-shallying, and so each of us busily dies.

So if Horace is still writing, his activity at the same time embodies a poetic ideal and reflects his awkward moral position: he reaches out towards philosophy, but his feet are planted in his own weakness.

Thus the bulk of *Epistle* 1 is a set of 'elementary teachings' (27):

> restat ut his ego me ipse regam solerque elementis.

I'm left to take charge of myself, and console myself, by these elementary teachings.

Its purpose is to identify the troubles for which philosophy is a cure: that is, very briefly, that people put material aims before moral ones, and that they are full of mental conflicts which stop them wanting anything, whether right or wrong, consistently. The theme of inconsistency brings us back to Horace as he described himself at the beginning of the poem. Here again he is in a state of confusion (97–100):

> ...quid mea cum pugnat sententia secum
> quod petiit spernit, repetit quod nuper omisit,
> aestuat et vitae disconvenit ordine toto,
> diruit, aedificat, mutat quadrata rotundis?

What about when my judgment fights against itself, when what it sought it rejects, what it just discarded it wants back, it is awash and out of sorts with life in its entire course, it tears down, it builds, and changes square to round?

and indeed the whole poem was directed as much at the poet as at other men. So philosophy is what he needs. Maecenas, who fails to recognize this, comes in again for gentle criticism: he shows himself as inconsistent as the rest of mankind, because he laughs at Horace's oddities of dress, grumbles about his ill-cut finger-nails, but does not react at all to the confusion in his soul. But the poet goes on to put his own aims in a clearer light, which also somewhat softens his criticism of Maecenas; as in the *Epistles* as a whole (cf. above on 7 and 8) tact in expression and rigour in thought go closely together. He offers an extreme version of the ideal of wisdom, in Stoic terms, but at once deflates it (106–8):

> ad summam: sapiens uno minor est Iove, dives,
> liber, honoratus, pulcher, rex denique regum,
> praecipue sanus—nisi cum pituita molesta est.

In sum, the wise man is second only to Jove. He is rich, free, honoured, beautiful, in short a king of kings; above all he is sound, except when he has a cold.

Even the complete sage is all-too-human; how much more must Horace go on sharing his weakness or sickness with other men. He will always be, like everyone who seeks wisdom, a beginner; and so studying philosophy does not set him on a different level from other men, including Maecenas. Moreover, he is still his patron's grateful friend (105):

> de te pendentis, te respicientis amici.

a friend who relies on you, who looks to you.

The ethics which Horace sketches in this programmatic *Epistle* combines a strong desire to live better with a shrewd and humorous sense of his own and everyone's fallibility. Likewise, it combines a firm rejection of Maecenas' pressures with warm gratitude to his patron. Horace's morality is a middle way. However, that does not mean a baggy compromise but a firm tension between idealism and realism. Indeed, as an exhortation to philosophy, a προτρεπτικὸς λόγος, *Epistle* 1 is a good deal closer to the problems of living than is Aristotle's famous *Protrepticus*; and being addressed to the writer himself, it is also more candid and more aware of human fallibility.[36]

The same self-critical element that pervades *Epistle* 1 finds expression again at the end of the book in *Epistle* 20.[37] This poem is

---

[36] *Epistle* 6 is also a kind of protreptic: see Kiessling-Heinze (1957: ad 6.29). But it is unusual as such in having a strong sceptical streak: cf. Sex. Emp. *Adv. Eth.* 110–40 who like Horace argues that to 'pursue intensely' (συντόνως διώκειν) any end at all is damaging, and applies this principle to different choices of goal, pleasure, fame or wealth. Thus here Horace is aware that even *virtus* can become a delusion if pursued to excess (15–16; the Stoics too saw this: see Kiessling-Heinze (1957: ad loc.)). So in his protreptics Horace does not, like Aristotle or Isocrates, impress and inspire the reader, but soberly points out, together with our need for right living, the difficulties that attend the search for it.

In general on the typical features of protreptics, see Düring (1961: 19–24); Hartlich (1889). For a lucid account of the argument of *Ep.* 6, see Courbaud (1914: 105–16).

[37] The end of the book, like the beginning, is a natural place for a programmatic poem; cf. Macleod (1973: 308). And to address or describe the physical book is a

addressed to the now complete volume as if it were a pretty slave-boy running away to make a fortune in the world out of its looks. The comparison between book and slave is brilliantly developed with a wealth of puns;[38] and the ironic inventiveness of the whole poem is as captivating as the slave hopes to be. At the same time the reader may well ask: how does this poem belong in a book devoted to ethics? And how can such a book be compared to a male prostitute?[39] Now any reader of Horace knows he is far from solemn or pompous; but his humour here, as usual, is more than a spoonful of honey to help down the bitter ethical pill: rather, it is the ethics. The joke is on Horace himself. He adopts the pose of the elder and better, warns the book of what is in store for it and finally turns his back on it with a laugh. But the fact remains that the volume is his work and his property; its escaping is a transparent fiction. Arrian uses the same fiction in the preface to his *Discourses of Epictetus*; but his purpose is to explain the unliterary manner of the work and by his modesty predispose the reader to receive it well.[40] Horace's book, by contrast, is 'brushed clean by the pumice of the Sosii' (*Sosiorum pumice mundus*, 2), just as Catullus' is 'freshly polished by dry pumice' (*arida modo pumice expolitum*, 1.2): the polished appearance of the book corresponds to the polish of the poems it contains. Further, by comparing his book to a beautiful slave-boy, Horace brings out its winsomeness: like all poetry, it is and should be designed to please (cf. *Ars Poetica* 338–46).[41] Horace, then, is far from quietly justifying a plain style as Arrian does, and as one might have expected from the would-be philosopher (cf. Sen. *Ep.* 75.1–7) or the writer of *sermones*

common way of saying something about the poetic character of its contents as a whole; besides Catullus 1, cf. Meleager *AP* 4.1; Cinna frag. 11 Morel; Ov. *Tr.* 1.1. For the poet as the delinquent slave, cf. *Ep.* 2.2.1ff.

[38] On these see Fraenkel (1957: 356–59). Note further on lines 17–19, Bonner (1972: 509–28).

[39] Cf. McGann (1969: 85).

[40] On the function of this preface, and for parallels to the notion of the escaping book, see the excellent remark of Wirth (1967: 149–61); note also Dover's commentary on Aristophanes, *Clouds* (1968: 270) (Addendum to p. xcviii).

[41] For humorous or sarcastic characterizations of poetry or style as sexually attractive see Ar. *Thes.* 130–3; Cat. 16; Lucr. 1.642–4; Pers. 1.19–21; Juv. 7.82–7, where the poet is the pander: this last passage is admirably discussed by Tandoi (1969: 103–22).

(cf. *Sat.* 1.4.39–63; 1.10.36–9).[42] Rather, in criticizing the book/slave, Horace is criticizing a part of himself, the vain author, anxious for publicity and admiration (cf. *Ep.* 2.1.219–28); and when he warns it (13)

> aut fugies Uticam aut vinctus mitteris Ilerdam

you will escape to Utica, or be sent to Ilerda in chains

that wittily transposes into the tone of this poem and the terms of its dominant metaphor the boast he makes for his own work in *Odes* 2.20.17–20, that he will be read and learned by heart from end to end of the known world.[43] Similarly, 'you groan at being paraded before few' (*paucis ostendi gemis,* 4) is the reverse of 'enough displayed' (*spectatum satis*) in 1.1.2, words with which Horace renounced poetry for philosophy. It goes with this that in the self-portrait which concludes the poem he is keen to cut a fine figure, telling the book to play down his family's standing in order to point up his own merits: Horace is doing what any author wants to do, sell himself. But because the poem stands back from this natural vanity and eyes it with humorous detachment, it embodies the philosophic self-criticism typical of Horace and essential to the *Epistles* as it was to the *Satires,* which is neither covert complacency nor voluptuous self-laceration. It is this quality that makes Horace a credible, agreeable, but also quite unsparing, moralist.

What has been said so far was meant to be comment on Horace's poetry as well as on his ethics. But it may be worthwhile to look more closely at one *Epistle,* trying to do more justice to the quality of expression in these poems; for though they are *sermones,* they have their own type of poetry no less rigorous and subtle than that of the *Odes.* A few final words, then, on *Epistle* 10.

The poem begins with a parody of a formal salutation:

> urbis amatorem Fuscum salvere iubemus
> ruris amatores.

We lovers of the country send greetings to Fuscus, the town-lover.

---

[42] On the *Epistles* as *sermones* see 2.1.250 (probably also 1.4.1); La Penna (1949: 14).

[43] Cf. Nisbet and Hubbard (1970: on *Od.* 2.20.14); and possibly the bird-image in line 21 ironically echoes *Od.* 2.20.9–12. Line 20 corresponds to 'pauperum sanguis parentum' in *Od.* 2.20.6–7, and line 23 to 'ego quem vocas, dilecte Maecenas' in *Od.* 2.206–7. In general on Horace's mockery of his own *amour propre* as a poet in the *Epistles,* see Macleod (1977: 373–5).

This device amuses; it also makes an initial statement of the contrast between town and country which runs through the poem. But what follows, while it stresses the difference between the two friends, also shows them affectionately attached as twins. The two sides of their relationship are joined in the metaphor of the doves (5, 'familiar old doves,' *vetuli notique columbi*); for doves are proverbially loving, but there are also two kinds of dove, one which stays at home and one which roams about.[44] The latter kind is what Horace is; and leaving the nest is an image of freedom, a notion now developed through the related language of kingship and slavery. The poet is as happy as a king when he has abandoned what others loudly acclaim as kings or great men are acclaimed,[45] or when he has become like a runaway slave: to be really a king, i.e. supremely happy or free,[46] Horace has escaped what is the real slavery, a taste for glory or luxury (8–11):

> quid quaeris? vivo et regno simul ista reliqui
> quae vos ad caelum fertis rumore secundo;
> utque sacerdotis fugitivus liba recuso,
> pane egeo iam mellitis potiore placentis

What, then? I come to life and take charge exactly by abandoning the things that you raise to the heavens with loud approval; like a priest's runaway slave I refuse sacrificial wafers. It is bread that I need now, heartier than honeyed cakes.

Now comes a spirited vindication of the country (12ff.):

> vivere naturae si convenienter oportet
> ponendaeque domo quaerenda est area primum
> novistine locum potiorem rure beato?

If life is to be lived in accord with nature, and first we have to find a site for building a house, do you know of a place better than the blissful countryside?

Vivere naturae . . . convenienter echoes the Stoic principle that a man, as a rational being, should be governed by his reason and accept his

---

[44] Kiessling-Heinze (1957) compare Varro *RR* 3.7.1–2.

[45] Cf. Stuiber (1954: 95–6 [s.v. 'Beifall']).

[46] Cf. *SVF* 1.216, 3.617. Further on kingship as supreme freedom, see Romilly (1963: 79–82) and Aesch. *PV* 49–50; and as supreme happiness Solon frag. 33w; Plat. *Gorg.* 470ᴅ–471ᴅ, 492ʙ; *Theag.* 125ᴇ–126ᴀ; Lucian, *Icarom.* 25; Arist. *Rhet.* 1371ᵇ 26.

place in the universe, which is likewise rational (ὁμολογουμένως τῇ φύσει ζῆν). But Horace adapts the doctrine to his own argument: *natura* here means man's natural needs and satisfactions which Epicurus took as the guide to right living; and these the country best fulfils.[47] From this proposition and from line 13 it follows that the country is the place to live. It turns out, then, that the runaway slave or wandering dove, Horace, has in fact found himself a home, and that in doing so he has achieved what every one by nature wants. So if lines 15–21 are at first sight merely a series of arguments designed to prove that the country is superior to the town, they are on closer inspection a way of suggesting what all human beings must find in order to live well. The country is in effect a symbol; and *Epistle* 11 reinforces the point that places are in the end indifferent to our happiness. In the country there is nothing violent or forced, so pleasures are genuine and untroubled; and the needs of the senses are appeased:

> est ubi plus tepeant hiemes, ubi gratior aura
> leniat et rabiem Canis et momenta Leonis
> cum semel accepit Solem furibundus acutum?
> est ubi divellat somnos minus invida cura?
> deterius Libycis olet aut nitet herba lapillis?
> purior in vicis aqua tendit rumpere plumbum
> quam quae per pronum trepidat cum murmure rivum?

Is there a place where the winters are milder, where a more pleasant breeze mellows both the Dog-star's rage and the attacks of the Lion, when he rages at being goaded by the sun? Is there a place where invidious worry interrupts sleep less? Does the grass smell worse, or shine any less, than marble tiles from Libya? Is the water that gushes from lead pipes in back alleys cleaner than what tumbles noisily down along a steep brook?

Thus even men who make themselves luxury houses try to find or to simulate a country setting for it (22–3); for (24–5)

> naturam expelles furca, tamen usque recurret
> et mala perrumpet furtim fastidia victrix.

---

[47] Cf. Kiessling-Heinze (1957: ad 10.12, 24); further Epic. *Basic Doctrines* 15 = *Vatican Sayings* 8; frags. 202–3, 468–9, 471, 477. Epicurus also commended country-life (frag. 570); cf. Lucr. 2.20–33, 5.1390–6. If, as Williams (1968: 596–7) suggests, Horace is punning in line 24 on *natura* as both 'great creating nature' (cf. Lucr. 1.629 etc.) and man's natural needs or desires, that has a background in Epicurus; and there is no merely comical sophistry here, any more than there is portentous dogmatism.

Expel nature with a fork, and still she will keep running back. And, before you know it, she will break through your foul disdain in triumph.

Perrumpet echoes *rumpere* in line 20: the piped water in town struggles in vain to break through the lead, whereas *natura* triumphantly breaks through our daintiness. So while *natura* avoids violence, it is also in its quiet way a conqueror (*furtim ... victrix*). Thus Horace revalues the language of superiority: 'kingship' in line 8 (*regno*) and 'conquest' in line 25 (*victrix*) are boldly associated with a peaceful and unassuming existence;[48] for that is really the supreme happiness and the irresistible goal.

The argument is developed by a further comparison (26–9):

> non qui Sidonio contendere callidus ostro
> nescit Aquinatem potantia vellera fucum
> certius accipiet damnum propiusve medullis
> quam qui non poterit vero distinguere falsum.

No more assuredly, and not any closer to his heart, will the man who knows nothing of an expert's comparisons between wool soaked in Aquinum's dye and Sidonian purple suffer harm than the man who cannot distinguish true from false.

What matters is to tell true from false: the connoisseurs who distinguish, or fail to distinguish, different grades of dye are both dealing with something whose whole purpose is to falsify.[49] 'True' here means true to our natural needs; and it is in the service of this kind of truth that Horace has revised the language of kingship and victory. This manipulation of conventional usage continues in the following lines. By running away from grandeur, our life can run ahead of kings': we win the race by opting out of the race (32–3):

---

[48] This kind of 'persuasive definition' is typically Stoic: see *Od.* 2.2.19–21 and Nisbet and Hubbard (1970: ad loc.). Note also Epic. frag. 476–7; Kiessling-Heinze (1957: on Hor. *Sat.* 2.2.15); Lucan 2.384–7.

[49] Cf. esp. Virgil *Georg.* 2.465, and in general the use of *fucus* and cognates; also Hor. *Ep.* 2.1.207: 'lana Tarentio violas imitata veneno'. *Imitata* in this context hints at Plato's condemnation of dramatic μίμησις; and *violas* evokes *violare* = μιαίνειν (note Virgil *Aen.* 12.67 with Homer *Il.* 4.141, 146). The general sense of the line recalls *Ion* 535D 2: κεκοσμημένος ἐσθῆτι ποικίλῃ, as 211–13 recalls *Ion* 535c 1–3.

For the thought of *Ep.* 1.10.26–9 Kiessling-Heinze compare Epic. frag. 548; for non-Epicurean parallels see La Penna (1949: 26).

fuge magna: licet sub paupere tecto
reges et regum vita praecurrere amicos.

Run from grandeur. You may live in a pauper's hut, but in your life you will
outdo kings and the friends of kings.

(*Fuge* here recalls *fugitivus* in line 10; and *reges... vita praecurrere*
recalls *vivo et regno* in line 8.) Conversely, the horse in the fable which
conquered by force (37, *victor violens*) was unable to cast off (38,
depulit) its rider or the bit; and so it was in an even worse plight than
when the stag was casting him out (35, *pellebat*) of their common
field. The victor, by winning, became a slave. The contrast to this is
freedom (40, *libertate*), which is to exploit limited means rather than
be exploited for the whole of life (41):[50]

serviet aeternum quia parvo nesciet uti.

He will forever be a slave because he doesn't know how to live on little.

This gives a further meaning to *vivere naturae... convenienter*: we
have to accept a modest wealth and status. This is, in fact, in
Epicurean terms the same as following our natural desires, since
these are always limited.[51] Horace again uses the word *convenire* to
make the point (42–3):

cui non conveniet sua res, ut calceus olim,
si pede maior erit, subvertet, si minor, uret

When a man's substance doesn't suit him, it's rather like a sandal sometimes:
if it is bigger than his foot, it trips him. If it's too small, it chafes.

Here there is another twist in the expression which makes the homely
comparison more than a platitude: it is not the shoe that has to fit us,
it is we who have to fit the shoe, our condition. Freedom is not the
same as unlimited scope for our whims.[52]

Finally, Horace turns directly to his addressee again. It is clear by
now that his apparent aim of proving the country better than the
town was only apparent. This is delicately brought out by the use of

[50] There is a certain tension between *aeternum* and *parvo*, and between *serviet* and
uti. The notion of freedom here has an Epicurean flavour (cf. Kiessling-Heinze (1957:
on line 40)).

[51] Cf. Epic. frag. 471–8.

[52] Cf. *Od.* 2.2.9–12 and Nisbet and Hubbard (1970: ad loc.).

comparatives (which are very numerous)[53] in the poem. In lines 14–20 they are used to commend Horace's preference for the country against the town; but it is a different kind of contrast, between genuine and conventional superiority, which really counts and to which the other comparatives, except the rather ironic *melior* and *minor* in lines 34–5, are related. Thus for Horace to get the better of the 'argument' with Fuscus would be as useless as it was for the horse to defeat the stag. The way in which the two friends should try to exercise control is by correcting each other's mistakes (44–8):

> laetus sorte tua vives sapienter, Aristi,
> nec me dimittes incastigatum[54] ubi plura
> cogere quam satis est ac non cessare videbor.
> imperat aut servit collecta pecunia cuique,
> tortum digna sequi potius quam ducere funem.

You will live wisely, Aristius, if you live happy with your lot. Nor will you send me away un-berated when I am caught piling up more than enough and never leaving off. Each man either controls the money he has gathered or is a slave to it. Money should follow the twisted rope, not to pull it.

Horace's whole poem was in a sense an admonition to Fuscus, and at this point he invites Fuscus to admonish him, if need be; but there will be need only if Horace forces wealth upon himself. *Nec me dimittes* is picked up by *cogere*, which is used here in its literal sense of 'gather' (*co-agere*) but carries as an overtone its normal sense 'compel'. Again paradoxes reinforce the argument: Horace is to be 'punished' only if he does not idle; and the man who 'gathers' (or 'compels') too much may well find that his 'collected' wealth 'lords it' over him. Once more, supremacy won by forcing nature is slavery; and the error which needs controlling is an excess of control.

The last two lines of the poem are utterly unobtrusive, but no less pregnant than the rest:

> haec tibi dictabam post fanum putre Vacunae,
> excepto quod non simul esses cetera laetus.

I was dictating these thoughts to you behind the crumbling shrine of Vacuna, happy in all ways except that you were not here with me.

---

[53] See lines 11, 14, 15, 18, 19, 20, 28, 34, 35, 39, 43, 45, 48.

[54] On this phrase, appropriate to Fuscus' profession of *grammaticus*, see Nisbet (1959: 74–5).

Vacuna was a Sabine goddess whom Varro identified with Victoria (see pseudo-Acro ad loc.); an inscription (*CIL* XIV.3485) records that the emperor Vespasian restored a temple of Victory near Horace's villa.[55] This interpretation of Vacuna must be in play here, given that the poem throughout employs in a bold and significant manner the language of victory and defeat. So these words are a further rejection of success as commonly conceived, in that the shrine of Victory is 'crumbling'. At the same time, they suggest that there is a better kind of success, which is indicated also by Varro's etymology for the name Vacuna: 'quod ea maxime hi gaudent qui sapientiae vacent'; the leisure and study implicit in the word *vacare*, or the philosophic 'victory', is precisely what Horace enjoys in the country, and at the shrine of Vacuna. The last line shows that Horace is what he tells Fuscus to be, happy (*laetus* in 44 and 50); *excepto quod non simul esses* points as well to another requirement for happiness, friendship, again a theme typical of Epicurus.[56] So happiness is not merely a question of living in studious retirement with our own needs or circumstances, but of taking pleasure in others' company when they are there, and so too of missing them when they are not. Friendship is a natural and necessary counterpart to freedom, the ideal which pervades this *Epistle*; for friendship is the affection we share with others and freedom the independence we have from them, when there is no attempt to dominate, to be 'king' or 'victor'. The wise man, then, does not become a 'winner' by avoiding all attachments, a point made more openly in the next *Epistle* (11.6ff.). And thus we rejoin the beginning of the poem, where Horace was no less fond of Fuscus because their tastes clashed.

In the *Ars Poetica* Horace envisaged a kind of poetry which would arise from both the study of ethics and the observation of life, which would at once instruct and delight its readers, which would, in short, embody in every sense the ideal of 'propriety' (esp. 309–44).[57] The immediate object of his words there is drama; but what he says of drama in the *Ars* is not meant to apply only to drama, and propriety

[55] Either Horace, by a small poetic licence, renamed the goddess of the temple Vacuna, or Vespasian renamed her Victoria, presumably because that divinity is closely associated with the emperor (cf. *ILS* III. 1, p. 555).

[56] See esp. frag. 174–5; *BD* 27–8; *VS* 13, 23, 52. Also Arist. *EN* 9.9.

[57] See esp. Cic. *Or.* 68–74. In general, Pohlenz (1933: 53–92 = 1965 100–39).

is a concept applicable to every form of writing, as to living itself. It goes with this that the practice of poetry makes moral demands on the poet (esp. *AP* 309ff.). The *Epistles* are poetry of an unusual quality because they scrutinize the pleasures, pains and problems of living against a standard, a standard represented by philosophy, and because the author's experience, more than anyone else's, undergoes that examination. For the same reasons they are peculiarly valuable as a historical document; for we understand more fully what life was like when we see, in the powerful light of an artistic recreation, how someone applied to his own existence a notion of what it was meant to be like.[58]

[58] I have been greatly helped by criticisms from Mr D. O. M. Charles and by previous conversation with him.

11

Poetry, Philosophy, and Letter-Writing in Horace *Epistles* 1

Stephen J. Harrison

Two long-running issues in the criticism of Horace's first book of *Epistles* now appear to be in a steady state: that of whether these twenty hexameter poems are in any sense 'real' letters, and that of whether Horace's professions of philosophical eclecticism in the programmatic *Epistles* 1.1 (13–19) are borne out by the collection. On the first issue, most would now agree that 'while the possibility remains that some of the *Epistles* were actually sent as letters, they are best judged as fictional discourse' and that these poems aim at 'a lively illusion of reality' (Kilpatrick 1986: xvii). On the second issue, Horace's lack of dogmatism seems to be re-established after attempts to make him more philosophically systematic, and he is now seen as an independent purveyor of familiar ethical generalisations.[1] These issues form the background to the questions addressed here. First, what kind of techniques does Horace use to present philosophical material (whatever it is) within the context of a collection of hexameter poetry? And second, how does Horace's fictionalised use of the letter-form (assuming that it is fictionalised) relate to ancient practice and prescription in the field of letter-writing? These issues will be dealt with separately in what follows, but as will emerge, they are crucially interrelated: letters were well-known as a means of presenting

---

[1] See e.g. Moles 1985, Mayer 1986, Rudd 1993a. Kilpatrick 1986 sees Horace as an Academic, McGann 1969 as an eclectic Stoic, but both these positions seem too dogmatic.

philosophy in the ancient world (note the extant epistles ascribed to Plato and Epicurus, and the lost epistles of Aristotle), and some of the techniques used in the presentation of philosophy in the *Epistles* have clear links with the prescriptions of ancient epistolographical theory.

1. POETRY AND PHILOSOPHY

The idea of putting philosophy into hexameter poetry was not of course original to Horace. Its history stretches back to Parmenides and Empedocles, and the *De Rerum Natura* of Lucretius had come out in the 50s BCE. There is clear evidence that Horace knew and used the work of Lucretius in the *Satires* and *Odes* as well as the *Epistles*,[2] but there are some important differences between the two poets. Horace deals not with the relatively recondite subject of Epicurean physics but with the central matters of ethics and personal conduct, common topics of educated conversation at Rome and closely applicable to everyday life; here, as has long been recognised, he is indebted to the *De Officiis* of Cicero, another publication of the previous generation, which tries similarly to apply the precepts of Greek ethics to the practice of Roman public and private life (McGann 1969: 10–14). There is also the question of dogmatism, intensity and grandeur: the doctrinaire missionary fervour and epic sublimity of Lucretius, though tempered at times by reflection and humour, is far from the mellow and humble protreptic persona adopted by Horace in the first book of *Epistles*.

Horace's presentation of philosophy in the first book of *Epistles* may be considered under two general headings: that of the poet's own self-representation as writer of the poems, and that of how the resources of hexameter poetry in particular are used in the exposition of ethics.

(i) Self-Presentation

The first and programmatic poem of *Epistles 1* gives the reader vital indications of the kind of philosopher Horace will be (*Ep.* 1.1.1–12):

---

[2] Cf. Rehmann 1969, Freudenburg 1993: 19.

Prima dicte mihi, summa dicende Camena,
spectatum satis et donatum iam rude quaeris,
Maecenas, iterum antiquo me includere ludo.
non eadem est aetas, non mens. Veianius armis
Herculis ad postem fixis latet abditus agro,
ne populum extrema totiens exoret harena.
est mihi purgatam crebro qui personet aurem:
'solve senescentem mature sanus equum, ne
peccet ad extremum ridendus et ilia ducat'.
nunc itaque et versus et cetera ludicra pono;
quid verum atque decens, curo et rogo et omnis in hoc sum.
condo et compono quae mox depromere possim.

Proclaimed by me in my first poetry, to be proclaimed in my last,
Maecenas, you seek to shut me up in my school/play of old.
Though already enough on show and presented with
    my retirement-sword.
My age, my mind are not the same. Veianius hung his arms
On Hercules' door and stays quiet hidden in the country,
To avoid begging the people so often from the arena's edge.
I have a voice which rings in my ear, now clean of dirt:
'Come to sense in time and loose the ageing stallion,
So that he doesn't stumble at the last and split his sides'.
So now I lay aside poetry and other playthings:
What is true and fitting is my care and request, I'm all for that.
I fashion/store and lay up/compose things to draw
    down in due course.

Horace here describes his turning to philosophy as the retirement of
a gladiator, who does not wish to enter again the *ludus*, playing on
the double sense of that word, which means both 'gladiatorial school'
and 'frivolous play' (West 1967: 23–4): the metaphorical message to
Maecenas is clearly that Horace will not write another book of erotic
Odes after the recent publication of *Odes* 1–3, and that he is keen to
put such frivolities behind him in his new ethical project. *Ludus* can
refer specifically to love as well as to erotic poetry, as it does in a
similar context at *Epistles* 1.14.36, *non lusisse pudet, sed non incidere
ludum*, 'I'm not ashamed to have played, but of not cutting the game
short' (cf. *TLL* 7.1789.32ff.); Horace is presenting himself as too old
both for love and for its poetry, as at *Odes* 3.26.1–2: *vixi puellis nuper
idoneus, | et militavi non sine gloria*, 'I have lived my life until recently

as one fit for girls, and I have campaigned not without glory' (cf. also *Odes* 1.5.13–16).

The image used there was of course the elegiac one of the *militia amoris*; here in the *Epistles* the same idea is presented through the image of the retired gladiator, a decidedly down-market and sordid version of the same metaphor (Veianius is not an elevated character—as a gladiator he was probably a slave). The rural retirement of the gladiator (*latet abditus agro*) reinforces the parallel with Horace the poet on his own Sabine *ager* (*Ep.* 1.16.4): Horace's pensive withdrawal to the country and its opportunities for philosophical reflection will be a major theme in *Epistles* 1 (cf. *Ep.* 1.7, 1.10, 1.14, 1.16). This lower tone is confirmed by the image of lines 8–9, where Horace's poetry is compared to a clapped-out nag, a reduced and comic version of the chariot of poetry;[3] Horace will have to slow down to a walk, suitable to the *Musa pedestris* of *sermo* (*Sat.* 2.6.17). Explicit allusion to philosophy comes at lines 10–12, where all poetry is renounced in favour of moral philosophy. The protestation is solemn, but tinged with not a little humour: Horace is after all renouncing poetry in the context of introducing a book of poems, a type of ironic fiction found elsewhere in his hexameter poetry (*Sat.* 1.4.41–2, *AP* 306). As in the opening image of the *ludus*, ambiguous language indicates this irony: *condo* and *compono* are technical terms for the storage or laying down of wine in a cellar, but both verbs can also refer elsewhere in Horace to the composition of poetry (Mayer 1994: 90).

So the first book of *Epistles* begins with a self-representation which is far from sublime, and with a renunciation of poetry in favour of morality which is strongly stated but cannot be literally true; the erotic and symposiastic themes of the *Odes* do largely disappear, but the collection is indubitably poetic. The apparent conversion to philosophy is at least partly a fiction for literary purposes, since philosophical concerns are far from absent from Horace's earlier writings.[4] The poet is not a 'born again' fundamentalist missionary

---

[3] For the chariot of poetry see e.g. Pindar *Ol.* 6.23, *P.* 6.23, *Isthm.* 8.68, Callimachus *Aetia* fr.1.25–8, Virgil *G.* 2.542, 3.18. Mayer 1994: 89 points out the link with Ibycus' presentation of himself as a superannuated race-horse pressed back into the competition of love: this link with archaic lyric is of course very fitting in a context where the lyric poetry of the *Odes* is being renounced.

[4] Here I agree with Mayer 1986 and Rudd 1993a against Macleod 1979, who takes the concept of conversion too literally.

in the Lucretian mould, but is able to joke about his new career as a poetic purveyor of philosophy to his friends. This combination of self-depreciating humour and enthusiasm in conveying his philosophical interests is a hall-mark of Horace's self-presentation in the first book of *Epistles*. This is confirmed by further examples. In *Ep.* 1.4 Horace writes to Tibullus,[5] advising his fellow-poet to enjoy the material benefits of his comfortable life while he may, despite the emotional traumas he writes about in his love-elegies (12–16):

> inter spem curamque, timores inter et iras,
> omnem crede diem tibi diluxisse supremum.
> grata superveniet quae non sperabitur hora.
> me pinguem et nitidum bene curata cute vises
> cum ridere voles Epicuri de grege porcum.

> Amid hope and concern, amid fear and anger
> Believe every day to have dawned your last.
> Pleasant will be the coming of the hour that's not expected.
> You'll come and see me, fat and shining with well-cared-for skin
> When you want to laugh at a porker from Epicurus' herd.

Once again this famous self-characterisation by Horace is clearly not an elevated one, and here again, as in the opening epistle, it is conjoined with earnest philosophical exhortations, here of an Epicurean kind no doubt suited to a hedonistic elegist.[6] Horace the philosophical teacher uses self-depreciation as a *captatio benevolentiae*.

Horace commonly presents himself in *Epistles 1* not as the great teacher and moral paragon but as a fallible fellow-pupil, while still urging a particular moral line. At the end of *Ep.* 1.6, Horace refers to his advice as no better than anyone else's, but encourages Numicius to take it if he knows nothing else better (67–8), while at the beginning of *Ep.* 1.17, in an equally prominent position, Scaeva is given instruction on the art of friendship, a philosophical subject in antiquity (see Powell 1995), but by a Horace who is still learning and who is like a blind man leading the way (3–4). Twice Horace, advocating the consistent moral life, alludes prominently to his own inconsistency (*Ep.* 1.8, 1.15.42–6), and the final poem of the book,

---

[5] So I think with Nisbet and Hubbard 1970: 368; for a more sceptical view on the identity of the Albius of *Odes* 1.33 and *Epistles* 1.4 see Mayer 1994: 133.

[6] As will be seen below, 1.4.13 translates an Epicurean precept.

although it is not concerned with philosophy as such, continues this modest self-presentation, in a direct contrast with the great closing claims for the poet made in *Odes* 2.20 and 3.30 (see Harrison 1988). The rationale behind this modesty both as poet and as teacher of philosophy is clear enough: Horace is evidently going to get further in interesting his friends in ethical topics by not posing as an omniscient sage. The humorous and fallible self-image of the poet as philosopher in *Epistles* 1 helps to convey its protreptic message in the most effective and acceptable way.

(ii) Poetic Packaging

I now turn to the advantages of poetry in general and of the hexameter in particular in Horace's presentation and packaging of philosophical material in *Epistles* 1. Two techniques will suffice here. One is the use of single-line *sententiae*, 'one-liners', through which the poet can encapsulate a thought in a single syntactical unit in one easily-memorable hexameter. There are many examples, of which the following list is merely a convenient selection:

1. *Ep.* 1.1.19   *et mihi res, non me rebus subiungere conor*
                 'I try to yoke events to myself, not myself to events'

2. *Ep.* 1.1.52   *vilius argentum est auro, virtutibus aurum*
                 'silver's inferior to gold, gold to good qualities'

3. *Ep.* 1.2.46   *quod satis est cui contingit nihil amplius optet*
                 'let he who has enough never wish for more'

4. *Ep.* 1.4.13   *omnem crede diem tibi diluxisse supremum*
                 'believe every day to have dawned your last'

5. *Ep.* 1.6.23   *hic tibi sit potius quam tu memorabilis illi*
                 'let him be a marvel to you rather than you to him'

6. *Ep.* 1.7.98   *metiri se quemque suo modulo ac pede verum est*
                 'it's a truth that each gauges himself by his own foot and measure'

7. *Ep.* 1.11.27   *caelum non animum mutant qui trans mare currunt*
                 'those who speed across the sea change climate, not their spirits'

8. *Ep.* 1.14.11   *cui placet alterius, sua nimirum est odio sors*
                 'he who likes another's lot naturally hates his own'

Stephen J. Harrison

9. *Ep.* 1.14.44   *quam scit uterque libens censebo exerceat artem*
'I'll rule that each of us should pursue the art he knows'

10. *Ep.* 1.16.17   *tu recte vivis, si curas esse quod audis*
'you live rightly, if you take care to match your reputation'

11. *Ep.* 1.17.10   *nec vixit male qui natus moriensque fefellit*
'he has lived no bad life who was born and died in obscurity'

12. *Ep.* 1.17.36   *non cuivis homini contingit adire Corinthum*
'not every man gets to go to Corinth'

13. *Ep.* 1.18.9   *virtus est medium vitiorum et utrimque reductum*
'virtue is a mean between opposite vices, far removed from either end'

These thirteen one-line *sententiae* divide into two types: those which express a very general philosophical or proverbial idea, and those which translate or adapt known moral precepts of Greek philosophers. Of the first type, 3 encapsulates the ideal of self-sufficiency (*autarkeia*) desiderated by most ancient philosophies, 6 the general idea that each man has his own individual measure, 7 refers to the common idea that travel does not ease the mind, 8 to the commonplace that each man dislikes his own lot and wants another (*mempsimoiria*) while 6, 9 and 12 are versions of known proverbs;[7] here it is worth recalling that ancient proverbs were often expressed in metrical units.[8] For each of the second type, we can trace a particular Greek prose source cast by Horace into verse, as follows:[9]

1. Cf. Aristippus in Diogenes Laertius 2.75 ἔχω … ἀλλ᾽ οὐκ ἔχομαι
2. Cf. Plato *Laws* 5.728a χρυσὸς ἀρετῆς οὐκ ἀντάξιος
4. Cf. Epicurus fr. 490 Us. (Plutarch *De Tranq.* 474C) ὁ τῆς αὔριον ἥκιστα δεόμενος … ἥδιστα πρόσεισι πρὸς τὴν αὔριον
5. Cf. Plutarch *De Tranq.* 470 d ζηλωτὸν εἶναι μᾶλλον ἢ ζηλοῦν ἑτέρους
10. Cf. Socrates in Xenophon *Mem.* 2.6.39 ὅ τι ἂν βούλῃ δοκεῖν ἀγαθὸς εἶναι, τοῦτο καὶ γενέσθαι ἀγαθὸν πειρᾶσθαι

---

[7] Cf. Otto 1890: nos. 221, 151 and 92 respectively.
[8] Cf. Otto 1890: xxxiii–xxxiv.
[9] All these parallels are collected by Kiessling and Heinze 1915.

11. Cf. Epicurus fr. 551 Us. λάθε βιώσας
13. Cf. Aristotle *NE* 2.6 1106b–1107a 'Έστιν ἄρα ἡ ἀρετὴ ... μεσότης
δὲ δύο κακιῶν, τῆς μὲν καθ᾽ ὑπερβολὴν τῆς δὲ κατ᾽ ἔλλειψιν

Thus it is clear that Horace is aware in the *Epistles* that hexameter verse adds an extra dimension to the presentation of philosophical precepts, enabling the poet to communicate philosophical views, whether general or particular, with epigrammatic point and neatness in a single regular and memorable unit not available to writers of prose.

A second resource offered by the poetic medium is that of imagery. Of course, prose texts and prose expositions of philosophy need not be poor in imagery (Plato's dialogues and Seneca's letters are good counter-examples), but the *Epistles* show that poetry, especially hexameter poetry with its long and rich tradition, offers greater opportunity for such ornament, and Lucretius had provided an important precedent for the extensive use of imagery in the poetic exposition of philosophy.[10] One particular technique which the *Epistles* share with Lucretius here is the use of analogy with the familiar and visual in giving expositions of non-visual philosophical ideas. A few examples. In the first poem Horace compares disorder of appearance and of soul (*Ep.* 1.1.94–100):

> si curatus inaequali tonsore capillos
> occurri, rides; si forte subucula pexae
> trita subest tunicae vel si toga dissidet impar,
> rides: quid mea cum pugnat sententia secum,
> quod petiit spernit, repetit quod nuper omisit,
> aestuat et vitae disconvenit ordine toto,
> diruit, aedificat, mutat quadrata rotundis?

> If I meet you with my hair done by a barber who cuts crooked,
> You laugh; if a worn shirt is under my smooth new tunic,
> Or if my toga parts unevenly, you laugh:
> What then, when my mind is at variance with itself,
> Spurns what it used to pursue, seeks again what it just dropped,
> Seethes and is at odds in the whole ordering of life,
> Demolishes, builds, changes square for round?

Here Horace comically implies that the elegant Maecenas is more interested in minor aberrations in Horace's dress and appearance than in major aberrations in his moral and internal state. The minute

---

[10] See still West 1969.

and everyday details of dress and haircut give the thought a strong visual element, and suggest that moral confusion is just as common a state as untidiness of dress, a significant disadvantage in polite Roman society, so forcing it on the reader's attention. Very similar is the briefer image at 1.10.42–3:

> cui non conveniet sua res, ut calceus olim,
> si pede maior erit, subvertet, si minor, uret.

> If a man's fortune doesn't fit him, it's like a shoe:
> Too big for his foot, it will trip him up in time,
> 	too small, it'll pinch him.

There discontent with one's material lot is aptly compared to an ill-fitting shoe, which will be uncomfortable if it is either too small or too big; again the sartorial detail brings the moral point home to the reader. Another instance is 1.18.84–5:

> nam tua res agitur, paries cum proximus ardet,
> et neglecta solent incendia sumere viris.

> For it's your concern when the neighbour's wall burns,
> And fires that are left alone usually grow in strength.

Here Horace advises Lollius to stick by friends who are attacked by others—he may be next, and will need their support in turn. This is reinforced by the vivid image of the burning house; in the close confines of a heavily inflammable Rome, conflagrations were all too common, and a neighbour's property in flames meant disaster for one's own.[11] All this is very similar to the technique by which Lucretius presents such invisible and arcane scientific matter as atomic motion through comparison in similes with things and events common in the visual life of late Republican Rome, most memorably public festivals or events in the theatre (cf. West 1969: 49–63).

The same can be said for the deployment of another image in the *Epistles*, the idea that philosophy is a cure for the soul just as medicine is a cure for the body. Again this is an image which begins in prose texts such as Democritus and Plato, but in *Epistles* 1 Horace uses it a number of times, taking advantage of the capacity of a poetry-book to continue and develop an image.[12] This medical

---

[11] See the material gathered by J. E. B. Mayor on Juvenal 3.7.
[12] See conveniently Bramble 1974: 35 nn. 2 and 3.

analogy appears prominently in the first and programmatic poem (1.28–37):

> non possis oculo quantum contendere Lynceus,
> non tamen idcirco contemnas lippus inungi;
> nec quia desperes invicti membra Glyconis,
> nodosa corpus nolis prohibere cheragra.
> est quadam prodire tenus, si non datur ultra.
> fervet avaritia miseroque cupidine pectus:
> sunt verba et voces quibus hunc lenire dolorem
> possis et magnam morbi deponere partem.
> laudis amore tumes: sunt certa piacula quae te
> ter pure lecto poterunt recreare libello.

> Just because you couldn't strain your eyes like Lynceus
> Doesn't mean that you should reject ointment when they're sore:
> And if you have no hope of the firm limbs of the champion Glycon,
> You should still keep your body free of knotty gout.
> You can always advance a little, even if you can't go any further.
> Your breast seethes with greed and wretched desire:
> There are words and expressions to soothe that kind of pain,
> And to dispel a great part of the disease.
> You swell with desire for glory: there are certain rites which
> can give you respite,
> When you've three times read your book in purity of heart.

Here the poet encourages Maecenas and the reader in general to make as much effort to cure their moral ills as they would to heal physical complaints. The illnesses named as analogies in lines 29–31 are familiar and everyday ones, inflamed eyes and gout; the poet then goes on to treat moral ills in terms of bodily metaphor, with some careful and elegant ambiguity—*fervet* can refer to simple feverish heat as well as spiritual warmth, *lenire dolorem* is as appropriate to the relief of physical pain as to mental soothing, while *tumes* can suggest malignant physical swelling as well as the metaphorical swelling of ambition (Mayer 1994: 95). *Ter pure* suggests a formula of magical or medicinal relief of a physical kind,[13] an idea continued in *recreare*, but *lecto... libello* points the surprise and the intentional ambiguity—the illness is one of the spirit, and its cure is a book, a text of philosophy, perhaps the very book which the poet is writing. The reader is being encouraged to read on in hope of a cure.

[13] Cf. conveniently Murgatroyd on Tibullus 1.2.54 and 1.3.25.

After this prominent introduction, the theme appears again in the next poem (1.2.51–3):

> qui cupit aut metuit, iuvat illum sic domus et res
> ut lippum pictae tabulae, fomenta podagrum,
> auriculas citharae collecta sorde dolentis.

> He who desires or fears is as much pleased by his house and wealth
> As painted pictures please a man with sore eyes or dressings the gouty,
> Or lyres please ears suffering from a blockage of dirt.

Once again the poet picks on everyday complaints, adding to the watery eyes and gout of the first epistle the pain of ears blocked with wax, arguing that they prevent the enjoyment of normal pleasures, and the point illustrated is similarly a trite one; the impossibility of pleasure for the rich man beset by cares is a favourite notion for Roman moralists.[14] Again, the point about moral health is effectively made through physical comparison and analogy. Equally effective is the image at 1.3.31–2, where the poet enquires of Florus whether the rift between Celsus and Munatius has been properly patched up, or whether it is still in operation:

> an male sarta
> gratia nequiquam coit ac rescinditur...?

> Or has your goodwill been poorly patched,
> So that the wound is mended in vain and then reopens?

Here the sundered friendship is clearly compared to an open wound where the stitches may or may not come together and heal; *sarta*, *coit* and *rescinditur* are technical terms of medicine.[15] The point is clearly an ethical one: the moral harm of quarrelling is like the physical harm of injury, and the reconciled friend is like the whole and healed body.

This link in imagery between physical and moral distemper is extended through another feature of the first book of *Epistles* already identified, the poet's detailed self-representation. Horace's own actual or potential ill-health is mentioned a number of times in the collection, and is linked from time to time with the unsatisfactory state of his mind. In 1.8, in a letter to Celsus, on campaign with Tiberius in the East, the analogy is fully explored (3–12):

---

[14] Cf. e.g. *Odes* 2.16.9–24, 3.1.17–24, 3.16.17–28; Seneca *Ep.* 84.11, 115.16, *Brev. Vit.* 2.4.

[15] Cf. *OLD* s.v. *sarcio* 1, *coeo* 5, *rescindo* 2b.

si quaeret quid agam, dic multa et pulchra minantem
vivere nec recte nec suaviter; haud quia grando
contuderit vitis oleamque momorderit aestus,
nec quia longinquis armentum aegrotet in agris;
sed quia mente minus validus quam corpore toto
nil audire velim, nil discere, quod levet aegrum;
fidis offendar medicis, irascar amicis,
cur me funesto properent arcere veterno;
quae nocuere sequar, fugiam quae profore credam;
Romae Tibur amem ventosus, Tibure Romam.

If he asks how I am doing, say that I promise many fine things
But live with neither virtue nor pleasure: not because
Hail has battered my vines or heat attacked my olives,
Or because my flock is sick in distant fields,
But because I am even weaker in mind than in my whole body,
And do not like to hear or learn any relief for my illness:
I take offence at my faithful doctors, rage at my friends,
Asking why they hasten to keep me from deadly lethargy;
I pursue what harms me, and avoid what I deem good:
Fickle as the wind, I love Tibur at Rome, Rome at Tibur.

Again, as elsewhere, the terms used are neatly ambiguous: *audire,
discere* and *quod levet aegrum* refer equally well to listening to med-
ically or spiritually curative advice, matching the balance in line 9
between *medicis* and *amicis* which suggests that friends try to do for
the mind what doctors try to do for the body, *veterno* in line 10 can
refer to physical conditions such as dropsy as well as mental lethargy,
and the pithy one-liner of line 11 presents a moral dilemma akin to
Aristotelian *akrasia* as well as a problem with daily diet and habits
(Mayer 1994: 177).

In 1.7, Horace's Sabine estate is used as a starting-point for more
general analogies between bodily and spiritual health. There Horace
claims health as a reason for staying on his estate rather than coming
to Maecenas in Rome; the opening, with its talk of the insalubrious
summer conditions in the city, stresses that physical risk is a main
factor in Horace's absence (1–13). But the rest of the poem, with its
exempla of the Calabrian host, the vixen in the corn-bin, and the
story of Philippus and Mena, makes it clear that the Sabine estate and
Horace's capacity to remain there represent more than physical

health. The estate and its gift through Maecenas' friendship allow Horace to remain healthy in spirit, that is to pursue an appropriate life-style of rural philosophical *otium* in dignified but grateful independence, and the poem ends with a generalising and proverbial 'one-liner' (see above) which stresses the ethical dimension (98 *metiri se quemque suo modulo ac pede verum est*).

The extension and variation of a type of imagery illustrating a philosophical idea to provide a link with a central theme of the whole collection is typical of the resources available for the exposition of ideas in a poetry-book. In fact, we have seen that discussion of the analogy between mental and physical health has also mentioned and included the two other aspects of the first book of *Epistles* which have been classified above as poetic techniques—the elaborate self-presentation of the writer and the use of 'one-liners', showing that the poet is in full command of a range of poetical strategies, and uses them in an integrated way towards the objective of his collection, the entertaining and informative presentation of ethical issues both to his immediate correspondents and to a larger readership.

2. LETTER-WRITING AND *EPISTLES* I

Here we turn to our second issue, that of whether the first book of *Epistles* is written with some consciousness of formal works on letter-writing; we shall see in due course that this links closely with our first issue of the poetic presentation of philosophy. Some influence on Horace from the epistolographical tradition is not improbable; Cicero's letters (especially those of recommendation) may show some awareness of it,[16] and it would only be natural for Horace to employ it in recasting *sermo* into epistolary mode in the first book of *Epistles*. The Greek works devoted to letter-writing collected in Hercher's *Epistolographi Graeci* are jejune and concerned almost entirely with epistolary typology, and insignificant here (Hercher 1873: 1–13); most important are the pages devoted to letter-writing

---

[16] See Keyes 1935, Cotton 1984 and 1985; for Cicero's (very general) awareness of various epistolary types see Hutchinson 1998: 7–9.

in Demetrius *On Style*, perhaps from the early Imperial period.[17] Similarities between Demetrius' precepts and Horace's practice in the *Epistles* could suggest knowledge on Horace's part of epistolographical theory, even if Demetrius' work were written much later, since ancient handbooks of this kind are notoriously tralatician, and even those who wish to assign a late date to Demetrius recognise that his treatise contains elements of much earlier doctrine. It is possible, of course, that Demetrius' precepts merely reflected literary practice in letter-writing, and that any links with Horace could be owed to Horace's knowledge of actual letters rather than of theory, but the striking nature of some of the resemblances suggest a more direct connection.

Demetrius begins his section on letter-writing (*On Style* 223–5) by asserting that the style of letters requires plainness (*ischnotes*), though this should also be combined with the more elevated quality of charm (*charis*). In support of this, he cites Artemon, editor of Aristotle's letters and certainly a pre-Horatian writer, to the effect that 'a letter may be regarded as one of the two sides in a dialogue'. This, like plainness of style, is one of the conventional recommendations of ancient epistolography (Cugusi 1983: 32–3). Here Horace fits the prescription, since most of the epistles in the first book are in effect his side of an exchange with the addressee, commonly an intimate with whom the poet might have regular contact and converse. More importantly, Artemon's view implies a colloquial stylistic level for letters, a view endorsed elsewhere in the epistolographical tradition (Thraede 1970: 27–61, Cugusi 1983: 33); of course, this is the natural register of Horatian hexameter *sermo*, making it a natural vehicle for letter-writing. Demetrius also stresses the small scale of the letter (228); in addition to mirroring the practicalities of ancient correspondence, brevity itself is another stylistic *topos* in epistolographical writing (Cugusi 1983: 34–6). Here we can see an interesting contrast between the *Satires* and the

---

[17] On the date see most recently Paffenroth 1994; I cite the translation of Demetrius by D. C. Innes in Russell and Winterbottom 1972. For Greek and Roman letter-writing cf. Thraede 1970 and Cugusi 1983. There is only one extant formal discussion of letter-writing in Latin from the ancient world, a few pages in the fourth-century *Ars Rhetorica* of C. Iulius Victor (see Halm 1863: 447–8), which uses Greek precepts but examples from Cicero.

first book of *Epistles*: the two books of *Satires* show an average poem-length of 119 lines (103 lines for Book 1, 135 for Book 2), the first book of *Epistles* one of 50 lines, dramatically different. The second book of *Epistles* and the *Ars Poetica* are of course rather longer, but there the epistolographical fiction is less immediately important; in *Epistles* 1 Horace is conforming more closely and consciously to the practice and prescriptions of letter-writing.

Further points made by Demetrius concern the content rather than the style of letters (227): 'A letter should be very largely an expression of character, just like the dialogue. Perhaps everyone reflects his own soul in writing a letter. It is possible to discern a writer's character in every other form of literature, but in none so fully as in the letter'. This aspect of self-revelation again fits Horatian *sermo* as a whole; Horace characterises his *Satires* as self-revelatory, following the tradition of Lucilius (*Sat.* 2.1.30–4), and we indeed hear much there about Horace's earlier and present life. It is even more a feature of the first book of *Epistles*; as Gordon Williams has noted, 'a most marked feature of the *Epistles* is the way in which the form invites, indeed compels, statements apparently autobiographical' (Williams 1968: 29). Horace continually presents the topics of his own life—his turning to philosophy (1.1), his literary studies (1.2), his social life (1.5), his friendship with Maecenas (1.7), the publication and reception of his poems (1.13, 1.19, 1.20), his life in the country (1.10, 1.14, 1.16), his health (1.7, 1.15), and of course the concluding self-description in the final poem (1.20.20–8). This relentless self-presentation recalls the intimate detail of actual correspondence such as Cicero's letters to Atticus; Horace relies here on the convention and practice of letter-writing as well as on the autobiographical element in Lucilian *sermo*. Here we can see a link with our earlier discussion of poetic self-presentation; the prominence of the writer himself in the first book of *Epistles* is both an effective protreptic tactic and an epistolary feature.

Most interesting of all in Demetrius' prescriptions for our purposes are those on the content of letters (230–2): 'We should also recognise that it is not only a certain style but certain topics which suit letters. Let me quote Aristotle, who is admitted to be an especially felicitous writer of letters: "I do not write to you on this; it does not suit a letter". If anyone writes on logic or science in a letter, he is writing something but certainly not a letter. A letter aims to be a brief token of friendship and handles simple topics in simple language. Its charm lies in the warmth of friendship it conveys and in its numerous proverbs. This is the only kind of wisdom a letter should have; for proverbs give popular sayings in everyday use. The man who is sententious and sermonises seems to have lost the letter's air of a talk and mounted the pulpit.' All these aspects apply closely to the first book of Horace's *Epistles*, and link up neatly with the poetical tactics discussed in 1 above.

First, the non-technical and simple nature of letters. This might appear to be paradoxical for a book of poems which includes a fair amount of philosophical doctrine, but in fact, as outlined at the beginning, Horace's exposition of philosophy in *Epistles* 1 is generalising, undogmatic and fundamentally concerned with ethics, the most popular part of philosophy which was of universal interest in his own day, and not with the grittier topics of logic or physics; it is interesting to note that the quotation from Aristotle in Demetrius specifically refers to science and logic being excluded as inappropriate to letters. Second, the link of letters and friendship. In one sense, this is simply an obvious comment on the means of intimate communication in a pre-telephonic age, but it is again worth noting that almost all the poems in the first book of *Epistles* are addressed to known friends of Horace, a difference from the *Odes* and even the *Satires*, that they contain particularly warm expressions of personal affection (e.g. 1.1.105, 1.10.1–5), and that friendship and its rightful conduct is a major topic in the collection (e.g. 1.7, 1.17, 1.18).

Third and perhaps most importantly, Demetrius' stress on the non-dogmatic and non-preaching role of the letter-writer, and his use of homely proverbs rather than technicalities and high-flown moral prescription, fits remarkably well with Horace's self-presentation in *Epistles* 1 as already discussed. Horace's humorous and self-deprecating role as author of moral protreptic in *Epistles* 1 is obvious from 1(i) above, but here we can see how it fits neatly into the conventions of letter-writing. The use of proverbs, too, can be plausibly connected with the 'one-liner' technique identified in 1(ii) above; not only does this technique resemble that of proverbial discourse with its pithy and memorable results (discussed, incidentally in ch. 9 of Demetrius *On Style*), but several of the 'one-liners' identified in *Epistles* I are, as already noted, themselves known proverbs. The homely and generalising wisdom of proverbs may also be appropriately compared with the overall strategy of *Epistles* 1 in proclaiming undogmatic and general ethical principles to which few would take exception.

3. CONCLUSION

In sum, I hope to have pointed to two features of the first book of Horace's *Epistles*, features which are crucially interrelated. First, I have indicated some of the strategies used by Horace to present his ethical material in hexameter poetry. Second, I have argued that some of the central features of Horace's treatment of his material are shared with ancient strictures on letter-writing, suggesting perhaps some knowledge on his part of epistolographical precepts in his epistolary practice.

POSTSCRIPT 2007

Of works which have appeared since I wrote this piece, Roland Mayer's commentary on *Epistles* 1 (1994) is very helpful on a number of points, and I have included references to it throughout; a few of the footnotes have also been updated. Beyond this, on philosophy in Horace's *Epistles* see now further Ferri 1993 and Moles 2007; Ferri 2007 is now a good starting-point on the key features of the *Epistles* as a whole. The relationship between Horace's *Epistles* and Roman epistolary theory has now been further investigated by De Pretis 2002 and Morrison 2007; on Roman epistolography more generally see further recently Trapp 2003, Edwards 2005 and Morello and Gibson 2007.

12

Horace and Aristippus: The *Epistles* and the Art of *Conuiuere*

Alfonso Traina

1. 'The only philosophical teacher by whom he seems personally attracted is the Cyrenaic Aristippus.'[1] Criticism has failed to appreciate Sellar's deft suggestion. The presence and importance of Aristippus in the works of Horace, especially in his *Epistles*, has in my opinion been under-appreciated, or at least not sufficiently analysed. In Horace's famous declaration of eclecticism at *Epist.* 1.1.18 (*nunc in Aristippi... praecepta relabor*, 'now I slip back... into the precepts of Aristippus'), Aristippus has generally been considered, since the time of the ancient scholiasts,[2] as a 'vulgar' substitute for Epicurus.[3] Only

---

[1] Sellar (1891: 42).

[2] Porphyr. *ad Epist.* 1.1.18: *quia Aristippus Epicureae princeps* ('because Aristippus was the originator of the Epicurean sect'); Pseudacr. ibid., p. 207 Keller: *Cyrenaicus fuit Epicureus* ('the Cyrenaic was an Epicurean').

[3] 'Vulgar' is the adjective used by Castorina (1965: 97). Setting aside the remarks of commentary writers, more or less along the same lines are: Kettner (1900: 47); Brakman (1921: 220); Dupouy (1928: 174); Rostagni (1937[1]: 93ff.; 1988[2]: 81), who thinks of Horace's ironic self-denigration; Zielinsky (1938: 85): 'son nom équivaut ici à d'Épicure'; Diano (1968: 14), but see below, n. 15; Gagliardi (1986: 66), who would take verses 18–19 *tout court* as a 'declaration of the Epicurean faith, in the spirit of a poetic hedonism'; Della Corte (1991: 62ff.): 'but perhaps he enjoys even more the hedonistic vice of Aristippus'; Michel (1992: 128); Oltramare (1926: 139) saw the author of *Epistles* Book 1 oscillating between popular Stoicism and the primitive hedonism of Aristippus, who is then, unexpectedly, presented on p. 148, in contrast to Diogenes, as the Horatian champion 'of true courage and of true virtue'. For Ferri (1993), who does not bring Aristippus into his discussion, the *Epistles* represent a return to Epicurus and Lucretius in the symbol of the *angulus*.

a few scholars have assessed his presence as a philosopher of *carpe diem* (see § 2 below), or of moral freedom,[4] in positive terms and spared him more than a few lines. And only one, the writer of a commentary on Book 1 of the *Epistles*, has devoted an article to Aristippus.[5] In it, however, there is no assessment of Aristippus' connection to the inspiration and thematics of the *Epistles* that would correspond to the debt of appreciation that Horace indicates he owes him. It will be worth our while, then, to re-examine the citations of the Cyrenaic philosopher in Horace, and to investigate the motives for their concentration in the *Epistles*.

2. Horace's citations of Aristippus are both explicit and implicit. The one citation that I would like to set aside at the start is that of *carpe diem*, since the ancestry of the phrase is claimed by both Epicurus and Aristippus.[6] The proverb that invites one to confine oneself to the present moment is so ancient and universal, and it is so common in Greek lyric poetry,[7] that it would be arbitrary to refer it back to a single, fixed philosophical source, especially in a poet who has made an open profession of his eclecticism (see § 4 below). And yet a careful examination of the pertinent texts, which are few and never terribly clear, pushes us more in the direction of Aristippus. This is so because Horace's *carpe diem*, as I have sought to demonstrate elsewhere,[8] is integrally connected to the rejection of the future: the poet closes himself off in the present not so much to enjoy its pleasures, but to defend the serenity that he obtains by keeping clear of the shadow (the *atra cura*, 'black care') cast by the uncertainty of chance and the certainty of death. The first and the last words of *Carm.* 1.11

---

[4] Marchesi (1940: 175–7 and 1946: 30–2); La Penna (1969: 948 and 1993: 256ff., 370ff.); Maguinness (1976: 172); Gigon (1977 and 1983; and see below, n. 58). Mandruzzato (1993[3]: 42–4); Romaniello (1984: 43ff.; and see next n.); Lana (1989: 161–4).

[5] Préaux (1977).

[6] Beyond a few scattered comments by Dilke (1996[3]: 26) and Traglia (1971: 43), the most thorough treatment to compare the sense of the present in Aristippus and in Horace is that of Gigon (1977) and, cursorily (1983: 20). Romaniello (1984: 33ff.) tacitly and uncritically repeats Gigon's theses, exaggerating their anti-Epicurean scope on the basis of 'a religious sense' in Horace that is completely foreign to Aristippus.

[7] Fontaine (1959); Del Grande (1965: 5–13); also, partially, Dilke (1966[3]: 26).

[8] Traina (1986[2]: 227–51) and (2005[17]: 8ff.).

are those not of an invitation, but of a prohibition: *tu ne quaesieris, scire nefas... quam minimum credula postero* ('do not ask, it is wrong to know... as for tomorrow, count on next-to-nothing'). It is precisely in this attitude towards the future that the teachings of Aristippus and Epicurus diverge. The former, to judge from two fragments, one passed down by Aelian (A 75 Giannantoni 1958 = IV a 174 Giannantoni 1983–5), the other by Athenaeus (B 28 G. 1958 = IV A 174 G. 1983–5), posited as the precondition for a serene state of mind focusing one's thoughts on today (ἐφ᾽ ἡμέρᾳ τὴν γνώμην ἔχειν) without agonizing about the past and worrying about the future (τῶν ἐπιόντων προκάμνειν).[9] The position espoused by Epicurus is more ambiguous and complex: the future, he says in his letter to Menoeceus 127, is neither entirely ours, nor is it entirely not ours.[10] But on the whole it is sufficiently explicit in recovering for the present either the memory of past pleasures or, in turn, the confident expectation of future pleasures. No shortage of these will befall the man who knows that his reasoning capacity (λογισμός or *ratio*) has the power to guarantee him the conditions of happiness.[11] Epicurean pleasure, unlike that proposed by Aristippus, is katastematic, collapsing together all dimensions of time, so that one's future is nothing more than today projected onto tomorrow. But it is precisely this confidence (ἐλπίς, *spes, expectatio*)[12] in the future that is unknown to Horace. With one exception: the future of the poet who will be immortalized by his verse: *non omnis moriar* ('I will not die completely').[13] But what of that other death, the

[9] Cf. Classen (1958: 188–90).

[10] To support *carpe diem* as Epicurean, Barbieri (1976: 480) is forced to surreptitiously lop off the end of the citation.

[11] Cf. Boyancé (1969: 46); Rist (1978: 117); and see the next n. The texts do not support Pesce (1958: 21) and (1981: 111ff.) in his claims about the Epicurean 'abolition' and 'negation' of the future.

[12] The texts are collected and discussed in Diano (1974: 259ff.).

[13] D'Anna (1979: 103–15) objects that for Horace the future is not always obscure, it is only sometimes uncertain. Precisely: because of this uncertainty one ought not count on it (cf., for example, *Carm.* 2.16.25ff.; *Epist.* 1.4.12–14), and this to me seems far from the optimistic reckoning of Epicurus, and therefore does not justify the assertion that '*carpe diem* is an Epicurean motif' (p. 106). The assertion is actually based on a Ciceronian text that attributes to the Epicurean *sapiens* the *exspectatio* of future pleasures (*Fin.* 1.62). Cf. now the fine analyses of Citti (1992) on 'hope' in Horace. Michel (1973: 331ff.), in treating the matter of time in Horace, has been too quick to take him as a champion of Epicureanism, especially in the *Epistles*, adding that in them Horace does not tire of congratulating himself for the protection that

one that inevitably awaits all men? The Epicurean does not fear it because he knows that it does not concern him. But Horace never said, as Lucretius once did, that 'for us death is nothing, and it has no relevance at all' (*nil... mors est ad nos neque pertinet hilum*). Rather, he exorcized it in all of his works by means of closing off time (*carpe diem*) and space (the *angulus*), through wine, friendship, and poetry.[14] But towards the end of his poetic testament, in the epistle to Florus, just as he was arranging to depart from the scene, he posed the question to himself once again: 'is your heart free from the terror of death?' (*caret tibi pectus... mortis formidine? Epist.* 2.2.206–7). Just as the sense of the future in Horace is unlike what one finds in Epicurus, so, too, his understanding of death is of a non-Epicurean stamp. And yet Epicurean elements are naturally not excluded from the composite wisdom of the poems, taken as a whole.[15]

3. But let us turn now to Aristippus. He is first caught sight of in the *Satires,* in the preaching of the Stoic Sterinius, as an *exemplum* of behaviour that differs from the avarice of Staberius: 'And did the Greek Aristippus do something like that? He ordered his slaves to cast aside his gold in the middle of the Libyan desert because they, sluggish from the load, were moving too slowly' (*quid simile isti* | *Graecus Aristippus? Qui seruos proicere aurum* | *in media iussit Libya, quia tardius irent* | *propter onus segnes, S.* 2.3.99–102). Is Aristippus' behaviour merely different from that of Staberius, or is it directly opposed? Is it to be commended or condemned? The question has kept commentators busy. But if we assume, as seems least controversial, that the question of verse 102, 'which of the two is more insane?'

has been accorded to him by Augustus and Maecenas, when it is actually in this work that such protection seems most problematic. A more analytical account is that of Deschamps (1983), who sees Horace's sense of time as a dialectic between the moment and extended time. But extended time is that of Roman history and of poetry's after-life.

[14] Traina (1986[2]: 253–67).

[15] See the excellent demonstration of Schwind (1965: 187–193), following the tracks of Oppermann (1938: 63–5); along the same lines, see Büchner (1970: 467), Bellardi (1975: 161), Gigon (1977: 446ff.), and now Grilli (1993: 38ff.), an article that unfortunately lacks a bibliography. Already Diano (1968: 17), in 'the sense of death that fills every pause', had pointed out an Epicurean limit to the idea of *carpe diem.* Terzaghi (1939: 81) also neatly defines the *carpe diem* motif as 'more pessimistic than Epicurean'.

(*uter est insanior horum?*), like that of verse 97, 'is he a wise man?' (*sapiensne?*), is neither posed by Horace nor by his interlocutor, Damasippus, but by Stertinius himself, following a pattern of diatribe that is common to all sermonizing, one must conclude that Aristippus' act is likewise a symptom of *insania*: it is set in opposition to the miserliness (φιλαργυρία) of the Roman Staberius,[16] along the lines of the antithetical pairs of insanity that were laid out in lines 50–1 ('one goes off to the left, the other to the right, but both stray from the path', *ille sinistrorsum, hic dextrorsum abit, unus utrique | error*) and exemplified at lines 56ff. and 64ff. The general tenet of verses 46ff. (all are mad, except the wise man) refers naturally to the Stoic *sapiens*, not to Aristippus. But at this point Stertinius abruptly concludes with: 'the example that solves one problem by means of another accomplishes nothing' (*nil agit exemplum, litem quod lite resoluit*, 103). The example does not fit because, against the best rules of dialectic, it responds to the question 'is Staberius' behaviour wise?' with another question: 'who is more insane, the one who subordinates everything to money, or the one who throws it all away?'[17] In fact Stertinius, or better, Horace, who manipulates him, is aware that the example does not fit, not so much from formal, logical reasons, but because in the tradition of diatribe, those 'conversations in the manner of Bion' (*Bionei sermones, Epist.* 2.2.60)[18] from which Horace draws, and from which both Lucilius (742M, cf. Garbarino 1973, 492) and Cicero (*Inv. rhet.* 2.176) drew on the subject of Aristippus, the anecdote was always reported as an example not of prodigality, but of Aristippus' mastery over money, of his tossing it aside when it became too heavy (*propter onus*).[19] This

---

[16] The ethnic opposition implied by the epithet *Graecus* is explained by Kiessling-Heinze with a reference to *Ars* 325.

[17] According to Kiessling-Heinze, ad loc., and already Heinze (1889: 26), the response to the last question should be to discredit the *auarus*. But from the Stoic point of view that is represented here by Staberius, if only for the sake of parody, all foolish acts are equal, all the more if they are antithetical. And into this opposition Lejay (1911: 379) saw emerge Horace's 'secret inclination' for the middle way; cf. also Plessis-Lejay (1957) ad *S.* 2.3.100.

[18] D.L. 2.77 supports a provenance for the anecdote in the diatribes of Bion; cf. Heinze (1899: 25); Lejay (1911: 374ff.). The anecdote is also recorded in the Suda.

[19] This does not authorize a change in the sense of Horace's question, as Oltramare (1926: 131) effected by surreptitiously confusing its terms: 'On peut donc se demander lequel est le plus fou de deux hommes dont l'un perd sa vie pour l'or et

corresponds to the Aristippean model of wisdom and of lifestyle that was handed down by the doxographical tradition (see below ¶7). It is this model that will be remembered, and according to which the poet of the *Epistles* will fashion himself.

4. It is not by chance that in the *Epistles* Horace's encounters with Aristippus become more frequent and more demanding.[20] His name is inscribed above the book's entryway, as it were, in the aforementioned profession of eclecticism, which we analyse here (*Epist.* 1.1.13–19):

> Ac ne forte roges quo me duce, quo Lare tuter;
> nullius addictus iurare in uerba magistri,
> quo me cumque rapit tempestas, deferor hospes.
> Nunc agilis fio et mersor ciuilibus undis,
> uirtutis uerae custos rigidusque satelles;
> nunc in Aristippi furtim praecepta relabor
> et mihi res, non me rebus subiungere conor.

And lest you ask me whose flag I fight under, and under what roof I keep myself safe: I have no master/trainer whose words I am forced to swear by. Wherever the storm blows me I wash ashore as a guest: first I become engaged in civic life, and I plunge into the waves as true virtue's guardian and stalwart protector. Then I furtively slip back, into the precepts of Aristippus, and I struggle to take charge of things, rather than have them take control of me.

Horace asserts his right to freedom of thought by means of a double emphasis in verse 14: one stylistic, in the negative hyperbaton that frames the verse (*nullius ... magistri*), and the other linguistic, in the syntactical hapax of *addictus iurare*. The word *addictus* here is not, as is asserted by some commentaries, the passive participle of *addico*, i.e. the word of the magistrate who makes over an insolvent debtor into the property of his creditor. Rather, as Obbarius (1837–47,

---

l'outre perd son or pour la vie.' In no verse does Horace talk of danger to Aristippus' life (Kiessling-Heinze speaks only of his 'leichte Unbequemlichkeit', and his situation is not terribly dissimilar from that described at Sen. *ad Helu.* 12.2). As to *in media Libya*, by some it is explained as a desert where the money tossed out helps no one (Kiessling-Heinze), by others as a land rich in precious metals (Lejay).

[20] Entirely gratuitous is the hypothesis of Ehwald (1901: 635), that in *Carm.* 2.3 Horace alludes to the kinetic pleasure of Aristippus, and thus he refers to the odes passage at *Epist.* 1.1.16ff. The *sententiae* of *Carm.* 2.3 are commonplace; cf. Nisbet-Hubbard ad loc.

ad loc.) asserted long ago, it is the passive (middle) participle of *me addico* ('I make myself a slave to'), the word of one who sells himself to the head of a gladiatorial troupe. With it, Horace continues the metaphor of the gladiatorial *ludus* introduced in line 2, punning on the double sense of *magister* ('teacher'/'troupe-master'). But *addictus* in this sense usually puts in the dative case a master (as at Petr. 117.5, *tamquam legitimi gladiatores domino corpora animosque addicimus*, 'just like genuine gladiators we are selling ourselves, body and soul, to a master') or a metaphorical owner, as at *Tusc.* 2.5 where Cicero opposes the dogmatism of those who are 'sold over to certain fixed opinions' (*certis quibusdam destinatisque sententiis addicti*) to his own Academic regard for probability: 'we ourselves... follow what is probable' (*nos... sequimur probabilia*). It is possible that Horace, a former student of the Academy (*Epist.* 2.2.45), is recalling Cicero in his first epistle.[21] And one certainly recalls a verse from his *Satires* (2.7.58) where he had referred to a gladiator with the technical term *auctoratus*, again in the passive middle voice ('hiring oneself out'),[22] and particularized by an infinitive that expresses the 'words of the sale contract' (*uerba auctoramenti*, Sen. *Ep.* 37.1), the juridical formula that attended the act of hiring oneself out: 'hired as a gladiator to be burned with rods and slaughtered by the sword' (*uri uirgis ferroque necari* | *auctoratus*). It is from here that the infinitive of our passage ('*iurare*' to swear) derives.[23] Its syntactic novelty increases the semantic pregnancy of *addictus* by keeping us aware of two meanings at once: both 'to become a slave' of someone, and 'to bind oneself' to do something. Translators choose between these two senses, but Turolla (even as he mistakes the metaphor) has carefully reckoned with the participle's double-sense: 'as a debtor become a slave, I am not constrained to swear by the words of any master.'[24]

[21] Alfonsi (1962) has added (though it was already signalled by Obbarius) a possible reference to *Tusc.* 4.7: *nos... nullis unius disciplinae legibus adstricti, quibus in philosophia necessario pareamus* ('we are bound by none of the laws of a single discipline, such as the ones that we are required to obey in philosophy'). Cf. Kilpatrick (1986: XVII), and see below §8.

[22] Cf. Pseudacr. ad loc., p. 191 Keller: *qui se uendunt ludo, auctorati uocantur* ('those who sell themselves to a [gladiatorial] school are called *auctorati*').

[23] More from this than from analogy with the passive *coactus* (Kiessling-Heinze), which may have been influenced at a paradigmatic level.

[24] Turolla (1962: 6 = 1968: 922). I substitute 'debtor' for the manifest typographical error 'creditor'.

Following this 'negative' representation of his intellectual independence, Horace provides a positive representation by way of a
different metaphor that arises in antithesis to the 'home-bound'
metaphor of verse 13: *quo lare tuter*, 'under what roof I keep myself
safe':[25] that of the sailor who does not stop in any particular place,[26]
but 'finds shelter as a guest' wherever the wind takes him.[27] The
variety of places where he puts in as guest is symbolized by an
(apparent) alternative, distributed evenly across two anaphoric dis-
tichs. The first of these is, implicitly, the Stoic alternative, characterized by two elements: participation in an engaged life, especially in
political life, and a belief in virtue as the only authentic good (*uera
uirtus*).[28] But already here there are sufficient undertones of irony to
warn us against taking him too seriously. The present verb *mersor*
('I plunge into') may include Horace's own republican past, but
certainly, spoken in 20 BCE, at the height of the Augustan regime, it
sounds more anachronistic than it does timeless. And the epithet
rigidus ('stalwart'), which Seneca will apply to the 'wisdom of the
Stoics' (*Stoicorum sapientia, ad Marc.* 12.4), and that recalls for us
Cicero's portrayal of Cato (who considered it shameful to 'change
one's thinking' [*mutare sententiam, Mur.* 62ff.] and against whose

---

[25] In support of *lar* as 'philosophical school', the commentary writers refer to the
Socratica domus of Carm. 1.29.14. But here *lar* has a connotation of protection that is
activated by *tuter*; cf. Plaut. *Merc.* 865. On the usage and sense of *tueor* and its
derivatives in Horace, cf. Traina (2005[17]: 23ff.). Marcucci (1993) offers nothing
substantially new.

[26] I do not believe that in *tempestas* there is also the sense of 'occasion', as
Castorina (1965: 96ff.) understood it, translated as such by Turolla (1962: 6 =
1968: 922), or that of Gagliardi (1988: 10): 'life's chances'. The word never has
these senses in Horace. Here the *uox media* is in the meteorological meaning of
'weather', as at *S.* 1.5.96 and at Cic. *poet. Fr.* 63Tr.; cf. Traina (1974[2]: 91ff.), and the
deft translation of Plessis-Lejay ad loc.: 'l'état du ciel'. And the verb rules it out as well:
it is *occasio rapitur*, not *rapit*; cf. *Epod.* 13.3ff., and Traina (1986[2]: 231ff.).

[27] Marchesi (1940) ad loc.; cf. also Perret (1967[2]: 150). One recalls Dido's pained
questioning of Aeneas at *Aen* 4.323: *cui me moribundam deseris, hospes?* ('to whom do
you leave me behind to die, oh guest?').

[28] Horace seems to be the first to supply an ethical sense to an alliterative *iunctura*
that had been used since the time of Ennius (*sc.* 300Vahlen[2]) in a military sense; on
which, see Le Bon (1937). But the memory of the military meaning remains in
Horace's *custos* and *satelles*, words that personify the *uirtus* of a military leader
(*dux*, cf. *quo me duce tuter* in verse 13). Seneca will activate this sense by opposing
to Epicurean *uirtus uoluptatum ministra* ('virtue that ministers to pleasures') Stoic
virtue that *ducere debet, imperare* ('must lead and issue commands', *Ben.* 4.2.1ff.).

inflexibility the orator proposed a 'certain moderation' [*quaedam mediocritas*] that comes very close to Horatian *mediocritas*), is under-cut by the definition of *uera uirtus* as a 'mid-point among vices' (*medium uitiorum*) at *Epist.* 1.18.8ff.[29] But there is no irony under-cutting the second alternative. Instead, it brings a surprise (ἀπροσδόκητον), because the pole we expect to oppose Stoic *uirtus* is the 'soft pleasure' (*mollis uoluptas*[30]) of the Epicureans. Instead we find neither Epicurus nor *uoluptas*. In fact, in the adverb *furtim* ('furtively', 'with no one noticing') of verse 18 some have wanted to see a definite allusion to λάθε βιώσας, as if to produce the sense of 'living outside of notice'.[31] But this is to force too much from the adverb that, we must not forget, governs (*re*)*labor* ('I slip back') and has an exact analogy in the furtive tears of *Carm.* 1.13.6–7: *umor et in genas | furtim labitur* ('without my noticing, tears glide across my cheeks').[32] *Furtim* denotes an action that escapes the notice of others and of the agent himself. With the first sense, Horace would have us understand that it is rather shameful to abandon the Stoic ideal for Aristippus. But, as we shall see, in the *praecepta* of Aristippus there is nothing to be ashamed of. With the second sense, supported by the *Odes* passage just cited, at play is the natural inclination of Horace, neatly interpreted by Marchesi: 'without my noticing,[33]

[29] Cf. also *Epist.* 1.6.15, and Marchesi (1940: VIII): 'On one principle Stoicism does not and cannot compromise: on the good as an absolute. There is one principle concerning which Horace never hesitates: in admitting the relativity of the good that, as such, must be contained within certain limits.' That, however, is more in keeping with the ethical system of the ancient Stoa, characterized by 'rationalism and dog-matism' [Wendland (1986: 65)] than with the later ethical system of Panaetius; cf. McGann (1969: 10ff.).

[30] A typical attribute of Epicurean philosophy; cf. the comment of Pease at Cic. *Nat. deor.* 1.113.

[31] Thus Préaux (1968) ad loc., and (1977: 396), *contra* Moles (1985: 56). Gigon (1977: 478); Dionigi (1980: 47); Grilli (1983: 268); to express the idea of λάθε βιώσας Horace uses *lateo* (*Epist.* 1.1.5), *latebrae* (*Epist.* 1.16.15), *fallo* (*Epist.* 1.17.10; 1.18.103); see below, §5. The exegesis of Stégen (1960: 10), whereby *furtim = raptim*, 'pour un temps', does not seem to have a solid linguistic basis. It is true that *furtim* may coexist with *raptim* (*TLL* s.v. 1642.68), but *raptim* ('in a rush') does not accord well with (*re*)*labor*.

[32] For this sense of *furtim*, in syntactical contrast to *arguens* ('revealing'), see Tescari (1967) ad loc.

[33] '*Nescio quomodo*' was the paraphrase of Dillenburger (1881) ad loc., translated by Sabbadini (1923²) ad loc. Kiessling-Heinze provides an apt comparison with Sen.

thus, naturally. And in fact it is his own nature that conveyed him to these precepts.'[34] One usually approaches *relabor* by way of a passage of Cicero, and one of Seneca.[35] But sufficient attention has not been paid to the play of the verbal prefixes. Seneca's Stoic interlocutor, who regards the movement from activism to *otium* as a loss of valour, emphasizes the notion of falling.[36] It will then occur to Seneca to explain to Lucilius that there is one type of *otium* that is higher than all *negotium*. In Cicero there is a movement opposite that of Horace, as a dislocation of the verbal prefix makes clear: Cicero is re-called (*re-uocat*) from Epicurus and Aristippus, back to virtue. But Horace slips back (*re-labor*) from virtue to Aristippus. If we want to express this with a single verb and the same prefix, Cicero *re-turns* to virtue and Horace to Aristippus,[37] each man according to the fundamental inclination of his own nature. And that is why I said that the alternative Horace proposes is only an apparent one.[38] The two poles are not on the same plane.[39] In reality he is presented as an

Ep. 22.16: *non animus nobis, non color constat, lacrimae nihil profuturae cadunt* ('our minds waver, complexions change, to no avail tears begin to fall'). Perhaps more opportune, for grieving as an irrepressible instinct, is *ad Helu.* 17.1.

[34] Marchesi (1940) ad loc. La Penna (1958²) oscillates between the two meanings. Stégen (1960: 10) objects: if Horace is not aware of his transition from austerity to a life of pleasure, how can he say that this alteration is the rule of conduct that he has chosen? But apart from the fact that the alteration is between Stoic dogmatism and the independence—not the hedonism—of Aristippus, Horace does not choose a rule of conduct (for which he actually goes searching), but rather he certifies his own natural incapacity to shut himself into a given philosophy.

[35] Cic. *Acad.* 2.139: *uideo quam suauiter uoluptas sensibus nostris blandiatur: labor eo ut adsentiar Epicuro aut Aristippo: reuocat uirtus* ('I see how sweetly pleasure entices our senses. I slip into agreeing with Epicurus or Aristippus, but virtue calls me back'); Sen. *ep.* 68.10: *otium commendas mihi? Ad Epicureas uoces delaberis?* ('Are you urging me to relax? Will you slip down to the sayings of Epicurus?').

[36] Cf. Cic. *Part. or.* 12: *aut a minoribus ad maiora ascendimus aut a maioribus ad minora delabimur* ('either we ascend from lesser to greater things, or we slip down from greater to lesser').

[37] Not to Epicurus, according to the thesis of Gantar (1972: 11ff.), who understands *relabor* as the return to an Epicurean past that can be dated to the aftermath of Philippi.

[38] And not in the sense of Courbaud (1914: 67) who, in his rather over-valued book, in order to defend the thesis of Horace's 'conversion' to Stoicism, interprets his declaration of eclecticism as an attempt to pacify his Epicurean friend. But cf. Mayer (1986: 63ff.); Gagliardi (1986: 66), and see above, n. 3 for the 'declaration of Epicurean faith'.

[39] Cf. Grilli (1993: 53): 'apparently Horace does not say what his preference is; only apparently, because anyone who knows the laws of ancient rhetoric knows that in a *controversia* one must put in the second position the thesis that is destined to prevail'.

Aristippean who is subject to episodic bouts of Stoic fancy. One might have already intuited this from the metaphor of the 'guest' that Horace applied to his vagabond philosophical travels. For it was Aristippus who said of himself: 'I am a guest everywhere' (ξένος πανταχοῦ εἰμι).[40]

Thus, Aristippus takes the place of the expected Epicurus. But which Aristippus? Horace tells us which one by synthesizing the *praecepta* of Aristippus' most famous saying: 'I possess, but I am not possessed' (ἔχω ἀλλὰ οὐκ ἔχομαι). But, considering how others had rendered it in Latin, he causes the saying to undergo a profound and meaningful shift.[41] The peremptory and proud assertion of the original has been toned down by being subordinated to the modal verb *conor* ('I try'), because for Horace wisdom is an ideal, and not yet something he possesses. And he knows, and wants Maecenas to know, that he has little time left to attain it.[42] Replacing the verb of possession, ἔχω ('I possess'), is a verb for domination, *subiungere* ('make subject to'). This was perhaps suggested by what Aristippus follows with in the version cited by Diogenes Laertius: ἐπεὶ τὸ κρατεῖν καὶ μὴ ἡττᾶσθαι ἡδονῶν ἄριστον, 'since the best of pleasures is being in charge and not being worsted/subjected', D.L. 2.75). The dry verbal antithesis of the Greek arrangement—active versus passive—in Horace shifts to a chiasmus of nouns, dative and accusative: *mihi res (non) me rebus*. But especially important is the substitution of the object: in numerous Greek and Latin sources[43] the object is, explicitly or implicitly, Lais, the prostitute, and therefore the pleasure (ἡδονή) with which Aristippus himself, in the passage just cited from Diogenes Laertius, glosses his epigrammatic saying. In Horace it is neither a woman nor pleasure that he claims to have renounced in his opening letter (*cetera ludicra pono*, 'I set aside other trifles', v. 10) and again in the near-contemporary letter to Florus (*anni | eripuere iocos, uenerem, conuiuia, ludum*, 'time has stolen away my fun, sex,

[40] Xen. *Mem.* 2.1.13 (IV A 163 Giannantoni 1983–5). Only a few have caught the cryptic citation: Marchesi (1940: 176), Préaux (1977: 397), Nickel (1980: 146), for whom Horace's Aristippus would derive primarily from Xenophon.

[41] Cic. *Fam.* 9.26.2: *habeo, non habeor a Laide* ('I possess, and am not possessed by, Lais'). Other texts are in Giannantoni 1983–5, IV A 95.

[42] For the *Epistles* one might speak in terms of his seizing the opportunity for wisdom, a *carpe diem* of *sapientia*; cf. *Epist.* 1.2.33–43; 1.3.28.

[43] IV A 95–6 Giannantoni 1983–5.

parties, and play', *Epist.* 2.2.55–6; *lusisti satis, edisti satis atque bibisti,* 'you've had your fill of play, of food and drink', *Epist.* 2.2.214, see below §8). Rather it is the bare, generic *res,* his 'circumstances'. To say with Gigon[44] that Horace has avoided as 'intolerably banal' the contrast between *uirtus* and *uoluptas,* and that for this reason he alludes to it indirectly by way of Aristippus' dictum about Lais, signifies a misunderstanding of the sense of Horace's re-elaboration: as spiritual advice the saying substitutes for the philosopher of active pleasure the philosopher of mastery over one's own life. And therefore the antithesis between virtue and pleasure, which is initially caught sight of, in actuality turns out to be a contrast between the rigidity of Stoic ethics, tightly focused on *uirtus,* and the flexibility of Aristippus, who adapts himself to, but is not subordinated to, *res.* This is a flexibility that a more rigid branch of Epicurean dogmatism, the dogmatism of *ipse dixit,* could not provide to Horace.[45]

5. Were we to have any doubts about this interpretation of the figure of Aristippus in Horace, the poet has thought to remove them for us in the second and more ample citation that concerns him at *Epist.* 1.17.13–32. In connection with the letter's theme, how best to conduct oneself with powerful men (*quo tandem pacto deceat maioribus uti,* 2), Horace introduces a second anecdote from the doxographical tradition, the dialogue between Aristippus and Diogenes. In it, two choices of life are contrasted, just as in the antithesis just analysed, this time with a Cynic standing in for the Stoic. But this antithesis stems from yet another alternative putting into play another choice of life, since dealing with powerful men is not inevitable for one who is content to live in the shadows: *neque diuitibus contingunt gaudia solis,* | *nec uixit male, qui natus moriensque fefellit* ('neither do the pleasures of wealth affect him, nor has he lived badly, whose birth and death have gone un-noticed', vv. 9–10). Certainly at stake here, exposed also at the level of syntactic modelling, is the Epicurean λάθε βιώσας.[46] One

---

[44] Gigon (1977: 478).

[45] Gantar (1972: 10); Grilli (1983: 268) and (1987: 18); Grimal (1958: 54), who cleverly notes how posing the problem of knowing what the good is, and what is true, 'is already to be unfaithful to Epicureanism, since it is to be unsure'. *Contra,* faintly, is Beck (1919); Abel (1969: 42f.).

[46] See Porphyr. ad loc.; cf. Degl'Innocenti Pierini (1992: 151ff.).

may agree with La Penna that 'the Epicurean ideal that Horace delineates here is certainly the option that he himself preferred'.[47] But it is not the one that he pursued. The 'sweet hiding-places' (*latebrae dulces*) of *Epist.* 1.16.15 conflict with the *officia* ('duties') of an *amicus* of the powerful (see below §8). In addressing Scaeva (just as when he addresses Lollius at *Epist.* 1.18.86ff.), Horace must have been thinking of himself.[48] Proving the point, though it requires little proving, is the clear connection of verse 35, *principibus placuisse uiris non ultima laus est* ('that one has gratified leading men is not the highest commendation') to the autobiographical statement of *Epist.* 1.20.23: *me primis urbis belli placuisse domique* ('I gratified leading men both at home and on the field of battle'). Therefore, even on this point Horace departs from the Epicurean path, leaving it for the path of Aristippus. Diogenes had said to Aristippus: *si pranderet holus patienter, regibus uti | nollet Aristippus* ('if Aristippus could put up with cabbage for lunch, he would not want to associate with kings', 13–14).[49] To which the Cyrenaic philosopher responded: *si sciret regibus uti, | fastidiret holus, qui me notat* ('if he knew how to associate with kings, the one who scolds me would despise cabbage', 14–15). Which of the two is right? Horace himself is quick to take sides in line 17 with *Aristippi sententia potior* ('Aristippus' opinion is more compelling'), and to justify that response (*namque*) in the next fifteen lines, summarized as follows: Aristippus goes on to say that if he *scurratur* 'plays the *scurra*',[50] he does so for himself (*mihi*, 'for myself'; cf. Horace's *sibi uiuere*, 'living for oneself', see below §8) and not, as Diogenes did, for the sake of

---

[47] La Penna (1985: 295).

[48] Lana (1989: 164) is right to insist on this.

[49] The word *regibus*, corresponding to τύραννοι of D.L. 2.68, evokes also the honorific title *patronus*; cf. *Epist.* 1.7.37, referring to Maecenas! *rexque paterque audisti coram* 'in your presence, you have heard me call you king and father.' See Gold (1987: 129); Nadjo (1989: 446).

[50] The *scurra* is a character-type that combines elements of the joker, the flatterer, and the parasite; cf. Lejay (1911: 551–3) and now Mazzoli (1987: 73–92), and La Penna (1993: 371–4). Malevolent eyes might regard as a *scurra* the *amicus* of powerful men; see Oltramare (1926: 148), and cf. *Epist.* 1.18.1–2: *metues, liberrime Lolli, | scurrantis speciem praebere professus amicum*, 'having claimed to be a friend, most candid Lollius, you will fear giving the appearance of a *scurra*'. It is thus for good reason that the verb is varied, and softened, two verses later: *officium facio*, 'I do my duty', which is to say the 'duty' of the *amicus* and the *cliens*; cf. Hellegouarc'h (1963: 159ff.).

public display (*populo*, for the common 'rabble', whom Horace never loved). Horace continues with a substantive characterization of Aristippus, *omnis Aristippum decuit color et status et res* ('any colour, position and circumstance suited Aristippus', lines 23ff.), that matches the description of D.L. 2.66: ἦν δὲ ἱκανὸς ἁρμόσασθαι καὶ τόπῳ καὶ χρόνῳ καὶ προσώπῳ ('and he had the ability to adapt himself to the place, the time, and the person').[51] The economic consequence of this adaptability is described in the next verse: *temptantem maiora, fere praesentibus aequum*; that is, he aspired for a better life when he could, but usually (*fere*) was content with the present (Porphyrio annotates *praesentibus* with τοῖς παροῦσιν), in other words, with what he had.[52] But this is the voice of Horace's own wisdom: he knows equally how to involve himself with powerful men (*S.* 2.1.76; 2.6.52) and how to make a meal of cabbage and beans (*S.* 2.6.64; *Carm.* 1.31.16ff.; *Epist.* 1.5.2). He is content with little; that is, with *paruum* (*S.* 2.2.1; *Carm.* 2.16.13; 4.9.45; *Epist.* 1.10.41) but not with *parum* ('not enough', the *importuna pauperies* of *Carm.* 2.10.7, the ode of *aurea mediocritas*), and with the *satis* ('enough') of so many verses, and the *quod nunc est* of *Epist.* 1.18.107. Thus we are familiar with Horace's wise pronouncements about *modus* ('limit'), but Aristippus too had said that one needed to accustom oneself to 'living on little' (ἀπὸ ὀλίγων ζῆν, IV A 76 Giannantoni 1983–5), and that 'the measure of riches ought to be sought in such a way that it is no more or less than what one needs in the present' (A 53 Giannantoni 1958 = IV A 78 G. 1983–5).[53]

The contrast between the flexibility of the Cyrenaic, Aristippus, and the rigidity of the Cynic, Diogenes, is captured in the symbol (and this too stems from the doxographical tradition[54]) of clothing (lines 26–32): no matter what mantle Aristippus dresses in, whether it is luxurious or stitched together from rags, he will always be himself. But Diogenes will always be constrained to dress in tatters,

[51] IV A 51 Giannantoni 1983–5. Porphyrio, ad loc., recalls Plato's assessment: ὦ 'Αρίστιππε, πάντα σοι πρέπει ('Oh, Aristippus, everything suits you').

[52] I prefer *fere*, along with the majority of editors, to what follows as more consonant with the image of Diogenes Laertius; cf. Préaux (1968) ad loc.; *contra*, for example, see D'Arbela (1934) ad loc.

[53] According to D.L. 2.72, he taught his daughter to despise excess (τοῦ πλέονος).

[54] Cf. IV A 34, 45, 56 Giannantoni 1983–5.

and to die from the cold. The Cyrenaic is an actor on the world's scene who knows how to recite any part (*personamque feret non inconcinnus utramque*, 'he will take up either part as nicely suited to him', *Epist.* 1.17.29) because he is synonymous with none of them. The Cynic, however, will always be the prisoner of his own mask. Horace was able to 'show the way' to Scaeva (*iter monstrare*, line 4), along the path trod by Aristippus, because this is the path that he himself had followed. At the end of his epistle to Florus he will offer an image of himself that, for one last time, reflects the image of Aristippus: *ego utrum | naue ferar magna an parua, ferar unus et idem* ('whether it's a big ship that carries me or a small one, the one inside it is always I, one and the same', *Epist.* 2.2.199–200).

6. That completes the inventory of Horace's citations of Aristippus. To be added to the list is one tacit encounter that Kiessling mentioned, subsequently taken up by Heinze:[55] the contrast between the one who feels ill and goes to the doctor, and the one who fails to recognize his spiritual malady and does not go to the philosopher. This was used twice by Horace in his *Epistles* (1.2.38 and 2.2.146), and has an exact counterpart in a saying of Aristippus, cited by Plutarch (*de cup. diu.* 3, IV A 73 Giannantoni 1983–5). The repeated allusion, if it is that, confirms the presence of Aristippus within the compass of the *Epistles*. And this, in fact, causes me to be suspicious about the Homeric Ulysses of *Epist.* 1.2.17–22, posited as an exemplar of *uirtus* and *sapientia*. Much current opinion makes him a Stoic.[56] Moles has introduced the idea of a Cynic Ulysses, and Gigante has recast him as an Epicurean, on the basis of texts of Philodemus that are not all terribly pertinent.[57] But what of his being an Aristippean?[58] We have some indication (IV A 55 Giannantoni 1983–5) that Aristippus took Ulysses as a model of life. This is worth crediting if we consider that the archetypal quality of Ulysses is, in keeping with the formulation of Scholes and Kellogg, that of his being 'always the master of the situation, no matter what the

---

[55] Kiessling (1889) ad loc.; Heinze (1889: 26ff.); and, naturally, Kiessling-Heinze ad loc.; discussion in Brink (1982: 362ff.).

[56] To mention certain names, aside from the commentators: Stanford (1963: 122ff.); Ronconi (1973: 67ff.); Grimal (1976: 40).

[57] Moles (1985: 35); Gigante (1990: 100ff.).

[58] Cf. Marchesi (1940: 191), and especially Gigon (1983: 72 and 240).

circumstance he appears in'.[59] It is, then, with the star that always stays above the waves, *rerum immersabilis undis* ('unsinkable in the waves of circumstance', *Epist.* 1.2.22), that Horace describes the hero, using a lexical *hapax* (*immersabilis*) that has no parallel in the formal epithets of Homer (in contrast to his nearly faithful translation of the first verses of the *Odyssey*).[60]

7. We can now ask to what extent Horace's Aristippus corresponds to the historical Aristippus, or at least to the Aristippus of tradition. The answer is made easier by the fact that, just as Horace once did, we ourselves draw on doxographical sources[61] that present Aristippus not so much as a systematic thinker—we are not even certain that he founded the Cyrenaic school—but as a master of wisdom, a 'virtuoso of the art of living'.[62] Like Epicurus, he is a master who presents himself in two aspects:[63] on the one hand he is an apologist for corporeal pleasures, and of the 'dolce vita' (φιλήδονος); and on the other, he advocates for a reasoned control (ἐγκράτεια) over pleasures and circumstances. It is precisely this second aspect that modern scholars privilege,[64] underscoring the need for 'inner freedom', the ἐλευθερία, that the Aristippus presented by Xenophon (*Mem.* 2.1.11, IV A 163 Giannantoni 1983–5) claims as a middle way between commanding and obeying. But the background of this idea lies squarely with Socrates.[65] This becomes relevant as soon as one

[59] Scholes and Kellogg (1970: 206).

[60] Ronconi (1973: 66). *Immersabilis* is a certain *hapax*. All the other Horatian epithets for Ulysses have counterparts in Homer: *duplex*, cf. Monteleone (1992: 85ff.); also *laboriosus, inclutus, patiens*; for the last of these see Massaro (1978), *contra* Horsfall (1993a: 60ff.).

[61] Gigon (1977: 451). The sources are predominantly of an anecdotal and apothegmatic type; see Giannantoni (1958: 75).

[62] Natorp (1895: 904); Gomperz (1950³: 666); Classen (1958: 191).

[63] This double-sidedness is reflected in Cicero: compare *Off.* 1.147 against *Fin.* 2.18–20 and *Tusc.* 2.15.

[64] Pohlenz (1973: 96–8): 'phronesis . . . is presupposed as necessary for a just conduct of life that aims to procure for a man a maximum measure of pleasure. By conferring upon him a superiority over the ephemeral stimulus of pleasure, it also guarantees him external independence and internal liberty.' Giannantoni (1985: 23); Lieberg (1958: 11); Humbert (1967: 250–72); Döring (1988: 62).

[65] In so far as, according to Pohlenz (1967: 11), Aristippus interpreted his teacher's call for an individual moral conscience in the sense that he needed to make them entirely self-reliant. On the Socratic aspects of Aristippus, see also Giannantoni (1958: 164), and Gigon (1983: 268).

remembers how often mention is made of Horace's 'Socratic' aspects,[66] in his continuous recourse to irony and self-doubt, two attitudes that were hardly congenial to the Stoics and Epicureans. To me it now seems clear that Horace subscribes to a Socrates who inclines more towards the flexibility of Aristippus than to the extremism of Antisthenes. But I would like to add one important fact: in the ancient sources, this spirit of independence is frequently realized by the philosopher's rapport with powerful men, in Aristippus' specific case, with Dionysius of Syracuse.[67] That which holds true for pleasures and circumstances, using them without becoming enslaved to them, holds true for one's momentary masters as well: even at court, Aristippus will always be his own master. For Aristippus, this was not an abstract saying, a mere piece of verbal wisdom. It was something he experienced in life. It was no accident that he had such influence on the poet of the *Epistles*.

8. Just as for Aristippus, so for Horace,[68] long recognized as fundamentals of the man's character have been his independence of spirit, and his need for freedom, perhaps instilled in him, as Heinze thought, by his freedman father.[69] We can see this, at a literary level, in the way he asserts his originality in approaching his Greek and Latin models at *Epist.* 1.19 (in the *libera uestigia* 'free tracks' of verse 21). We encountered it as a declaration of eclecticism in regard to the teachings of specific philosophical schools,[70] an eclecticism that was certainly confirmed by his training (*institutio*) at the Academy, and that Cicero (*Acad.* 2.120) defined in terms of *libertas*.[71] And we encountered it as an aspiration towards self-sufficiency, or αὐτάρκεια, the liberty of one who desires no more than what he has, and who is content with little.[72] But Horace subscribes to a

[66] In particular, Gantar (1972: 23ff.), who quotes Anderson's reference to Horace as 'the Roman Socrates'; Grimal (1976) and (1978: 8); Mayer (1986: 72); but already in the eighteenth century, Algarotti (1990 [1791]: 60).

[67] Pohlenz (1963: 98); Humbert (1967: 256ff.).

[68] Sellar (1924: 41); Bréguet (1954) is both detailed and elusive. Also now Pucci (1988).

[69] Heinze (1960³: 130).

[70] Maguinness (1976).

[71] It took an uncurable autoschediast like Paratore (1960⁵: 241) to define this as an 'incurable spirit of cultural snobbism'.

[72] For an in-depth analysis of Horatian αὐτάρκεια and its contradictions, see La Penna (1969: 140ff.) and (1980: 71–5), and more succinctly (1990: 10).

'little' that can be accounted 'enough' (see above §5). And it is here
that his moral and economic αὐτάρκεια came into conflict. The *otia
liberrima* ('leisurely diversions, utterly free') that Horace, writing to
Maecenas at *Epist.* 1.7.36, would not have exchanged for the riches of
Arabia, came at a price. And the person to whom he needed to pay
that price was Maecenas. While the poet's relationship to his powerful friend and protector was a problem that dogged Horace for his
entire career, the problem perhaps reached its furthest point, very
close to the breaking-point, in the period of the *Epistles*.[73] In composing his first book of letters, then, Horace wrote his own *De
beneficiis.*

Here we need to make a brief stop to clear the terrain of a question
that has received a great deal of scholarly debate, concerning the
autobiographical basis of the *Epistles*.[74] The question, when it is
figured as an antithesis between the factual 'I' and the poetic 'I', is
insoluble, especially in the case of ancient writers. But between these

---

[73] On the relationship between Horace and Maecenas, an informed and balanced
overview is that of Lefèvre (1981). Some new insights are in Petronio (1991). Among
earlier works of note are Meister (1950), treating the difference between *clientela* and
conuictio, and Reckford (1959); less incisive are Noirfalise (1950) and (1952), and
Desch (1981), whose version of such relationships is a bit romantic. Outside the
mainstream are Eckert (1961), who emphasizes the 'religious' basis of their friendship; going too far in the opposite direction is Van Ooteghem (1946), who errs also in
presupposing an antithesis between the Stoicism of the *Epistles* and the Epicureanism
of Maecenas; and Gigon (1977: 471), who asserts an affinity between the lifestyles and
literary tastes of the two friends (but one thinks of Maecenas' desire for luxury, and
his lingering neotericism). Special attention has centred on *Epist.* 1.7, where the
relationship problem is interwoven with that of the autobiographical or fictional
character of the letter (see next n.): specifically Gunning (1942), Hiltbrunner (1960),
Büchner (1962), Drexler (1966), who writes in the shadow of Heinze (1960). And
recently Horsfall (1993a).

[74] The two opposed theses, one that sees in the events of the *Epistles* only the
excuse for moral lessons, and the other, more widespread, that sees in them a
reflection of lived experience, are partial and therefore not irreconcilable; cf. recently
Gagliardi (1988: 12) whose bibliography is to be supplemented, at least, by Becker
(1963) and Maurach (1968), and now Pizzolato (1989: 160) and (1993: 143).
Certainly Horace is presented as a teacher of life to his young friends (*Epist.* 1.17.3:
disce...; a study of performativity in the *Epistles* would be interesting), but on the
basis of his own experience (*Epist.* 1.18.87: *expertus*). This marriage between intro-
spection and advocacy, which will next be evident in Seneca, cf. Traina (1987[4]: 130),
was neatly grasped by Heinze (1960: 305). One must not undervalue the conditioning
effects of addressees, who neither allow Horace to invent, nor do they allow him to
say, everything.

poles there is a median position in the narrating 'I'. When we identify these other 'I's' with the narrated 'I', we both can and must end up not with the man himself, and his actual activities, but with the image of them that the narrator has given us to consider. Such is the 'reality' that the poetry provides. What relationships and feelings may have held between Horace and Maecenas, in their various phases, we will never know, even for our near total lack of historical documentation. But we do know that Horace has 'constructed' in all of his works a history of these relationships, presenting himself as a *conuictor* and *amicus* ('companion' and 'friend') of a protector, to whom he owed his economic independence (the only means available to Horace given his situation and the societal conditions of his time),[75] and therefore the very possibility of devoting himself to poetry. But there was a payment to be made, an obligation of gratitude,[76] not just in one's feelings. This extended to the point where the burden of gratitude did not threaten the actual benefits of independence, and of *se ipsum seruare* ('self-preservation', *Epist.* 1.2.33) and of *sibi uiuere* ('living for oneself'), as Horace says in his letter to Lollius, as he sets out to plan the rest of his life (*mihi uiuam | quod superest aeui, Epist.* 1.18.107–8).[77]

When he writes the first book of the *Epistles* (and perhaps this will also apply to the epistle to Florus, which shares with the first book many of the same 'autobiographical' elements, in the sense described above),[78] Horace has crossed into his forties (*Epist.* 1.20.26–8). He feels old, sensing especially that his inspiration as a lyric poet has been spent. As would have happened to Virgil, had he lived longer, Horace will fill the break from writing poetry (the grand creative act that dispels death) by pursuing philosophy, which is not only the art of living well, but also—as the Horatian Seneca[79] will tell us many times—that of preparing for death, and of dispelling the fear it

---

[75] Recently treated in Gold (1987).

[76] On the especially cautious verbal manifestation of such gratitude, see Hewitt (1940–1).

[77] On the motif of *sibi uiuere*, see Dupouy (1928: 165ff.), and especially Drexler (1966: 140ff.).

[78] Cf. Pasoli (1965), with whom I am not altogether in agreement; for example, concerning Horace's passing from *ludus* to *sermo*. But this needs another discourse.

[79] Grimal (1978: 7): 'Horace annonce Sénèque, et le prefigure.'

inspires (*formido, Epist.* 2.2.207–10). The entire first book of the *Epistles* is, in this sense, a protreptic,[80] and a choice of life: the first epistle is the inverse image of the proem of the *Odes*,[81] just as the leave-taking of *Epist.* 1.20 allusively contrasts the farewell of *C.* 3.30. But Maecenas called the poet back to erotic lyric—the *ludus* ('play') that is both lyric song and its object, *amor*[82]—just as, at another time, he had called him back to iambic poetry (*Epod.* 14), placing it as an obstacle (*Epist.* 1.1.23–5) between Horace and *sapientia*. In this sense, the entire first book, and not just the first epistle, is also a *recusatio*, both direct and indirect, the longest and most difficult that the poet would address to Maecenas. The invitation of the poet's powerful friend to return to the poetry of the past is, in the seventh epistle,[83] encapsulated inside an invitation to return to the unhealthy

[80] Bignone (1937), naturally, recognized in it echoes of Aristotelian protreptic. See also La Penna (1956: 192–5), and next n.

[81] Inasmuch as the βίος θεορητικός of the lyric poet is replaced by that of the philosopher; cf. Ghiselli (1983²: 37–49); also La Penna (1963) and Setaioli (1973). Unnoted, it seems, is the fact that the connection between the two works is allusively underscored by the elaborate stylization of the opening apostrophes to Maecenas: *Maecenas, atauis edite regibus,* | *o et praesidium et dulce decus meum* ('Maecenas, born of ancient kings, and, oh, my protector and sweet pride', *Carm.* 1.1.1–2), versus *Prima dicte mihi, summa dicende Camena* | ... *Maecenas* ('Maecenas, sung by my first Muse, again to be sung by my last', *Epist.* 1.1.1–3). Such stylizing is certainly more understandable in lyric than in the prosaic register of *sermo* (cf. *Carm.* 2.17.3 and 3.29.3 versus S. 1.1.1; 1.3.64; 1.6.1; 1.6.47; 2.1.16; *Epist.* 1.7.15; 1.19.1), as Dilke (1966³: 27) has observed.

[82] Cf. the combination of poetry and amore at *Epist.* 1.1.10: *uersus et cetera ludicra pono* ('I set aside verses and other trifles'); also 2.2.55–7: *anni* ... *eripuere iocos, uenerem, conuiuia, ludum;* | *tendunt extorquere poemata* ('the years have stolen away games, sex, parties and play; they are trying to wrench away poetry'), and 1.14.36: *nec lusisse pudet, sed non incidere ludum* ('the disgrace is not in having played, but in not putting an end to play'). Horace's rejection is not so much of lyric in general, but of erotic lyric; the point is well made by Gigon (1977: 477), and see already Cima in Pascoli (1895: LXXXI), though the hypothesis of Pascoli himself is quite sophisticated. And I would consider reasonable McGann (1969: 97ff.), who senses here a polemic against the generic flavour of the day, elegy; cf. Otis (1945). For Virgil, cf. Conte (1992: 162ff.). By keeping quiet about civic lyric poetry, which is not *ludere* but *canere*, and which had been a substantial part of his aeolic lyric programme, Horace leaves the door open for a possible future of the *uates*. However I cannot agree with Pizzolato (1989: 179) and (1993:145), who folds into *ludus* civic poetry as well.

[83] An arrangement important to the architecture of Book 1 (apart from the proem and the book's last poem) must be read in the hexads that culminate in Maecenas (2–7, 14–19) and Augustus (8–13): thus I modify the proposal of Préaux (1968: 6ff.); another proposal and bibliography in Dilke (1981: 1837–42).

environs of Rome: the book's first invitation focuses on Horace's psychological well-being (*Epist.* 1.1.94), the second on his physical health (*Epist.* 1.7.3ff.). A return, both temporal and spatial, would be possible only with the return of youth (*Epist.* 1.7.25–8) and its attributes: sound health, desire, poetry. If Maecenas cannot restore (*reddas*, 25) these to Horace, Horace can serenely (*laetus*) return to Maecenas the gift that he gave him (*donata reponere*, 1.7.39). The moral problem of αὐτάρκεια is thus realized in the very real problem of 'cultivating an influential friend' (*cultura potentis amici*): the 'art of living',[84] for a *conuictor* ('companion', lit. one who 'lives with') of Maecenas, becomes the art of 'living with': that is, with the powerful,[85] but also with friends (*Epist.* 1.8.9 and 17; 11.9; 20.25), and with oneself (cf. the *secum pugnare*, 'do battle with oneself', of *Epist.* 1.1.27). If in his *Epistles* Horace stresses the symptoms of his neurosis (cf. *Epist.* 1.1.97–100; 8.7–12; 11.28),[86] he does so also to emphasize his urgent need for psychic healing, for the *fomenta* ('poultices') of *caelestis sapientia* ('heavenly wisdom', *Epist.* 1.3.26ff.). Such are the reasons behind his poetic *recusatio*. Within this frame one understands how the Horace of the *Epistles* rediscovered in Aristippus a wisdom that was rooted in a lived experience, and that was missing from Socrates, from the Stoic masters, and from Epicurus. Already in 1934 Max Pohlenz beautifully intuited and condensed the idea in a footnote: 'Horace felt a kinship with Aristippus in the internal freedom that he maintained in his encounters with his powerful protector.'[87]

---

[84] The happy formulation has given titles to at least two works: Grimal (1964) and Gagliardi (1988).

[85] Maecenas, but also with Augustus, whose personal relations with the poet in this period are well attested by the biography of Suetonius.

[86] Traina (1986²: 249ff.) and (2005¹⁷: 6ff.); Canali (1988: 18ff.); La Penna (1993: 282); Lana (1993: 96): *contra* Lembo (1989: 133–5), who returns to the traditional image of a harmoniously balanced Horace. While living within limits might be the basis of his 'programme of serenity', to propose a programme is not the same as to realize it; cf. Traina (1993).

[87] Pohlenz (1970: 131).

13

Poetry, Philosophy, Politics, and Play: *Epistles* 1

John Moles

Scholars disagree over the philosophical and political aspects of *Epistles* 1. While earlier generations (represented by Heinze, Courbaud and Fraenkel) talked freely of 'philosophical conversion' and Macleod, Kilpatrick, Ferri and Harrison still see the book as philosophical, Williams, Mayer and Rudd deny it even formal philosophical status, although both Rudd and Mayer project Horace as a moralist.[1] Similarly, where Williams and Mayer see unequivocal praise of Augustus and Maecenas, Seager, Lyne and Oliensis detect disengagement, even disaffection.[2] These questions entail general questions about Roman poetry: the relationships between literature and life, between *persona* and person, between literature and politics and between poet, patron and addressee.

This chapter[3] argues that the *Epistles* are both formally and profoundly philosophical; that the philosophical and political interrelate;

I thank: helpful seminarians at LILS (16/2/1996) and NECROS (23/11/1998); David West for oral sparrings; and Francis Cairns and the editors for criticism of written versions.

[1] Kiessling-Heinze (1970: 370); Courbaud (1914: 36); Fraenkel (1957: 308); Macleod (1979a); Kilpatrick (1986); Ferri (1993); Williams (1968: 1–6); Mayer (1986), endorsed by Galinsky (1996: 253, 419); Mayer (1994, esp. 39–47); Rudd (1993b).

[2] Williams (1968: 14, 19–22); Mayer (1994: 143, 174, 205); Seager (1993: 34–5); Lyne (1995: 144–57); Oliensis (1998a: 154–65, 168–81).

[3] Inchoate earlier treatments on which I draw: Moles (1985); (1995).

and that the poems express some tensions, ambiguities and reservations in Horace's attitudes both to public life and to Maecenas and Augustus, tensions which inform a wide-ranging and radical debate about the pros and cons of engagement in, or withdrawal from, that public life.

PHILOSOPHICAL POETRY

Epistles 1.1.1–19 (English trans. KF):

> Prima dicte mihi, summa dicende Camena,
> spectatum satis et donatum iam rude quaeris,
> Maecenas, iterum antiquo me includere ludo?
> non eadem est aetas, non mens. Veianius armis
> Herculis ad postem fixis latet abditus agro,
> ne populum extrema totiens exoret harena.
> est mihi purgatam crebro qui personet aurem:
> 'solue senescentem mature sanus equum, ne
> peccet ad extremum ridendus et ilia ducat.'
> nunc itaque et uersus et cetera ludicra pono:
> quid uerum atque decens, curo et rogo et omnis in hoc sum:
> condo et compono quae mox depromere possim.
> ac ne forte roges, quo me duce, quo lare tuter:
> nullius addictus iurare in uerba magistri,
> quo me cumque rapit tempestas, deferor hospes.
> nunc agilis fio et mersor ciuilibus undis
> uirtutis uerae custos rigidusque satelles,
> nunc in Aristippi furtim pracepta relabor
> et mihi res, non me rebus, subiungere conor.

My first Muse spoke of you, Maecenas, and so, too, will my last. Now that I have had my fill of entertaining, and have just now been awarded the retired fighter's sword, you seek to shut me again inside my old school. My age isn't what it was, nor is my mind. Veianius nailed his arms to the doorpost of Hercules' temple, and he hides tucked away on his farm, so that he won't have to beg the crowd, again and again, to release him. Someone's voice keeps ringing in my ear, though I've rinsed it many times: 'be reasonable and release that ageing horse while the time is right, lest he should stumble to the finish, a laughingstock, panting for breath.' And that is why I am now setting aside verses and other playthings. My concern is with what is true and fitting; that's what I ask, and it is what I am all about. I am storing up and arranging things that I may at some point fetch from storage. And lest you should ask me whose flag I am fighting under, and under what roof I keep myself safe: I have no master/trainer whose words I am forced to swear by. Wherever the storm blows me I wash ashore as a guest: first I become engaged in civic life, and I plunge into the waves as true virtue's guardian and stalwart protector. Then, without noticing, I slip back, into the precepts of Aristippus, and I struggle to take charge of things, rather than to have them take control of me.

When Maecenas requests more of the same (3), Horace likens his previous poetical activity to a gladiatorial *ludus*: that was his old school, he has retired and put all that aside (10 *ludicra* ∼ 3 *antiquo . . . ludo*). His new activity (11),[4] necessarily also a *ludus*, seems to be philosophy, an activity appropriate for those of mature age (4). *rogo* evokes philosophical 'enquiry' (what more philosophical question than 'What is truth?'). *decens* has a triple philosophical aspect: firstly, 'the neuter sing. of adjectives . . . is turned into a noun to provide philosophical technical terms';[5] secondly, *qua* participle, *decens* is an even closer calque upon the Greek *prepon* ('fitting') than the customary *decorum*; thirdly, as we shall see, at least retrospectively, *decens* glosses the specifically Panaetian understanding of *prepon*. And *omnis in hoc sum* suggests the absoluteness of philosophical conversion.

Since the metaphorical gladiatorial *ludus* subdivides into individual *ludi* (14), the same applies to philosophy. Thus far *ludus* and cognates have four applications: (a) the *ludus* of gladiatorial combat; (b) the rejected *ludus/ludicra* of Horace's previous poetry; (c) the *ludus* of philosophy; (d) individual philosophical *ludi*. To these we may add a paradoxical (e). Inasmuch as Horace's philosophical *ludus* is still expressed in poetry, some association between *ludus* and poetry remains (I shall return to this). Horace's polysemous exploration of 'play' will be a key element in the structure, imagery and argument of 1.1 and of the whole book.

---

[4] Freudenburg (1993: 29) reverses the argument, as do those who see 16–17 and 18–19 as glossing Horace's Stoic and Epicurean odes.
[5] Mayer (1994: 90).

The treatment of individual philosophies acquires definition in 13–19. The philosopher Aristippus is explicitly named in 18. His polar opposite (16–17) is also a philosopher: the orthodox Stoic, 'active' in political life (*agilis* ∼ *praktikos*), emblematic of virtue in a strong sense (*uirtutis uerae* ∼ 11 *uerum*), and imaged in terms of warfare (*custos*) and 'hardness' (*rigidus*).[6] A good reason for (sometimes) attaching philosophical labels to poetry is that they are one of Horace's own thematic categories, whether explicit (18–19) or implicit (16–17).[7]

Numerous allusions underpin the philosophical texture. Line 5 *latet abditus* glosses the Epicurean tag 'live unnoticed' (λάθε βιώσας). Line 7 evokes Socrates' *daimonion* ('guiding spirit'), appropriately 'deterring' Horace from poetry. Maecenas' anticipated question in 13 assumes Horace's adhesion to some philosophical master. The sectarian religious imagery of 13 *quo lare tuter* suggests philosophical exclusiveness. Line 14 echoes the Academic non-commitment of Cicero, *Tusculans* 4.7: 'let each man defend what he thinks, for judgments befit free men, and we will hold to a standard, though bound to the laws of no single school' (*sed defendat quod quisque sentit: sunt enim iudicia libera, nos institutum tenebimus nullisque unius legibus disciplinae adstricti*), and contrasts with the Epicureans' oath to their master's doctrines. Line 15 echoes *Academica* 2.8: '(they cling) to whatever school they have been swept to, as if by a tempest' (*ad quamcumque sunt disciplinam quasi tempestate delati*). Line 15 *hospes* glosses Aristippus' claim to be a *xenos* ('guest') everywhere (Xen. *Mem.* 2.2.13). Line 17 *custos* and *satelles* image virtue as a king, glossing Stoic 'kingship'. Line 18 adapts *Academica* 2.139: 'I see how sweetly pleasure entices our senses. I am slipping into agreeing with Epicurus and Aristippus' (*uideo quam suauiter uoluptas sensibus nostris blandiatur: labor eo ut adsentiar Epicuro aut Aristippo*); 18 *furtim*, echoing 5, nicely characterises Epicureanism. Line 19 glosses, via the yoking metaphor, Aristippus' boast 'I have, but I am not had' (Diog. Laert. 2.75).[8] The combination of that yoking metaphor, of

---

[6] Mayer (1994: 92) and cf. (e.g.) the sparkling exploration of this complex of ideas in Sen. *Ep.* 33.

[7] Not discussed by the sceptical Rudd (1993b: 67–71).

[8] Excepting the interpretation of 5 (confirmed by 16.15 *latebrae dulces*: pp. 325–6 below), this material is garnered from Préaux (1968), K-H (1970) and Mayer (1994).

the horse metaphor for Horace's rejected earlier poetry (8–9) and of
the name 'Aristippus' (= 'best at horses' or 'best horse') recalls the
contrasting horses of *Phaedrus* 246bff. And beneath the polarity
of 16–19 lies Hercules' choice between Virtue and Vice/Pleasure
and their corresponding roads, a choice put to Aristippus (*Mem.*
2.1.21–34) and alluded to in *Academica* 2.139. Although the primary
contrast in 17–19 is between an unchanging conception of virtue and
a flexible ideal, virtue-vice, hard-soft and virile-effeminate contrasts
are also latent. Given this Aristippean colouring, 3 *includere* must be
read (retrospectively) as including a (prospective) gloss on Aristippus' refusal to 'shut himself into' (*Mem.* 2.1.13) any *politeia*.

Horace's deployment of his immense philosophical erudition[9]
accommodates different levels of readership: philosophically erudite
readers can enjoy the depth and ingenuity of allusion, but the main
philosophical divisions are spelled out, and all readers can understand both the need for some form of philosophy and the difficulties
of putting it into practice.

The conclusion that the *Epistles'* subject matter is philosophy
might be supported by certain (admittedly controversial) generic
considerations.[10] But the general conclusion is sure. Yet the standard
objections to it[11] require consideration, since they illuminate the
complexity of Horace's engagement with philosophy and indeed of
the very activity of philosophising.

OBJECTIONS TO A PHILOSOPHICAL READING

(a) The first objection is the alleged *naïveté* of supposing that
Horace had had a philosophical conversion, especially given his
earlier philosophical poems. But the latter factor does not preclude

---

[9] Denied by Rudd (1993b: 67).

[10] e.g. the influence of the philosophical letter (Dilke (1981) 1844, 1846) and other
philosophical modes (Harrison (1995b: 48–57)); Lucretian influence (Ferri (1993));
the *Epistles'* status as *sermones*, with debatable links to *Bionei sermones* (*satura*) and
'diatribe': cf. variously Horsfall (1979); Rudd (1979); Brink (1982: 254, 299–300);
Braund (1992: 25, 31 n. 61); Muecke (1993: 2–4).

[11] Culled from Williams (1968: 1–7); Mayer (1986; 1994: 39–47); Rudd (1993b:
64–5, 67, 77, 82–3).

a broad distinction between non-philosophical and philosophical matter, no doubt exaggerated to suit the rhetoric of conversion, and the main point foists upon philosophical interpreters a crude biographical model to which they are not committed.

But this objection does point an important question: the relationship between literature and life. No one still believes that the *Epistles* are 'real letters'[12] and many stress the presence of motifs from the *Satires,* a linkage strengthened by their common status as *sermones.*[13] Yet Maecenas, like all the addressees, is a real person, and the subtlety of Horace's allusions to addressees' characteristics and interests is well recognised.[14] Whatever the truth of Horace's self-description in 94–7, Maecenas' fussy reactions suit a notorious fop; Maecenas *was* Horace's patron; he *did* request poems; Horace *was* pressured into producing *Odes* 4.[15] In short, if, on the question of the relationship between the *Epistles* and real life, the theoretical possibilities are: (i) elaborate, self-conscious, fictionality; (ii) literal truth; and (iii) poetic truth à la *Poetics* 9 (allowing a degree of historicity—real people, broadly historical circumstances and events), then the world of the *Epistles* includes all three and rather more of (ii) than many moderns concede. If we do not attribute some substantive truth to that world, Horace's proffering of his own life-experience and his fitful moral progress through the text will fall flat. For the poems to engage the reader emotionally, socially and morally, there must be some recognisable relationship between 'Horace' (the literary construct) and Horace (the 'real person').

This point is reinforced by the *sphragis* of the last poem, Horace's farewell to his book (20.19–28):

> cum tibi sol tepidus plures admouerit aures,
> me libertino natum patre et in tenui re
> maiores pennas nido extendisse loqueris,
> ut, quantum generi demas, uirtutibus addas;
> me primis urbis belli placuisse domique,

---

[12] Williams (1968: 1–30) vs. Fraenkel (1957: 308–63); De Pretis (1998) (sophisticated reformulation).

[13] Kilpatrick (1986: 2–6); Braund (1992: 25); Freudenburg (1993: 28–9); Johnson (1993a: 4–5, 114–15); Lyne (1995: 186–7); n.10 above.

[14] Nisbet (1959); McGann (1963); Allen (1970); Harrison (1992); Jones (1993); Johnson (1993a: 11 n. 4, 11–17); Lyne (1995: 146–7).

[15] So I believe: Suet. *Vita Hor.,* Loeb ed. 2.486.

> corporis exigui, praecanum, solibus aptum,
> irasci celerem, tamen ut placabilis essem.
> forte meum siquis te percontabitur aeuum,
> me quater undenos sciat impleuisse Decembres,
> collegam Lepidum quo dixit Lollius anno.

Once a milder sun has brought more ears to hear you, tell them that I am the son of a freed slave, and that in my slender means I stretched out wings bigger than my nest, thus to add as much to my valour as you take away from my status. Tell them that I found favour with the city's leaders in war and in peace, that my stature is slight, hair prematurely grey; that I am sun-baked and quick to anger, but such a one as can be easily appeased. If someone perchance asks you how old I am, know that I filled out Decembers eleven times four in the year that Lollius called Lepidus his colleague.

Line 23 echoes 17.35 'to have found favour with princely men' (*principibus placuisse uiris*), of Aristippus, who, as we shall see, there represents one side of Horace. Epistles 1, 7 and 19 (to Maecenas), 9 (to Tiberius) and 13 (on Augustus' receiving the *Odes*)[16] attest that worldly success. And 26–8 ring with 1.4: Horace has indeed changed; he is ageing. His allegedly new interest in philosophy is psychologically and chronologically plausible. An inevitable gap remains between writer and text (a gap upon which 1.20 itself elegantly plays), but the two connect.

(b) The second objection claims that Horace cannot be maintaining a distinction between poetry and philosophy: his words scan; he *is* writing poetry. There are self-conscious thematic overlaps with the *Satires*. Any poetry-philosophy distinction in favour of the latter is challenged by the opening of Epistle 2: Homer tells us what is fine, what is base, what is useful, what is not, more clearly and better than Chrysippus and Crantor (1–5). Epistle 4's and Epistle 13's allusions to *Satires* and *Odes* respectively bring those poetic types closer to the *Epistles*. Epistle 12 (to Iccius) intertexts with *Odes* 1.29.[17] And Horace's defence of his poetry in Epistle 19 centres on *Odes* and *Epodes*.

Now it is clearly true that Horace presents the *Epistles* as both different from some or all of his previous poetry and as part of his whole poetic corpus, the latter emphasis predominating in the

---

[16] Moles (1995: 168).
[17] Putnam (1995).

second half of the book. Yet the paradox of the *Epistles'* being *both* poetry *and* not-poetry but philosophy is created and emphasised in 1.10–11:

> nunc itaque et uersus et cetera ludicra pono:
> quid uerum atque decens, curo et rogo et omnis in hoc sum.

And that is why I am now setting aside verses and other playthings. My concern is with what is true and fitting; that's what I ask, and it is what I am all about.

These lines of verse make a polar opposition between verse and all other playthings *and* philosophy; *uersus* cannot be restricted to lyric, since this excludes the *Satires* and the term can include poetic *sermo*: hence 10–11 do not appeal to the prosaic status of *sermo* (as many argue), but to the simple idea that philosophy is something distinct from poetry—cf. Socrates and Plato[18] (simple, though of course highly paradoxical when the text propounding it is itself poetry).

Now if the *Epistles'* subject matter is philosophy, they themselves must constitute a philosophical text. Horace says so: 12 *condo* and *compono* ('store/write' and 'arrange/compose') are literary terms. The *Epistles* are Horace's own 'store-house' now that he has 'put aside' *uersus et cetera ludicra* (12 *compono* ∼ 10 *pono*). And when in 23–5 Horace envisages the eventual possibility of *total* commitment to philosophising (25 *agendi* ∼ 16 *agilis* and 25 *nauiter* ∼ 15),[19] rather than the make-shifts of 14–19, and when he says *restat ut his ego me ipse regam solerque elementis* (27), *his . . . elementis* must gloss the *Epistles*. This reading receives confirmation from 20.17–18: 'this also awaits you, that stammering old age will find you in the back streets teaching boys their ABC's' (*hoc quoque te manet, ut pueros elementa docentem | occupet extremis in uicis balba senectus*). There the book will be reduced to teaching *elementa* of an even more 'elementary' kind. Similarly, while within the sickness metaphor the 'book chastely read three times' (*ter pure lecto . . . libello*) of 37 is the booklet of spells used in propitiatory rites, outside the metaphor it is the *liber* which will make Horace's readers 'pure',

---

[18] Thus e.g. McGann (1969: 35); Macleod (1977: 360; 1979a: 16); Harrison (1995b: 49–50); Moles (1995: 162).

[19] Cf. Maltby (1991: 406) for *nauus'* association with ships.

i.e. the *Epistles*. Furthermore, Epistle 1 rings with Epistle 20: Horace's own *liber* frames and instantiates the teachings of the collection. It is not true that Horace never recommends philosophical texts;[20] he does: his own. Beneath the irony, wit, self-depreciation etc., the implicit claims for the philosophical potential of the *Epistles* are huge, although to derive maximum benefit both Horace and his readers will have to re-read the poems repeatedly (*ter lecto...*).

The paradox of the *Epistles'* being *both* poetry *and* not-poetry but philosophy still requires explanation. Of course, once Horace the poet decides to write philosophy, he is committed to that paradox. But this does not *explain* it. One factor is that the *Epistles'* place in his whole poetic corpus helps to make Epistles 19 and 20 into a general *apologia pro vita sua*, and some aspects of that *vita* (e.g. Horace's ability *primis urbis... placuisse*, 20.23) antedated the alleged conversion of 1.10–11, yet show one possible philosophical road. Another factor is that both the writing and reception of poetry function as a sort of metaphor for a range of moral behaviour in life. We shall see something of this in Epistles 3 and 4, and it is an important aspect of Epistle 19.[21] Nor is it just a matter of metaphor: Horace moves progressively through the book towards a more philosophical conception of poetry. More radically still, some such paradox is inherent in the best philosophical writing itself. On the one hand, such writing is superior to other types of writing such as poetry, because of its philosophical commitment and rigour; on the other, it has an inevitable relationship with such writings; again, even to write about philosophy is a poor substitute for the real thing. The ambiguity of Horace's presentation of the *Epistles*—poetry-not-poetry, of enormous value, merely an elementary propaedeutic—is paralleled in writings that are indubitably philosophical, such as Plato's.

The same applies to Horace's fizzing wit and irony; many of the greatest ancient philosophers are witty and ironic (most relevantly, Socrates, Aristippus, Plato and Diogenes). It was the Socratic *daimonion* that caused Horace's conversion (7) and Socrates is important to Horace's self-presentation[22]—or *persona*. For although 7 *personet*

---

[20] *Pace* Mayer (1994: 124); cf. also 1.37 ∼ 2.1–2 (p. 313); 18.96ff. (pp. 330–1).
[21] Macleod (1977: 360, 363ff.).
[22] Macleod (1979a: 21); Mayer (1986: 72); Johnson (1993a: 88–9).

means 'sounds through', Horace here acknowledges the decisive influence of an identifiable philosopher; there is (as we shall see) a general Panaetian influence upon the epistle; Panaetius made much of *persona*-theory; and later in the collection Horace himself exploits Panaetian *persona* theory.[23] *personet*, therefore, introduces, precisely, Horace's Socratic *persona*. Then, Horace's irresolute changes of philosophical position (15–19) humorously recall Socrates' wanderings in search of knowledge (Pl. *Ap.* 22a) and his encounters with the Roman people in the colonnades (70ff.) suggest Socrates' debates in the *agora*. The epistle even sketches a certain rudimentary Socratic *elenchos*: Horace 'asks' what is true (11), Maecenas may 'ask' who Horace's philosophical master is (13), the Roman people may 'ask' Horace why he does not share their judgements and tastes (70), it is one of the aims of philosophy to teach one to 'respond' to Fortune (68): a 'response' underpinned by Socratic *elenchos*.

Socrates, too, was the paradigm of 'the laughing philosopher'. The epistle is full of allusions to laughing (*rideo*), whether justified (9, 10, 91) or misplaced (95, 97, cf. 101). Moreover, in 59–60 Horace cites the children's game of 'kings' as pointing the right moral lesson: 'but boys, in their play, say "you will be king, if you do what's right"' (*at pueri* <u>ludentes</u> 'rex eris' aiunt | 'si recte facies'). On a banal level, this gives the term *ludus* a sixth application, that of literal children's 'play' or 'games'. But the appeal to the *ludus* of *pueri* as a moral standard is polysemous. The implicit etymological connection (more prominently trailed in 2.67–8) between *puer* and *purus*[24] underpins a central paradox, which, *mutatis mutandis*, unites the thoughts 'now I am become a man, I have put away childish things' (10 *ludicra*, cf. 3) and 'except you become as little children you cannot enter the kingdom of God' (59). To begin the quest for virtue, at whatever age (26), one must become as *purus* as a *puer*. Thus the children's *ludus* is at least potentially philosophical, so that *ludentes* suggests not just philosophy as a *ludus* but *ludus* as a way of doing philosophy. Thus *ludentes* glosses Socratic 'play' (*paizein*)[25] (the seventh application of *ludus*). And since the concept of *ludus* here appears in juxtaposition

---

[23] McGann (1969: 10–12, 22–3).
[24] Maltby (1991: 506).
[25] Kindstrand (1976: 47–8, 192).

with *pueri*, the collocation *pueri ludentes* glosses the Socratic/Platonic pun *paideia/paidia*: 'play' is a thing for children (*paides*) but children point towards right moral behaviour—true 'education' is a form of play.[26] *Ludus* thus acquires an eighth application: 'education'. Even a ninth: Horace also suggests a punning allusion to the moral/philosophical idea of 'serious play' (*spoudaiogeloion*), the vehicle used by Socrates, and after him, the Cynics, and the satirical Horace himself, for philosophical teaching.[27] Thus the phrase *pueri ludentes* is itself complexly and brilliantly philosophical. And intimates a potential clarification of the paradox of 10–11: poetic 'play' will yield to philosophical 'play', or, rather, to 'philosophical play' expressed in poetic form.

The tenth application of *ludus* is to the 'school' that children attend, imaged in 53–69. Horace imagines Janus teaching both young and old the supreme value of wealth. Then he himself appeals to the children's jingle (59–62) to suggest a better lesson. This further application of *ludus* explains the challenge of Epistle 2: the poem is a protreptic to philosophy, and in a protreptic one returns to school, to the beginnings of moral wisdom, the teaching of Homer. This stance, which philosophers themselves could take (Antisthenes, Plutarch etc.), is not Horace's final word but the first step in one's philosophical career. A poem which comes after Epistle 1 sequentially is anterior to it logically (because Epistle 1 sketches the whole philosophical process), a point made by the interaction between 2.1–2 'I have re-read the writer of the Trojan War' (*Troiani belli scriptorem . . . relegi*) and 1.37 *ter pure lecto . . . libello. relegi* is 'pre-cut' by *ter lecto*. The *Epistles'* philosophical potential *exceeds* Homer's.

The complex and intricate 'play' element does not erase the *Epistles'* philosophical seriousness, but there is an implicit challenge to readers to penetrate the 'play' to that underlying seriousness. They may fail. The rich philosophical potential of pure *pueritia* at school may degenerate into a dismal and familiar reality: 20.17–18 'this also awaits you, that stammering old age will find you in the back streets teaching boys their ABC's.' The hopes of 1.27 may never be fulfilled.

---

[26] e.g. Pl. *Leg.* 2.656c; Dio Chrys. 4.30; Chris Rowe cites also Heraclitus fr. 52 αἰὼν παῖς ἐστι παίζων, πεσσεύων· παιδὸς ἡ βασιληίη ('Time is a child playing a game of draughts; the kingship is in the hands of a child').

[27] Kindstrand (1976: 47–8).

Reading/interpreting/implementing philosophy requires unremitting commitment and effort by both poet and readers.

There is the possibility even of an eleventh application of *ludus:* 'playing a part';[28] lines 2–3 are not far from this and the idea of the Socratic *persona* (7) helps.

This analysis may seem to give insufficient value to the self-depreciation which overlays Horace's philosophical self-assertion. There are indeed several aspects to that self-depreciation (including the needs to respond tactfully to Maecenas and to explore the inevitable shortfalls from philosophical precepts), but self-depreciation, whether real or assumed, is an essential part of the Socratic tradition. Socrates, notoriously, knew nothing. The Socratic philosopher teaches and learns in a reciprocal relationship with his pupils: hence the interaction between Socrates, his *daimonion* and Horace (7), between 7 *purgatam* and 37 *pure*, between Horace's ear (7) and his readers' ears (40).[29] Horace's self-depreciation simultaneously ingratiates, challenges and teaches.

(c) The third objection is that 14–19 are philosophically unorthodox in the refusal to enlist under one master and in the appeal to Aristippus, who had no contemporary followers. Yet on *one* level Horace's eclecticism (problematic but useful term) must be taken seriously, because it parallels his refusal to be 'included within any (poetical) *ludus*' (3). Such admitted eclecticism is rare in ancient philosophy but not unknown,[30] and there is a carry-over from 7: no ancient philosopher more truly exemplified the principle *nullius addictus iurare in uerba magistri* ('I have no master/trainer whose words I am forced to swear by') than Socrates. Similarly, as we have seen, 15–19 playfully echo Socrates' famous wanderings in search of knowledge at the start of *his* philosophical career. Moreover, as already noted, the wording of 14 extends to philosophy at large the

---

[28] Cf. *OLD* s.v. *ludo* 6b.

[29] I suspect that, especially after the anagrammatic play with 'Maecenas' (1–3), 7 *purgatam ... personet aurem* also recalls *Flaccus* (as also 4.15–16 *me pinguem et nitidum bene curata cute uises | cum ridere uoles Epicuri de grege porcum* (Moles (1995: 167)), cf. *Epod.* 15.12; *Sat.* 1.9.20; 2.1.19), Horace's improved aural status not so much *glossing* his existing cognomen as 'renaming' him Q. Horatius *Socrates.* The humour of 4.16 will be enhanced by Horace's relapse into his customary 'flaccidity'.

[30] e.g. Lucian, *Demon.* 5.

eclecticism that is found *within* Academicism. As for Aristippus, contemporary philosophy could still allude to him and discuss his ethics (as did Panaetius and Cicero).[31] Finally, to be philosophically unorthodox is, logically, to be philosophical (no mere sophistry, as will become clear).

On another level, however, Horace's eclecticism is vulnerable: he is making a complete hash of his philosophical options. When he tries Stoicism, 'I plunge in', *mersor ciuilibus undis* (16);[32] then 'furtively I slip back', *furtim ... relabor* (18): compared with the Stoic ideal, however ironised, 'Aristippeanism' is a 'furtive' second best, not the '*best* philosophical horse'. Some scholars[33] have seen Aristippus as Horace's ideal: he is not, he is simply one possibility. Here his attractions are recognised but formally decried; conversely, in 1.17 he wins the debate against Diogenes over whether or not to associate with 'kings', in which respect he does reflect Horace's own view and practice, but then in 1.18 Aristippus' own claims are implicitly criticised (he is too much the *scurra*: 2–4). Nor does the irony of 1.1.16–17 and 108[34] entail Horace's dismissal of orthodox Stoicism: on the contrary, he has the highest respect for it (1.16), although it is not, ultimately, for him personally.[35] Thus the eclecticism of 14–19 can be read alternatively as a serious eclecticism, to be justified as the book progresses, or as an eclecticism destined for refutation: one particular philosophy may after all hold the key to right living. But, however read, Horace's assumed eclecticism has obvious structural advantages, allowing the relatively unprejudiced exploration of a range of philosophical alternatives.

(d) The fourth objection is that the *Epistles* are about life, not philosophy. But the dichotomy is false. The *Epistles* are about 'living rightly' (*recte uiuere*, 60) as interpreted by different philosophies. The fact that a few Epistles resist philosophical categorisation does not undermine the book's philosophical classification. General,

---

[31] Cic. *Off.* 1.148; 3.116.

[32] Moles (1995: 163).

[33] Traina (1991); Rudd (1993b: 82–3); Mayer (1994: 44).

[34] Where *pituita* presumably includes an allusion to Horace's *lippitudo* (~29; cf. *Sat.* 1.5.30–1), i.e., dramatically speaking, Horace himself is still (unsuccessfully) aspiring to orthodox Stoicism (~16–17).

[35] For 1.16 and Horace's ultimate Epicureanism, see discussion below.

non-doctrinaire, moralising is found extensively in philosophers such as Cicero, Seneca, Musonius and Plutarch and in the popular philosophical writings of the Cynic tradition, of which Horace was in some respects heir.[36]

In sum, the *Epistles'* subject matter is philosophy; they themselves constitute a philosophical text; and they register—indeed enact—many of the problematics of writing philosophy.

PHILOSOPHICAL ARGUMENTS AND STRUCTURE

The next question to consider is the philosophical argument of 1.1, beginning with its ambiguous Stoic *color*. Lines 16–17 imply that orthodox Stoicism is 'best' and the flavour of 68–9 'or he who is there to admonish and ready you to respond to arrogant Fortune freely, standing on your own two feet?' (*an qui Fortunae te responsare superbae | liberum et erectum praesens hortatur et aptat?*), on the gains available from philosophy, is heroically Stoic.[37] The poem ends (106–8) by endorsing the Stoic *rex*, the 'answer' to the question of *recte uiuere*, though that endorsement is finally ironised.

But there are counter-elements. There is much that is objectively consistent with the moderated Stoicism of Panaetius: *decens* (11), which *could* gloss Panaetian *prepon*; the eclecticism of 14–19; the appeal to Aristippus; the idea that some progress is better than none—32 *could* gloss the Panaetian concepts of *profectus* and *proficiens*; the modest definition of *uirtus* in 41–2; the awareness of individual difference as frustrating universal norms (80–93); the ironisation of the sage. Should we, then, add a Panaetian label to our existing collection of orthodox Stoic, Aristippean and Epicurean? McGann, in his seminal philosophical investigation, claims: '*decens*...can in Rome at this time, less than a quarter of a century after the publication of *De officiis*, point in one direction only, to the ethics of Panaetius'. This is perhaps exaggerated, but Panaetius certainly comes into the frame with the parallel definition of philosophy

---

[36] Heinze (1889); Fiske (1920); Muecke (1993: 2–8).
[37] Johnson (1993a: 42); 1.68–9 also ∼16.73–9 and 1.17∼16.67 (p. 326).

in 2.3 ('what is lovely, what is foul, what is useful, and what is not', *quid sit pulchrum, quid turpe, quid utile, quid non*), so only a little retrospective reading (which 1.37 entails) activates his presence in 1.11. There is, then, a tension in the poem's Stoic *color*. While formally the Stoic elements push towards an orthodox Stoic solution, sub-elements advocate more modest, and pluralist, Panaetian goals.[38]

And there are other elements. Partly in their own right (5), partly through Aristippus, the Epicureans 'lurk' (appropriately) in the background. Aristippus himself represents both a certain conception of pleasure and philosophical flexibility. The Socratic element promotes the claims both of non-doctrinaire pluralism and of dialectical pursuit of truth. Orthodox Stoicism re-emerges really only in Epistle 16, but it provides a convenient, indeed the obvious, initial standard of virtue with (as it were) a capital 'v'. All other elements conduce better to the exploration in subsequent poems of a range of philosophical alternatives, to Horace's own developing pluralist philosophical *persona* and to ever more direct engagement between philosophy and life.

Hence the final philosophical aspect of Epistle 1: its architectural role. While there are many organising principles in this most intricate of poetry-books,[39] the philosophical one is primary. Horace's basic procedure is to provide preliminary sketches of the main figures of the philosophical landscape, which he then tries out on the real people of the *Epistles*, himself included, matching temperament to philosophical choice, in a series of dramatic situations, whose individual rationales and interlocking permutations are characteristically explored through recognisable philosophical positions. The concepts of *ludus* and *persona* help to articulate this shifting scenario.

Lines 16–19 institute a complex polarity between orthodox Stoicism/virtue/consistency and Aristippus/adaptability/pleasure, a polarity resolved and not resolved by the description of the *sapiens* at the poem's end: *qua* ironic, this description suggests the Panaetian perspective otherwise implicit in the poem; the Epicureans are also in play, partly through their implicit association with Aristippus.

---

[38] McGann (1969: 10–12 (quotation from 10)); Moles (1985: 37–8).
[39] Maurach (1968); McGann (1969: 33–87); Johnson (1993a: 66–71).

Epistle 2 deploys a similar polarity, between Virtue/Wisdom/Odysseus (17–22), implicitly linked with the addressee Lollius, and Pleasure/Folly/Companions/Phaeacians (23–31), and it ends by compromising between the two (70–1). This compromise looks like Panaetian *profectus*, and the initial philosophical formulation (3) is definitely Panaetian. By analogy with Epistle 1 Odysseus' virtue must be broadly Stoic (or Cynic), as confirmed by the link between 2.22 *immersabilis* ('unsinkable') and 1.16 *mersor* ('I plunge/sink into') (Odysseus and Horace are 'swimming' in the same philosophical 'sea'). One naturally reads the opposing Pleasure as vulgar Epicurean, as confirmed by the link between 2.26 *sus* ('sow') and 4.16 *Epicuri de grege porcum*. The lurking Epicureans of Epistle 1 replace Aristippus as the polar opposite of Virtue, though their portrayal, unlike Aristippus', is now straightforwardly negative.[40] And the foppish Maecenas of Epistle 1 now looks rather Epicurean (2.29∼1.94 ff.).[41]

Epistle 3 is difficult, but 3.5 asks if Florus (the addressee) and his friends are behaving like Phaeacians/vulgar Epicureans, and the poem's unifying thought is that true wisdom involves concord/friendship with oneself, one's fellows, one's *patria* and the *cosmos* (28–9). This is Stoic and indeed directly Panaetian (*De off.* 1.50–8).[42] The argument works with the same essential polarity as Epistles 1 and 2, though Panaetian Stoicism now appears in a loftier light. Epistle 4 recycles that polarity yet again but this time favours Epicureanism (notwithstanding Horace's ironic self-description) over Albius' austere Stoicism.[43] Favourable redefinition of Epicureanism continues in Epistle 5 addressed to the Epicurean Torquatus: Augustus' birthday allows a busy man to implement Epicurus' advice of 4.13.[44]

So much, for now, for the *Epistles'* philosophical architecture. To change the figure, in this poetic corpus the dramatic situations are the skin and tissue, the philosophies the bones and sinews.

[40] Detail in Moles (1985: 36–9; cf. 1995: 164), also Eidinow (1990: 566).

[41] As he probably was: Cairns (1995: 124).

[42] Moles (1995: 164–6).

[43] Moles (1995: 167); for Jones (1993: 8), Albius is 'not looking at things philosophically': rather, his philosophy is criticised.

[44] For the Epicureanism see McGann (1969: 44–6); Moles (1995: 167); Eidinow (1995).

PHILOSOPHY AND POLITICS

Epistle 1 foregrounds programmatically the questions of political participation, linked to choice of philosophy, and of the moral well-being of the *patria*. But the central social/political question of the poem itself is Horace's relationship with Maecenas. Maecenas is Horace's alpha and omega, a compliment reflected in the structure of both poem (1, 105) and book (Epistle 1~19), though in both cases the ring that is Maecenas is outflanked by other, and larger, concerns.[45] Maecenas tries to restrict Horace to his old poetic *ludus*; Horace responds with the *Epistles*, which are something new. Reproof jostles with compliment. It is paradoxical that the *Epistles* can give Maecenas freedom (69) when he seeks to restrict Horace's (3); that he laughs at Horace's unkempt habits (95, 97), not the things that are truly *ludicra* (10); that he remains Horace's *tutela* ('protection,' 103), when Horace seeks a *tutela* elsewhere (13). Can it really be true that Horace still 'looks to' Maecenas (105), when he himself no longer wants to be 'looked at' (2)? Is he really still 'dependent' on Maecenas (105), when he himself wants freedom from his old poetry to concentrate on philosophy and freedom even within philosophy? Horace tries to bring Maecenas within the philosophical process by extensive second-person-singular addresses, some of which must at least include Maecenas.

The compliments remain, including the compliment of being able to take public reproof, yet with all the urbanity and joking Maecenas' attitudes are objectively criticised, and he is implicitly on probation.[46] Maecenas the *laudandus* is an addressee in a philosophical book most of whose addressees are criticised or admonished. And 'figured-speech' theory[47] admits criticism through compliment.

Epistle 3 warns against strife among young careerists in a military camp, who risk the 'disturbances of foolish kings' (*stultorum regum ... aestus*) of *Iliad* and *Odyssey* (2.8); broaches the possibility of poetic

---

[45] Lyne (1995: 72–3, 139, 155).
[46] Similarly: McGann (1969: 34–7); Johnson (1993a: 9, 55–6); Lyne (1995: 144–50).
[47] Ahl (1985).

commemoration of Augustus' *res gestae* (7); and elevates devotion to the *patria* (29). The apparently slight and urbane epistle to Tibullus contains one jarring allusion: 4.3 'to write something to surpass the smaller works of Cassius of Parma' (*scribere quod Cassi Parmensis opuscula uincat*). As in Epistle 3, poetic rivalry functions partly as a metaphor for civic strife. The Epicurean Epistle 5 celebrates the birthday not of Epicurus but of Augustus: implicitly the good king, who in Epicurean political thought can be the guarantor of Epicurean quietism.[48] No tension here between Epicureanism and Augustanism or between country and city. Epistle 7 reintroduces Maecenas, complaining that Horace has stayed away for a month rather than the promised five days; compliments and endearments abound but Horace maintains his position (metaphorically and literally). Panaetian relativism allows individuals to choose what is right for them (44, 98; cf. Cic. *Off.* 1.110), here, for Horace, a form of rural Epicureanism.[49] In Epistle 10 Horace's happiness at the crumbling shrine of Vacuna, Sabine goddess of victory whose name suggests *uacare*, pointedly subverts worldly values, and in Epistle 11, with the right attitude of mind, happiness is available at Ulubrae for Bullatius (29).[50] By contrast, in Epistle 12 imperial successes and bumper crops in Italy point the unreasonableness of Iccius' discontent with his managership of Agrippa's estates (25ff.). Epistle 13 commemorates Augustus' receiving the *Odes* a few years before: like Epistle 9 and others it advertises Horace's connections with the court. Still, Augustus is nowhere addressed, as he himself was to complain (Suet. *Vita Hor.*, Loeb ed. 2.486), and, unlike Maecenas (1.1), he is not formally 'first and last': even in his own poem he comes in the second and penultimate lines.[51]

In the majestic and philosophically rigorous Epistle 16[52] Horace is on his farm (1–16), master (2, 10) of his simple natural bounty and 'safe' in his Epicurean retreat: 15 'these sweet hiding places', *hae*

---

[48] Fowler (1989b: 129ff.).

[49] Broadly 'anti-Maecenas' readings of 7: Johnson (1993a: 9, 43–4); Seager (1993: 34); Lyne (1995: 150–5); Oliensis (1998a: 157–65).

[50] Macleod (1979a: 27); Ferri (1993: 112–13).

[51] Note also Oliensis' gloss (1998a: 182) on Augustus' failure to secure Horace's secretarial help: 'Horace chose to write letters on his own account [i.e. the *Epistles*] and not on the emperor's.'

[52] I intend fuller treatment elsewhere.

latebrae dulces ∼ 1.5 'he hides tucked away', *latet abditus*; *dulces* glosses Epicureanism,[53] 16 *incolumem* that 'security' (*asphaleia*) obtained by Epicurean 'withdrawal' (Epic. *KD* 14). The addressee, Quinctius, is politically active in Rome (17–79). The poem operates with a *rus*/Epicurean—Rome/Stoic contrast, hence the latter's appeal to Stoic doctrines: only the wise man is happy (20), virtue and vice are absolutes and vice is rejected through love of virtue, not fear of punishment (52–4), and all sins are equal (56).

What, within this Roman context, does *recte uiuere* mean? Who is *beatus*, or *sapiens* and *bonus*? Worldly honours are no criterion: they can exaggerate a man's worth (if he is flattered as if he were Augustus) or be removed at the donor's whim (34). ('Who he?' one wonders, and, at least retrospectively, the answer must be: 'Augustus'.)[54] Loss of worldly honours does not degrade a virtuous man. Is the *bonus*, then, the man who does good public service (40)? Not necessarily, for his household and neighbourhood may know that he is base within (a common philosophical contrast between outer and inner). The absolute materialist (67) has deserted the post of Virtue (contrast the Stoic ideal of 1.17). The captured deserter should not be killed but sold as a slave, when he can usefully become a shepherd, ploughman, or whatever: although the complete materialist is a moral slave his immoral activity has some commercial benefit for society.[55] This section highlights the qualities of the polar opposite of the moral slave, the truly free man, who, as the last lines of the poem emphasise, may face loss of all his possessions, imprisonment or even death (1.16.73–9).

> uir bonus et sapiens audebit dicere 'Pentheu,
> rector Thebarum, quid me perferre patique
> indignum coges?' 'adimam bona.' 'nempe pecus, rem,
> lectos, argentum: tollas licet.' 'in manicis et
> compedibus saeuo te sub custode tenebo.'
> 'ipse deus, simulatque uolam, me soluet.' opinor,
> hoc sentit 'moriar'. mors ultima linea rerum est.

The good and wise man will have the courage to say: 'Pentheus, King of Thebes, what undeserved punishment are you compelling me to tolerate and

---

[53] Cf. e.g. *Carm.* 2.7.28 (Moles (1987: 70)); 3.2.13 (Pinsent (1976)).

[54] Support from 33–5∼18.111–12 (of Jupiter).

[55] Thus Mayer (1994: 229).

suffer?' 'I will take away your goods.' 'Go ahead, certainly, away with my flock, my estate, the couches and the silver!' 'I will have you shackled, legs and arms, and kept by a cruel guard.' 'God himself, as soon as I choose, will release me.' I suppose he means 'I will die.' Death is the finish line for all things.

These lines adapt the scene between Pentheus and Dionysus from Euripides, *Bacchae* 492–8. Philosophical exegesis of literary passages is commonplace; that Epictetus also uses this scene[56] suggests a common Stoic source. The move from 'real life' to 'myth' imitates a concluding philosophical *muthos*. The scene also provides a concrete dramatic representation of 1.68–9 'or he who is there to admonish and ready you to respond to arrogant Fortune freely, standing on your own two feet?' (*qui Fortunae te responsare superbae | liberum et erectum praesens hortatur et aptat*). It also crowns the philosophical argument. The *uir bonus et sapiens* is finally revealed (outer and inner united), the criterion being his unflinching response to tyranny. Whereas Epicurean retreat gives 'safety' and autonomous self-'mastery', Stoic engagement risks collision with a tyrannical 'external' *dominus*. But it is impossible for the tyrannical *rector* to degrade the man of virtue, whose virtue and freedom are underwritten by the freedom of suicide. Horace transmutes Euripides into pure Stoic doctrine, reinforced by the notion of 'the god within' (78–9): in Euripides Dionysus simply says: 'the god will free me from imprisonment', whereas Horace's exegesis makes Dionysus mean: 'I can release myself by suicide.'

The closing *sententia*—'Death is the last line of things' (like the line at the end of a race)—is no mere banality. For the man of virtue, it is consolatory: untimely death as a necessary response to tyranny is no evil since we all die sometime; for the tyrant, it is admonitory: you can compass the death of the man of virtue, but you gain nothing, since you yourself have to die. For such Stoic insouciance there are (again) good parallels in Epictetus, e.g. when (1.25.22) the philosopher Demetrius says to Nero: 'you threaten me with death but nature threatens you'. Further, as applied to a pursuer of the philosophical *rectum*, the image of the *line* fittingly adorns a *noble* death. There is still another implication, again applicable both to man of virtue and

[56] 1.1.22–4; 29.5–8.

tyrant, though again in different ways: 'you can't take it with you': *rerum* also interacts with 75 *rem* and 68 *re* (both of property). Lastly, the image of the line achieves a final modification of the poem's architecture: if the poem works, as it were, horizontally, with a polar opposition between Epicureanism and Stoicism, then, as it were, vertically, all polar oppositions are resolved in death, though the Epicurean and Stoic attitudes to death are of course different, and this also is part of the densely condensed meaning.

What are the consequences for political interpretation? Formally set in legendary Thebes, the heroic final scene must also play in contemporary Rome, the setting of the whole Stoic section. Not only is the scene the culmination of the argument, but Thebes itself can function as a metaphor for civil-war Rome. It is so used by Virgil and Ovid, and, as we shall see, by Horace himself in 18.41ff. Also relevant is the Pindaric/Theban *color* of Epistle 3, with its warnings against intestinal and fraternal strife.[57] Further, the word *rector* (4) recalls Cicero's conception of the *rector*, which envisaged Pompey and was in some sense fulfilled by Augustus,[58] who is within the frame of the poem. This *rector*, however, is the antithesis of *recte uiuere*. Thus the concluding *muthos* implies an analogy between the political status of Pentheus and that of Augustus, 'monarch'[59] and in certain contexts, from certain focalisations, also 'tyrant'. Ancient theories of 'figured speech' easily accommodate such radical implications. No coincidence, then, that Epictetus (also) applies the Euripidean scene to tyrannical emperors.

Does the man of *uirtus* suggest any specific allusions? Certainly not to the materialistic[60] Quinctius, for whom the point of the scene is the extremely high stakes risked by his Stoic political engagement under the new monarchy. But Cato Uticensis and Brutus must qualify:[61] Cato who committed suicide rather than endure the clemency of Augustus' father and whom Horace introduces as a paragon of Stoic virtue in a thematically related later poem (19.12–14); Brutus, Horace's erstwhile *imperator*, who had recognised Stoic

---

[57] Hardie (1990); Hubbard (1995).
[58] e.g. Cic. *Rep.* 2.51.1; Ov. *Tr.* 2.39.
[59] Millar (1973).
[60] McGann (1969: 74); Lyne (1995: 147).
[61] Armstrong (1989: 129–31 (important)).

affiliations, whose last words before his suicide denounced Octa-vian,[62] and who cannot be excluded from the *primi* of 20.23 (*me primis urbis belli placuisse domique*). But also Horace himself, for, while, dramatically speaking, Horace here plays the Epicurean role, it is Horace the poet who voices this existential struggle between Stoic virtue and Caesarian tyranny. Despite all the material benefits show-ered on him by Augustus and Maecenas, in an ultimate sense the poet-philosopher remains morally and politically free, inspired by the examples of Cato and Brutus and by Stoic ethics at their most magnificently uncompromising. Nor does its tremendous moral power exhaust the poem's political quality. DuQuesnay has persua-sively argued that some of Horace's poetry shows detailed inner knowledge of the political thinking of Augustus and his *consilium*;[63] by contrast, this poem contemplates unflinchingly one of the new dispensation's supreme costs: the death of men of true *uirtus*. Had it been written under Tiberius or any of the later 'tyrant'-emperors, the poem would not, perhaps, have been in this respect very remarkable; that it was written early in Augustus' reign and by a poet so closely involved with the imperial court is eloquent testimony to Horace's political acumen.

The worldly and practical Epistle 17 reshuffles the cards. The players are Panaetians, Epicureans, Aristippeans and Cynics. The aim is *maioribus*, even *regibus*, *uti* (2, 13, 14), clearly recalling Epistle 16, though *reges* now include patrons as well as kings. As in 16 Epicurean withdrawal is a legitimate and virtuous option (9~36). Cynicism's claim to a virtuous but independent life within the city is refuted by the flexible and Panaetian Aristippus. It is virtuous and onerous *principibus placuisse uiris* (35), and honour and reward rightly attend such success. There are strong shades of one side of Horace here: perhaps, after all, orthodox Stoic heroics are avoidable, even without Epicurean withdrawal. So Epistle 18 explores the prob-lem of successful social engagement with the great. Cynic behaviour *within* society is merely boorish and does not confer *uirtus*, but you must not be an unprincipled parasite. You can be a true *amicus* of the great, thereby attaining 'virtue, the mean of vices' (*uirtus ... medium*

---

[62] 'Stoic': Moles (1987: 64–5); 'last words': Plut. *Brut.* 51.1 with Moles (1983: 773).
[63] e.g. DuQuesnay (1995).

uitiorum, 9).[64] How? On Bowditch's[65] attractive 'figured-speech'
reading, Horace's mature poetic *ludus* plays dangerously with the
covert realities of Augustan Rome—Augustus' supremacy as *dux* and
patronus, loss of *libertas,* the intestinal nature of Actium—as a way of
warning the young and excessively *liber* Lollius. But on any reading
the tone is grim enough: 86–7 'those who haven't tried it think it
pleasant to court a powerful friend. Those who have tried it will
dread it' (*dulcis inexpertis cultura potentis amici:* | *expertus metuet*), a
sentiment, incidentally, applied by Pindar fr. 110 to war.

But 'among other things you will read and make enquiry of
learned men' (*inter cuncta leges et percontabere doctos,* 96). Although
simultaneous with cultivation of powerful *amici,* this activity is
preferable: to be a friend to yourself, to be Horace's friend, matters
more.[66] That the *docti* are at least primarily philosophers is
confirmed by many things:[67] 96's echo of *Academica* 2.1.2 ('partly
in making enquiry of experts, partly in reading of military achievements', *partim in percontando a peritis, partim in rebus gestis legendis*)
and 4 (same process in philosophical matters); the Socratic *percontabere* (contrasting with the nosy 'enquirer' of the body of the poem
and ringing with Horace's Socratic *elenchos* of Epistle 1); the contrast
with Iccius' high-flown philosophical interests; the thematic echoes
in 98–9 of Epistles 14, 6 and 16 (all strongly philosophical); the Stoic
mediocriter utilium; the question of 100; the Aristippean 102; and the
Epicurean 103. And the *docti* must include Horace, Lollius' present
counsellor, the ironic *docendus* of Epistle 17, then pointedly revealed
as *doctus* (17.16), the poet of the *liber* with such vast philosophical
potential (1.36–7). And seventeen lines after 18.96 Epistle 19 begins:
'If you believe old Cratinus, my <u>learned</u> Maecenas' (*Prisco si credis,
Maecenas <u>docte</u>, Cratino*). As at the book's beginning, Maecenas is
doctus in poetry, not in the *doctrina* of 18.96–103, or, if the latter,
only because he has *learned* (become *doctus*) from Epistles 1–18.
Poets, then, are included only to the extent that Horace himself is a
philosophical poet, promoting a philosophical conception of poetry.

---

[64] Epistles 17 and 18: Moles (1986: 43–6 (rather misrepresented by Rudd (1993b: 69 and 86 n. 20))).

[65] Bowditch (1994).

[66] McGann (1969: 80); Jones (1993: 10).

[67] Moles (1995: 170 (controverting Mayer (1994: 254))) adapted.

Lollius must choose which philosophy suits him best. Then he must keep at it: philosophising never stops. Back once more to Epistle 1: the cure is philosophy. But from Socratic non-commitment and the relativism which exists within Academicism, Panaetianism and Aristippeanism, Horace has fashioned a relativism which allows individual choice between philosophies: an original and creative philosophical move, and one based on a simple but profound psychological truth: individual personality greatly influences—and should influence—philosophical, political and intellectual choices. For Horace himself, now, the Epicurean way is most suited, it cannot be for ever (104 *quotiens*), because we are none of us completely free—only the *liber* is *liber* (Epistle 20),[68] but may it last at least a year (109). Maecenas will have an even longer wait than Epistle 7 requested. Indeed, Horace's final praise of Maecenas is conditional upon Maecenas' approving of Horace's philosophical talk, upon his allowing Horace greater freedom, and upon his trying himself to become a better person.

Is, then, *Epistles* 1 'anti-Augustan' (robustly useful term)? Are the praises of Maecenas in Epistles 1, 7 and 19 (praises themselves not unequivocal), of Augustus in Epistles 5 and 13, and of patriotism in 3 sapped by the Epicurean 7, by the Stoic heroics of 16 and by the grimness of 18? Augustus did not find the *Epistles* sufficiently complimentary.[69] But, logically, deconstruction must work both ways: such is the interactive economy of the circular book. And the pleas of 3 for concord seem real enough, while 5 floats the possibility of reconciliation between praise of Augustus and Epicureanism within Rome. Augustus could not get angry. Nevertheless, along with Horace's pride in 'pleasing the *principes*' and his insistence that each must choose his own philosophical road goes recognition of the increasing dangers of cultivation of the mightiest *amicus* (Epistle 18), of the fact that under him the truly virtuous may have to die to preserve their virtue (Epistle 16), and of the ever-greater attractions of Epicurean withdrawal (Epistles 7, 16, 18). The social and political backdrop to the *Epistles*' exploration of the range of philosophical choices is not inert: Horace registers the ever-sharper challenges of the new monarchy. Ultimately, Epicurean withdrawal is where

[68] Johnson (1993a: 69).   [69] Suet. *Vita Hor.* Loeb ed. 2.486–8.

Horace's own heart lies. But this is a conditional Epicureanism, non-doctrinaire, and untainted by the smugness which disfigures ortho-dox Epicureanism and enfeebles its intellectual processes. In import-ant respects, Horace's Epicureanism is better than the real thing. Here, too, so far from rejecting philosophy or even just moving outside it, Horace shows himself to be a philosopher and a thor-oughly useful one.

But individuals must make their own philosophical choices. They must balance one philosophical position against another. They must read and re-read the text, much of whose complexity derives from the poems' kaleidoscopic shifts of viewpoint, which create an inter-active dynamic which itself constitutes a kind of Socratic dialectic. And they must constantly interface this complex text with the com-plexities of life. The *Epistles*, then, are what they claim to be: both formally and profoundly philosophical, although to gauge their full philosophical profundity readers are required to penetrate the poems' polysemous 'play' in an act of interpretation which itself unites the aesthetic, the moral and the philosophical and itself promotes their philosophical growth, if, that is, they are prepared to do so (20.17–18).

Part III

Horace's *Epistles*, Book Two and the *Ars Poetica*

14

Horace's Letter to Augustus

Friedrich Klingner

For Karl Reinhardt on Feb. 14th 1951

If, after all of the efforts that have been spent to explain them, Horace's late hexameters (three letters chiefly: to Florus, to the Pisones, and to Augustus) remain difficult and mysterious even today, the blame for this has little to do with the poems' contents, with their ideas and historical realities, and nothing at all to do with the details of their language and style. On all of these topics, save for the provenance of specific poetic doctrines, sufficient light has been shed. Things turn murky as soon as one asks about the meaning and intention of each of the three epistles, and about how their verse groups, materials, and ideas, all alternating in dazzling array, are connected and unified. That is, the trouble starts if one asks whether there is order and unity in them at all. The problems encountered by interpreters of the *Ars Poetica* are well known: on what is its unity based, and what is its conceptual plan? Answers deviate greatly. The idea that the poem is an *ars*, a systematic doctrine that could be used as a procedural guide to creation, was given up long ago. The title 'Ars Poetica', passed down since the time of Quintilian, is based on this misunderstanding. It is well known that this epistle is a *sermo*, an informal conversation, like the others.[1] While it is unclear to what extent traditional schemes of didactic literature have influenced the work's overall progression and arrangement, what is clear is that the poem reflects a high culture of conversation among select friends, and that its topics are interwoven less simply than one would expect.

---

[1] For Horace's letter to the Pisones, see Klingner (1964: 352–405).

The latest of these three works, namely the letter to Augustus, in recent decades has received the least attention. It may have been the last poem that Horace wrote. The following samples will demonstrate just how far opinions about the meaning and intention of this piece can differ. In his commentary on the *Ars Poetica*, A. Rostagni tried to see the letter to Augustus as a belated defence of the *Ars Poetica*. According to Rostagni, the letter's main thoughts, its basic opinions about old and new poetry, and its artistic rules were the same as before; but Horace had by now undertaken to justify these maxims, and to demonstrate that they served a patriotic goal, and that they were suitable for lifting Latin poetry up to the level of Greek masterpieces.[2] O. Immisch sees Horace responding to the literary programme of the emperor, especially to his efforts to support stagecraft. And, in this respect, he naturally has Horace deliver a prognosis that is less than favourable.[3] Villeneuve approves of the idea, but he goes even farther by posing the question of whether the letter to Augustus was not actually a eulogy of the craft of those poets whose rise he had celebrated near the end of his first book of satires.[4] R. Heinze is more cautious when he judges that the letter was 'a quasi-report that Horace dispatched to the *princeps* about the actual state of poetry as its appointed advocate. He does not point out poetry's achievements, but problems that need to be dealt with, and that can only be overcome if insightful judges take charge, especially Augustus himself.'[5] Finally, W. Wili recently called the letter a bible of literature for its time, asserting elsewhere that it was the Romans' most important attempt 'in its day to sever the bonds between ruler and poet, between visual and auditory art'.[6]

In its design and structure, the *Ars* is rather more difficult to understand. In this respect the poem has much in common with many other works of the period. Since Scaliger's Tibullus edition of 1577, editors and critics have consistently missed the overall plan of these poems and, depending on time and character, they have summarily broken the received whole into its parts, and rebuilt it according to a plan that

[2] Rostagni (1930: xviiff.); quote by Villeneuve (1934: 145).
[3] Immisch (1932: 143f.).
[4] Villeneuve (1934, 146).
[5] Kiessling-Heinze (1957: 198).
[6] Wili (1948: 264, 310).

makes sense. In some cases they deleted problems, and in others they did not clear the chaos, rather they explained it according to the formula of Homeric criticism as arising from the compositional process. And thus they broke the poems into their historical components. Even in 1869, no less than O. Ribbeck himself would try his hand at healing the epistle to Augustus according to Scaliger's method.[7] After line 101 he inserted lines 73–85 from the *Ars Poetica*, then he continued with line 102 of our poem, following that with lines 32–3, then lines 108ff. But he rejected lines 114–17, instead postulating that several lines had been squeezed out by them. He then tacked on lines 118–24, then adding lines 391–407 from the *Ars Poetica*. From that point on he let the epistle to Augustus continue undisturbed, save at lines 260–3, which he erased as a 'gush of stammered words'.[8]

Soon after, in 1871, J. Vahlen challenged this violent practice. With calm understanding, and with no particular theory to prove, he proceeded through the poem by taking it in sections, one block at a time. His treatises are arguably the best written on the poem.[9] Nearly as good is R. Heinze's commentary from 1914, with his introduction on the epistle to Augustus surpassing even Vahlen. While Vahlen had observed connections only of a narrowly circumscribed kind, Heinze began taking into account the relationship between larger parts. Since Heinze's commentary, nothing new of real significance has emerged.

The general question about the formal art of Roman poems of the classical period has come up again recently in a book by E. Howald on the nature of Latin poetry.[10] He denies that these works share a homogenous artistic form, or a uniform arrangement. He rather has them consist of individually worked 'blocks', so to speak, parts that are interchangeable and actually juxtaposed rather than integrally related to one another. And indeed, as long as one recognizes 'composition' only in an arrangement that derives by analysis from an over-arching concept, one must reach the same conclusion. For a long time now I have attempted to show that the structure of these creations is considerably less simple, but at the same time quite exact

---

[7] Ribbeck (1869); taken up by Vahlen (1871).
[8] See Vahlen (1871: 490).
[9] Klingner (1964: 411 n. 6).
[10] Howald (1948).

and identifiable, and that an art, subsequently lost, of combining spontaneity and calculation was at work in them. This art still needs to be rediscovered. It is in this sense that the attempt presented here aims to enlarge upon two earlier works where I treated the letters to Florus and to the Pisones.[11]

Leaving aside the introductory lines 1–4 and 5–17, which excuse the poet and praise the emperor, the following topics lend themselves to being picked up at first glance by readers who want to know only what the letter is about. I quote Schanz–Hosius: 'thus disparaging the tendency to admire the old poets at the expense of the new ones, he touches on his age's poetic fever, but not without pointing out the positive side of the disease; he laments the ruin of dramatic art... and finally he recommends that the emperor cultivate the writing of poetry as the best means of heralding great deeds.'[12] One is right to think that these topics could have been more lucidly and consistently developed, and that they could have been put in a clearer relationship to one another. Especially in the lines that deal with archaism and dilettantism, the poem's pieces are shoved together, and the reader recognizes neither their point nor their message. With certain verse groups, such as lines 93–102 and 139–44, one cannot be certain whether they adhere to what precedes or to what follows.

Here, as Heinze clearly saw, the notion of *sermo* as relaxed conversation comes into its own. But the art of conversation that operates here is one that modern readers find hard to grasp, and that they treat with a sense of stunned inner regard. Its culture is one of complete discretion; a discretion that prefers allusions and playful pretence to direct statements.

Both the letter to Florus (2.2) and the letter to the Pisones begin in a 'Socratic' mode. The letter to Augustus has a fairly oblique beginning as well. But is it Socratic? For a conversation with Augustus, that is hardly what we would expect. A completely different beginning is needed. Horace chose to begin with an apology, and from there things follow as if on their own: the letter-writer steals time from the emperor, consumed as he is with heavy and important duties.

---

[11] Klingner (1964: 321–4; 352–405). On the *Ars poetica*, see in particular Steidle (1939).

[12] Schanz and Hosius (1935: 132).

The term 'duties' leads into a wider-ranging discussion of the fortunes that befall the benefactors of mankind: until they die, they are pursued by envy. Despite appearances, this does not lead into a compassionate lament for the hard lot of Augustus, who has already been exalted by being named among the εὐεργέται who share in divine honours. Rather, the apology foregrounds verses that deliver a different message, telling Augustus that he enjoys in life honours that others held only in death.

After the apology, grateful words are addressed to the busy and distressed emperor. The style reaches very high, and what is said is, at first, self-sufficient. A denouement is felt. What will come next?

The lines praising Augustus describe a state of happy fulfilment, such as had never before been seen on earth. Diffused throughout the passage are notions of time's fulfilment, and of an all-embracing concord.

At this point another thought arises to move the argument along, but it is hardly what the lines preceding have led us to expect: the happy state of affairs under Augustus, free from the usual jealousies, and the capacity for correct assessment that comes with Augustus' fulfilled age, are now missing in all other respects (18–22):

> Sed tuus hic populus sapiens et iustus in uno
> te nostris ducibus, Caesar, anteferendo,
> cetera nequaquam simili ratione modoque
> aestimat et, nisi quae terris semota suisque
> temporibus defuncta videt, *fastidit et odit.*

All that is current is despised. Since people now completely favour the past (*fautor veterum*, 23), there is a failure to connect with the present. Given what was said previously about time's fulfilment, the princeps-addressee has little choice but to take sides with the speaker. In fact, reading between the lines, he is indirectly implicated: *tua, Caesar, aetas.*

An example follows to help us sort out the public's failure to relate to the present: *sic fautor veterum, ut duodecim tabulas, foedera antiqua et similia*

> dictitet Albano Musas in monte locutas.

As mentioned above, this is, first of all, just an example. And it certainly derives from the terrain of literature. That it is a caricature is proven by the language, the hyperbolic manner of expression, and the parting representation in burlesque of Rome's staid and honourable old lawgivers as new Hesiods on the Muses' mountain home. An outburst of surprised laughter necessarily follows to confirm that an understanding is shared.

With this, the conversation has made a sudden turn. It has become a debate about literature, arguing in favour of the arts of the present day. By means of the previous lines, these arts have been tacitly connected to the idea of time's fulfilment under Augustus. Opposing the contemporary arts are the *fautores veterum*.

The debate begins with dialectical banter, a show of shadow-boxing. The speaker handles his materials deftly and with cheek, twisting his evidence in ways that, given the age of the debate, were probably not new. In lines 28–30 we find an analogy with Greek literary history, and the problematic idea of 'the ancients'. The former is treated in an off-hand manner, in lines that are largely characterized by everyday comparisons and a colloquial style (asyndetic, short elements, and paratactic main clauses instead of subordinate *si*-clauses). The second argument has the well-known form of the 'pile-analogy' or *sorites* paradox. It unfolds as a Socratic dialogue of about ten lines, playful throughout, and featuring a comical parting image (47):

> dum cadat elusus ratione ruentis acervi

This is capped off by a pair of absurdities: the calendar as the benchmark of worth, and the funeral as its source!

It is on this note that the dialectical banter of lines 28–49 concludes, as the notion of the *fautor veterum* with which we began has at last returned in a comical, grotesque form (49):

> miraturque nihil nisi quod Libitina sacravit.

These words cast a certain light on the ancient poets, who are now named in succession, each with his own title of honour that makes it difficult for us to take them seriously. The titles are stale and quaint, their routine use both harmless and funny. Ennius is called *sapiens et fortis* (50), exactly as the elder Scipio (Barbatus, consul in 298) on the oldest of the Scipionic inscriptions.[13] He is a 'second Homer' (*alter*

---

[13] CIL I² 7. 2 *fortis vir sapiensque.*

Homerus), and as such he can feel secure enough in his critics' attitude to be unconcerned about what may come of his splendid Pythagorean dream.[14] Referred to here is the contrivance at the beginning of the *Annales*, where the poet claims: 'I am Homer in a new body'—surely a bit thick in Horace's opinion. Naevius is an author almost modern: an idea just as thick. Then other authors appear in the popular form known as *syncrisis*, as criticism's highest titles and comparisons are generously distributed among the old masters of the previous century. These are the poets Rome recognizes right now as her own. The imbalance is emphasized by the expression *Roma potens* (61), referring to a Rome that now stands on a higher plane than it stood before, the Rome of Augustus! *Ad nostrum tempus* (62): as if everything stopped with the second century, and 'our' time has no relevance!

With the words *ad nostrum tempus* we catch a glimpse of the poet's perspective. We think back to the introduction, where the Augustan age is treated as a time of fulfilment and happiness, but the right of the present is not immediately advocated.

The fight against his opponents here differs from what it was before, shifting from the tones of dialectic to mime. The grand poets of antiquity, and those who paved the way for them, are loaded with their full, comic weight, most noticeable in the mocking line: *ad nostrum tempus Livi scriptoris ab aevo*. Comical and hyperbolic, the argument here scrapes the barrel's bottom: as if only Livius Andronicus

---

[14] R. Heinze has connected the lines that talk about Ennius (50–2) with those that follow concerning Naevius (53–4). As follows: Ennius claims to be a new Homer. But the claim is, in fact, faulty. For Naevius is still in the hands of the audience. 'If Ennius' poem succeeded in bringing his vision's promises to fulfilment, he would have to play Homer's role in Roman literature. That is, he would be its archegete, and his predecessors could all be forgotten. But is it not Naevius, scorned by Ennius, who is in everyone's hands and on everyone's mind?' Horace's words do not support the idea that his verses on Ennius concern the status of Homer and Ennius as archegetes, and hence, indirectly, the displacing of predecessors. And the context demands something different. Holding lines 50–62 together is the concept of a nonsensical 'amazement' (*mirari*) towards the old poets. Pertaining to this are the ridiculous titles of honour they are assigned (*Ennius, et sapiens et fortis et alter Homerus*), and the sloppy thoughtlessness of the critics who feel so confident in their vulgar judgements. On such terms as these, Ennius can feel confident as well. No one calls his boasts, spoken in such full, round tones, into question. People still read even his predecessor, Naevius. This was rightly seen already by Vahlen (1871: 467).

still needed to be mentioned! The verse moreover draws this section of the letter to its famous close, and offers a place to pause.

From line 63 on the tone becomes quite different. Up to this point the poet's only opponents have been the *fautores veterum*. The downside of blind enthusiasm came briefly into sight already at the beginning of this section (21ff.): *nisi... suis... temporibus defuncta... fastidit et odit.* There the problem of despising the merits of one's own time arose in another sphere, regarding human merit generally, and especially the great public benefactors. The problem was raised but not pursued. But now we approach the matter again, and enthusiasm for the old poets turns polemical. Horace, moreover, takes the issue farther, and his argument grows more serious and more detailed.

But here, just as he prepares to launch a more vigorous attack, he becomes tolerant and polite: *Interdum volgus rectum videt* (63). Whereas the error is captured in a single word (65 *errat*), the imagined consensus is embraced by ample verbal expression (*et sapit et mecum facit et Iove iudicat aequo,* 68).[15] The conciliatory tone continues in 69–70: *non equidem insector delendave carmina Livi esse reor,* as if to say 'I am not as nasty as I appear to be.' Here, of course, the irony is obvious: it is his piety towards his old teacher that causes him to be so conciliatory. Those old texts are thereby shifted into the terrain of an unhappy school-life. Amid these ironic and pleasant turns, the poet himself has secretly entered the scene: *mecum facit* (68), *non equidem insector delendave... reor* (69ff.). In what follows he takes a still more active role: *miror* (72), and even: *indignor* (76). By now he is beyond having fun. His attitude borders on rage.

The polemical harshness of both sides reaches its climax in lines 88–9: *ingeniis non ille favet plauditque sepultis, nostra sed inpugnat, nos nostraque lividus odit.* An alleged love for the old masters is unmasked as ill-will towards contemporary poetry.

In retrospect one can see with what superior skill the argument has been conducted. The hatred against all things new is set out in the beginning, right after the praise for Augustus, but as yet without any reference to the poet: (21f.) *nisi quae terris semota suisque temporibus*

---

[15] Heinze is without justification in taking v. 68 *Iove iudicat aequo* as a reference to the judgement of Augustus.

defuncta videt, fastidit et odit. But then the core of the problem is set aside, the better side of the public's hostile demeanour is pointed out, and their preference for the old authors is examined as neutrally as possible. This examination leads imperceptibly to a more serious clash. Up till now the people have been referred to as *fautor veterum* (23), adhering to the literary credo *antiquissima quaeque... optima* (28f.). The poet's opponents are said 'to admire nothing that hasn't been hallowed by Libitina' (*miratur... nihil nisi quod Libitina sacravit,* 49). But now, when the same motif and words arise again with *veteres ita miratur* (64), the downside of such admiration becomes obvious: *ut nihil anteferat, nihil illis conparet* (65). In other words, they are hostile towards anyone who dares to hold a different opinion. Meanwhile, as things turn serious, Horace's own critical standards come into view. Gradually his opponents are unmasked. In the end, all that is left of them is their sheer malevolence against contemporary art, a malevolence that is just one part of a general malevolence against modern-day achievements, from which only Augustus has been spared. Thus, the goal foreshadowed in the beginning by *fastidit et odit* (22) has been reached. But we now know where that malevolence is directed, and that it takes aim at the speaker in a very personal way: *nostra sed inpugnat, nos nostraque lividus odit* (89).

What exactly happens in this more serious clash? As mentioned above, the speaker comes out with his own standards, and he says what bothers him about the old poets: outmoded vocabulary, too many constructions that are jarring and loose. These are objective criticisms of artistic failings. His opponents, on the other hand, are not objective. For them, individual lines and expressions that are well-turned are enough to recommend the complete work. They do not reproach a work for its artistic mistakes, for example, because of a crude style (76 *crasse*) or a lack of witty and cheerful refinement (77 *inlepide*)—and here the reader recognizes Horace's own artistic ideal. They criticize it because it has been written recently. Objective criticism they reject as impertinent, and for their authorities they appeal to the great stage actors of the Sullan era, Aesop and Roscius. They become agitated and rude (80). And the reason for this demeanour? They are mentally lazy, comfortable with the caprice of false authority. They make no room for new things because they are stubborn. The crowd's caprice is unmasked completely when they take refuge in

absurdities and praise the *Salian Hymn*, a laughable affectation that
demonstrates not a love for ancient poets, about whom they are
completely ignorant, but jealousy and hatred towards all that is
new and 'ours'. That is what this is all about, says Horace, in language
that is uncharacteristically vehement.

At this point the tension in the argument decreases, with the final
verse contributing the catchphrase 'hatred of the new' (*novitatis invi-
dia*). Were the Greeks to have allowed the same to happen in their day,
Horace continues, such literature as is generally approved and read
today, what we would call 'the classics', would not exist. Here the
poem seems to return to the dialectical cross-examination that we
observed before. Looking to the Greeks becomes an instrument of
insight, just as before in verse 28, where Greek literature was used as
an example. It is as if this were, by now, enough to refute the hatred of
contemporary art, having exposed that hatred as, at heart, a bias
favouring the ancient poets. And meanwhile it shows that here we are
exiting the circle that closes by bringing us back to the issue of malevolent hatred. Where we are headed next is not easy to recognize. The fight
against the ancient poets' advocates is pursued no further, and the fight
against their hatred of all things current is dropped as well. Mention of
the Greeks turns out to be a transition. That their mention certainly
entails more, and that it touches upon crucial matters as yet unspoken,
will be made clear in due course.

At first it looks as if we will be treated to a simple description of how
classical literature developed, long ago, in Greece, and how it was
enabled and encouraged by a boundless readiness to be open to new
things. But in fact the speaker-rogue[16] has switched roles, to that of an
honest old Roman who grumpily describes how the blossoming of the
arts among the *Graeculi* and their readiness to accept new things looks
in his eyes: once they stopped waging war among themselves, they
took up puerilities, every second something new (102):

> hoc paces habuere bonae ventique secundi;

This is what comes of peace and prosperity! *Positis nugari Graecia bellis
coepit et in vitium fortuna labier aequa* (93f.). This approximates a well-
known, dour idea that the common crowd necessarily degenerates if

---

16 See Vahlen (1871: 475, 506).

they are not kept under tight constraint. They adore playing silly games (*nugari*), sinking into vice (*in vitium labi*). Fans of the *fabri*,[17] workers in marble, ivory or bronze, they jump from one thing to the next like children, or even a little girl. Such are the speaker's emphatic means of characterizing the scene.

Under the guise of an honest old gentleman, Horace contrasts the nugatory play of the *Graeculi* with a serious, Roman way of life, completely old-fashioned, serious and unmusical (103–7):

> Romae dulce diu fuit et sollemne reclusa
> mane domo vigilare, clienti promere iura,
> cautos nominibus rectis expendere nummos,
> maiores audire, minori dicere, per quae
> crescere res posset, minui damnosa libido.

This, he says, is the way it was for a long time: *dulce diu fuit et sollemne*.

What is his point? Is it that such a style of life kept poetry and all manner of twaddle from developing—in which case one would have to regard ironically Horace's own grudge against these backwater cultural habits?[18] No. Instead he has his good old Roman realize, with astonished disapproval, that similar circumstances have now actually broken out in Rome, in a popular craze for poetry.[19] The poet's own return to lyric—what we find collected in the fourth book of the *Odes*—is presented to Augustus as a part of this mild epidemic madness (111–13). In the end, the indignant Roman, whose role Horace adopts, is completely justified in being upset about the city's clueless dilettantes.

Barely has Horace let out the keywords *novitas invisa* in line 90, when he changes cheekily into the role of someone who condemns the current age—and we need to keep in mind that this is the age of Augustus. He describes the current blossoming of the poetic arts from the standpoint of a conservative gatekeeper. He is not the type to excuse himself for preferring ancient poetry, but an even grimmer old-Roman. He has little-to-no use for poetry, just as Cato the Censor. It is as if Horace was thinking of the old censor's words:

---

[17] The humble word is chosen on purpose; see Klingner (1964: 358 n. 2).
[18] *Ars* 323–32.
[19] *Carmen de Moribus* fr.2 (p. 83 Jordan).

'Poetry was not held in high esteem. If someone had to do with it or went to banquets or orgies, he was called a dawdler.'[20] Where else does one find feasting and writing poetry joined so tightly to living a frivolous life?

Having had a laugh at this fine mess, Horace leads Augustus forward, step by step, still jesting at first, to the observation that poets are a special, and not completely scornful case (118–19):

> Hic error tamen et levis haec insania quantas
> virtutes habeat, sic collige.

His statements are, at first, modestly negative: *vatis avarus | non temere est animus* (119–20). Then positive propositions follow: after all, the poet does no one any harm. He is frugal, even useful, perhaps not in war, but certainly in peace—that is, if one deems poetry, for all its triviality, relevant to matters of true importance. Its usefulness is narrowly limited at first: it begins in the schoolroom, where it is with poetry that children are taught language, proper language. Then the thought becomes gradually more elevated: the poet's teachings have a moralizing effect on the mind. And, in the end, poets give voice and form to pious prayers, by means of which—as recently in the Secular Games—choruses invoke the help of the gods (138):

> carmine di superi placantur, carmine Manes.

But to what end all these ironic jests? First off, and in the most general of terms, these ironies exist for their own sake. For here, in the poet's darting about his topic, in his shifting of registers of tone from playful to serious, we have characteristics that let us feel, like nothing else, the free-wheeling disposition of Horatian *Sermo*. This is the life-blood of Horace's satires and epistles. But something else is at work as well, something belonging to the subtleties of such social politesse.

In Plato, when the conversation approaches a subject that is especially dear to his heart, Socrates happily dodges into play, doing

---

[20] Vahlen (1871: 480), and Heinze ad 102, have made it highly likely that Lachmann was right, and that v. 101 must have originally come after 107. The question in 101 *quid placet aut odio est, quod non mutabile credas?* is consistent with astonished questions elsewhere: *Carm.* 1.29.10ff. *quis neget arduis pronos relabi posse rivos... cum tu... libros... mutare loricis... tendis?* Verg. *Ecl.* 8.26f. *Mopso Nysa datur: quid non speremus amantes? iungentur iam grypes equis...* [v. 101 is probably apocryphal].

so with particular rogueishness. This deserves further consideration, for something similar seems to be happening here in Horace. Of the phoney advocates of the ancient poets he said: *nos nostraque lividus odit* (89). Just before that, in lines 63–89, he had become more forthcoming with his own person, his art, and his own standards of judgement. Then, midway in the next section, with good-natured irony, he reckons his own relapse into lyric as part of the craze for new poetry (111 *ipse ego...*). He ends by reminding us of the choirs at religious festivals, all but naming his *Carmen Saeculare*. Here, then, the poet's own art is more present than elsewhere in the epistle. It would be pushy for him to proceed directly, so he sidesteps into jest, again here more than anywhere else in the poem. Whoever takes his point—and he obviously assumes that Augustus will—understands that his discussion of contemporary poetry in the end concerns his own *Carmen Saeculare* and his late lyric. Thus here, under a cover of irony that the poet wields against himself, things turn quite serious, perhaps more serious than anywhere else in the poem.

But ahead of this development we have lines 90–2:

> quod si tam Graecis novitas invisa fuisset
> quam nobis, quid nunc esset vetus? Aut quid haberet
> quod legeret tereretque viritim publicus usus?

It was said above that these lines seem to mark the beginning of a battle against malevolent attitudes that now stand exposed, and against a hatred that would suppress Horace's own contemporary art. It was further suggested that we expect him to launch into a dialectical back-and-forth, as he did before in the fight against the craze for ancient poets, telling us, in sum, that the ancient poets had once been modern, too. And since that fight is apparently not pursued, the conversational shift that we encounter in these lines has the look of a transitional motif. But if, in what follows, it is the poet's own art, a matter that concerns him directly, that stirs his stylized attack against a backwater primitivism in Rome, as well as his own jesting self-defence; if a connection is made between his own concerns and those of Augustus; if, behind an ironic façade, the seriousness of the preceding lines (63–89) continues apace, or is perhaps even increased, so that the theme that was touched on in the praise of Augustus, concerning the jealous hatred of the merits of

Horace's own age, is still active, one should see in the lines that set the open-mindedness of the classical Greeks against the nasty intransigence of the Romans an allusion to an unspoken thought, and one should perhaps pursue this thought to its conclusion: perhaps, Horace might have said, were he to allow himself to express such a thought, perhaps there is something from our own day that deserves to be valued as highly as those old Greek poets, whom we all read. Our stubborn bourgeois are straining to suppress the glory of our own age.

If such a thought stands behind his words, as the context suggests, and even demands, Horace wins his point. And if he wants his words to clear a path for the kind of art that he himself subscribes to, he has succeeded. Subsequent generations were raised no longer on Ennius, but on Vergil.

The passage just analysed (93–138) is the most difficult part of the epistle. It concerns the craze for innovation among the Greeks, their passion for art, and Rome's staying put in an old and uninspired style of life. It also treats a recent turn of events in Rome, and the current, widespread craze for poetry among Romans. And finally, it concerns the value of the poetic arts. Thus, to summarize even more tightly, these lines, which are only loosely connected to what precedes (as I will show in a moment), contain a humorous attack against contemporary poetry followed by its serio-comic defence. Ernst Hohl might well have described this as one of the 'blocks' out of which, according to his theory, Roman poets of the age assembled their poems. Something similar had already been suggested by O. Immisch, when he explained the structure and progression of the *Ars Poetica* as a matter of individual 'eclogues' (his expression) set in succession. But this is hardly the case to be made for the lines considered here. First of all, one cannot be sure whether the individual verse-groups, even as designated ('the history of the Greek arts', or 'the history of the persistence and collapse of Roman discipline and order', and so on) are not 'blocks' unto themselves, connected one to the next in ways that are not at all clear. Moreover, given what our analysis has turned up so far, we would be right to resist this idea on the grounds that, although the attack against the current scene of poetry, as well as poetry's defence, have a loose formal connection to what precedes, they are deliberately set out in such a way that, in fact,

the relationship is not forced upon the reader; so that all that went
before is wrapped up within them, in the notion of *inuidia* that dogs
not Augustus but the poetry of his age, and in the concept of that
poetry's belonging to the age of Augustus. Here as elsewhere in the
works of this poet, inherent in transitions that seem random is an
inner unity: spontaneity is guided by a hidden artistic design. The
listener (or reader) he strings along in a series of playful turns, never
letting him see where his promptings will take him, keeping him
primed for the pleasures of surprise. Such an art belongs certainly to
the most advanced culture of conversation.

Associative connections, apparently random transitions, stringing
the audience along: these all can be found in the lines that follow as
well (139ff.). But first, to finish his defence of the poet and his art, he
adds a broad conclusion that encompasses the heavens and the
underworld:

> carmine di superi placantur, carmine Manes

Here our thoughts rise from trifles to matters of highest import, in a
sentence that is both meaningful on its own, and more than just one
last link in a chain of evidence: it can be prised free of its connections
to the preceding apology and give rise to a new chain of thoughts.
And, in fact, it is with this sentence that the poem's momentum shifts
in another direction. *Carmine di superi placantur, carmine Manes.*
First of all, this exemplifies a general truth, or it at least gives the
appearance of doing so. For we are subsequently told in lines 139–44
how in ancient times farmers used to placate their country gods with
festivals after the harvest (*Tellurem porco, Silvanum lacte piabant,*
143): poems, too, were employed (145ff.). But we are now in a new
context. In fact, the issue now concerns the origins of drama; more
precisely, of comedy. The history of comedy is described along the
lines of a well-known pattern that I need not discuss here. Hardly is
the history here for its own sake. Primarily it sets us on towards what
follows. It says that the exuberant and frolicksome ridicule of Rome's
Ur-comedy, the Fescennine Verses, had its origin in those rustic
festivals. This freedom later got out of hand, and those affected
or threatened by verbal assault (ὀνομαστὶ κωμωδεῖν) officially
banned it. Once *malum carmen* and *maledicere* within poetry were
forbidden, when verbal assault was regarded as taboo, people were

forced by fear of an ancient and gruesome death penalty to switch to 'blessing' (*bene dicere, bene dicere*) and 'delighting' (*delectare*).[21]

I think there can be no doubt that here Horace plays with the double meanings of *malum carmen/bonum carmen, maledicere/bene dicere*, just as he did in the closing lines of *S. 2.1*. There, when the satirist is warned by the jurisconsult, who draws his attention to a purported law from the Twelve Tables legislating against *malum carmen* ('disparaging song'/'bad poetry'), he responds with: 'yes, that may well be the case, but my own poems are not *mala* but *bona*.' With that joke, the legal case dissolves into laughter. Thus, in the turn towards polite speech in line 155 (*ad bene dicendum*), there is also a first step towards the artistic refinement that follows those crude beginnings. A further step in this direction can be found in lines 156–7:

> Graecia capta ferum victorem cepit et artis
> intulit agresti Latio.

In the depiction of the process that follows, the coarse and rustic character of the ancient Italians is underscored in ever more drastic terms (157–9):

> sic horridus ille
> defluxit numerus Saturnius et grave virus
> munditiae pepulere.

Grave virus is the stinging and pungent sweat of a unkempt person. One recalls from the *Ars Poetica* (297ff.) how the figure of an unkempt man who refuses to shave or cut his nails is used to describe someone who despises *ars* (τέχνη), i.e. cultivated art. One should not be surprised to find the same metaphorical language here, for the topic concerns *ars* and the lack of *ars*. And, indeed, in the lines that follow it becomes clear why the past situation is envisioned as so vividly present, even when the progress towards refinement is described as something that began in the peasant festivals of a distant past. Horace does not intend to talk about the history of culture or

---

[21] With this, a poorly understood law of the Twelve Tables has been connected to the demise of Old Comedy in Athens and, in any event, to the famous troubles that Naevius experienced in Rome because of the barbed and mocking passages of his comedies, and other mocking poems. See Beckmann (1923: 64ff.).

theatre (159–60): *in longum tamen aevum | manserunt hodieque manent vestigia ruris* (∼ *rusticitatis*). This is why he has gone so far back in time, and the topic of the next line takes up from there: Greek art has indeed been influential, but it was late in arriving. Along with tragedy came a disposition for the sublime and forceful, for tragic *animus* and daring. But because there was no understanding of the dignity of the artist's own toil, much remains to be done. What is lacking is not the poet's inborn power and disposition (*natura*, φύσις), but his technical ability (*ars*, τέχνη). These skills are just as lacking for Roman tragedy as they were for comedy. Plautus serves to exemplify how much Italian popular burlesque still inheres in Roman comedy, how little heed it pays to the rules of modesty, and how sloppy its verses are. Here avarice is the evil that blocks the development of an authentic art (170–6).

The unfinished journey of Roman stagecraft; the lingering residue of a pre-artistic state; the grave defect of Roman poetry, in its failure to perceive the majesty of hard effort, and of skills that are carefully controlled: these have emerged as the central themes of lines 139 (*agricolae prisci...*) to 176 (*securus, cadat an recto stet fabula talo*). Although a history was laid out, the whole of it was aiming towards a present where the evils exposed have yet to be exorcized.

The letter's subsequent progression shows that there is nothing random about the poet's choosing stagecraft to exemplify all other genres. For what follows is a satire on the current state of the theatre in Rome, with specific reference to viewers, and to the way public plays are produced to suit popular tastes.

Immisch would probably call this a new 'Ekloge', and Howald a new, loosely added 'Block', drawing attention to its abrupt beginning (177–80):

> Quem tulit ad scaenam ventoso Gloria curru,
> exanimat lentus spectator, sedulus inflat:
> sic leve, sic parvum est, animum quod laudis avarum
> subruit aut reficit.

Along these same lines, one could also maintain that the satire on the contemporary theatre is only tangentially related to the technical deficiencies of Roman dramatic works. But, in truth, the beginning does not come entirely out of the blue, for Horace had just named

avarice as the reason why, in Plautus' case, comedy failed to develop
into a true form of art in Rome (175–6):

> Gestit enim nummum in loculos demittere, post hoc
> securus, cadat an recto stet fabula talo.

So it is when *avaritia* impels a man to write for the stage. His
counterpart we have in the *laudis auarum* of line 179. One might
have thought that things would improve once the evil's cause should
fall away. But no. Once one becomes dependent on the spectator, all
is lost. The masses hold sway, and they prefer animal fights and
boxers to poetry. The affluent and educated, whom one might
otherwise trust, are not much better. Even they do not seek the
work of poets, but empty pageantry. Drama amounts to theatrical
revue. What follows is a fairly nasty satire on the vacuous pomp of
the theatre, and on the dull, gaping people in the stands, and the
noise that drowns out every word. The jesting scene sublimates a
deep-seated hatred of such mass events.

One cannot therefore claim that these lines about the contemporary theatre have only a tangential connection to those concerning the
deficiencies of Roman dramatic works. Thoughts about why works of
genuine art could not develop in the Roman theatre lead straight on
to thoughts about why they are so hard to find in general.
Consequently, one has to acknowledge that there is an inner cohesion
to all the lines that treat issues of dramatic poetry (139–213). In the
end, the picture Horace paints of this branch of poetry is hardly
favourable, so he defends himself against the charge of malevolence
by tendering praise to the poets of drama. This is praise that, in truth,
only confirms what he said before. For lauded here are the powers of
enchantment that belong to dramatists who are poets, and these are
the very artists whom the theatre business prevents from emerging.

In what follows next we turn from questionable stagecraft to the
art of those poets who prefer to be read rather than to 'put up with an
insolent spectator's foul mood'. Obviously, towards this branch of art
Horace is as resolutely sympathetic as he is grudging towards the
theatre. But he makes the opposite assumption regarding his addressee. Right after he praises the genuine poet of drama, he begins
(214ff.): 'But please, spare some small concern for those who prefer
to entrust themselves to readers.' There follows a concession, as if to

someone resisting slightly, when for ten lines it is admitted that taking care of these people is an annoying task. They make it hard for one to care. They are obtrusive, thin-skinned, tactless in reciting aloud, and prone to whine that no one understands the finer details of their art. Lastly, they are ridiculously demanding. All of this is true, Horace says, and again he good-naturedly includes himself. Nevertheless, he says, it is good to take care of them—and here one can see how aware he is of his own situation, in the way he must kindly coax his addressee, the emperor: these poets are, one might say, the temple guardians of the emperor's majestic virtue. It is through their work that moral virtue and inner strength become visible, as through facial expressions portrayed on statues of bronze. And it is crucial that the emperor's sublimity not be entrusted to an unworthy poet. With a bad poem, the ink rubs off, blurring the splendour of praiseworthy deeds.

Along the by-way of lines 232–44 this word of warning turns into a point of pride for Augustus. That happens by way of a flattering and detailed counter-image: Alexander the Great certainly knew how to find the greatest painters and sculptors, and these were the only ones he would allow to portray him. But, possessing no critical judgement of poetry, he entrusted himself entirely to a single poet, Choerilus. Augustus can be glad, then, because he knows full well that his own judgement was right, and his inner-self well represented, in the works of Vergil and Varius.

The epistle to Augustus could have ended here. It began by noting a lack of balance in the assessment of Augustus and the poetry of his age. This issue, as troublesome, difficult, and lamentable as it is, the letter handles with a certain seriousness, but also with cheer, as a 'conversation' in letter form demands. Now, in ending the letter, Horace has us think back to a precious and happy rapport between Augustus and the poetry of his age, to a relationship that was honourable, and that guaranteed him eternal renown. Thereby, Augustus is ranked with Alexander, just as in the beginning he was ranked with the great, divinized benefactors: Romulus, Bacchus, Castor, Pollux, and Hercules. One can see how beginning and ending are falling into place.

But Horace does not stop here. Deploying a Pindaric idea, he casts the emperor and the poetic arts as relying on one another. This lets

Augustus claim to have achieved something difficult and valuable that even Alexander could not achieve: namely, despite being raised so high above everyone else, as he was at the beginning of the epistle, Augustus has managed to have his true essence suitably portrayed in works of poetry. This thought touches the outer limit of what a *sermo* can contain; Horace cannot end it here. For every time he rises a little higher within the genre, he studiously calls himself back to the level of a cheerful and well-mannered conversation. Above all else, he takes pains not to end on a difficult or pretentious note. Most times he ends with a joke. His three large literary letters all follow that rule. Here, in the letter to Augustus, the funny turn at the end stems, almost by necessity, from the deeply serious thought that precedes: Vergil and Varius are named as the artists who represented Augustus' inner-character to the world. One then has to ask: 'But what about Horace?' And it is right here that we should expect the rogue's withdrawal. Through the conventional form of a polite refusal, Horace can now add the final strokes to the picture he began in the letter's opening lines, to his portrait of Augustus, summarizing in a few loftily styled lines the splendour and glory of his deeds, and the peace of his rule. That done, he can hole up and hide away behind his own inability, the thing that keeps him from getting involved himself, much as he would love to, in producing epic images of the emperor. Only now does this *recusatio* make a graceful turn, when Horace imagines what would happen if he were to allow himself to lapse, with every good intention, into impudence, and to approach the majesty of Augustus: the picture that precedes these lines is now undone, in a burlesque of the Pindaric ideal. The laughable lines of an affectionate but tactless 'praise-dispenser', he says, settle into the ears of readers and listeners more obstinately than do serious words. Contrasting the *expressi voltus per aenea signa* (248), such poetry resembles an unintentionally funny and cheap wax portrait of a commoner. Such a gift is an utter embarrassment to the one who receives it. In the end, both man and poem are sold off as so much scrap paper that will end up in the spice shop, along with all the other literary trash.

Just as things are becoming awkward for him, when he can no longer address the matter at hand in a serious way without becoming indiscreet, because he is himself implicated, Horace steps away with an ironic jest. One remembers the same technique from the middle of the poem. Again, what remains unspoken is no less important than what is articulated.

In retrospect, after its individual stages are understood, the letter's overall progression no longer appears as random and confused as it might well seem to the casual reader.

Augustus merits high esteem, but the poetry of his age does not. This is the idea that Horace took up in the beginning, putting Augustus and the contemporary arts in close association. Detractors vigorously disparage these arts, first disguised as fans of ancient poets, then with undisguised hostility. Horace has much to say to them, cloaking his words in irony, but still in a way that his addressee, Augustus, also sees himself drawn into the game. Especially at the end of the verses where Horace's *Carmen Saeculare* is indirectly referenced (132–8), Augustus will recognize that these words address him, and that they seriously concern his own work.

Once things have got that far, then it is in accordance with general taste and, I might add, with the taste of Augustus, to devote one's thoughts and care first and foremost to dramatic art, i.e. to the theatre.[22] The thoughts of the poem also seem to move in this direction. After a short delay, Horace's judgement gradually comes out: the dramatic arts in Rome have failed to pan out, and necessarily so. One should understand this judgement as deriving from a touchy moment in the epistle's situation, and one should not insist that certain works that Horace is likely to have appreciated, such as Varius' *Thyestes*, written and performed fifteen years earlier, or perhaps Ovid's *Medea*, be specifically and expressly excepted.

After brushing this aside, Horace directs his thoughts back to the genuine art of his day, and to its close relationship to Augustus.

---

[22] Vahlen (1871: 486) thinks that Horace, after rejecting the rights of the old poets and after pointing out the Romans' resentment against poetry out of principle, must now elaborate on the development of Roman poetry in order to point out the deficiencies of the old poets and 'the circumstances that were at work to keep them from reaching the perfection that is now applied to them willingly and without any justification'. This is contradicted by the fact that the subsequent verse-group talks only about drama, not about poetry in general, and hence it concerns the judgement of the Roman theatre. But one thing is certain: that the progression of thought goes some distance initially, namely up to the example of Plautus (170–6), into the terrain of performances implicated in the barbarism of the old times. In that respect the lines work backwards as well as forwards, as often happens in Horace.

One should think this a sensible and straightforward course for the poem: the first movement, ending in a noticeable fermata, goes to about the middle (138). In it, *inuidia* is countered by a defence of contemporary art. The second movement fills the poem's second half. Here poetry for reading is set against the theatre, and the period's true art confronts the 'half-art' of the stage.

Perhaps here, in the idea of half-art, we have the key term that leads beyond a recognition of this movement's structure to an insight into its unity of thought and attitude. Dramatic poetry is regarded as hazardous because it has not become, nor can it become, a genuine form of art in contemporary Rome. The entire history of the Roman theatre (139–65) is laid out solely to demonstrate how drama progressed towards art, but got stuck halfway, in the zone of half-art. The critique of Plautus (168–76) concerns his lack of art. The ridicule of the current theatrical scene (177–207) takes aim solely at the art-eschewing barbarity of its spectacles. On the other side is the poetry that should occupy Augustus' caring thoughts. Representing this kind of poetry are Varius and Vergil. Their art is characterized as genuine by contrast with that of Choerilus, Alexander's epic poet, and his *inculti versus et male nati* (233), and through the idea of Alexander's inability to judge artistic quality, at least regarding poetry (241–4).

Thus, in preferring poetry meant for reading to poetry performed on stage, Horace has no other concern than art. To him, what matters is not subject or attitude, but art itself. This explains his rejection of mass spectacles in the theatre as well. For in matters of art, he holds to the belief that all that is loud and overstuffed and crude is hostile to art. This is an essential element of his credo's Callimachean foundation.

In the first part of the poem the same belief is at work. Why is the preference for the old poets wrong? Is it because their works no longer offer an expression that is adequate to the current age? Is it because they give voice to ideals that are passé? No. It is because of their artistic deficiencies; because they have so much that is unruly and loose; because they offer only momentary flashes of beauty, in individual words and lines, while churning along with much that is lacklustre, muddy and formless. It comes down to this: nothing is to be fitted into the words and verse that is crude (76: *crasse*, one of the many echos of the Callimachean formula παχὺ γράμμα) or inelegant (77 *inlepide*). All of which agrees quite nicely with what Horace has

thought all along about the older arts in Rome, as in his critique of
his predecessor, Lucilius, at *S*.1.4.9–13:

> Nam fuit hoc vitiosus: in hora saepe ducentos
> ut magnum, versus dictabat stans pede uno;
> cum flueret lutulentus, erat quod tollere velles;
> garrulus atque piger scribendi ferre laborem,
> scribendi recte: nam ut multum, nil moror.

Link this assertion to like passages in the *Sermones, Epistulae,* and even
the *Ars Poetica*, and you have the makings of a unified theory of art. The
Callimachean foundation, as I have just called it, becomes obvious.[23]

It is this conviction about art that makes sense of Horace's demeanour towards Rome's ancient poets, and towards contemporary
art, in the letter to Augustus. He does not advocate the modern-day
arts because it is now his turn, and that of his fellow artists, to
demand their place in the sun, but because art has only now come
into its own; only now is a poem formally shaped not just here and
there, but as a complete structure from beginning to end. At issue
here are matters of art, not of persons. It is this very art, demanding
and majestic, that he defended against ignorance, unruliness, and
conceit in the letter to the Pisones. Ultimately, his mockery of
dilettantism in Rome (108–17) feeds on the same zeal for the rigours
of art, and perhaps no other passage in the letter to Augustus so
closely approximates the letter to the Pisones (*ars* 379–82).[24]

In the *Ars Poetica*, it is with arrogant dilettantes and would-
be poets that Horace has to deal as an advocate of true art. In
the letter to Augustus he deals sometimes with those who hate
poetry, especially contemporary poetry, and sometimes with fans of
the theatre which, in Rome, can never achieve the status of genuine
art. The dilettantes are treated only incidentally. But in both
poems the situation of the speaker is the same: as the advocate of
art's rigours and the toils of the artistic craft, he fancies himself
surrounded and harassed by creatures who are uninspired and hostile
to art. The relationship between the poet Horace and his Roman
environment is comparable to that of Callimachus and his

---

[23] See Klingner (1964: 432–55).
[24] See Klingner (1964: 392ff.).

adversaries with their βασκανίη: art that is genuine and pure is set off from surroundings that are malevolent and ignorantly antagonistic.

In both cases the poet is in agreement with a few select friends from the intellectual elite of Rome. Here it is Augustus who, as we know, has invited himself into this company as a partner in such a *sermo*. It is explicitly acknowledged that his ability to judge poetry rightly places him among the insightful and the initiated. And one has to deem Horace lucky in being able to trust that the first man of Rome had what it took to understand and enjoy the art of conversation, such as we have defined it. Without his partner's understanding smile, or a laugh that not only follows but gets the jump on the conversation's twists of thought and changes in tone, without a shared, advanced culture of conversation—even if this is restricted to a small circle— such structures cannot develop. And yet, one cannot help but wonder whether Augustus was capable of giving the advocate of pure art the full measure of approval that Horace subscribes to him. In one of its sections, at least, the epistle seems intent upon pulling Augustus away from his own amateur enthusiasms over to Horace's own side: there, where the poet reveals his resentments against Roman theatre.

But this last issue no longer pertains to the poem's intellectual unity, which, to summarize one last time, lies in a certain artistic mindset and intent, and in the relationship that these have to the world at large. Rather, the issue draws us into the poem's historical situation. We know from Suetonius' biography of Augustus that Augustus liked watching performances of all sorts: 'He made no secret of his being enthralled by a desire to watch, and he confessed it openly.' 'He surpassed all others in the frequency, variety and splendour of his spectacles.' The colourful details that Suetonius spreads across three chapters on this topic (43–5)[25] perfectly elucidate Horace's satire on the Roman theatre, and they inform his request that care be taken also for those who write for readers in order to fill the new Palatine library with masterpieces. Without putting undue emphasis on this contrast, one recognizes here that there is a slender limit to the accord between poet and emperor.

[25] There one can read about festivals where actors of all languages performed on various stages, about performances in the forum, in the amphitheatre, in the circus, in the *comitium*, in the campus Martius, and along the banks of the Tiber (Aug. 43.1). Obviously, set against these performances, the theatre as a site of dramatic art played

A final observation follows from this, concerning the relationship between the poem and its age. The poem begins as an argument against antiquated tastes, and then turns briefly to an apology for contemporary poetry. But upon closer inspection, it presents itself as the words of the last man standing from the past; words that are spoken not only in surroundings that are largely hostile to art, but amid poetry that, with Ovid, has already become alien to what is here defended as 'our' art. The young people around Tiberius, whom we encounter in the first book of letters, and who apparently regarded Horace as an authority, have, at any rate, produced nothing that will stand the test of time. But this is not to say that Horace, having become aware of these historical conditions, intends the letter as a eulogy lamenting the poetic profession to which he belonged. His request to Augustus speaks to his conviction that it might still be possible to keep working on the ground already gained. But, in truth, his letter remains the last utterance of great Augustan poetry.

the tiniest of roles. Augustus, in fact, had a preference for the recklessly crude jokes of the popular spectacles: *spectavit autem studiosissime pugiles et maxime Latinos, non legitimos atque ordinaritos modo, quos etiam committere cum Graecis solebat, sed et catervarios oppidanos, inter angustias vicorum pugnantis temere ac sine arte* (45.2). *Solebat etiam citra spectaculorum dies, sie quando quid invisitatum dignumque cognitu advectum esset, id extra ordinem quolibet loco publicare, ut rhinocerotem apud Saepta, tigrim in scaena, anguem quinquaginta cubitorum pro comitio* (43.4). *Quodam autem muneris die Parthorum obsides tunc primum missos per mediam arenam ad spectaculum induxit superque se subsellio secundo collocavit* (43.4). One imagines that this exotic pomp was visually spectacular. The emperor rewarded outstanding performances, and for contests he gave prizes in the Greek manner. He took a personal interest in persons who performed in spectacles of all sorts, exercising care and strict oversight (45). One easily becomes unsettled by reading this when mindful of those places in the epistle where this same carefree *Schaulust* is degraded (185–8):

> media inter carmina poscunt
> aut ursum aut pugiles; his nam plebecula gaudet.
> verum equitis quoque iam migravit ab aure voluptas
> omnis ad incertos oculos et gaudia vana.

Included among the outlandish displays derided by Horace are exotic animals, the giraffe and the white elephant. In short, his satiric description vividly elucidates what Suetonius will later report, without any reproach, about the lavishness of Augustan spectacles.

This is of course only one side of the coin. Elsewhere (89.3) Suetonius says: *ingenia saeculi sui omnibus modis fovit. recitantis et benigne et patienter audiit, nec tantum carmina et historias, sed et orationes et dialogos. componi tamen aliquid de se nisi et serio et a praestantissimis offendebatur admonebaturque praetores, ne paterentur nomen suum commissionibus obsolefieri.* This approximates what Horace touches on, in his own way, in lines 214–70.

15

Una cum scriptore meo: Poetry, Principate and the Traditions of Literary History in the Epistle to Augustus

Denis C. Feeney

On the first day of fighting at Philippi, the watchword and battlecry for the tyrannicides' army was the inspiring 'Libertas'.[1] It is probable, however, that the twenty-two year old Horace did not hear it—as if in anticipation of the confused failure to come, the tickets with the watchword were still being passed along to the officers when Brutus' legions spontaneously hurled themselves against the forces of Caesar opposite.[2] Returning to Rome after the eventual catastrophe of the Republican cause, Horace carried on his fumbled engagement with

A number of friends have assisted me in the writing of this essay. Pride of place goes to Tony Woodman, who has been as acute and penetrating a reader as ever. It is a pleasure to thank Kirk Freudenburg not only for his comments on this piece, but for many years' conversation about Horace, and for making it possible for me to read his illuminating forthcoming work. I thank also Alessandro Barchiesi, Joe Farrell, and Stephen Hinds for their generous correspondence. Finally, Michèle Lowrie gave me searching comments and helped me out of a big impasse at the end; her article Lowrie (2002) comes at many of the same issues from a different, Ciceronian, angle, and my essay should be read in tandem with hers. Warm thanks to audiences at Cambridge, London, Oxford and Victoria, BC, who heard various versions of these arguments. This essay is the working out of a paragraph in Feeney (1992), my first attempt at exploring the relationship between the politics of Augustan poets and the poetics of Augustus. There I commented on Horace's 'acute sensitivity to the transformations of *libertas* under the triumvirate and Principate' (9), and asked why Horace's *Epistle to Augustus* represented the history of literature and of censorship as coextensive at Rome.

[1] Dio 47. 43. 1.
[2] Plut. *Brut.* 41. 2.

libertas as he tackled the two genres, one archaic and Greek, one only a century old and Latin, whose entire *raison d'être* consisted in the exercise of unrestrained outspokenness; as has often been remarked, his *Epodes* and *Satires* make a major theme out of why and how they do not live up to their generic trademarks in the unparalleled political environment of triumviral Rome.[3]

The transformations of the conditions for speech in the ever-changing Principate continued to engage the poet throughout his career, as he and his near coeval, Caesar Augustus, remade their respective traditions. In what is very probably his penultimate work, possibly his last, the *Epistle to Augustus*, Horace addresses the man against whom he fought thirty years before, each of them now supreme in his own field. They have both reached their position of classic status in a surprisingly short time and from beginnings which had promised any outcome but this. Revolutionaries in their twenties, now, in the summer of 12 BCE, at the age of 50 for Augustus and 52 for Horace—suddenly, as it must often have seemed to them both—they were the established order.[4] Horace's *Epistle* to the *Princeps* simultaneously analyses and enacts the interplay between the new poetry and the new Principate, and my main purpose in this essay is to chart the strong 'gravitational pull' exerted by this pair's bonding.[5]

In tackling 'the place of the poet ... in contemporary society',[6] 'il rapporto fra poetica e potere',[7] Horace is certainly continuing his career-long interest in the possibilities of speech in the given political

---

[3] Briefly, Fitzgerald (1988) on the *Epodes*; Henderson (1998a: ch. 3) and Freudenburg (2001: ch. 1) on the *Satires*; for a different interpretation, see DuQuesnay (1984), Galinsky (1996: 57). We return to this theme below.

[4] Henderson (1999: 102–3); cf. Nisbet (1995a: 390) on Horace as one of the 'three great literary innovators' of the 30s (along with Virgil and Sallust).

[5] 'Gravitational pull' is the phrase of Freudenburg (2002b), capturing the energy created by the relationship between Horace and his addressees. Cf. Oliensis (1998a) for the different 'faces' Horace assumes with different readers, esp. 7–13 on the complementary ways of addressing Augustus in *Epist.* 2.1 and Florus in *Epist.* 2.2; and Henderson (1999: 206–7) on language in Horace's *Sat.* 1.9 'in its contemporary ("Bakhtinian") understanding as a saturated dialogism ...—a matter beyond individualizing "characterization" or ethopoeia; rather, the valorization of a topology of social/political relations'.

[6] Williams (1968: 73).

[7] Barchiesi (1993: 150). My debts to Barchiesi's analysis of the interplay between the realms of 'poet and *Princeps*' will be evident (Barchiesi (1993) and (1994)). Habinek (1998: 9) promises that his methodology will be an advance on Barchiesi's,

and social environment, but in this Epistle there is a new dimension, for now he is attempting to contextualise this long-standing interest within the field of literary history. This represents a challenge, for us as well as for him. For us, the limits of literary history, and especially of the claims to explanatory power of its various contextualisations, are a topical problem; and Horace's experiment may provide us with a salutary test-case. For Horace, the experiment is even more difficult, since his inherited traditions of literary history and criticism do not afford him any models for such a politically informed inves-tigation of the social status of poetry.[8] The poem treats us, then, to the spectacle of Horace struggling with a recalcitrant literary-critical tradition that barely gives him the purchase he needs. Yet he persists in the struggle, for, as we shall see, Horace needs to construct for himself some kind of critically informed sense of the social condi-tions for poetry at Rome before he can engage with a situation without precedent in Rome—a quite novel political and poetical power and preeminence, implicated in and defining each other, and joined together in the immortality of posterity as they both knew they would be.[9] The momentum of this Epistle shows how Augustus and Horace depend upon each other for the immortality they both covet so much. It is Horace and his poetic peers 'who will eventually be in control of the *Princeps*' posthumous fate', as the *aeditui* of the temple of Virtus.[10] Conversely, it is now Augustus who is in charge of

but I do not think he delivers: as will emerge in this essay, I agree rather with, e.g., Felperin (1990) and Perkins (1992) in being unpersuaded that it is possible to 'relate the ideology of the text to the material circumstances of ancient society', as Habinek professes to be able to do (loc. cit.).

[8] Cf. Brink (1982: 566), to which we return below. Although I disagree with much of the analysis of Habinek (1998: 93–102), I concur strongly in wanting to take seriously 'the very form of literary chronology that structures the body of the letter' (93).

[9] For Augustus' angle, see the fragment of his *Epistle to Horace* preserved by Suetonius' *Life of Horace*, in which Augustus wonders why Horace hasn't yet ad-dressed an *Epistle* to him, asking 'Are you afraid that it will be a black mark against you with posterity that you look like a friend of mine?' (*an uereris ne apud posteros infame tibi sit, quod uidearis familiaris nobis esse?*).

[10] Feeney (1998: 114) on *Epist.* 2.1.6 and 229–31; Augustus is unique in being honoured as divine while he is still present here on earth (*praesenti tibi maturos largimur honores,* 15), but what will guarantee his divinity when he is no longer *praesens*?

access to the libraries, housed in his temple of Apollo (214–18). They each control the temple that will guarantee the other's immortality.

The two men's shared and mutually implicated hopes of immortality are only one example of numerous points of identity between them, tokens of the inextricability of their spheres of eminence. At the end of the poem, famously, addresser and addressee are collapsed together in the phrase which provides my title, when Horace puts himself into Augustus' shoes as the object of panegyric and fantasises about being consigned to oblivion by and together with the inept person writing about him (264–70). This culminating identification is hinted at already in the first sentence of the poem, which offers the obverse, with its glimpse of the *Princeps* as a super-artist or super-critic, 'adorning' and 'emending' the state (*res Italas . . . moribus ornes,* | *legibus emendes* (2–3).[11]

The poem's very first line signals the most obvious point of identity, with the emphatically placed *solus*, 'alone', at the end, describing Augustus. Undecidable as the issue of the Epistle's dating must ultimately remain, there is much in favour of the often canvassed date of 12 BCE, not least the consideration that this was the year when Augustus did indeed find himself definitively alone at the summit of affairs.[12] On 6 March of that year Augustus claimed the one prize left and was elected by 'a multitude from the whole of Italy' to the office of *pontifex maximus* which had finally been vacated by Lepidus' recent death.[13] Two weeks later he heard that M. Agrippa, just arrived in Campania from Pannonia, was seriously ill; rushing to see him, he found already dead the man who had been his right hand for thirty years, his son-in-law, father of his adopted sons, colleague as consul (twice) and as quindecimuir (and doubtless

[11] On 'the ruler as artist', see Fowler (1995: 252, 254); Alessandro Barchiesi and Tony Woodman both remind me that the phrase *res Italas* can refer to subject-matter (as that of the shield of Aeneas, Verg. *Aen.* 8.626). The *Epistle*, then, is an extreme case of Horace's typical adaptation of his poetry to the qualities of his addressees, on which see Nisbet (1995a: 1–5; 2002); Armstrong (1993) on the importance of the Pisones as the addressees of the *Ars poetica*.

[12] Brink (1982: 552–4). In connecting Horace's description of Augustus as *solus* with the death of Agrippa, I follow Syme (1939: 392) and (1978: 173), despite Brink (1982: 554 n. 3) and Rudd (1989) ad loc.; cf. Habinek (1998: 92–3).

[13] *Res gestae* 10.2.

other, undocumented, priesthoods), joint holder of supreme *imperium* and *tribunicia potestas*.[14]

In his own sphere, the poet was just as isolated, the sole survivor of his generation. For him the crucial year will have been 19 BCE, when he had lost Virgil, Tibullus, and (probably) Varius.[15] Some two decades before writing to Augustus, at the beginning of his career, when closing the first book of *Satires*, Horace had presented a battery of names, fellow-composers and readers, a crowd of individuals representing the new wave which Horace was hoping to catch. As Horace's fellow-composers we are shown Fundanius, Pollio, Varius, Virgil (*Sat.* 1.10.40–5), and thirty-five lines later as his ideal audience we meet Plotius, Varius and Virgil again, together with Maecenas this time, then Valgius, Octavius, Fuscus, both Visci, Pollio again, Messalla and his brother, Bibulus and Servius, Furnius, and 'a good number of others, learned men and friends of mine too, whom I discreetly skip' (*compluris alios, doctos ego quos et amicos | prudens praetereo*, 87–8). There is a striking contrast with the later Epistle, from which the Satire's throng of sympathetic and cooperative peers has vanished. Of all those names from the Satire only two return in the Epistle, Virgil and Varius (*Epist.* 2.1.247)—and they are dead.[16] The poet is left alone with the *Princeps*, who had been 'discreetly skipped' in the Satire, or masked by the nearly homonymous Octavius (*Sat.* 1.10.82). Before, there had been many estimable poets. Now, there is only one.[17] Before, there had been many people whose judgement counted. Now, there is only one.[18] Horace's like-minded contemporaries are gone, and, as we shall see below, the judgement of those who are supposedly professionally qualified to

[14] Dio 54.28.2–3; on Agrippa as Augustus' virtual co-regent at the time of his death, see Reinhold (1933: 98–105), *CAH*[2] 10.97. I follow the edict of Barnes (1998: 144) in eschewing the phrase *maius imperium*.

[15] Wili (1948: 341), Klingner (1950: 32), Brink (1982: 559); on the 'watershed' in Roman literary history represented by this year, see Brink (1982: 546).

[16] Brink (1963: 208–9).

[17] Apart from this footnote, I am as silent as Horace is about (i) Propertius, who may have been no more than eight or nine years younger, and (ii) the great figure of the next generation, Ovid. Does Horace's awareness of these (and other) figures lie behind the frequent first person plurals of the poem, as Michèle Lowrie suggests to me (89, 117, 214, 219)?

[18] Oliensis (1998a: 12) brings out very clearly how, within *Epistles* 2 as a book, 'Horace's only "patron" is Augustus'.

judge, the *critici*, is exposed as valueless by Horace, their criteria systematically lampooned; now, the important *iudicia*, no longer 'merely' literary-critical, are those of Augustus (*tua... iudicia*, 245), and it is inclusion in his library on the Palatine that determines survival.[19] Horace's contrasts between these two literary *sermones* highlight the novel isolation he occupies in 12 BCE—an isolation which mirrors that of the *Princeps*.[20] In the Epistle he further highlights his exposed position by the affinities he constructs with literary-historical traditions, for the Epistle presents wide views over literary and social history of a kind that are absent from the Satire. We shall be examining his engagement with his literary-historical traditions in more detail shortly; at this stage, we need only remark how this literary-historical context puts a great deal of pressure on Horace's exposed isolation, calling attention to the fact that he alone is being mentioned and discussed. The point is that the histories and canons of his tradition regularly restricted their attention only to authors who were already dead. The presence of Virgil and Varius in the Epistle is acceptable on these terms, but that of Horace is anomalous. It is well known that Quintilian, a century later, did not discuss living authors in his survey of the canons, and in this restriction he is openly following the Hellenistic scholars Aristarchus and Aristophanes.[21] In the generation before Horace, Cicero says quite explicitly that in his survey of Latin oratory down to his own time he will not discuss living authors (*Brut.* 231): the evaluation of living

---

[19] Cf. the valuable observations of Horsfall (1993b: 60–3) on *Epist.* 2.1.216–18, together with Oliensis (1998a: 193). Note how earlier in the poem the people, if they agree with Horace about the ancients, are 'using their head, siding with me, and giving a *iudicium* with the favour of Jupiter' (*et sapit et mecum facit et Ioue iudicat aequo*, 68). For a minor-key anticipation of this theme, note *Sat.* 2.1.82–4. Tony Woodman points out that there is a big shift from the end of *Odes* 1.1, with its important stress on the *iudicium* of Maecenas (*quodsi... inseres*, 35).

[20] As Kirk Freudenburg puts it to me, Horace's solitude is partly historical 'fact', partly self-construction as he is 'sucked into the imperial vortex'.

[21] *Inst.* 10.1.54; cf. 1.4.3 and 10.1.59 for other mentions of canonical procedure, with 2.5.25–6 on contemporary models; on the canons, Pfeiffer (1968: 203–8), Jocelyn (1979: 74–5), Scotti (1982). At *Tr.* 2.467–8 Ovid alludes to the canonical suppression of living authors' names; cf. Vell. Pat. 2.36.3. As Kirk Freudenburg points out to me, the clearest example of Quintilian's self-denying ordinance is at *Inst.* 10.1.96, where he mentions the recently deceased Caesius Bassus as a prominent lyricist, adding that he is surpassed by living talents, whom he leaves anonymous.

orators is skilfully entrusted to the other speakers, Atticus (Caesar, 252–3), and Brutus (Cato, 118, Metellus Scipio, 212, Marcellus, 249–50).[22] When Pollio opened his new library in the Atrium Libertatis in the 30s, Varro—appropriately enough for the author of a book called *Imagines*—was the only living writer who had a bust there (Plin. *HN* 7.115). This was because he was 'too old to envy',[23] for envy was the enemy of the living author, as Horace makes very clear in the opening section of the Epistle (especially 86–9).[24]

Alive, and hence out of the reckoning according to the traditional critical procedures of the kind he engages with in the Epistle, Horace yet finds himself at a fascinating juncture in the history of literary history, for he is in the unprecedented position of belonging to the first generation of authors to be school-texts in Rome while they were still alive.[25] In the middle 30s BCE, in *Satires* 1.10, he can ask an adversary with scorn if he 'wants his poetry to be dictated in the cheap schools' (74–5), although this anticipates by a few years our first secure independent evidence for the teaching of contemporary poets in Roman schools.[26] Certainly by 20 BCE, when he releases the first book of *Epistles* to its public, the two-edged fate of being in the curriculum stares him in the face (1.20.17–18).[27] A classic in his own lifetime, his reception out of his control, he is imitated by others, pawed over by the uncomprehending, the object of envy, plagiarism, and inevitable misreading. Isolated as he now is when he writes to Augustus, he can observe the distortion of his and his peers' accomplishments, mordantly contemplating, for example, the collapse

[22] Douglas (1966: ix).

[23] Nisbet (1995b: 403); also as a compliment to the original plan of Pollio's leader, Julius Caesar, who had charged Varro with the task of organising a library (Horsfall (1993b: 59).

[24] Already in the fourth century, the prominent tragedian Astydamas had enviously observed of his three great predecessors that 'they have the advantage of time, for envy does not touch them': Astydamas 60 *TrGF*, T 2a. Here, of course, is a cardinal point of difference which Horace identifies between himself and Augustus, whom he represents as uniquely beyond envy even before his death (5–17).

[25] Bloomer (1997: 67).

[26] Suet. *Gramm.* 16. 3, with the important discussion of Kaster (1995: 188–9).

[27] Oliensis (1995) and (1998a: 174–5) on Horace's 'conflicting impulses toward elitism and popularization'. This interest in Horace's simultaneous lust for and dread of popularity is more valuable than the monocular focus on his elitism in Habinek (1998: esp. 99–102).

into pat neoteric cliché of the hard-won aesthetic victories of his generation, in which they had reworked and upgraded the Callimacheanism of the neoterics, making it a suitable engine for their grander ambitions.[28] Now, with a heavily ironic first-person plural he pictures the poets of the day recycling the hackneyed jargon as they lament that people don't notice 'our "toils", and our poems "spun with fine thread"' (*cum lamentamur non apparere labores | nostros et tenui deducta poemata filo*, 224–5; Pope catches the mood brilliantly in his *Imitation*: 'we...lament, the Wit's too fine | For vulgar eyes, and point out ev'ry line', 366–7).

Already in *Epist.* 1.19 Horace had openly shown his anger and hilarity at the antics of those who misunderstood the multi-layered nature of his art in their attempts at imitation (esp. 19–20). The third poem in that collection is a much more indirect piece of advice and exemplification, offered to the young Florus as a model of how to deal with the neoteric inheritance as one element in a manifold tradition. The worthy Florus is a member of the *cohors* of Tiberius, travelling somewhere in the East (*Epist.* 1.3.1–5). Perhaps he is covering the same ground as Catullus had covered some thirty-five years earlier, in the last years of corrupt Republican provincial government, when he had gone to Bithynia in a very different kind of *cohors*, with a very different kind of governor, Memmius.[29] Florus may be at the Hellespont (4), like Catullus visiting his brother's tomb;[30] perhaps he is in Asia (5).[31] The deft allusions to the earlier poetic *cohors* signal the enormous social and governmental gulf that had opened up in the intervening generation, an object lesson in how to work dynamically with neotericism.[32] As

---

[28] Feeney (1993: 45); to the references there, add Syme (1939: 255) and Brink (1963: 166–70, 195, 214), which I should have cited; compare Farrell (1991: esp. ch. 7), Nisbet (1995b: 395–6), and Zetzel (2002). The pan-Callimachean tendency that Horace consistently skewers persists strongly in modern criticism.

[29] See Catull. 10.5–12 and 28.9–10 for the rapacity and cynicism of the operation.

[30] Catull. 68.97–100, 101.1–2.

[31] Catullus is leaving the plains of Phrygia and the fertile land of Nicaea to see the famous cities of Asia (*linquantur Phrygii, Catulle, campi | Nicaeaeque ager uber aestuosae: | ad claras Asiae uolemus urbes*, 46.4–6); Horace suppresses Phrygia and transfers the fertility and plains to Asia (*an pingues Asiae campi collesque morantur?*, 5). Tony Woodman suggests another Catullan touch, in the link between *Epist.* 1.3.2 (*scire laboro*) and Catull. 67.17 (*scire laborat*).

[32] In *Epist.* 1.13, addressing Tiberius, he will give us an object lesson in how to talk to the leader of the *cohors*—very differently from the way Catullus talked to Memmius (28.9–10).

Horace moves on to discuss the poetic projects of Florus and his friends,
he illustrates the perils of imitating the classics of ancient Greece and
contemporary Rome, likewise giving lessons in how to do it properly as
he goes. His own dextrous reworking of Pindar in the course of this
poem, illustrated by Hubbard, casts a pall over the Pindaric attempts of
Titius (10–11).[33] Further, as Hubbard points out, 'Horace very well
knew what could be done in Latin with Pindar, and he had done it
himself in the sapphics of *Odes* 1.12 and the alcaics of *Odes* 3.4';[34] this
perspective suddenly gives Horace's politeness at line 12 a distinctly
feline tone, as he enquires 'How is Titius getting on? *Is he keeping me in
mind?*' (*ut ualet? ut meminit nostri?*). The dangers of plagiarism are
the explicit subject of the next lines, where Celsus is warned to look to
his own stocks and keep his hands off the writings in the temple of
Apollo Palatinus (15–17). Finally, in addressing Florus himself, Horace
treats us to a delightful reworking of a living Roman classic from
Apollo's temple, transforming his addressee into one of the bees from
Virgil's fourth *Georgic* (21–7).[35] The Epistle as a whole is a showpiece for
the confident artist's creative engagement with poetry from Classical
Greece and from neoteric and contemporary Rome—including his
own.

If we return to 12 BCE, eight years later, Virgil is now dead, and
Horace is now even more exposed in his novel status as the only
living classic, who cannot be accommodated by the received wisdom
of the critical tradition. How does he position himself and his
achievement when writing to Augustus, his counterpart as a living
classic, prematurely divine, who cannot be accommodated by the
received wisdom of the political tradition?[36]

His fundamental tool for the analysis of the unique position he
now occupies in the Rome of Augustus is literary history, a literary
history which he contextualises within historical and social

[33] Hubbard (1995: 220–1): 'he is . . . teasingly showing how to make use of Pindar,
and by no means in Titius' way'.

[34] Hubbard (1995: 220).

[35] West (1967: 30–9). Kirk Freudenburg (2002b) comes to analogous conclusions,
arguing that in both Epistles Florus' status as a lawyer is a focus for the themes of
legitimate ownership of poetic property.

[36] Horace describes the divine honours paid to the living Augustus as *maturos*
(15): is that 'occurring at the proper time, timely' (*OLD* s.v. 7) or 'occurring before
the proper or usual time, premature, early' (*OLD* s.v. 9)?

frameworks to a surprising degree. I say 'surprising' because, as I remarked at the beginning of this essay, Horace's critical traditions offered him very little to go on by way of such frameworks. As Brink astutely observes, when remarking on the two motifs of Horace's theorising in this poem (the 'technical', on the one hand, and the 'human, social, political, religious and moral', on the other): 'clearly the models of Horace's literary theories did not provide him with a notion that unified these two large groups of subjects'.[37]

What, then, did he have at his disposal? It is well known that 'the historical study of literature in antiquity was very rudimentary by modern standards'.[38] There was rather more of it than one might think: the Peripatetics in particular wrote voluminously on the histories of various forms, especially drama, compiling lists of victors, chronologies, and lives of authors;[39] and the Romans carried on the tradition, with Accius' prose *Didascalica* and the verse works of Porcius Licinus and Volcacius Sedigitus taking up questions of authenticity and chronology, before we reach the crowning researches of Varro.[40] Still, we lack systematic attempts at historically informed literary history, of the kind that aims at what Williams calls an 'understanding of the relationship of author and genre to the historical environment'.[41] As Williams goes on to point out, their oratorically based theory had no more to offer than ' "canons" or lists of the great' and 'survey in an antiquarian fashion'.[42]

The history of Roman literary history shows three exceptions standing out clearly against this broad background: Cicero, preeminently in the *Brutus*; Tacitus, in Cicero's footsteps, in the *Dialogus*;[43] and Horace in our Epistle, likewise, as far as I can see, profoundly influenced by Cicero. Horace responds to the gaps in his tradition's capacities in two ways. First, he lampoons the conventional procedures of canons and

[37] Brink (1982: 566).

[38] Russell (1981: 159); cf. Williams (1978: 270–1).

[39] Leo (1901: 99–107), Podlecki (1969), Russell (1981: 159–68). The masterpiece of Pfeiffer (1968) scandalously skips straight from Aristotle to Alexandria: Richardson (1994).

[40] Rawson (1985: 267–81), Kaster (1995: xxiv–xxviii) (both Greek and Roman).

[41] Williams (1978: 270).

[42] Williams (1978: 271).

[43] See Fantham (1996: 18, 45–7), for the importance of Cicero and Tacitus in this regard.

lists and antiquarian survey, exposing their inadequacy as a tool of thought, often precisely on the grounds of their lack of historical sense; second, he attempts to chart ways of thinking about the place of poetry in Roman cultural history which will help him plot the new conditions of writing in the new regime. I shall deal first with the more straightforward, negative, side of his strategy, before turning to the much more problematic question of what his constructions of literary history can and cannot achieve.

First, then, his attacks on the conventional unhistorical critical procedures. After his introduction, Horace opens his attack on the archaists, who revere only the antique, with 18–27, 'one long and flexible sentence';[44] the long and flexible period is itself a demonstration of his superiority, for this periodic technique is not to be found in the pages of the *ueteres* (the 'ancients').[45] In 28–33 he keeps up the attack on those who think the old is good, but brings in a vital extra point when he claims that his adversaries praise the old on analogy with Greek literary history: in Greek literature the oldest is the best, so it must be true of Roman literature too. His hostility to this unthinking and unhistorical use of cross-cultural analogy is extremely deep. He sees it as purely mechanical, and in 28–9 he ridicules it by going back to one of the first images used to lampoon mindless comparison-making, the weighing scale of Aristophanes' *Frogs* (1365–410).

At 50ff., and especially 55ff., he explodes the whole revered procedure of the κρίσις ποιημάτων ('judgement/criticism of poems') as carried on by the κριτικοί ('critics')—the transliteration *critici* which he uses in 51, instead of the native Latin calque, *iudex*, has a derisorily hypertechnical, jargony tone.[46] He is attacking many targets at once in these lines: first, the whole enterprise of the comparison of Greek and Roman authors; second, the ranking of authors in a canon; third, the summary encapsulation of an author with a telling word or phrase.

[44] Brink (1982: 59).
[45] Cf. Norden (1927: 376–8) on Virgil as the first transposer of periodic prose style to verse. Horace has a very similar moment at *Sat.* 1.10.56–64, illustrating the gap between his technique and Lucilius'.
[46] Brink (1982) ad loc.: '*criticus*, in place of Latin *iudex*, occurs twice only in Republican and Augustan Latin—in this passage and at Cic. *Fam.* 9.10.1' (the Cicero passage is also highly ironic and tongue-in-cheek: Brink (1982: 418–19)).

He is, in other words, attacking the entire underpinning of what we later see as Quintilian's procedure in *Inst.* 10.1.46–131, a procedure which in Roman literary history goes back at least to Volcacius Sedigitus, whose scholarly poem *De Poetis* included a ranking of the Roman comic poets, from Caecilius Statius as Number One to Ennius as Number Ten.[47] In line 3 of that fragment Volcacius uses the Latin word for κρίσις, *iudicium* ('judgement/criticism') to justify his canon, just as Quintilian later uses *iudicium* of the process of making a canon selection (1.4.3; 10.1.54, 60). To Horace this kind of procedure is not a proper use of the judging faculty: proper *iudicium* is what the *uulgus* are delivering if they agree with Horace about the *ueteres* (68); the poem will at the end, as I have already noted, return to the *iudicia* that now really count, those of Augustus (245).

Horace derides the thumbnail one-word summing up of an author's essential characteristics: Pacuvius is *doctus*, Accius is *altus*, Caecilius has got *grauitas*, and Terence has got *ars* (56–9). It is sobering to remind ourselves how many people still think they are doing criticism when they come up with this sort of thing.[48] Most importantly, Horace derides the comparison of Roman authors with Greek: Ennius is *alter Homerus, ut critici dicunt* (50–1);[49] Afranius is Menander, Plautus is Epicharmus (57–8). In order to appreciate Horace's originality here, we have to remind ourselves of how fundamental a tool the σύγκρισις ('comparison') was for literary critics, within the Greek tradition and across the two traditions.[50] Horace will have none of it. In this Epistle such συνκρίσεις ('comparisons') are made in order to be ridiculed, as here, or else the συνκρίσεις are negative: Virgil and Varius are *not* Choerilus, at the end of the poem, as Augustus is *not* Alexander (229–47).[51] At the root of his objection to the comparison-mentality is his conviction, ultimately inherited from Cicero, that the historical

[47] Conveniently in Courtney (1993: 93–4).
[48] Pope's Note at this point in his *Imitation* is wonderful: 'The whole paragraph has a mixture of Irony, and must not altogether be taken for Horace's own Judgement, only the common Chat of the pretenders to Criticism'; cf. Brink (1982: 104).
[49] Not the least of the problems in these very difficult lines on Ennius is that it was not just the critics who claimed Ennius as *alter Homerus*, but Ennius himself (despite Brink (1982: 95–6)).
[50] Leo (1901: 149–50); Focke (1923); Petrochilos (1974: 144–62); Vardi (1996).
[51] At least, so far as taste is concerned, as Michèle Lowrie reminds me: for Augustus' *imitatio Alexandri*, see n. 93 below.

patterns of Rome and Greece are distinct and cannot be compared to each other without absurd distortion.[52]

At the end of the section about the fans of the *ueteres*, Horace narrows down, finally, to himself (*nostra... nos nostraque*, 89). But then he veers away, and moves into his panorama of first Greek and then Roman cultural history, which will eventually take us all the way down to the present day and the resumption of his direct address to Augustus (214–18). Here we may take up the second, constructive, side of his reaction to his literary-critical tradition, for it is here that he embarks on his elusive literary history, which circles around and around the issues of the status of poetry in Rome since its inception, in order to create a background that will put his own contemporary status in perspective.

It is important to be clear about what Horace is and is not doing as a literary historian, for if we do not place his attempts properly we run the risk of claiming too much or too little for him. It is plain that Horace is not writing cultural and literary history for its own sake (whatever that means). What interests him is poetry now, his poetry, in Augustus' Rome;[53] whatever he writes about the Greek and Roman cultural past arises from his apprehension of his own position in contemporary Rome, which colours his whole retrospective view, and inevitably focuses teleologically on the present. In many important respects, therefore, Horace's literary history resembles what Perkins, following Nietzsche's essay *On the advantage and disadvantage of history for life*, calls 'critical' literary history, which 'does not perceive the literature of the past in relation to the time and place that produced it, but selects, interprets and evaluates this literature only from the standpoint of the present and its needs'.[54] In other words, like all literary history, it is very bad history.[55]

[52] I realise that these claims about Horace's attitude to cross-cultural comparison will seem odd to those who believe that he regularly casts himself as another Alcaeus, for example; but see Feeney (2002) for Horace's attitudes to σύνκρισις, and for his debt to Cicero's literary histories (although the subject of Horace's debts to Cicero deserves a book).

[53] Klingner (1950: 22–3).

[54] Perkins (1992: 179); cf. Barchiesi (1962: 43), Hinds (1998: ch. 3, esp. 63).

[55] Perkins (1992); an important discussion of these issues in Hinds (1998: ch. 3), with focus on Hor. *Epist.* 2.1.50–75 at 69–71; cf. Goldberg (1995: 5–12). Of course, at some level, the teleological interestedness described by Perkins is true of any history: Martindale (1993: 17–23).

For all that, Brink goes too far when he claims that 'the relativities of modern historical thought are wholly alien to these absolute judgements ... [T]his kind of "history" is literary judgement or theorizing applied to the past.'[56] On the contrary, Horace is perfectly capable of seeing the historically relativistic point that what is now archaic was modern in its day (*Epist.* 2.1.90–1),[57] and it may be that he applies this insight to his judgement of Ennius' attempt to supplant Naevius (50–4);[58] he is perfectly capable of saying that if Lucilius were alive now he would not be the same author (*Sat.* 1.10.67–71).[59] Fundamentally, he has learnt well the Ciceronian lesson that the relative conditions of Roman literary history are very different from those of Greek—this is, as we have seen, the basis of his objection to a great deal of his literary-critical tradition, with its unthinkingly unhistorical apparatus of cross-cultural analogy, and we shall see shortly how profound are the differences Horace constructs between Greek and Roman culture.

There is, then, a more historically informed sense at work here than is often allowed, even if modern scholars are quite right to remark that the result does not look very much like what most modern practitioners of literary history produce. I take this lack of overlap with modern practice, however, to be a merit of Horace, principally because I agree with Perkins (1992) in regarding as illusory the causal or explanatory value of the Zeitgeist contextualisations offered by conventional literary history (whether of the Old or New Historical variety). We cannot explain (in any rigorous sense of the word) the way any given literary text is shaped by its contexts, because it is impossible to know what kind of causal relationship we might be talking about: the nexus of cause and effect is irrecoverable,[60] and the number of contextualisations to be taken into account is insuperably large.[61] And Horace is not given to such explanatory or

---

[56] Brink (1982: 566).

[57] Klingner (1950: 18), Hinds (1998: 55).

[58] White (1987: 233–4), Hinds (1998: 69–70).

[59] Cf. Cicero on Thucydides (*Brut.* 288); for Horace's Ciceronian apprehension of such matters, see Barchiesi (1962: 66 n. 300).

[60] For a devastating general attack on history's claims to explain causes, see Veyne (1984: 87–105, 144–72).

[61] For the inadequacies of literary historical contextualisation, see Perkins (1992: ch. 6, esp. 128): 'How can an essay or book adequately display the intricate, manifold involvement of a particular text in the hugely diverse context that is thought to

causal contextualisations—indeed, as we shall see, at a certain level the production of poetry at Rome is to him an anomalous, even unaccountable phenomenon, and a great deal of his literary history is devoted precisely to highlighting how out of place poetry is at Rome, rather than to explaining the circumstances of its production.

What historical contextualisation *can* do, however imperfectly, is alert us to a set of possibilities (if always at the expense of closing off others) by organising and creating patterns out of the data-bank of the past: as Paul Veyne puts it, 'Historians of literature and historians per se, including sociologists, do not explain events . . . They explicate them, interpret them.'[62] Horace needs to have *this* set rather than another, and I am trying to explicate the motivations he constructs in this poem, without implying that the set Horace identifies for his purposes is historically the 'right' or only possible one. My own historical situating in this essay, in other words, tracks and responds to Horace's (more 'gravitational pull'), and does not purport to explain why Horace's text is the way it is rather than some other way. From this perspective, it becomes more clear why Horace's own position in Augustus' Rome is what lies behind his entire project of literary history; in following what he says about the position of poetry in the life of Rome, we will need to keep that teleological aim as clearly in view as Horace did. Underlying everything is his apprehension of the possibilities and constraints that go to shape what he can say in poetry, an apprehension which he expresses, in different ways throughout his work, from the *Epodes* on, and which culminates here, in his address to the *Princeps*.

We see this apprehension powerfully at work throughout the Epistle, most openly in his account of the origins of Roman literary history. The entire section begins with Greece's cultural acme after

determine it? Moreover, any context we use for interpretation or explanation must itself be interpreted. In other words, the context must be put in a wider context, which itself must be interpreted contextually, and so on in a recession that can only be halted arbitrarily.' Cf. Felperin (1990: esp. 142–69) (a critique of New Historicist contextualisation in particular); Martindale (1993: 13); Goldberg (1995: 19–26); Fowler (2000b: x–xi, 174). Naturally, it is in practice impossible to write about literature without one kind of contextualisation or another, as my own essay shows (Martindale (1993: 14–15)): the question is how much weight to put on their explanatory or causal value.

[62] Veyne (1988: 178).

the Persian wars, and is rather flippant and tongue-in-cheek in its characterisation of Greek nature (93–102); the beginning of the Roman section after that is similarly flippant and tongue-in-cheek, drifting from a general picture of how different pre-literate Rome was from Greece down to the current mania for poetry (103–117). For our purposes, looking ahead to the conclusion, the key Horatian antithesis to perceive in this juxtaposition is that between, on the one hand, the 'naturalness' of poetry in Greece, part of a whole range of artistic activities that the Greeks take to with the natural spontaneity of a child, even an *infans* (99), and, on the other, the isolation of poetry in Rome as the only cultural pursuit, undertaken by the fickle people on a whim (103–10): in the early part of the Epistle Horace had used the idea of Romans excelling at other Greek arts (painting, playing the cithara, wrestling) as a self-evident absurdity to cap an *argumentum per impossibile* (32–3). Tragedy in Greece is presented as the offshoot of a natural predisposition which manifests itself in other, related, ways (athletics, sculpture, painting, music); in Rome, poetry is an unmotivated and unique cultural phenomenon, represented as being at odds with what Brink calls the 'national psychology, attuned in Rome to enduring institutions of commerce and law'.[63] For all that, Horace can eventually claim a place—however ironically at first—for the value of the poet to the educational and religious life of the city (118–38). This section climaxes in the central panel of the poem, with 131 lines on either side, an idealised and freefloating image of the social function of choral lyric, which clearly, yet entirely indirectly, looks to Horace's own *Carmen Saeculare*, performed five years before at the Ludi Saeculares (132–8).[64]

At 139 Horace resumes, backtracking to the origins of Roman literature, moving into an historical register which is rather different from what preceded—the very fact that he offers us *two*, rather different, Roman literary histories is itself a sign of his nuanced historicism, for this tactic acknowledges that there is not one single story to be told about this question, any more than about any other.[65] Again, we must recognise that Horace's historical register

---

[63] Brink (1982: 142–3).

[64] The anomalous nature of this single performance's social function, however, emerges clearly from Barchiesi (2002).

[65] As Michèle Lowrie put it to me.

does not overlap with that of many modern literary historians: commentators quite rightly stress that Horace in this second historical section does not supply definite dates, when he might easily have done so, but instead uses apparently specific but actually recalcitrant phrases such as *Graecia capta* (156) and *post Punica bella* (162).[66] Horace is interested in very broad and tenacious cultural movements, which do not fit into neat demarcations of time; his refusal to pin down one particular moment as the decisive impact of Greece on Rome brings him close to a view canvassed by Hinds (in 'deliberately overstated terms'), casting Rome's 'Hellenizing revolutions' 'as recurrent but essentially static renegotiations of the same cultural move'.[67]

The start of this section concerns the beginnings of Roman literature. Even before the impact of Greece in line 156 Horace shows some kind of compositions taking place in Rome, and it is notorious that the very start of this enterprise is enmeshed in state regulation according to his presentation: at 145–55 we are told that *licentia* and *libertas* got out of hand and had to be curbed by law. The history of Roman literature, then, is for all intents and purposes co-extensive with the history of the state's regulation of it. This stance is especially striking in someone who, as I stressed at the start, had begun his career in the two genres, Greek and Latin, which had the exercise of *licentia* and *libertas* as their *raison d'être*. The regulation of expression that Horace is talking about in the *Epistle to Augustus* is not just the origin of Roman literature, but the origin of Horace's career—a very deep aetion, then.

We may of course accuse him of bad faith in deliberately creating a Roman literary history without a golden age, with no predecessors who were not hampered by legislation and constraints upon their speech. It is important, however, to go on from there to see how the Epistle develops this long-standing preoccupation of his. In the *Epodes* and *Satires* he had been obsessed with the strange figure

---

[66] Brink (1982: 184–5); Porcius Licinus, e.g., could be more specific: *Poenico bello secundo*... (fr. 1, Courtney (1993)). Alessandro Barchiesi points out to me that *Graecia capta* is a particular tease because it resembles so closely triumphal labels that are chronologically specific (*Achaia capta, Corintho capta*).

[67] Hinds (1998: 63 with 82); cf. Brink (1962: 192) on *Epist.* 2.1.161–3: 'a tendency rather than a date'; Rudd (1989) on 156–7.

he cut as an impotent follower of outrageously frank predecessors, becoming a pioneer in a new mode of unavoidably polite and (self-) restrained expression;[68] in the first book of *Epistles* he had shifted tack, taking up more explicitly the philosophical interest in παρρησία, freedom of speech, turning his book into a test case in the post-Classical shift in register of παρρησία, as public outspokenness has become domesticated into the urbane frankness of private individuals.[69] In the *Epistle to Augustus* he is writing 'directly' to the figure who embodies the public transformations against which he has played out this long dialectic, and he is confronting, not exactly head-on, the problem of how the two of them can negotiate with each other.[70] The major theme of the close of the poem will be the difficulties Augustus faces in getting the poetry he deserves and the difficulties Horace faces in providing it,[71] and Horace takes the debate into Augustus' realm of public display in order to begin closing in on that theme. For it is commonly remarked upon that when Horace talks about Roman literary history after the Greek invasion he focuses on the drama, and quickly focuses even more specifically on the aspect of spectacle and display—signalled in advance by the mimetic *aspice*, 'look', with which he introduces Plautus (170)—from where he leads up to the eventual antithesis between spectacle and private reading that begins the poem's finale (*uere age et his, qui se lectori credere malunt | quam spectatoris fastidia ferre superbi, | curam redde breuem*, 'Come on now, pay some brief

---

[68] On the *Epodes*, see Schmidt (1977), Fitzgerald (1988) and Oliensis (1991), with Watson (1995), who professes to take issue with these scholars' conclusions about Horace's impotence, but who to my mind actually ends up confirming and taking even further their picture of Horace's inversion of the epodic voice. On the *Satires*, see DuQuesnay (1984), Kennedy (1992: 29–34), Freudenburg (1992: 86–92, 102, 209), Muecke (1995), Henderson (1998a: ch. 3) and (1999: ch. 8), and especially Freudenburg (2001: 15–124).

[69] Hunter (1985); cf. Freudenburg (1993: 86–92) on the influence of Philodemus' concept of παρρησία in the *Satires*, and Armstrong (1993: 192–9) for the *Ars*; on παρρησία in general, see Scarpat (1964). See Johnson (1993) for *libertas* as the dominant theme of *Epistles* 1.

[70] We should remind ourselves that Horace had never addressed a poem to Augustus until the Fourth Book of *Odes*, published only the year before: Brink (1982: 536), Feeney (1993: 54), on the oddity of the sole apparent exception, *Odes* 1.2.

[71] Barchiesi (1993: 155–8).

attention to those who prefer to entrust themselves to the reader rather than to put up with the pickiness of the arrogant spectator', 214–16).

It is the compulsion to engage with Augustus' world, and the resulting momentary assimilation of Augustus' world of display to Horace's world of poetry and criticism, that helps explain the interest—so often seen as puzzling—in Roman dramatic perform-ance in this penultimate section of the poem (177–213). Certainly, there are other important factors at work, well enumerated by Williams.[72] But I wish to concentrate on the dialectic Horace con-structs between his world of art and Augustus' world of public display; and here, to set up our conclusion, we return to the themes of the beginning of the essay, for to Horace his and Augustus' worlds define each other, by repulsion as much as by attraction.

Habinek likewise locates Horace's interest in spectacle within a promisingly political framework, but, following his book's procrus-tean programmatic obsession with the binary antithesis between elite and mass, he systematically misreads Horace's argument on this score: 'What troubles Horace about spectacle is that it . . . appeals to the least common denominator within the population. . . [T]he *Letter to Augustus* articulates a new set of oppositions, pitting elite against masses. . .'[73] This is precisely incorrect. Horace criticises the appeal

---

[72] Williams (1968: 73). In connection with Williams' point about the heavy emphasis on drama in the post-Aristotelian critical tradition, note Horace's play on two key Aristotelian concepts, ὄψις, 'spectacle', and μίμησις, 'imitation/representa-tion'. Following Aristotle in seeing ὄψις as the least artistic of all the aspects of drama (*Poet.* 1450b16–18, 1453b1–8; cf. Edwards (1993: 105)), Horace says that the pleasure in contemporary drama has all gone from the ear to the uncertain eyes (*ab aure . . . ad incertos oculos*, 187–8; remember that his own poetry will engage both the ears and eyes of the *Princeps*, *Epist.* 1.13.17). In line 195, with his description of a giraffe (*diuersum confusa genus panthera camelo*), Horace acts out for us just how uncertain the eyes can be: you really cannot tell what you are looking at when you are looking at a giraffe, and the intricate and ultimately uncategorisable grammar mimics this visual uncertainty, as is shown by the intricate grammatical exegeses of Brink (1982) and Rudd (1989) ad loc. (Rudd: 'one cannot be sure'). At the end of this section the key Aristotelian concept of μίμησις receives attention (205–7): 'Everyone is clapping. Has the actor said anything yet? Of course not. What is making them clap, then? *lana Tarentino uiolas imitata ueneno.*' But this too is mere ὄψις; the only μίμησις taking place on the Roman stage is a dyed cloak *imitating* the colour of violets.

[73] Habinek (1998: 99). This binarism leads him also to say some very strange things about the 'vulgar' and 'nonelite' nature of the *imagines* alluded to at the end of the poem (264–5): 99, 102.

of spectacular drama not just to the *plebecula* ('wee plebs') in 186 but also (*quoque*) to the *eques* in 187. Pope, in the 'Advertisement' to his *Imitation*, puts his finger, as usual, on the right point: '*Horace* here pleads the Cause of his Contemporaries, first against the Taste of the *Town* . . . ; secondly against the *Court* and *Nobility* . . .'[74]

Crucially, of course, Pope goes on to say—'and lastly against the *Emperor* himself'.[75] As Barchiesi puts it, Augustus is at once student and teacher in this poem,[76] and Horace's didacticism is close to the surface as he develops the momentum that will lead to his explicit contrast between public display and literature for reading (214–18). In Horace's poem the world of the popular theatre overlaps with the world of public display and pageantry, as he gives us a glimpse of what recent scholars have called the 'political theatre' of the Principate.[77] Already in the *Satires* Horace had merged the two worlds in his description of Scipio and Laelius withdrawing from the mob and the stage (*a uulgo et scaena, Sat.* 2.1.71).[78] In this section of the Epistle, his presentation of the theatre is dotted with vocabulary and imagery appropriate to politics: the playwright who competes on the public stage is like a politician competing for votes, dependent on the whim of the onlooker (177–80); the audience is split like an historian's public assembly, with the ignorant many outnumbering the virtuous and high-born few (183–4); Roman spectacles are like triumphs, with which the *ferus uictor* ('savage victor', 156) is still obsessed (189–93: note especially 193, *captiuum portatur ebur, captiua Corinthus*, 'captured ivory is carried along,

---

[74] So, very clearly, Brink (1982: 220): 'Even the *equites* share the prevailing grossness of taste.'

[75] Though he misplaces the reason for Horace's difference with the Emperor ('who had conceived them [i.e., Horace and his contemporaries] of little Use to the Government'). For varying accounts of Horace's differences with Augustus' taste for spectacle and theatre, attested in Suet. *Aug.* 43–5 and 89.1, see Klingner (1950: 32), Fraenkel (1957: 395–6), La Penna (1963: 148–62), Brink (1982: 562–5).

[76] Barchiesi (1993: 152): 'insieme discente e maestro'.

[77] Hopkins (1983: 14–20), Edwards (1993: 110–19), Bartsch (1994); cf. Fowler (1995) on Augustus' aestheticising of politics.

[78] Cf. Cic. *Brut.* 1.9.2, tibi nunc populo et scaenae, ut dicitur, seruiendum est, and Cic. *Lael.* 97, *in scaena, id est in contione*, with the note of Powell (1990: ad loc.) for material on 'the comparison of a public meeting with a theatrical performance'.

captive Corinthian bronze'[79]). This is a world of public judgement and competition from which Horace always removes himself;[80] but it is one that means a great deal to Augustus, not merely because he has a well-known taste for the old Roman comedy, but because in his new Rome the theatre has 'an outstanding importance...as a substitute for public life'.[81] It is an arena in which he takes an active interest, recovering the discriminations between the orders, stamping out the mixed seating of the slack last days of the Republic, with all its overtones of *libertas*, so as to make the theatre a template for his 'whole hierarchic vision of the society of the Roman Empire'.[82]

Horace appears to have his doubts about the desirability and feasibility of this enterprise.[83] Indeed, one of the reasons, perhaps, that Horace objects to this world of pageantry and display is that, as an *eques* who is *caelebs* ('a bachelor'), he may have been legally barred by his addressee's marriage and theatre legislation from attending the theatre at all. The evidence is indirect, but suggestive, that senatorial and equestrian bachelors were barred from the *ludi* for a period of some years, from perhaps as early as 22 BCE.[84] Before this period, it appears that Horace had been entitled to sit in the equestrian order's Fourteen Rows along with Maecenas (*ludos spectauerat una*, 'he had

[79] On the sack of Corinth in 146 BCE as an event that the Romans consciously constructed as a major turning-point in Greek–Roman relations, see Purcell (1995: esp. 143).

[80] *Sat.* 1.10.39, 72–7; *Epist.* 1.19.41–5.

[81] Schnurr (1992: 156).

[82] Rawson (1991: 509, 543). On the implications of the seating arrangements, cf. Kolendo (1981) and Schnurr (1992): Horace alludes to the separate seating of people and knights in 186–7, and in *Epod.* 4.15–16 he had used the violation of the *Lex Roscia* as an emblem of the dissolution of order. The relationship between the poet's art and the performances staged by the *Princeps* is likewise fundamental to Ovid's argument in his *Epistle to Augustus* (*Tr.* 2.279–84, 497–520): Barchiesi (1993: 167).

[83] This is part of the problem with the performance genres of drama or oratory— as Cicero says repeatedly in his oratorical works (e.g., *Brut.* 183–9), and as Horace says in the *Ars* (153), if the people do not respond properly to performance, it is bound to flop: Mayer (1995: 291–4). The political and the critical traditions both say you have to pay attention to the *uulgus* but both have serious qualms about it.

[84] Discussions of the evidence (Suet. *Aug.* 44.2, *CIL* 6. 32323.56–7, Mart. 5.41.8, Dio 54.30.5) in Rawson (1991: 525–6), canvassing various dates between 22 and 18, and Schnurr (1992: 159), suggesting the *Lex Iulia de maritandis ordinibus* of 18. Nicholas Purcell has kindly discussed with me the pitfalls of any secure reconstruction of the scope of any such ban, and the problems of whether Horace would have qualified as an *eques* of the right status to be covered. His caution has been salutary.

watched the show along with him', *Sat.* 2.6.48);[85] writing in 12, he
may be commenting on the spectacular dimension of a great theatrical world which he cannot actually see.

Whether or not this is the case, he certainly does not regard the
public as educable, and, as he shows when he begins the concluding
section at 214ff., he wants to retreat even from this more regulated
public world into a world of readership, instructing the *Princeps* to
accompany him if he wishes his regime to leave an enduring literary
legacy: *uerum age et his, qui se lectori credere malunt | quam spectatoris
fastidia ferre superbi, | curam redde breuem, si munus Apolline
dignum | uis complere libris*, 'Come on now, pay some brief attention
to those who prefer to entrust themselves to the reader rather than to
put up with the pickiness of the arrogant spectator, if you want to fill
up with books your dedication worthy of Apollo', 214–17.

Augustus should be more Horatian, it seems. At this most didactic
moment in the Epistle, with its *age* plus imperative leading into the
culminating instructions for the *Princeps*, we see more clearly than
anywhere else in the poem that Horace's discourse is not simply
mimicking or tracking that of Augustus.[86] Certainly, he is compelled
by the 'gravitational pull' of his addressee into a particular kind of
dialectic, and comparison with his other literary-critical epistles
throws this power-relationship into relief:[87] if, for example, you are
talking drama to the Pisos, as Horace is in the *Ars*, you might not find
yourself pulled into a political and spectacular realm of imagery and
thought, but if you are talking drama to Augustus, it appears, you
will. Brink, consequently, regularly calls attention to the differences
in this respect between our Epistle and the *Ars*, remarking that the
Ars 'does not explicitly dilate on the historical situation of poetry in
its own time', and 'avoids the political entanglements that cause
strains and stresses in the letter to Augustus';[88] we may acknowledge
the justice of his point, even if we do not follow him in marking the

[85] See Muecke (1993: ad loc.) and on *Sat.* 2.7.53; cf. Wiseman (1971: 71–2) on
Horace's equestrian status.
[86] A modification of the Lucretian formula *nunc age* + imperative (Brink (1982:
ad loc.)); cf. Barchiesi (1993) on Horace's didacticism in the Epistle.
[87] Again, 'gravitational pull' is the phrase of Freudenburg (2002b), a powerful
study of this effect in the correspondence of Horace and Florus.
[88] Brink (1982: 567, 571); cf. La Penna (1963: 171 n. 1); White (1993: 132).

Ars up and the *Epistle to Augustus* down accordingly. Nonetheless, what we are watching in the Epistle to Augustus is part of a dialogue, with the poet both reacting to and applying pressure; as Oliensis puts it, 'Horace's poems are not detached representations of society but consequential acts within society'.[89] Brink's 'strains and stresses' are the result of the friction generated as Horace and Augustus inter- change the roles of teacher and student: at this point, Horace's reservations about the value of spectacle are not just those of a literary critic, and when he moves into instructions on how rulers and poets should conduct relations, he is at once responding to and moulding one of the ruler's most dear concerns, his current and posthumous image.

   Santirocco well remarks that 'Augustus has been co-opted to the poet's own agenda', with the first of his Horatian roles being to stand in, 'as the object of the people's admiration', for 'the contemporary poet who deserves to be judged by the same critical standard'.[90] The interplay between the roles of addressee and addresser becomes a strange identity by the end of the poem, as Horace finally puts himself in Augustus' shoes and becomes the one who has a writer attached to him, running the risk of being commemorated in igno- miny *una | cum scriptore meo*, 267–8. The main lever he uses to get into this position is the long-lived conundrum of what Hunter, in an outstanding discussion of Theocritus 16, calls 'the doubleness of the patronage relationship', an issue that goes back to Simonides and Pindar, for whom 'poet and patron need each other, and are in much the same boat'.[91] The boat will carry poet and patron down the river

[89] Oliensis (1998a: 2–3); cf. Kennedy (1992: 40–2), Santirocco (1995), Feeney (1994: 347): 'The poets are not mirroring something that is a given, but participating in a social praxis as they make their constructions'.

[90] Santirocco (1995: 243).

[91] Hunter (1996: 105, 97); cf. Lowrie (2002) and for Horace's use of this Pindaric trope in the *Odes*, see Lowrie (1997: 107–8). Theocritus 16 is as important to Horace at the end of this *Epistle* as it is in *Odes* 4 (on which see Barchiesi (1996: 13–17, 25–9)). I am not concentrating on the problems of remuneration; briefly, it is instructive to juxtapose Oliensis (1998a: 194–7) on the different kinds of 'gifts' in this closing section with Hunter (1996: 105) on the ambiguities of χάριτες ('both "poems" and the "favour" or "pay" which those poems bring') and τιμή ('as well as "honour"..."pay" or "public office"'). Note how Horace's *dona Musarum* (243) modulates into the loaded word *munera* (246, 267), a word which carries all of the meanings listed by Hunter for his key Greek terms, except for 'poems'—plus, in addition, 'funeral rites', with which his poem ends.

of time together, as objects of reverence, envy, or ridicule.[92] A failure of Augustus' taste in fostering poets will make him a laughing-stock, as happened to Alexander, whose taste in painting, sculpture and classical poetry was not matched by his taste in contemporary poetry (232–44).[93] If the poet fails, the risk for both is colossal, as the closing allusion to Catullus 95 makes clear:[94] poet and *laudandus* alike will be ranked with the infamous sheets of Volusius, wrapping paper, consigned to death.

The concluding section, in which Horace skirmishes with these huge topics, is an advertisement for his classic status, as a master who dominates every aspect of his tradition. He begins with a ringing allusion to Ennius in line 229, showing that—whatever he may have said about the *ueteres* earlier in the poem—he knows that a Roman poet writing about praise and poetic apotheosis cannot avoid engaging with the poet of the *Annales* and the *Scipio*.[95] From this point on, the close of the poem outdoes even *Epist.* 1.3 in being an object lesson in how to use allusion to all the important layers of tradition simultaneously: Classical Greek (Simonides and Pindar), Hellenistic Greek (Theocritus), archaic Roman (Ennius), classics of the previous Roman generation (Cicero and Catullus) and the current one (Virgil and, no doubt, if we had more of him, Varius).[96]

[92] Cicero is the focus for the anxieties of ridicule here (256, and 262–3): see Barchiesi (1993: 157) and Lowrie (2002).

[93] Such I take to be part of the point of 241–4, where Horace says that Alexander was such a bad judge of contemporary poetry that you would swear he had been born in Boeotia: apart from the allusion to the proverbial stupidity of Boeotians, we should note that Boeotia was the home of Pindar, and when Alexander sacked Thebes in 335 he killed or enslaved everybody except for priests, *xenoi* of the Macedonians, and the descendants of Pindar, and destroyed every building except for the house of Pindar (Plut. *Alex.* 11.6; Arr. *Anab.* 1.9.10). As Alessandro Barchiesi reminds me, Augustus had his own problems of how to imitate models correctly: on his imitation of Alexander, see Galinsky (1996: 48, 167–8, 199–200).

[94] Barchiesi (1993: 158).

[95] *est operae pretium* looks to Enn. *Ann.* 494–5 and *op.inc.fr.* ii Skutsch; cf. Barchiesi (1962: 66, 69–70) for Horace's admiration for Ennius, and Hinds (1998: 15) for the way Ovid acknowledges the canonising power of Ennius' apotheosis of Romulus. Even in the earlier denunciation of the craze for the archaic, Horace had been careful to close his demolition of the *critici* by saying that the *ueteres* are not to be condemned altogether just because their defenders are idiots: see Hinds (1998: 70–1) on Horace's tribute to Livius Andronicus in 2.1.69–75.

[96] Space forbids detailed exemplification: besides the commentaries, see n. 91 for Pindar, Simonides, and Theocritus as models for the problems of praise and patronage; n. 95 for Ennius; n. 92 for Cicero; n. 94 for Catullus.

This parade of credentials is impressive, clinching the author's right to rank with Virgil and Varius. Still, once we have admired the credentials Horace parades here, we need to stand back and ask what it is that he actually delivers with them. The poem is full of things Horace cannot or will not do (tragedy, comedy, and especially panegyrical epic), although its principal argument is that he is the last member of a literary movement that has carried Roman poetry to a peak that matches the eminence of the restorer of the state. The poem ends with a strange, yet typically Horatian, mixture of confidence and incapacity, and we may conclude our analysis by using Horace's literary histories as a way of bringing this simultaneous sense of power and helplessness into focus.

First of all, the power and importance of poetry receive strong attention. The *Princeps*, for his part, wants to foster poetry, even if he needs instruction in how to do it consistently, and the poem closes by being acutely self-conscious that poet and *Princeps* will live together in this medium. The apprehension of poetry's power is highlighted, as regularly in Horace's late poetry, by its superiority to the visual arts, of painting, or sculpture.[97] Poetry is more expressive of character than these other arts (248–50); above all, throughout the closing section the immortalising power of poetry is the focus, and here Horace continues to assert, as he had in his *Odes*, that words on papyrus are a more potent form of commemoration than the apparently more durable and impressive medium of statuary.

If we bring to bear the perspective provided by Horace's literary histories, however, another dimension comes into play, which is now not necessarily an enabling one for the poet. Behind the antithesis between poetry and sculpture or painting there regularly lies another antithesis, that between Roman and Greek.[98] The Greek Alexander is perfectly at home as a connoisseur of the painter Apelles and the sculptor Lysippus (239–41): 'in this field, Greeks

---

[97] Important discussions in Hardie (1993: esp. 121–2, 133–5), and Barchiesi (1996: 12–13, 21) (on *Carm.* 4. 8). Note how *uidendis artibus* (242) picks up all the Aristotelian objections to the pleasure gained by the uncertain eyes in the section on spectacle (187–8).

[98] Exactly as in Anchises' speech in Virgil's Underworld (*excudent alii spirantia mollius aera* | ... *uiuos ducent de marmore uultus, Aen.* 6.847–8).

are still unchallenged'.[99] The radical Roman ambivalence to the Greek visual arts, and to the general culture they typify, is plain over the Epistle as a whole. Earlier in the poem painting was one of the Greek arts singled out for traditional ridicule (32–3); we have already noted Horace's scorn for the parade of Corinthian sculpture (193);[100] and the whole range of Greek culture is presented as the product of decadence and fickleness (93–8); yet the cultural energy that produced these arts is admired—the Greeks do it because they *enjoy* it (*gauisa*, 98)—and the arts are part of a coherent cultural drive, whereas in Rome they are not.[101] We remember that Horace's literary history showed poetry in Greece as one manifestation of a general tendency; at Rome, by contrast, poetry is always being, as it were, written against the grain, at odds with the national character,[102] legislated against, misunderstood by the public, the only one of the *artes* to be cultivated.[103] Against the background of Horace's literary histories, the isolation of poetry as the only part of Greek μουσική to find anything like a secure home in Rome is all the more accentuated—a paradox about Roman Hellenisation with which most modern literary historians would agree.

This uniqueness makes the poet powerful, because he is the sole figure in his domain, and weak, because he is isolated. One may see why Horace's last three projects are concerned with the writing of poetry. He is gradually writing himself, or being written, into a corner. On the conventional dating, after this Epistle, only the *Ars poetica* remains.[104]

[99] Barchiesi (1996: 21), on this theme in *Carm.* 4.8, where Parrhasius and Scopas are the paradigms.

[100] If sculpture is what it is: Brink (1982: 431–2).

[101] Cf. Wallace-Hadrill (1988: 232): 'Greek παιδεία, as far as we can see, was socially undifferentiated, belonging to, even defining, the world of the leisured. It was part of the Roman response to a threat to introduce sharp differentiation.' It is very poignant to see a Roman lyricist including the playing of the cithara as one of the things one cannot imagine a Roman doing properly (*psallimus*, 33).

[102] Even when the Romans do have a natural affinity (for tragedy, 165–6), it keeps getting overridden by their lack of capacity for *ars* (167). It is instructive to compare Roman historians' defence of their writing in a political and martial society: Kraus and Woodman (1997: 17).

[103] The untethered memory of the public performance of the *Carmen Saeculare* stands out as the exception (132–8): again, see Barchiesi (2002) for the significance of that exception.

[104] Cf. Brink (1982: 522, 559–61), on the options facing the later Horace, either 'to continue the political motif' (559), or else 'the three long literary epistles' (560).

16

Horace, Augustus, and the Question of the Latin Theatre

Antonio La Penna

I do not propose in this article to bring in new evidence, but to follow up on certain results that were arrived at by Otto Immisch in his commentary on Horace's *Ars*.[1] His work, along with the commentary of Rostagni, is one of the most productive contributions to the aesthetic history of the ancient world.

It is well known that the problem of the Latin theatre is discussed in Horace's epistle to Augustus (*Epist.* 2.1). I will attempt to trace out the development of its argument here. First Horace states, by way of a premise, that he will be brief, because Augustus, burdened as he is with such important tasks, has little time to listen to him (lines 1–4).[2] He therefore weaves a brief panegyric of the emperor, whose merits the Roman people recognize completely, since they worship him as a god even before his death (5–17).

As an introduction, this panegyric is skilfully adapted to the epistle's fundamental motif: the people are right to worship the emperor, but they do not judge all matters with the same discretion. For example, they judge very badly in preferring rough-hewn archaic literature to contemporary literature (18–27). It can be said that among the Greeks the best writers are the old ones. But if we should

---

[1] Immisch (1932).

[2] The tone of the letter's proem is much clearer if one keeps in mind that it was actually Augustus who demanded that Horace write the verse epistle (Suet. *Vita Hor.*).

proceed to apply this analogy as an absolute law, to what an absurd end we would come! (28–33). And moreover, how does one set the criterion of a poet's worth in relation to his antiquity? Shall we say that one poet is better than another because he was born one month, or one year, earlier? (34–49). The Roman people now award the highest value to the archaic poets, to Ennius, Naevius, Pacuvius, Accius, Afranius, Plautus, Caecilius, and Terence (we should note here that already attention has turned chiefly to the theatre): 'Mighty Rome learns them (that is, the poets just listed) by heart, and they watch them in the theatre, packed to capacity' (*hos ediscisit et hos arto stipata theatro | spectat Roma potens*, 60–1).

In fact, Horace continues, what good one can find in these archaic poets is an occasional brilliant word or gracious verse. But not one of their works is completely resistant to tasteful critique, though such critique may cause our elders to scream, they who were always so thrilled by Aesop and Roscius, the great actors of their youth (50–89). Moreover, if the Greeks had had the same terrible hatred towards innovation, they would never have created anything new and original, and they would not have given us the great works that we have from them (90–102). While they were creating these great works, constantly revamping their literary style, Romans were thinking of nothing but work and money and the law, etc. And it was precisely their love of innovation that turned them towards literary pursuits: 'the fickle populace have changed their thinking, and they hotly pursue just one passion: that of writing' (*mutauit mentem populus leuis et calet uno | scribendi sudio*, 108–9).[3]

This pursuit then became exaggerated, so that now everyone thinks he can scribble out lines of verse. In other professions, even those that are less noble, a certain competence is required: 'Qualified or unqualified, it doesn't matter: we write poetry' (*scribimus indocti doctique poemata passim*, 117).

At this point, however, Horace thinks he should excuse this literary insanity: the poet finds in writing verse an innocent distraction from bitter reality, but he does no one any harm. In fact he is useful to

---

[3] This notion that the love of innovation is important for the development of poetry is the central thread of lines 90–117. It is this same notion that Horace defends with regard to neologisms at *Ars* 46ff.

society, especially in his role as a moral and religious poet (118–38). Verses 118–38 are obviously a digression: Horace wanted to reaffirm the concept of poetry's moral utility in a letter wherein he has been defending implicitly his own work as a poet of satire and lyric. With verse 139 we return to the problem of archaic literature. Horace has condemned it. And he has also, in verses 108–17, condemned the fundamental vice that has tenaciously held over from archaic literature and still remains, to some extent, in contemporary literature: slapdash writing. He now resumes his case: how, and with what defects, did Latin literature come into being? It was initially the rough and unstructured literature of farmers: religious songs, fescennine songs. The latter of these degenerated into such licence that the law had to intervene to restrain it.[4]

True Latin literature begins after the conquest of Greece, through Greek influence: 'Greece, when captured, captured its fierce conquerer' (*Graecia capta ferum uictorem cepit*, 156). Even so, the defect persists. Greek influence did not eliminate altogether the primitive roughness: 'but even so traces of rusticity remained for a long time, and they still remain today' (*sed in longum tamen aeuum | manserunt hodieque manent uestigia ruris*, 159–60).

The Latins have not learned sufficiently from the Greeks how to file a work smooth (139–67). This lack of polish, then, is especially serious in the case of comedy. Look at Plautus. What carelessness marks his dramatic construction and his style! It matters little to him if his comedy stays on its feet or feebly stumbles over itself. He thinks only of filling his pockets (168–81). It is true that the dramatic poet has an ailment that bedevils him: the bad taste of the mob, *plebecula* (186), whom he needs to strive to please. This tasteless mass is tyrannical: if the spectacle does not gratify them, if the knights are at all out of step with their tastes, they clamour for an animal show. And so the theatre has been reduced to a series of empty and imposing choreographical parades that dazzle the eyes of stupid

---

[4] One thinks here of another charge against archaic poetry: what a beautiful recommendation it has in its *licentia*, while poetry should be a teacher of morality! I do not think that this interpretation is spot-on. In reality Horace is little concerned with fescennine verse. He keeps his aim on the authors of lines 50ff., whom the archaizers elevated to the stars. Moreover, how do we explain the reference to archaic religious poetry (lines 139–44)?

crowds. If Democritus were to show up among us, he would laugh not at the show on stage, but at the spectators (182–207). Horace, at any rate, is not against the dramatic arts *per se*. He would delight in a theatre that had substance, and that would stir up the emotions and awaken the imagination (208–13). One sees that from verse 168 on the poet's attention is concentrated entirely on the problem of the contemporary theatre.

Now, Horace continues, seeing that contemporary theatre produces no serious poetry—on the contrary, given the wretched taste of the Roman public, it presents conditions that are hostile towards its own development—to what other poetry should the emperor turn his attention? To poetry that is intended for reading, and that is the fruit of painstaking labour (214–16):

> Uerum age et his, qui se lectori credere malunt
> quam spectatoris fastidia ferre superbi,
> curam redde breuem.

But, come now, give a modicum of attention to those who prefer to entrust themselves to a reader rather than to subject themselves to the disdain of a haughty viewer.

It is only poets of this type that the emperor can entrust with his fame to deal with it worthily (214–44). Up to this point, moreover, Augustus has followed no other criterion: his judgement has been infinitely superior to that of the masses. He has entrusted himself to poets such as Virgil and Varius. Horace, too, would sing of the glory of Augustus if he had the strength for it (a commonplace of the *recusatio*, 244–59). But, in fact, making poetry requires strength of mind. Praise for a great man that is rendered in bad poetry will completely damage his reputation. It will end up as so much paper in the *uicus Tuscus,* in the marketplace, to be used for wrapping pepper and incense and goods of that type (260–70).

The logical development of the epistle, as we see above, presents no serious difficulties.[5] Certainly one need not think that Horace is, like

---

[5] I might have spared myself the summary and analysis of the epistle, if its structure were not so vigorously discussed; see, for example, Oltramare (1905: 411–25). In reality there is much less reason to discuss the structure of this poem than there is to discuss that of the problematic *Ars.*

390 Antonio La Penna

a professor, setting out to deduce and mark all of his logical transitions. One can consider this work a subtle literary satire (Horace is a satiric poet even in the *Ars*). And here Horace, as in all of his satires, maintains a pace that is brisk and agile, 'cinched up higher than we are' (*altius ac nos praecinctus*, *S*. 1.5.5–6, even if he wasn't so brisk in his travels). And yet there are logical transitions not hard to find, and the epistle suggests itself to us as an organic whole. The whole of it is tethered to a polemic against archaizing poetry that lacks polish in the name of poetry that is highly wrought. But the polemic becomes ever more concrete, and it shows its true face as it nears its conclusion (from verse 168 on): it is poetry for reading, the refined and precise poetry of literary circles, that is contrasted against the more popular literature of the theatre (there is no need to get into *S*. 1.10 here). This epistle, just as the *Ars,* but even more so, has behind it a precise problem of literature that belongs to the Roman culture of its day.

But against whom is this polemic aimed? At verse 81 Horace named the *patres* ('fathers' or 'elders'), men of the preceding generation, who were attached to the theatre of the second century BCE, and who were enthusiastic fans of the great actors of those plays, Aesop and Roscius. These old men think it shameful to yield to modern styles and to abandon the passions of their youth. Everyone will think of Cicero, who often expressed his deep passion for archaic plays, and for those who stood for conservative values in his day. Horace, although perhaps unconsciously, is continuing the debate that took place between Cicero (who represents, naturally, a certain social and intellectual current in Rome) and the neoteric poets. He is, on this point, in agreement with the neoterics—in fact the poetic principles of Callimachus owe much to the *Ars* of Horace for their continued vitality.[6] This is a polemic, therefore, aimed at a sector of Roman high society that was attached to the literary traditions of the second century BCE. The continued relevance of this tradition is easy to explain: for Cicero, archaic dramatic productions, along with the *Annales* of Ennius, are the great national poetry of the Roman people. Virgil, with one strand of Augustan poetry, in a certain sense, and within certain limits, wanted to continue that tradition. Augustus

[6] Cf. *Ars* 289ff., 386ff.

uses the tradition as one of the levers of his conservative political platform.

Most often Horace attacks in a contemptuous tone the taste of the Roman people, and of the ignorant masses. These masses are, to be more exact, the *plebecula* ('rabble') that corrupt the theatre with their coarse tastes. Such a polemical stance is clear for those who recall other passages in Horace. In the tenth satire of his first book he defends his own highly wrought poetry, savoured by a select circle of friends, against the slipshod poetry of others that finds favour with a larger public, and he compares himself to the actress Arbuscula, who despised the catcalls of the plebs and haughtily contented herself with the applause of the knights: 'it's enough for me that the class of knights applaud me' (*satis est equitem mihi plaudere*, *S.* 1.10.76). In the section of the *Ars* that is devoted to the music of the theatre (202–19), Horace assigns blame for the corruption and over-elaboration of this art that followed upon the first great Mediterranean conquests of Rome, to the tastelessness of the rough Latian farmers (*Ars* 212–15):[7]

> Indoctus quid enim saperet liberque laborum
> Rusticus urbano confusus, turpis honesto?
> Sic priscae motumque et luxuriem addidit arti
> Tibicen traxitque uagus per pulpita uestem.

For what aesthetic sense was that (old-time Roman) to have untaught, a bumpkin on his day off, a concatenation of country and city, decent and base? Thus the flute-player added lascivious movements to his pure old art, and he let his costume drag ramblingly across the stage.

The passage immediately following at *Ars* 220–50 treats the matter of satyr plays. Here I will leave aside the question of the relationship of this passage to ancient aesthetics and the history of the Roman theatre. What seems certain to me is that here Horace is treating his own ideal of comic poetry, a poetry that is refined and free of all triviality.[8] The rabble's favourite gags (and here Horace is probably

---

[7] Cf. the commentary of Immisch (1932: 131ff.).

[8] The concern here is not just for an ideal comic poetry, but for a more general stylistic ideal. It is this very ideal that Horace pursued in his *Sermones* and *Epistulae:* a refined comic sense, urbane, and free of vulgarity and bombast. In those poems Horace's satiric vocabulary is familiar, but his style is at once familiar and noble. This is a matter of establishing a characteristic middle tone. It would be interesting to study the formation of that tone in both Greek and Latin literature.

thinking of Plautus without naming him) offend the refined tastes of
the knights (248–50):

> Offenduntur enim quibus est equus et pater et res,
> nec, si quid fricti ciceris probat et nucis emptor,
> aequis accipiunt animis donantue corona.

Men of good lineage, of property and horse find (these low comic tricks)
offensive. And they do not warmly receive, and award the crown to, what
those who snack on toasted chick-peas and nuts approve of.

The polemic takes a turn, polite and veiled, against even Augustus.
We know that Horace (and there is sufficient evidence for this in his
works) was polite, but by no means servile. There is nothing strange,
then, in the idea that he might have allowed himself to issue a critique
against Augustus. Certainly Horace had to agree with the emperor at
some level on his inclinations that were specific to literature—and
here we will leave aside the bigger question of his agreement with the
emperor's political tendencies. Augustus loved a style that was serious, clear, *elegans et temperatum* ('elegant and measured'), without
excessive ornamentation and, above all, not *recherché*.[9] For example,
he made fun of the farfetched and obscure style of Maecenas.[10] In his
letters he shunned gravity and approximated a tone of *sermo cotidia-
nus* ('everyday conversation'). But it is precisely on the matter of the
theatre and archaic poetry that Augustus' ideas must have differed to
some extent from those of Horace. Augustus enjoyed the shows of
low-brow artists.[11] That is, he enjoyed exactly those shows that the

---

[9] On the style of Augustus, of which we have an example in the *Monumentum
Ancyranum*, cf. Suet. *Aug.* 86ff., and Malcovati (1928: XV–XXVI).

[10] Suet. *Aug.* 86.3. Maecenas was the right hand of Augustus in his literary politics,
owing to his numerous connections in the world of letters. But it is probable that all
of the literary, stylistic, and ideological tendencies that belong to this political agenda
come from Augustus. The style of Maecenas, as his fragments attest, is laughably
distant from the tendencies that are dominant in Augustan literature. Augustus was
much greater than his ministers.

[11] Suet. *Aug.* 43ff., especially 45, 74, 99. See the passages cited by Immisch (1932:
157). Also Ovid Trist. 2.509ff. *inspice ludorum sumptus, Auguste, tuorum... haec tu
spectasti spectandaque saepe dedisti... luminibusque tuis, totus quibus utitur orbis,
scaenica uidisti lentus adulteria* ('examine the cost of your own plays, Augustus... you
have watched these spectacles and you have often staged them to be watched...
relaxing, you have beheld staged adulteries with your eyes, the very ones that the
whole world uses').

Roman plebs loved and that Horace despised. Augustus delighted in the plays of Old Comedy and he staged them often for the Roman populace.[12] Perhaps the sharp Italian 'vinegar' of archaic literature dressed the fescennine verses that he wrote (according to the testimony of Macrob. *Sat.* 2.4.21). Unfortunately we can say nothing of his effort at tragedy, entitled the *Aiax*, only that he lacked the will to finish it, and so he destroyed the draft. To his friends who wanted to know of his play's status he responded that 'Ajax had fallen on his own sponge'.[13]

There is a contrast more serious and significant. Behind the epistle to Augustus and the *Ars poetica* stands an Augustan programme of restoring the Latin theatre. I am in no position to make a demonstration of it here. Several have already made this observation, and the study that does it most clearly is that of Immisch.[14] Why undertake to restore the theatre? Because the theatre was the most popular form of literature. It wielded influence among not only persons of the middle classes, who were cultivated to some degree, but also the plebs.

In his social politics Augustus sought to achieve a balance, and a collaboration, between the classes, aiming skilfully, but with a clear conservative purpose, towards a compromise between opposing forces.[15] The powers of the aristocracy were limited, but aristocrats always preserved the highest place in the social hierarchy. They maintained administrative control over a certain block of provinces. And although the knights were no longer able to use tax-farming as a means of robbing at will, the doors of a vast and highly mechanized bureaucracy were open to them. Those in the middle classes sought to protect themselves by attempting to slow down the economic process that was pushing towards the destruction of the small economic stake they possessed. Their attempt, over time, was doomed to fail, but for a while they managed effectively to slow its advance. For the unemployed and hungry plebs, Augustus adopted an unfortunate remedy, the free distribution of moneys and grain, and the staging of spectacles in the

[12] Suet. *Aug.* 89. Immisch (1932: 156).
[13] Suet. *Aug.* 85.3.
[14] Immisch (1932: 143ff.).
[15] Cf. the chapter dedicated to Augustus in Rostovtzeff (1926).

theatre and circus (naturally this could only happen because Rome was positioned atop the imperial hierarchy: the provinces in fact paid for the plebs of the capital).[16] Augustus sought to do all he could with the classes to keep them balanced against one another as self-contained organic units.

Rome's middle classes form the central axis of this politics of balance and compromise. It would take us too far afield here to research in detail just how much this orientation might help us interpret the literature of the Augustan age. But it is easy to see how the abandonment of neoteric poetry, refined and obscure, learned and literary, for a poetry more open, more clear, and more human might agree with the political tendency I have pointed to. The poet of the *Eclogues* and *Georgics* tells in his *Aeneid* of the sorrows and dreams of rustic Evander. At the same time he addresses the sorrows and aspirations of a crowd of *agricolae* who have been shattered by civil war, and who yearn for the workaday peace of their tiny farms. Tibullus, a minor poet, is in line with the same trend. Horace never misses an opportunity to censure the manic opulence of Rome's rich and elite. His own personal philosophy, which has little fanciful speculation in it but much of real life, is an adaptation of all that Romans and Italians of the middle classes might usefully extract from various Hellenistic philosophies: the golden mean, the manly renunciation of excess, and so on.

With this I do not wish to say that Augustan poetry is entirely of this type. On the contrary! Virgil's loftiest poetry issues from a tragic mask. And Horace's philosophical equilibrium is always rather shaky. He borders on lonely disappointment in his old age. At times he is even desolate. But this means that contemporary poetry, deep inside itself, escapes from Augustan politics. We think that it escapes from what that compromise was hiding.[17]

In addition to the trends just mentioned, the great poetry of the Augustan period was poetry of the schools and recitation halls. It

---

[16] *Mon. Anc.* 15. Augustus cares about presenting himself as the protector and benefactor of the plebs. One recalls the rioting of the plebs during the famine of 23 BCE. Augustus quelled the violence by assuming for himself the care of the grain supply.

[17] For an interpretation of the *Aeneid* in this sense, compare Paratore (1944: 148ff.), a book that is rich, for all of its unstable effervescence.

was, moreover, overly attached to neotericism, the experience of which it continued to actively assimilate and preserve. For Virgil, Theocritus and Apollonius of Rhodes count for much more than do Hesiod and Homer. One need not recall how much the elegiac poets and Horace himself owe to the neoteric currents of Alexandria. To be heard and interpreted, Augustan poetry required cultured knowledge and refinement of the highest order. Not that it was short on human feeling. On the contrary, to be enjoyed, this strain of human feeling required hard effort. It was a poetry much more popular than neoteric poetry, but not as popular as Augustus would have liked, because literature awakened around him the consensus and the energies of a wide swathe of the Roman populace, including the lower classes. Thus theatre became a necessity.

The decadence of the Roman theatre was precisely the result of written literature's meagre popularity. The most popular poet in Rome was Plautus, whose talent, while profoundly Italian, was nurtured by the Greek theatre and developed at a time when the Roman people were still sufficiently united in their zest for grand military conquests. This was a time when the economic process that arose from these conquests had not yet produced a vast proletariat among the Roman populace, and the ferocious class wars and the political crisis that began with the Gracchi and ended with Augustus.

It is well known that the Scipionic Circle already worked out a sense of *urbanitas*, a literature of the cultured elite. Thus we have Terence as the follow-up to Plautus. The literature that extends from Ennius to Accius obviously aims ever more at an elite audience. And by the end of the second century BCE we already see the emergence of a neoteric spirit that will stamp its profound mark on the literature of the first half of the next century.

In every way the poetry of the second century BCE, especially that of the theatre, still touched all strands of the Roman populace. Plautus, touched up and refashioned, would often revisit the Roman stage. Cicero is not only a reader, but a spectator of his favourite poets. The age of Augustus knows only two theatrical successes, the *Thyestes* of Varius and Ovid's *Medea*. These are successes, moreover, that will find no further life beyond their own time. For Augustus, therefore, the restoration of the national theatre was the central problem of his literary politics. He had good reason to reward the *Thyestes* as richly as he did.[18] His zest for Old Comedy thus resurfaces in a new light. The emperor's programme had to involve poets who were insulated by patronage, even Horace.

In the epistle to Augustus Horace says no to the emperor. The poetry that the emperor should care about is that which is highly wrought and intended for readers, and for readers of taste. Horace's position will change, at least up to a certain point, in the *Ars*.[19] Here he will implicitly approve of the programme of the theatre's restoration.[20] But, in approving of it, he will do all he can to bring it back to the poetic ideal that he has always pursued. That is why so many of the motifs of the epistle to Augustus will be reintroduced in the *Ars*: the condemnation of the archaic theatre, of popular enthusiasms, and of shoddy workmanship. Virgil, in emulating the great poets of Greece, still holds Ennius in high regard. Horace recommends studying the Greeks day and night, but he finds nothing to save in Archaic drama. He exhumes satyr drama because it represents, as we have said, an ideal of aristocratic comic practice that is a far cry from plebeian farce.

Horace not only expresses his own personal convictions, but he interprets broadly, consciously or not, the predilections of contemporary literary circles and of the cultured classes. Thus the *Ars* may hold in it an era's last will and testament. It presents to us, in the face of the Augustan programme and its need for a literature that was widely heard by the people, the limit that literature of the age hesitated to cross, and that it was unable to cross.

The reason that this limit could not be crossed is clear to the modern historian, and perhaps a mind as sharp as the one that conceived the *Dialogus de Oratoribus* may have already discovered it: popular national drama could not be revived precisely because Augustus' social solution was not a healing or recovery, but a compromise that hardened the blood of Rome's wounds without healing

---

[18] According to the *didascalia* of both cod. Par. 7530 and Casanatensis 1086, the prize was a million sesterces.

[19] The assertion presupposes that the *Ars* was written after the epistle to Augustus. On this chronology, see the Appendix below.

[20] It was clear already to Lejay (1903) that the *Ars* pursues an ideal of dramatic poetry that was not yet realized in the Latin world. He took issue with Boissier (1898), who thought that the *Ars* reflected images of the dramatic poetry of the Augustan age.

them. To have a theatre like that of Plautus and Ennius you need, as a prerequisite, a citizenry and a society like the ones they had in their day: still healthy, and not yet shaken and split by one of the most ferocious economic and political crises that history has seen. Dramatic poetry in Latin died shortly after the Gracchi, just as great oratory died with the Republic.

And it was never revived in Rome, just as literature that was truly popular was never revived.[21] Although there is perhaps still much further clarity to be had by subjecting the evidence to the light of the social history of the empire, this is not the place to trace the development of pagan Latin literature in the empire all the way to the feckless neotericism of the so-called *poetae novelli*, and to the playthings of the professor-poet, Ausonius, and the gilded ornaments of the court poet, Claudianus.[22] Everyone will concede that, until the emergence of Christian literature, Latin literature will have no wide hearing among the people at large. The attempt made by Augustus, in the end, was a clear failure, and history has generally taken sides with Horace.

If all that I have argued to this point is soundly based, Horace's epistle to Augustus is a key to interpreting the development of Latin literature.

APPENDIX: THE CHRONOLOGY OF THE *ARS* AND THE EPISTLE TO AUGUSTUS

All that I have said above about the *Ars* coming after the epistle to Augustus obliges me to make a defence of my chronology.

It will be useless to analyse once again the poem's references to contemporary events and persons. Not one of these allows us to posit

---

[21] It is a near-universal opinion that the tragedies of Seneca were not staged. However those of Pomponius Secundus were staged (Tac. *Ann.* 11.13). Quintilian judges him quite favourably at *Inst. or.* 10.1.98. But his plays must have been harshly received by the people, given that Claudius in 47 had to take measures against popular licence on the occasion of their being staged in the theatre.

[22] While correcting page proofs I now have in my hands Paratore's *Storia della letteratura latina*, which marks a step forward in this regard.

a secure date, since none prevents us from dating the poem after 13 BCE, that is, the date of the epistle to Augustus and Book 4 of the *Odes*.[23]

Immisch's dating of the *Ars* to 20–19 BCE, that is, just prior to the death of Virgil, is based primarily on the argument, not new, that in the *Ars* hardly any space is devoted to epic poetry, and no mention is made of Virgil as the poet of the *Aeneid*.[24] In reality other omissions just as great remain to be explained. And they are best explained by what Immisch, in his excellent commentary, aims to demonstrate; namely, that the *Ars* is not a teaching handbook, careful and complete, but a treatise. It is, at the same time, a polemical work that is linked to a particular literary problem, the renovation of the Roman theatre. It is a defence of a particular poetic sensibility. Moreover, it is known that from Aristotle on dramatic poetry had assumed the dominant place in discussions of poetry to the disadvantage of other genres. In the end, the slight bit of room given to epic poetry, and the poem's silence regarding Virgil, would be strange, even aside from these factors, so soon after the death of the poet. Why wouldn't Horace, just as Propertius did, announce the arrival of that glorious poem? In fact, when Horace was writing the *Ars*, the problem of national epic was no longer current.

Perhaps we can take a point of departure less insecure for dating the *Ars* from the pages that Rostagni has dedicated to the question.[25] From a comparison of the motifs shared between the *Ars* and the epistle to Augustus, he deems it possible to conclude that the former does not 'summarize and repeat (as is the common opinion of many) the "material" that was laid out' in the latter, but that, on the contrary, the latter is 'not only a development of, but an apologia for' the former. He therefore dates the *Ars* a little before the epistle to Augustus; that is, to 14–13 BCE. Though we might expect a detailed

---

[23] I think that the observations of Lejay (1902: 361ff.) are still valid on this point.

[24] Immisch (1932: 7).

[25] Rostagni (1930: XVI–XIX). Those who are willing to wander through labyrinthine hypotheses, as gratuitous as they are labyrinthine, can read the slight article by Smith (1936: 163–6). He thinks that the *Ars* was composed between 23 and the end of 22 BCE, then set aside for a decade, then finally corrected and dedicated to the Pisones and published after 13. Everyone is satisfied this way. Horace would have then applied to his own work the principle of *nonum prematur in annum* ('hold [the work] back for nine years').

comparison of motifs and parallel passages, Rostagni does not go into the details.

I do not think that a comparison of parallel motifs would produce any secure result. To assert that certain motifs in the *Ars* are taken up and developed in the epistle to Augustus is no more legitimate than to say that motifs developed in the epistle to Augustus are recapitulated in the *Ars*. This has to be taken as a general treatise. It therefore must not give excessive development to any parts with respect to the whole. And, moreover, across its entirety it aims at an elegant and ripe concision (the famous 'eclogistic' procedure).

Let's look at some specific instances. A motif that is shared by both epistles is the polemic against those who are enthusiastically devoted to archaic literature. This is a central topic in the epistle to Augustus, as we have seen. At *Ars* 258–74 there unfolds a brief argument about the use of the iambic trimeter, that it was used by the archaic poets with too much licence and negligence, and that it was jumbled with other verse types. Can anything be concluded from this about one epistle's coming before the other? One may conclude that the epistle to Augustus supports with ample demonstration a polemic that is set alight by a single passage of the *Ars*. But one can make the counter reply that the *Ars* limits to a single case the application of an idea that is amply developed in the epistle to Augustus.

Nearly the same argument can be made in the case of another shared motif, the comparison between the development of Greek literature and Latin literature. In the epistle to Augustus the comparison is very important and detailed (lines 90–102 treating the Greeks, lines 103–117 treating the Romans). In the *Ars* the comparison is developed first in relation to dramatic poetry (lines 275–94, with the same conclusion being reached in both epistles: to put effort into Greek texts, to polish like the Greeks), and then in lines 323–32, a comparison between the practical and mercantile spirit of the Romans and the natural genius and harmony of Greek poetry. In neither case does one epistle necessarily presuppose the other.

In lines 114–17 of the epistle to Augustus Horace develops a satiric motif: anyone who wants to practise a professional skill, such as that of a helmsman, a physician, or a carpenter, considers it necessary to possess certain talents and training. But when it comes to poetry no one has any scruples about scribbling out lines. The motif is developed in the *Ars* more amply and with a number of examples (lines 408–18). This serves to demonstrate that poetry requires art just as much as it requires natural talent. It will be said, then, that the *Ars* gives fuller treatment to an idea that occurs in the epistle to Augustus. An objection arises: but the comparison is better suited to the *Ars* (where it at least presents a minimum of difficulty). One could continue to argue this way *ad infinitum*. Discussions that concern the chronology of Sophocles and Euripides are equally endless, because there is no way to fix the chronology other than by internal comparisons from one tragedy to another.

The argument that Rostagni and others have drawn from Suetonius' *Vita Horati* is just as weak. Augustus, *post sermones quosdam lectos* ('after he had read some of [Horace's] *Sermones*'), complains in a letter to the poet that he has never addressed a composition in that genre to him, and so Horace writes to him the verse epistle that we are discussing here. The *sermones* that Suetonius speaks of are surely the epistles. Everyone agrees on this. But one need not accept that the *Ars Poetica* was among these *sermones*. The epistle to Florus, according to Rostagni himself, precedes the epistle to Augustus, and among the epistles of Book 1 there are some (1, 2, 7, 16, 17, 18) of considerable length.

It seems to me that we are left with one important argument for dating the epistle to Augustus ahead of the *Ars*. This letter, we have seen, is predicated on the opposition between the poetry of the theatre, on the one hand, and poetry for reading, on the other. Its conclusion is that the emperor ought to direct his care towards poetry for reading. Not that Horace rejects the theatre altogether. But this concession is only briefly glimpsed (in lines 208–13) before we pass on to the letter's substantial point: the defence of poetry that is, so to speak, closed off from public view. The *Ars*, in turn, is predicated entirely on this concession, which turns into an acceptance of a programme of dramatic poetry, then a battle over it. Horace's case is clear: a poet of satire and lyric, he writes no drama himself. He is oriented towards the theatre simply as poetry's gadfly and advocate. And in the end he deems the *spectatoris fastidia superbi* ('haughty spectator's disdain') acceptable for the poet.

If, however, we were to allow for the idea that the *Ars* precedes the epistle to Augustus, we would have to think that Horace, as a poet within a literary coterie, embraced, if only in his own way, the Augustan programme to revive the theatre, but that he then thought better of this and turned back to poetry for reading, distancing himself from Augustus. Anyone can see just how much less probable this second hypothesis is (I speak here of probability because I do not, of course, pretend to have split the knot).

It is not my intention here to throw into doubt the identification of Piso the father with the Lucius Piso of Porphyrio. The pages of Rostagni that reconstruct the entire literary milieu surrounding Lucius Piso Caesoninus, a scene with which Horace would have had fruitful contacts, seem to me to rank among the highlights of his work.[26] This is a work of Italian philology that, quite rightly, enjoys a larger European resonance. But it is clear that the identification it proposes for the Piso of the *Ars* stirs up much less difficulty the later one puts the date of the *Ars*.

[26] Rostagni (1930: XIX–XXXIV).

17

Towards a Reading of Horace's Epistle to Julius Florus (*Epistles* 2.2)

Elio Pasoli

Horace's epistle to Julius Florus, whether because of its bulk or its theme, has traditionally been classed with the letters to Augustus (*Epist.* 2.1) and to the Pisones (called the *Ars poetica* since antiquity[1]) as a 'literary' epistle. As a consequence, the letter is usually read and studied more for its points of contact with those other 'literary' epistles, and for one of its sections—a limited portion in respect to the whole (17 verses out of 216) containing Horace's demands for an unexceptional poetic style—than it is for its own sake. However, in my judgement, a close reading of the epistle to Florus can easily demonstrate that this letter differs actually quite profoundly from the other two long epistles that deal with questions of literature. In those letters, even more in the epistle to the Pisones than in the epistle to Augustus, the discussion is nearly overwhelmed by matters literary, exquisitely so, and technical. In them one looks, first of all, for Horace's poetic credo, the ideology to which he bound his poetic considerations in the last years of his life. But a pronounced character of spiritual withdrawal, and an active, penetrating lyricism that stems from the poet's complete withdrawal to the written page characterizes the long confession to his young friend, Julius Florus. This is a

---

[1] The title *Ars poetica* or *De arte poetica liber* was known and used already by Quintilian. For the documentation and for a discussion of the question, see chapter 5 of Pasoli (1964a).

withdrawal that Horace himself had discovered in Lucilius, as Aristoxenus had found it in the older Greek lyric poets.[2] There, in those other two 'literary' epistles, poetic worth is located primarily in the rudiments of what G. della Volpe has felicitously defined a 'poetics of realism'.[3] An ideology of literature, and the adherence to a literary programme that is in some measure 'global' in the *Ars poetica* and *au courant* in the epistle to Augustus, guarantee to these texts a significance and a relevance that one associates, in great measure, with their 'theoretical' contents. And at the same time—this generally happens in works where the criticism in question is being crafted by a poet—each letter's significance, to a greater extent in the epistle to Augustus, and lesser in the *Ars poetica*, surpasses its theoretical content. Another case has to be made in the case of the epistle to Florus, because here even the sections that are more strictly literary, and in particular lines 109–25, possess a value that is above all not absolute, but functional. They serve as component parts of a state of mind that is multiform and complex; a state of mind that, for six years, from 23 to 17 BCE, caused Horace to detach himself from the creation of poetry in the lyric mode of the *Odes*—for him the equivalent of staying away from poetry altogether, for from the standpoint of theory he regards as true poetry only that which is devoted to artistic rules in the very manner of the *Odes*—in order that he might dedicate himself to *sapientia* ('wisdom'), to a search, not always easy or successful, for an interior balance that is obedient to the principles of *autarkeia* and *mesotes* ('self-rule' and 'moderation'). This is a state of mind that, even when the poet was subsequently pressured by an invitation from Augustus to celebrate by means of an official *Carmen* the *ludi saeculares* of 17 BCE, and then again when he turned to composing Book 4 of the *Odes*, left evident

---

[2] Hor. *S.* 2.1.30–4, 'way back then he used to entrust his secrets to his books as though they were trusted companions. He would make straight for them, having no other recourse, whether things went badly or well. And so we have the old man's entire life splayed out before us as if represented on a votive tablet.' Horace's position relative to Lucilius is considered by the scholiasts Porphyrio and pseudo-Acro (ad loc.) as similar to that of Aristoxenus to Sappho, Alcaeus, and Anacreon. On this question, see Brink (1963: 172–4, with n. 2). Horace's statement, with all of its implications for his character, at once both literary and human, is effectively discussed by Fraenkel (1957: 150–3).

[3] Della Volpe (1964: 9–11).

Elio Pasoli

traces on the singer's voice.[4] That voice was clearly no longer the same.

Because the epistle to Florus was written, as far as we can tell, towards the end of 20 BCE, at the centre of a spiritual crisis that is known as the *intervallum lyricum*, in a certain sense, the letter gets to the heart of that crisis by revealing its motivations and its evolution, giving a faithful image of Horace's state of mind at the centre of his *intervallum lyricum*.[5] Thereby the epistle serves up an obvious paradox. For at the same time as it undertakes to distance Horace from lyric poetry and to document his progress away from it, the epistle ends up being 'lyrical' in the highest degree, if by lyricality one understands the outpouring of one's inner life, and the writer's abandoning himself, without reticence or cover, to the written page. Lyricality, that is, in its modern conception, not that it was understood this way already in the ancient world, nor by Horace in particular. But in any case the poetry of this letter is deeply valid in ways that extend beyond its usefulness in documenting certain of Horace's ideas about literature, and for the details it provides in its depiction of the poet's career. Richard Heinze, in an essay that is memorable, despite sometimes going too far in the extremism of certain of its assertions, maintained that the most pronounced characteristic of *Epistles* Book 1—to which the epistle to Florus should quite clearly be joined, in that it is intimately linked to them by its date of composition, its tone and contents—is that of its being a spiritual autobiography.[6] Its protreptic character, dedicated to the

---

[4] Suetonius' biography of Horace puts it this way: '[Augustus] so approved of his writings...that he commissioned him to write not only the *Carmen Saeculare*, but also the victory of his step-sons, Tiberius and Drusus, over the Vindelici. To this end he forced him to add a fouth book to his three books of *Carmina* after a long break (from lyric).' Even if we do not take these statements literally, there can be no doubt that the pressures applied by the princeps himself, as well as by the general climate of the Augustan era, were weighty factors in pushing Horace to return to the genre of lyric after six years of inactivity. On the relations between Augustus and the larger Augustan climate and Horace in the last period of his life, see my interpretation of the epistle to Augustus, Pasoli (1964a: 196–225).

[5] Against the hypothesis of Vahlen (1878), according to which the epistle is to be dated to 18 BCE, strong arguments both internal and external point to a date near the end of 20 BCE, just before the publication of the first book of *Epistles*, or actually contemporaneous with them. See my discussion of this at Pasoli (1964a: 60–4).

[6] Heinze's *Horazens Buch der Briefe* was originally published in *Neue Jahrbücher* 43 (1919: 305ff.) then republished in a selection of Heinze's writings edited by E. Burck

instruction of others, especially to those young men who will constitute the next generation of statesmen (a group to which Julius
Florus himself belongs, as do many other of the correspondents to
whom Horace addresses his epistles[7]), is certainly in keeping with
this first characteristic, but it is secondary to it. If it is in fact certain,
as Heinze himself recognized, that Horace's personal experience both
could and should serve to lead others along the same path, especially
the young, it is nonetheless true that a straightforwardly lyrical
outpouring of such personal experience is a preponderant feature
of the letter to Florus, often to the point of displacing entirely its
protreptic aims.

As an aside I wish here to recall the awkwardness of the position
recently taken by C. Becker, who, engaging in a polemic against
Heinze's interpretation, has asserted that the *sapientia* of the
Epistles is entirely of an abstract kind, and that the epistles are not
linked to any particular situations and experiences of the author, and
that the precepts they contain are universal and detached from any
contingent circumstances.[8] That Heinze might have been essentially
right is actually demonstrated by the conclusion of the epistle to
Florus. There the protreptic intent, implicitly declared by Horace
before he begins his long meditation (line 145), largely gives way to
the poet's full confession, to a conversation with himself first, then
with his own conscience.[9] In a few quick strokes his conscience
destroys the security that Horace had just seemed to attain by putting
before him a conclusion that has the feel of a definitive and final
sentence. That sentence concerns not Florus, but only Horace. For it

---

(1938: 236–54). The latter has now been reproduced in the appendix to Kiessling-
Heinze vol. III (1961) 367–80.

[7] Horace also dedicated *Epist.* 1.3 to Julius Florus. Porphyrio annotates the first line
of that letter as follows: 'this Florus, a scribe (by which he seems to mean "secretary" of
Tiberius), was a writer of satires. Satires of his were selected from Ennius, Lucilius, and
Varro' (which signifies that, in addition to writing satire himself, Florus edited an
anthology of the great writers of satire). In 21 BCE he was in the *cohors* that accompanied Tiberius to Asia. Both of Horace's epistles to him stem from the period of that
expedition, the first (1.3) a little after his departure, in the last months of 21 or the first
months of 20, and the second (2.2), as we have said, towards the end of 20.

[8] Becker (1963).

[9] I maintain that in the last part of the epistle, from lines 205 to the end, it is the
conscience of Horace that speaks.

is Horace who is near the end of his life, the moment when 'it is time to leave' (*tempus abire... est*, 215). This is certainly not true of Florus, who at that time has a full life ahead of him.

As far as I am concerned, then, there is no doubt that the epistle to Florus, at the same time as it represents the acme of Horace's detachment from poetry, and the sense of disgust and ill-health that it provokes in him, turns out to be a work that is poetically rich and full. This is the basic antinomy that dominates all the epistles of Horace, works that the poet intended as 'conversations crawling along the ground' (*sermones... repentes per humum*, Epist. 2.1.250, referring to the style to which he had deliberately lowered them), and yet managed nonetheless to make profoundly and singularly valid as poetry. And although I cannot fully share the opinion of E. Turolla, who seems to see in the epistles of the first book the high-point of Horatian poetry, in any case I believe that the actual poetic substance and worth of these epistles should be considered in inverse proportion to the 'disengagement' from poetry that Horace wanted them to represent.[10] For him, these epistles were to be accounted 'verses' rather than poetry, a meditation conducted in the prosaic manner of a monochord hexameter, and thus distinct from poetry. And yet to us they appear a work of highest poetry. The 'pattern' for making poetry, that is, the 'verse' (the concrete expression of Jakobson's 'poetic function'[11]), which on its own does not constitute poetry, but without which there can be no poetry, becomes for Horace a living, breathing 'example' of poetry. Even when he no longer wishes to be one, he remains a poet.

Is Horace, then, a poet in spite of himself in his *Epistles*? One can concede to this up to a certain point. But one cannot ignore the fact that in his *Epistles*, even as he is deliberately constrained within the

---

[10] Turolla (1963). See esp. his *Introduzione alla lettura di Orazio*, pp. CXII–CXXX, and *Introduzione alle Epistole*, 869–915 (esp. 875ff.) and 906–8.

[11] I am recalling here the suggestive statements and terminology of Roman Jakobson in his recent essay 'Linguistics and Poetics'. There he studies the connections between linguistics and poetics, and analyses with strict scientific rigour the essence and structure of the poetic function. The essay, originally published in English in 1960, appears in French translation as R. Jakobson (1963). *Essais de linguistique general*, trans. and intro. N. Ruwet (Paris). It appears as chapter XI of the book, under the title 'Linguistique et poétique', pp. 210–48. For the issues under consideration here, see esp. pp. 221ff.

limits of his *sermo pedester*, his 'conversations crawling along the ground', and while he is deliberately distant from lyric's loftiness of tone, Horace nonetheless deploys with his usual, signature mastery many of the procedures that a more modern and established criticism recognizes as constituting, in essence, the poetic function. To restrict ourselves to the epistle to Florus, we see that here, as always, Horace proves himself the master of 'clever arrangement' (*callida iunctura*). This is not the place for a detailed analysis of the problems that come with interpreting the 'vexed' expression of the *ars* lines 46–8: 'Even when you are sparing and cautious in plaiting your words together you will have said something remarkable if by a clever arrangement you have made something new of a familiar word' (*in uerbis etiam tenuis cautusque serendis | dixeris egregie, notum si callida uerbum | reddiderit iunctura nouum*).[12] Suffice it to say that, in order to clarify and interpret this passage in its correct sense, modern concepts concerning the elements that constitute the poetic function seem to be extremely useful. In short, it seems to me that Horace wanted, in his own way, to say that a word that, on its own, has a purely 'denotative' function (to use the terminology of C. Brooks and R. P. Warren, by now nearly universal and, for the most part, felicitous[13]), when it is inserted into a fixed context takes on a further 'connotation' that renders it, in essence, poetic and therefore, in the final analysis, 'new'. Naturally a variety of expressive procedures are included in Horace's assertion, and those who have interpreted his

---

[12] There exists an entire literature on this expression and its interpretation. In addition to the principle commentaries on Horace, I will here make mention of Cupaiuolo (1942), which contains a rich and thorough review of earlier interpretations, and a very recent essay by M. Ruch (1963), which offers nothing new. Basically all interpretations, with one exception, to which I will return shortly, can be referred to one of two camps: (1) those who believe that Horace is speaking of the *compositio uerborum*, the 'pairing of words' or 'style' (this seems unlikely given that at this point in the *ars* Horace is quite obviously speaking about poetic vocabulary, of individual terms), and (2) those who think (as, most recently, Ruch) in terms of limit-concepts, obvious cases of oxymoron, such as *concordia discors*, or the like. This hypothesis is made problematic by the fact that expressions of this type are proportionally rare in Horace, and they are not the sort to justify the importance that has been attached to the precept. Deviating entirely from these is the interpretation of A. Rostagni (1930), who thinks that *serendis* derives from *sero* 'to sow seeds' or 'plant' instead of 'weave', and he decides that Horace is alluding to this metaphor.

[13] Brooks and Warren (1952). On this work, see Della Volpe (1964).

words here have perhaps erred in wanting to reduce his expression to
the definition of just one single process. Hence we are left with the
fact that none of the explanations that have been advanced has
produced a satisfying result. And one must also consider that
Horace was unable to think of these expressive procedures in the
same terms of scientific exactitude that we use to define and catalogue them. Still, in my opinion, it is certain that he had an intuitive
concept of these procedures, and that he put them into practice. After
all, what does the well-known *arte allusive*[14] amount to if not the
most learned application of the aforementioned 'connotative' procedures? Horace certainly is not the only classical poet to employ a
poetics based on such procedures (thus C. Del Grande is right to
recognize a similar allusivity in the poetry of Virgil;[15] and the same
assessment should be given to that of Propertius[16]). But, among the
ancients, he deserves a special place for having produced a theoret-
ical-didactic analysis of these procedures, in addition to having
masterfully put them into practice.

Only a detailed commentary on the long epistle to Florus could
permit an informed and useful analysis of the poetic processes it
contains. But that would be out of place here. And, at any rate, I have
elsewhere provided a commentary that is sufficiently detailed.[17] We
will therefore limit ourselves here to a number of significant
examples.

Always in his poetry, but especially in the *sermo* of his maturity,
Horace avails himself, lavishly and with expert skill, of the technique
of the idea-word as key to a section of poetry, or even to a composition in its entirety. The fundamental theme of this epistle, that which
gives it its poetic unity beyond its evident division into two large
sections (first lines 1–140, where Horace no longer feels the need to
compose 'engaged' poetry, that is lyric poetry, and he explains his
reasoning to his young friend; then lines 141–216 describing his
search for *sapientia*, meditating on life and the best way to live it,

---

[14] The delightful expression is that of Giorgio Pasquali (1951), but the assessment
is deemed universally valid and certain; cf. the bibliographical appendix of A. La
Penna in his recent new edition of Pasquali's *Orazio Lirico* (1964: 813).

[15] Del Grande (1960: 131).

[16] See Pasoli (1956: 16–19).

[17] Pasoli (1964a: 60–117).

with thoughts of death not far off), can be synthesized as follows: his advanced age and the inkling of death have taken from Horace his relish for 'play' (*ludus*), and that includes, quite specifically, poetry. This sends him into reflection, into the realm of *sapientia*, to show precisely that no form of *ludus*, beginning specifically with poetry, is suitable (πρέπει) for a man of his age. All of this is clearly affirmed by the poem's conclusion. There the poet's conscience subjects him to a pitiless interrogation for proudly feigning to have already achieved *sapientia*. It finds him in good shape on just one point, namely, the mind's detachment from riches, but still enslaved by all the more usual and dangerous vices and human prejudices that are obstacles to *sapientia*. Seeing that he does not know how to live well, his conscience finally urges him in lines 213–16 to depart from the world's scene, which by rights belongs to the young, for whom *ludus* is suitable.

Sapientia, ludus, and a life that is nearing its sad decline: these are, in sum, the three mainstays of the letter's poetic essence. The second two of these themes accompany one another already in lines 55–7 ('The years as they pass despoil us of pleasures, one at a time. They have snatched away jests, sex, parties, and play. Now they are trying to wrench away my poems. So what am I to do?').[18] The first of these themes (*sapientia*), appears as a subtle play on words in line 128, at the close of the section where Horace claims that the arduous, but necessary, demands of his poetic style, along with the worries provoked by conceiving them theoretically and toiling to put them into practice, cause him to experience a very real and special brand of torture. For along with the value of 'having artistic judgement (discernment)', and of one's 'being familiar with the laws of poetic style', wisdom appears as a motif of torment: 'to be wise and bare my teeth' (*sapere et ringi*, 128). This creates, by way of anticipation, a contrast between foolish *sapientia* and that which will be set against it in line 141, by the contrastive separation produced by *nimirum* ('it's no wonder', 'naturally'), and by the manifest sense that here the

---

[18] In listing the reasons why Horace cannot continue to write poetry and play an active role as a poet, these lines do not register as terribly important. But McGann (1954: 349 and 358) has rightly observed that these verses already anticipate the epistle's bitter conclusion.

epistle's entire second section is being given its title: 'naturally it is to my advantage to possess wisdom and, by tossing frivolities aside, to concede to children the play that suits their age' (*nimirum sapere est abiectis utile nugis,* | *et tempestiuum pueris concedere ludum, Epist.* 2.2.141–2).[19] This 'entitling' of the epistle's second section already contains the themes of the conclusion that are, as we have said, the poem's cardinal themes: wisdom, play, and the advancing of age that renders play unsuitable (*intempestiuus*). These cardinal concepts are nevertheless strongly implied at various stages of Horace's composition. The obvious intent and effect of this is to produce a consistent poetic unity on a conceptual plane that is also repeatedly recalled on an expressive plain, to the point where the two aspects or movements fuse into a single identity.

I have already mentioned above the importance of verses 109–25 to the overall economy of the poem. These are the only lines that are distinctly and technically literary in their contents. But at the same time they are endowed with an important and pronounced 'lyric' purpose. McGann was wrong to take them as a digression, because their function is absolutely vital. In these lines Horace carries to extremes his conviction that making a *legitimum ... poema* (109), 'poetry according to the rule of art', is a difficult undertaking, a special brand of torture. The explicit passion that he displays in these verses, and his unrelenting commitment to explaining statements so strict about the means of creating the lexicon and style of poetry, appear to be linked directly to the state of mind he is in at that moment. Ever since the tenth satire of his first book (35 BCE[20]) Horace was convinced that the creation of true poetry required tremendous creative effort, to the point of the poet's own physical

---

[19] The adverb *nimirum* serves up an obvious connotation that extends well beyond its normal range, for here the word's original etymological sense is brought to mind with a view towards specializing its adverbial function. Poetry, which generally avoids connections with prose, makes use of them for the sake of a poetics of realism. Here it is with the aim of presenting the sense of a 'true' *sapientia* that opposes the false. For the etymology of *nimirum* from *ni* (= *non*) <*est*> *mirum*, see Marouzeau (1910: 152). For a rival case, see Hofmann-Szantyr vol. II (1964), where it is less plausibly maintained that the word derives from *nil* <*est*> *mirum*. For the 'poetics of realism', see Della Volpe (1964: 71), and Calboli (1962–3: 98–100).

[20] For the dating and, more generally, for points of contact between the literary criticism of the *Satires* and that of the *Epistle*, see Pasoli (1964b).

pain and exhaustion.[21] But now, at the very point where he explains in minute detail and with technical precision what exactly this creative force ought to consist of, he shows himself incapable of tolerating that pain, and he actually wishes to swear off poetry because of it. Here, once again, a poetics of realism seems to demand laws of its own, because the very passage that is specifically more 'technical' and apparently also (according to an errant concept that is trumped by its own poetical packaging) less poetic, seems maximally endowed with poetic qualities that come with the writer's being so deeply committed to the principles he poses. The style of the passage, in keeping with the author's ideological and emotional engagement, rises markedly from the mid-level tone of Horatian *sermo* generally, and of this letter in particular, because at the same time as he lays out the requirements of a style that is technically irreproachable, Horace provides (as he is wont to do, and this has long been noted by different critics[22]) the practical and immediate example of the very style that his statements designate. The passionate 'lyricality' of the passage steadily ascends to a climax, and so, too, its style: by playing cleverly on the sustained metaphor of the censor (in respect to his own verses, the poet must be, as it were, a censor, exercising all the usual duties of this magistrate) and by introducing the metaphor of a river that is clear but, even more, impetuous, there is a steady elevation of tone up to the conclusion of lines 124–5.[23] These lines, functioning as an exasperated precis of the entire passage ('he will have the look of someone now at play, now in agony, like the one who dances first the part of the satyr, then the bumpkin Cyclops', *ludentis speciem dabit et torquebitur, ut qui | nunc Satyrum, nunc agrestem*

---

[21] Hor. *S.* 1.10.69–71: '[Lucilius] would file a great deal from himself, and he would prune back all that sweeps past the perfect finish. And in fashioning verse he could repeatedly scratch his head and gnaw his nails to the quick.'

[22] Marouzeau (1926b: 60; and 1926a: 110ff.), and Cupaiuolo (1942: 22).

[23] It is useful to note here just how much of his own originality Horace delivers in his deployment here of an over-used metaphor of Callimachean origin, in order to affirm that the style of the true poet ought to be, in addition to clear, strong-rushing and beneficial to the community, causing his native vocabulary to be enriched: the ideology of the poet's 'duty' as social and communal, in addition to its being artistic, powerfully and substantially reactivates a typical Alexandrian *topos*. For the metaphor, see Callim. *Hymn to Apollo* 108ff., 'abundant is the flow of the Assyrian river, but its waters sweep along a great deal of mud and refuse'.

Cyclopa mouetur) nicely round off the climax. And, at the same time, they prepare for, and justify in advance, the declaration that Horace makes in the lines immediately following. Namely, before he comes to talk of the difficult and discouraging work that awaits the poet who is aware of what his art's theoretical rationale demands, he manages to say, 'I would rather seem a crazed and incompetent writer, so long as I enjoy my own faults, or so long as they at least delude me' (*praetulerim scriptor delirus inersque uideri,* | *dum mea delectent mala me uel denique fallant,* 126–7). And this, although it is an unusual declaration for Horace (it seems to stand apart from his critical-poetic attitudes elsewhere), serves principally to anticipate the contrast, already hinted at earlier, between false and useless knowledge and true knowledge; between that pleasant but dangerous form of folly that comes of being unaware of one's actual artistic task—an unawareness instanced by the pleasant folly of the citizen of Argos, on whom the story of verses 128–40 turns—and the awareness of how life should be lived. The need for this awareness is proclaimed in verse 141, at the beginning of the second section of the epistle.

The crucial verses of the section we are now considering, lines 109–25, are the two final lines. Their structure merits special attention. On the plane of denotation, the comparison with a pantomime who executes a dance nicely illustrates the concept of *souplesse*, giving an impression of the grace, the agility and ease that the work of a true poet should give. One sees just how appropriate are the verbs chosen for 'playing' and 'turning' (*ludentis* and *torquebitur*). In their literal sense, these define the pantomime's activities (he dances and turns himself about), and in a figurative sense they are applicable to the creator of poetry.[24] But a good deal of meaning happens also at the level of connotation: *torquebitur* in fact evokes, whether in the case of the pantomime or the poet, the idea of torture, while *ludentis* evokes, just as much for the one as for the other, the idea of the fluency and agility that must hide the creator's tremendous toil. It is from this toil that the impression of fluency and ease actually arises. And further mediating the use of *ludere* beyond its denotative significance within its immediate context is its allusion, by way of a shared terminology,

[24] For *ludere* in the sense of 'dance', cf. Horace himself *ad Carm.* 2.12.19, with the commentary of Tescari (1947) ad loc.

to one of the work's cardinal themes: that is, to poetry as a kind of *ludus* that isn't worth the trouble of torment. Can it possibly escape our notice that in these lines, by way of several 'clever joinings' (*callidae iuncturae*), Horace has given a new and fuller sense to the most common of words, *ludere* and *torqueri*? The *callida iunctura*, therefore, amounts to what we call, in modern terminology, 'connotation'; that element, in other words, in which a substantial part of the poetic function resides.

Roman Jakobson, in the essay already cited, has shown just how large a part of the poetic function can reside even in tropes and in grammatical figures of speech. He makes the point as follows: 'the resources of poetry disguised in the morphological and syntactic structure of language, in short the poetry of grammar and its literary product, the grammar of poetry, have seldom been recognized by critics. And they have been almost entirely overlooked by linguists. On the other hand, creative writers have frequently known to take full advantage of them.' The Russian scholar has elsewhere demonstrated the 'obligatory' character of the grammatical categories (or 'normative', to start from the terminology of Gramsci[25]) by going deeply into the viewpoint of F. Boas.[26] He concludes that 'an actual a-grammaticality deprives a statement of its semantic information', and he demonstrates through a refined analysis of Antony's funeral elegy for Caesar in Shakespeare's *Julius Caesar* how the dramatic force of the opening of this discourse issues primarily from the way in which Shakespeare plays with the grammatical categories and constructions. I am certain that classical poetry also presents a wealth of instances where the grammatical function is decided by the poetic expression. Abundant examples of this type have been illustrated by me in my commentary on the epistle to Florus, cited previously. Therefore it will be enough for me here to point out one example that is particularly significant because in it the connotation is made more rich and effective precisely by a syntactic function that is not initially evident. Horace writes: 'you should neither refuse to spend money, nor agonize over making more. But instead, as when you were a boy

---

[25] Gramsci (1953: 195–205). See also Della Volpe (1964: 175).
[26] Jakobson (1959: 139–45), published subsequently in Jakobson (1963: 197–206) under the title 'La notion de signification grammaticale selon Boas'.

on the loose at Spring Break, you should enjoy that small bit of welcome time by tearing into it' (*neque sumptum | inuitus facias neque plura parare labores, | ac potius, puer ut festis Quinquatribus olim, | exiguo gratoque fruaris tempore raptim*, 195–8).

The image is not only precious in its poetic worth, but also utterly 'modern'. The wise man ought not to preoccupy himself with amassing riches for the future, but put himself in the same condition of spirit that he had as a boy. He was overjoyed, then, at having five consecutive days of spring vacation, free from school.[27] Seeking only to enjoy those days of freedom completely, he did not worry about the impending return to school. To live life that way, the way a child lives his vacation, that is wisdom's precept. It is a precept from which poetic ideas and images that are alive even for us (as in the image of that little child) do not seem far removed. Quite clearly, there are two terms in the Horatian expression in which the poetic function is concentrated and polarized: *puer* ('boy') and *olim* ('once upon a time'). The term *puer*, placed via hyperbaton at the beginning of the comparison, puts us directly into the milieu and world that the poet wants to create. The comparative element *ut* ('as') causes us to understand that we are not dealing with actual reality, but only a comparison. Although to a certain degree it diminishes the intensity and lyric concentration of the image, it stands behind the image's key-word (*puer*) in a position that is weak and secondary. The other key term, *olim*, is positioned at the very end of the verse, and also at the end of the entire comparison, in order to set in relief the distance in time, a distance that in Horace, who is now mature and feels himself in decline, provokes an acute nostalgia for an age he can no longer recover, and for a disposition of mind that he finds very difficult to recover. Thus, as was already observed in the case of *nimirum*, the etymological content of the adverb *olim* (connected to *olle*, an archaic form of *ille* and denoting distance in time[28]) is refreshed and underscored to produce a more pregnant poetic intensity. This is a goal towards which its particular placement also aims.

---

[27] The vacation days of the *Quinquatrus* festival are comparable, both in terms of when they fell [19–23 March] and their duration, to our Easter vacation. This observation I owe to Bione (1952) ad loc. In commenting on the same line, Bione also makes mention of the syntactic characteristic of verse 197, which I discuss above.

[28] Ernout-Meillet (1959–60: 460).

In sum, the cardinal terms of the image, *puer* and *olim*, open and close the image by corresponding to its extremities. But the two terms are interrelated above all at the level of grammar, since *puer* here has a predicative function, and that function is made clear precisely in the presence of *olim*. Without it, in fact, *puer* could be taken as the subject of the comparative expression, with its own revelatory function. But it is precisely the predicative function of the word that intensifies the image's poetic qualities by substituting for an anonymous generic example ('the way a child acts during the spring holiday') a direct reference to the youth of the interlocutor himself ('the way you used to act when you were a child'). Thus a grammatical element, such as the syntactic predicative function of *puer*, becomes a component of the poetic charge of the entire image that is anything but secondary. And this syntactic function is revealed by *olim*. This word thus, in addition to its own proper denotation, and the connotation that accrues to it by its pronounced position at the end of both the verse and the image, also takes on a further connotation: namely, that of revealing the syntactic function (connotative in turn for its own sake) that hides in *puer*.

I could continue my analysis, an effort that, I think, would bear fruit. But I think I have already shown in some measure through these observations how great is the 'lyric' concentration of this epistle, and just how much of that concentration can be grasped by a reading that is not only attentive to some of the poem's more subtle and penetrating expressive processes, but conducted in harmony with several of the chief principles of recent linguistic and aesthetic criticism.[29]

---

[29] On the epistle to Florus, available now are the fine observations of Castorina (1965: 148–50).

18

Writing to/through Florus: Criticism and the Addressee in Horace *Epistles* 2.2

Kirk Freudenburg

In the course of his long career as a poet and critic at Rome, Quintus Horatius Flaccus, better known to us as Horace (65–*c*.8 BCE.), wrote three verse-letters of exceptional length on matters pertaining to literature and the profession of poets in his day. Although these letters to friends, *Epistles* 2.1 (to Augustus), *Epistles* 2.2 (to Florus), and the *Ars Poetica* (to the Pisones), are now commonly taken as a set and referred to as his 'literary epistles', the second of these, to Florus, has long stood out from its companions as easily the least 'literary' of the set. Its theoretical discussion is slight. And since it addresses a man of relatively little account, on matters that are, at least on the surface, more personal and autobiographical than they are literary and/or political, the letter to Florus has tended to play a role secondary to that of its more famous book-companions in the study of the Augustan literary and political life.

It is the purpose of this essay to crack open new areas of interest in this letter by demonstrating the 'political' that hides inside the 'literary' and 'personal' in *Epistles* 2.2, even in matters as patently personal as the poet's growing tired of writing, and his obsessing over the legacy he intends to leave to his heir. The poem's one most readily extractable portion of literary theory (lines 106–25) I will make the centerpiece of this demonstration by showing how the theory of these lines is deeply invested in, and expressive of, a very specific Augustan rhetoric of late 19–early 18 BCE. In undertaking these demonstrations I make frequent nods towards the letter to Augustus and to the excellent recent studies of that poem by Alessandro Barchiesi and Denis Feeney. Their analyses, in tandem with the political insights of Oliver Lyne and Ellen Oliensis, and the expert historical and formal studies of Ross Kilpatrick and Niall Rudd, have greatly influenced what I have to say in this essay. My own contributions to this scholarship will be primarily of an observational kind, namely in the drawing of new parallels between known historical facts and a given political rhetoric and the speaker's expressed point(s) of view. Working from these (primarily narratological) observations I will argue for a much tighter political setting as the backdrop of the poem, in the period of frantic building and purging that preceded the heralding of Rome's 'new age' in 17 BCE. With this backdrop in place, I will introduce a different set of politically expressive, even 'satirical', options for reading the poem's many personal and literary lessons.

The first lines of Horace's *Epistle to Florus* suggest that a letter has made its way to Rome from the east. The year is 18 BCE.[1] The future emperor Tiberius is stationed with his troops in the far north-east of Rome's empire, sent there two years before to install a friend of the Roman state, Tigranes II, on the throne of Armenia, and thereafter to recover the standards lost by Crassus at Carrhae.[2] The commission is his first real test as a statesman and general. And thus, in time-honored fashion, he gathers up and brings with him a select group of friends to advise him, and to help him pass the wee hours of a long journey as a decent Roman in the company of other young men of impressive pedigree, promise, and style. Within this constellation of privileged travel-companions is a certain Julius Florus, by name a budding 'Julian Flower'. A talented young civil servant (a *scriba*, just as Horace once was) and poet, it turns out that this man is the closest

---

[1] Dates for *Epistles* 2.2 have been proposed from as early as late 20 BCE, Rudd (1989: 13), to as late as 11 BCE, Krüger (1869: 300). I follow Vahlen's generally accepted date of 18 BCE, without accepting his assertion that Florus and Tiberius are, by this time, stationed in *Gallia Comata*; see Vahlen (1923: 58–9). Instead I side with Kiessling-Heinze (vol. III, 1959: 244), contending that Tiberius does not make his way back to Rome with Augustus in October of 19 BCE, but that he stays in the east as *legatus* through the following winter. For recent support of the idea, see Kilpatrick (1990: 15 with n. 4).

[2] See Suet. *Tib.* 9.1, 14.3, and Dio 54.9.4–5.

thing to a son and poetic heir that the old bachelor Horace will ever have.[3]

In the letter to which *Epist.* 2.2 responds, Florus has chided his old friend for being sluggish in responding to his letters, and for failing to deliver what Horace dubs the 'awaited songs' (*exspectata carmina*, 25). In lines 1–25 of *Epist.* 2.2 Horace addresses Florus with an allegorical tale told to defuse the complaints expressed in that lost (quite possibly imaginary) letter. I paraphrase: 'it's as if a slave-dealer had sold you a slave, Florus, telling you up front that the boy was good for just a few things, dinner-party fun, mostly, but not terribly useful for anything else; truth be told, the boy is lazy, and has been known to run off for fear of his master's whip. So, Florus, it was with eyes wide open that you bought this flawed product (*prudens emisti vitiosum*, 18). And yet you complain to me about my sluggishness, as if I didn't tell you up-front that I, the slave in this story, was lazy, no, worse, "nearly crippled" (*prope mancum*, 21) when it comes to the duties you expect of me. Moreover you complain that I am like some lying Parthian, promising "songs" that I refuse to deliver (*exspectata ... carmina* mendax, 25). Just you give me a minute, Florus, and I will tell you why you are not to expect them any time soon.' And so the poem proceeds with the extended swearing-off of lyric that is its first half.

This introductory tale is commonly taken as a fairly standard gesture of apology, i.e. the letter-writer's excusing himself for failing to write *before* moving on to the 'real business' of the poem.[4] In this

---

[3] The scholiasts tell us that Julius Florus wrote satire, or that he edited an anthology of the satires of Ennius, Lucilius, and Varro: Porphyrion notes in his introduction to *Epist.* 1.3, the earlier of Horace's two letters to Florus: 'This Florus was a scribe and a writer of satires. He selected his satires from Ennius, Lucilius, and Varro.' At *Epist.* 1.3 line 24, Horace refers to Florus as a writer of *amabile carmen*, a reference that I, along with Rudd, and others, believe pegs him as a writer of lyric song (as Pindaric lyric, see n. 24 below). Thus, taken together, the scant evidence we have suggests that Florus should be regarded not simply as a particularly dear young friend of an aging poet (thus someone deserving of two letters rather than one); rather, he is a youthful mirror-image of Horace himself; as it were, the son he never had, and thus worthy of one of those standard advice letters from sage Roman father to impressionable young son. For *carmina* as lyric verse, see Pasoli (1964a: 73) and Rudd (1989: 13).

[4] For example, Lyne (1995: 188): '(*Epist.* 2.2.) is structured rather like *Epistle* 1.3: it takes a polite interest in the preoccupations of Florus, before delivering its explicit message.'

paper I will make a different case for these lines, arguing that they are very much about the poem's 'real business'. For not only does the opening allegory introduce certain moral and literary themes to be developed later as the letter proceeds (esp. the problem of 'owning' and 'using' what has previously belonged to someone else—see below), but, more importantly, the story gives readers of the poem a secure purchase on the mindset from which its lessons on literature and life are produced. It is in the sensing of the peculiarities of that mindset that certain curious pressures are applied to the ways in which we receive and value the didaxis of the letter itself.

But before I move on to these demonstrations of mindsets and themes necessarily interacting, I want first to provide bigger reasons for our caring about the poem's formal properties and its several narratological tics by setting out for my readers' critical inspection certain, potentially disquieting, ironies that inhere in the poem's opening slave-allegory, and that, once sensed, put a good deal of political spin on our reading of the poem's lessons on literature and life. For operating inside these lessons one can hear the tell-tale sounds of a tendentious, and highly specific, 'Augustan' rhetoric of what counts as literature *now*, in 18 BCE, and how life *now*, for poets, is to be respectably lived, as never before in Rome, in an age when the poet's pursuits are (increasingly) never purely literary.[5] Specifically, I want to begin by dwelling on what might be called the 'imperial demeanor' of the young Florus' complaint. His demands are two-fold, and very specific: 'I want a letter from you, Horace. Why don't you send one? I also want more "songs" (*carmina*).' My question about this is simple: who does this *really* sound like? Note the way in which Horace has us think of letter writing here as a quasi-official 'duty' or public office with *talibus officiis* in line 21; and consider, too, what one might call the 'physiology' of his refusal in the claim that he is 'nearly crippled,' *prope mancum*, when it comes to his fulfilling a duty of that sort, as if his spirit were willing but his body weak.

From here we move back in time several years to 23 BCE, the year of Horace's own triple-triumph in the publication of his *Odes* Books 1–3. This year was, in most other 'non-poetic' respects, a

---

[5] This is, by now, an old saw of postmodern theory. An excellent recent expression of the idea is that of Currie (1998: 73–95).

nerve-wracking time both for the Roman state, and for Augustus in his personal life: Marcellus, the emperor's young nephew, died in 23; the conspiracy of Varro Murena was discovered in the same year and noble Romans brought to justice;[6] but perhaps most disturbing of all was the emperor's near-fatal illness. So sick was he, the historians tell us, and so sure of dying, that he gave his signet ring to Agrippa as an indication of where the succession would go. But after many weeks of languishing and many prayers prayed on his behalf, Augustus recovered, helped along by the miracle cure of his Muse, Antonius Musa, who prescribed a new-fangled cold-water therapy that would become his signature cure.[7]

At this point Horace makes a brief appearance in the political story of 23 BCE.[8] For in the year of his grave illness, Augustus had trouble keeping up with many of his official duties. In a now famous letter to Maecenas, the original of which was once inspected and directly quoted by Suetonius, Augustus requests that Maecenas send Horace away from his 'parasitic' table to his 'kingly' one so that he might do his part for emperor and country (as well as for himself) by becoming his *ab Epistulis* in charge of writing letters to friends (*scribendis epistulis amicorum*).[9] Horace politely declined the offer of that 'office' (*officium*), a refusal not easily carried out since it risked ruining his relationships on many fronts. But Augustus took no offence, and in subsequent letters (Suetonius knows a whole series of them, and he quotes several) the emperor makes a grand show of *clementia* to prove to Horace (and to whatever incidental audiences that these letters might have had) that he bears no grudge. Now, although Horace's letter refusing the offer is never quoted by Suetonius, included in his account of Augustus' 'think nothing of it' response are clear indications that Horace refused the task of letter writing by

[6] For the dating of the conspiracy to late 23 BCE rather than 22 (Dio 54.3), see Lyne (1995: 190 n. 16).

[7] For issues of the succession and Musa's cure, see Dio 53.30; cf. Suet. *Aug.* 81.

[8] I date the letter to 23 BCE based on Augustus' describing himself as <u>nunc occupatissimus et infirmus</u> (see next n.).

[9] Suet. *Vit. Hor.* 18–23: 'Augustus also offered him the post of letter-writer, as he signifies by writing to Maecenas as follows: "previously I was up to the task of writing letters to friends myself. But now, since I am sick and so incredibly busy, I desire to seduce our friend Horace away from you. He will come, then, away from your parasitic table to my regal one, and he will help me in my letter-writing." '

citing precisely *his own* ill health; that is, 'I cannot write your letters, Augustus, because I, too, am sick.'[10]

And thus, there is a distinct irony to be sensed in Horace's taking up, what else, but letter-writing, a book of letters to friends, no less, as his next big poetic project in that same year. This is an irony that inheres in every letter he writes in that book, a curious tension we are set with sensing and making something of in our reading of those letters, especially when within them the poet makes such a deliberate point of his being sick and out-of-sorts and in need of time away from Rome and, especially, from the demands that Maecenas is putting on him for a return to lyric: Augustus cannot write letters when sick. Horace, when sick, must write them. Not for Augustus, as requested, but for himself.[11]

Demands put upon Horace for letters, for Augustus' letters, and for more lyric poems, brood over his epistles. Suetonius tells us that when Augustus read certain of these 'conversations' with his friends (a reference to *Epistles* Book 1) he was deeply offended that Horace had not seen fit to address a letter to him.[12] By making this complaint, Suetonius says, he 'squeezed out' (*expressit*) the letter that begins *cum tot sustineas, Epist.* 2.1, the *Letter to Augustus*.[13] But along

---

[10] Suet. *Vit. Hor.* 23–9: 'And not even when he (Horace) refused did he (Augustus) grow angry at him or cease lavishing him with his friendship. I have appended a few extracts from letters still extant to prove my point: "Consider any privilege of my house yours for the taking, just as if you belonged to my household. For you'll have acted rightly and with good sense, since I wanted to live on close terms with you, if only your health would allow it (*si per valitudinem tuam fieri posit*)."'

[11] I have argued elsewhere that his letters to friends are a means of charting his own very 'Augustan' convalescence, curiously miming the emperor's drawn-out search for renewed health and a return to public life. They are his philosophic *diludium*, a space between his lyric efforts that will stabilize and empower him for his lyric's 'expected' return. See Freudenburg (2002).

[12] The phrasing of Augustus' response (see next n.) is telling, because generically specific: *quod videaris familiaris* ('that you should seem my friend') suggests that he has read a collection of letters *ad familiares* (like those of Cicero) in which he himself has not been addressed *as* a *familiaris*. For the problem of naming Augustus as a 'friend' in that book, see Freudenburg (2002: 138–40).

[13] Suet. *Vit. Hor.* 43–9: 'But after reading certain of the Conversations (*Sermones*) he complained that they contained no mention of him, as follows: "know good and well that I am enraged at you because in the several writings you've produced in this genre you do not talk with me first and foremost. Or are you afraid that future generations will regard it as a scandal that you seem to be my *familiaris*?" And thus he squeezed out a poem addressed to himself, the one that begins "since you, all by yourself, bear burdens so many and so great."'

with that demand, Suetonius suggests (and he seems still to be working from original correspondence here, though he does not cite it directly) Augustus had been pushing for a return to lyric. But clearly not lyric of just any sort, but some grand, flag-waving poems to celebrate the military victories of his step-sons, Drusus and Tiberius, as well; that is, he wanted a bit of Pindaric 'fat' to grease the wheels of his increasingly sticky succession.[14] Thus, under the surface of these requests we get the distinct impression that the love-poet of *Odes* Books 1–3, as much as he may have been loved a few years before, is apparently not being asked back. He is not useful for the immediate purposes that Augustus has in mind; so he is not missed, nor is his return being actively sought.[15]

Such are the unseen ironies of Horace's choosing to write letters to friends precisely when he chose to write them: his every letter to a friend in *Epistles* Book 1 counts as a letter *not* written for Augustus (whether to him, as *familiaris*, or on his behalf, as his *ab epistulis*). Now considering all of this—that is to say, now that I am so much the more convinced that standard prosopographical methods cannot tell us all we need to know, I want to restart my investigation into *Epist.* 2.2 by once again asking the question with which I began: 'who, in fact, is this letter's addressee, Julius Florus?' In other words, what do we make of his resembling Augustus so uncannily in the demands he makes, hounding the poet with 'where is my letter Horace? And what about those *Carmina* you promised you would write? When can I expect them to see the light of day?'

Perhaps the most obvious point to be drawn from Florus' Augustan demeanor is that, in its own indirect way, the *Epistle to Florus* can be read, at another level, as a letter to Augustus, i.e. the letter that he complained of not receiving after the publication of Book 1. For, insofar as the letter responds to two distinct pressures that Augustus himself had put upon Horace, it has the power to draw

---

[14] Suet. *Vit. Hor.* 38–43: 'So thorough-going was his approval of his writings, and so certain was he that they would last forever, that he enjoined upon him to write not only the *Carmen Saeculare*, but the victory of Tiberius and Drusus over the Vindelici. And to this end he compelled him to add a fourth book to his three-volume *Carmina* after a long break.'

[15] I follow Lyne (1995: 188–90) in connecting this change in expectations to the poet's abandonment of lyric.

Augustus into its field of focus and to include him as an un-named addressee.[16] For one can easily imagine how Augustus might snap to attention and prick up his ears upon hearing precisely what it is that Florus wants from Horace. But there is a certain narratological advantage to be beheld in Horace's directing these 'Augustan' questions through Florus, and then, in turn, in directing the answers back to him. For this allows Horace to speak openly and aggressively, and thus to be as crass and cynical and abrupt as he, in fact, is in this letter.[17] In short, he both confronts (at one level) and avoids (at another) the incredibly tricky issue of presuming to instruct Augustus about matters of literature and life—a very difficult task. And thus he shows himself already involved with, and skirting, that famous 'insegnare ad Augusto' problem that Alessandro Barchiesi has so beautifully shown in operation in the *Epistle to Augustus*.[18]

But I want now to look at the earlier of the poet's two letters to Florus, an earlier, smaller letter in Book 1, his *Epist.* 1.3, in order to identify and qualify the literary issues that both letters address. In so doing, I hope also to show that these lessons, given the highly patterned packages in which they are wrapped, possess a remarkable potential for producing further addressees for themselves; that is, for suggesting that other audiences hide in their margins, in addressees unnamed but 'sensed' nearby and by no means (as we have seen with Augustus above) hard to find. Augustus, we shall see, is a strong gravitational presence throughout the *Letter to Florus*. And I hope further to expand our options for 'who is speaking to whom' in this poem by having us question the perfectly reasonable assumption that these lessons are, in fact, directed simply 'from' Horace 'to' Florus, just as their title, *The Epistle to Florus,* suggests they are. Instead I want to insist that the poem's addressees themselves (and here I am

---

[16] Here I am obviously indebted to the excellent recent work by Oliensis (1998a) on the multiple 'overhearing' audiences that listen to Horace's poems.

[17] Oliensis (1998a: 11): 'The situation decorously suppressed from the one epistle thus resurfaces in the other. Given that *Epistles* 2.2 is designed to be overread by Augustus, the de facto dedicatee of the collection, we could say that the epistle to Florus functions as an oblique and nonactionable rebuke of Horace's imperial complainant. Or at least it enables Horace to play at, and to play out, a combination of compliant servility and self-assertive disobedience that he could not perform to the emperor's face without risking his own face.'

[18] See Barchiesi (1993: 149–84).

424   *Kirk Freudenburg*

obviously including addressees explicitly named as well as others not named, but strongly sensed as 'ghostly intertextual presences') exert a strong pre-emptive 'interference' on the nature of the lessons that are taught to them.[19] That is to say, they inhabit the role of teacher/writer by working an unseen 'prefigurative' force on the lessons they are taught. Florus, I argue, is thus not simply the blank 'recipient' of Horace's lessons. Nor, for that matter, does Horace address him with lessons that are intertextually 'innocent' (i.e. not in dialogue with, and shaped by, other highly patterned discourses that can be readily detected in the peculiar tics of their expression) and, simply put, *from* expert *to* ephebe. Rather Florus is, in some sense (and I think this is all remarkably demonstrable), the source from which Horace's lessons spring, and the mind from which they are, at least to some degree, produced.

Both *Epist.* 1.3 (of 20 BCE) and the larger letter to Florus (of 18 BCE) have us imagine the addressee off on campaign with Tiberius, and both use that occasion to dwell not on the day-to-day concerns of Roman military life, but on issues of who owns what—a theme that I take, in both cases, to refer to poetic ownership.[20] This is easy enough to see in the case of *Epist.* 1.3 because the issue of plagiarism

[19] For 'ghostly intertextual presences,' see Currie (1998: 81).
[20] The end of *Epist.* 2.2 suggests that the poet's legacy has been much on his mind: at line 145 Horace invites Florus, and those who read with him, to listen in on a series of lessons that he directs from himself towards himself as part of his search for wisdom and self-improvement: 'I tell these things to myself and go over them in silence' (*mecum loquor haec tacitusque recordor*). The series of maxims that follow concern primarily issues of property ownership and making use of one's wealth in good measure rather than stockpiling it for another's use, especially that of a greedy heir. Given their timing, these lessons have perhaps as much to do with the social and political demands put on Horace by Augustus' political legacy as it does with Horace's own private concerns over what he intends to use up and/or leave to his heir. For in 18 BCE, the year in which Horace writes these words to Florus (see n. 1 above), all unmarried members of Rome's highest orders were abruptly forced to think seriously about their unmarried status and their testamentary desires in the wake of Augustus' legislation on marriage. Galinsky (1996: 130) points out that: 'the *Lex Julia de maritandis ordinibus* made marriage and remarriage mandatory for men from the ages of twenty-five to sixty...the childless or unmarried could not inherit nor could they leave an inheritance to anyone except for blood relatives to the sixth degree, otherwise the state became the sole beneficiary.' That Horace should address the matter of his own legacy (see previous n.) in a letter of that same year is, I suggest, significant. In the end, he will leave everything to Augustus, his sole heir, not by testament, but by word of mouth (see Suet. *Vit. Hor.* 67–70).

is one of the poem's explicit themes. In lines 15 and following Horace asks Florus how another mutual friend, Celsus Albinovanus (later the addressee of *Epist.* 1.8), is getting along on campaign. Celsus, he lets on, has repeatedly been warned by Horace to keep his hands on his own property and to avoid adding luster to his poems with *furtivis coloribus* (line 20), splashes of colour he has stolen, like so many tail-feathers from a peacock, from other poets. Horace follows his warning to Celsus by asking Florus how he himself is getting along: 'And what about your own daring enterprises? What beds of thyme are you busy flitting about (*quae circumvolitas agilis thyma*)? Your talent isn't puny, nor is it uncombed and shaggy with unsightly growth.'

Waved under our noses in these lines, for our olfactory consider-ation, is an image strongly redolent of another poet's poetry, and of flowers nipped from a distant field. The figure of the bee-poet is most distinctly reminiscent of Pindar, who figured himself as a flower-nipping bee at *Pyth.* 10.54, and when Horace uses the same image again at *Carm.* 4.2.25–32 he does so with explicit reference to Pindar.[21] But David West has shown that the specific striping of the bee in line 22 (*non incultum ... et turpiter hirtum*) derives not from Pindar but from Virg. *Georgics* 4.96–9 (*namque aliae turpes horrent*), describing bees that are shaggy and unkempt.[22] Thus the metaphor as we encounter it in *Epist.* 1.3, like the bee it has us imagine, is well-travelled, and distinctly redolent of flowers nipped in the thyme-beds of other poets. It has flitted its way into this poem from Pindar's distant field, by way of Virgil's garden (and perhaps other places as well). And by thus retaining those remembered colors and scents (distinctly, but in certain small measures, mixing just so much of this with whiffs of that), that deeply redolent image teaches a crucial lesson to Florus (and to us) about how one can re-deploy other poets' materials in a way that is not heavy-handed (as the outright 'theft' of well-feathered Celsus), but multi-layered, subtle, and thus capable of producing something truly unique and one's own.

Celsus, all decked out in borrowed feathers, does not get it. Clearly. But what about Florus? The question still remains as to whether these

---

[21] For the metaphor's basic Pindaric underpinnings and its many further uses after Pindar, see especially Davis (1991: 134–8) and Hubbard (1995: 221).

[22] West (1967: 31–4).

lessons perhaps take issue with him as well. He is, after all, a 'flower' by name, the compiler of a florilegium of satire as well as a composer of a certain brand of *amabile carmen,* quite possibly lyric.[23] As such, his works are necessarily bright with remembered colors and redolent of distant scents. Is he, perhaps, just as guilty as Celsus of 'stealing' bits of poetry that he simply writes down and calls his own? Florus, in fact, knows all about such matters. Or at least he should know about them because, according to what follows at *Epist.* 1.3.23–4, not only is he skilled in composing *amabile carmen* (likely a reference to Pindaric 'praise' poetry[24]), he also takes the winner's ivy (perhaps here yet another Pindaric image) for arguing cases at court, as well, and, as Horace puts it, for 'giving rulings on matters of civil law' (*civica iura respondere*). Florus, in other words, is a 'budding' juris-consult, an expert in all the tiny and painfully tedious technicalities of who owns what in ancient Rome.[25] And this, I think, goes a long way towards explaining why Horace opens his larger *Epistle to Florus* the way he does, by arguing, in essence, that if anyone should know whether or not an illegitimate sale was transacted, whether Horace has sold Florus flawed goods, knowing they were flawed, Florus should know. He is a jurisconsult, and he makes it his business to know such things. And that talent of his, on the rise in *Epist.* 1.3, and fully operational in *Epist.* 2.2, has made him one of the brighter flowers in Tiberius' bouquet.

One can see something of the quasi-contractual and legalistic makeup of the proem of *Epist.* 2.2 (the slave-sale allegory paraphrased above) by consulting legal sources, such as *P. Turner* 22 (CE 142) documenting the sale of a slave from one owner to another:

[23] The bee's flower-gathering may actually hint at Florus' work as a florilegist.

[24] The phrase *amabile carmen* is calqued from *melos charien* of *Pyth.* 5.107. The bee-nipping metaphor derives from Pindar's tenth *Pythian Ode* (line 54). The strong Pindaric coloring of these lines suggests that Florus is not a writer of lyric songs generally, but of Pindaric lyric, that is, to songs that will win him the desired *amicitia* of his general, Tiberius, by celebrating his victories in the east. For a fuller accounting of *amabile carmen* as a distinctly Pindaric expression, see Hubbard (1995: 221–2) and Mayer (1994: 129).

[25] The pun is un-pardonable. But Horace clearly keeps us mindful of it. Florus, for him, represents the next generation, young, flourishing, involved in activities that he is now too old for, or too jaded to engage in; cf. Galinsky (1996: 31–2) on the moneyer Aquillius Florus punning his own name by representing a flower on the obverse of a denarius of 19 BCE.

In the consulship of L. Cuspius Rufinus and L. Statius Quadratus, at Side, before L. Claudius Auspicatus, demiurge and priest of the goddess Roma, on 26 Loos. Pamphilos, otherwise known as Kanopos, son of Aigyptos, from Alexandria, has purchased in the marketplace from Artemidoros, son of Aristokles, the slave girl Abaskantis, or by whatever other name she may be known, a ten-year-old Galatian, for the sum of 280 silver denarii. M. Aelius Gavanius stands surety for and guarantees the sale. The girl is healthy, in accordance with the Edict of the Aediles . . . is free of liability in all respects, is prone neither to wandering nor running away, and is free of epilepsy . . . [26]

By including this document, I do not intend, in any way, to give the impression that I am an expert on Roman civil law. And yet I think there is a point to be made about my not being an expert, and yet feeling the need to provide these materials as useful comparanda. Namely this: the opening slave-sale allegory of *Epist.* 2.2 makes special demands on readers by putting us in a highly technical world where we do not often have to go in Horace.[27] Some scholars know their way around this territory, and others, most (I include myself here), do not. And yet in *Epist.* 2.2 we are required to activate whatever technical legal sensitivities we might possess and keep them at-the-ready from start to finish. Why should this be the case?

Perhaps the most obvious point to be made is this: knowing what *Epist.* 1.3 tells us about Florus' legal expertise, as well as his poetic ambitions, goes a long way towards explaining the inordinate stress in the larger letter addressed to him put upon matters legal and military, especially as these can be seen to operate at the dead-theoretical center of that poem in the discussion of what constitutes a *poema legitimum*, literally (if not perversely) a 'poem according to the law' (line 109), as if poetry were somehow analogous to, say, a marriage sanctioned by law and thus capable of producing 'legitimate' children. That, after all, is the primary, technical application of the adjective in Roman legal parlance: it is applied to contracts, and to marriages, wives, and children.[28] Just how, and how much, this matters we shall consider below.

---

[26] The translation is that of Bradley (1994: 8).

[27] On the 'legal flavour' of the slave-sale allegory, see Rudd (1989: 13). Cf. the thick legalese of lines 158–79, on which see Brink (1982: 367–70).

[28] These are by far the most common uses of the term in legal sources; see *OLD* s.v. *legitimus* 2; and *TLL* s.v. *legitimus* II.A.1.a, and II.A.2.

428 *Kirk Freudenburg*

The idea figuring poetry as somehow 'legally' acceptable, as if somehow bound by the laws of the state, is rare elsewhere in the works of Horace. Nowhere else does it appear in such blunt terms, and without apology.[29] Thus, to explain the idea and, in a sense, to render it less presumptuous and off-putting, commentators routinely refer their readers to the first two lines of *Sermones* 2.1, where Horace complains that some in his reading audience have faulted him for 'stretching' his work 'past the law's limit' (*ultra* | *legem tendere opus*). Now although I have no doubt that these lines do introduce the notion of a 'generic law', though they clearly refer us to a very real law of libel as well, I think that we are perfectly within our rights to question whether either instance counts as a straightforward expression of Horace's own theoretical mindset. For here, too, in fact, in that one other clear reference in Horace to poetry as somehow 'legitimate,' the narratological scenario we have to imagine is that of the poet addressing himself to a legal expert. In this case, to the most famous jurisconsult of his day, Trebatius. I think this matters terribly.

Put simply, this is a notion that tends to crop up in certain, highly specific narratological contexts as a *condition of* those contexts. One should perhaps hesitate, then, to push the idea of law-abiding poetry too far as an uncomplicated expression of Horace's own everlasting critical beliefs. For much of what is so often taken as run-of-the-mill literary 'history' and 'theory' in Horace (especially here, in his so-called 'literary epistles') is anything but the stable set of fixed and, as it were, transcendental ideas that they are commonly taken to be. Rather, in all of his works, but especially in these, I see Horace actively conceptualizing and mobilizing his literary-critical ideas from one moment to the next. Or, to steal a phrase from Stephen Hinds, who has neatly argued a similar case for the literary histories of Statius,

---

[29] A 'generic law' (*operis lex*) for tragedy is implied in a later poem, at *AP* 135. But here, too, we have to reckon with the speaker's thick legalese (e.g. esp. in lines 256ff.: *iura paterna*, 256; *artis crimine turpi*, 262; *iudex*, 263; *peccata*, 266; *culpam*, 267; *legitimumque sonum*, 274, etc.) and his strong penchant for treating poetic 'judgment' as a quasi-legal exercise, analogous to that of a jurist or censor. The mindset from which the speaker speaks is that of a wizened old Catonian who has set himself with 'judging' the current poetic scene and passing on to a younger generation of writers his years of infallible knowledge.

Martial, and others, Horace's ideas about literature are expressed 'for the particular purposes of particular poems, and even for the particular purposes of particular moments in particular poems.'[30] The idea of poetry as somehow 'legitimate' is toyed with elsewhere in Horace. But in the *Letter to Florus*, that is, in a poem addressed to a young jurisconsult, an expert in notions of the same type, the idea has a full and impressive life of its own. And in that impressive new life of the idea we can detect the gravitational pull exerted by the letter's addressee (a force unseen in itself, but obvious in its effects). Without saying a thing, just by being Florus (i.e. as constructed before our eyes by Horace), the addressee exerts a profound influence on the narrative and figurative habits of the poem. Most letters, of whatever kind, show these gravitational effects to some degree, with the writer responding to the addressee by actively shaping his/her discourse to conform to the addressee's well-known concerns and obsessions.[31] That narrative tug is evident in the letters of Horace, all of them, and it is especially apparent in his letters of Book 2, where the poet routinely shapes his theoretical discussion in a way that anticipates, conforms to, and/or speaks from within his addressees' military, censorial, and/ or legalistic mindsets. Ross Kilpatrick, for one, has commented on these anticipatory effects as they appear in the proem to *Epist.* 2.2, treating them as a whimsical performance put on for his addressee, to show them to be of like minds.[32] I think this is a fine idea. But I want to make a slightly different case for how these gestures might be read, and I especially want to insist that they are there from beginning to end in this poem, not just in its proem, and that they influence nearly everything that is said even in those parts of the poem that are commonly regarded as 'straightforward theory'.

My point, in its simplest and most extreme form, is this: the letter to Florus is focalized *through* Florus, or at least warped, to some degree, by *his* obsessions and legal mindset, shaped by *his* ways of

---

[30] Hinds (1997: 187–207).

[31] In my own case, I know that my email messages to Dan Hooley reek of fine scotch, and e-notes to John Henderson are spiced with provocative nonsense. My nonsense, not his, and that's the important point. The more highly defined the personality, the stronger the pull. This is clear from the letter to Augustus (no one stronger, or more distinct, than he!).

[32] See Kilpatrick (1990: 17).

shaping *his* world. And thus the theoretical tenets of the poem need
to be read with that distortion in mind; that is, not as 'straight'
didaxis from a sage and steady poet-critic straight to us, his poem's
'intended' eavesdroppers, with the letter's addressee serving as a mere
conventional device.[33] Rather, they must be taken as lessons figured
through another mindset, shaped Florus' way not just to create
conditions ideal for his receiving them (this is where I differ from
Kilpatrick) but to invite us, the letter's outside eavesdroppers, into
that alien mindset, and to have us imagine how poetic matters are
construed therein—exotically, idiotically, or otherwise.

But all of this, quite obviously, raises a crucial question regarding
the take-home value of these epistolary lessons as lessons on poetry,
always clearly 'Horatian', but never 'simply' his own. What do we
make of their exotic figurings, and of their being, so often, and so
uncharacteristically, dogmatic and glib? Are they put to us simply as
Horace's 'treatise on poetry,' ours to take away and use as his way of
thinking and 'what he says,' the stuff of anthologies and companions
to ancient lit.? Or might these lessons, in some cases, be delivered in
their strange, figurative packages to suggest just how strange and
disorienting the world of the addressee's figuring is? For example, in
construing poetry bound by laws and quasi-censorial oversight—I
will return to the censor analogy shortly—is there no discomfort in,
and no irony to, the lesson put to us that way? If so, is there perhaps a
lesson behind the surface lesson *per se*, interfering with it, in the irony
that we have to work to defuse and/or ignore? That is, a lesson about
applying one way of thinking, legal and censorial, to another sphere
of endeavor where it simply does not belong?

These same questions can be asked of the poet's capsule autobiography in lines 26–54, where he compares his career to a soldier's life:
he is a veteran of many wars, he says, now worn out, though
handsomely rewarded, by his years of 'regal' service (i.e. in the pay
of 'king' Maecenas).[34] Having raked in a good deal of booty, he sees
no reason to continue fighting. Where does this extreme cynicism
come from, and how do we reckon with its unhappy marriage to a

[33] Not that didaxis and literary criticism are ever perfectly 'straight' ('pure theory').
[34] The phrase *praesidium regale* must, in some measure, refer to *Odes* Books 1–3; cf.
C. 1.1.1–2 *Maecenas atavis edite regibus | o et praesidium;* see Oliensis (1998a: 13 with n. 18).

lesson on poetry and life, in a letter advising the ephebe what it will take for him to become a real poet, and an heir worthy of his father? Commentators are routinely taken aback by the soldier-for-hire analogy, shocked that the poet should speak so openly of his work's mercenary aims.[35] Elsewhere he is careful to underplay these aims or deny them altogether.[36] So this is a most unusual exposé. Certainly the idea of poetry as military service is common enough in Horace, but here the stress is heavily on the drudgery of the enterprise, and the gross cupidity of the entrepreneur.

Yet here again the gravitational effects of Florus need to be considered. For it is he, after all, not Horace, who is off cruising Rome's military frontier to make a killing in the company of his latter-day Lucullus, Tiberius.[37] He has been introduced for our consideration as the poet-entrepreneur in this story, determined to get ahead with his poems and his sage legal advice, just as Horace once did with Brutus, then with Maecenas. Recently Denis Feeney has shown that the entourage of *Epist.* 1.3, that earlier letter, has the decidedly sinister look of quite another poetic crew, the *cohors* of Memmius in Catullus poems 10 and 28—and never has literature known a more rapacious and jaded crew than that, unless perhaps we recall historical descriptions of the infamous entourage of Lucullus himself.[38] So the analogy, intertextually cued, is anything but flattering to Florus. And so I ask: is this just a bit of fun made at Florus' expense, or is there a serious point being made as well? He, the addressee, is at the dead-center of that Catullan cluster of entrepreneurial spirits in 1.3, determined to catch his general's ear, and perhaps to take in a bit of hard-won booty by means of his *amabile carmen*. So whose voice do we hear issuing from that 'auto'-biography of *Epist.* 2.2, in the figure of a jaded old soldier, *Lucullus'* soldier? Lucullus, too, we should recall, went off to fight in Parthia, and this is anything but

---

[35] e.g. Oliensis (1998a: 12–13) explains that the poet's senior status in relation to his addressee soothes the sting of this exposé.

[36] The sudden darkening of the poet's perspective on his lyric enterprises is a principle theme of the first lines of *Epistles* Book 1; on the disturbing contours of the *lyrica/ludicra* analogy that introduces the book, see Freudenburg (2002: 123–5).

[37] L. Licinius Lucullus directed a lengthy Roman counter-offensive against the Parthians in the Mithridatic Wars (88–70 BCE). His armies had the reputation of being undisciplined and rapacious.

[38] For allusions to Catullus 10 and 28 in Hor. *Epist.* 1.3, see Feeney (2002a: 176).

an incidental connection between the old general and the new (Tiberius). The soldier who follows him (in Horace's story) does so for the sole purpose of sweeping up great piles of cash. Once he has the money, he wants nothing to do with the war and his old profession, even though that war, the story makes clear, is only half-won (here is another connection with Lucullus). Whose world do these ideas about poetry, and the fine art of bilking great men of their excess cash *through* poetry, draw us into? From what mindset are they produced?

Some of these same questions are worth asking of the *Epistle to Augustus* (12 BCE) as well, for here again, as Alessandro Barchiesi has shown, the 'division of labour' between teacher and student is continually transgressed.[39] With Augustus we realize that there is a new pressure put upon poets to be publicly relevant, and to somehow march in step with his political/social program—we have seen some evidence for this already above. That pressure is evident not only in the way that Horace tells his peculiar life-story in *Epist.* 2.2, but in his version of Rome's literary history later in *Epist.* 2.1. Although it stands up as respectable literary history in many respects (most of what is said in this poem, as Brink shows, can be traced to earlier Roman and Greek critics), this particular version of Rome's literary history contains much potential for confusion and/or offence in what it leaves out, and what it stresses, even the several odd metaphors it uses to imagine the workings of poets and their craft.[40] To mention just two such challenges to our transcendentalizing the precepts of the poem, and of finding in them nothing more than standard bits of Greek theory rendered in Latin, there is the striking manner in which the critic underscores, in the second of his back-to-back

[39] The decisive, pioneering study of these narratological-*qua*-political issues in *Epist.* 2.1 is Barchiesi (1993 = 2001); cf. esp. the latter, p. 81: 'The peculiar complexity of *Ep.* 2.1 can be ascribed to a basic tension: here Augustus is both student and teacher. The text teaches Augustus . . . the basis for a new literature . . . the text in turn learns from Augustus, since the political model of the Principate influences the form of the new poetry for the new times. The division of labour made between politics and literature allows Horace to teach the Princeps, but this division is continually transgressed, since the poets need to learn how to speak to and of Augustus, and to do so they have to learn from him.'

[40] Rudd (1989: 36) sees similar potentials for confusion and/or offence in some of the more extreme theoretical ideas espoused by the *Ars Poetica*.

histories of Roman literature, the strong and unquestioned influence of censorship at the beginning of Rome's literary history.[41] Feeney observes: 'it is notorious that the very start of this enterprise is enmeshed in state regulation according to his presentation: at 145–55 we are told that *licentia* and *libertas* got out of hand and had to be curbed by law. The history of Roman literature, then, is for all intents and purposes co-extensive with the history of the state's regulation of it.'[42] This particular tale of *libertas* degenerating into *licentia*, however uncomfortably it may reside in a treatise on literary history, bears an uncanny resemblance to a certain ubiquitous rhetoric of the twenties and teens, promoted by Augustus to bolster his on-going efforts to check the powers of the senatorial aristocracy. Galinsky writes (with my emphases): 'the excess of *libertas had degenerated into license* (*licentia*); the reaction to it is the redefinition of *libertas* in terms of *securitas*. *The concept was pervasive*; its attestations include Dio's summary of Augustus' reign (56.43.4), the Alexandrian sailors who cheered him on the eve of his death (Suet., *Aug.* 98.2), and the obverse of a denarius with the most comprehensive of Roman numismatic legends.'[43]

Similarly off-putting, but highly suggestive, in *Epist.* 2.1 is the way in which the critic treats the Roman *vates* as, at best, a kind of schoolteacher and giver of precepts. According to the dour portrait drawn of him in lines 118–38, his worth derives from chastening the city's youth, and training them in the songs and rites of the gods.[44] Brink has shown that much of the language of this description, as well as its main division of poetry into two acceptable types, comes not from Aristotle or Neoptolemus, but from Plato at his most utopian and censorial (the lines are strongly reminiscent of Cato the censor as well). The resemblances to Plato he regards as both pronounced and 'impressive'. He concludes: 'in discussing the poet

---

[41] My thinking on this matter has been fundamentally influenced by Feeney (1992a: esp. 9) treating the problem of beginning the history of Latin literature with the history of censorship. For a fuller treatment of these issues see Feeney (2002a).

[42] Feeney (2002a: 182).

[43] Galinsky (1996: 54–5).

[44] On the poet as teacher in lines 126–8, see Brink (1963: 201): 'it is *paideia* with a small *p*, *paideia* for *paides*.'

who is *utilis urbi* Horace has largely spoken of educational matters. The philosophers' strictures upon poetry have been rejected by implication. But while delimiting the field of poetry he has also moralized it. In the utopian setting of the *Republic* Plato had restricted poetry to hymns to the gods and songs of praise of heroes. In the educational context of this part of the poem the same two topics have been admitted, religious *carmina* and poems commemorating *recte facta,* and nothing besides that has any moral connotation.'[45]

Here again, in accounting for the oddities of Horace's lessons, we may well have to reckon with the gravitational pressure of the addressee in order to understand just how, and to what purpose, Horace now takes such a distinctly Platonic/censorial view of the poet's function in society. This may also help explain why the poet is so preternaturally obsessed with loud, militaristic theater-productions and hymnic shows in *Epist.* 2.1, to the exclusion of nearly all other kinds of literary work. For the scant evidence we have regarding Augustus' own critical ideas concerning the place of literature in 'his' society suggests that he may well have taken precisely this 'preceptive' and 'exemplary' view of the poet's public role.[46]

---

[45] Brink (1963: 202). For a full reckoning of the specifically Platonic character of these lessons, see Brink (Vol. III, 1982: 155–79 *passim* and 429–30).

[46] For Augustus as a stylist, and his attitudes towards literature generally, see Lyne (1995: 30 and 189–90). The most valuable ancient evidence is that of Suet. *Aug.* 85–9. Near the end of his discussion of Augustus' literary and stylistic habits (89.2), Suetonius asserts, on the evidence of letters that he had himself read, that: 'in reading the writers of both tongues there was nothing for which he (Augustus) looked so carefully as precepts and examples instructive to the public or to individuals (*praecepta et exempla publice uel priuatim salubria*); these he would often copy word for word, and send to the members of his household, or to his generals and provincial governors, whenever any of them required admonition' (trans. J. C. Rolfe, *Suetonius,* vol. I (London and New York, 1914) 258). Augustus' own summary of the legislation passed on his initiative at *Res Gestae* 8.5 expresses a strikingly similar view of the paradigmatic and educational functions of law: 'by new laws passed on my initiative I brought back into use many exemplary practices of our ancestors (*multa exempla maiorum*) that were disappearing in our time, and in many ways I myself transmitted exemplary practices to posterity for their imitation (*multarum rerum exempla imitanda*)', trans. Galinsky (1996: 129). Much the same rhetoric operates inside Ovid's account of the razing of Vedius Pollio's urban mansion in 7 BCE (to be replaced at Augustus' own expense by a public garden and the Portico of Livia) at *Fasti* 6.645–8: 'Caesar took it upon himself to tear down such an enormous building and to destroy the riches of which he had become the heir. That is the way to carry out the work of

But all of this raises a large problem for the poem's speaker. For in addressing himself to Augustus, Horace has us imagine a world in which the vast majority of his own poems do not belong, and where he himself does not qualify as the relevant, chaste, preceptive, and publicly valuable poet that *Epist.* 2.1 constructs as 'his(?)' Platonic ideal.[47] The one big exception to the rule is his *Carmen Saeculare*, wherein he nearly fits the narrow confines of preceptor and *choregos*.[48] But he makes clear in lines 76–89 that this, his one most obvious foray onto Augustus' public stage, as an announced player in his public relations show, was regarded as much too modern by the likes of the Stoicizing, archaizing critics of the poem. There he constructs them, his deluded detractors, as 'this crowd of yours' (*hic tuus populus*), meaning Augustus' crowd. That is, they are somehow to be reckoned as *his* arbiters of what counts as real poetry in Rome. They must be thought, in some measure, to be dancing to his beat. But the evidence of *Epist.* 1.19 indicates that the problem goes back much farther, to 20 BCE, if not to 23, when *Odes* Books 1–3 were first published. For strangely, as Horace tells it, these poems (which we commonly assume to have been instant 'classics') were both praised and vilified not by different readers, but by the same readers waxing critical in different contexts: *laudet ametque domi, premat extra limen iniquus* (36). The reaction is most unusual and hard to make sense of. For it is by far the more common situation, often represented in Roman literature, that one has to grit one's teeth in public and

---

Censor and that is the way to set examples (*sic agitur censura et sic exempla parantur*) when the judge himself does what he asks others to do', trans. Galinsky (1996: 187). Much of this thinking, I suggest, is distilled in the theorizing of *Epist.* 2.1, especially in the idea of the *uates* as a writer of works through which 'the moral habits and minds of illustrious men are manifest' (*mores animique uirorum clarorum apparent*, *Epist.* 2.1.249–50)—as if that is all that the likes of Virgil and Varius were good for! Lyne (1995: 191 n. 26) is alert to the way in which Augustus' own expectations inhere in the theoretical attitudes expressed by these lines: 'The way Horace describes Virgil's and Varius' functions...so clearly fits many Horatian Odes that Horace must want to remind Augustus and us that he too has done his bit.'

[47] Referring to the critical stance adopted in lines 145–55, Feeney (2002a: 182) observes: 'this stance is especially striking in someone who, as I stressed at the start, had begun his career in the two genres, Greek and Latin, which had the exercise of *licentia* and *libertas* as their *raison d'être*.'

[48] On the description of the *vates* at *Epist.* 2.1.132–8 as a specific reference to the writer of the *Carmen Saeculare*, see Putnam (2000: 130–2).

applaud what one hates (cf. the scenarios of Persius 1 and Juvenal 1, both based on Horace), if only to vilify it later at home. 'Home' is where one's true feelings can be expressed. And in Horace's case these domestic expressions are, by his accounting, highly complimentary and enthusiastic. So why not in public? Why should the same readers feign dislike of his poetry, but only while others are watching them in the act of criticism? The answer has to be that there is some unusual pressure (whether real or invented by Horace we cannot tell) 'out there' in the literary-critical world of Augustus' Rome as it is presented for our consideration in *Epist.* 1.19 and 2.1. This is the pressure to be seen valuing poetry of certain kinds (morally uplifting, exemplary, castigating luxury, etc.) and castigating others (playful, pleasure-loving, amatory, etc.). For the questions that many still ask of Horace's *Carmen Saeculare* may well have been those that were posed (for the benefit of Augustus' overhearing) after it was performed in 17 BCE: 'why no Golden Age, Horace? And why are you so cagey about proclaiming everything perfect now, with Augustus, our shimmering god-on-earth?'[49] Some of these same 'public' criticisms may well have been leveled against the *Odes* 1–3. And even the panegyrics of Book 4 are not immune from charges of being overly self-indulgent and/or indirect. Below we will see that such public criticisms of Horace have their clear mirror image in Augustus' own (need to be seen) castigating the senate in 19–18 BCE.[50]

[49] On these as pressing questions still, see Barker (1996: 434–46).

[50] Galinsky (1996: 54–7) points out that one of the main props of Augustus' political program, from a very early time, and a key to his longevity, was his championing the cause of the non-political classes of Italy against the old, entrenched senatorial oligarchy of Rome; cf. esp. Wiseman (1971: 8–12). As a *vindex libertatis* in that sense, I maintain, it is crucial that Augustus be seen consistently in the act of chastising the senate. This he does on several occasions, but most notably in the first weeks of 18 BCE (see below) as part of a bigger project of 'purging' Rome and setting everything in a new (old) order before announcing the onset of a new *saeculum* in 17. Thus, my one small criticism of Galinsky's excellent studies of Augustus' moral legislation is that they do not sufficiently take into account the way in which one role (that of *vindex libertatis* for an Italian majority) *necessitates* the other (that of moral reformer and chastiser of the senate). Instead, Galinsky consistently reckons the motives behind the moral legislation of Augustus in terms of his attempts to manifest 'the spiritual and moral superiority of the ruling classes of Italy and Rome' in order to justify Rome's right to expand her empire through military conquest; see Galinsky (1981: 138); cf. Galinksy (1996: 128–40).

By now it is clear that much of this way of imagining and talking about literature in *Epist. 2.*1 comes not simply 'from' Horace 'to' us, however that might be imagined to work, but from a mindset, highly attuned to the ways in which art was conceived of and used by the imperial regime, if not by Augustus himself.[51] Theoretical ideas, in other words, are prefigured by, and expressive of, a certain highly-charged rhetoric of the teens. They have been 'looped through' that rhetoric before being delivered to us, so their narratological trajectory is more that of a knot than a line. If not always, then at least, certainly, sometimes. For as Denis Feeney has clearly shown, the poet and princeps are never clearly distinguishable in the *Epistle to Augustus*. They exist as conditions of one another. And because their blurring is so complete from beginning to end, huge obstacles stand in the way of our ever finding therein Horace's own univocal and politically un-enmeshed 'Art of Poetry'.

But perhaps that was the wrong thing to look for in *Epist.* 2.1 in the first place. Maybe that was never the point. The better option, I believe, and this poem's best way of speaking in a fuller voice that both expresses a given rhetoric and questions it, is not to solve the theoretical problems it presents, nor to loosen its narratological knots, but to allow these problems to express themselves in full, and thus to interfere with the way we read. For in doing so we are wont to ask questions not just of the poem, but of ourselves as its critics: how do we react to being put in that alien, but still familiar landscape? Just how disoriented do we feel? And even more, how do we feel about Horace's now sounding so responsible, censorial, and relevant? The lyric playboy of the *Odes* (esp. Book 1), has disappeared, with the old bachelor's being made, finally, to grow up, become responsible, and produce something 'legitimate'.

Having explored the problem of the 'Augustan' contouring of the poem's critic in *Epist.* 2.1, I want now to consider how some of these same gravitational effects might be traced in the theoretical tenets of

---

[51] I am not the first to see this. Oliensis (1998a: 213 n. 25) argues that: 'recalling that Augustus undertook massive public works along these lines, exercised censorial powers to purge the senate of what Suetonius terms the unseemly and low-born mob that had infiltrated its ranks, lavished gifts on individuals, and contributed enormous sums directly to the treasury, we may surmise that Horace's poet-benefactor is ultimately modeled on the emperor himself.'

the *Epistle to Florus*; for example, in that one most readily extractable portion of 'literary theory' that comes in the poem's middle, at lines 106–25:

> Ridentur mala qui componunt carmina; uerum
> gaudent scribentes et se uenerantur et ultro,
> si taceas, laudant quicquid scripsere beati.
> At qui legitimum cupiet fecisse poema,
> cum tabulis animum censoris sumet honesti;
> audebit, quaecumque parum splendoris habebunt
> et sine pondere erunt et honore indigna ferentur,
> uerba mouere loco, quamuis inuita recedant
> et uersentur adhuc inter penetralia Vestae;
> obscurata diu populo bonus eruet atque
> proferet in lucem speciosa uocabula rerum,
> quae priscis memorata Catonibus atque Cethegis
> nunc situs informis premit et deserta uetustas;
> adsciscet noua, quae genitor produxerit usus.
> uemens et liquidus puroque simillimus amni
> undet opes Latiumque beabit diuite lingua;
> luxuriantia compescet, nimis aspera sano
> leuabit cultu, uirtute carentia tollet,
> ludentis speciem dabit et torquebitur, ut qui
> nunc Satyrum, nunc agrestem Cyclopa mouetur.

Those who compose songs badly are laughed at, but they take pleasure in writing badly and they revere themselves for it. And if you should say nothing to them, they themselves will praise whatever they, in their state of bliss, have written. But if someone wants to produce a poem that is legitimate, he must take up the law-tables and mind of a well-born censor when he writes. Those lacking distinction, and yet others who are frivolous and considered unworthy of office, these words he will have the daring to remove from their station, even though they are unwilling to leave and even to this day linger inside Vesta's inner sanctum. A man of good standing himself, he will unearth long-lost words for the people's use, and he will expose to the light of day lovely terms for things that were once recalled by Rome's ancient Catos and Cetheguses but now lie fallen beneath unsightly neglect and lonely old age. New words fathered by usage he will adopt. Strong and flowing, just like a pristine river, he will pour out wealth and he will bless Latium with rich language. Words over-grown he will prune back, and words too rough he will smooth with wholesome cultivation. Those without virtue he will remove. And all the while he is being tortured he will have the look of someone at play, like a dancer who plays first a satyr, then an oafish Cyclops.

Here the notion of the poet's 'law-abiding poem' (*legitimum poema*) is developed in full, and the point is clearly not to unhinge the metaphor from its origins in the laws of the state, and thereby to soften it; rather, connections with the laws of the state are actively and emphatically developed in the picture of the poet/critic as a 'censor' charged with fashioning poems that are in strict keeping with the laws of the state. He needs, as it were, to make 'good citizens' out of them: un-serious riff-raff (*sine pondere*, line 112[52]) and those unworthy of 'office' (*honore*) he removes from his poetry's senate-list. In the layout of this idea Horace elaborately separates 'whatever' (*quaecumque*) in 111 from its punchline, 'words' (*uerba*), in line 113 to keep us guessing, just for a moment, as to whether we are to think of reprehensible 'activities' or 'words'. In 115–18 we see the poet/critic replacing that riff-raff with ancient words of decent pedigree; as it were, from the noblest of old Roman families whose fortunes have fallen on hard times. The language of 118 has us imagine these forgotten old words as once-grand buildings, fallen down and in need of repair. The dutiful poet/censor brings them back to their former glory.

The question I ask of this funny picture is, does it not have a distinctly familiar look to it? Let's keep going: line 119 suggests that the censor will recognize a few new words (*noua*) that have common 'usage' (*usus*) as their 'father' (*genitor*).[53] A few 'new men', in other words, *noui homines* of dubious background but proven utility (words like the man, Agrippa, if such can be imagined), will be allowed into the senate house of this poet's books. But, as lines 121–3 make clear, the self-censoring poet (here further troped as a farmer digging and pruning and watering his well-kept field, thus filling out the analogy with Cato, the farmer-censor[54]) will crack down on luxury (*luxuriantia compescet*) applying sumptuary

---

[52] i.e. lacking *grauitas*.

[53] Rudd (1989: 138): 'As the censor admits new members, the poet will admit new words.'

[54] The agricultural imagery of vv. 121–3 is unmistakable, esp. in references to a well-watered Latium that 'pours forth riches' (*fundet opes*); to 'overgrowth (*luxuria*); and to the censor's work as 'cultivation' (*cultus*).

legislation to his verbal expression. Moreover, he will keep hot-heads (*nimis aspera*) in check, and notions lacking virtue and brave civic purpose (*uirtute carentia*) will be removed from the list altogether.[55] And he will do it all with a smile on his face to hide the agony of his mammoth linguistic toil.

Now these are funny notions, certainly. But not just that. They are, at least potentially, 'satiric,' able to scandalize as well as to inform and/or delight. For in them we are invited to see the poet as the mirror-image of not just any old censor, certainly not in 18 BCE anyway, but of the princeps himself. For Augustus was, at this very time, doing exactly what these lines talk about: building up fallen old buildings and families; beautifying the city and its people by initiating moral reforms, passing sumptuary laws, keeping family lines, and the senate, noble and clean, and seriously restricting who could do what. Dio records that in response to the electoral violence of the first weeks of 19 BCE, Augustus allowed himself to be elected to the position of 'supervisor of morals' for five years.[56] He began cleansing the city in that year by introducing legislation against electoral corruption and by passing certain sumptuary measures on lavish expenditures at dinner parties.[57] In the first weeks of 18 BCE he took upon himself what was once one of the republican censor's principal duties, a *lectio senatus,* in which he attempted to bring the number of senators down to 600 by removing those whom he deemed 'useless' and/or 'unworthy' on social and moral grounds.[58] In the process he found it necessary to offer financial assistance to certain members of Rome's highest orders 'who lived upright lives' but whose fortunes fell short of the basic property requirement.[59] The result of these efforts, according to Galinsky, was that 'the Senate...was composed of a minority, at least after 19 BCE, of

---

[55] Galinsky (1981: 139–40) points out that the mantra of Augustus' *lectiones senatus*, whereby he introduced certain new men to the order, and discarded many others, was his returning the senate to its *prisca uirtus*.

[56] Dio 54.10.5 mentions no refusal on Augustus' part in 19 BCE; *Res Gestae* 6.1 suggests that he refused the office (but this is perhaps a reference to the refusal of 22 BCE, recorded by Dio 54.2.1), preferring instead to use 'his powers as a tribune to carry out the requisite legislation', Galinsky (1996: 101).

[57] Galinsky (1996: 102).

[58] For the *lectiones senatus* of 29 and 18 BCE, see Wiseman (1971: 10–11).

[59] Dio 54.17.3–4.

old-style *nobiles* and a majority of ascending *novi homines* who came mostly from the municipalities of Italy.'[60] Thus the senate, as it was being remade by Augustus, has its mirror-image in the poet-censor's carefully regulated vocabulary, mixing just so much of the old and noble with a healthy infusion of the useful and new.

All of the Republican censor's old-time functions, that of moral reformer and watchdog, the keeper of Rome's lists of citizens and senators, as well as the city's chief builder and restorer of its fallen buildings, even the keeper of its aqueducts as the man in charge of the quality and security of the city's water supply (remember that *that* was one of the censor's duties too, and thus it is clearly written into the poet's job description in lines 120–1), all of these same functions are inscribed in the image of the poet in these lines.[61] Funny, certainly. But because Augustus, as we know, was so actively doing all of these same things at the very moment when this poem was written, and, in fact, he had been about most of them at least since 22 BCE when he made a great show of refusing the office of censor for life,[62] I have to believe that the analogy is more than just a casual reference to censorship generally; rather, this image, as Horace paints it, has the power to draw us into the Herculean world of Augustus' aggressive refashioning of Rome. We see one enterprise reflected inside the other in a curious double-image: the princeps inside the poet, and the poet matching his every 'theoretical' thought to the princeps' every 'political' move.

Now how does all of this fit into the larger letter from which I have extracted it as a sample? How, for example, can these same alien pressures be observed to work an effect upon the poem's most famous (and disputed) scene, in the recitation contest of lines 90–105? Here the complaint, later taken up and much amplified by Persius and Juvenal, is that all public criticism in Rome is now dead. Great battles are staged in Augustus' library on the Palatine hill, in

---

[60] Galinsky (1981: 139).

[61] On the censor as builder of roads, public buildings, and caretaker of the city's water-supply, see Suolahti (1963: 60–6).

[62] See Dio 54.2.1–3 makes clear that although Augustus refused the title of censor, he possessed the full powers of that office and subsequently performed many of the duties that belonged to that office. On Augustus' frustrated attempts to revive the censorship of the Republic in 22 BCE, see Suolahti (1963: 500–5).

recitations featuring the greatest of living Roman writers (i.e. now
that Virgil, Varius, and Tibullus are dead), even the likes of Horace
himself, and perhaps Propertius.[63] The noise of the battle can be
heard from far off (*procul audi*, 95). Blows are struck, first by this
combatant, then by that. The battle outlasts the day, and continues
on into the night (*lento Samnites ad lumina prima duello*, 98). But
then something amazing happens: when the dinner-bell sounds the
contest is over, and everyone goes home a winner, fittingly canonized
by the (quasi-military) cognomen that they fought for, and won: 'you
call me Alcaeus, Propertius, and I will call you Callimachus.'
Everyone is happy, brilliant, gifted, and, it seems, utterly beyond
criticism. For that is how the show is set up to operate. Like the
gladiator contest it resembles, it is a pandering spectacle that plays
well to the crowds (*supplex populi suffragia capto*, 103). As criticism,
however (real war), it amounts only to so much stagey critical noise.

Clearly Horace is still very much in the role of the jaded old soldier
in these lines. But the main observation I would like to make about
this scene has to do not with his perspective *per se*, but how, within
that perspective, he continues to develop certain themes and metaphorical gambits that he introduced in the section that immediately
precedes it (the larger description of 'noisy Rome' in vv. 65–86),
doing so in a way that makes the activities of poets in the second
scene analogous to that of the construction-workers (and their
mules) in the first: both are frantically 'battling' within their respective plains of war (one at the bottom of the hill, the other at the top)
to get the emperor's projects built, and his libraries filled. Thus, the
point of view is again that of a jaded mercenary, but his jadedness, in
this case, has to do not with his being tired of writing *per se*, but with
what that writing now entails in Rome, in the wake of Augustus'
aggressive, and newly focussed, refashioning of the city in 22–18 BCE.
These scenes are thus the 'glue' that connects the poems two halves,
linking the poet's mercenary autobiography of lines 26–64 to his
strangely 'Augustan' theoretical musings of lines 106–25 (the famous
poet-as-censor passage that I have discussed in detail above).

---

[63] On the deaths of Virgil, Tibullus and (probably) Varius as factors in Horace's
isolation on the poetic scene of the teens BCE, see Feeney (2002a).

The basic question that Horace asks Florus in lines 65–86 is how he is supposed to meditate quietly on his lyric projects when there is so much business to be attended to in Rome, and so much bustle and noise to be battled against? In line 71 he complains of having to cross the entire *interualla* (literally the 'space between the pallisades' of a military camp) that separates the Quirinal hill from the Aventine in order to visit a sick friend. The word is highly suggestive, for it likens the low-lying areas of the city to a war zone. The description that follows in lines 71ff. develops the figure in full. For to his interlocutor's happy suggestion that the streets of Rome are now swept clean and wide open for quiet meditation (71), Horace counters with a description of the city as a crowded military camp running in high gear, with mules and contractors racing supplies here and there (*festinat calidus mulis gerulisque redemptor,* 72); siege engines 'hurling' stones and huge beams into place (*torquet nunc lapidem, nunc ingens machina tignum,* 73); funerals 'wrestling', dogs 'fleeing', pigs 'attacking', and so on. The scene of his embattled life in these lines will become the backdrop to Juvenal's third satire, a poem written in the madhouse of Rome, and delivered in a volume loud enough to be heard. But that is precisely the question that Horace puts to Florus in lines 79–80. In essence: 'Just how loud am I going to have to scream to get heard in all this racket!?' he asks in lines 79–80. 'And just how lovely is that lung-busting song likely to be?'

Thus, it is with remarkable consistency that this speaker, whether in setting his eyes on the valley between the hills, or peering inside the glimmering new precinct of Apollo atop the Palatine, sees vast, wide open spaces (*interualla . . . haud sane commoda*; *purae . . . plataea*; *uacuam . . . aedem*) that are being aggressively 'battled' over, and filled not only with clutter and noise, but with new works, both architectural and poetic, that are the point of the battles themselves: filling the city with sky-high buildings, and clogging its streets with siege-engines and supplies, are veritable 'armies' of contractors and mules; up above, we have seen, are the poets, producing just as much racket, and in conditions that are equally combative, and wearying. It is crucial that we see just how much the building contractors racing about in the valley below resemble the poets laying siege to the citadel above. For it is clear that the perspective we are being invited to take of their efforts is consistent from one scene to the next. Their shared figuring suggests that the two activities are, to this viewer's mind, of like kinds. The first glimpse we have of the Apollo precinct's libraries thus straddles the perspectives of poet and building-contractor, seen as 'a job/work (*opus*) marvelous to see, engraved (*caelatum*) by/for the nine muses.' That is, the libraries have been crafted not just *by* the muses, but *for* them, as a space for them to occupy, and awaiting their arrival. Next, in the phrase *uacuam Romanis uatibus aedem* (94) we consider the emptiness of the edifice, with the double sense of *uacuam* suggesting that the space is both 'open to' poets, and, as yet, 'empty of' them. Thus we are given a sense of how much of the job remains to be done. When can the new tenants, the Muses, move in? Just how quickly will the construction-workers, the poets, complete that library, all so close to being done but the finish-work, the books themselves? Their construction-noise can be heard from far off. 'Alcaeus goes over here, right? And what about this one? Who's he? Mimnermus? Anybody seen Callimachus?'

Such is the noise heard to emanate from within the Apollo temple's precinct walls. This scene, just as the one that precedes it, puts us squarely inside the world of Augustus' aggressive remaking of Rome, letting us feel the pressure felt by many, from the poets at the top of the hill to the mules at the bottom, to get the emperors projects built and his library (especially lacking on the Latin side) filled. Thus the concern of both scenes, I suggest, is not so much with life in Rome *per se* as it is with life in Augustus' Rome, in the busy last days of an old, outmoded *saeculum* that would soon (by way of much hammering, purging, and polishing) give way to the new (the *Carmen Saeculare* is securely dated to June of 17 BCE).[64] In lines 106–25, then, we see this same pressure applied to theory itself, experienced as a set of censorial guidelines (the contractor's checklist) for getting the job done to the owner's satisfaction, responsibly, on time, and with every detail tastefully expressive of Augustus' own way of expressing himself.

The knee-jerk criticism that finds Horace naming his opponent Callimachus, and his opponent calling him Alcaeus, tells of the

---

[64] On the moral legislation of 19–18 BCE as a deliberate preparation for the opening of a new *saeculum* in 17 BCE, see Galinsky (1996: 101–2 and 128–30); and Putnam (2000: 49).

pressure put upon poets to fill specific, pre-fashioned slots on the shelves of the library's Latin wing.[65] Described this way, the critical scenario of lines 90–105 helps us imagine just how hard it must have been in late 19 to early 18 BCE for any budding Florus to flower into a poet of his own making in a setting where rich rewards were at hand for anyone willing to become someone else, i.e. Rome's best approximation of a Pindar, Callimachus, or whomever, by way of direct and obvious imitation. It is thus with a much keener sense of the political hurdles that Florus faces in finding a voice he can call 'his own' that we return at the end of the letter to the issue with which it begins; that is, to Florus' failing to 'own' what was sold to him. Ross Kilpatrick has recently argued that Florus does not want just any old letter from Horace. Rather he wants a letter of criticism. For the scenario we are to imagine is that Horace's young imitator has sent him a poem, or perhaps a set of poems, that he wants his older father-figure to criticize and review.[66] This I regard as a brilliant suggestion, for it helps make sense of the letter's second half where the discussion turns (at lines 87ff.) from Horace's refusal to write songs to the issue of criticism itself, with the poet insisting that criticism has to come from inside yourself because the critical 'scene' in Rome is dead, a magnificent, stylish, noisy show that is utterly devoid of substance. What you really need, he insists, is a censor inside yourself; or, to put a satirical spin on the idea, you need to swallow Augustus whole. Thus, the first half of the letter addresses one complaint, that of the missing songs, and the second half the other complaint, that of the missing 'critical' letter.

What helpful feedback, then, does Horace offer to his young friend? The 'ownership' theme that began *Epist.* 2.2 resurfaces again at the end of the poem, bringing with it some of the same questions we have just asked about who we imagine this teacher to be, and the ultimate 'take-home' value of his lessons. In lines 141–45 Horace tells Florus that whenever he is tempted to write more of those playboy songs from his youth, and to play at nonsense rather than wisdom, the censor inside of him kicks in and he gives himself a good talking to. Everything, then, from line 146 to the end of the poem are the

---

[65] For the challenge of filling the library's empty shelves, see Horsfall (1993b: 58–67).

[66] See Kilpatrick (1990: 29–30).

poet's words of wisdom to himself, a scolding put to the poet by none other than the censor inside himself. This is the voice, he says, that all poets must listen to 'silently' inside (*haec tacitusque recordor,* 145) now that Rome's critical scene is so meaningless and loud.

But here again, in the lessons that follow from here to the end, Horace takes us into his addressee's world so completely that it is hard to keep track of where these lessons issue from, and to whom they presume to speak. These scoldings are thus easily seen to criticize not only the speaker himself (as lessons to himself), but Florus as well, and thus to provide Florus with that long-awaited letter critiquing his work and commenting on his capacity as a potential heir.

For example we see in lines 158–65 that Horace is again trying his hand at the jusrisconsult's art, that is, Florus' art, by explaining to him the technicalities of property-transfer insofar as these have a bearing upon one's own contentment. He argues: 'If what one sells with weighing scale and cash is one's own, there are certain things, if you trust legal-experts, that shift owners by being used. The field that feeds you is your own. Orbius' estate-manager regards you as his master when he hoes the fields that will soon give you grain. You hand over cash and receive grapes, chickens, eggs, a jug of cheap wine. And, of course, in that way, little by little you are purchasing the field.'

He goes on in this vein for several more lines. Not terribly convincing, I suspect, and one wonders just how this argument will have been received by his legal-expert friend: you buy some eggs, you own the farm? Since when? But as the discussion proceeds, Horace brings in an Epicurean notion he has relied on before, the kernel of which is that he does not really believe in the existence of 'ownership' in the first place, since, according to Epicurus, nothing can ever be truly 'one's own.' Rather, he argues that ownership *per se* is delusional, since ours is only a momentary *usus* ('use' or 'enjoyment') of the things we provisionally call our own. And thus, he continues in lines 174–9:

> permutet dominos et cedat in altera iura.
> sic quia perpetuus nulli datur usus, et heres
> heredem alternis uelut unda superuenit undam,

quid uici prosunt aut horrea? quidue Calabris
saltibus adiecti Lucani, si metit Orcus
grandia cum paruis, non exorabilis auro?

(sc. the property you now call your own) changes owners, and it passes into someone else's control. And thus, because no one has the right of enjoying/ using forever, and one heir follows upon another like wave upon wave, what good are your storage-barns and granaries? What good are groves that stretch all the way from Lucania to Calabria if Orcus harvests the big with the small, and cannot be swayed by gold?

This is a standard Cynic/sometimes-Stoic/sometimes-Epicurean *topos,* like so many similar 'ownership' aphorisms encountered in the diatribes of Lucretius, Bion, and in Horace himself. But Horace has given the theme a poetic spin that I am unable to trace in its previous uses, and in that way, in his unique 'using' of the motif, he has made the *topos,* momentarily, 'his own'. For, as he finishes off his discussion of ownership in lines 174–9, Horace incorporates a small lesson in the ways of making poetry one's own, by cueing us to the previous ownership of the very verses that talk about ownership, verses that he now calls 'his own': like honey wafting with the scent of the original thyme or sage that went into its making, these lines carry the distinct scent of earlier verse, specifically of lines 970–1 of *De Rerum Natura* Book 3: 'thus, one this always rises from another, and life is granted to no one as a possession, but to all for their use' (*sic alid ex alio numquam desistet oriri/vitaque mancipio nulli datur, omnibus usu*). But those lines in Lucretius already bear the scent of an earlier flower in Lucilius fr. 777W: 'since I know that nothing is granted to mortal man in life that is his own' (*cum sciam nihil esse in vita proprium mortali datum*). And there is no telling where Lucilius might have had it from.

But that perhaps is the point: the saying is, after all, an aphorism, and a fairly common one at that, so it defies being assigned strictly to one author or one school.[67] It is attested in various forms over a broad range of philosophical and literary sources. As such, the

---

[67] Brink (1982: 369): 'that *mancipium* and *usus* had become a commonplace in this kind of saying is shown by their appearance in the *Sententiae* of Publ. Syr. 593...H. himself had so used *proprius* and *cedere usum,* very affectingly, at *S.* II.2.130ff., where the speaker is the dispossessed farmer Ofellus.'

maxim's pliable, 'hereditary' character is strangely illustrative of its sense; for, like the field it describes, the saying has no fixed owner: it 'passes into the use' now of one author, now of another, with specific deployment constituting all that any individual writer, and only momentarily, can claim as 'his own'. Thus, I maintain, in his peculiar rendering of the motif here at the end of *Epist.* 2.2, Horace has done much more than just ply us with an allusion to Lucilius *via* Lucretius (and who knows what others). He has shown Florus, in very real terms, how 'poetry proceeds through the processing of poetry'.[68] This is a lesson that apparently Florus needs to learn, for we have seen Horace teach him this in the intertextual image of Pindar's bee nipping flowers from Virgil's field, then making its way into a verse-letter of Horace. And we remember that it is he who, according to the slave-allegory that began the poem, has complained of failing to control the property he was sold, the fun-loving slave who looks so much like a book of Horatian love-lyrics, with his 'smattering of basic Greek', and a penchant for dinner-party 'song?'[69] How can you really 'own' a slave like that when he keeps shirking the new hard work you want to put him to, and reverting to his old bad habits?

As we have seen above, the criticism that Florus demands from Horace is right there under his nose. I think it is there already in *Epist.* 1.3 in a whole series of intertextual cues that invite us all to observe how specific words and images 'picked' from other poets' fields can be re-deployed in a complex, multi-layered way, to express new ideas, thereby to become the poet's 'own' through his unique 'using' of them. But the question remains, can Florus see any of this? Does this man of the flowers know anything of sniffing them? Can he sense, for example, that the farmer's copper pot put on to boil in the

---

[68] Henderson (1995: 107). Consider, too, the way Horace leads into the ownership *topos* in lines 141–51 by figuring his epistolary work as a kind of anti-lyric medication; his means to wisdom and sanity, something he uses (*sapere est utile*) for his own benefit, having cast aside the games of his youth. In other words, the epistle itself is an object of *usus*, the field that feeds him, and that slowly he renders into his own.

[69] *quin etiam canet indoctum sed dulce bibenti* ('and what's more he sings song untaught, but sweet for the drinker'). Recently Oliensis (1998a: 9) has made an excellent case for the double-nature of this slave, arguing that he resembles the slave-book of *Epistles* 1.20 and the cupbearer of *Odes* 1.38: 'The slave of *Epistles* 2.2 is thus an apt figure for both the letter and the lyrics that are the objects of Florus' frustrated desire.'

chill of night (*sub noctem gelidam lignis calefactat aënum*, 169) recalls
a very specific set of images from *Georgics* 1 lines 287–97 (*Multa adeo
gelida melius se nocte dedere... Volcano decoquit umore | et foliis
undam trepidi despumat aëni*)? Does he sense the irony of Horace's
heating that pot not with Virgil's personified 'Vulcan' but with a
much more 'elemental' Lucretian raw material (*emptis... lignis*)?
Does he see how, by mixing and layering these images into one
another, Horace has produced something quite new? And how
about when Horace re-personifies the elemental stuff a few lines
below, in an aphorism strong in 'Lucretian overtones'?[70] As expressed
in lines 175–9 the aphorism might even be thought to risk sounding
too much like a stolen bit of Lucretius were it not for that image of
the grim reaper, Orcus, mowing down the great with the small in
lines 178–9. This is precisely the kind of thinking about death,
conceived as some menacing underworld force, that Lucretius in-
veighs against repeatedly in his *De Rerum Natura*. For he names
Orcus only three times in that poem, and always only to insist that
'he' doesn't really exist, and that you are a pathetic fool if you think of
death as 'Orcus' coming up from hell to mow you down. Not once
does he personify fire as Vulcan; for him, fire is always about *ligna*,
'raw materials', as are words and poems.[71]

These are just a few samples of the criticisms that Florus needs to
hear, in memories snatched from earlier poetry, and creatively re-
deployed for new purposes and effects. Rather than follow these
examples with more of the same, I want simply to conclude by saying
that the *Epistle to Florus* is well matched to the letter that has been its
book-companion since antiquity, the *Epistle to Augustus*. Both
poems, I hope to have shown, not just the latter, are capable of
addressing Augustus. For both present us with Horace's peculiar set
of personal and theoretical preoccupations from a jaded period, late
in his career, but they do so in a way that invites us to consider how
these preoccupations might themselves be conditioned by, and fully

---

[70] Rudd (1989: 144): 'the whole of the preceding passage, from 158–79, has strong
Lucretian overtones'; cf. Brink (1982: 367): 'thus the section that begins in a humorous manner ends in a serious "Lucretian" vein.'

[71] The poplar tree in 170 that fixes the border dividing one man's field from the
next 'recalls Virgil's beeches in the same position'; see Brink (1982: 377), referring to
E. 9.9: *usque ad aquam et ueteres, iam fracta cacumina, fagos.*

capable of addressing, very real pressures that are being applied to the poet's interior 'personal' and 'theoretical' worlds from the outside world of Augustus' Rome. By focusing in this paper on some of the narrow and relatively old-fashioned figurative, thematic and narratological problems that, I think, these poems present, I hope to have addressed, in some small way, the problem of how old formalism can itself be made to say something new, helping us comprehend the full conundrum of poetry as politics in Rome, and politics as art.

19

Fashioning Men: The Art of Self-Fashioning in the *Ars Poetica*

Ellen Oliensis

The author projected by the *Ars poetica* is, more or less by definition, an authority on the poetic art, a master performer who has earned the right to instruct others.[1] What will concern me in this chapter is less the overt aesthetic content of this instruction than the social lessons that are packaged within it. On the one hand, the *Ars* is a profoundly normative textbook that not only describes but helps enforce the rules of the game the Piso brothers are about to enter. This game, like the *ludus* Horace declines to reenter at the start of *Epistles* 1, involves social as well as poetic performance; Horace is teaching the Piso brothers how to fashion their selves as well as their poems. On the other hand, the *Ars* in no way guarantees that these young men will emerge as winners. As Horace recurrently remarks, success depends on a player's ability not merely to follow the rules (by composing a well-formed iambic line, for example) but, more importantly, to improvise a performance within them and some- times to break them. The sense of decorum that enables such im- provisations is something that can be advertised, as it is throughout

---

[1] The date of the *Ars* and the identity of Horace's Pisones remain controversial. While certainty on this score is not essential to the argument of this chapter, I follow (e.g.) Rudd (1989: 19–21) and Armstrong (1993: 199–202), who argue for a date of around 10 BCE and identify Horace's senior Piso with Lucius Calpurnius Piso Pontifex (son of the patron of Philodemus). My reading of the *Ars* is much indebted to Armstrong's demonstration of the way the poem is shaped to suit Horace's young, aristocratic, and potentially arrogant Pisonian audience; see Armstrong (1993: 203–16).

the *Ars,* but that cannot be taught. What Horace teaches the Piso brothers is finally not what to do or not to do but what he can do and they cannot.

Horace's disquisition on the art which is the source of his authority (social and poetic) is addressed to an audience that boasts conventional social advantages Horace cannot claim, and this conjunction of subject matter and audience produces an extremely volatile blend of authority and deference: a 'masterwork' which is also a study in self-defacement, an educational essay which is also an exercise in antididaxis. The *Ars poetica* presents a face-off between Horace's poetic authority and his audience's social prestige. And although Horace repeatedly defers to his aristocratic audience, he triumphs over them in the end—triumphs, indeed, by deferring. The monstrously indecorous figures that frame the *Ars* (and that will also frame my discussion) may be ridiculous, but they enjoy the last laugh.

FASHIONING MEN

The social side-effect, as it might be termed, of Horace's poetic instruction is most readily discerned in the famous opening lines of the *Ars poetica.* While this opening can be and generally has been read simply as a statement of poetics, such a reading is maintained only at the cost of ignoring the surprising form this statement takes. The educational content of Horace's negative *exemplum* is in fact highly overdetermined (*Ars* 1–5):

> Humano capiti ceruicem pictor equinam
> iungere si uelit et uarias inducere plumas
> undique collatis membris, ut turpiter atrum
> desinat in piscem mulier formosa superne,
> spectatum admissi, risum teneatis, amici?

If a painter wished to join a human head to a horse's neck and to plaster all kinds of feathers on limbs gathered from all over, so that a woman beautiful on top ended foully in a black fish—let in for a viewing, could you hold back a laugh, my friends?

To represent the vice of aesthetic incoherence, Horace could have proceeded any number of ways. He might have had his painter depict a body with disproportionate limbs (a tiny head on a thick neck) or with ill-assorted limbs in another arrangement (a fish body on human feet). As it stands, the painting contains the profiles, blurred but unmistakable, of thoroughly familiar monsters, in particular the horse-man Centaur and fish-woman Scylla.[2] Moreover, although Horace's *ut*-clause superimposes one profile upon the other, retroactively specifying the 'human head' of line 1 as the head of a beautiful woman (who is 'beautiful', it follows, only from the neck up),[3] this syntactical logic is countered by the powerful descriptive coherence of the final figure—a figure reminiscent, as commentators note, of Virgil's biform Scylla, fair maiden above and sea-monster below (*pulchro pectore Virgo | pube tenus, postremo immani corpore pistrix, Aen,* 3.426–7). Rhetorically if not syntactically, Horace's pictured mermaid displaces the centaur-like figure of the opening lines. And it is at this moment that the description thickens and the tone darkens into disgust: *turpiter atrum.* In the end it is the female who makes manifest the gap between form and deformation, outside and inside, surface and depths, fair beginnings and foul endings.

In this scene of viewing, both roles are sexually specified. The emergence of a figure marked as female precipitates the emergence of an audience marked as male—Horace's masculine 'friends' (*amici, Ars* 5). The spectacle of the female monster will cause these friends, Horace predicts, to emit an irrepressible laugh. But this involuntary expenditure of masculine energy is figured as a sign of solidarity, not impotence. Horace's long-awaited main clause establishes both syntactical and sexual order by subjecting the female figure to the scrutiny of a group of men. The opening of the *Ars* is thus an episode in the history of the construction of what is now commonly termed the 'male gaze'. Indeed, if the sexual dynamic of this Horatian scene has passed unremarked, one reason is that it matches the norms of European pictorial representation so precisely as to be invisible.

---

[2] See Brink (1971: 85). As remarked by Frischer (1991: 74–85), Horace's art criticism positively invites a suspicious reading, since this style was favored not only by the imperial circle but also, it seems, by Horace himself (the Sabine villa identified as Horace's was decorated with griffins and sphinxes).

[3] So Rudd (1989: 150); Brink (1971: 86).

It is not by chance that the first word of Horace's *Ars* is 'human', followed by the complementary noun 'head'. To be human is, as it were, to keep one's head, which means to maintain the natural and manly superiority of the head in relation to the rest of the body. The best commentary on the hierarchy that supports the opening of the *Ars* is provided by Cicero, not in his rhetorical writings but in his *De officiis*, a treatise on social and moral propriety addressed to his son at school in Athens.[4] Like the monster in Horace's painting, Ciceronian 'human nature' is defined by division: 'The essential character of the soul is twofold. One part is centered in the appetite (in Greek ὁρμή), which carries a man off this way and that way, the other part in reason, which teaches and makes plain what should be done and what avoided. And so it comes about that reason governs, appetite obeys' (*Off.* 1.101). The implicit metaphor is elaborated in the paragraph that follows: appetites are like horses which must be curbed and guided by reason, the prudent charioteer (102). Nature and reason together militate against behavior that is, in Cicero's instructive collocation, 'indecorous or effeminate' (*natura ratioque . . . cavet . . . ne quid indecore effeminateve faciat*, 14). To be a man means to maintain control of one's lower 'animal' appetites.

Cicero goes on to map this hierarchy directly onto the human body: 'Nature herself seems to have had an excellent plan [*rationem*] for our body: she placed our face and the rest of our figure, which has a respectable appearance, in full view, but covered and hid away those parts of the body which, dedicated to nature's needs, would have been misshapen and foul to see' (*Off.* 1.126–7).[5] Human modesty, *verecundia*, is thus but the imitation of nature: 'what nature has concealed, all those who are of sound mind keep out of sight' (*quae enim natura occultavit, eadem omnes qui sana mente sunt removent ab oculis*, 127). Cicero's judgment on the 'misshapen and foul' parts of the body (*deformem . . . atque turpem*) corresponds to Horace's judgment on the 'foul' ending (*turpiter, Ars* 3) that deforms his fair or 'shapely' female (*formosa*, 4). What Cicero helps us see is that the

---

[4] For a juxtaposition of the *Ars* and the *De officiis* in the service of a reconstruction of Panaetius, see Labowsky (1934).

[5] The male genitalia form a notable exception to Cicero's rule of natural concealment. Are these parts then to be imagined as less 'misshapen and foul' than their female counterparts?

guffaw of Horace's male friends is provoked not only by the incoherence of the painting but also by the sight of the genital fishtail it exposes to view. The body that conceals its ugliness, by contrast, provides Cicero with a model for the decorous or well-composed life (*Off.* 1.98):

ut enim pulchritudo corporis apta compositione membrorum movet oculos et delectat hoc ipso, quod inter se omnes partes cum quodam lepore consentiunt, sic hoc decorum quod elucet in vita movet approbationem eorum quibuscum vivitur ordine et constantia et moderatione dictorum omnium atque factorum.

For as the beauty of a body with well-composed limbs draws the gaze and gives pleasure on just this account, that all the parts harmonize together with a certain charming effect, so this propriety which shines out in a person's life, draws the approbation of those among whom that life is spent, on account of the good order and consistency and restraint of all [his] words and deeds.

Whereas the indecorously exposed body resembles the Horatian monster, this beautiful body is its very antitype.[6] Neatly composed of harmonious limbs, its indeterminate sex modestly concealed, this body earns the applause of the spectators as the Horatian monster earns their ridicule. It is almost as if Horace had designed his monster to illustrate the hideous consequences of a lapse of decorum, in the broad Ciceronian sense of a revolt of animal appetite against the dominion of reason. In the Horatian declension, the priority of the human head is undermined by the centrifugal energy of the lower body parts. 'Humanity' is restored when the men put their heads together, chasing the animal back into hiding with a volley of communal laughter.

The opening scene of Horace's *Ars* thus summons the Piso boys to join the social and sexual community to which they 'naturally' belong. And the summons is forcefully framed. To withhold assent to Horace's rhetorical question is to position oneself outside the community of *amici*, in the company of the derided monster; to assent (the path of least resistance) is to accept the values of that community and to earn a place within it. The scene is part of what the sociologist Norbert Elias has termed the 'civilizing process', the

---

6 For the parallel, cf. Grimal (1988: 12).

process whereby people 'seek to suppress in themselves', and thereafter in their children, 'every characteristic that they feel to be
"animal".[7] The suppression of everything 'animal', a category that
is always expanding, maintains the distance not only between the
child and the adult but also between the lower classes and the social
elite. As Pierre Bourdieu remarks in his study of distinction, 'the
denial of lower, coarse, vulgar, venal, servile—in a word, natural—
enjoyment, which constitutes the sacred sphere of culture, implies an
affirmation of the superiority of those who can be satisfied with the
sublimated, refined, disinterested, gratuitous, distinguished pleasures forever closed to the profane'.[8] The correlated oppositions that
define the opening scene of Horace's *Ars*—between the head and the
tail, top and bottom, human and animal, male and female, reason
and appetite, modesty and obscenity, sanity and insanity; beauty and
ugliness, closure and disclosure, form and deformity—all serve to
create and maintain a distinction between the knowing spectators
and the foolish spectacle, the empowered subjects and the disenfran-
chised, vulgar object. The monster of the *Ars* is set up like a carnival
duck for the Pisones to shoot down, as an exemplary exercise in
elementary *humanitas*.

FASHIONING GENTLEMEN

The laughter of the Pisones targets the inept painter along with his
monstrous painting. Every portrait—every work of art—reflects on
its maker, and the aim of art is to direct one's own performance. If
Horace, himself no playwright, devotes so much of his *Ars* to dramatic proprieties, one reason is that drama, more directly than epic
or lyric, offers embodied models for acting in public.[9] For Horace as

---

[7] Elias (1978: 120 and *passim*). Erasmus' *De civilitate morum puerilium*, extensively discussed by Elias, is an interesting offshoot of Horace's *Ars*.

[8] Bourdieu (1984: 7).

[9] The putative interest of the *maior juvenum* in drama (so, for example, Kilpatrick
(1990: 57)) is not a sufficient justification; nor do I find convincing in isolation
Dupont's suggestion (1985: 335–41) that Horace is developing a program for a
revived Augustan theater. For a mix of explanations see Williams (1968: 349–53).

for Cicero, life is essentially a theatrical performance. Whether his venue is the forum, the stage, the dinner table, or the bookroll, the performer who wants to succeed must anticipate the spectator's critical eye. The arts of poetic and social 'deportment' alike involve rigorous self-scrutiny and ever more subtle refinements, what Horace terms the 'work of the file' (*limae labor, Ars* 291) and Cicero describes as a kind of fine-tuning. As Cicero advises his son, it is not the obvious breaches of decorum (*quae multurn ab humanitate discrepant, Off.* 1.145) but the almost imperceptible false notes in our behavior that require our particular vigilance: 'Just as an expert generally takes notice when a lyre or flute is even slightly out of tune, so we ought to see to it that nothing in our life is out of tune, all the more because harmony of actions is much more important and more valuable than harmony of tones.'[10] The literary critic is likewise distinguished by his capacity to distinguish the slightest *faux pas*. 'Not just anyone,' Horace reminds his tutees, 'has the judicious eye to spot an ill-measured poem' (*non quivis videt immodulata poemata iudex, Ars* 263). In Rome's uncivilized infancy, the meters and the witticisms of a Plautus may have won praise; but critics today will judge those judgments harshly, 'granting that we know, you and I'— and the poet's conspiratorial plural politely assumes that the Pisones already possess the knowledge that he is in the process of imparting—'the difference between refinement and rusticity, and that we can recognize, with tapping finger and listening ear, the sound of poetry that obeys the laws of prosody' (*si modo ego et vos | scimus inurbanum lepido seponere dicto | legitimumque sonum digitis callemus et aure, Ars* 272–4). The art of discrimination is the prerequisite to success on the social stage, for poets as for senators.

Horace's implicit identification of poetic with social performance may help explain not only the emphasis on drama but the deemphasis of comedy within the *Ars*. To write comedies, in this

---

[10] This Ciceronian passage is reworked by Castiglione (1959: 96–7). Castiglione's courtier also draws social lessons from Horace's aesthetics; compare, e.g., Castiglione (1959: 55) with Hor. *Ars* 240–2 (on the inimitability of seemingly imitable effects), Castiglione (1959: 58) with Hor. *Ars* 60–9 (on the mutability of words). For a stimulating reading of the *De officiis* as a proto-courtly text, see Narducci (1984: 203–29); on the progressive refinement of the standards of urbanity in this period, see Ramage (1973: 64–76).

metaphorically charged atmosphere, would be tantamount to acting like a character out of a comedy. And as Cicero reminds his son in the *De officiis*, the dignity of our human character accords best with what might be called a tragic demeanor: 'Nature has not fashioned us such that we seem made for playing and joking, but for sobriety rather, and pursuits of greater weight and importance' (*neque enim ita generati a natura sumus ut ad ludum et iocum facti esse videamur, ad severitatem potius et ad quaedam studia graviora atque maiora, Off.* 1.103). Cicero's social distinction between dignity and frivolity finds its literary counterpart in Aristotle's *Poetics*, where tragedy and comedy are associated with two distinct classes not just of characters but of poets, 'more elevated' and 'more base' respectively.[11] Within the *Ars*, the personified genres are similarly contrasted (*Ars* 89–92):

> versibus exponi tragicis res comica non vult;
> indignatur item privatis ac prope socco
> dignis carminibus narrari cena Thyestae:
> singula quaeque locum teneant sortita decentem.

A comic theme doesn't want to be set out in tragic verse; so too the dinner of Thyestes feels slighted if it is recounted in poetry that is informal and better suited to the [comic] sock. Let everything keep the proper place allotted to it.

Assisted by the etymological and semantic proximity of 'decorum' and 'dignity', Horace's personifications assimilate Comedy and Tragedy to the humble and noble characters with which they are respectively peopled (so Comedy expresses herself bluntly, in a single hexameter closed by two monosyllables, while Tragedy's manner, as if combating Horace's comically mundane handling of the 'dinner of Thyestes', is more elevated and roundabout). And while this discussion of diction accords the two genres almost equal treatment, comedy is elsewhere largely driven from the field.[12] The 'proper

---

[11] See *Poet* 1448b, on the primitive poetry of praise and blame, from which Aristotle derives tragedy and comedy (1449a). My text of *Ars* 89–92 below follows Klingner (1959).

[12] Characters such as Ixion and Io (124), subjects such as the Trojan war (129) and the vengeance of Atreus (186), conventions such as the *deus ex machina* and the moralizing chorus (191–201): these are the stuff not of comedy but of tragedy.

place' of the Pisones is in the company of the severe gods and heroes, not the jesting commoners.

As the opening scene of the *Ars* suggests, Horace is engaged in teaching his pupils how to fend off laughter—not how to elicit it. (Imagine Horace teaching the Piso boys to be comedians; imagine their father's reaction to such a course of instruction.) The comic function is absorbed into the discursive framework of the *Ars*, which stages aesthetic vices for the amusement and benefit of Horace's Pisonian audience. Within the *Ars*, accordingly, laughter is regularly the sign not of comic success but of artistic failure.[13] This does not mean, however, that humor is entirely off limits for a 'class' poet or for a gentleman. Cicero makes allowances for moderately comic interludes in the sober business of life, deeming some indulgence in 'playing and joking' (*ludo... et ioco*) permissible, after the demands of 'weighty and serious affairs' (*gravibus seriisque rebus*) have been met, so long as the style of joking is 'not extravagant or unrestrained, but gentlemanly and urbane' (*non profusum nec immodestum, sed ingenuum et facetum, Off.* 1.103). Within the *Ars* it is not comedy but the satyr play that provides the theatrical equivalent of Cicero's decorous comic relief. Like Cicero, Horace stipulates that the shift from sobriety to play (*vertere seria ludo, Ars* 226) should be accomplished, as in the earliest satyr plays, with no impairment of *gravitas* (cf. *incolumi gravitate iocum temptavit,* 222). A certain decorum is to be observed when the gods and heroes of tragedy, 'conspicuous a moment before in regal gold and purple' (*regali conspectus in auro nuper et ostro,* 228), join the company of the 'laughing' satyrs (*risores,* 225—the one instance of aesthetically sanctioned laughter in the *Ars*). Tragedy will never lose a sense of her own dignity, even when transferred to the satyric stage (231–3):

> effutire levis indigna Tragoedia versus,
> ut festis matrona moveri iussa diebus,
> intererit Satyris paulum pudibunda protervis.

---

[13] The rule is proved by one apparent exception: although Horace claims that poets must have the power to 'lead the spirit of the audience wherever they wish' (*quocumque volent animum auditoris agunto, Ars* 100)—to laughter, that is, as well as tears—he proceeds to treat laughter not as a legitimate dramatic goal but as a form of spontaneous criticism aroused by an inept tragedy (*aut dormitabo aut ridebo,* 105). On the didactic function of laughter within the *Ars*, see Kilpatrick (1990) 38, 52–3.

Above spouting trivial verses, Tragedy will be somewhat shamefaced, like a matron bidden to dance in honor of a holiday, when associating with lascivious satyrs.

It is the same individuals, in Cicero and in Horace, who condescend on occasion from (tragic) gravity to (satyric) levity. The relation between the passages is reinforced by Horace's concluding simile, which aligns tragedy with the work-day, the satyr play with the holiday—despite the fact that tragedy, like all forms of drama in antiquity, was actually performed *festis diebus*. The final simile might be rewritten, with a Ciceronian emphasis, as follows: the Roman matron, like her husband, customarily behaves with the sobriety of a character in a tragedy; it is only on special occasions that she lightens up enough to join the ritual dance—never failing, however, to preserve her dignity and her distance from the commoners and slaves who crowd the city of Rome as well as the comic stage.[14] So the Piso boys must learn to act in a manner that befits their station.

FASHIONING POETS

To the extent that the *Ars* is a Horatian *De officiis* in aesthetic dress, it is of a piece with the social and moral fashioning of the young in which Horace elsewhere represents the poet as engaged. As Horace implies when he advises the older Piso brother to 'carry away and keep in mind' his fatherly instructor's words of wisdom (*hoc tibi dictum tolle memor, Ars* 367–8), the detachable *dicta* of the *Ars* are designed to travel with Horace's youthful addressees as part of their equipment for living. They are thus akin to the *dicta* with which Horace's father fashioned his young son (*sic me formabat puerum dictis, S.* 1.4.120–1), to the memorably versified bits of moral wisdom that Horace elsewhere bestows on young friends, and to the 'well-known models' with which the model poet of Horace's letter to Augustus 'equips the rising generation' (*orientia tempora notis instruit exemplis, Ep.* 2.1.130–1). Similarly nourishing and normalizing old

---

[14] Cf. Elias (1978: 16), linking the courtier's 'good form' with the forms of classical French tragedy.

chestnuts, seeds of the *mos maiorum,* are contained in the versified prayers memorized by 'unmarried girls and chaste boys' (*castis cum pueris ignara puella mariti, E.* 2.1.132)—prayers which, in the manner of Horace's own *Carmen saeculare,* not only solicit the gods' favor for Rome but help insert the choral performers into the legal and moral order of Augustan Rome. As we have seen, the moment of shared laughter at the start of the *Ars* normalizes the Piso boys along broadly similar lines, inviting them to assume their reserved places in society.

But the *Ars* is of course something other and more than a Horatian *De officiis.* In the course of the *Ars,* Horace treats the poetic performance not only as a metaphor for but as a particular species of social performance. As David Armstrong has pointed out, the *Ars* effectively extends the Republican educational practice of 'informal tutelage', a practice designed to produce lawyers and politicians and generals, men equipped to rule their own households and the state, to the production of poets.[15] Horace argues for such an extension in his letter to Augustus, where he contrasts Rome's utterly practical past, when a man would open his house at dawn to clients seeking legal advice (*reclusa | mane domo vigilare, clienti promere iura, Ep.* 2.1.103–4) and would 'learn from his elders and teach his juniors how to increase a fortune and decrease expensive desires' (*maiores audire, minori dicere per quae | crescere res posset, minui damnosa libido,* 106–7), with her utterly frivolous present (108–10):

> mutavit mentem populus levis et calet uno
> scribendi studio; pueri patresque severi
> fronde comas vincti cenant et carmina dictant.

The fickle populace has changed its disposition and burns with enthusiasm for writing and for nothing else; sons and stern fathers dine with garlands on their heads and recite poem after poem.

Whereas in the old days experience was respected and the young heeded the wisdom of their elders, the present age fails to discriminate between the generations, and 'stern fathers' act as foolishly as their sons. Other professions, Horace complains, have their acknowledged, licensed practitioners (114–16); but just crown your head

---

[15] See Armstrong (1994: 202).

with a garland, and you can call yourself a poet, the match for any other: 'everywhere you look, schooled and unschooled alike, we're writing poems' (*scribimus indocti doctique poemata passim,* 117). In the *Ars,* Horace aims to separate sons from fathers and the unschooled from the schooled by instituting a system wherein Romans will 'learn from their elders and teach their juniors' not only how to make a tidy fortune but how to compose a proper poem.

What Horace purports to be fashioning in the *Ars* is, after all, not model citizens but model poets; his *dicta* teach not how to live but how to write.[16] Whereas Horace elsewhere insists on the moral value of measure (*modus*), in the *Ars* he writes, and at some length, about literal verse 'measures'—the hexameter, the elegiac couplet, the iamb, the spondee (73–82, 251–62). Conversely, the competing claims of candidates for political office, satirized in Horace's first Roman ode (*C.* 3.1.9–14), make way here for the competing claims of poets vying for 'election' before a kind of 'centuriate assembly' of readers (*Ars* 341–4).[17] In *Epistles* 1.2 Horace recommends Homer's exemplary Ulysses to the attention of his young friend Lollius (*quid virtus et quid sapientia possit utile proposuit nobis exemplar Ulixen, Ep.* 1.2.17–18). But in the *Ars* the instruction derived from the arch-poet is of a very different kind: 'As for the exploits and grim battles of kings and generals, Homer has shown in what meter they may be described' (*res gestae regumque ducumque et tristia bella | quo scribi possent numero, monstravit Homerus, Ars* 73–4). It is no longer Homer's characters but Homer himself who provides a pattern to imitate.

Such transformations may suit the didactic project of the *Ars,* but they also draw attention to its fundamental impropriety. Ulysses may offer Lollius a shining example of virtue and wisdom. But is the blind bard of Chios a suitable role model for the Piso boys? Shouldn't these boys be studying not how to represent *res gestae* but—following the example of the tough *puer* celebrated in Horace's second Roman ode—how to perform them? Again, it is all very well to garner every vote (cf. *omne tulit punctum, Ars* 343) from one's readers. But is this the kind of glory the Piso boys should be pursuing? Should they

---

[16] On Horace's transfer of the rules of 'right living' (*recte vivere*) to the sphere of 'correct writing' (*recte scribere*), see Becker (1963: 64–112).

[17] See Brink (1971: 356–8).

really be devoting themselves to the poetic shadow rather than the sociopolitical substance of a senatorial career? It is by no means obvious that poetry is a socially acceptable career for well-born boys such as these. A diversion, yes, a form of polish, even an intensely cultivated side-interest, but not a career. The father of the Piso boys may have been a patron of poets, but he also had a very distinguished public record, and one may presume that he expected his sons to follow in his footsteps. Thus he might have had some sympathy for the father whose hilariously philistine rebuke would one day be recollected (in verse, naturally) by his incorrigibly literary son, the poet Ovid: 'More than once my father said to me "why are you exerting yourself in a useless profession? Homer himself left no fortune"' (*saepe pater dixit 'studium quid inutile temptas?* | *Maionides nullas ipse reliquit opes',* Tr. 4.10.21–2). Ovid's wealthy equestrian father voices the materialistic perspective Horace derides within the *Ars* when he contrasts Greece's 'greed' for glory (*praeter laudem nullius avaris, Ars* 324) with Rome's focus on money management (*cura peculi,* 330), a skill that literally pays off. A loftier version of the same prejudice is expressed by Virgil's Anchises when he famously instructs Rome to leave the arts of sculpture, oratory, and speculative science to others and to concentrate instead on the practical art of empire-building (*tu regere imperio populos, Romane, memento* | *(hae tibi erunt artes), Aen.* 6.851–2). When Horace holds out the vision of a Rome as renowned in the arts of language as in the arts of war (*nec virtute foret clarisve potentius armis* | *quam lingua Latium, Ars* 289–90), he is operating on the highly polemical assumption that Rome would value or should value aesthetic mastery as well as, and perhaps even as highly as, her imperial sway.[18]

It is Rome's misvaluation of the art of poetry Horace argues, that has kept her from achieving preeminence in the field of letters. Rome's poets are 'offended' by what Horace calls 'the time-consuming labor of the file' (cf. *si non offenderet unum* | *quemque poetarum limae labor et mora, Ars* 290–1); they will not condescend to labor over their creations, like the lowly artisan who sweats to give his statues the requisite finish. The roots of this prejudice are exposed in *Satires* 2, where Horace, adopting the perspective of his detractors,

---

[18] Cf. Brink (1971: 321).

often figures art as the recourse of those who have been handicapped by fortune.[19] Those who believe that art does nothing more than supplement (and thus signal) a deficiency will shun art as inherently degrading. Instructed by Horace, the Pisones will know better. The poem in a state of nature cries out for cultivation (291–4):

> vos, o
> Pompilius sanguis, carmen reprehendite quod non
> multa dies et multa litura coercuit atque
> praesectum decies non castigavit ad unguem.

Sons of Numa's blood, censure the poem that many a day's blotting has not pruned and polished and corrected ten times over down to the last detail.[20]

Aesthetic labor is not occasionally but always called upon to smooth the rough surface of the newly created poem. The poem that has not been thus corrected by its maker deserves to stand corrected by its readers. In this context, Horace's comically inflated apostrophe to the 'sons of Numa's blood' serves as a friendly warning. No matter how purple their blood, in the field of poetry the Pisones must bow to the claims of lowly *ars*.[21]

This message is amplified by Horace's satiric sketch of the contemporary crush of 'mad poets', would-be geniuses who decline to use the file not only on their poems but on themselves (*Ars* 295–301):

> ingenium misera quia fortunatius arte
> credit et excludit sanos Helicone poetas
> Democritus, bona pars non unguis ponere curat,
> non barbam, secreta petit loca, balnea vitat.
> nanciscetur enim pretium nomenque poetae,
> si tribus Anticyris caput insanabile numquam
> tonsori Licino commiserit.

Because Democritus believes that inborn talent is more of a blessing than miserable art and refuses to admit sane poets to Helicon, a good number of men don't trouble to trim their nails or their beard, they hunt out remote lairs and avoid the baths. For a man will win the name and reputation of a poet, if he never entrusts his head to Licinus the barber—a head that three townfuls of hellebore will never restore to sanity.

---

[19] See Oliensis (1998a: 51–60).
[20] This translation follows D'Angour (1999).
[21] So Armstrong (1994: 209).

Such a poet equates the flamboyant absence of art with the indisputable presence of genius and the condition of his body with the
condition of his poetry; he cultivates a shaggy exterior, one
uncoerced and uncastigated by the refinements of razor, file, or
bath, in the hope of validating his claim to the glory that belongs
to the poet of *ingenium*. But the redundancy of the parallel phrases
'three townfuls of hellebore' and 'Licinus the barber' (*tribus
Anticyris... tonsori Licino,* phrases linked by alliteration and conson-
ance, and similarly placed within their respective lines) suggests that
what ails his 'incurable head' is, after all, nothing that a visit to the
barber couldn't cure. By severing the conventional semiotic link
between scruffiness and brilliance, the absence of surface polish and
the presence of deep genius, Horace exposes the long-nailed ranter as
a creature meriting not awe but ridicule. The poem that has not been
perfected *ad unguem* ('to the nail') will earn its creator the same
treatment.

It is altogether to be expected that the author of the *Ars poetica*
should champion the art of poetry. What could not perhaps have
been predicted is the extent to which Horace's arguments are saturated with the discourse of class distinctions. According to the view
that Horace is ridiculing, *ingenium* is *fortunatius*—not simply
'attended by good fortune' but 'of higher status' or perhaps 'wealth-
ier'—than 'poor, base art' (*misera arte, Ars* 295).[22] Elsewhere Horace
may pretend to concede the nigh-equivalence of 'census-rating and
inborn talent' (*censum ingeniumque, S.* 2.1.75) and to acknowledge
that he ranks below the great Lucilius in both respects—as if the
one inferiority automatically entailed the other. But within the *Ars*
he labors with some consistency to break the connection between
these two terms. One of his most effective weapons is a tactfully
collusive irony, as when he rallies to the defense of the gentleman who
'doesn't know how to compose verses' but 'ventures to do so all the
same' (*qui nescit versus tamen audet fingere, Ars* 382). And why
should he not? 'He's a free man—a freeborn gentleman—and, be it
noted, with the census-rating of a knight—and clear of all vice' (*liber
et ingenuus, praesertim census equestrem* | *summam nummorum,*

---

[22] While *fortunatius* may evoke *Tyche* (so Brink [1971: 330]), the main resonance
here is social.

vitioque remotus ab omni, 383–4). The man who is *ingenuus,* endowed by birth with the standing of a gentleman, assumes that he is therefore also *ingeniosus,* endowed by birth with the talents of a poet; and if he is himself 'clear of all vice' to which the censors might object, surely his poems are 'correct' enough to pass, without further ado, the censorious critic. If the Pisones harbor the belief that their social qualifications automatically qualify them to write poetry, Horace politely sets them straight by assuming that they will join him in mocking the absurdity of such a belief.[23]

Within the *Ars,* poetic and social status tend to be not merely divided but opposed. Not only is it not the case that the well-born and well-to-do are automatically guaranteed the status of poets in good standing; it sometimes seems as if the traditional criteria of status at Rome were substantial barriers to the achievement of poetic distinction. The rich poet, so Horace asserts, will have trouble finding an honest critic to comment on his work before he releases it to the world (*Ars* 419–21). Indeed, the richer he is, the more trouble he is likely to have telling a true from a false friend (422–5). Horace develops the point in an admonitory skit, set at the dinner table, with the poet in the role of a patron attended by a well-fed and wildly appreciative parasite (426–30)—the only audience, Horace implies, with which this poet's work is likely to make a hit. Only the poet who submits his work to a disinterested professional critic (to Horace, for example) can hope to produce authentic poetry. Horace further demotes the rich amateur by likening him to an auctioneer (419–21):

> ut praeco, ad merces turbam qui cogit emendas
> adsentatores iubet ad lucrum ire poeta
> dives agris, dives positis in faenore nummis.

Like an auctioneer who ropes in a crowd to buy his merchandise, a poet who is rich in land, rich in money loaned out at interest, invites yes-men to come and collect their cash reward.

As Niall Rudd comments, the point of comparison here is that both men tempt their respective audiences with the promise of a bargain— wares at good prices in one case, a dinner purchased with a few

---

[23] Similarly Armstrong (1994: 213).

compliments in the other.[24] And yet the points of difference are still more striking. It is an impoverished professional, not a wealthy dilettante, who might naturally be imagined as thus hawking his poetic merchandise. The fluent auctioneer has less in common with the gullible host than with his flattering parasites—men who know how to turn words into substantial profit.[25] The role-reversal that is written into the simile suggests that the rich amateur is not only handicapped in his poetic endeavors but potentially degraded by them.

A central claim of the *Ars poetica* is that it is not the wealthy amateur but the master author who truly merits, regardless of his census-rating, the title of patron and benefactor. His gifts are linguistic; he is a word-coiner who confers a wealth of language on the entire community of Latin speakers, 'enrich[ing] his inherited stock of speech' (*sermonem patrium ditaverit, Ars* 57). This benefaction is also celebrated in Horace's second letter to Florus, where Horace describes how the model poet 'will pour out his wealth and bless Latium with the riches of his tongue' (*fundet opes Latiumque beabit diuite lingua, Ep.* 2.2.121). Such a poet performs the linguistic equivalent of an exalted civic service. In the letter to Florus, he is likened to an 'honorable censor' (*censoris... honesti,* 110) who expels words that do not deserve their place of distinction (111–14), restores fine old words that have fallen on hard times (115–18), and adopts new words as needed (119). In the *Ars,* his linguistic creations are linked with the achievements of Roman technology: the creation of a harbor, the transformation of marsh into arable land, the rechaneling or agricultural 'education' of a river (*Ars* 63–8). The context is elegiac—what Horace insists on here is not the permanence but the perishability of everything man-made—but the implicit equation redounds nonetheless to the poet's credit.[26]

---

[24] See Rudd (1989: 219).

[25] On the figure of the *praeco,* see Oliensis (1998a: 164).

[26] Recalling that Augustus undertook massive public works along these lines, exercised censorial powers to purge the senate of what Suetonius terms the 'unseemly and uncivilized mob' (*deformi et inconditia turba, Aug.* 35) that had infiltrated its ranks, lavished gifts on individuals, and contributed enormous sums directly to the treasury, we may surmise that Horace's poet-benefactor is ultimately modeled on the emperor himself. See Dio 52.42; Aug. *RG* 8.2, 15–18; Rudd (1989: 161); Millar (1977:

It is not only society at large but the poet who stands to benefit from his linguistic gifts. As he makes his fortune, the poet also makes himself. The metaphorical identification of 'new words' with 'new men' that is forged in the epistle to Florus, where the censor-poet is described as 'admit[ting] new words' (*adsciscet noua, Ep.* 2.2.119) to his linguistic Senate, also underlies Horace's discussion of neologisms in the *Ars*. If your subject matter should require it, Horace remarks, you will be granted the license to coin new words, so long as you exercise that license with discretion and derive your words from a Greek source. But as the indignant question that follows suggests, this license is not universally conceded (*Ars* 53–9):

> quid autem
> Caecilio Plautoque dabit Romanus ademptum
> Vergilio Varioque? ego cur, acquirere pauca
> si possum, invideor, cum lingua Catonis et Enni
> sermonem patrium ditaverit et nova rerum
> nomina protulerit? licuit semperque licebit
> signatum praesente nota producere nomen.

But why will Romans grant to Caecilius and Plautus what they deny to Virgil and Varius? Why, if I am capable of adding a little to the stock of words, am I evilly eyed, when the tongue of Cato and Ennius enriched our native language and brought forth new names for things? It has been and always will be our right to produce words stamped with the mark of the present.

The topic of the neologism opens up the quarrel between the ancients and the moderns, and the image of the new word as a new coin figures this quarrel in social terms as a conflict between established families and arrivistes, old money and new money.[27] Long-dead poets constitute a kind of hereditary nobility of poetry, this nobility being 'inherited', as it were, not from the past but from the future—from the canonizing passage of time, which has given their names

189–93). The absence of such imperial figurations of the poet's role in Horace's epistle to Augustus may indicate Horace's sense that even a metaphorical claim of parity could be taken as an affront to the emperor's dignity.

[27] The conservative sentiment is well expressed in a seventeenth-century French work (Francois de Callières, *Du bon et du mauvais usage*, Paris, 1694), quoted by Elias (1978: 110), which deplores a 'bad turn of phrase, which began among the lowest people and made its fortune at the court, like those favorites without merit who got themselves elevated there in the old days'.

and their neologisms the patina of accepted currency. Contemporary poets, by contrast, have no stock of years to authenticate their claims to poetic authority. They are 'new men' on the poetic scene, and as such they and their innovative words encounter the same social prejudice as political newcomers struggling to make their names. As the prominence of proper names in Horace's discussion of the neologism suggests, the poet's name (*nomen*) depends on the poet's words (*nomina*)—the poet makes his name in part by exercising his right to coin words. As Horace stresses in the simile that follows, moreover, the invention of new words is not only a matter of the new poet's self-promotion but part of a natural cycle. Old words die, and new words arise to take their place (*Ars* 60–2):

> ut silvae foliis pronos mutantur in annos,
> prima cadunt, ita verborum vetus intent aetas,
> et iuvenum nitu florent modo nata vigentque.

As the forests change their leaves from swift year to year, the first of them fall, so the old age of words passes away, and those just born flourish like the young and are strong.

In one respect, the simile seems to be at cross-purposes with Horace's theme. Whereas the preceding lines champion such distinctive and distinguished proper names as Caecilius, Plautus, Virgil, and Varius, the famous Homeric simile that Horace is reworking here ('As the generations of leaves, so the generations of men', etc., *Il.* 6.145–9) eradicates all such distinctions, arguing that names mean nothing since all men are equally doomed to oblivion. The Homeric allusion signals Horace's acknowledgment of the leveling force of death, an acknowledgment fully articulated in the ensuing passage, which opens in the leveling first-person plural (*debemur morti nos nostra-que, Ars* 63) and closes by drawing out the implications for poets of the general mortal law: 'things made by mortals will pass away; still less will the honor and influence of speech continue to flourish' (*mortalia facta peribunt,* | *nedum sermonum stet honos et gratia vivax, Ars* 68–9). Horace's deference inheres in the recognition that it is not only speech but Horatian *sermo*, including the *Ars*, that is destined to fade.

Still, deference tempers but does not muffle the self-authorizing ring of Horace's newly reminted Homeric coin. Unlike Homer's,

Horace's simile is in effect not elegiac but assertive, moving from death to life and from age (*vetus... aetas, Ars* 61) to youth (*iuvenum,* 62). Moreover, the simile does not, as we might have expected, signal the senior poet's recognition that a fresh generation, represented by 'youthful' aspirants such as the Piso boys (*iuvenes,* 24), is arising to take his place. It is Horace himself, the senior but also the modern poet, who is aligned here with the young upstarting word. Indeed, if the Pisones appear anywhere in this simile, it is on the other side. Although Horace's simile may seem to flatter his strong young addressees, it effectively pits the newly arisen poet against his establishment audience. Thus it may have been the social reverberations of the Homeric simile that appealed to Horace at this particular juncture in his *Ars.* 'Why do you ask me about my lineage, magnanimous son of Tydeus?' asks Homer's Glaucus, meaning that identifying marks such as the patronymic are irrelevant, however glorious and distinguished one's lineage may be, since every generation is destined to fall and to be replaced. That Horace invokes this famous image of the fragility of names just after insisting on the primacy of the poet's name suggests the diminished value of genealogy as a measure of a name's currency. A name as old and distinguished as that sported by Numa's purported descendants may be supplanted, in the 'natural' course of things, by a new name such as Horace's own.

THE IMMORTAL LEECH

If the aesthetic and social lessons of the opening of Horace's *Ars* are readily absorbed, Horace's last lesson, incorporated in the figure of the 'mad poet', is more difficult to apprehend. Although the oppositions that structure the opening recur, the stakes have been raised, and the pressure increased. Whereas the opening scene contained deviance within the person of the inept painter, it is Horace himself, no other artist intervening, who authors the grotesque composite figure—joining the metaphor of a leech to the simile of a bear—that deforms his poem's end. And whereas the monstrous painting is framed on one side by the 'human head', on the other by Horace's sensible *amici,* nothing supervenes to contain or control the final image of the poem. Horace's *Ars* as a whole thus repeats the trajectory of the monstrous painting, moving from top to bottom, from head to tail-end, from human to animal, from *humano* to *hirudo,* its mocking echo. We are left to make of this monstrous design what we can, without the assistance of the author, who drops off just when we may feel we need him most.

Here is the passage *(Ars* 453–76):

> ut mala quem scabies aut morbus regius urget
> aut fanaticus error et iracunda Diana,
> vesanum tetigisse timent fugiuntque poetam
> qui sapiunt; agitant pueri incautique sequuntur.
> hic, dum sublimis versus ructatur et errat,
> si veluti merulis intentus decidit auceps
> in puteum foveamve, licet 'succurrite' longum
> clamet 'io cives!' non sit qui tollere curet.
> si curet quis opem ferre et demittere funem,
> 'qui scis an prudens huc se deiecerit atque
> servari nolit?' dicam, Siculique poetae
> narrabo interitum. deus immortalis haberi
> dum cupit Empedocles, ardentem frigidus Aetnam
> insiluit. sit ius liceatque perire poetis.
> invitum qui servat idem facit occidenti.
> nec semel hoc fecit, nec si retractus erit iam
> fiet homo et ponet famosae mortis amorem.
> nec satis apparet cur versus factitet, utrum
> minxerit in patrios cineres, an triste bidental
> moverit incestus: certe furit, ac velut ursus,
> obiectos caveae valuit si frangere clathros,
> indoctum doctumque fugat recitator acerbus;
> quem vero arripuit, tenet occiditque legendo,
> non missura cutem nisi plena cruoris hirudo.

As with a man afflicted by a repulsive rash or jaundice or frantic wandering inflicted by angry Diana, men of sense are afraid to touch a mad poet and flee him; reckless children follow after and harass him. Suppose, as he weaves along with his head in the clouds, belching his poems, he falls down into a pit or a well, like a bird-catcher intent on blackbirds; though he yell loud and long 'Ho, fellow-citizens, help, help!' no one will bother to pull him out. If someone should bother to come to his aid and let down a rope, 'How do you know he didn't throw himself down there on purpose and doesn't want to be saved?' I'll say; and I'll recount the death of the Sicilian poet. Longing to be thought an immortal god, frigid Empedocles jumped into the flames of Etna. Grant poets the right and the license to die. If you save a man against his will, you've as good as killed him. This isn't the first time he's done this; if you pull him out, don't expect him to join the human race and give up his yearning for a celebrity death. It's not quite clear why he keeps turning out poems. Did he piss on his father's grave, or disturb the sanctity of a somber shrine? At any rate, he's mad and, like a bear strong enough to break the confining bars of his cage, he puts everyone to flight, schooled and un-schooled alike, this merciless reciter; but if he catches a man, he holds him tight and reads him to death, a leech that won't let go until it's full of blood.

The family resemblance between this portrait and the painting that heads the *Ars* is unmistakable. *Nec...fiet homo:* like the human-headed monster, fledged but not airborne, the mad poet aspires to rise above the human condition and ends up far below it. Although his head is in the clouds, his belched-out poetry is a product of the belly; although he hopes to be counted among the gods, he is counted, by sensible men at least (*qui sapiunt, Ars* 456), among the beasts. In Ciceronian terms, he is devoid of the distinctively human faculty of *ratio*, hence incapable of self-restraint; his all-too-visible animal appetite is held in check only by the external imposition of a cage. His accelerating devolution reaches its nadir in the last word of the poem, *hirudo:* a blood-sucking leech, a tail that is all mouth, pure appetite. As the description of the painting moves from head to tail and from centaur to mermaid, so the bear (*ursus*, masculine) ends up a leech (*hirudo*, feminine), a cousin of the mermaid's black fishtail and a graphic or pornographic image of the female sex. Following the lead of Shakespeare's King Lear, who identifies women's nether parts with 'the sulphurous pit', we can recognize this voracious leech as a trans-formation of the devouring Etna into which Empedocles leaped.[28]

While the mad poet brings to life the monstrous painting, he also recalls the aspiring genius who shuns the barber and the baths in the hope of gaining entrance to Helicon (*Ars* 295–301). The poet at the

---

[28] *King Lear* IV vi. 124–9 (as if conflating the opening and close of the *Ars*): 'Down from the waist they are Centaurs, | Though women all above; | But to the girdle do the gods inherit, | Beneath is all the fiend's. | There's hell, there's darkness, there is the sulphurous pit; | Burning, scalding, stench, consumption.'

end of the *Ars* outdoes this ill-groomed confrere not just by letting his hair grow but by transforming himself (with the help of Horace's simile) into a shaggy bear, the very model of poetic unkemptness. But he resembles him in that he is, for all his feigned unsociability, a creature of society to his very core. His erratic behavior is artfully calculated for its effect on an audience to which he only pretends to be indifferent. Horace's Empedocles knew just what he was up to when he took his famous leap: he wanted men to believe he was a god (*deus immortalis haberi*, 464). So too, when the purportedly absent-minded poet 'falls' into a well, the accident may be calculated (cf. *prudens*, 462) to advertise his credentials: 'Inspired bard available, suitable all occasions, permanent position preferred.' The final image of the *Ars* thus encapsulates one of the central arguments of the poem—that beneath his rough exterior, a shaggy bear may be a slick operator, a leech that is as smooth as smooth can be.[29]

The conjunction of bear and leech, bristling *ingenium* and slippery *ars*, describes perfectly a type familiar to us from Horace's satires. Consider, for example, Horace's description of the singer Tigellius in *Satires* 1.3. Deaf to the requests of his patron, the young Caesar, Tigellius would launch into song only when the fancy struck him (*si collibuisset*, S. 1.3.6), but then he was irrepressible: 'he'd sing out with his "Hail, hail Bacchus!" from the first course to the last—now in falsetto, and now in the deepest tone the lyre sounds' (*ab ovo | usque ad mala citaret 'io Bacche!' modo summa | voce, modo hac resonat quae chordis quattuor ima*, 6–8). Tigellius presumably believes that he proves his *ingenium* by thus flouting the norms of moderation. A true poet, he might argue, cannot sing to order but must await the stirrings of his god (whom Tigellius here summons with the ritual cry of the devotee); and once possessed or 'enthused', he is at the god's mercy—not his patron's. This does not mean, of course, that he scorns the fine food and wine his talents have earned.

Another less genial relative of the bear-leech is the unnamed hanger-on of *Satires* 1.9, a man who likewise prides himself on the

---

[29] Brink (1971: 431) notes that the metaphor of the leech is 'established in Roman comedy for financial blood-sucking' and 'is probably proverbial' but is careful to dissociate Horace's 'poetic *hirudo*' from this unsavory company.

copious fluency of his versification (*nam quis me scribere pluris | aut citius possit versus? S.* 1.9.23–4). Attaching himself to Horace (*usque tenebo,* 15) in the hope of winning access to Maecenas, he offers Horace a practical demonstration of his verbal stamina (*cum quidlibet ille | garriret,* 12–13). When Horace breaks in to ask if he has any surviving relatives, his companion replies that he has none: 'I've laid them all to rest' *omnis composui* (28)—a phrase that could also mean 'I've versified them all.' 'Finish me off,' Horace moans to himself, *confice* (29)—meaning at once 'kill me' and 'write me'. This was, he recollects, the doom foretold by a Sabellian fortune-teller when he was a boy: 'a chatterer will some day consume him; if he has sense, let him shun talkative men when he reaches maturity' (*garrulus hunc quando consumet cumque: loquaces, | si sapiat, vitet, simul atque adoleverit aetas,* 33–4). As if anticipating the end of the *Ars,* Horace here represents an endless flow of speech 'exhausting' or 'eating up', leech-wise, the very substance of the addressee.

But there is another candidate for the role of the murderously exuberant versifier within the *Ars* itself. In the most literal and immediate sense it is Horace—Horace, who clings and clings to his readers for all of 476 lines (more lines by far than any other poem in the Horatian corpus) before dropping off into silence—who is the leech of the *Ars poetica.* The final image, a quintessentially Horatian self-depreciation, holds the place of an ironic closural apology: 'but I've kept you too long, I'm really a terrible pest, you must be utterly drained.'[30] The blood-filled leech is thus a grotesque variation on the familiar closural figure of 'satiety'. At the end of his first satire, for example, Horace underscores the self-reflexive closural potential of this figure by comparing life to a meal and correlating the sated dinner-guest (*satur, S.* 1.1.119) with the fulfilled or completed poem (*satis,* 120).[31] The same set of associations underpins the magnificent close of *Epistles* 2.2 (214–16):

---

[30] The end of the *Ars* thus resembles what Fiske (1920: 89) characterizes as the 'abrupt and witty endings sometimes coupled with ironical mockery of the satirist himself', of Horace's satires. On the affinities between the *Ars* and *S.* 2, see Frischer (1991: 87–100).

[31] See Freudenburg (1993: 192–3).

lusisti satis, edisti satis atque bibisti:
tempus abire tibi est, ne potum largius aequo
rideat et pulset lasciva decentius aetas.

You've played your fill, you've eaten and drunk your fill; it's time for you to leave—or else, when you've drunk more than you should, the younger generation, in whom wildness is more becoming, will laugh at you and kick you out.

The epistle inevitably illustrates its own lesson, rehearsing the Apollonian injunction 'nothing too much' by curbing its own excessive tendencies (to extend the poem beyond this point would be to invite the ridicule and abuse with which the aging drunkard is threatened). In these poems the poet makes his quest for a proper, measured conclusion emblematic of the broader ethical problem of living within one's mortal limits. But this larger context is sheared away at the finale of the *Ars poetica*. The author and his audience are here not fellow banqueters who share an ethics and aesthetics of satiety; the audience is itself the feast, its blood supplies the poet's liquor.[32] In this perfectly self-reflexive figure, closure coincides with the separation not of poet and poem (a fiction that leaves space for moral reflection) but of sated poet and exhausted audience. If Horace earlier specifies this audience as 'Numa's blood' (*Pompilius sanguis*, *Ars* 292), one reason for the specification may be that the leech is by nature partial to blue blood. The founding *iunctura* of the *Ars poetica* is perhaps this juncture of lowly Horatian leech and illustrious Pisonian host.[33]

Horace, who repeatedly boasts of his rise from humble origins to a high destiny and of the success with which he attached himself to the most important men of his day,[34] is after all a shining example of the social value of consummate artistry. But it would be falling into

---

[32] The *plena cruoris hirudo* complements the *conviva satur* of *S.* 1.1, completing the Lucretian doublet *satur ac plenus* (3.960); earlier in the same passage Lucretius favors *plenus* (*cur non ut plenus vitae conviva recedis?* 3.938).

[33] The semantics of *iunctura/iungere* encompass social as well as verbal conjunctions; cf. *S.* 1.3.54 (*haec res et iungit iunctos et servat amicos*); *Ep.*1.5.25–6 (*ut coeat par | iungaturque pari*).

[34] Most notably in the capsule autobiographies of *S.* 1.6, *C.* 2.20, and *Ep.* 1.20. The boast is telling whether or not Horace's depiction of his 'humble origins' is accurate; on Horace's status see Armstrong (1986); Williams (1995).

the trap set by Horace's irony simply to identify him with his leech. If the poets Horace derides are leeches in bear's clothing, Horace is a powerful bear concealed within a leech's smooth skin. The bold claims of *Epistles* 1.19, where Horace presents himself as a legislator and model (on a par with Homer and Ennius) for the 'servile herd' of his imitators, are put into practice in the final passage of the *Ars*, which demonstrates conclusively that while the 'mad poet' may appropriate the trappings of *ingenium*, Horace has the real thing.[35] And insofar as Horace addresses his *Ars* not to the freedmen or impoverished gentlemen who might be eager to imitate his social and literary success, but to a prominent Roman family, his *Ars poetica* is less an instruction manual than a warning or a boast. The civil war not only disordered the *ordines* of Roman society; it also changed the very rules of the social game. From here on in, the conventional forms of distinction, centered on military and political achievement, will always be shadowed if not obscured by the dominant figure of the *princeps*. In the future, the poet's status may be worth more than the senator's. If Horace dissimulates his power, masquerading as a mere sane critic, a leech, or as Bernard Frischer suggests a lowly *grammaticus*,[36] the disguise may be designed to deflect the invidious accusations of hubris that this message might be expected to attract.

It is not surprising, then, that Horace's *Ars poetica* offers no recipe for either social or literary distinction. Although Horace teaches what can be taught, although he supplies some of the rules, some of the fundamentals, with which a practicing poet must in fact be equipped, it is, in the end, the art that cannot be taught that holds the key to Helicon. It is the very audacity with which Horace breaks his own rules, defies his own prescriptions, for example with the unimaginable figure of the bear-leech with which his poem does not so much finish as break off or break out, that distinguishes Horace from all would-be imitators. In fact the bear-leech is an excellent example of that 'metaphysical wit' famously disparaged by Samuel Johnson as 'a kind of *discordia concors*, a combination of dissimilar images', in which 'the most heterogeneous ideas are yoked by violence together'.

---

[35] Cf. Brink (1971: 516): the final passage 'fascinates because it is written from inside the experience which it professes to ridicule'.
[36] See Frischer (1991).

With this yoking, Horace constructs a metaphor which at once demonstrates and represents his own *ingenium.* It is well known that Horace does not discuss metaphor within the *Ars poetica.* One reason is that metaphor by its very nature falls outside the scope of his didactic poem—we have it on good authority (that of Aristotle, followed by Cicero) that metaphor, being 'a sign of innate talent', 'cannot be learned from another' *(Poet.* 1459a).[37] Another reason may be that metaphor is inherently inimical to Horace's decorous scheme, which requires that everything remain in its proper, literal place *(singula quaeque tocum teneant sortita decentem, Ars* 92). The social implications of metaphorical dislocation are drawn out in Cicero's *De oratore,* where 'proper' words, words which are 'born almost at the same moment' as the things they name, are contrasted with words 'used metaphorically and stationed where they are not at home, so to speak' *(quae transferuntur et quasi in alieno loco collocantur, De or.* 3.149). These latecomers should not be too bold or brash. Indeed, a metaphor should be polite, even bashful, 'so as to seem to have been escorted into a place that does not belong to it, not to have broken in, and to have entered by permission, not by force' *(ut deducta esse in alienum locum, non irruisse atque ut precario, non vi venisse videatur,* 3.165).

Within the *Ars,* the gap left by metaphor is partly filled by the inherently more decorous figure of *iunctura,* the art of verbal arrangement.[38] *Iunctura,* which Horace discusses in tandem with the neologism, is another way of achieving novelty. It is a means at once of making a familiar word strange and of setting oneself apart from the crowd: 'your diction will be distinguished if a clever conjunction makes a known word new' *(dixeris egregie notum si callida verbum | reddiderit iunctura novum, Ars* 47–8). Horace returns to the topic when pronouncing on the diction appropriate to the satyr play (240–3):

---

[37] Similarly Arist. *Rh.* 1405a; Cic. *De or.* 3.160 (one reason why we delight in metaphor is that it is *ingenii specimen...quoddam*). On the unteachability *of ingenium,* cf. Brink (1963: 258).

[38] For *iunctura* as 'the "refreshment," which may or may not be metaphorical, of ordinary words in a pointed context', see Brink (1971: 139).

> ex noto fictum carmen sequar, ut sibi quivis
> speret idem, sudet multum frustraque laboret
> ausus idem: tantum series iuncturaque pollet,
> tantum de medio sumptis accedit honoris.

The poem I'll aim for will be fashioned out of familiar materials, such that
any poet might hope to do as well, but will only sweat and sweat and struggle
in vain when he attempts the same feat: such is the power of connection and
yoking, so great the distinction accorded that which is drawn from the
common stock.

It is surely not an accident that this boast occurs within Horace's
discussion of the satyr play, that middling genre which has clear
affinities, in style and pitch if not in substance, with Horace's satires.[39] In the fashioning of a poem as of a gentleman, it is easy enough
to make a silk purse out of silk, harder to achieve the same result with
a sow's ear. What distinguishes the poet is the art by which he
transforms the familiar and commonplace (*notum, medium*) into
something novel and distinguished. Nor does Horace explain how
such effects—effects that others will discover that no amount of labor
can reproduce—are to be achieved. The art of 'connection and
yoking' here inherits the mysterious, unteachable, and inimitable
power and distinction typically associated with *ingenium* and its
chief exponent, metaphor.

The indecorous combination of leech and bear at the end of the
Ars both demonstrates and represents the power—the aggressive
meekness, the deferential authority—that forever takes us by surprise. The poet who begins the *Ars* by penning the monster in ends by
letting it out of its cage. The anti-closural impulse extends to the
closural figure of 'satiety', which here expresses not philosophical
resignation (the diner's readiness to depart the banquet of life) but a
violently antic resistance to the force of time. The finale of the *Ars* is
littered with grave sites—the 'well or pit' (*Ars* 459), the 'flames of
Etna' (465), the 'father's ashes' (471). But in the end it is not the poet
who plunges to his death. It is rather the reader who succumbs to the
embrace of the bear, the kiss of the leech. The shocking final image
suggests that the leech, like the poet who elsewhere claims that he will

---

[39] So Perret (1964: 165–6); Innes (1989: 264).

'grow forever fresh in the praise of future generations' (*usque ego postera | crescam laude recens, C.* 3.30.7–8), may indeed win a kind of immortality from the blood of its readers. Horace ends not by laughing with his friends but by making a face at them—and by making his face at their expense.

References

Journal abbreviations follow those in *L'Année Philologique*.

ABEL, K. H. (1969). 'Horaz auf der Sache nach dem wahren Selbst', *A&A* 15: 29–46.

ACOSTA-HUGHES, B. (2002). *Polyeideia: The Iambi of Callimachus and the Archaic Iambi Tradition*. Berkeley: University of California Press.

ADAMS, J. H. (1982). *The Latin Sexual Vocabulary*. Baltimore: Johns Hopkins University Press.

ADDISON, J. (1705). *Remarks on Several Parts of Italy in the Years 1701, 1702, 1703*. London: J. and R. Tonson.

AHL, F. M. (1976). *Lucan: An Introduction*. Ithaca: Cornell University Press.

—— (1984). 'The art of safe criticism in Greece and Rome', *AJP* 105: 174–208.

—— (1985). *Metaformations: Soundplay and Wordplay in Ovid and Other Classical Poets*. Ithaca: Cornell University Press.

—— (1988). 'Ars est caelare artem (art in puns and anagrams engraved)', in J. Culler (ed.), *On Puns: The Foundation of Letters*. Oxford: Basil Blackwell.

ALFONSI, L. (1962). 'Orazio, Epist. I, 1, 14', *Latomus* 21: 616–17.

ALGAROTTI, F. (1990). *Saggio sopra Orazio*. Venosa: Editore Osanna.

ALLEN, W., JR. (1970). 'The addressees in Horace's first Book of Epistles', *Studies in Philology* 67: 255–66.

ANDERSON, W. S. (1955–56). 'Poetic fiction—Horace *Serm.* 1.5', *CW* 49: 57–9.

—— (1963a). 'The Roman Socrates: Horace and his Satires', in J. P. Sullivan (ed.), *Critical Essays on Roman Literature, Vol. II: Satire*. London: Routledge & Kegan Paul, 1–37 (= Anderson (1982) 13–49).

—— (1963b). 'Pompey, his friends and the literature of the first century BC', *University of California Publication of Classical Philology* 19: 1–87.

—— (1972). 'The form, purpose and position of Horace's *Satires* I, 8', *AJPh* 93: 6–13.

—— (1974). 'Autobiography and art in Horace', in G. K. Galinsky (ed.), *Perspectives of Roman Poetry*. Austin: University of Texas Press, 33–56.

—— (1982). *Essays on Roman Satire*. Princeton: Princeton University Press.

—— (1984). 'Ironic preambles and satiric self-definition in Horace *Satire* 2.1', *Pacific Coast Philology* 19: 35–42.

ANDRÉ, J.-M. (1967). *Mécène: Essai de biographie spirituelle*. Paris: Les Belles Lettres.

ARDIZZONI, A. (1963). 'Considerazioni sulla struttura del libro die Giambi di Callimacho', in *Miscellanea di Studi Alessandrini in memoria di Augusto Rostagni*. Turin: Bottega d'Erasmo.

ARMSTRONG, D. (1964). 'Horace's *Satires* I, 1–3: a structural study', *Arion* 3: 86–96.

—— (1986). 'Horatius eques et scriba: *Satires* 1.6 and 2.7', *TAPhA* 116: 255–88.

—— (1989) *Horace*. New Haven: Yale University Press.

—— (1993) 'The addressees of the Ars poetica: Herculaneum, the Pisones and Epicurean Protreptic', *MD* 31: 185–230.

—— (2004). 'Horace's *Epistles* 1 and Philodemus', in David Armstrong, Jeffrey Fish, Patricia A. Johnston, and Marilyn B. Skinner (eds.), *Virgil, Philodemus, and the Augustans*. Austin: University of Texas Press, 267–95.

ASTBURY, R. (1985). *Terentius Varro: Saturarum Menippearum Fragmenta*. Leipzig: Teubner.

ASTIN, A. E. (1967). *Scipio Aemilianus*. Oxford: Oxford University Press.

AUSTIN, R. G. (1964). *P. Vergili Maronis Aeneidos liber secundus*. Oxford: Oxford University Press.

AXELSON, B. (1945). *Unpoetische Wörter*. Lund: Gleer University Press.

BADIAN, E. (1989). 'The *Scribae* of the Roman Republic', *Klio* 71: 582–603.

BAKHTIN, M. (1986). 'Introduction to extracts from "The problem of speech genres" ', in G. S. Morson (ed.), *Bakhtin: Essays and Dialogues on his Work*. Chicago: University of Chicago Press.

BALSDON, J. P. V. D. (1969). *Life and Leisure in Ancient Rome*. London: Bodley Head.

BARBIERI, A. (1976). 'A proposito della satira II, 6 di Orazio', *RAL* 31: 481–507.

BARCHIESI, A. (1993). 'Insegnare ad Augusto: Orazio, Epistole 2, 1 e Ovidio, Tristia II', *MD* 31: 149–84 (= (2001), in M. Fox and S. Marchesi (trans.), *Speaking Volumes: Narrative and Intertext in Ovid and Other Latin Poets*. London: Duckworth).

—— (1994). *Il poeta e il principe. Ovidio e il discorso augusteo*. Rome: Laterza.

—— (1996). 'Poetry, praise and patronage: Simonides in Book 4 of Horace's *Odes*', *CA* 15: 5–47.

—— (2001). 'Horace and Iambos: the poet as literary historian', in A. Cavarzere, A. Aloni, and A. Barchiesi (eds.), *Iambic Ideas: Essays on a Poetic Tradition from Archaic Greece to the Late Roman Empire*. Lanham, Md.: Rowman and Littlefield.

BARCHIESI, A. (2002). 'The uniqueness of the Carmen Saeculare and its tradition', in T. Woodman and D. West (eds.), *Poetry and Politics in the Age of Augustus*. Cambridge: Cambridge University Press, 107–23.

—— and CUCCHIARELLI, A. (2005). 'Satire and the poet: the body as self-referential symbol', in Kirk Freudenburg (ed.), *The Cambridge Companion to Roman Satire*, Cambridge: Cambridge University Press, 207–23.

BARCHIESI, M. (1962). *Nevio epico*. Padua: Cedam.

BARDON, H. (1956). *La littérature Latine inconnue. Tome II. L'époque impériale*. Paris: Klincksieck.

BARKER, D. (1996). 'The Golden Age is proclaimed? The *Carmen Saeculare* and the renascence of the Golden Race', *CQ* 46: 434–44.

BARNES, W. R. (1988). 'Horace *Sermones* 1.5.104', *Prudentia* 20.1, 57–9.

BARTHES, R. (1981). *Le grain de la voix: entretiens 1962–80*. Paris: Seuil.

BARTSCH, S. (1994). *Actors in the Audience: Theatricality and Doublespeak from Nero to Hadrian*. Cambridge, Mass.: Harvard University Press.

BAUMAN, R. A. (1985). *Lawyers in Transitional Politics*. Munich.

BEARE, W. (1964). *The Roman Stage*. 3rd edn. London: Methuen.

BEATLES, THE (1965). *Rubber soul*. Hayes.

BECK, H. K. (1919). *Das Verhältnis des Horaz zum Epikureismus*. Diss. Rostock.

BECKER, C. (1963). *Das Spätwerk des Horaz*. Göttingen: Vandenhoeck & Ruprecht.

BECKMANN, F. (1923). *Zauberei und Recht in Roms Frühzeit*. Diss. Münster.

BELLARDI, G. (1975). 'Di alcuni motivi oraziani. Ipotesi di lettura attuale', *A&R* 20: 159–64.

BENEDETTO, A. DI (1980–1). 'La *Satira* Oraziana 1. 9 nelle interpretazioni più recenti', *Helikon* 20–1, 385–410.

BÉRANGER, J. (1953). *Recherches sur l'aspect idéologique du principat*. Basel: Schweizerische Beitrage zur Altertumswissenschaft.

BERNARDI PERINI, G. (1975). 'Aceto italico e poesia luciliana. Hor. *Sat*. 1.7', in *Scritti in onore di C. Diano*. Bologna: 1–24.

BERNSTEIN, M. A. (1992). *Bitter Carnival. Ressentiment and the Abject Hero*. Princeton: Princeton University Press.

BINDER, G. (1971). *Aeneas und Augustus: Interpretationem zum 8. Buch der Aeneis*. Meiseheim am Glan: Anton Hain.

BIONE, C. (1952). *Commento al libro delle Epistole*. Milan.

BLOOMER, M. (1997). *Latinity and Literary Society at Rome*. Philadelphia: University of Pennsylvania Press.

BODEL, J. (1999). 'The *cena Trimalchionis*', in H. Hofmann (ed.), *Latin Fiction: The Latin Novel in Context*. London: Routledge, 38–51.

BODENHEIMER, A. R. (1984). *Warum? Von der Obszönität des Fragens.* Ditzingen: Reclam.

BODOH, J. J. (1970). 'Unity in Horace "Sermo" 1.1', *AClass* 39: 164–8.

BOGAERT, R. (1963). *'est tibi mater* . . . ? (Horace, *Sat.* 1, 9, vv. 26 ss.)', in *LÉC* 31, 159–66.

BOISSIER, G. (1898). 'L'art poétique et la tragédie romaine', *RPh* XXII: 1–17.

BOLL, F. (1913). 'Die Anordnung im zweiten Buch von Horaz' Satiren'. *Hermes* 48: 143–5.

BOLLACK, J. (1969). 'Les Maximes de l'Amitié', *Actes du VIIIe Congrès Association Guillaume Bude.* Paris: Bude, 221–36.

BONNER, S. F. (1972). 'The street teacher: an educational scene in Horace', *AJPh* 93: 509–28.

BOURDIEU, P. (1984). *Distinction: A Social Critique of the Judgement of Taste* (trans. Richard Nice). Cambridge, Mass.: Harvard University Press.

BOWDITCH, L. (1994). 'Horace's poetics of political integrity: *Epistles* 1.18', *AJP* 115: 409–26.

BOYANCÉ, P. (1969). *Épicure.* Paris: Presses Universitaires de France.

BRADLEY, K. (1994). *Slavery and Society in Rome.* Cambridge: Cambridge University Press.

BRAKMAN, C. (1921). 'Horatiana I', *Mnemosyne* 49: 209–22.

BRAMBLE, J. C. (1974). *Persius and the Programmatic Satire.* Cambridge: Cambridge University Press.

BRAND, D. (1991). *The Spectator and the City in 19th Century American Literature.* Cambridge: Cambridge University Press.

BRAUN, G. (1877–8). 'La originaria nazionalità di Orazio', *Archeografo triestino*, 5: 247–82.

BRAUND, S. H. (1992). *Roman Verse Satire.* Oxford: Oxford University Press.

BRÉGUET, E. (1954). 'Horace, un homme libre', in *Collection Latomus* 22, *Hommages Niedermann.* Brussels: 82–9.

BRINK, C. O. (1962). 'Horace and Varro', *Varron* (Fondation Hardt Entretiens 9), Vandoevres-Geneva: 175–206.

—— (1963). *Horace on Poetry 1: Prolegomena to the Literary Epistles.* Cambridge: Cambridge University Press.

—— (1971). *Horace on Poetry, 2: The 'Ars Poetica'.* Cambridge: Cambridge University Press.

—— (1982). *Horace on Poetry, 3: Epistles Book II.* Cambridge: Cambridge University Press.

BROOKS, C. and WARREN, R. P. (1952). *Understanding Poetry.* New York: Henry Holt.

BROUGHTON, T. R. S. (1968). *The Magistrates of the Roman Republic.* Vol. 2. 2nd edn. New York: American Philological Association.

Brower, R. A. (1959). *Alexander Pope: The Poetry of Allusion*. Oxford: Clarendon Press.

Brown, M. (1993). *Horace, Satires I*. Warminster: Aris and Phillips.

Brown, P. and Levinson, S. (1987). *Politeness. Some Universals in Language Usage*. Cambridge: Cambridge University Press.

Brown, R. D. (1987). *Lucretius on Love and Sex: A Commentary on De Rerum Natura IV, 1030–1287*. Leiden: E. J. Brill.

Brunt, P. A. (1965). 'Amicitia in the Late Republic', *PCPS* 191: 1–20.

—— (1971). *Italian Manpower 225 B.C.–A.D. 14*. Oxford: Oxford University Press.

Buchheit, V. (1968). 'Homerparodie und Literarkritik in Horazens Satiren I 7 und I 9', *Gymnasium* 75: 519–55.

Büchner K. (1940). 'Der siebente Brief des Horaz', *Hermes* 75: 64–80 (= (1962). *Studien zur römischen Literatur* 111: 139–57).

—— (1961). 'Horaz, S. 1, 9, 44', *RCCM* 3: 3–15 (= (1962). *Horaz. Studien zur römischen Literatur. Bd. III*. Wiesbaden: Steiner, 113–24).

—— (1962). *Horaz*. Wiesbaden: Steiner.

—— (1970). 'Horace et Épicure', in *Actes du VIIIe Congrès Association Guillaume Bude*. Paris: Bude, 457–69.

Burton, G. P. (1975). 'Proconsuls, assizes and the administration of justice under the empire', *JRS* 65: 92–106.

Byron, George Gordon, Lord (1970). *Poetical Works*. Oxford: Oxford University Press.

Calboli, G. (1962–63). 'Nuovi contributi allo studio della sintassi latina', in *Quaderni dell'Istituto di Glottologia di Bologna* VII: 91–105.

Cairns, F. (1995). 'Horace's first Roman Ode', *PLLS* 8: 91–142.

Calogero, G. (1960). *La conclusione della filosofia del conoscere*. New expanded edition. Florence: Sansoni.

—— (1962). *Filosofia del dialogo*. Milan: Edizioni di Comunità.

Cameron, A. (1995). *Callimachus and his Critics*. Princeton: Princeton University Press.

Canali, L. (1988). *Orazio: annie fuggiaschi e stabilità di regime. Horatiana* 3. Venosa.

Canter, H. V. (1930–1). 'Venusia and the native country of Horace', *CJ* 26: 439–56.

Carter, J. (1970). *The Battle of Actium*. London: Hamish Hamilton.

Castiglione, B. (1959). *The Book of the Courtier* (trans. Charles S. Singleton). New York: Doubleday. Orig. publ. 1528.

Caston, R. R. (1997). 'The fall of the curtain (Horace Sat. 2.8)', *TAPhA* 127: 233–56.

CASTORINA, E. (1965). *La poesia di Orazio*. Rome: Edizioni di storia e letteratura.

CATAUDELLA, Q. (1950). 'Filodemo nella Satira I, 2 di Orazio', *PP* 5: 18–31.

CAWS, M. A. (ed.) (1993). *City Images: Perspectives from Literature, Philosophy, and Film*. New York: Gordon & Breach.

CÈBE, J.-P. (1966). *La caricature et la parodie dans le monde romain antique des origines a Juvénal*. Paris: Bibliothèque des Écoles Françaises d'Athènes et de Rome.

CHADWICK, H. (1978). s.v. 'Gewissen', in *RAC* 10: 1056.

CHAMBERS, R. (1984). *Story and Situation: Narrative Seduction and the Power of Fiction*. Manchester: Manchester University Press.

CHIARO, D. (1992). *The Language of Jokes. Analysing Verbal Play*. London: Routledge.

CITRONI, M. (1989). 'Musa pedestre', in G. Cavallo, P. Fedeli, and A. Giardina (eds.), *Lo spazio letterario di Roma antica*. Vol. 1. Rome: Salerno, 311–41.

—— (1991). 'Satira, epigramma, favola', in F. Montanari (ed.), *La poesia latina: forme, autori, problemi*. Rome: La Nuova Italia Scientifica.

—— (1993). 'Gli interlocutori del sermo oraziano: gioco scenico e destinazione del testo', in *Atti del convegno nazionale di studi su Orazio*. Turin, 95–127.

CITTI, F. (1992). 'Hor. *Ars* 172, e della speranza in Orazio', *Orpheus* 13: 261–77.

—— (1994). *Orazio, L'Invito a Torquato: Epist. 1.5. Introduzione, testo, traduzione e commento*. (Scrinia, 6) Bari: Edipuglia.

CLASSEN, C. J. (1958). 'Aristippos', *Hermes* 86: 182–92.

—— (1973). 'Eine unsatirische Satire des Horaz? Zu *Sat.* 1,5', *Gymnasium* 80: 235–50.

—— (1988). 'Satire, the elusive genre', *Symbolae Osloensis* 63: 95–121.

CLAUSEN, W. V. (1964). 'Callimachus and Latin poetry', *GRBS* 5: 181–96.

—— (1972). 'On the date of the First Eclogue', *HSCP* 76: 201–5.

—— (1976). 'Catulli Veronensis Liber', *CPh* 71: 37–43.

CLAUSS, J. J. (1985). 'Allusion and structure in Horace *Satire* 2.1: the Callimachean response', *TAPhA* 115: 197–206.

CLAYMAN, D. (1976). 'Callimachus' Thirteenth Iamb: the last word', *Hermes* 104: 29–35.

—— (1980). *Callimachus' Iambi*. Leiden: Mnemosyne.

CLOUD, J. D. (1989). 'Satirists and the law', in S. H. Braund (ed.), *Satire and Society in Ancient Rome*, Exeter Studies in History. Exeter: Exeter University Press, 49–67.

486   *References*

CLOUD, J. D. (1996). '*XII Tabulae*', in M. Crawford (ed.), *Roman Statutes*, Vol. 2. London: Inst. of Classical Studies (BICS University Press 64).

COFFEY, M. (1989). *Roman Satire*. 2nd edn. London: Methuen (first published 1976).

COHAN, S. and SHIRES, L. M. (1988). *Telling Stories: A Theoretical Analysis of Narrative Fiction*. London: Routledge.

COLEMAN, R. (1977). *Vergil, Eclogues*. Cambridge: Cambridge University Press.

CONNOLLY, W. E. (1984). 'The politics of discourse', in M. Shapiro (ed.), *Language and Politics*, Oxford: Blackwell, 139–67.

CONNOR, P. (1987). *Horace's Lyric Poetry: The Force of Humour*. Berwick, Victoria: Aureal Publications.

CONTE, G. B. (1991). *Generi e lettori*. Milan: Mondadori.

COPLEY, F. O. (1969). *Latin Literature. From the Beginnings to the Close of the Second Century AD* Ann Arbor: University of Michigan Press.

CORBETT, P. B. (1986). *The Scurra*. Edinburgh: Scottish Academic Press.

COTTON, H. M. (1984). 'Greek and Latin epistolary formulae: some light on Cicero's letter writing', *AJPh* 105: 409–25.

—— (1985). '*Mirificum Genus Commendationis*: Cicero and the Latin letter of recommendation', *AJPh* 106: 328–34.

COURBAUD, E. (1914). *Horace: sa vie et sa pensée à l'époque des Épîtres*. Paris: Hachette.

COVA, P. V. and MANZONI, G. E. (1993). *Voci orazione*. Brescia : La Scuola.

COURTNEY, E. (1993). *The Fragmentary Latin Poets*. Oxford: Clarendon Press.

CROOK J. A. (1967). *The Law and Life of Rome*. London: Thames and Hudson.

—— (1996). 'Political history, 30 BC to AD 14', in *CAH*, vol. 10. 2nd edn. Cambridge: Cambridge University Press, 70–93.

CROWLEY, T. (1989). 'Bakhtin and the history of the language', in K. Hirschkop and D. Shepherd (eds.), *Bakhtin and Cultural Theory*. Manchester: Manchester University Press, 68–90.

CSILLAG, P. (1976). *The Augustan Laws on Family Relatives*. Budapest: Akademiai Kiado.

CUCCHIARELLI, A. (2001). *La Satira e il poeta: Orazio tra Epodi e Sermones, Biblioteca di materiali e discussioni per l'analisi dei testi classici* 17. Pisa: Giardini.

CUGUSI, P. (1983). *Evoluzione e forme dell'epistolografia Latina*. Rome: Herder.

CUNNINGHAM, I. C. (1971). *Herodas: Mimiamboi*. Oxford: Clarendon Press.

CUPAIUOLO, F. (1942). *A proposito della 'callida iunctura' oraziana.* Naples: Arti Grafiche Torella.

CURRIE, M. (1998). *Postmodern Narrative Theory.* New York: Palgrave Macmillan.

D'ALESSIO, G. (1996). *Callimacho: Inni Epigrammi, Ecale* (vol. 1) and *Aitia, Giambi e altri Frammenti* (vol. 2). Milan: Rizzoli.

DALZELL, A. (1956). 'Maecenas and the poets', *Phoenix* 10: 151–62.

DAMON, C. (1995). 'Greek parasites and Roman patronage', *HSPh* 97: 181–95.

—— (1997). *The Mask of a Parasite: A Pathology of Roman Patronage.* Ann Arbor: University of Michigan Press.

DAMROSCH JR., L. (1987). *The Imaginative World of Alexander Pope.* Berkeley: University of California Press.

D'ANNA, G. (1979). 'Ancora sul motivo oraziano del "carpe diem" ', *AMArc* 3.7: 103–15.

D'ARBELA, E. (1934). *Orazio,* Epistole. Naples.

D'ARMS, J. H. (1981). *Commerce and Social Standing in Ancient Rome.* Cambridge, Mass.: Harvard University Press.

DAUBE, D. (1951). '*Ne quid infamandi causa fiat*: the Roman law of defamation', in *Atti del congresso internazionale di diritto romano e di storia del diritto, 1948.* Vol. 3. Milan, 411–50.

DAWSON, C. (1950). 'The Iambi of Callimachus: a Hellenistic poet's experimental laboratory', *YCS* 11: 1–168.

DE PRETIS, A. (1998). ' "Epistolarity" in the First Book of Horace's *Epistles*', Diss. Bristol.

—— (2004). *'Epistolarity' in the First Book of Horace's Epistles.* Piscataway, NJ: Gorgias Press.

DE WITT, N. W. (1939). 'Epicurean Doctrine in Horace', *CP* 34, 127–34.

DEGL'INNOCENTI PIERINI, R. (1992). '*Vivi nascosti*: riflessi di un tema epicurreo in Orazio, Ovidio, Seneca', *Prometheus* 18: 150–72.

DELACY, P. (1941). 'Cicero's invective against Piso', *TAPhA* 71 (1941), 49–58.

DEL GRANDE, C. (1960). *Bologna e la cultura dopo l'unità d'Italia.* Bologna: Zanichelli.

—— (1965). 'Poetica dei motivi', *Vichiana* 2: 150–72.

DELLA CORTE, F. (1991). 'Orazio come lirico', in *Orazio Le Opere I.* Rome: Istituto Poligrafico e Zecca dello Stato (Libreria dello Stato), 5–91.

DELLA VOLPE, G. (1964). *Critica del gusto.* 2nd edn. Milan: Feltrinelli.

DESCH, W. (1981). 'Horazens Beziehung zu Maecenas', *Eranos* 79: 33–45.

DESCHAMPS, L. (1983). 'Il tempo di Orazio ossia dal tempo perduto al tempo ritruvato', *Orpheus* 4: 195–214.

DESSEN, C. (1968). *Iunctura Callidus Acri: A Study of Persius' Satires.* Urbana: University of Illinois Press.

DESY, P. (1988). 'La traversée de l'Apennin par Horace', *Latomus* 47: 620–5.

DIANO, C. (1968). 'Orazio e l'epicureismo', in *Saggezza e poetiche degli antichi.* Venice: Neri Pozza, 13–30.

—— (1974). *Scritti epicurei.* Florence: L. S. Olschki.

DIHLE, A. (1966). s.v. 'Ethik', *MC* 6: 646–796.

DILKE, O. A. W. (1966). *Horace: Epistles Book I.* London: Bradda Books.

—— (1981). 'The interpretation of Horace's *Epistles*', in *ANRW* II, 31.1: 1837–65.

DILLENBURGER, W. (1881). *Horati opera omnia.* Bonn: Marcus.

DIONIGI, I. (1980). 'L'epistola I, 1 di Orazio e il proemio del De otio di Seneca', *BStudLat* 10: 38–49.

DOBLHOFER, E. (1966). *Die Augustuspanegyrik des Horaz in formalhistorischer Sicht.* Heidelberg: Carl Winter Universitätsverlag.

—— (1972). *Rutilius Namatianus, De reditu suo siue Iter Gallicum.* Heidelberg: C. Winter.

—— (1980). 'Gedanken zur Cena Cocceiana', *Informationen zum altsprachlichen Unterricht* 2: 52–67.

DÖRING, K. (1988). *Der Sokratesschüler Aristippos und die Kyrenaiker. Akademie Wissenschaft Mainz, Abh. der geistes- u. sozialwiss. Klasse,* I.

DORSCH, J. (1904). *Mit Horaz von Rom nach Brindisi.* Prague: Haase.

DOUGLAS, A. E. (1966). *M. Tulli Ciceronis Brutus.* Oxford: Clarendon Press.

DOVER, K. J. (ed.) (1968). *Clouds.* Oxford: Clarendon Press.

DREXLER, H. (1966). *Die Entdeckung des Individuums.* Salzburg: Müller.

DREW, P. and WOOTTON, A. (eds.) (1988), *Erving Goffma:. Exploring the Interaction Order.* Oxford: Polity Press.

DRUMANN, W. and GROEBE, P. (1899). *Geschichte Roms in seinem Übergangs von der republikanischen zur monarchischen Verfassung.* 2nd edn. Berlin: Borntraeger.

DRYDEN, J. (1900). 'A discourse concerning the original and progress of satire' (1693), in W. P. Ker (ed.), *Essays of John Dryden.* Oxford: Clarendon Press, 15–114.

DUDLEY, D. R. (1967). URBS ROMA. *A source book of classical texts on the city and its monuments selected and translated with a commentary.* Aberdeen: Aberdeen University Press.

DUNCAN, J. S. and DUNCAN, N. G. (1992). 'Ideology and bliss: Roland Barthes and the secret histories of landscape', in T. J. Barnes and J. S. Duncan (eds.), *Writing Worlds: Discourse, Text and Metaphor in the Representation of Landscape.* London: Routledge, 18–37.

DuQuesnay, I. M. Le M. (1984). 'Horace and Maecenas: the propaganda value of *Sermones* I', in T. Woodman and D. West (eds.), *Poetry and Politics in the Age of Augustus*. Cambridge: Cambridge University Press, 19–58.

—— (1995). 'Horace, *Odes* 4.5: *Pro reditu Imperatoris Caesaris divi filii Augusti*', in Harrison (1995a), 128–87.

Dupont, F. (1985). *L'Acteur-Roi, ou, Le théatre dans la Rome antique*. Paris: Les Belles Lettres.

Dupouy, A. (1928). *Horace*. Paris: B. Grasset.

Düring, I. (1961). *Aristotle's* Protrepticus. *An Attempt at Reconstruction*. Göteborg: Almqvist & Wiksell.

Dylan, B. (1964). *Another side of Bob Dylan*. New York.

—— (1965). *Bringing it all back home*. New York.

—— (1971). *More Bob Dylan greatest hits*. New York.

—— (1997) *Time out of mind*. New York.

Eagleton, T. (1986). *William Shakespeare*. Oxford: Blackwell.

Earl, D. (1961). *The Political Thought of Sallust*. Cambridge: Cambridge University Press.

—— (1967). *The Moral and Political Tradition of Rome*. Ithaca: Cornell University Press.

Eckert, K. (1961). 'O et praesidium et dulce decus meum (Horazens Freundschaft mit Maecenas als eine Seite seiner Religiosität)', *WS* 74: 61–95.

Edwards, C. (1993). *The Politics of Immorality in Ancient Rome*. Cambridge: Cambridge University Press.

Ehlers, W. W. (1985). 'Das "Iter Brundisinum" des Horaz (*Serm*. 1.5)', *Hermes* 113, 69–83.

Ehwald, R. (1901). 'Horaz carm. II 2 und 3', *Philologus* 60: 635.

—— (2005). 'Epistolography', in S. J. Harrison (ed.), *A Companion to Latin Literature*. Oxford: Blackwell, 270–83.

Eidinow, J. S. C. (1990). 'A note on Horace, *Epistles* 1.1.26 and 2.2.75', *CQ* 40: 566–8.

—— (1995). 'Horace's Epistle to Torquatus (*Ep*. 1.15)', *CQ* 45: 191–9.

Elias, N. (1978). *The History of Manners* (trans. Edmund Jephcott). New York: Pantheon. Orig. publ. 1939.

Empson, W. (1974). *Some Versions of Pastoral*. 2nd edn. New York: New Directions.

Ernout, A. and Meillet, A. (1959–60). *Dictionnaire étymologique de la langue latine*. 4th edn. Paris: Klincksieck.

Evenepoel, W. (1990). 'Maecenas: a survey of recent literature', *AncSoc* 21: 99–117.

Fairclough, N. (1989). *Language and Power*. Harlow: Longman.

FANTHAM, E. (1972). *Comparative Studies in Republican Latin Imagery.* Toronto: University of Toronto Press.

—— (1996). *Roman Literary Culture: From Cicero to Apuleius.* Baltimore and London: Johns Hopkins University Press.

FARELL, J. (1991). *Vergil's Georgics and the Traditions of Ancient Epic.* Oxford and New York: Oxford University Press.

FEDELI, P. (1994). *Q. Orazio Flacco: Le Opere II, Le Satire.* Rome: Istituto Poligrafico e Zecca dello Stato (Libreria dello Stato).

—— (1997). *Q. Orazio Flacco: Le Opere II, Le Epistole, L'Arte Poetica.* Rome: Istituto Poligrafico e Zecca dello Stato (Libreria dello Stato).

FEENEY, D. C. (1992). '*Si licet et fas est*: Ovid's *Fasti* and the problem of free speech under the Principate', in A. Powell (ed.), *Roman Poetry and Propaganda in the Age of Augustus.* London: Bristol Classical Press, 1–25.

—— (1993). 'Horace and the Greek lyric poets', in N. Rudd (ed.), *Horace 2000: A Celebration. Essays for the Bimillenium.* Bristol and Ann Arbor: University of Michigan Press, 41–63.

—— (1998). *Literature and Religion in Rome: Cultures, Contexts, and Beliefs.* Cambridge: Cambridge University Press.

—— (2002a). '*Una cum scriptore meo*: poetry, Principate and the traditions of literary history in the Epistle to Augustus', in A. J. Woodman and D. C. Feeney (eds.), *Traditions and Contexts in the Poetry of Horace,* Cambridge: Cambridge University Press, 172–87.

—— (2002b). 'The odiousness of comparisons: Horace on literary history and the limitations of synkrisis', in M. Paschalis (ed.), *Horace and Greek Lyric Poetry.* Rethymnon: Rethymnon Classical Studies: 7–18.

FELDMAN, L. H. (1993). *Jew and Gentile in the Ancient World: Attitudes and Interactions from Alexander to Justinian.* Princeton: Princeton University Press.

FELPERIN, H. (1990). *The Uses of the Canon: Elizabethan Literature and Contemporary Theory.* Oxford: Oxford University Press.

FER, B. (1993). 'The hat, the hoax, the body', in K. Adler and M. Pointon (eds.), *The Body Imaged: The Human Form and Visual Culture since the Renaissance.* Cambridge: Cambridge University Press, 161–73.

FERRI, R. (1993). *I dispiaceri di un epicureo. Uno studio sulla poetica delle epistole oraziane.* Pisa: Giardini.

—— (2007). 'The *Epistles*', in S. J. Harrison (ed.), *The Cambridge Companion to Horace.* Cambridge: Cambridge University Press, 121–31.

FIELDING, H. (1967, 1st American edn.). *Joseph Andrews.* Middletown: Wesleyan University Press.

References 491

References 491

FISKE, G. C. (1920). *Lucilius and Horace: A Study in the Classical Theory of Imitation*, University of Wisconsin Studies in Language and Literature 7. Madison: University of Wisconsin Press.

FITZGERALD, W. (1988). 'Power and impotence in Horace's *Epodes*', *Ramus* 17: 176–91.

FOCKE, F. (1923). 'Synkrisis', *Hermes* 58: 327–68.

FONTAINE, J. (1959). 'Les racines de la sagesse horatienne', *L'Information Littéraire* 11: 113–24.

FOWLER, D. P. (1989a). 'First thoughts on closure', *MD* 22: 75–122.

—— (1989b). 'Lucretius and politics', in M. Griffin and J. Barnes (eds.), *Philosophia Togata*. Oxford: Oxford University Press, 120–50.

—— (1995). 'Horace and the aesthetics of politics', in S. J. Harrison (ed.), *Homage to Horace: A Bimillenary Celebration*. Oxford: Oxford University Press, 248–66.

—— (2000a). 'The didactic plot', in M. Depew and D. Obbink (eds.), *Matrices of Genre*. Cambridge, Mass.: Harvard University Press, 205–20.

—— (2000b). *Roman Constructions: Readings in Postmodern Latin*. Oxford: Oxford University Press.

FRAENKEL, E. (1957, repr. 1970, 11th edn.). *Horace*. Oxford: Oxford University Press.

FRAISSE, J.-C. (1974). *Philia: la notion d'amitié dans la philosophie antique*. New York: Oxford University Press.

FRANK, T. (1920). 'Heliodorus-Apollodorus. Horace *Serm.* 1.5.2', *CPh* 15: 393.

FREUDENBURG, K. (1990). 'Horace's satiric program and the language of contemporary theory in *Satires* 2.1', *AJPh* 111: 187–203.

—— (1993). *The Walking Muse: Horace on the Theory of Satire*. Princeton: Princeton University Press.

—— (1995). 'Canidia at the feast of Nasidienus (Hor. Sat. 2.8)', *TAPhA* 125: 207–19.

—— (1996). 'Verse-technique and moral extremism in two satires of Horace (*Sermones* 2.3 and 2.4)', *CQ* 46: 192–206.

—— (2001). *Satires of Rome: Threatening Poses from Lucilius to Juvenal*. Cambridge: Cambridge University Press.

—— (2002a). '*Solus sapiens liber est*: recommissioning lyric in Horace's *Epistles* Book One', in A. J. Woodman and D. C. Feeney (eds.), *Traditions and Contexts in the Poetry of Horace*, Cambridge: Cambridge University Press.

—— (2002b). 'Writing to/through Florus: sampling the addressee in Horace *Epistles* 2.2', *Memoirs of the American Academy in Rome*, 47: 33–55.

FREUDENBURG, K. (2006). 'Playing at lyric's boundaries: dreaming forward in Book Two of Horace's *Sermones*', *Dictynna* 3: 135–72.

FRIER, B. W. (1985). *The Rise of the Roman Jurists*. Princeton: Princeton University Press.

FRISCHER, B. (1982). *The Sculpted Word: Epicureanism and Philosophical Recruitment in Ancient Greece*. Berkeley: University of California Press.

—— (1991). *Shifting Paradigms: New Approaches to Horace's Ars Poetica*. Atlanta: Scholars Press.

FUSSELL, P. (1965). *The Rhetorical World of Augustan Humanism*. Oxford: Clarendon Press.

GABBA, E. (1970). *Appiani Bellorum Ciuilum Liber V*. Florence: Nuova Italia.

GAGLIARDI, D. (1986). 'Ironia e saggezza in Orazio', in D. Gagliardi (ed.), *Studi su Orazio*. Palermo: Palumbo, 61–74.

—— (1988). *Un'arte di vivere (Saggio sul I libro delle Epistole oraziane)*. Rome: Ateneo.

GAISER, K. (1981). 'Platone come "kolax" in una letter apocrifa (13a Epist.)', *Scandalion* 4: 71–94.

GALINSKY, K. (1981). 'Augustus' legislation on morals and marriage', *Philologus* 125: 126–44.

—— (1996). *Augustan Culture: An Interpretive Introduction*. Princeton: Princeton University Press.

GANTAR, K. (1972). 'Horaz zwischen Akademie und Epikur', *ZAnt* 22: 5–24.

GARDNER, M. (ed.) (1967). *The Annotated Snarkl*. Harmondsworth: Penguin.

GARGIULO, T. (1981). 'PHerc. 222: Filodemo sull'Adulazione', *CErc* 11: 103–27.

GARNSEY, P. (1970). *Social Status and Legal Privilege in the Roman Empire*. Oxford: Oxford University Press.

GELZER, M. (1968). *Caesar: Politician and Statesman*. Oxford: Blackwell.

GHISELLI, A. (1983, 2nd edn.) *Orazio Ode 1.1: saggio di analisi formale*. Bologna: Pàtron.

GIANNANTONI, G. (1958). *I Cirenaici*. Florence: G. C. Sansoni.

—— (1983–85). *Socraticorum reliquiae*. 3 vols. Rome: Edizioni dell'Ateneo.

GIBBON, E. (1814). 'A minute examination of Horace's journey to Brundisium, and of Cicero's journey into Cilicia', in J. H. Sheffield (ed.), *Miscellaneous Works*, IV. New York: AMS Press, 335–54.

GIGANTE, M. (1993). *Orazio: una misura per l'amore*. Venosa: Edizioni Osanna.

—— (1966). *Memoirs of My Life*, ed. G. Bonnard. New York: Funk & Wagnalls.

GIGON, O. (1977). 'Horaz und die Philosophie', in O. Gigon and L. Straume-Zimmermann (eds.), *Die antike Philosophie als Maßstab und Realität*. Zürich and Munich: Artemis & Winkler Verlag.

—— (1983). *Problemi fondamentali della filosofia antica*. Naples: Guida Editori.

GOFFMAN, E. (1972). *Encounters: Two Studies in the Sociology of Interaction*. Harmondsworth: Penguin.

GOLD, B. K. (1987). *Literary Patronage in Greece and Rome*. Chapel Hill: University of North Carolina Press.

GOLDBERG, S. M. (1995). *Epic in Republican Rome*. Oxford: Oxford University Press.

GOLDHILL, S. (1991). *The Poet's Voice*. Cambridge: Cambridge University Press.

GOMPERZ, T. (1950, 2nd edn.). *Pensatori greci II*. Florence: Nuova Italia.

GOWERS, E. (1993a). *The Loaded Table: Representations of Food in Roman Literature*. Oxford: Oxford University Press.

—— (1993b). 'Horace, *Satires* 1.5: an inconsequential journey', *PCPS* 39: 48–66.

—— (2003). 'Fragments of autobiography in Horace *Satires* 1', *ClAnt* 22.1: 55–91.

—— (2005). 'The restless companion: Horace, *Satires* 1 and 2', in Kirk Freudenburg (ed.), *The Cambridge Companion to Roman Satire*. Cambridge: Cambridge University Press, 48–61.

GRAMSCI, A. (1953). *Letteratura e vita nazionale*. 3rd edn. Turin: Einaudi.

GRAY, E. W. (1975). 'The crisis in Rome at the beginning of 32 BC', *PACA* 13: 15–29.

GREEN, R. P. H. (1991). *Ausonius, Mosella*. Oxford: Clarendon Press.

GRENADE, P. (1950). 'Le mythe de Pompée et les Pompéiens sous les Césars', *REA* 52: 28–63.

GRIFFIN, J. (1984). 'Augustus and the poets: "*Caesar qui cogere posset*" ', in F. Millar and E. Segal (eds.), *Caesar Augustus: Seven Aspects*. Oxford: Clarendon Press, 189–218.

—— (1993). 'Horace in the Thirties', in N. Rudd (ed.), *Horace 2000: A Celebration. Essays for the Bimillenium*. Bristol and Ann Arbor: University of Michigan Press, 1–22.

GRIFFIN, M. (1995). 'Philosophical badinage in Cicero's letters to his friends', in J. G. Powell (ed.), *Cicero the Philosopher: Twelve Papers*. Oxford: Oxford University Press: 325–346.

GRILLI, A. (1983). 'Orazio e l'epicureismo', in J. Cabañero and J. Reta (eds.), *Corollas philologicas : in honorem Josephi Guillén Cabañero*. Salamanca: Universidad Pontificia de Salamanca, 267–92.

GRILLI, A. (1993). 'Orazio e il pensiero filosofico', in P. V. Cova and G. E. Manzoni (eds.), *Voci orazione*. Brescia: La Scuola, 29–40.

GRIMAL, P. (1943). *Les jardins romains à fin de la république et aux deux premiers siècles de l'empire*. Paris: E. de Boccard.

—— (1958). *Horace*. Paris: Éditions du Seuil.

—— (1976). 'Étude de quelques notions philosophiques dans l'oeuvre d'Horace', *Atti V Conv. Oraz.*: 37–50.

—— (1978). 'La philosophie d'Horace au premier livre des *Épîtres*', *VL* 72: 2–10.

—— (1988). 'L'éclectisme philosophique dans l' "Art Poétique" d' Horace', in A. Ceresa-Gastaldo (ed.), *I 2000 anni dell' Ars Poetica*. Genoa: Istituto di Filologia Classica e Medievale, 9–26.

GROSSMITH, G. and W. (1945). *The Diary of a Nobody*. Harmondsworth: Penguin. First publ. 1892.

GRUBE, G. M. A. (1965). *The Greek and Roman Critics*. Toronto: University of Toronto Press.

GRUEN, E. S. (1974). *The Last Generation of the Roman Republic*. Berkeley: University of California Press.

GRUPP, H. (1953). *Studien zum antiken Reisegedicht*. Diss. Tübingen.

GUNNING, J. H. (1942). 'Der siebente Brief des Horaz und sein Verhältnis zu Maecenas', *Mnemosyne* 10: 303–20.

HABINEK, T. (1998). *The Politics of Latin Literature: Writing, Identity, and Empire in Ancient Rome*. Princeton: Princeton University Press.

HADAS, M. (1930). *Sextus Pompey*. New York: AMS Press.

HALM, C. (1863). *Rhetores Latini minores*. Leipzig: Teubner.

HANSLIK, R. (1937). 'Untersuchungen zu dem ersten Satirenbuch des Horaz', *Comm. Vind.* 3: 19–31.

HARDIE, P. (1990). 'Ovid's Theban history: the first "anti-*Aeneid*"?', *CQ* 40: 224–35.

—— (1993). '*Ut pictura poesis*? Horace and the visual arts', in N. Rudd (ed.), *Horace 2000: A Celebration: Essays for the Bimillenium*. Bristol and Ann Arbor: University of Michigan Press, 120–39.

HARRIS, R. (1990). 'On freedom of speech', in J. E. Joseph and T. J. Taylor (eds.), *Ideologies of Language*. London: Routledge, 153–61.

HARRIS, W. V. (1979). *War and Imperialism in Republican Rome*. Oxford: Clarendon Press.

HARRISON, G. (1987). 'The Confessions of Lucilius (Horace *Sat.* 2. 1. 30–4): a defense of autobiographical satire?', *ClAnt* 6: 38–52.

HARRISON, S. J. (1992). 'Fuscus the Stoic: Horace *Odes* 1.22 and *Epistles* 1.10', *CQ* 42: 543–47.

—— (ed.) (1995a). *Homage to Horace: A Bimillenary Celebration*. Oxford: Oxford University Press.

—— (1995b). 'Poetry, philosophy and letter-writing in Horace *Epistles* 1', in D. Innes, H. Hine, and C. Pelling (eds.), *Ethics and Rhetoric: Classical Essays for Donald Russell*. Oxford: Clarendon Press, 47–61.

—— (ed.) (2005). *A Companion to Latin Literature*. Oxford: Blackwell.

—— (ed.) (2007a). *The Cambridge Companion to Horace*. Cambridge: Cambridge University Press.

—— (2007b) 'Horatian self-representations', in S. J. Harrison (ed.), *The Cambridge Companion to Horace*. Cambridge: Cambridge University Press.

HARTLICH, P. (1889). *De exhortationum a Graecis Romanisque scriptarum historia et indole*. Leipzig: Hirzel.

HARVEY, R. A. (1981). *A Commentary on Persius*. Leiden: Brill.

HATIM, B. and MASON, I. (1990). *Discourse and the Translator*. London: Longman.

HEINZE, R. (1889). *De Horatio Bionis imitatore*. Inaug. Diss. Bonn: Typis C. Georgi.

—— (1919). 'Horazens Buch der Briefe', *NJA* 43: 305–15.

—— (1938). *Vom Geist des Römertums*. Leipzig: Teubner.

—— (1960). *Die Augusteische Kultur*. 3rd edn. Darmstadt: Wissenschaftliche Buchgesellschaft.

HELLEGOUARC'H, J. (1964). *Le vocabulaire latin des relations et des partis politiques sous la république*. Paris: Les Belles Lettres.

HENDERSON, J. (1975). *The Maculate Muse: Obscene Language in Attic Comedy*. New Haven: Yale University Press.

HENDERSON, J. (1976). *Anecdote and Satire in Phaedrus: Commentary and Discussion*. Oxford DPhil Thesis.

—— (1989). 'Satire writes "woman": *Gendersong*', *PCPS* 35: 50–80; revised and reprinted in J. Henderson (ed.), *Writing Down Rome: Satire, Comedy, and other Offences in Latin Poetry*. Oxford: Clarendon Press.

—— (1993). 'Be Alert (Your Country Needs Lerts): Horace, *Satires* 1.9', *PCPhS* 39: 67–93.

—— (1994). 'On Getting Rid of Kings: Horace, Satire 1.7', *CQ* 44: 146–70.

—— (1995). 'Pump up the Volume: Juvenal *Satires* 1.1.1–21', *PCPhS* 41: 101–37.

—— (1998a). *Fighting for Rome: Poets and Caesars, History and Civil War*. Cambridge: Cambridge University Press.

—— (1998b). 'Valleydiction: Virgil, *Eclogue* 9', *PVS* 23, 149–76.

—— (1998c). *A Roman Life: Rutilius Gallicus on Paper and in Stone*. Exeter: University of Exeter Press.

HENDERSON, J. (1999). *Writing Down Rome: Satire, Comedy, and other Offences in Latin Poetry.* Oxford: Clarendon Press.

HENDRICKSON, G. L. (1900). 'Horace, *Serm.* 1.4: a protest and a programme', *American Journal of Philology* 21: 121–42.

—— (1916). 'Horace and Valerius Cato', *CP* 11: 249–69.

—— (1917). 'Horace and Valerius Cato II', *CP* 12: 77–92 and 329–50.

HERCHER, R. (1873). *Epistolographi Graeci.* Paris: Didot.

HERDMAN, J. (1981). *Voice without Restraint: Bob Dylan's Lyrics and their Background.* Edinburgh: Harris Press.

HERTER, H. (1951). 'Zur ersten Satire des Horaz', *RhM* 94: 1–42.

HEWITT, J. W. (1940–41). 'The gratitude of Horace to Maecenas', *CJ* 36: 464–72.

HILTBRUNNER, O. (1960). 'Volteius Mena. Interpretationen zu Hor. *epist.* 1, 7', *Gymnasium* 67: 289–300.

HINDS, S. (1997). 'Do-it-yourself literary tradition: Statius, Martial and others', *MD* 39: 187–207.

—— (1998). *Allusion and Intertext: Dynamics of Appropriation in Roman Poetry.* Cambridge: Cambridge University Press.

HODGE, R. (1990). *Literature as Discourse.* Cambridge: Blackwell/Parallex.

—— and KRESS, G. (1988). *Social Semiotics.* Cambridge: Polity Press.

—— and —— (1993) *Language as Ideology.* 2nd edn. London: Routledge.

HOFMANN, J. B. and SZANTYR, A. (1964). *Lateinische Grammatik.* Vol. II. Munich: Beck.

HOLLIS, A. (1977). 'L. Varius Rufus, *De Morte* (Frs. 1–4 Morel)', *CQ* 27: 187–90.

HOLQUIST, M. (1986). 'Answering as authoring: Mikhail Bakhtin's translinguistics', in G. S. Morson (ed.), *Bakhtin: Essays and Dialogues on his Work.* Chicago: University of Chicago Press, 59–71.

—— (1990). *Dialogism: Bakhtin and his World.* London: Routledge.

HOLST, H. (1925). *Die Wortspiele in Ciceros Reden.* Oslo: Some.

HOOLEY, D. (2007). *Roman Satire.* Cambridge: Blackwell.

HOPKINS, K. (1983). *Death and Renewal.* Cambridge: Cambridge University Press.

HOPKINSON, N. (1988). *A Hellenistic Anthology.* Cambridge: Cambridge University Press.

HORSFALL, N. (1976). 'Ad Iuv. I. 40', *Mnemosyne* 28: 422.

—— (1979). 'Horace: *Sermones* 3', *LCM* 4: 117–19.

—— (1981a). 'Poets and patron', *Publication of the Macquarie Ancient History Association* 3, 1–24.

—— (1981b). 'Some problems of titulature in Roman literary history', *BICS* 28: 103–14.

—— (1993a). *La villa sabina di Orazio: il galateo della gratitudine. Una rilettura della settima epistola del primo libro*. Venosa: Osanna.

—— (1993b). 'Empty shelves on the Palatine', *G&R* 40: 58–67.

HOWALD, E. (1948). *Das Wesen der lateinischen Dichtung*. Zürich: Rentsch.

HOWES, C. (1986). 'Rhetorics of attack: Bakhtin and the aesthetics of satire', *Genre* 10, 25–43.

HUBBARD, M. (1970). *A Commentary on Horace: Odes Book I*. Oxford: Oxford University Press.

—— (1995). '*Pindarici fontis qui non expalluit haustus*: Horace, *Epistles* 1. 3', in S. J. Harrison (ed.), *Homage to Horace: A Bimillenary Celebration*. Oxford: Oxford University Press, 219–27.

HUMBERT, J. (1967). *Socrate et les petits socratiques*. Paris: Presses Universitaires de France.

HUNTER, R. L. (1985). 'Horace on friendship and free speech (*Epistles* 1.18 and *Satires* 1.4)', *Hermes* 113: 480–90.

—— (1996). *Theocritus and the Archaeology of Greek Poetry*. Cambridge: Cambridge University Press.

HUTCHINSON, G. O. (1998). *Cicero's Correspondence: A Literary Study*. Oxford: Oxford University Press.

HUZAR, E. G. (1978). *Mark Antony: A Biography*. Minneapolis: University of Minnesota Press.

ILLUMINATI, L. (1938). *La satura odeporica*. Società Anonima Editrice Dante Alighieri: Albrighi, Segati & co.

IMMISCH, O. (1932). *Horazens Epistel über die Dichtkunst*. Leipzig: Dieterich, 1932.

INNES, D. C. (1989). 'Augustan critics', in G. A. Kennedy (ed.), *The Cambridge History of Literary Criticism*. Vol. 1: *Classical Criticism*. Cambridge: Cambridge University Press, 245–73.

JAKOBSON, R. (1959). 'Boas' view of grammatical meaning', in R. Jakobson (ed.), *World and Language: Selected Writings*. Vol. 2. The Hague: Mouton: 489–96.

—— (1963, repr. 2003). *Essais de linguistique general* (trans. N. Ruwet). Paris: Les Editions de Minuit.

JAL, P. (1963). *La guerre civile à Rome*. Paris: Presses Universitaires de France.

JARDINE, L. (1996). *Reading Shakespeare Historically*. London: Routledge.

JAWORSKI, A. (1992). *The Power of Silence: Social and Pragmatic Perspectives*. London: Sage.

JOCELYN, H. D. (1979). '*Vergilius cacozelus* (Donatus *Vita Vergilii* 44)', *PLLS* 2: 67–142.

JOHNSON, T. and DANDEKER, C. (1990), 'Patronage: relation and system', in A. Wallace-Hadrill (ed.), *Patronage in Ancient Society*. London: Routledge, 219–45.

JOHNSON, W. R. (1993). *Horace and the Dialectic of Freedom: Readings in Epistles 1*. Ithaca: Cornell University Press.

JOHNSTON, D. (1999). *Roman Law in Context*. Cambridge: Cambridge University Press.

JONES, F. (1993). 'The role of the addressees in Horace, *Epistles*', *LCM* 18: 7–11.

KAMBYLIS, A. (1965). *Die Dichterweihe und ihre Symbolik*. Heidelberg: Carl Winter Verlag.

KASSEL, R. and AUSTIN, C. (1986). *Poetae Comici Graeci*. Berlin: Novi Eboraci.

KASTER, R. A. (1995). *Suetonius: De grammaticis et rhetoribus*. Oxford: Clarendon Press.

KEANE, C. (2006). *Figuring Genre in Roman Satire*. Oxford: Oxford University Press.

KELLY, J. M. (1966). *Roman Litigation*. Oxford: Clarendon Press.

KENDON, A. (1988). 'Goffman's approach to face-to-face interaction', in Drew and Wootton (1988), 14–40.

KENNEDY, D. F. (1992). ' "Augustan" and "Anti-Augustan": reflections on terms of reference', in A. Powell (ed.), *Roman Poetry and Propaganda in the Age of Augustus*. London: Bristol Classical Press, 26–58.

KENNEY, E. J. (1982). 'Books and Readers in the Roman World', *CHCL* 2: 3–32.

KERKHECKER, A. (1999). *Callimachus' Book of Iambi*. Oxford. Oxford University Press.

KERNAN, A. B. (1959). *The Cankered Muse*. New Haven: Yale University Press.

KETTNER, G. (1900). *Die Episteln des Horaz*. Berlin: O. R. Reisland.

KEYES, C. W. (1935). 'The Greek letter of introduction'. *AJPh* 56: 28–44.

KIENAST, D. (1969). 'Rom und die Venus vom Eryx', *Hermes* 93: 478–89.

KIESSLING, A. (1915–30). *Q. Horatius Flaccus*. 3 vols. Leipzig: B. G. Teubner.

KIESSLING, A., and HEINZE, R. (1921). *Q. Horatius Flaccus. Satiren*. 5th edn. Berlin: Weidmann.

—— and —— (1957) *Horatius Flaccus. Briefe*. 5th edn. (ed. E. Burck). Berlin: Weidmann.

—— and —— (1959). *Q. Horatius Flaccus: Satiren*. 7th edn. (ed. E. Burck). Berlin: Weidmann.

—— and —— (1961). *Q. Horatius Flaccus: Satiren*. 8th edn. (ed. E. Burck). Berlin: Weidmann.

KILPATRICK, R. S. (1986). *The Poetry of Friendship: Horace, Epistles I.* Edmonton: Alberta University Press.

—— (1990). *The Poetry of Criticism: Horace Epistles II and Ars Poetica.* Edmonton: Alberta University Press.

KINDSTRAND, J. F. (1976). *Bion of Borysthenes: A Collection of Fragments with Introduction and Commentary.* Uppsala: Almqvist & Wiksell International.

KLINGNER, F. (1931). 'Virgil als Bewahrer und Erneuerer', *Gymnasium* 42: 123–36.

—— (1950). 'Horazens Brief an Augustus', *SBAW* 5: 1–32.

—— (1964). *Studien zur griechischen und römischen Literatur* (ed. K. Bartels). Zürich: Artemis Verlag.

—— (1967). *Virgil.* Zürich: Artemis Verlag.

KNOCHE, U. (1982, 4th edn.). *Die römische Satire.* Göttingen: Vandenhoeck and Ruprecht.

KOESTERMANN, E. (1971). *C. Sallustius Crispus: Bellum Iugurthinum.* Heidelberg: Carl Winter Verlag.

KOLENDO, J. (1981). 'La répartition des places aux spectacles et la stratification sociale dans l'Empire Romain: à propos des inscriptions sur les gradins des amphithéâtres et théâtres', *Ktèma* 6: 301–15.

KORNSTEIN D. J. (1996). *Kill All the Lawyers? Shakespeare's Legal Appeal.* Princeton: Princeton University Press.

KRAUS, C. D. and WOODMAN, A. J. (1997). *Latin Historians (Greece & Rome New Surveys in the Classics No. 27).* Oxford: Oxford University Press.

KRÜGER, G. T. A. (1869). *Des Q. Horatius Flaccus Satiren und Episteln.* Leipzig: B. G. Teubner.

LABATE, M. (1981). 'La satira di Orazio: morfologia di un genere irrequieto', in M. Labate (ed.), *Orazio, Satire.* Milan: Biblioteca Universale Rizzoli, 5–45.

—— (1993). 'I generi letterari a Roma: tra retorica grammatical e poetica', in S. Settis (ed.), *Civiltà dei Romani. Vol. IV: Un linguaggio commune.* Milan: Electra.

—— (1996). 'Il sermo oraziano e i generi letterari', in H. Krasser and E. A. Schmidt (eds.), *Zeitgenosse Horaz: der Dichter und seine Leser seit zwei Jahrtausenden.* Tübingen: Gunter Narr Verlag, 424–41.

LABOWSKY, L. (1934). *Die Ethik des Panaitios: Untersuchungen zur Geschichte des Decorum bei Cicero und Horaz.* Leipzig: Meiner.

LAFLEUR, R. A. (1981). 'Horace and *onomasti komodein*: the law of satire', *ANRW* 2. 31. 5. 1790–1826.

LANA, I. (1989). *Il libro delle Epistole di Orazio.* Turin: G. Giappichelli.

—— (1993). *Orazio: dalla poesia al silenzio.* Venosa: Osanna.

La Penna, A. (1949). 'Schizzo di una interpretazione di Orazio, partendo dal primo libro delle Epistole', *ASNP* 18: 14–48.

—— (1950). 'Orazio, Augusto e la questione del teatro latino', *Annali della Scuola Normale Superiore di Pisa* XIX: 143–54.

—— (1956). 'Due note sulla cultura filosofica delle Epistole oraziane', *SIFC* 27–8: 192–201.

—— (1958). *Orazio, Satire ed Epistole*. 2nd edn. Florence: Sansoni (first published 1957).

—— (1963). *Orazio e l'ideologia del principato*. Turin: Einaudi.

—— (1968). *Orazio: Tutte le opere*. Florence: Sansoni.

—— (1969). *Orazione e la morale mondana europea*. Florence: Sansoni.

—— (1981). 'Persio e le vie nuove della satira latina', in F. Bellandi (ed.), *Persio: Satire*. Milan: Rizzoli, 5–78.

—— (1990). 'L'intellettuale emarginato nell'antichita', *Maia* 42: 3–20.

—— (1993). *Saggi e studi su Orazio*. Florence: Sansoni.

Latacz, J. (1980). 'Horazens sogenannte Schwätzersatire', *AU* 23: 5–22.

Le Bon, M.-T. (1937). 'La "vera virtus" chez Horace', in AA. VV., *Études Horatiennes*, Paris: Les Belles Lettres, 141–6.

Leach, E. (1971). 'Horace's *Pater Optimus* and Terence's Demea: autobiographical fiction and comedy in *Serm.* 1.4', *AJP* 92: 616–32.

—— (1999). 'Ciceronian "Bi-Marcus": correspondence with M. Terentius Varro and L. Papirius Paetus in 46 BCE,' in *TAPhA* 129: 139–79.

Leeman, A. D. (1958). 'The good companion (Ennius *Ann.* 234–251 Vahlen)', *Mnemosyne* 11: 318–21.

—— (1982). 'Rhetorical status in Horace, *Serm.* 2.1', in B. Vickers (ed.), *Rhetoric Revalued*. Binghamton, NY: Center for Medieval & Early Renaissance Studies, State University of New York, 159–63.

Lefèvre, E. (1981). 'Horaz und Maecenas', *ANRW* 2.31.3: 1987–2019.

—— (1993). *Horaz: Dichter im augusteischen Rom*. Munich: Beck.

Legman, G. (1972). *Rationale of the Dirty Joke: An Analysis of Sexual Humour*. Vols. I–II. London: Cape.

—— (1978). *No Laughing Matter: Rationale of the Dirty Joke: Second Series*. London: Cape.

Leith, D. and Myerson, G. (1989). *The Power of Address. Explorations in Rhetoric*. London: Routledge.

Lejay, P. (1902). 'La date et le but de l'Art poétique d' Horace', *Revue de l'Instruction Publique en Belgique* 45: 361–86.

—— (1903). 'La date et le but de l'Art poétique d' Horace', *Revue de l'Instruction Publique en Belgique* 46: 153–85.

—— (1911). *Oeuvres d'Horace, Satires*. Paris: Hachette.

—— (1966). *Q. Horati Flacci Saturae*. Hildesheim: Georg Olms.

LELLI, E. (2004). *Critica e polemiche letterarie nei Giambi di Callimaco.* Alessandria [Italy]: Edizioni dell'Orso.

—— (2005). *Callimachi Iambi XIV–XVII.* Rome. Edizioni dell'Ateneo.

LEM, S. (1979). *A Perfect Vacuum.* London: Secker & Warburg.

LEMBO, D. (1989). 'L'Orazio delle *Epistole* e i suoi critici ovvero "umano, troppo umano"', *Orpheus* 10: 127–40.

LENNON, J. (1974). *Walls and bridges.* Hayes.

LEO, F. (1901). *Die griechisch-römische Biographie nach ihrer literarischen Form.* Leipzig: Teubner.

LEWIS, R. G. (1966). 'Pompeius' freedman biographer: Suetonius, *De Gramm. et Rhet.* 27 (3)', *CR* 16: 271–302.

—— (2006). *Asconius: Commentaries on Speeches by Cicero.* Oxford: Oxford University Press.

LIEBERG, G. (1958). 'Aristippo e la scuola cirenaica', *RSF*: 3–11.

LIEBESCHUETZ, J. H. W. G. (1979). *Continuity and Change in Roman Religion.* Oxford: Oxford University Press.

LISTER, C. (1991). *Between Two Seas: A Walk down the Appian Way.* London: Secker & Warburg.

LITTLEWOOD, C. (2002). '*Integer ipse?* Self-knowledge and self-representation in Persius *Satires* 4', *Phoenix* 56: 59–63.

LONG, A. A. and SEDLEY, D. N. (1987). *The Hellenistic Philosophers.* Cambridge: Cambridge University Press.

LOWE, W. H. (1979). *Horace, Sermones, Book 1. A Study.* Diss. Brown University.

LOWRIE, M. (1997). *Horace's Narrative Odes.* Oxford: Clarendon Press.

—— (2002). 'Horace, Cicero and Augustus, or the poet statesman at *Epistles* 2.1.256', in T. Woodman and D. Feeney (eds.), *Traditions and Contexts in the Poetry of Horace.* Cambridge: Cambridge University Press, 158–71.

—— (2005). 'Slander and horse law in Horace, Sermones 2.1', *Law and Literature* 17: 405–31.

LUDWIG, H. (1968). 'Die Komposition der beiden Satirenbücher des Horaz', *Poetica* 2: 304–35.

LYNE, R. O. A. M. (1978). 'The Neoteric poets', *CQ* 28: 167–87.

—— (1995). *Horace: Behind the Public Poetry.* New Haven: Yale University Press.

MCCARTNEY, E. S. (1918–19). 'Puns and plays on proper names', *CJ* 14: 343–58.

MCGANN, M. J. (1954). 'Horace's epistle to Florus', *RhM* 97: 343–58.

—— (1963). 'Vinnius Valens, son of Vinnius Asina?', *CQ* 13: 258–9.

—— (1969). *Studies in Horace's First Book of Epistles.* Brussels: Latomus.

McGann, M. J. (1973). 'The three worlds of Horace's *Satires*', in C. D. N. Costa (ed.), *Horace*. London: Routledge and Kegan Paul, 59–93.

McGinn, T. (2001). 'Satire and the law: the case of Horace', *PCPhS* 47: 81–102.

Macleod, C. (1973). 'Catullus 116'. *CQ* 23: 304–9.

—— (1976). 'Callimachus, Virgil, Propertius and Lollius (Horace, Epistles 1.18.39–66)', *ZPE* 23: 41–3.

—— (1977). 'The poet, the critic, and the moralist: Horace, *Epistles* 1.19', *CQ* 27: 359–76.

—— (1979a). 'The poetry of ethics: Horace, *Epistles* I', *JRS* 69: 16–27.

—— (1979b), 'Ethics and poetry in Horace's *Odes* (1.20; 2.3)', *G&R* 26: 21–9.

MacMullen, R. (1967). *Enemies of the Roman Order*. Harvard: Harvard University Press.

MacNeice, L. (1966). *The Collected Poems*. London: Faber.

Maguinness, W. S. (1938). 'Friends and the philosophy of friendship in Horace', *Hermathena* 51: 29–48.

—— (1976). 'Der Eklektizismus des Horaz', in G. Maurach (ed.), *Römische Philosophie*. Darmstadt: Wissenschaftliche Buchgesellschaft, 169–89.

Malcovati, E. (1928). *Imp. Caesaris Aug. operum fragmenta*. Turin: Paravia.

Maltby, R. (1991). *A Lexicon of Ancient Latin Etymologies*. Leeds: ARCA.

Mandruzzato, E. (1993). *Orazio, Le lettere*. Milan: Rizzoli.

Marchesi, C. (1940). *Orazio, Satire ed Epistole*. Milan and Messina: Principato.

—— (1946). 'Orazio', in *Voci di antichi*. Rome: Edizioni Leonardo, 25–40.

Marchesi, I. (2005) 'In memory of Simonides: poetry and mnemotechnics chez Nasidienus', *TAPhS* 135.2: 393–402.

Marcucci, S. (1993). '*Ac ne fores roges quo me duce, quo lare tuter* (Hor. *epist.* I,1,13)', *Maia* 45: 173–86.

Mariotti, S. (1951). *Lezioni su Ennio*. Pesaro [Italy]: Federici (3rd edn. 1991, Urbino: QuattroVenti).

Marouzeau, J. (1910). *La phrase à verbe 'être'*. Diss. Paris.

—— (1926a). 'L'example joint au précepte', *RPh* 52: 110–11.

—— (1926b). 'La leçon par l'exemple', *REL* 14: 58–64.

Marshall, A. J. (1976). 'Library resources and creative writing at Rome', *Phoenix* 30: 252–63.

Martindale, C. (1993). *Redeeming the Text: Latin Poetry and the Hermeneutics of Reception*. Cambridge: Cambridge University Press.

Marx, F. (1904). *C. Lucilii Carminum Reliquiae*. Leipzig: Teubner.

Massaro, M. (1978). 'Un'incertezza di lettura in due passi oraziani (patiens/sapiens)', *A&R* 23: 173–86.

MAURACH, G. (1968). 'Der Grundriss von Horazens erstem Epistelbuch', *AClass* 11: 73–124.

MAYER, R. G. (1986). 'Horace's *Epistles* I and philosophy', *AJPh* 107: 55–73.

—— (1994). *Horace: Epistles I.* Cambridge: Cambridge University Press.

—— (1995). 'Horace's *Moyen de Parvenir*', in S. J. Harrison (ed.), *Homage to Horace: A Bimillenary Celebration.* Oxford: Oxford University Press, 279–95.

MAZUREK, T. (1997). 'Self-parody and the law in Horace's *Satires* 1.9', *CJ* 93: 1–17.

MAZZARINO, S. (1968). 'Aspetti di storia dell' Appia antica', *Helikon* 8: 174–96.

MAZZOLI, G. (1987). 'Etimologia e semantica dello scurra plautino', in S. Boldrini and F. Della Corte (eds.), *Filologia e Forme Letterarie, Studi off. a F. Della Corte II.* Urbino: Università Degli Studi di Urbino, 73–82.

MEISTER, K. (1950). 'Die Freundschaft zwischen Horaz und Maecenas', *Gymnasium* 57: 3–38.

MERRILL, W. A. (1905). *On the Influence of Lucretius on Horace.* Berkeley: University of California Press.

MICHEL, A. (1979). 'Quelques aspects de la conception philosophique du temps à Rome: l'expérience vécue', *REL* 57: 323–39.

—— (1992). 'Poésie et sagesse dans les odes d'Horace', *REL* 70: 126–37.

MILLAR, F. (1973). 'Triumvirate and Principate', *JRS* 63: 50–67.

—— (1977). *The Emperor in the Roman World.* London: Duckworth.

MITCHELL, C. (1952). *Hogarth's Peregrination.* Oxford. Clarendon Press.

MITSIS, P. (1988). *Epicurus' Ethical Theory: The Pleasures of Invulnerability.* Ithaca: Cornell University Press.

MOLES, J. (1983). 'Some "last words" of M. Iunius Brutus', *Latomus* 42: 763–79.

—— (1985). 'Cynicism in Horace *Epistles* 1', *Proceedings of the Liverpool Latin Seminar* 5: 33–60.

—— (1986). 'Cynicism in Horace *Epistles* I', *PLLS* 5: 33–60.

—— (1987). 'Politics, philosophy and friendship in Horace *Odes* 2,7', *QUCC* 25: 59–72.

—— (1995). 'Review of Mayer, R. (1994) *Horace Epistles Book I*', in *BMCRev* 95.02.37.

—— (2002). 'Poetry, philosophy, politics and play: *Epistles* I', in T. Woodman and D. Feeney (eds.), *Traditions and Contexts in the Poetry of Horace.* Cambridge: Cambridge University Press, 141–57.

—— (2007). 'Philosophy and ethics', in S. J. Harrison (ed.), *The Cambridge Companion to Horace.* Cambridge: Cambridge University Press, 165–80.

Momigliano, A. (1942). rev. of L. Robinson, *Freedom of Speech in the Roman Republic*, *JRS* 32: 120–4.

Mommsen, Th. (1877). 'Die pompeianischen Quittungstafeln des L. Caecilius Jucundus', *Hermes* 12: 88–141.

Monteleone, C. (1992). *Stratigrafie esegetiche*. Bari: Edipuglia.

Moore, T. and Carling, C. (1988). *The Limitations of Language*. Basingstoke: Macmillan.

Morello, R. and Morrison, A. D. (eds.) (2007). *Ancient Letters: Classical and Late Antique Epistolography*. Oxford: Oxford University Press.

Morrison, A. D. (2007). 'Didacticism and epistolarity in Horace *Epistles* 1', in R. Morello and A. D. Morrison (eds.), *Ancient Letters: Classical and Late Antique Epistolography*. Oxford: Oxford University Press: 107–32.

Morson, G. S. (ed.) (1986), *Bakhtin: Essays and Dialogues on his Work*. Chicago: University of Chicago Press, 91–7.

Mras, K. (1936). 'Horaz als Mensch und als Dichter', *WS* 54: 70–85.

Muecke, F. (1993). *Horace, Satires II*. Warminster: Aris & Phillips.

—— (1995). 'Law, rhetoric, and genre in Horace, *Satire* 2.1', in S. J. Harrison (ed.), *Homage to Horace: A Bimillenary Celebration*. Oxford: Oxford University Press, 203–18.

—— (2007) 'The *Satires*', in S. J. Harrison (ed.), *The Cambridge Companion to Horace*. Cambridge: Cambridge University Press, 105–20.

Murley, C. (1939). 'Lucretius and the history of satire', *TAPhA* 70: 380–95.

Musurillo, H. A. (1955). 'Horace's journey to Brundisium—fact or fiction?', *CW* 48: 159–62.

Nadjo, L. (1989). *L'argent et les affaires à Rome des origines au IIe siècle avant J.-C.* Louvain and Paris: Peeters Publishers.

Narducci, E. (1984). 'Il comportamento in pubblico (Cicerone, *de officiis* I 126–149)', *Maia* 36: 203–29.

Nash, W. (1985). *The Language of Humour: Style and Technique in Comic Discourse*. London: Longman.

Natorp, P. (1895). 'Aristippos', in *RE* III, 902–6.

Nesselrath, H.-G. (1985). *Lukians Parasitendialog: Untersuchungen und Kommentar*. Berlin: de Gruyter.

Newman, J. K. (1967). *Augustus and the New Poetry*. Brussels: Latomus.

Nickel, R. (1980). 'Xenophon und Horaz', *Gymnasium* 87: 141–50.

Nicolson, H. (1944). 'Horace's progress from Tome to the Adriatic, based on the journey to Brundisium', *Spectator* 172.21: 1.

Niebuhr, B. G. (1848). *Vorträge über römische Geschichte*. Berlin: G. Reimer.

Nisbet, R. G. M. (1959). 'Notes on Horace, *Epistles* 1', *CQ* 9: 73–6.

—— (1961). *Cicero: In Pisonem*. Oxford: Oxford University Press.

—— (1978). 'Felicitas at Surrentum (Statius, *Silvae* II, 2)', *JRS* 68: 1–11.

—— (1984). 'Horace's *Epodes* and History', in T. Woodman and D. West, (eds.), *Poetry and Politics in the Age of Augustus*. Cambridge: Cambridge University Press, 1–18.

—— (1995a). *Collected Papers on Latin Literature* (ed. S. J. Harrison). New York: Oxford University Press.

—— (1995b). 'The survivors: old-style literary men in the triumviral period', in R. G. M. Nisbet (1995a), 390–413.

—— (2002). 'A wine-jar for Messalla: Carmina 3.21', in T. Woodman and D. Feeney (eds.), *Traditions and Contexts in the Poetry of Horace*. Cambridge: Cambridge University Press, 80–92.

—— and HUBBARD, M. A. (1970). *A Commentary on Horace: Odes Book I*. Oxford: Oxford University Press.

—— and —— (1978). *A Commentary on Horace: Odes Book II*. Oxford: Oxford University Press.

NOCK, A. D. (1933). *Conversion: The Old and the New in Religion from Alexander the Great to Augustine of Hippo*. Oxford: Oxford University Press.

NORDEN, E. (1905). 'Die Composition und Litteraturgattung der Horazischen Epistula ad Pisones', *Hermes* 40: 481–528.

—— (1915). *Ennius und Vergilius*. Leipzig: Teubner.

—— (1927). *P. Vergilius Maro: Aeneis Buch VI*. 3rd edn. Leipzig: Teubner.

NOIRFALISE, A. (1950). 'Horace et Mécène', *LEC* 18: 289–303.

—— (1952). 'L'art de réussir auprès des grandes d'après les *Épîtres* d'Horace', *LEC* 20: 358–63.

NUSSBAUM, M. C. (1994). *The Therapy of Desire: Theory and Practice in Hellenistic Ethics*. Princeton: Princeton University Press.

O'HARA, J. J. (1996). *True Names: Vergil and the Alexandrian Tradition of Etymological Wordplay*. Ann Arbor: University of Michigan Press.

OLIENSIS, E. (1991). 'Canidia, *Canicula*, and the decorum of Horace's *Epodes*', *Arethusa* 24, 107–38.

—— (1995). 'Life after publication: Horace, *Epistles* 1.20', *Arethusa* 28: 209–24.

—— (1998a). *Horace and the Rhetoric of Authority*. Cambridge: Cambridge University Press.

—— (1998b). '*Ut arte emendaturus fortunam:* Horace, Nasidienus, and the art of satire', in T. Habinek and A. Schiesaro (eds.), *The Roman Cultural Revolution*. Cambridge: Cambridge University Press, 90–104.

OLTRAMARE, O. (1905). 'L'épître d' Horace à Auguste, son objet et sa disposition', in *Mélange Nicole*. Geneva: W. Kundig et Fils, 411–25.

—— (1926). *Les origines de la diatribe romaine*. Lausanne: Payot.

OPPERMANN, H. (1938). 'Horaz als Dichter der Gemeinschaft', in *Probleme der augusteischen Emeuerung: Auf dem Wege zum nationalpolit* (Gymnasium 6). Frankfurt: M. Diesterweg, 61–75.

OTIS, B. (1945). 'Horace and the Elegists', *TAPhA* 76: 177–90.

OTTO, A. (1890). *Die Sprichwörter und sprichwörtlichen Redensarten der Römer*. Leipzig: Teubner.

PALMER, A. (1883). *Q. Horatius Flaccus. Satires* (2nd edn. 1885). London: Macmillan.

PAPPENROTH, K. (1994). 'A note on the dating of Demetrius' *On Style*', *CQ* 44: 280–1.

PARATORE, E. (1944). *Virgilio*. Rome: Firenze.

—— (1950). *Storia della letteratura latina*. Florence: Firenze.

PASCOLI, G. (1895). *Lyra Romana*. Livorno: Tip. di R. Giusti.

PASOLI, E. (1956). 'Nota introduttiva per una lettura di Properzio', *Nuova Rivista di Varia Umanità*, fasc. 4: 16–19.

—— (1964a). *Le epistole letterarie di Orazio*. Bologna: Pàtron.

—— (1964b). 'Spunti di critica letteraria nella satira oraziana', *Convivium* 32: 449–78.

—— (1965). 'Per una lettera dell'epistola di Orazio a Giulio Floro (*Epist.* 2.2)', *Il Verri* XIX: 129–41 (= (2000). E. Pasoli, A. Traina, and R. C. Melloni (eds.), *Tre poeti tra repubblica e impero (Lucrezio, Catullo, Orazio)*. Bologna: Pàtron, 101–13).

PASQUALI, G. (1920). *Orazio lirico*. Florence: Le Monnier (repr. 1966, ed. A. La Penna).

—— (1951). *Stravaganze Quarte e supreme* (Collezione di Varia Critica, 5). Venice: Neri Pozza.

PEARCE, T. E. V. (1970). 'Notes on Cicero, "In Pisonem" ', *CQ* 20: 309–21.

PEASE, A. S. (1963). *M. Tulli Ciceronnis De Diuinatione*. Darmstadt: Wissenschaftliche Buchgesellschaft.

PECHEY, G. (1989). 'On the borders of Bakhtin: dialogisation, decolonisation', in K. Hirschkop and D. Shepherd (eds.), *Bakhtin and Cultural Theory*. Manchester: Manchester University Press, 39–67.

PELLING, C. (1996). 'The triumviral period', *CAH* 10. 2nd edn. Cambridge, 1–69.

PERKINS, D. (1992). *Is Literary History Possible?* Baltimore and London: Johns Hopkins University Press.

PERRET, J. (1959, repr. 1967). *Horace*. Paris: Hatier.

—— (1964). *Horace* (trans. Bertha Humez). New York: New York University Press.

PESCE, D. (1958). *Il pensiero stoico ed epicureo*. Florence: Nuova Italia.

—— (1981). *Introduzione a Epicuro*. Bari: Laterza.

PETROCHILOS, N. K. (1974). *Roman Attitudes to the Greeks*. Athens: National and Capodistrian University of Athens, Faculty of Arts.

PETRPONIO, G. (1991). 'Il mecenatismo', *Problemi*: 4–23.

PFEIFFER, R. (1949). *Callimachus*. Oxford: Clarendon Press.

—— (1968). *History of Classical Scholarship: From the Beginnings to the End of the Hellenistic Age.* Oxford: Oxford University Press.

PINSENT, J. (1976). 'Horace, *Odes* 3.2.13', *LCM* 1: 84.

PISANI, S. (1953). *A New Guide to Rome and its Environs.* Rome: E. Verdesi.

PIZZOLATO, L. F. (1989). 'L'amicizia con Mecenate e l'evoluzione poetica di Orazio', *Aevum(ant)* 2: 145–82.

—— (1993). *L'idea di amicizia nel mondo antico classico e cristiano.* Turin: Einaudi.

PLAZA, M. (2004). '*Solventur risu tabulae*: saved by laughter in Horace (*S.* 2.1.80–6) and Apuleius (*Met.* 3.1–2)', *C&M* 54: 353–8.

—— (2006). *The Function of Humour in Roman Verse Satire: Laughing and Lying.* Oxford: Oxford University Press.

PLESSIS, F. and LEJAY, P. (1957, 1st edn. 1911, repr. Hildesheim: Olms, 1966). *Oeuvres d'Horace.* Paris: Hachette.

POCOCK, J. G. A. (1984). 'Verbalising a political act: towards a politics of speech', in M. Shapiro (ed.), *Language and Politics.* Oxford: Blackwell, 25–43.

PODLECKI, A. J. (1969). 'The Peripatetics as literary critics', *Phoenix* 23: 114–37.

POHLENZ, M. (1965). *Kleine Schriften, I* (ed. H. Doerrie). Hildesheim: Olms ((1939). *NGG* N.F. 3: 151–98).

—— (1973). *La Stoa I.* Florence: La Nuova Italia (first published 1959).

POLLOCK, G. (1988). *Vision and Difference: Femininity, Feminism and the Histories of Art.* London: Routledge.

PORT, W. (1926). 'Die Anordnung in den Gedichtbüchern der augusteische Zeit', *Philologus* 81: 280–306, 427–68.

POSNER, R. (1988). *Law and Literature: A Misunderstood Relationship.* Cambridge, Mass.: Harvard University Press.

POWELL, J. G. F. (1990). *On Friendship and the Dream of Scipio.* Warminster: Aris & Phillips.

PRÉAUX, J. (1968). *Horace, Epistulae, Liber Primus.* Paris: Presses Universitaires de France.

—— (1977). 'Horace et Aristippe', in *Mélanges Senghor.* Dakar: Nouvelles Editions Africaines, 395–400.

PUCCI, J. (1988). '*Voces liquatae*: a re-reading of Horace's *Ode* 3, 29', *Ramus* 17: 75–89.

PUELMA PIWONKA, M. (1949). *Lucilius und Kallimachos: Zur Geschichte einer Gattung der hellenistisch-römischen Poesie.* Frankfurt am Main: V. Klostermann.

PURCELL, N. (1983). 'The *Apparitores*: a study in social mobility', *PBSR* 51: 125–73.

PURCELL, N. (1995). 'On the sacking of Carthage and Corinth', in D. Innes, H. Hine, and C. Pelling (eds.), *Ethics and Rhetoric: Classical Essays for Donald Russell*. Oxford: Clarendon Press, 133–48.

PURDIE, S. (1993). *Comedy: The Mastery of Discourse*. Hemel Hempstead: Harvester Wheatsheaf.

PUTNAM, M. (1995). 'From lyric to letter: Iccius in Horace *Odes* 1.29 and *Epistles* 1.12', *Arethusa* 28: 193–208.

—— (2000). *Horace's* Carmen Saeculare: *Ritual Magic and the Poet's Art*. New Haven: Yale University Press.

QUASTHOFF, U. M. (1989). 'Social prejudice as a resource of power: towards the functional ambivalence of stereotypes', in R. Wodak (ed.), *Language, Power and Ideology: Studies in Political Discourse*, Amsterdam: Benjamins, 181–96.

RABE, H. (1913) *Hermogenis opera*. Leipzig: Teubner.

RADKE, G. (1989). 'Topographische Betrachtungen zum Iter Brundisinum des Horaz', *RhM* 132: 54–72.

RAMAGE, C. T. (1868). *Nooks and By-Ways of Italy*. Liverpool: E. Howell.

RAMAGE, E. S. (1973). *Urbanitas: Ancient Sophistication and Refinement*. Norman: University of Oklahoma Press for the University of Cincinnati.

RAMBAUX, C. (1971). 'La composition d'ensemble du Livre I des *Satires* d'Horace', *RÉL* 49: 179–204.

RAUH, N. K. (1989). 'Auctioneers and the Roman economy', *Historia* 38: 451–71.

RAWSON, E. (1975). 'Caesar's heritage: Hellenistic kings and their Roman equals', *JRS* 65: 161–74.

—— (1985). *Intellectual Life in the Late Roman Republic*. London: Duckworth.

—— (1991). '*Discrimina ordinum*: the *lex Julia theatralis*', in E. Rawson, *Roman Culture and Society: Collected Papers*. Oxford: Clarendon Press, 508–45.

RECHMANN, W. (1969). *Die Beziehungen zwischen Lukrez und Horaz*. Diss. Freiburg am Breisgau.

RECKFORD, K. J. (1959). 'Horace and Maecenas', *TAPhA* 90: 195–208.

—— (1997). 'Horatius: the man and the hour', *AJPh* 118: 583–612.

REED, L. (1972). *Transformer*. London.

REINHOLD, M. (1933). *M. Agrippa*. Geneva, NY: W. F. Humphrey Press.

RIBBECK, O. (1869). *Horatius' Episteln mit Einleitung und kritischen Bemerkungen*. Berlin: Decker.

—— (1883). *Kolax: Eine ethologische Studie*. Leipzig: S. Hirzel.

RICHARDSON, N. J. (1994). 'Aristotle and Hellenistic scholarship', in *La Philologie grecque à l'époque hellénistique et romaine* (Fondation Hardt Entretiens 40). Vandoevres-Geneva, 7–27.

RICHMOND, J. (1978). 'Catalepton 9', *Mus. Phil. Lond.* 3: 189–201.

RIGNALL, J. (1992). *Realist Fiction and the Strolling Spectator.* London: Routledge.

RIST, J. M. (1978). *Introduzione a Epicuro.* Milan: Mursia.

ROHDICH, H. (1972). 'Die 18. Epistel des Horaz', *RhM* 115: 261–88.

ROLF, J. C. (1914). *Suetonius* (2 vols., Loeb Classical Library Series). Cambridge, Mass.: Harvard University Press.

ROMANIELLO, G. (1984). *Poesia etico-religiosa di Orazio.* Latina: Phos.

ROMILLY, J. DE (1963). *Thucydides and Athenian Imperialism.* Oxford: Blackwell.

RONCONI, A. (1973). *Interpreti latini di Omero.* Turin: Bottega d'Erasmo.

ROSENMEYER, T. G. (1985). 'Ancient literary genres: a mirage?', *Yearbook of Comparative and General Literature* 34: 74–84.

ROSTAGNI, A. (1930). *Arte poetica di Orazio. Introduzione e commento.* Turin: Chiantore.

—— (1937). *Orazio.* Rome: Edizioni Roma (= (1988). Venosa: Edizioni Osanna).

ROSTOVTZEFF, M. I. (1926). *The Social and Economic History of the Roman Empire.* Oxford: Oxford University Press.

RUCH, M. (1963). 'Horace et les fondements de la "iunctura" dans l'ordre de la création poétique (*A.P.*, 46–72)', *REL* 41: 246–69.

RUDD, N. (1960). 'The names in Horace's *Satires*', *CQ* 10: 161–80.

—— (1961). 'Horace's encounter with the bore', *Phoenix* 15: 90–6.

—— (1966). *The Satires of Horace.* Cambridge: Cambridge University Press.

—— (1976). *Lines of Enquiry: Studies in Latin Poetry.* Cambridge: Cambridge University Press.

—— (1979). '*Epistles* and *Sermones*', *LCM* 4: 149.

—— (1982). *The* Satires *of Horace.* 2nd edn. London: Bristol Classical Press.

—— (1986). *Themes in Roman Satire.* Norman: University of Oklahoma Press.

—— (1989). *Horace: Epistles Book II and Epistle to the Pisones ('Ars Poetica').* Cambridge: Cambridge University Press.

—— (1993a). 'Horace as moralist', in N. Rudd (ed.), *Horace 2000: A Celebration. Essays for the Bimillenium.* Bristol: University of Michigan Press, 64–88.

—— (1993b). *Horace 2000: A Celebration. Essays for the Bimillenium.* Bristol: University of Michigan Press.

RUFFELL, I. A. (2003). 'Beyond satire: Horace, popular invective and the segregation of literature', *JRS* 93: 35–65.

RUSSELL, D. A. (1981). *Criticism in Antiquity.* London: Duckworth.

—— and WINTERBOTTOM, M. (1972). *Ancient Literary Criticism.* Oxford: Oxford University Press.

SALLER, R. P. (1982). *Personal Patronage under the Early Empire.* Cambridge: Cambridge University Press.

SALLMANN, K. (1974). 'Die seltsame Reise nach Brundisium. Aufbau und Deutung der Horazsatire 1, 5', in U. Reinhardt and K. Sallmann (eds.), *Musa iocosa (Festschrift for A. Thierfelder).* Hildesheim: Olms, 179–206.

SALMON, E. T. (1967). *Samnium and the Samnites.* Cambridge: Cambridge University Press.

SANTIROCCO, M. S. (1995). 'Horace and Augustan ideology', *Arethusa* 28: 225–43.

SARTRE, J.-P. (1965). *Nausea.* Harmondsworth: Penguin.

SAVAGE, J. J. H. (1960). 'Flentibus amicis. Horace, *Sat.* 1.5.93', *CB* 36: 3–4.

—— (1962). 'The Cyclops, the Sibyl and the poet (Horace *Sat.* 1.5.51–70)', *TAPhA* 93: 410–42.

SCARPAT, G. (1964). *Parrhesia. Storia del termine e delle sue tradizione in latino.* Brescia: Paideia Ed.

SCHANZ, M. and HOSIUS, C. (1935). *Geschichte der römischen Literatur,* Vol. 2. 4th edn. Munich: Beck.

SCHLEGEL, C. (2005). *Satire and the Threat of Speech: Horace's Satires Book 1.* Madison: University of Wisconsin Press.

SCHLEGOFF, E. A. (1988). 'Goffman and the analysis of conversation', in P. Drew and A. Wootton (1988), 89–135.

SCHMIDT, E. A. (1977). '*Amica vis pastoribus*: Der Iambiker Horaz in seinem Epodenbuch', *Gymnasium* 84, 401–23.

SCHNURR, C. (1992). 'The *lex Julia theatralis* of Augustus: some remarks on seating problems in theatre, amphitheatre and circus', *LCM* 17: 147–60.

SCHRIJVERS, H. (1993). 'Horace moraliste', in Walther Ludwig (ed.), *Horace: L'Oeuvre et les imitations, un siècle d'interpretation* (Entretiens sur l'Antiquité Classique 39). Geneva: Fondation Hardt, 41–90.

SCHRÖTER, R. (1967). 'Horazens Satire 1,7 und die antike Eposparodie', *Poetica* 1: 8–23.

SCHWIND, G. (1965). *Zeit, Tod und Endlichkeit bei Horaz.* Diss. Freiburg.

SCODEL, R. (1987). 'Horace, Lucilius, and Callimachean polemic', *HSPh* 91: 199–215.

SCOTT, K. (1929). 'Octavian's propaganda and Antony's *de sua ebrietate*', *CP* 24: 133–41.

—— (1933). 'The political propaganda of 44–30 BC', *PAMAAR* 11: 7–50.

SCOTTI, M. (1982). 'I "canoni" degli autori greci', *Esperienze Letterarie* 7: 74–91.

SEAGER, R. (1972). *Tiberius*. London: Methuen.

—— (1979). *Pompey: A Political Biography*. Oxford: Blackwell.

—— (1993). 'Horace and Augustus: poetry and policy', in N. Rudd (ed.), *Horace 2000: A Celebration. Essays for the Bimillenium*. Bristol: University of Michigan Press, 23–40.

SEDLEY, D. (1976). 'Epicurus and his professional rivals', in J. Bollack and A. Laks (eds.), *Études sur l'epicurisme antique*. Publications de l'Université de Lille III: 119–60.

—— (1998). *Lucretius and the Transformations of Greek Wisdom*. Cambridge: Cambridge University Press.

SEECK, G. A. (1991). 'Über das Satirisch in Horaz' Satiren, oder: Horaz und seine Leser, z.b. Maecenas', *Gymnasium* 98: 534–47.

SEECK, O. (1902). *Kaiser Augustus*. Bielefeld and Leipzig: Velhagen & Klasing.

SELLAR, W. Y. (1891). *Horace and the Elegaic Poets*. Oxford: Clarendon Press.

SETAIOLI, A. (1973). *Il proemio dei Carmina oraziani*. Florence: Olschki.

SHACKLETON BAILEY, D. R. (1965). *Cicero's Letters to Atticus*. Vol. 1 (Cambridge Classical Texts and Commentaries 3). Cambridge: Cambridge University Press.

—— (1981). *Cicero: Epistulae ad Quintum fratrem et M. Brutum* (Cambridge Classical Texts and Commentaries 22). Cambridge: Cambridge University Press.

—— (1982). *Profile of Horace*. London: Duckworth.

SHATZMAN, I. (1975). *Senatorial Wealth and Roman Politics*. Brussels: Latomus.

SHOTTER, J. (1993). *Cultural Politics of Everyday Life: Social Constructionism, Rhetoric and Knowing of the Third Kind*. Buckingham: Open University Press.

SIDER, D. (1997). *The Epigrams of Philodemus: Introduction, Text and Commentary*. Oxford: Oxford University Press.

SILK, E. T. (1966). 'The god and the searchers for happiness', *YCS* 19: 235–50.

SIMON, C. (1991). *The best of Carly Simon*. New York.

SIRAGO, V. A. (1958). 'Lucanus an Apulus?', *AC* 27: 13–30.

SKUTSCH, O. (1963). 'The structure of the Propertian *Monobiblos*', *CP* 58: 238–9.

—— (1968). *Studia Enniana*. London: Athlone.

—— (1969). 'Symmetry and sense in the *Eclogues*'. *HSCP* 73: 153–69.

—— (1985). *The Annales of Q. Ennius*. Oxford: Oxford University Press.

SMITH, R. E. (1951). 'The law of libel at Rome', *CQ* 1: 169–79.

SMITH, W. K. (1936). 'The date of the Ars Poetica', *CPh* 31, 163–6.

SNYDER, J. M. (1980). *Puns and Poetry in Lucretius' De Rerum Natura.* Amsterdam: Grüner.

SOMMARIVA, G. (1980). 'La parodia di Lucrezio nell' *Ars* e nei *Remedia* ovidiani', *A&R* 25: 123–48.

SONNENSCHEIN, E. A. (1898). 'The nationality of Horace', *CR* 12: 305.

SORNIG, K. (1989). 'Some remarks on linguistic strategies of persuasion', in R. Wodak (ed.), *Language, Power and Ideology: Studies in Political Discourse.* Amsterdam: Benjamins, 95–113.

STAHL, H.-P. (1974). 'Peinliche Erfahrung eines kleinen Gottes: Horaz in seinen Satiren', *A&A* 20: 25–53.

STANFORD, W. B. (1963). *The Ulysses Theme.* Oxford: Blackwell.

STÉGEN, G. (1960). *Essai sur la composition de cinq Épîtres d'Horace (I, 1, 2, 3, 11, 15).* Namur: Maison d'Editions ad. Wesmael-Charlier (S.A.).

STEIDLE, W. (1939). *Studien zur Ars poetica des Horaz.* Würzburg: Aumühle, K. Triltsch.

STERNE, L. (1993, 6th edn.). *Tristram Shandy.* Hertfordshire: Wordsworth Editions.

STUIBER, A. (1954). s.v. 'Beifall', in *RAC* 2, 95–6.

SUOLAHTI, J. (1955). *The Junior Officers of the Roman Army in the Republican Period: A Study on Social Structure.* Helsinki: Suomalainen Tiedeakatemia.

—— (1963). *The Roman Censors: A Study in Social Structure.* Helsinki: Suomalainen Tiedeakatemia.

SYME, R. (1939). *The Roman Revolution.* Oxford: Oxford University Press.

—— (1964a). *Sallust.* Berkeley: University of California Press.

—— (1964b). 'Senators, tribes and towns', *Historia* 13: 105–25.

—— (1978a). *History in Ovid.* Oxford: Oxford University Press.

—— (1978b). 'Mendacity in Velleius', *AJPh* 99: 45–63.

TAIT, I. M. (1941). *Philodemus' Influence on the Latin Poems.* Diss. Bryn Mawr.

TALBERT, R. J. A. (1984). *The Senate of Imperial Rome.* Princeton: Princeton University Press.

TANDOI, V. (1969). 'Il ricordo di Stazio "dolce poeta" nella sat. VII di Giovenale', *Maia* 21: 103–22.

TANNEN, D. (1989). *Talking Voices: Repetition, Dialogue, and Imagery in Conversational Discourse.* Cambridge: Cambridge University Press.

TATUM, J. (1998). '*Ultra legem:* law and literature in Horace, *Satires* II 1', *Mnemosyne* 51: 688–99.

TAYLOR, L. R. (1968). 'Republican and Augustan writers enrolled in the equestrian centuries', *TAPhA* 99: 469–86.

TAYLOR, T. J. (1992). *Mutual Misunderstanding: Scepticism and the Theorizing of Language and Interpretation*. London: Routledge.

TERZAGHI, N. (1939). *Orazio*. Milan: Bietti.

TESCARI, O. (1947). *Commento a Odi ed Epodi*. 4th edn. Turin: Società Editrice Internazionale.

TESTORELLI, E. (1977). *Analisi stilistica della Satira 1,5 di Orazio*. Lugano: Gaggini-Bizzozero.

THEY MIGHT BE GIANTS (1990). *Flood*. New York.

THRAEDE, K. (1970). *Grundzüge griechische-römische Brieftopik* (Zetemata 48). Munich: Beck.

TRAGLIA, A. (1971). 'L'epicureismo di Orazio', *Horatianum, Atti III Conv. Or.*: 41–54.

TRAINA, A. (1974). *Vortit barbare*. Rome: Edizioni dell'Ateneo.

—— (1986). 'Semantica del carpe diem', in *Poeti latini (e neolatini) I*. Bologna: Pàtron, 227–51.

—— (1987). *Lo stile 'drammatico' del filosofo Seneca*. 4th edn. Bologna: Pàtron.

—— (1991). 'Orazio e Aristippo. Le *Epistole* e l'arte di convivere', *RDF* 119: 285–305.

—— (2005). *Orazio, Odi ed Epodi*, trans. E. Mandruzzato, introd. A. Traina. Milan: Rizzoli.

TRAPP, M. B. (2003). *Greek and Roman Letters*. Cambridge: Cambridge University Press.

TREGGIARI, S. (1969). *Roman Freedmen during the Late Republic*. Oxford: Clarendon Press.

—— (1973). 'Cicero, Horace and mutual friends: Lamiae and Varrones Murenae', *Phoenix* 27: 245–61.

TUPET, A. M. (1976). *La magie dans la poésie latine*. Paris: Les Belles Lettres.

TUROLLA, E. (1962, repr. 1963, 1968). *Orazio, Le Epistole*. Turin: Loescher.

TURPIN, W. (1998). 'The Epicurean parasite: Horace, *Satires* 1.1–3', *Ramus* 27.2: 127–40.

ULMER, G. L. (1989). *Teletheory: Grammatology in the Age of Video*. London: Routledge.

USHER, S. (1965). '*Occultatio* in Cicero's speeches', *AJPh* 86, 175–92.

VAHLEN, J. (1871). 'Horatius' Brief an Augustus', in *Zeitschr. f. d. österr. Gymnas.* 22 (= Vahlen [1911] *Gesammelte Philologische Schriften*, Vol. 1, Leipzig and Berlin, 461–511).

—— (1878). 'Über Zeit und Abfolge der Literaturbriefe des Horatius', in *Monatsberichten den Berliner Akademie*, 688–704 (=Vahlen [1923] *Gesammelte Philologische Schriften*, Vol. 2, Leipzig and Berlin, 46–61).

VAHLEN, J. (1874). 'Zu Horatius' Brief an Florus', in *Zeitschrift f. d. österr. Gymnas.* 25 (= Vahlen [1911] *Gesammelte Philologische Schriften,* Vol. 1, Leipzig and Berlin, 511–15).

VAN OOTEGHEM, J. (1946). 'Horace et l'indépendance', *Latomus* 5: 185–8.

VAN ROOY, C. A. (1966). *Studies in Classical Satire and Related Literary Theory.* Leiden: Brill.

—— (1968). 'Arrangement and structure of Satires in Horace, *Sermones,* Book I, with more special reference to Satires 1–4', *AClass* 11: 38–72.

—— (1970a). 'Arrangement and structure of Satires in Horace, *Sermones,* Book I: Satires 4 and 10', *AClass* 13: 7–27.

—— (1970b). 'Arrangement and structure of Satires in Horace, *Sermones,* Book I: Satires 5 and 6', *AClass* 13: 45–59.

—— (1971). 'Arrangement and structure of Satires in Horace, *Sermones,* Book I: Satire 7 as related to Satires 10 and 8', *AClass* 14: 67–90.

—— (1972a). 'Arrangement and structure of Satires in Horace, *Sermones,* Book I: Satires 9 and 10', *AClass* 15: 37–52.

—— (1972b). 'Horace, *Sat.* I,1 and I,6 and the topos of cardinal vices', *Antidosis* (Festschrift W. Kraus), *WSt* Beiheft 5: 297–305.

—— (1973). ' "*Imitatio*" of Vergil, *Eclogues* in Horace, *Satires,* Book I', *AClass* 16: 69–88.

VAN SICKLE, J. (1978). *The Design of Virgil's Bucolics.* Rome: Ateneo.

—— (1980). 'Augustan poetry books', *Arethusa* 13.1 (Buffalo, NY: SUNY Press).

VARDI, A. D. (1996). '*Diiudicatio locorum*: Gellius and the history of a mode in ancient comparative criticism', *CQ* 46, 492–514.

VEYNE, P. (1984). *Writing History: Essay on Epistemology,* trans. M. Moore-Rinvolucri. Manchester: Manchester University Press.

—— (1988). *Roman Erotic Elegy: Love, Poetry, and the West,* trans. D. Pellauer. Chicago: University of Chicago Press.

VICKERS, M. (1977). *Pericles on Stage: Political Comedy in Aristophanes' Early Plays.* Austin: University of Texas Press.

VILLENEUVE, F. (1934). *Horace, Epîtres.* Paris: Les Belles Lettres.

VOLTAIRE (1759). *Candide, ou l'Optimisme.* Paris: Sirène.

WALLACE-HADRILL, A. (1981). 'Family and inheritance in the Augustan marriage laws', *PCPhS* 27: 58–80.

—— (1982). '*Civilis princeps*: between citizen and king', *JRS* 72: 32–48.

—— (1988). 'Greek knowledge, Roman power', *CP* 83, 224–33.

—— (1990). 'Introduction'; 'Patronage in Roman society: from Republic to Empire', in A. Wallace-Hadrill (ed.), *Patronage in Ancient Society.* London and New York: Routledge, 1–13; 63–87.

References   515

WALLACH, B. P. (1976). *Lucretius and the Diatribe against the Fear of Death.* Leiden: Brill.

WATSON, L. C. (1995). 'Horace's *Epodes*: the impotence of *iambos?*', in S. J. Harrison (ed.), *Homage to Horace: A Bimillenary Celebration.* Oxford: Oxford University Press, 188–202.

WATSON, P. (1984). 'Love as civilizer: Ovid, *Ars Amatoria*, 2.467–92', *Latomus* 43: 389–95.

WEHRLI, F. (1944) 'Horaz und Kallimachos', *MH* 1: 67–76.

WEIHER, A. (1913). *Philosophen und Philosophenspott in der attischen Komödie.* Diss. Munich.

WEINSTOCK, S. (1971). *Divus Julius.* Oxford: Clarendon Press.

WENDLAND, P. (1986). *La cultura ellenistico-romana nei suoi rapporti con quidaismo e cristianesimo.* Brescia: Paideia Editrice (trans. from German first edition [1912] Tübingen: Mohr).

WEST, D. (1967). *Reading Horace.* Edinburgh: Edinburgh University Press.

—— (1969). *The Imagery and Poetry of Lucretius.* Edinburgh: Edinburgh University Press.

WIGODSKY, M. (1972). *Vergil and Early Latin Poetry* (*Hermes Einzelschriften* 24). Wiesbaden: F. Steiner.

WILI, W. (1948). *Horaz und die augusteische Kultur.* Basel: Schwabe & Co.

WILKES, J. J. (1969). *Dalmatia.* Cambridge, Mass.: Harvard University Press.

WILLIAMS, G. W. (1968). *Tradition and Originality in Roman Poetry.* Oxford: Oxford University Press.

—— (1969). *The Third Book of Horace's Odes.* Oxford: Clarendon Press.

—— (1972). *Horace* (*Greece and Rome* New Surveys in the Classics No. 6). Oxford: Oxford University Press.

—— (1978). *Change and Decline: Roman Literature in the Early Empire.* Berkeley and Los Angeles: University of California Press.

—— (1982). 'Phases in political patronage of literature in Rome', in B. K. Gold (ed.), *Literary and Artistic Patronage in Ancient Rome.* Austin: University of Texas Press, 3–27.

—— (1995). '*Libertino Patre Natus*: true or false?', in S. J. Harrison (ed.), *Homage to Horace: A Bimillenary Celebration.* Oxford: Oxford University Press, 296–313.

WIMMEL, W. (1960). *Kallimachos in Rom. Die Nachfolge seines apologetischen Dichtens in der Augusteerzeit.* Wiesbaden: Steiner.

—— (1962). *Zur Form der horazischen Diatribensatire.* Frankfurt: Klostermann.

WIRTH, TH. (1967). 'Arrians Erinnerungen an Epiktet', *MH* 24: 149–89.

WIRZUBSKI, C. (1950). *Libertas as a Political Idea at Rome.* Cambridge: Cambridge University Press.

WISEMAN, T. P. (1971). *New Men in the Roman Senate: 139 BC–AD 14.* Oxford: Oxford University Press.

—— (1982). '*Pete nobiles amicos*: poets and patrons in Late Republican Rome', in B. K. Gold (ed.), *Literary and Artistic Patronage in Ancient Rome*. Austin: University of Texas Press, 28–49.

—— (1988). 'Satyrs in Rome? The background to Horace's *Ars Poetica*', *JRS* 78: 1–13.

WISTRAND, E. (1958). *Horace's Ninth Epode and its Historical Background.* Göteborg: Almqvist & Wiksell (= (1972). in E. Wistrand (ed.), *Opera Selecta*. Stockholm: Swedish Institute in Rome, 289–350).

WHITE, P. (1974). 'The presentation and dedication of the *Silvae* and *Epigrams*', *JRS* 64: 40–61.

—— (1978). '*Amicitia* and the profession of poetry in Early Imperial Rome', *JRS* 68: 74–92.

—— (1993). *Promised Verse: Poets in the Society of Augustan Rome*. Cambridge, Mass.: Harvard University Press.

WITTE, K. (1923). *Der Satirendichter Horaz*. Erlangen: self-published.

WOODMAN, A. J. (1977). *Velleius Paterculus: The Tiberian Narrative (2.94–131)* (Cambridge Classical Texts and Commentaries 19). Cambridge: Cambridge University Press.

—— (1983). *Velleius Paterculus: The Caesarian and Augustan Narrative (2.41–93)* (Cambridge Classical Texts and Commentaries 25). Cambridge: Cambridge University Press.

YARDLEY, J. C. (1973). 'Sick-visiting in Roman elegy', *Phoenix* 27: 283–8.

YAVETZ, Z. (1969). *Plebs and Princeps*. Oxford: Oxford Univeristy Press.

ZETZEL, J. E. G. (1980). 'Horace's *Liber Sermonum*: the structure of ambiguity', *Arethusa* 13: 59–78.

—— (1981). *Latin Textual Criticism.* New York: Arno. (Diss. Harvard University 1972).

—— (2002). 'Dreaming about Quirinus: Horace's *Satires* and the development of Augustan poetry', in A. J. Woodman and D. Feeney (eds.), *Traditions and Contexts in the Poetry of Horace*. Cambridge: Cambridge University Press, 38–52.

ZIEGLER, H. (1891). *Cleomedes.* Leipzig: B. G. Teubner.

ZIELINSKI, T. (1938). *Horace et la société romaine du temps d'Auguste.* Paris: Les Belles Lettres.

ZIJDERVELD, A. C. (1979). *On Clichés: The Supersedure of Meaning by Function in Modernity.* London: Routledge and Kegan Paul.

Acknowledgements

Permission to reprint the following items is gratefully acknowledged:
James Zetzel, 'Horace's *Liber Sermonum*: the structure of ambiguity', *Arethusa* 13 (1980), 59–77.
DuQuesnay, I. M. Le M. 'Horace and Maecenas: the propaganda value of *Sermones* I', in T. Woodman and D. West (eds.), *Poetry and Politics in the Age of Augustus* (Cambridge: Cambridge University Press, 1984), 19–58.
M. Labate, 'Il sermo oraziano e i generi letterari', in *Zeitgenosse Horaz: der Dichter und seine Leser seit zwei Jahrtausenden* (Tübingen: Gunter Narr Verlag, 1996), 424–41.
W. Turpin, 'The Epicurean parasite: Horace, Satires 1.1–3', *Ramus* 27.2 (1998), 127–40.
Gordon Williams, *Libertino Patre Natus*: true or false?', in S. J. Harrison (ed.), *Homage to Horace* (Oxford: Oxford University Press, 1995), 296–313.
E. Gowers, 'Horace, Satires 1.5: an inconsequential journey', *PCPS* 39 (1993), 48–66.
J. Henderson, 'Be alert (your country needs lerts): Horace, Satires 1.9', *Proceedings of the Cambridge Philological Society* 39 (1993), 67–93.
R. Scodel, 'Horace, Lucilius, and Callimachean polemic', *Harvard Studies in Classical Philology* 91 (1987), 199–215.
Jeffrey Tatum, '*Ultra legem*: law and literature in Horace, *Satires* II 1', *Mnemosyne* 51 (1998), 688–99.
C. Macleod, 'The poetry of ethics: Horace *Epistles* I', *JRS* 69 (1979), 16–27.
S. J. Harrison, 'Poetry, philosophy and letter-writing in Horace *Epistles* 1', in D. Innes, H. Hine, and C. Pelling (eds.), *Ethics and Rhetoric: Classical Essays for Donald Russell* (Oxford: Oxford University Press, 1995), 47–61.
A. Traina, 'Orazio e Aristippo. Le *Epistole* e l'arte di convivere', *Poeti Latini (e Neolatini): Note e Saggi Fiologici IV* (Bologna: Pàtron Editore), 161–86.
J. Moles, 'Poetry, philosophy, politics and play: *Epistles* I', in A. J. Woodman and D. C. Feeney (eds.), *Traditions and Contexts in the Poetry of Horace* (Cambridge: Cambridge University Press, 2002), 141–57.
F. Klingner, 'Horazens Brief an Augustus', *Sitzungsberichte der Bayerischen Akademie der Wissenschaften* 5 (Munich: Verlag der Bayerischen Akademie der Wissenschaften, 1950), 1–32.
D. C. Feeney, '*Una cum scriptore meo*: poetry, Principate and the traditions of literary history in the Epistle to Augustus', in A. J. Woodman and D. C.

Feeney (eds.), *Traditions and Contexts in the Poetry of Horace* (Cambridge: Cambridge University Press, 2002), 172–87.

A. La Penna, 'Orazio, Augusto e la questione del teatro latino', *Annali della Scuola Normale Superiore di Pisa* XIX (1950), 143–54.

E. Pasoli, 'Per una lettera dell'epistola di Orazio a Giulio Floro (*Epist.* 2.2)', *Il Verri* XIX (Milan: Edizioni del Verri, 1965), 129–41.

K. Freudenburg, 'Writing to/through Florus: sampling the addressee in Horace, *Epistles* 2.2', *Memoirs of the American Academy in Rome* 47 (2002), 33–55.

E. Oliensis, 'The art of self-fashioning in the Ars poetica', in *Horace and the Rhetoric of Authority* (Cambridge: Cambridge University Press, 1998) 198–223.